Making Progress

Making Progress

Essays in Progress and Public Policy

Edited by C. Leigh Anderson and
Janet W. Looney

LEXINGTON BOOKS
Lanham • Boulder • New York • Oxford

LEXINGTON BOOKS

Published in the United States of America
by Lexington Books
A Member of the Rowman & Littlefield Publishing Group
4720 Boston Way, Lanham, Maryland 20706

PO Box 317
Oxford
OX2 9RU, UK

British Library Cataloguing in Publication Information Available

Library of Congress Cataloging-in-Publication Data

Making progress: essays in progress and public policy / edited by C. Leigh Anderson and Janet W. Looney.
p. cm.
Includes bibliographical references and index.
ISBN 0-7391-0490-X (alk. paper) – ISBN 0-7391-0491-8 (pbk.: alk. paper)
1. Policy sciences. 2. Progress. I. Anderson, C. Leigh, 1960– II. Looney, Janet W., 1959–

H97.P764 2002
320'.6—dc21 2002028301

Printed in the United States of America

™ The paper used in this publication meets the minimum requirements of American National Standard for Information Sciences—Permanence of Paper for Printed Library Materials, ANSI/NISO Z39.48–1992.

Betty Jane Narver
1934-2001

whose passion was people and the belief that
human progress is not only possible but imperative

Contents

Preface

Making Progress: Essays in Progress and Public Policy is an outgrowth of a year-long exploration into the nature of progress, a joint effort of the Daniel J. Evans School of Public Affairs and the Glaser Foundation. The central goal of our project was to provoke and facilitate a broad-based discussion on the meaning of, measurement of, and necessary conditions for progress. This ambitious effort included an educational video and public lectures by speakers such as President Jimmy Carter, Senator George Mitchell, Jane Goodall, and Doris Kearns-Goodwin.

This book is distinguished from its many predecessors on progress by its focus on policy. Many of us believe that public policy should reflect a vision of a better future, and that great leaders and good policy can even help to shape it. The success of this process depends on our individual and collective ability to respond to at least three challenges which we explore as themes throughout the book: knowledge, universality, and complexity.

First, concerns about the dangers of certain types of knowledge, such as nuclear fission and the human genome, challenge the Enlightenment idea of progress premised on human discovery. Public policy plays a role in promoting, spreading, and determining the ownership of this knowledge. Most important for public policy at this juncture, we believe, is to know thyself. By knowing ourselves, our limits, and our possibilities, we can better design institutions that promote progress—perhaps fostering wiser decisions about our relations with others, for example, and our ability to make use of technology and preserve the environment.

Second, universal definitions of progress, across time or across cultures, are largely elusive. There are some common principles of progress, such as eliminating hunger, eradicating disease, and promoting justice. But a plurality of views, within and across cultures and generations, ensures differing judgments about the nature of any event—whether capital punishment, for example, constitutes justice. Without some common understanding of what principles or events constitute progress, public policy will inevitably create winners and losers. Individuals often evaluate their own progress, not absolutely, but gauged relative to others. This has implications for cultural relativism and the imposition of values, and perceptions of equality and how policies distribute the benefits of progress.

Finally, complex problems may demand complex institutions. Complexity allows individuated choice and form via specialization with these component parts integrated through common (i.e. universal) principles. Unfortunately, although specialization in both biological and economic systems can promote growth and progress, inherent in specialization are a variety of risks. Common examples would include the unintended consequences and vulnerability to environmental change, whether natural or economic. But there are also political risks. For example, when our elected and non-elected officials understand too little about the complicated issues at hand, policy-making devolves to adjudication of the competing claims of specialists, many of whom are in the employ of wealthy special interest groups. For citizens the incomprehensibility of our systems and policies makes us susceptible to the partial truths offered by proponent and opponent alike, and weakens our ability to hold our officials accountable.

We begin with an overview chapter that offers several propositions on the relationship between progress and policy—the institutions that govern how individuals relate. This chapter draws heavily on the insights of our contributing authors. Our overview is followed by three chapters that introduce definitions of progress and public policy, indicate how progress is measured for policy purposes, and discuss some of the major difficulties to implementing progress.

Scholars have traditionally defined measures of progress within three broad domains: "moral, aesthetic, and intellectual sensibilities,"[1] social relations, and material wealth and technical capacity. Accordingly, we have organized the remaining chapters into three domains, beginning with the individual and working outwards: *progress in ourselves*, which includes evolution, religion, and literature; *progress in relation to others*, which includes collective action, social relations and ethnopolitical warfare; and *progress in our material and physical world*, which includes science, economic wealth, technical capacity, and the natural environment.

Our approach to the book reflects our belief in the value of differentiation bound by common principles—complexity. With latitude as to form, each author was given the common task of discussing the meaning of progress in his or her field and the conditions necessary for progress to occur. The result is that each domain contains a mix of fairly formal academic chapters and more informal shorter essays that broadly discuss progress in the field. Each domain concludes with examinations of progress in particular policy areas including bioethics, education, international development, the media, information technology, and environmental sustainability. These policy discussions illustrate the complexity and politics of the rhetoric of policy, particular policies that have either promoted or retarded progress as defined, the role of leadership as proactive or reactive, and avenues for better policy processes or instruments.

Making Progress is the only book we know of that attempts to systematically explore the relationship of public policy to the idea of progress. We have tried to set current views in their historical context, marry theory and practice, and call upon practitioner and academic. We believe it will be of interest to scholars and the public whose lives are touched daily by public policy, and the policy-makers, advocates, analysts and voters who are helping to craft those policies in the name of progress.

With few exceptions, these book chapters were written prior to the tragic events of September 11th, 2001. For some of us, our illusion of progress has been shaken: how we would define progress and our assessment of what progress we had made as a country, or in the world. For others of us, our vision and measures of progress remain intact, but our belief in how we need to act on that vision, including the role of public policy, has changed. To acknowledge these events we asked Senator Daniel J. Evans to write a post-September 11th foreword.

We would like to thank the Glaser Foundation for its generous support and vision of the Progress Project, Rob Glaser and Martin Collier for their belief that there is a different way to do business, David Harrison for his unwavering optimism and bounty of ideas, Marc Lindenberg for his support and leadership, Hollie Sheriff for her exceptionally careful review and preparation of all the chapters, and the many individuals at the Daniel J. Evans School of Public Affairs who worked on this project and helped to shape this vision. We would also like to thank all the members of the University of Washington and Evans School community, and others like them, who devote their professional lives to teaching, researching and practicing public policy to promote progress.

Editors post-script: On May 17th, 2002, Marc Lindenberg, Dean of the Evans School, lost a short but brave battle with lung cancer. His approach to his illness reflected his approach to life: devoid of cynicism, full of optimism, insistent that individuals can make a difference, and confident that always, progress is possible. His legacy will continue with the Marc Lindenberg Center for Humanitarian Action, International Development, and Global Citizenship at the University of Washington, and in the hearts, minds, and resolve of the many people he touched.

Notes

1. Raymond Gastil, *Progress: Critical Thinking about Historical Change* (Westport: Conn.: Praeger, 1993).

Foreword

Daniel J. Evans

Progress is an elusive concept. A prime dictionary definition is "A movement toward a goal or a further or higher stage."

For many, the measurement is wealth, for others, societal health, and for some, progress is unsettling, even frightening.

Thousands of years ago, wandering nomads formed family groups and then tribes, brought together by the need to join efforts to survive. Hunting, farming and eventually manufacturing required shared work and group talent. Human aggressive tendencies led to conquest, revolution, and eventually the building of empires, none of which proved eternal. The dominant bonds that create and unite nations are race, ethnicity, religion, tradition, and conquest.

Few nations celebrate their diversity, rich ethnic and religion mixtures, and traditions of citizen participation in every facet of their existence. In the United States, the glue which holds us together is neither race nor religion, but an idea, a set of principles, a constitution for the ages. People now throughout the world struggle to emulate this remarkable example of individual freedom and self-governance.

This progress toward human freedom was matched by malevolent progress in the efficiency and horror of warfare. Threats of nuclear holocaust, made vivid by the destruction of Hiroshima and Nagasaki, stalled aggressors. Nasty tribal and ethnic conflicts continued but most of the world grew—in both material and human progress.

Suddenly, on September 11, 2001, our complacency and confidence were shattered. Terrorism, the malignant weapon of radicalism, had been distant and puzzling, but now was upon us in devastating force. No nation, no army, no uniforms, just a ghostly band of intruders—using our icons of material progress as weapons against us.

Our economy plunged deeper into recession and our individual rights were trimmed away in the drive to capture terrorists or in the name of eliminating terrorism. Progress by all of its measurements seemed threatened.

Just a week earlier Congress quarreled over social security "lock boxes," network news anchors chortled over a Congressman's peccadilloes, fatuous talk show hosts ranted about waste in government, and most citizens listened to none of the above but enjoyed a satisfying season of baseball.

But now a remarkable transformation transpired. Citizens volunteered money, blood, and support in stunning amounts for the victims. For everyone there was a reawakened perception of governmental skills. In an era of reduced taxes and weakened government, it was the public sector that responded valiantly.

New York fire and police departments were new national heroes. Mayor Giuliani and President Bush gave inspired leadership to the nation. It was not corporate or union leaders, not political pressure groups, not talkshow hosts or television anchors, but these same public employees we love to deride who did their duty magnificently.

Is there a message in the madness of September 11th, the citizen response, and progress?

I think so. It is that government works pretty well. We all think taxes are too high but seldom add up the benefits which come from that investment. Taxes are the price we pay for living in an organized society. Military forces helped sustain our free world and win the Cold War. That's a pretty good return on investment. We enjoy the finest network of interstate and local highways of any country on earth. Our water and sewer systems work effectively and our fire and police protection is dependable. Our children enjoy a free education and participate in the broadest system of public colleges and universities in the entire world. We all look forward to Social Security benefits and Medicare, enjoy the national parks which preserve our heritage and control land use to prevent callous misuse of resources, and depend on the Center for Disease Control to prevent outbreaks of infectious diseases. The list is much longer.

Each of these is the product of human effort and organization guided by government. They are the product of good policy.

Human progress depends on a free society bound together by a code of conduct that nurtures innovation, embraces diversity, and respects public service. Only then will human and scientific progress flourish.

Introduction

C. Leigh Anderson and David A. Hennes

> We cannot point to a single definitive solution of any one of the problems that confront us—political, economic, social, or moral, i.e., having to do with the conduct of life. We are still beginners, and for that reason may hope to improve. To deride the hope of progress is the ultimate fatuity, the last word in poverty of spirit and meanness of mind.
>
> Peter B. Medawar [1]

These words, spoken over thirty years ago, continue to inspire our belief that we can improve our lives, the lives of our close families, friends, and neighbors, and the lives of distant strangers. Our particular interest in this process centers on the role of policy in promoting that progress—that is, what are the right institutions for progressive change and what processes are most likely to yield them? In addressing this question, we begin with the assertion that policy matters, and that the pace and magnitude of progress has varied in each of three domains: progress in ourselves, in our relations with others, and in our material and natural world.

In our appeal to the various contributors to this book we suggested several themes that we believe both challenge policy makers in promoting progress, and characterize the processes or outcomes that are generally identified as progressive: specialization and differentiation, universality, complexity, and knowledge. What we received in return has sufficiently formed our views and emboldened us to advance four propositions on the relationship between progress and public policy: (1) Progressive policy allows experimentation that promotes differentiation of knowledge, technique, and organizational structure; (2) Progressive policy enables universality by disseminating, redistributing, and contesting ideas, knowledge, and opportunities; (3) Progressive policy embodies complexity—the means to resolve the tension between the diversity and specialization driving progress and the universal adoption of the changes necessary to realize progress; and (4) Progressive policy requires self-knowledge. We develop these ideas drawing support from the authors in this book who offer the insights of their disciplines, interdisciplines, and life's work and experience.

The Domains of Progress

We begin by dividing progress into three domains: progress in ourselves, in our relations with others, and in the material and natural world.[2] Though these are obviously not mutually exclusive, we are interested in knowing whether the answers to our initial questions vary in a meaningful way among these domains. Most authors have discussed the role of institutions in progress from their disciplinary perspective, such as psychology or economics. Within each domain, however, we have also asked some authors to approach the question by focussing on a particular policy area, such as education. As figure 1 suggests, these policy chapters, in particular, span all three domains.

The Domains of Progress and Public Policy

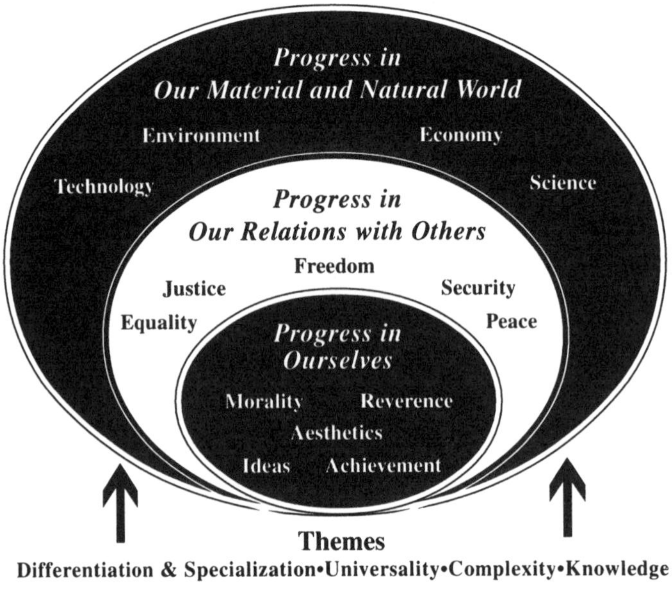

As defined here, progress in ourselves is the domain of ideas, intuition, creativity, conscience, morality, reverence, aesthetics, enlightenment, and achievement. It is the domain of self-expression. Accordingly, policies that affect religion, ethics, art, music, literature, innovation, and exploration will directly affect this domain. Our authors in this domain discuss the biological limits to progress in ourselves, progress in religion, and progress in literature. Our policy focus is on bioethics because of the tension it highlights over knowledge and morality—a central tenet in the history of progress,[3] and on education for its central role in equipping each individual to reach their potential.

Progress in our relations with others is the domain of collective action, cultural regression, stagnation or advance, social organization, genocide, war, and international development. If, as some believe, progress in human nature is unobtainable because of original sin or biological limits, then progress depends more heavily on the institutions that govern us. Our authors discuss institutional and cultural maturity and conflict. Our policy chapters focus on nongovernmental organizations (NGOs) as an alternative organizational form to effect change and the media as the interpreters of progress, or lack thereof.

Finally, progress in our natural and material world is the domain of science, technology, economics, and environmental change. Our authors discuss progress in the natural sciences and poverty alleviation. Our policy chapters focus on information technologies, where institutions are challenged to keep up with the staggering pace of change, and environmental sustainability, which contrary to historical views, is considered requisite for progress in many of the chapters that follow.

Parameters of Discussion

At the outset, we need to make a distinction between progress as process and outcome, and progress as belief system or ideology. Progress as process and outcome is the more pragmatic view that human activity and natural change occur in certain ways and yield certain outcomes that according to various, often subjective, criteria are deemed beneficial, particularly to humans but also to other species and the physical environment. Generally these processes and outcomes are therefore judged to be superior to previous processes and outcomes. As such they are believed to be susceptible to improvement towards maturity, or even capable of perfectibility. Progress as a belief system or ideology, on the other hand, goes beyond the description and classification of processes and outcomes (of change) as progressive or not. It implies inquiry into the existence or validity of the concept of progress and further into the philosophy of progress as a cultural principle.

We do not in this chapter seek to confirm or refute relativist critiques of the concept of progress. Indeed, we take as a given that defining progress is one of the greatest challenges to achieving more and faster progress. Nor do we seek to answer questions concerning the imperfectability of man as the object of divine creation. To the extent that this view exists, however, it fundamentally affects the possibilities for policy. In chapter 1 Patrick Dobel and Leigh Anderson discuss the four main historical views of flow and progression—cyclical, fallen, contingent, and linear—and how they can relegate policy to a limited role of, for example, delaying the inevitable or seeking to minimize society's downfall. We do not recount the history of the idea of progress, or dwell on the positions and propositions of various philosophers regarding its validity, but refer the reader to this volume's "Select Readings on Progress" for several excellent books that do.[4]

This book, while not leaving the latter issues completely unexamined, focuses more on progress as process and outcome, and the specific role of public policy in that endeavor. Though we do not debate the idea of progress, we refer to several early scholars to place our ideas and this volume in an historical context. We begin with a working assumption that progress is a valid concept for assessing the changes that have occurred and are occurring in the world—in individuals, groups, within populations or species, and as the result of human activity or of natural physical processes. Given the broad representation of contributors to this book, however, we do not wish to represent this view as one that is necessarily shared by all.

Progress in Our Three Domains

Definitions of "progress" have been discussed extensively and well in earlier literature.[5] We use the word simply to mean change (the descriptive component) for the better (the normative component), and allow each author to expand or refine that definition as they choose.[6] Ruth Schwartz Cowan and Robert Heilbroner, for example, mention choice as a criterion for progress: "Perhaps what people mean—or ought to mean—when they talk about progress is not improvements in comfort and well-being, but rather increases in the number and range of choices. By that standard, progress has certainly occurred."[7] Several authors share their concepts of differentiation or specialization of form (consistent with having choice), and the universality of knowledge or attributes. These concepts support Martin Daly and Margo Wilson's assessment of progress in evolutionary history according to several different definitions, all of which involve growth: in complexity, in intelligence or understanding (i.e., of the environment in which one must survive), and in cooperative action and expanding spheres of common cause.

Early writers on progress often enthusiastically held that progress had occurred in all domains. For example, John Adams, one of the founding fathers of the United States, wrote:

> The arts and sciences, in general, during the three or four last centuries, have had a regular course of progressive improvement. The inventions in mechanic

> arts, the discoveries in natural philosophy, navigation, and commerce, and the advancement of civilization and humanity, have occasioned changes in the condition of the world, and the human character, which would have astonished the most refined of nations of antiquity.[8]

Benjamin Franklin echoed that "I have been long impressed with the same sentiments you so well express, of the growing felicity of mankind, from the improvements in philosophy, morals, politics, and even the conveniences of common living, by the invention and acquisition of new and useful utensils and instruments, that I have sometimes almost wished that it had been my destiny to be born two or three centuries hence."[9]

The First World War, however, and several events that followed in the twentieth century, shook many people's faith in the idea of progress. Since then more scholars have tended to assert the possibility of progress in our material world, the third domain, but to express skepticism of progress in the first two domains: in ourselves and in our relations with others. As ethicist Ruth Macklin observed more than twenty years ago, "It is wholly uncontroversial to hold that technological progress has taken place; largely uncontroversial to claim that intellectual and rhetorical progress has occurred; somewhat controversial to say that aesthetic or artistic progress has taken place; and highly controversial to assert that moral progress has occurred."[10]

Hubert Locke's essay on "Faith and the Future" lends a similarly cautionary note to this volume, pointing out the contrary evidence and position that history and previous religionists have brought to bear on the subject of progress. Locke identifies one source of religion's unease about progress in the possibility of mortal humans affecting change in world conditions. He writes, "At one level, adherents are admonished to do works of compassion and justice.... But at another level, there is cynicism—and in several instances, Divine cautions—about thinking that mortals have the capacity to bring about improvement in the world."[11]

Perhaps in illustration of such divine cautions, Charles Tilly, in his contribution on progress in contentious politics, describes a continuum of countries from capitalist democracies to countries or regimes that combine a concentration of coercive means with domestic authoritarianism or beyond to those in which a dispersion of coercive means and violence "has infested domestic politics." Tilly is forced to conclude that "nowhere along that continuum can we speak of progress in contentious politics. In sheer levels of political violence, the world has actually regressed since 1940."[12]

The picture is not completely hopeless, however. Daniel Chirot, discussing ethnic warfare and genocide, acknowledges the paucity of progress but also describes a more positive view that such atrocities will diminish over time as human knowledge and experience progress and as we establish policies and institutions that serve to reduce ethnic conflict. In support of this view Chirot writes, "In short, it is possible to point to types of organization, behavior, and ideology that mitigate the retribalization of the modern world. It is particularly in societies that try to adhere to Enlightenment ideals of free exchange, democracy, and individualism that the strongest resistance can still be found to accepting a world of warring tribes."[13]

But progress in ourselves remains elusive, despite Locke's belief that religion has imposed "a continual challenge or demand that individuals live lives of higher and nobler purpose, accompanied by a set of moral norms that indicate what "higher" and "nobler" mean."[14] Religion's vision and exposition of the goals of human conduct and existence offer an alternative conception of progress. Locke suggests the religious view of progress is one of capacity or potentiality, rather than the limitless, continuous notion of the enlightenment. He cites Paul Tillich's conception, which would view progress as "a process of maturation" and would involve acquiring "deeper understanding of man's essential nature in individual and social relations."[15] Locke acknowledges as indisputable, scientific and technological advancements in our mastery of the natural world, but points out the incompleteness and inconsistencies of such mastery when it comes to human behavior and moral progress and therefore questions any declaration of general progress.

Most authors of the chapters that follow agree that there has been scientific and technological advancement over virtually any time period one would care to examine. They, like Locke, however, question whether in the absence of progress elsewhere, those achievements constitute real progress. Andrew Gordon and Tom Martin, Mihaly Csikszentmihalyi, and others raise the question: progress toward what end and at what expense? Alex Inkeles notes that despite our material progress

> There is a significant audience which does not accept the conclusion that these numerous and diverse changes in the human condition suffice to prove that we are enjoying ever wider and deeper *progress*. They question whether, within the longer life we have been granted, we enjoy more affection and love; whether we can count on being treated with respect, shielded from ridicule and degradation; whether we can savor a strong sense of community or must accept being isolated and alone; whether we feel more or less empowered; whether life brings more joys or more sorrow; or, whether we feel *in sum more or less satisfied and happy* than those who came before us, or even than we ourselves felt a decade ago.[16]

These authors point out that what really matters is not technological progress according to some abstract definition or measure, but technological progress in support of the betterment of humans and other forms of life on this planet.

There are two aspects to this ambivalence over technological progress. The first is whether technical or material progress alone constitutes progress, or whether human betterment requires progress in all domains—wider and deeper progress. Working up Maslow's hierarchy of needs, physiological needs (water, food, and shelter) require progress in our material and natural world. Intimacy needs (friendships and familial relationships) and safety needs (protection, predictability, and order) rely on progress in our relations with others, and esteem needs (self-respect, recognition) and self-actualization needs (fulfilling one's potential) fall in the domain of progress in ourselves.[17] Progress, or at least the "deeper progress" Inkeles and others speak of, may require moving further up the ladder of needs. Progress in our material world has not, as originally envisioned by several Enlightenment thinkers, trickled down (or up, in this case) to the social and moral realms.[18]

The second aspect of this ambivalence is that most changes do not bring universal benefits, especially when there are harmful side effects. Change implies a movement from the status quo, and it is unlikely that everyone will perceive this change as positive. Cowan writes that "progress needs to be made as complex, subtle and nuanced as life itself is. The same event can look both good and bad to two different beholders; indeed, it can look both good and bad to *the same* beholder; indeed, it can *be* both good and bad, both progressive and retrogressive, at the same time."[19] As Gordon and Martin remind us, "It depends on where you sit."

Albert Jonsen, in his description and exploration of progress in access to lifesaving medical technology and the role of bioethics, plainly lays out the progress dilemma: benefit against harm. He corroborates others' views that by certain measures scientific and technological progress in the past century is unquestionable, but explores further the questions raised by Gordon and Martin regarding the distribution of benefits and harm from technological changes and Csikszentmihalyi regarding the relative rates of advance between scientific and technological knowledge and our capacity to control such knowledge.

One of the more pronounced side effects of material progress has been the toll on our natural world. In contrast to historical definitions of progress as man's domination over nature, sustainability is a recurring theme throughout these chapters. San Ng and Marc Lindenberg discuss shifts in international development paradigms in the 1990s away from simple economic growth to ideas of sustainable development, which includes the environment. Inkeles, Csikszentmihalyi, and Elinor Ostrom include natural resource sustainability in their visions of progress. Richard Zerbe argues that policies that extend empathy to creatures other than humans characterize culturally progressive societies. Alison Cullen and Chris Bretherton's chapter is devoted to environmental sustainability as a goal of progress. Their chapter is not a dark prophesy of the limits to growth, reminiscent of the 1970s when the environmental movement gained momentum, but rather takes stock of our planet's resources and argues that environmental progress will require better information, changing values, and exploiting opportunities.

Instead of generating harmful side effects, universal benefits may be elusive simply because they have not been universally distributed. Scott Montgomery notes that the spread of scientific discovery "has not brought with it, in a glittering wake, any specific improvements in human welfare, practically speaking, nor in a more rational distribution of opportunity, privilege, health, wealth, and happiness."[20]

In sum, most of the authors that follow agree that there has been extensive technological and scientific progress over virtually any time period in human history. But there are several cautions that the pace and magnitude of progress in our material world too frequently out distance progress in the other two domains and that this very technical progress—unsupported by moral and cultural progress—threatens to undermine overall progress. What then, is the role of policy in managing this imbalance?

The Role of Policy in Progressive Change: Assertions

In our view, progressive change is a function of the presence or absence, in isolation or in combination, of a variety of enabling or constraining attributes. In broad terms these attributes are the product of either biology or culture. Human progress is, essentially, the process of improving and increasing our understanding and control over these attributes. Of particular importance to our overall inquiry into policy and progress are two questions, which lead us to two assertions. The first is whether and how institutions and public policy affect progressive change? The second, to what extent is human nature the product of social formation and experience, and therefore susceptible to institutional influences, versus being the product of nature (i.e., human evolution)?[21]

Our assertions are first, public policy does affect progressive change through its ability to create or alter incentives and thereby human behavior, and second, human nature, while not immutable, is not changed on any meaningful timescale for affecting progress through this means. We hold more to the view expressed by philosopher Mortimer Adler[22] on the theory of progress in a dialectic of history: "The progress which the successive stages of history represent resides in the quality of human institutions rather than in the nature of man. If more economic justice or greater political liberty is achieved, it is not because the later generations of men are born with a nature more disposed to goodness or virtue, but because better institutions have evolved from the conflict of historical forces."[23]

Producing institutions that enable progress in a large number of areas depends on our ability to understand the constraints under which the institutions must work. If human nature is fixed, absolutely or according to any meaningful time frame, then policy must reflect and work with this reality and not be swayed by the false promises of utopian ideals.

Biological Constraints: Is Human Nature Mutable?

There have been several periods when "The concept of controlling human behavior, even shaping human nature, to ensure that men would pursue their own secular happiness efficiently became familiar."[24] Drawing on his two categories of progress scholars, Nisbet wrote that "progress as freedom" writers dealt with individuals as they actually are, whereas for "progress as power" thinkers, freedom is inseparable "from the creation through absolute power if necessary of a new type of human being."[25] From a contemporary perspective, the authors gathered here, when they address the subject, provide a two-sided message. On the one hand, human nature is the product of, and therefore limited by, evolutionary processes. On the other hand, there may be more to our initial evolutionary endowments than previously represented and these endowments might be pressing humans toward social progress. Daly and Wilson suggest that human nature has evolved under selection and as outcomes of that evolutionary process humans exhibit psychological attributes involving social comparison (equity) and in and out-group formation, or an us-versus-them capacity, which allows for moral consideration (justice) and alliance formation (cooperation) with other individuals or groups. Moreover, these attributes have contributed to the survival of the species. Others suggest similar conclusions:

> Countless studies of animal species, whose instinctive behavior is unobscured by cultural elaboration, have shown that membership in dominance orders pays off in survival and lifetime reproductive success.
>
> E. O. Wilson[26]

> In addition, various types of altruistic behavior, among the adult and elderly members of human and nonhuman animal groups that on the surface may not seem to be related to reproductive success per se (Simonds 1974, 128-133), have been demonstrated to add to the survival of the group.
>
> Abhijit Guha[27]

> Extreme advance in the ability to perceive and react to the environment is perhaps the most fundamental characteristic which marks off Homo sapiens from all other animals. Symbolic language, complex social organization, control over the environment, the ability to envisage future states and to work toward them, and values and ethics are developments made possible by the human's greatly developed capacity to obtain and organize information about the state of the environment.
>
> Francisco J. Ayala[28]

Even Darwin, whose theory of biological evolution was not intended to translate to social progress "does affirm that man 'is capable of incomparably greater and more rapid improvement than is any other animal.'"[29]

It is also the case, however, that the evolutionary development of these attributes has taken place over millennia and many generations. To put this in concrete terms, Daly and Wilson regularly use the term "geological time." Any progress on social issues of concern that would be based on change in human nature would likely require millennia more and continued evolutionary pressure for a sustained change in our nature. Such sustained pressure could be aided by some major biological innovation that is currently at work or the presence of pressure from some co-evolving species or from within our own species.

Nature is full of surprises, however, and regressive pressures could also appear or be at work, leading human nature away from justice, or cooperation, for example.[30] No guarantees are part of the

> blind, creative, Darwinian process. Evolution's arrow (if such a thing exists) does not point toward the abolition of pain and suffering. Evolution by selection *invented* pain and suffering as motivational devices that encourage fitness-promoting behavior. Neither does the evolutionary process tend to produce an ever-increasing stock of human happiness.... Like suffering, pleasure is regulated and is *fleeting by design*, because chronic satisfaction would be counterproductive for an organism whose prospects for increasing its expected future fitness must ever entail striving after goals as yet unattained.[31]

Social Constraints: The Role for Policy

Regardless of the answer to the question of the mutability of human nature, overemphasizing human evolution fails to capture all the dimensions of progress. Although all forms of progress arguably involve the biological attributes of individuals, progress relies on for its existence and propagation myriad intellectual and physical relationships with natural and cultural environments, and most significantly those among humans. These relationships are governed and played out according to formal and informal rules and customs. Institutions, which include public policy, are these rules that define and regulate the societal order in which individuals learn, think, promote their ideas, form groups, coordinate actions, take risks, resolve differences, and produce progress.

We are asserting that there is now and always has been, albeit under different names, a role for policy in the creation of progressive change. As William Zumeta reminds us, "that the goal of collective action, or public policy, is to help a society achieve or improve according to some standard of performance, either by remedying felt problems or taking advantage of opportunities."[32] This view, of course, varies considerably from some philosophers of progress—including Adam Smith, William Godwin, and Herbert Spencer—who believed that progress, as individual freedom, implied no government and in some cases, no civil collective action.[33] The "staunch cultural relativist, A. L. Kroeber, remarked about cultural progress: 'The deep-seated, blind and intricate forces that shape culture, also mold the so-called creative leaders of society as essentially as they mold the mass of humanity. Progress, so far as it can objectively be considered to be such, is something that makes itself. We do not make it.' (Kroeber 1923: 133) Darwin's idea of evolutionary progress is very similar to this notion of gradual transformation without any controlling agency."[34]

At the other extreme, exemplified by the views of Hegel, Marx, and Rousseau, were philosophers who believed that progress was achieved, indeed defined, via the power of the perfect state, even at the expense of individual freedom.[35] Others, such as John Stuart Mill, while stressing progress as individual freedom, conceded a government role in distributing wealth, but not producing it.[36] "Saint-Pierre's arguments depended on the power of human reason, correctly focused and directed, to devise policies for ensuring human happiness. His system involved punishments and rewards to channel behavior toward useful pleasure and away from antisocial vice and depended on the support of strong governments."[37]

Institutions may be formal or informal and are distinct from organizations. An organization is a group of people brought together for a common purpose—one component of which is inevitably the creation of institutions—and institutions are the governing principles, laws, and rules in which the people within an organization function.[38] Thus, the Congress, the Court, the Church and the Tribe are not institutions in this construct, but the Constitution, federal, state and local law, Vatican II, and cultural norms are. Public policies are institutions. Moreover, though we tend to think of public policy as most directly being the realm of government, as Dobel and Anderson note, it is the product of "a coordinated pattern of actions across the society" involving all individuals.[39] Csikszentmihalyi, Zerbe, and Gordon and Martin refer to "memes," or the cultural traits handed down between generations. A subset of these memes could perhaps include and be considered a culture's most fundamental institutions.

Our view is that the processes of human induced creation and change occur within a cultural sub-context of institutions. Institutions enable and constrain human behavior. They create incentives and disincentives for individuals, families and organizations, among other things, to form themselves, and invest their time and resources (or not depending on the prevailing institutions) in the activities from whence progress comes. Creating, eliminating, or altering institutions results, via a change in constraints and incentives, in changes in behavior and consequently affects the rate and direction of progressive change. Absent certain policy influences, such as assigning and protecting property rights, support for the efficient and free flow of information, taxation, and resource allocation toward research institutes and education, the rate of idea creation, development, dissemination and adoption, and therefore the speed of progressive change, slows measurably. For example, as Zumeta notes in this volume "Where a strong commitment [to education] exists, it is usually codified in constitutions, laws and funding arrangements."[40]

To be clear, this institutional sub-context does not exclusively determine or guarantee individual or group behavior, let alone progress, but it is present in virtually every action and decision made by humans today. Several authors remind us of the often subtle complementary interworkings of policies that are necessary to achieve progress. Discussing the role of public investment in education and beneficial economic outcomes Zumeta writes, "investments in education by themselves do not guarantee any salutary outcome unless they are accompanied by complementary investments and policies, including efforts to stimulate exports or other sources of private sector growth."[41]

Political and economic institutional differences between the economically advanced and less advanced nations are more and more frequently called out as explanatory factors in the relative conditions of these nations.[42] Others describe how the wrong institutions can have and have had disastrous effects, altering incentive structures to the point of war or complete resource destruction. John Adams recognized the importance of getting institutions right: "The institutions now made in America will not wholly wear out for thousands of years. It is of the last importance, then, that they should begin right. If they set out wrong, they will never be able to return, unless it be by accident, to the right path."[43]

We further assert that this institutional framework holds across cultures and time. Early agrarian communities, bound by kinship and religious precepts, were no less enabled or constrained by an institutional framework than more modern communities. The differences are ones of formality and complexity of the institutional environment, but not in the existence of institutions. Similarly across the globe, with perhaps some extreme exceptions, individuals and communities, organizations, tribes and nations all operate according to some set of formal and informal rules.

Assuming then that the biological attributes of human nature are practically fixed, progressive change will vary according to cultural attributes, particularly with the quality and appropriateness of the prevailing institutions. Based on these assertions we return to our original questions: what institutions enable progressive change, and what processes are most likely to yield them? We acknowledge that to answer these questions for the manifold problems we face and cultures in which we face them would be to provide a road map to progress in all three domains, and could well be considered a utopian vision.

A Theory of Progressive Change: Propositions

The authors that follow present a broad picture of what progress is, or might be considered to be, and where progress has occurred or has not. There are also glimpses into which institutions have been enabling and which have not. Finally they provide a number of insights into what sorts of necessary conditions, organizational structures, and processes enable progressive change and what sorts do not. Although by no means an exhaustive description of their insights or of the processes and nature of policy and progress, we have gathered what we perceive to be the dominant themes under four categories: specialization and differentiation, universality, complexity, and knowledge.[44] There is significant overlap among the workings of these four terms, in that the first two are processes that yield the latter two.

We offer the following propositions summarizing the themes and their role in both promoting and characterizing progress, and evidence to support them from the chapters that follow. Specifically, we propose:

> 1. Specialization and differentiation. These are the two fundamental processes driving progressive change in most human and natural systems.

Progressive policy allows experimentation that promotes differentiation of knowledge, technique, organizational structure, and institutions. Specialization and differentiation can also lead to regressive outcomes if unconstrained.

> 2. Universality. Progress is often not recognized until the change is "universally" expressed or adopted by a population.

Progressive policy enables universality by disseminating, redistributing and contesting ideas, knowledge, and opportunities. Relative imbalances, inequities, overspecialization, and outright blockages in the distribution of knowledge and progressive change diminish and, in some cases, nullify the spread of progress in and among all domains.

> 3. Complexity. Progressive systems are often complex: they promote diversity and change via specialization and differentiation and simultaneously disseminate and mediate what is often a disruptive change.

Progressive policy and organizational structures embody the means for efficient and equitable resolution of the tension between the diversity and change that represents progress and the universal adoption of change that makes progress so. Such systems, whether small or large, and singular in focus or of general purpose, embody complexity. They are often the product of human institutions, which need to adapt in complexity to the complexity of the problem for which they are designed. They also tend to be stable and sustainable. Progressive policies and systems reach maturity and full effect because they embody sustainability, in a self-regulating way or according to natural constraints, not maximization.

> 4. Know Thyself. Knowledge, particularly self-knowledge, remains the engine of progress and the source of beneficial and appropriate policy.

Progressive policies require self-knowledge. The world abounds with change, but we are confronted with evidence that most of it does little to resolve what might be considered Earth's most intractable physical and cultural problems. At the root of many of those problems lies the nature and behavior of humans. Of the greatest importance for progress in ourselves and in our relations with others, and for controlling progress in technology and the material world, is greater knowledge, and thereby control, of ourselves, our nature and behavior, both as individuals and as participants in collective action problems.

1. Specialization and Differentiation

A variety of circumstances and processes, including purposeful experimentation, experience, and chance association, yield advances in knowledge, technique, organizational structure, technology, and institutions. Among the more systemic of these are specialization and differentiation. Biologically, specialization and differentiation create diversity and the subsequent ability or inability of species to withstand shocks, adapt to changes, and compete. Modern social and physical sciences and engineering have also undergone extreme specialization among subfields to yield our current immense stocks of knowledge and technical capacities. Economically, it is a driver of trade, wealth, knowledge, and technical capacity. Through specialization individuals and countries are able to concentrate their abilities to their advantage. In *The Wealth of Nations* in 1776, Adam Smith described the extraordinary production made possible by dividing the work of pin manufacturing into specialized tasks. Workers would develop heightened skills at their task, allowing them as a group to produce far more pins than had each made the entire pin themselves.

Specialization and differentiation occur in all areas of human endeavor. As stand alone works, individual creations of literature, music, or art are difficult to imagine along a continuum of progress. But as Charles Johnson describes in his essay the forms and subjects of art do change and can be assessed in terms of progressive criteria. Just as Daly and Wilson and Csikszentmihalyi consider processes and definitions involving differentiation and complexity, so too Johnson writes of the differentiation in form of the novel that occurred in the eighteenth and nineteenth centuries. He attributes much of this change to environmental factors in which authors and readers found themselves throughout the period. As if discussing the evolution of a species, Johnson briefly describes the evolution and dominant ascendance of the short story complete with ancestral predecessors and related but now minor "short prose" cousins. He further suggests that "characterization in twentieth century fiction advances beyond much of what appeared in nineteenth century literature, where too often characters were defined one-dimensionally by a single, dominant emotion or trait ... and thereby left much to be desired in terms of human complexity."[45]

Historically, Herbert Spencer, strongly influenced by Darwin, is most associated with the idea of differentiation as a theory of social progress.[46] In 1857 Spencer wrote:

> Now, we propose in the first place to show that this law of organic progress is

aries will provide a clear view of the world as it really is, not as it appears through the lens of ideology and religious dogma, or as a myopic response solely to immediate need."[52]

Montgomery describes how the production of scientific knowledge has evolved to its current state as a complex system of specialized fields and sub-fields funded by industry, government, and private foundations, and directed by a blend of government, industry, universities, institutes, and scientists themselves. Analogously to the capital creating market system and perhaps the political and judicial systems, the knowledge creating scientific system works within a set of institutions that don't, or can't, quite control the process and products of the system. As Jonsen points out, scientific practices and discoveries also frequently put society in uncomfortable ethical positions. And as Montgomery carries forward, the questions are not just ethical, but socio-political and therefore policy questions:

> At base, progress in natural science increases the span of human power, and this power has many possible dimensions, even those that extend beyond the simple dichotomy of Promethean fires and Pandoran boxes. There is no simple formula for understanding, predicting, or even controlling the direction of progress in natural science as a supra-national phenomenon of mind, nor is there ever likely to be—despite centuries of attempts by individuals, groups, and governments to do so.[53]

Montgomery identifies the desire, and legitimacy in a democratic system, of policy makers and the public to understand scientific knowledge sufficiently to enable intelligent decision making. He also doubts that a sufficiently universal understanding of much of scientific knowledge will ever occur, due to the difficulty and volume of the subject area. He doubts whether even scientists can have a good command of all the key concepts and basic principles of science. This is an issue not only of understanding the parts but also the whole. Montgomery asserts, "Specialization, in other words, has also meant that there is no longer any fixed, single definition of the material world, one scale of reality into which all others can be collapsed."[54] He contends science, at least, is not headed for some fundamental unity.

The effect of this on policy making is profound as our elected and non-elected policy makers, including our scientists, all too frequently understand too little about the specialized issues at hand. Policy making under these circumstances becomes adjudication of the competing claims of specialists, many of whom are in the employ of wealthy special interest groups. For citizens the incomprehensibility of biological and environmental systems and policies all but ensures confusion over whom to trust and what the best solution is. It also makes citizens susceptible to the partial truths offered by proponent and opponent alike.

Despite this Montgomery also makes a counterclaim to the idea that specialization leads to ever-greater difficulties in understanding the work of others, suggesting that specialization has also "led to an increasing amount of cross-fertilization as well as divergence."[55] These views illustrate the subjective neutrality, as well as the tension inherent, in these processes. Fortunately, specialization and differentiation are not the only processes at work. There are also processes of dissemination, integration, and rejection that are necessary for change to become universally adopted.

2. Universality

Universality is the integrating counterpart to the diversity created through differentiation and specialization. From an evolutionary perspective Daly and Wilson use the term fixation to describe the state of universal expression of an attribute within a population. From a cultural perspective universality implies the active adoption of changes and the modification of behavior. As Cullen and Bretherton argue, the fruits of progressive change are "achievable only through billions of everyday decisions in its favor by individuals, populations and leaders in all sectors."[56] Universality is intended to capture the process by which individuals come to embody or live by a common set of principles or attributes that then express themselves within an entire population. It is particularly relevant to our ability to define and measure progress or what principles, events, and conditions represent progress.

Progress does not occur, we are arguing, unless the benefits or advantages of a progressive change or attribute spread universally among a population. Public policy affects universality in every domain through its role in establishing rules, setting standards, resolving disputes, and building consensus, channeling resources, providing access to education, information and experiences, protecting and preserving ideas, and allowing for choice. Universality is dependent on the interplay of several processes: dissemination and integration, equality, and relativism.

Dissemination and Integration

Dissemination refers to the spread of moral, ethical, political, and other principles for conducting our affairs, delivering information about benefits, costs, and risks for making decisions, and the fundamental transmission of the world's stock of knowledge or the latest finding from one generation or individual to the next to again begin the cycle of differentiation and change.[57] Dissemination is a necessary, but not sufficient process for universality, which also depends on integration. Across cultures there are large differences in capacities to disseminate, evaluate, and adopt new information and changes. Formal and informal institutional differences in the form of systems supporting education, the media, the arts, industry, and other sectors, play an important role in the critical process of determining which progressive changes gain traction (that is, lead to integration) and which do not.

Johnson effectively identifies three conditions whose presence stood in the way of the development of the novel, simultaneously pointing to the ways in which institutions in a variety of settings have or have not changed to permit this very same development: the widespread illiteracy of the population, the belief that knowledge or an understanding of the workings of the world can come through experience as opposed to revelation, and finally a mass market for stories about the lives of classes other than the elites. Today, although the place of the novel at least in most cultures is firmly established, there are still constraints to the dissemination of art. From a policy perspective Johnson leaves us with the admonition to continue to provide public support to authors, and presumably to all artists. The plea is not to simply guarantee a supply of entertaining fiction or guarantee an income to minor talents, but rather to ensure that "ephemeral fashions and social whims"[58] as directed through the marketplace do not replace critical standards for which work can exist and which cannot. Without support we risk preempting the creation of major works of art.

Johnson's example points to the fundamental importance of public policies aimed at providing education: "Condorcet stresses the importance of educating every possible individual in the laws and techniques of science [and the arts] in order to spread scientific knowledge and discovery as widely in the world's population as is possible."[59] "And Malthus is one with Adam Smith, Godwin, and Condorcet in emphasis upon the indispensable role that must be played by education: education through schools made available by political government for the entirety of the people."[60] As Richard Brandon notes, we are now realizing that learning begins at birth and "the 'pre-school' years constitute a vital first step in a continuous process of learning and development."[61] Zumeta lists the "social spillover" benefits from educating the populace as: improved labor force capacity to innovate and adapt to change including the adaptations necessary for technological change and economic growth; gains in tolerance or acceptance of others different from oneself; creation of larger markets for artistic and cultural productions; and improved capacity to understand complex systems and relationships such as those between human societies and the natural world."[62]

Other examples of necessary institutions for broad and open dissemination of progressive change abound: protection of property rights, free markets, freedom of association and movement, and freedom of the press to name but a few. The institutions enabling free dissemination of information, ideologies, goods, and the other byproducts of progressive change, once again, are a necessary but insufficient condition to guarantee progress. Cullen and Bretherton note that "In today's world, we obtain information from such diverse sources as conversation, television, the Internet, schools, pricing schemes, and government mandated labels."[63] But despite a multiplicity of sources, they lament the paucity of information about the environment that is disseminated, relative to the amount of scientific research that takes place. Increasingly the media are the prime disseminators of current information. As Margaret Gordon observes, the media's role in deciding what to report, and how to report it, becomes even more critical with the specialized and sheer volume of information available.

But, Margaret Gordon warns, we can no longer count on the press "to educate people about the news of the day." It is true that "journalists have access to more information than most of the rest of us, and we count on them to sift, filter, and review it and to summarize for us what is most important." But, "When scientists hold conflicting views, the mass media find it hard to assess their judgment and credentials, and those with more sensational claims of hazard are likely to be featured."[64] Cullen and Bretherton likewise believe that "the media cover scientific and technological findings, simplifying complex issues skillfully, [but] they often focus on controversy, sensation and extremes in order to maintain an audience."[65] This tendency can lead to a misallocation of scarce time and resources toward the sensational problems at the expense of what the body of information available at the time might indicate as the real problem.

These points raise a number of issues concerning how producers of information, technology or other kinds of progressive changes decide which are worth disseminating and which individuals or groups are appropriate to receive the change. The interactive journalism experiments described by Margaret Gordon are designed to "reconnect" the news media with an alienated public by providing readers, viewers, and listeners with the information they want and need for participating in civic life and governance at both the national and local levels. This means that the news may be increasingly varied from community to community, and person to person as online forms and web sites allow almost complete personalization. Ostrom makes similar points regarding the value of local knowledge and approaches in defining and resolving many collective action problems, suggesting the relevant population is frequently smaller or more localized than we have a tendency to believe. An institutional regime for managing forest lands, for example, need not be, and perhaps should not be, national in scope. This large-scale approach increases the likelihood that policy will be less appropriate for the local conditions and that the costs associated with disseminating and adopting the regime will be higher. Margaret Gordon and Ostrom agree that for further progress to be realized the lessons from local experiments need to be disseminated, adapted, and adopted elsewhere when appropriate. Margaret Gordon predicts, "If the changes in the cultures of newsrooms discussed here continue to broaden so that they include the largest markets and to deepen so that they regularly incorporate daily news coverage—not just special projects—the impacts could increase geometrically, and they could be profound."[66]

Equality

In the historical idea of progress some measure of equality has been essential, if not for reasons of morality or compassion, then for the theoretical possibility of achieving the perfection of man. According to Condorcet, when the benefits of human reason are distributed to every member of the race, then we can speak of the perfection of mankind. Progress requires "the abolition of inequality between nations" as well as "the progress of equality within each nation."

More recent commentators such as twentieth century economist Henry George tend to be less concerned with visions of perfectibility, and more concerned with equity as an issue of resource distribution. "Why," George asked, "amid all the incontestable evidences of the progress of mankind, does the misery of the poor increase almost in direct proportion to progress in technology, science, government, the arts, and so many spheres of the social order?"[67] In this volume, Brandon defines progress as "reducing the disparities in levels of well being among different groups of children and families."[68] Philosophers have differed on how equal equality should be in pursuit of progress. Rousseau wanted to end all inequality: "If it is good to know how to deal with men as they are, it is much better to make them what there is need that they should be. The most absolute authority is that which penetrates into a man's inmost being, and concerns itself no less with his will than his actions."[69] Other philosophers, such as Marx and Hegel, expressed their dedication to complete equality, both in access and outcomes, in the doctrines of socialism.

Others argued for preserving some differences: "It is not absolute, total equality that Condorcet seeks and predicts for the future; not a levelling of human beings for its own sake.... [Condorcet] took note of the importance of preserving the possibility of those inequalities which will be 'useful to the interest of all.'"[70] Like the founding fathers, his concerns were about inequality of wealth, condition, and instruction. Condorcet writes, "It will behoove us, then to show that these three sorts of real inequality are bound to diminish continually, without, however, disappearing altogether; for they have natural and necessary causes which it would be absurd and dangerous to wish to destroy; nor could we even attempt to destroy their effects entirely without opening up more fruitful sources of inequality, without giving to human rights a more direct and fatal blow."[71] "The equality that he forsees is not a sterile uniformity, but a 'condition in which everyone will have the knowledge necessary to conduct himself in the ordinary affairs of life, according to the light of his own reason.'"[72] Likewise, Mill hoped "that the gross inequalities among individuals and also nations would through the continuation of progress eventually disappear, leaving only those inequalities which are natural and creative."[73] It is these very inequalities, we suggest, that give rise to specialization and differentiation.

For all of these writers, equality extended beyond material wealth to knowledge, values, and access. Zumeta argues that some commitment to equity in allocating educational opportunities is essential "because education is so fundamental to individual and societal welfare and aspirations."[74] But Brandon reminds us of how far away we are from international equity as disparities grow among countries in measures of child well-being and access to early learning opportunities.[75] Condorcet's confidence in the future destiny of man rested on his belief that not only European science and technology but also the high moral principles recently discovered in France will be disseminated around the globe by modern communication.[76] Muhammad Yunus, in this volume, holds out similar hopes that the universal spread of information technology will alleviate poverty and reduce disparities among nations. Gordon and Martin, however, make clear that the distribution of technology or its benefits is not now, and has never been, universal. One explanation for this is the workings of the market, which relies on price signals for its distributional logic. They, like Montgomery and others, also point to the role of scarce governmental or private philanthropic dollars as a major obstacle to greater distribution in the face of market failure. But they also look to society and governments to organize themselves and create the appropriate rules to allow greater sharing of the benefits.

Relativism

People's willingness to integrate and follow a set of guidelines is often a function of their feelings of equity and fairness—how they perceive their situation relative to others.[77] Dobel and Anderson note that individuals tend to assess their progress both over time, against their own baselines, and across space, relative to others. As Daly and Wilson note, humans engage in social comparison.[78]

Absolute material progress, aspired to by many, has not brought the expected returns in happiness. In 1960 Inkeles found that "national populations had a culturally fixed tendency to report themselves as happy or unhappy, and a rise in the standard of living was not automatically reflected in an increase in the proportion who reported life satisfaction." Inkeles offers an example from Richard Easterlin, who found that despite a per capita income in 1987 five times as great as 1957, the typical Japanese respondent reported themselves to be no happier or more satisfied with life. Money can buy happiness, Easterlin seems to be saying, but only if the amounts get bigger and other people aren't getting more.[79] More recently, research in behavioral economics has supported the idea that individuals have "reference-based preferences" and assess their well being "by changes in circumstances, not merely absolute levels."[80]

Our inability to establish absolutes, or universal definitions of progress (or the pace at which we establish universality) might stand as the greatest constraint to achieving more progress more rapidly. In his thoughtful contemporary book on historical change, Raymond Gastil concludes that "As long as relativism reigns unadorned as a universal solvent of values, individual and collective, neither progress nor any other system for overcoming despair can be a success."[81] This is due in part to the fact that the benefits and costs of progress are never fully known, fully articulated, fully perceived, fully accepted, or evenly distributed across all populations. And yet achieving integration, or "universal" adoption, of a progressive change within populations or subpopulations does occur and is a necessary part of the process of progress.

One of Western society's mechanisms for dealing with differing values around change is through established, protected institutional means of sharing information, educating the populace, public deliberation, and decision making that frequently culminates in policy creation. Part of this process is the process of society finding its common core values and translating them into society's informal and formal institutions: "Values come to us through a variety of ways, including through experience, by rote learning, and from friends and leaders we esteem. Shifts in values bring about profound changes not only in decision making at every level, but also in our perception of the costs and benefits of these changes ... the combined values of multiple individuals collectively influence institutional decision making."[82]

Jonsen cites the field of bioethics as an example of this process: "Bioethics is the study of the moral ambiguity of medical progress."[83] He points out how articulating ethical issues, "such as respect for the individual and fairness in distributing the goods of a community,"[84] helps shape public debate and policy formation. In addition to often times providing a vocabulary and forms of argument to enable discussion of complex ethical and medical issues by researchers, practitioners, policy makers, and patients, bioethicists provide a specialized knowledge that might alternatively serve to counterbalance, articulate, legitimate, and translate the viewpoints of participants in the debate. Their role is predicated on the philosophical notion of fallibility and the fact of "reasonable pluralism" among us.[85] Good, progressive policy reflects these conditions by deliberating and resolving the diverse moral and other views of participants into a practical solution given the conditions of the day.

Ruth Macklin, and Zerbe in this volume, further emphasize the place of moral and ethical principles in defining progress. Macklin's principles are based on humaneness (intolerance to pain and suffering) and humanity (recognition of the inherent dignity, basic autonomy, and intrinsic worth of human beings); Zerbe's on a similar set of universal human rights consistent with empathy. Both argue that cultures that design institutions to further these principles are more progressive than cultures that do not:

> If humans have a demonstrable psychological need for a degree of individual freedom—the preservation of their autonomy and dignity—then a society that ensures or promotes such freedom and dignity in its laws and moral beliefs is more morally progressed than one which fails to secure these needs for its members. Similarly, a society that tolerates less pain and suffering of its members by ensuring that no one starves or lacks necessary medical care is more morally progressed than one that allows even the basic human needs to remain unsatisfied.[86]

Chirot, writing on genocide, identifies the potential within the ideal of individualism for making individual rights supercede group rights, thus making it more difficult, or even immoral, for whole groups to be treated as indivisible enemies. The historical record, however, reveals the difficulty of overcoming the tension between the drive of a dominant, perhaps larger group to achieve universal control and adoption of its ethos and legitimacy, and that of a minority group to differentiate itself. Moreover, because of the sway of individual leaders and the control of information and knowledge, institutional frameworks and ideologies that might alleviate such tensions, even if generally agreed to among large segments of a population, may not be implemented. Chirot contends, "We know what works to lessen ethnic conflict, but we do not know how to make certain that the right policies are applied when leaders, ruling ideologies, or popular opinion reject such solutions.[87]

Some would argue that all states—though not all individuals—are willing to accept at least a core set of rights and binding duties. The global community has spent the last fifty years painstakingly writing compacts that define an emerging consensus upon issues as diverse as human rights and war crimes. These rights are listed in the human rights treaties as "non-derogable" and include prohibiting the use of force, genocide, racial discrimination, crimes against humanity, and trade in slaves and piracy.[88] Of course, as Christina Cerna observes, "A state's ratification of an international human rights instrument is not sufficient evidence that the state, in fact, observes the provisions of that instrument...[but] evidence of a state's intent to be legally bound by the provisions of that instrument."[89]

The process of formally recognizing a set of human rights, described by Ng and Lindenberg, has been fitful, but reflects the possibility of a global ethic that can frame thinking on many issues. As an example, Ng and Lindenberg discuss a new rights-based approach (RBA) informing international development NGO activities, which is given formal status through the international legal system. The RBA was inspired by Nobel laureate Amartya Sen's "capability" approach to poverty alleviation, that stresses equipping individuals with the ability to lead the life they value. Two hundred years later, this echoes Condorcet's "condition in which everyone will have the knowledge necessary to conduct himself in the ordinary affairs of life, according to the light of his own reason." The legal framework of human rights may give current development practitioners, using a Rawlsian metric of progress that requires improving the lives of the worst off, the missing vehicle for achieving universality.

Whether or not a rights-based approach to development ultimately achieves some progress by reducing disparities and alleviating poverty remains to be seen. But as Daly and Wilson conclude, we have "not been selected to tolerate relative disadvantage." Inequitable access to resources motivates people to change their situations by both individual and collective action. The authors see hope for social progress because we resent injustice, precisely because the Darwinian process favors those who look out for their own interests and those of their family.

Achieving universality is perhaps the most difficult task in achieving progress. The forces of specialization and differentiation persist as resources continue to be allocated toward the development of the new to gain advantage and solve problems. For progress to occur the mass of these changes must be put into effect and evaluated and their benefits must be spread to the relevant population in a way that the group feels is equitable. As the discussion above indicates this occurs, to the extent that it occurs, through countless organizations held together in overlapping systems of institutional rules and principles. It is by combining these two forces—differentiation and universality—that complexity emerges.

3. Complex Institutions for Complex Problems

To this point we have discussed specialization and differentiation, two of the fundamental processes of progressive change, and universality and dissemination, the complementary processes enabling the integration of change into our lives. These processes are systems, which, in many respects, defy complete description. What we assert, however, is that they work according to principles and rules. For natural systems these principles and rules are the laws of nature, for human-created systems they are captured in what we are defining as formal and informal institutions. Regardless of scale or place in the great mix of systems that populate our existence, whether considered individually or in their entirety, some of the most progressive of these systems embody complexity.

From Specialization to Complexity

Spencer, Darwin and other early writers referred more often to specialization and less often to complexity. Although specialization yields the differentiated forms, ideas, and processes that make up complexity, it does not by itself create complexity. Complexity is intended to capture notions of higher degrees of web-like interdependence among and within systems, processes, and forms involved in change. Complex systems consist of specialized but integrated components. Complexity is formed, and progress occurs in part, when the outcomes of individual lineages of differentiation are integrated with others to form new plateaus from which further differentiation will occur. This notion of higher orders of interdependence and integration manifests itself in systems and forms with higher functionality, stability, flexibility, responsiveness, adaptability, and survivability. Thus, even as subsystems may become more specialized, due to their integration into higher systemic orders, the overall system becomes more sustainable. Complex systems are characterized by and enable richness, abundance and diversity within the physical or temporal limits of their resources. Examples abound, the human body, the earth's ecosystems and its atmosphere, the market, the computer, the automobile, the United States Constitution, democracy, plastic, and cities to name only a few.

The image of innumerable differentiation processes occurring simultaneously, producing a multitude of outcomes, which are in turn rejected or integrated into multiple layers of pre-existing or newly formed systems, subsystems, and forms suggests complexity. It also suggests how different outcomes can be viewed as both progressive or not, depending on one's perspective or level of analysis. It is possible to argue, for example, that at one level the lineages of specialization, differentiation, and integration that have yielded the automobile and its mass production are complex and represent progress. From a higher level perspective, however, several of the automobile's attributes are poorly integrated into the earth's ecosystems, implying that those systems are not as sustainable or progressive as they could be. Both conclusions can be true and may simply point to a future time when the processes of differentiation and innovation yield a superior, complex, and more highly integrated form of transportation.

Complexity in the sense intended here should not be confused with disorder and chaos, or impenetrability and inefficiency. Each complex form or system is often highly ordered and might work according to some fairly simple principles and processes. It can also be made up of some fairly simple component pieces upon analysis, but as an integrated operating whole, producing multiple effects, it may defy complete understanding or description. The sum is greater than the parts. The multiple levels at which most systems are integrated and the degree of interdependence with other systems produces an almost exponential growth in possible outcomes. A good example of this is the United State Constitution, which as an institution provides the structure and rules for a government and society that is founded on relatively simple principles, processes, and component pieces, such as the balance of powers and freedom of speech, election of representatives and the securing of property rights via the registration of patents, and the three branches of government and church and state. Yet even to describe the full diversity of the organizations and activities, let alone the effects, which the Constitution enables is impossible.

Heilbroner's paper describes the development of another complex system: capitalism. The market is complex in its makeup of component subsystems, coordinating inputs and relationships, transferring information, and creating value, and in its ability to adapt to a variety of social and political environments. It is integrated via a fairly simple set of individual incentives and exchange rules (property rights) that are commonly understood by the participants. Heilbroner points out that capitalism has evolved, for example, with the public sector as a counterweight and guide to the private sector. In support of the notion of flexibility, adaptability, and diversity, he notes the presence in all capitalisms of differentiated national cultures. Similarly, in answering the question of the capability of capitalism to give rise to a progressive society, Heilbroner identifies its potential to develop "in more than one socio-political direction."[90] In the end, however, it is not clear that we currently possess the knowledge to expand the potential of capitalism beyond its primary function of economic growth.

Complexity of Institutions

There is considerable overlap and evidence within the chapters that progressive institutions will both embody and enable the development of a complexity that helps to ensure robustness and adaptability, but that is also appropriate for the culture, groups, and individuals who must live with them and for the diverse conditions in and for which they must be used. Institutions should create an environment in which the discontented problem-solver (i.e., nearly all humans) is encouraged to experiment with differentiated forms and solutions while simultaneously providing the means to disseminate and judge the outcomes. This does not imply institutional structures that purposefully lead to the mindless pursuit of change and complexity for complexity's sake—though we have that too. It rather implies establishing institutions that create greater individual opportunity and choice commensurate with the problems faced and in accord with fundamental natural and cultural principles.

It also implies that complex problems are more likely to require complex institutions to manage them. As Ostrom writes, "Studying [locally created common-pool resource management] rule systems leads to a recognition of the complexity of situations that individuals face and the consequent complexity of the rule systems they devise."[91] These locally created rule systems meet the test of cultural and problem-specific appropriateness. To the extent that they are also solving the problem, they are successful and could be considered progress.

In general, Ostrom argues the way to progress is through ongoing experimentation in policy and practice. More specifically, it is through repeated innovation and practice by decentralized groups more than policy analysis by the center that progress occurs. Ostrom indicates that in the United States at least in the latter half of the twentieth century and at least in the areas of education and common-pool resource management, we have trended toward centralization and consolidation of organizations, policy decision making, and experimentation. Zumeta likewise argues that for education, "decentralization can increase academic autonomy and at least the potential for innovation and rapid responsiveness."[92] He notes that the federal government's efforts towards standardized testing may conflict with efforts to expand local school choice. For early child education, Brandon believes that "the American predilection for parental choice in education and in the nurturing of young children makes progress toward universality more likely to come from providing financial access to a diverse set of providers than from instituting a single state or national service system."[93] Cullen and Bretherton provide similar evidence describing how centralized command and control regulations can "[stifle] innovation by prescribing technology rather than performance standards."[94] They point out, however, that these are slowly being replaced by incentive-based programs that recognize a firm's advantages in identifying the means of reducing their own pollution. The Front Porch Forum described by Margaret Gordon is an experiment in public journalism designed to encourage civic participation and the responsiveness of the local media to citizen concerns. Ng and Lindenberg emphasize the decentralization of NGOs to allow for flexibility and experimentation in overseas field offices.

Ostrom suggests that the trend toward centralization has begun to reverse itself as the perceived benefits of order, simplicity, and effectiveness driving such an approach have fallen victim to its shortcomings, principally a level of complexity insufficient to meet the needs of the differentiated environments in which the policies are applied: "These common-sense assumptions, however, lead to proposals to improve the operation of political systems that have had the opposite effect. By removing decisions about the ways to innovate, adapt, and coordinate efforts from those who are directly affected, these policy reforms have created institutions that are less able to respond to the problems for which they were created."[95]

This centralization parallels what Janet Looney refers to as the "top-down" model of implementation. She also concludes that the exclusive focus on central decision makers leaves little room for program innovation by other players, such as frontline service deliverers or local governments. Fundamentally, the centralized or "top-down" approach fails to take full advantage of the knowledge of the decentralized individuals and groups, thus stunting the process of differentiation and experimentation that could be occurring. Progress is more likely to occur when differentiation and experimentation occurs among what Ostrom describes as a polycentric system, or a more complex system of multiple, individuated centers at multiple levels—be they individuals, firms, or NGO field offices—and when better channels exist to share information on the results of this experimentation

> Polycentric systems are themselves complex, adaptive systems without one central authority dominating all of the others. Due to the redundance and rapidity of this trial-and-error learning process, a polycentric system has a higher probability (than either a fully decentralized or a fully centralized system) to avoid major disasters and eventually to discover rules that work relatively well. Because polycentric systems have overlapping organizations, information about what has worked well in one setting can be transmitted to others who may try it out in their settings.[96]

Looney, quoting Richard Elmore, notes these "bottom-up" models rely on "communications and compliance linkages"—the integration of the specialized units. They assume that "the closer one is to the source of the problem, the greater is one's ability to influence it; and the problem-solving ability of complex systems depends not on hierarchical control but on maximizing discretion at the point where the problem is most immediate."[97]

The emergence of nonprofits or NGOs within the civil sector to address the seemingly intractable problem of poverty in international development is an example of organizational differentiation and specialization leading to an evolving complexity both organizationally and institutionally. The more monolithic traditional development agencies such as the World Bank and International Monetary Fund have been repeatedly criticized for practicing "one-size-fits-all" approaches to development. Yunus argues that not only do these organizations not foster differentiated responses consistent with local conditions, they direct their efforts overseas towards inappropriately creating organizations and institutions in their own image. The civil sector, which as described by Ng and Lindenberg "encourages the pursuit of individual interests," is by nature more differentiated and they have been able to foster grassroots support, credibility, and local accountability that allows more experimentation.

Looney reminds us, however, that both top-down and bottom-up models of implementation have been subject to criticism. Devolution, the newest iteration of decentralization, tries to combine the best of both worlds: locally-based solutions evaluated by common program performance and outcome goals. This allows for complexity: individuated form, responsive to irregularities in local preferences and constraints, and governed by integrating principles.

Individual and Societal Complexity

Part of Csikszentmihalyi's prescription for progress in ourselves is to acknowledge the evolutionary processes of differentiation and integration, and the resulting complexity that increases the survivability of individuals and species. He then translates that over to a cultural context. Culturally, Csikszentmihalyi calls for an individual whose "consciousness is uniquely individuated, yet whose desires, goals, and actions are in harmony with each other."[98] Through complexity individuals and society will achieve control of themselves and social phenomena, like the advance of technology and economic growth. Progress will result from humans' own reigning in of their undesirable behaviors, curbing unproductive incentives and re-channeling dangerous impulses.

Zerbe's view is in many respects an alternative statement of Csikszentmihalyi's assertions but points to a means for achieving complexity through helping individuals gain "a firmer sense of self, a heightened sense of differentiation," and thereby "a greater sense of empathy with others."[99] It is this capacity to understand and to empathize that allows individuals and cultures to successfully contest and accommodate differences in religious, philosophical, and moral beliefs as well as more superficial legal, political, and day-to-day differences. Of singular importance to the development of a mature culture is the rule of fair law coupled with the culture's understanding and appreciation for its role in solving collective action problems. Basic cultural attributes, such as cooperation and trust, are enabled by laws or other cultural institutions that are perceived as fair. Extending trust and empathy internationally is the litmus test of cultural maturity and would be supported by a unified body of law and custom.

4. Know Thyself

The rule of fair law, empathy, individual and collective security, control of technology, sustainable use of natural resources, eradication of poverty, cooperation—these are the progressive goals that remain within our sight but often beyond our grasp. We have developed complex systems of institutions and organizations aimed at expanding our control and improving our knowledge in order to achieve these goals, yet every generation seemingly is pressed to overcome similar obstacles to peace, justice, security, health, and well-being. As the work in this volume and many previous works on progress make clear, knowledge is the catalyst of human progress. For progress in many of the areas we care about the most, which generally take the form of collective action problems, the most important form of knowledge is captured in the ancient precept inscribed on the temple at Delphos: *Know Thyself.*

Through scientific inquiry we have made unquestionable progress in describing and understanding ourselves physically and the world in which we live. This progress, albeit incomplete, extends even to the workings of the brain and is almost complete enough to allow humans to alter human evolution at the cellular level. This knowledge has provided tremendous improvements in our ability to treat injury and disease and to preserve life. It has equally allowed us to manipulate the resources at our disposal to provide a level of physical comfort unparalleled in human history. Our knowledge promises even greater control and advances in the future.

In spite of these gains, however, there is some doubt whether across the hundreds of generations of human evolution, humans are better able to know and regulate their own emotions and behavior. In short, we as a species may still be in denial or ignorant of our true nature and therefore of understanding why we do the things we do, both good and bad. Despite the progress in understanding ourselves from evolutionary biology and other bio-physical sciences, "both ethics and political science lack a foundation of verifiable knowledge of human nature sufficient to produce cause-and-effect, predictions and sound judgments based on them."[100] We perhaps still do not see clearly the world around us, and our place in it. Delusional, fearful and destructive behaviors founded in ignorance and a lack of self-regulation, may condemn us to an inefficient and sub-optimal use of life's energy and this world's resources. Consequently, progress in ourselves and in the other domains might be on a lower historical trajectory than it otherwise could be.

These assertions serve as working assumptions and challenges for authors such as Zerbe and Csikszentmihalyi. Zerbe draws on evolutionary biology and psychology to define cultural progress in terms of a culture's maturity and ability to support its members' individual and social development. More mature and progressive cultures have a greater capacity to peacefully and productively accommodate and support the diverse or differentiated beliefs and attributes of individuals within that culture and of other cultures. This collective capacity is achieved by effectively promoting individual self-awareness and thereby understanding one's relationships with others and the natural world. A realistic view of one's place in the world ultimately enables empathy for other beings. Thus, individual and cultural maturity mutually support each other.

Csikszentmihalyi suggests the first step and a necessary condition for future individual and social progress is for humans to better understand the evolutionary or biological basis and nature of our own, often self-destructive, behavior. Specifically he cautions us that for real progress to occur our cultural memes[101] must keep pace with and even anticipate our technological capabilities and creation. As discussed above, however, our current institutional systems encourage specialization in and the application of resources toward technological advancement, perhaps to a greater degree than the development of countervailing integrative institutions or memes.

Gordon and Martin similarly argue that information technology, like all technology, operates within the moral frame we provide. They speak to the necessity of knowing ourselves and using that knowledge to improve our social organization and institutions, so that technological advances are better directed toward progressive ends. They emphasize one element, the need for "sensitive and enlightened deliberative processes," as necessary for developing policy prescriptions that would balance our desires to corral "destructive forces while also unleashing creative potential and furthering opportunities for human communion."[102]

Keeping pace and providing a moral frame captures the essence of the imbalances and tensions in knowledge and institutions and explains why progress is often slow to materialize. "Locke, Hume, and Kant insist that a study of the human mind should precede all other studies in order to save men from fruitless disputes concerning matters beyond their capabilities for knowledge."[103] We are always at the edge of our knowledge and capabilities, and it is not surprising that developments in one field remain unlinked to those in another, or that we should frequently find one aspect of our creation in conflict with another. Nor, perhaps, should we find it surprising that once discovered, resolutions or solutions often require years to form and implement. Montgomery points out how provisional and speculative scientific discovery frequently is, and he could well include most other areas of knowledge. This is the case, in part, because history shows that scientific developments and theories have often required large amounts of time to coalesce and amass sufficient corroborative evidence.

Parallel developments and synthesis of complementary knowledge and technique are crucial to progress and these, in turn, depend on the varied processes of human learning. Several authors provide insight into the way we learn and how discoveries materialize. Gordon and Martin, for example, recount how in a single conversation the association of previously unassociated knowledge—of electricity and communicating information—by William Morse, produced the contingent progress of telegraphy.

Johnson describes how, over time, through the progressive changes in artistic representation and theme, we have also expanded our knowledge of ourselves, including our social, work, and personal relations. He suggests the availability of ideas, stories, descriptions, and alternative perspectives from authors of all cultures serves to increase our knowledge and promote progress. He provides the example of late-twentieth century American literature as a period in which alternative social perspectives have appeared and helped to transform American's understanding of themselves and their society.

Cowan offers the example of her own experiences with doctors and medical practices to show how an individual can integrate new knowledge and experience into an existing framework of knowledge, belief, and practice. Her example illustrates not only the development of complexity within an individual but also the role of self-knowledge in progress. Although she might not truly empathize with the doctors she describes, she nonetheless was able, with the right knowledge, to understand the value of their actions for her and other women.

Solving Collective Action Problems

Elinor Ostrom's chapter focuses our attention on human behavior, social organization, and policy creation. In this regard she echoes the views of others that the most essential knowledge we can possess is an understanding of our own behavior: "It is essential that we recognize the limits of all individuals—citizens and public officials alike."[104]

Ostrom establishes a strong link between understanding human behavior and improving public policy. She argues that advances in this regard require the freedom to formulate and pursue questions about human behavior and raise concerns about guardedly specialized academic disciplines being an obstacle to improving our understanding of human behavior. To the extent that disciplinary focus deters such pursuits by enforcing rigidity on the types of questions that are valued, then it impedes progress.[105]

The value of unfettered inquiry into the nature of human behavior is realized in the results of the experimental research record. For example, despite the current application of behavioral postulates to the contrary, this record supports the view that humans frequently cooperate despite the presence of measurable individual benefits from pursuing one's narrow short-term self-interest. Or that "humans do not possess the cognitive capabilities assigned to them in most policy analyses, but that they frequently overcome their cognitive limitations by adopting effective heuristics."[106] From these and other findings Ostrom suggests that we should change the simple model of human behavior that we use in policy analysis to recognize that there are several different types of behavior and that humans, while striving to do the best they can, are nonetheless fallible and do not have perfect foresight. Policy making under these conditions calls for experimentation over time in an attempt to optimize outcomes. This model contributes to her view that we need to look to more locally based policy making systems as opposed to nationally or centrally based systems. Locally based systems rely on the knowledge and experience of those most involved with the conditions, stakeholders, resources, and constraints. They are in a better position to experiment and measure the results, then respond with the next experimental iteration.

Thus, from knowledge of self comes better institutions and ways of organizing ourselves to solve collective action problems. From better institutions and social organization comes better knowledge for solving collective action problems. Ostrom emphasizes, in particular, the means to achieve such social learning, or knowledge creation:

> For social learning to occur, overlapping arenas as well as highly parallel structures (multiple units of government operating at the same level) are needed so that information about successful innovation can be more rapidly diffused. Thus, ... polycentric systems—those organized at multiple scales with considerable autonomy and diversity at each scale—are more likely to continue progress in the next millennium by more effective organization for contestation and learning.[107]

As with all approaches, however, policy makers need to experiment and learn when one approach is preferred over another. For many policy areas Ostrom's model of polycentric systems would presumably yield higher levels of experimentation, greater knowledge, and faster progress. For other areas, however, it is not clear how to apply such a model. Tilly and Chirot's chapters on contentious politics and ethnopolitical warfare, genocide, and massacres highlight the importance of the dynamic between beliefs (or knowledge), institutions, and behavior and how little we actually know about forming and controlling them (i.e., ourselves) to prevent regress or to yield progress.

Although experimentation with differing institutions for the peaceful resolution of conflicts between ethnic groups and nations would seem an obvious priority, Tilly infers from his own conjectures, among other things, that "pacification and democratization are only likely to occur through external shock (e.g., defeat in war) or internal struggle (e.g., revolution)."[108] If true, then it is unclear whether this is an area where experimentation is relevant, even though the need for greater self-knowledge on the part of political leaders and affected groups is evident.

Their examples also highlight the idea that knowing thyself does not necessarily imply the elimination of the biologically and culturally derived conditions and attributes that lead to genocide, for example, but rather to their control. Chirot's chapter makes brutally clear the role of biologically determined attributes, knowledge, and institutions as causal agents in ethnic massacres and warfare, but also in preventing such acts. Although enabled by our biological capacities for, among other things, fear and discrimination, ultimately it is the control and manipulation by military and political leaders of group knowledge and perceptions that play off of the biological capacities, and that leads one group to believe that it must eliminate another, or face elimination itself.

The catalytic role of leaders and political entrepreneurs in fomenting action by individuals and groups of followers also supports Ostrom's point concerning the importance of adding different types of actors to our behavioral models. In the context of contentious politics, any policy prescriptions aimed at changing behavior in such a way as to reduce destruction and increase participation will necessarily have to consider the behavior of a very broad array of behavioral types. Even then, Chirot warns us that "the modern notion that we can remedy social ills by carefully planned public policy means that we are bound to fall again into the trap of adopting simplistic ideologies that will lead to new totalitarian nightmares."[109] It would be naïve to think that destructive actors, either within or across ethnic groups, are all motivated by the same beliefs or goals, or that they are responding to existing institutional or other stimuli in the same way, and that they would therefore similarly respond to a single set of policy changes. Not surprisingly, the most progressive institutions have been those that are resilient to the individual.

Conclusion

Our frustration in achieving moral and social progress should not lead us to abandon reason and knowledge. The chapters that follow provide a variety of perspectives on progress and public policy. From our perspective identifying and measuring progress is a human phenomenon, as is most creation and destruction, but one which affects all living beings. As such the primary obstacles to progress are developing humans' knowledge of their own behavior, its motivations and consequences, integrating this knowledge with fundamental natural and cultural systems, and developing a higher order of control over the same. An essential ingredient is developing systems within and between ourselves and between ourselves and the material and natural world that promote diversity and accommodate progressive change. John Rawls captures the essence of the challenge within our systems of moral philosophy and institutions. He argues that at least in a democracy, and we would suggest elsewhere,[110] reasonable pluralism will be the norm:

> A democratic society is not and cannot be a community, whereby a community I mean a body of persons united in affirming the same comprehensive, or partially comprehensive, doctrine. The fact of reasonable pluralism, which characterizes a society with free institutions makes this impossible. This is the fact of profound and irreconcilable differences in citizens' reasonable comprehensive religious and philosophical conceptions of the world, and in their views of the moral and aesthetic values to be sought in human life.[111]

Holding our biological attributes constant, it is through public policies and other institutions and self-knowledge that we create the complexity of character and form, and integrative means necessary to hold society together despite our profound and irreconcilable differences.

Notes

1. Peter B. Medawar, *The Hope of Progress—A Scientist Looks at Problems in Philosophy, Literature and Science* (New York: Anchor Books, 1972). Originally from his 1969 Presidential Address to the British Association on "The Effecting of all Things Possible." Also quoted in John T. Edsall, "Progress in Our Understanding of Biology," in *Progress and Its Discontents*, ed. Gabriel Almond, Marvin Chodorow, and Roy Harvey Pearce (Berkeley: University of California Press, 1982), 159.

2. These categories were influenced by the very helpful discussion of progress in Raymond Gastil, *Progress: Critical Thinking about Historical Change* (Westport, Conn.: Praeger, 1993).

3. Robert Nisbet, *History of the Idea of Progress* (New York: Basic Books, 1970), 7.

4. We have relied heavily in this chapter on Nisbet's, *History of the Idea of Progress*. We would also like to acknowledge our debt to the superb collection of essays edited twenty years ago by Gabriel Almond, Marvin Chodorow. and Roy Harvey Pearce, *Progress and Its Discontents*. Their volume, especially the chapters on science and the arts, has allowed us to over-sample authors in the social sciences regarding our particular concern with public policy and the role of institutions in progressive change.

5. See, for example, J. B. Bury, *The Idea of Progress* (New York: Dover Publications, 1932); Nisbet, *History*; W. Warren Wagar, ed., *The Idea of Progress Since the Renaissance* (New York: Wiley, 1969); Gastil, *Progress: Critical Thinking*; and Almond, Chodorow, and Harvey Pearce, *Progress and Its Discontents.*

6. Ruth Macklin, "Moral Progress," *Ethics* 87, no. 4 (July 1977): 373; Francisco J. Ayala, "The Evolutionary Concept of Progress," in *Progress and Its Discontents*, ed. Gabriel Almond, Marvin Chodorow, and Roy Harvey Pearce (Berkeley: University of California Press, 1982), 109.

7. Ruth Schwartz Cowan, "Perhaps Progress Really is our Most Important Product: A Feminist Contemplates the Twentieth Century," 329, chapter 19 of this volume.

8. From Nisbet, *History*, 199.

9. From Nisbet, *History*, 200.

10. Macklin, "Moral Progress," 370. Also quoted in Nannerl O. Keohane, "The Enlightenment Idea of Progress Revisited," in *Progress and Its Discontents*, ed. Gabriel Almond, Marvin Chodorow, and Roy Harvey Pearce (Berkeley: University of California Press, 1982): 24.

11. Hubert Locke, "Faith and the Future: Religion and the Problem of Progress in the New Millennium," 89, chapter 6 of this volume.

12. Charles Tilly "Progress and Contentious Politics," 239, chapter 14 of this volume.

13. Daniel Chirot, "Ethnopolitical Warfare and Massacres: Is There Progress?" 219, chapter 13 of this volume.

14. Locke, "Faith and thc Future," 89.

15. Locke, Faith and the Future," 89.

16. Alex Inkeles, "Two Steps Forward and One Step Back: An Assessment of Progress in the Twentieth Century," 29, chapter 2 of this volume.

17. A. Maslow, "A Theory of Human Motivation," *Psychological Review* 50, (July 1943): 370-96. See Randy Brians, "Subjective Well being and the Pursuit of Progress: Insights from the 1995-97 World Value Survey," MPA degree project, Daniel J. Evans School of Public Affairs, University of Washington, Seattle, 2000; and Macklin, "Moral Progress," for more on Maslow's hierarchy and progress.

18. These observations concur with those of Almond, Chodorow, and Harvey Pearce who conclude that the linkages between material, moral, and social progress envisioned by Condorcet and other original Enlightenment writers on progress have not been realized. See Almond, Chodorow, and Harvey Pearce, *Progress and its Discontents*, 11.

19. Cowan, "Perhaps Progress," 329.

20. Scott L. Montgomery, "Progress and the Natural Sciences: Issues and Perspectives," 297, chapter 17 of this volume.

21. Daly and Wilson write of this distinction as being between "nativism" and "empiricism"—the latter being derived from experience of the outside world gathered over the course of a lifetime. See Martin Daly and Margo Wilson, "Progress and Evolution," 67, chapter 4 of this volume.

22. Adler, author of *The Great Works*, was himself a true believer of universality and progress, advocating that all citizens be able to access and understand the ideas of the great philosophers.

23. Mortimer J. Adler and William Gorman, ed., *The Great Ideas—A Syntopicon of Great Books of the Western World* (Chicago: William Benton, 1952), 439.

24. Keohane, "The Enlightenment Idea," 33.

25. Nisbet, *History*, 238.

26. E. O. Wilson, "The Biological Basis of Morality," *Atlantic Monthly* 281, no. 4 (April 1998): 67.

27. Abhijit Guha, "The Darwinian View of Progress: Comment on Sen," *Population and Development Review* 20, no. 4 (Dec 1994): 861.

28. Ayala, "The Evolutionary Concept of Progress," 122.

29. Adler and Gorman, *Great Ideas*, 440.

30. Rousseau claims that "the faculty of self-improvement is one distinction between man and brute. . . . But he also thinks that this faculty is the cause of human decline as well as progress." Adler and Gorman, *Great Ideas*, 440.

31. Daly and Wilson, "Progress and Evolution," 67.

32. William Zumeta, "Progress and Education: Supporting the Realization of Human Aspirations," 139, chapter 10 of this volume.

33. William Godwin was perhaps the most extreme in this realm, believing that even cooperation was counter to progress. "From these principles it appears that everything

that is usually understood by the term cooperation is in some degree an evil ... all supererogatory cooperation is carefully to be avoided, common labor and common meals." See Nisbet, *History*, 190, 212, 229.

34. Guha, "The Darwinian View," 861.

35. For Marx, of course, the state would eventually whither away.

36. Nisbet, *History*, 227.

37. Keohane, "The Enlightenment Idea," 33.

38. Our institutional perspective is most directly informed by Douglass C. North, *Institutions, Institutional Change, and Economic Performance* (New York: Cambridge University Press, 1990).

39. James E. Anderson, *Public Policy Making*, 3d ed. (New York: Holt, Rinehart and Winston, 1984), 3-5.

40. Zumeta, "Progress and Education," 139.

41. Zumeta, "Progress and Education," 139.

42. See for example, Douglass C. North, "Institutions, Ideology, and Economic Performance," in *The Revolution in Development Economics*, ed. A. Dorn, Steve H. Hanke, and Alan A. Walter (Washington, D.C.: The Cato Institute, 1998), 95-107.

43. Nisbet, *History*, 199.

44. Nor are these the primary theses of any single chapter, or necessarily the only themes that could be derived from this volume.

45. Charles Johnson, "Progress in Literature," 101, chapter 7 of this volume.

46. Darwin himself thought that "Von Baer has defined advancement or progress in the organic scale better than anyone else, as resting on the amount of differentiation and specialization of the several parts of a being." Adler and Gorman, *Great Ideas*, 437.

47. From Nisbet, *History*, 234, quoting Herbert Spencer, *Progress: Its Law and Cause*, 1857.

48. Nisbet, *History*, 227.

49. Jerome H. Buckley in *The Triumph of Time* details the impact of the idea of progress on Victorian literature. Nisbet, *History*, 176-7. (Jerome H. Buckley, *The Triumph of Time: A Study of the Victorian Concepts of Time, History, Progress, and Decadence* (Cambridge: Belknap Press of Harvard University Press, 1966).

50. Bernard D. Davis, "Fear of Progress in Biology," in *Progress and its Discontents*, ed. Gabriel Almond, Marvin Chodorow, and Roy Harvey Pearce (Berkeley: University of California Press, 1982), 183.

51. Andrew C. Gordon and Tom Martin, "Information Technology and Progress," 343, chapter 20 of this volume.

52. Edward O. Wilson, "Back from Chaos" *The Atlantic Monthly* 281, no. 3 (March 1998): 52.

53. Montgomery, "Progress and the Natural Sciences," 297.

54. Montgomery, "Progress and the Natural Sciences," 297.

55. Montgomery, "Progress and the Natural Sciences," 297.

56. Alison Cullen and Christopher Bretherton, "Progressing toward Environmental Sustainability," 379, chapter 22 of this volume.

57. Although important for both physical and cultural progress, we are focused here on cultural progress.

58. Johnson, "Progress in Literature."

59. Nisbet, *History*, 210

60. Nisbet, *History*, 220.

61. Richard N. Brandon, "Young Children: The First Step in Progress," 125, chapter 9 of this volume.

62. Zumeta, "Progress and Education," 139.

63. Cullen and Bretherton, "Progressing toward Environmental Sustainability," 379.

64. Davis, "Fear of Progress in Biology," 183.

65. Cullen and Bretherton, "Progressing toward Environmental Sustainability," 379. M. Gordon views this sensationalism as stemming, in part, from the drive for profits in the media business, especially in the United States. See, Margaret T. Gordon, "Free Press, Profit Margins, and Democratic Governance: Is There a Fatal Flaw?" chapter 16 in this volume.

66. M. Gordon, "Free Press," 267.

67. Nisbet, *History*, 205.

68. Brandon, "Young Children," 125.

69. Nisbet, *History*, 241.

70. Nisbet, *History*, 210.

71. Nisbet, *History*, 211.

72. Keohane, "The Enlightenment Idea," 36.

73. Nisbet, *History*, 228

74. Zumeta, "Progress and Education," 139.

75. Brandon, "Young Children," 125.

76. Keohane, "The Enlightenment Idea," 36.

77. For references on social preferences, see Matthew Rabin, "A Perspective on Psychology and Economics," Department of Economics, University of California, Berkeley, Working Paper No. E02-313, February 2002; Matthew Rabin, "Psychology and Economics," *Journal of Economic Literature* 36 (March 1998): 11-46.

78. Daly and Wilson, "Progress and Evolution," 67. This social comparison may explain why the press has found it profitable to increasingly "include sensationalized and personalized stories about celebrities," and "the exploits of the rich and famous, drawing the attention of more and more 'common' men, and women." See M. Gordon, "Free Press," 267.

79. J. Patrick Dobel and C. Leigh Anderson, "Progress and the Promise of Public Policy," 3, chapter 1 of this volume.

80. Rabin, "A Perspective," 19. For more references, see Rabin, "Psychology and Economics;" and Michael McBride, "Relative-income Effects on Subjective Well-being in the Cross-section," *Journal of Economic Behavior and Organization* 45, no. 3 (July 2001): 251-278.

81. Gastil, *Progress: Critical Thinking*, 11.

82. Cullen and Bretherton, "Progressing toward Environmental Sustainability," 379.

83. Albert R. Jonsen, "Paradoxical Progress: Medical Advances and Moral Anxiety," 113.

84. Jonsen, "Paradoxical Progress."

85. John Rawls, *Justice as Fairness A Restatement*, ed. Erin Kelly (Cambridge, Mass.: The Belknap Press of Harvard University Press, 2001), 3.

86. Macklin, Moral Progress, 378.

87 Chirot, "Ethnopolitical Warfare," 219.

88. Christina M. Cerna, Universality of Human Rights and Cultural Diversity: Implementation for Human Rights in Different Socio-Cultural Contexts," *Human Rights Quarterly*, 16, no. 4 (1994): 744.

89. Cerna, "Universality," 748.

90. Robert Heilbroner "Progress: An Economist's View," 319.

91. Elinor Ostrom, "Achieving Progress in Solving Collective-Action Problems," 165, chapter 11 of this volume.

92. Zumeta, "Progress and Education," 139

93. Brandon, "Young Children," 125.

94. Cullen and Bretherton, "Progressing toward Environmental Sustainability," 379.

95. Ostrom, "Achieving Progress," 165.

96. Ostrom, "Achieving Progress," 165.

97. Economic theory might change and extend this maxim slightly to read: "The greater is one's ability to influence outcomes subject to variability, the greater should be that person's claim to the residual values of those outcomes." See, for example, Yoram Barzel, *Economic Analysis of Property Rights* (New York: Cambridge University Press, 1989).

98. Mihaly Csikszentmihalyi, "The Meaning of Progress in the New Millennium," 79.

99. Richard O. Zerbe, Jr., "Is There Cultural Progress?," 191, chapter 12 of this volume.

100. Wilson, "The Biological Basis," 64.

101. Csikszentmihalyi, "The Meaning of Progress," 79, contextually defines memes as customs, laws, and religious prohibitions, which in this example allowed members of previous civilizations "to limit the negative effects of the novelties they invented." Zerbe, "Is There Cultural Progress?," 191, attributes the term to the evolutionary biologist Richard Dawkins and provides a fuller definition as the cultural attributes, such as ideas, technologies, or religious or political philosophies, that are passed on through time and across cultures.

102. A. Gordon and Martin, "Information Technology," 343.

103. Adler and Gorman, *The Great Ideas*, 442. Molecular biologist Gunther Stent believes that we may have arrived at the end of progress, because of the mind-matter paradox. "Thus, as far as consciousness is concerned, it is possible that the quest for its physical nature is bringing us to the limits of human understanding, in that the brain may not be capable, in the last analysis, of providing [an] explanation of itself." Richard John Neuhaus, "The Idea of Moral Progress," *First Things: A Monthly Journal of Religion and*

Public Life 95 (August 1999): 21.

104. Ostrom, "Achieving Progress," 165.

105. Individuals across several disciplines share this concern. In economics and psychology, for example, see Rabin, "A Perspective;" Rabin, "Psychology and Economics;" Daniel Kahneman and Amos Tversky, ed. *Choices, Values, and Frames* (New York: Russell Sage Foundation, 2000), and George Loewenstein and Jon Elster *Choice Over Time* (New York: Russell Sage Foundation, 1992).

106. Ostrom, "Achieving Progress," 165.

107. Ostrom, "Achieving Progress," 165.

108. Tilly, "Progress and Contention Politics," 239.

109. Chirot, "Ethnopolitical Warfare," 219.

110. The veneer of social and economic homogeneity under non-democratic rule, as we have seen in post-communist societies, may stifle, but does not eliminate the diversity of individual religious, philosophical, moral, and aesthetic views.

111. John Rawls, *Justice as Fairness*, 3.

Section I—Defining, Measuring, and Implementing Progress

Chapter 1

Progress and the Promise of Public Policy

J. Patrick Dobel and C. Leigh Anderson

> Good government implies two things: first, fidelity to the object of government, which is the happiness of the people; secondly, a knowledge of the means by which that object can be best attained.[1]
>
> James Madison

Public policy encompasses the ways societies choose to pursue aspirations for the common good. Crafting public policy involves making choices amid conflict. The choices force political actors and societies to think hard about the possibilities before them and to envision alternatives and futures among which they can choose. These choices arise where visions of the future meet the realities and constraints of power, knowledge, resources, institutions, values, and culture. Public policy is made at this intersection of choice and possibility.

Although "progress" is a relatively new word in the English language, dating from the seventeenth century,[2] the western concept of human progress has profoundly influenced how people see the possibilities of policy as well as shaped the politics and rhetoric that inform public policy debates. In this chapter we endeavor to describe the relationship between progress as an idea—as a theory of change—and progress as an outcome of the goals, methods, and organizations of public policy.

The stakes involved in policy conflicts driven by a vision of progress are high. When international nongovernmental organizations (NGOs) and the Chinese government battle over the placement and costs of a major dam that will transform the agriculture of an area but displace hundreds of local communities, the conflict centers around definitions of progress. When fundamentalist Muslim rulers close schools for women in Afghanistan, or debates arise over banning female genital cutting, the conflict centers on a concept of progress confronting a traditional conception of social order. When nations ban trade in hormonally treated animals or question genetically modified organisms, they are, economics aside, questioning scientific advances as progress. Throughout the world, issues revolving around human rights, technology, and environmental sustainability, pit claims of progress versus a variety of different views on the role of society and policy.

This chapter discusses progress as an idea and how that ethos affects policy options. We begin by discussing how the role and scope of policy has been influenced by four historical ideas of change—cyclical, fallen, contingent, and linear—and how these views shape the possibilities for action. The role of policy is limited, for example, in a society that predominantly views itself as forever fallen from a golden age, or that views change as random. These historical views lead us to the current understanding of change—the modern ideal of progress, which postulates that through applying knowledge and reason humans can improve their basic welfare. This axiom greatly enhances the promise of public policy—the possibility of promoting progress coupled with the responsibility of reacting appropriately to ideas of progressive change from its citizens. At a minimum, believing that progress is possible creates a policy imperative to provide a set of institutions within which individuals can seek change that is consistent with views of societal progress.

We follow by examining public policy and its goals, methods, and organizations. We define and measure progress by the goals we set, yet no state has escaped debates about what constitutes progress in a society and whether such progress is desirable. At a minimum, by introducing a fundamental debate about the range of historical possibilities for a society, progress challenges the status quo. Politics and debate rage over what (the goals), how (the methods), and who (the individuals and organizations) are the proper engines of progress.

Public Policy and Historical Ideas of Change

There are no universal public policies for all times and places. At any point in time each society possesses a unique distribution of political, economic, and social power. Institutions of rule, production, and religion exist at a particular historical moment suffused with the culture, values, symbols, technologies, and self-understandings of that time. Within this moment people have an understanding of what the historical possibilities of change and action are. The memories of the culture, the pattern of authority, and the internalized norms and identities of the social order all intensely affect how people view their futures and possibilities. These, in turn, impact the nature of public policy and what it might seek to accomplish.

Policy depends upon both knowledge of the issues and a diagnosis of the range of possibilities before the policy makers. It involves not only problem solving, but also taking advantage of opportunities to further the common good. Policy makers grapple with the available knowledge, gather resources, and build the power base and institutions to accomplish their goals. At a deeper level, however, these activities are hemmed in by the historical understandings of the culture that provide the people, elites, and policy makers with a series of frames by which to perceive and analyze the world around them.[3] This understanding of history becomes one of the prime ways by which individuals and societies give meaning to their lives and status.[4] Often these meanings exist within a self-conscious creation of traditions to legitimize the existing structures of power.

This view of history affects how public policy is envisioned. Past historical understandings identify grievances, success, victims, and enemies, and categorize the moral reality of cause and effect and blame and praise for the present state of affairs. At the same time, the view of the flow of history brings forth possibilities for the future. Four main ways of viewing historical flow traditionally influence understandings of the possibilities of policy—cyclical, fallen, contingent, and linear.

Cyclical views of history, common among Renaissance thinkers, see certain inevitable tendencies of society that cannot in the long run be resisted.[5] The evolution of society and government move through a patterned cycle of birth, growth, and decay. While improvement can take place within the cycle, especially from the birth to maturity of a society or country, decay is inevitable. Fundamental dimensions of social and public life are not transformed in the cyclical view, but limited growth and change is possible. Any changes for the good are doomed to be sporadic and temporary. After the upward curve of increasing prosperity and safety, the inevitable direction of change becomes one of corruption of the social order and its values. Increasing inequality, external threats, and internal unrest fate a society to decline into anarchy and chaos.[6] With luck, a new beginning will emerge from the destruction, and the cycle begins again.

Such a predictable and bleak succession presents public policy with limited possibilities that are tied to their place in the cycle. In the cyclical view, public policy most often resembles a rearguard action against decay. The government strives to hold off the inevitable before resigning to the ultimate decline that afflicts all human institutions.[7] John Stuart Mill noted, "though most men in the present age profess a contrary creed, believing that the tendency of things, on the whole, is toward improvement; we ought not to forget that there is an incessant and everflowing current of human affairs toward the worse."[8] History pushes strongly against great visions of change and transformation or of any notion of ongoing progress that improves the lives of everyone.

Many societies understand history as a state bedeviled by human society's fall. Their cultures exist in the shadow of a once perfect Garden of Eden or Golden Age. This shadow casts a pall over all great possibilities of change for the social and political order. The golden age defines a time of human harmony, even perfection where people lived in concord with nature and their divine order. Injustice caused by huge inequality, the anger of divinities, or disasters wrought by nature did not exist in the world. For some reason, humans lost their place in the garden and the golden age ended. At best, the fallen world permits moments of happiness or stability that are interludes in an otherwise relentless world.

If the fall suffuses human nature and affects it with limitations as the notion of original sin suggests, then political imagination becomes very stunted. Since the glory of the golden age can never be achieved again, public policy possibilities may be even more limited than with a cyclical view that permits the possibility of growth. In the fall view, humans left on their own create a world "nasty brutish and short."[9] At best they seek security and protection from enemies and each other. This security becomes paramount; later some justice might be possible if strong law and authority keep the fallen state of humans and nature at bay. The all powerful state of Thomas Hobbes' *Leviathan* presents one solution to the problem of fallen humans struggling and warring with each other and their intractable nature.[10] Periodic movements might grow from the society, sometimes from the masses, sometimes from the elites, to restore the golden age and bring about salvation. But the notion of change suggests a backward almost mystical longing for a never to be discovered time.

The fall theme takes a different variation in the notion of a founding. Classical political theory extols the idea of the lawgiver and founding of a society. Like the stories of Romulus and Remus founding Rome or the first dynasties of China, they extol the virtues and wisdom of the founders.[11] Often founders have divine help in creating the state as in the Greek or Chinese founding stories or in creating laws handed down from a divine order. Whatever the reality, the historical moment of the founding of the state fixes a moment of idealized virtue, wisdom, and clarity about law and order. Most states slowly accrete festivals and chronicles to augment the stature of the foundings and trace the lineage of their rulers to the founders. In these societies, the attributes and world of the founders become totems of value and political direction. New or conquering dynasties will seek to marry into old lines to buttress their claims to power. The future is often interpreted as a slow but relentless devolution from the purity of the founding moment. Possibilities are confined to the past and restoring lost virtue rather than moving into the future with its great possibilities.

Interwoven among the strands of cyclical, fallen, and founding views of history lies a "realistic" conception that can exist in any culture. This view sees history as contingent and without a set direction or meaning—things happen. No direction, no pattern, and no deities control history. Humans make their own history interacting with random accidents of natural disaster, plagues, or chance meetings with other civilizations, some stronger, some weaker. Machiavelli and Renaissance scholars called it a world of "fortuna." Ancient Chinese and Greek political theory held such realist theories as do postmodern and other recent thinkers. In such a world, the strong rule and the weak suffer what they must.[12] Like nature itself, nothing is static and at most individuals or societies fight to stay in place against the relentless tide of nature and genetics.[13] Even small, hardy, and adapted hunter-gatherer groups remain constantly on the verge of disaster if the environment changes.[14]

Facing an unplanned, random, and sometimes catastrophic world, policy as a rational purposive activity has profound limits in the contingent view. Public policy becomes a reactive enterprise with societies trying to maintain integrity and security amid ceaseless change. Success is measured in momentary achievements of equilibrium or wealth that enable a society to weather significant encounters with human or natural disasters. Public policy does not become a means of forward progress so much as the methods by which people consolidate and protect their achievements and prepare for the next event. Policy must ultimately focus upon developing wealth and the human and technological strength to sustain the society in an unstable world racked with accident and chance. It may involve an incessant need to expand against enemies to both protect itself and gain wealth and power as practiced by most traditional empires.

The least common view of history takes the cycle and turns it into a straight line. History takes a single forward direction. This linear movement has within it the seeds of the modern idea of progress because it presumes that human well-being gradually and definitely improves over time.[15] "What the idea means, as we have seen, is first and foremost that humanity is advancing toward some goal continuously, inexorably, and necessarily."[16]

One common variant of this version focuses upon the individual. The person moves through life seeking to achieve a state of moral perfection as demanded by the divine order. It involves study and discipline that culminates in achieving human bliss or perfection in the afterlife. It lies at the heart of the Judeo-Christian tradition as well as in Islam and many Indo-Aryan myths. A variation on this view of progress through life involves individuals obeying God's mandates in a monotheist tradition. The ideal of "Pilgrim's Progress" moves one closer to God through living up to the obligations of, and cooperating with, God's law.

The wider implications of this linear view are revealed when the society must adhere to a plan or direction. The contract between Yahweh and the Israelites introduces this idea into human history and culture. This contract postulates a relationship, direction, and future for the society and people of Israel. If they keep God's commandments, Yahweh will aid them in achieving a holy land, a homeland, and a place to stay and flourish. All their actions then become interpreted by this basic contract and direction. Saint Augustine continued this insight by arguing that humans and God can cooperate with each other in building *The City of God* through the future.[17] While the cities (of man) are not ultimately the end, they can contribute to the unfolding of God's planned reconciliation with humanity—ending the age old battle between the forces of light and darkness. States and public policy can contribute by creating conditions of peace to enable God's word to spread. They can also ensure the best world for people by building their own laws on the foundations of God's laws and creating a religious republic. But in the end, public policy is epiphenomenal to the historical movement beneath the wars and glories of empires and civilizations. Moved by providence, social forces, or divine will, history advances at its own enigmatic pace and direction to increase humanity's welfare.

Modern Views of Change

Modern theories of progress possess two unique attributes that contribute to their power as ideologies of change. First, in their most strident forms, concepts of progress embody a theory of inevitable or inexorable change. As Hegel argued, "Progress is an historical necessity, and it reaches an historic consummation."[18] The theory postulates an overarching historical movement to improve the physical and moral status of humanity, and that nothing permanently stops this movement. Despite temporary setbacks and even cycles of decay—the dialectic of history—progress continues, on net, to improve material and moral well-being. Christian providence, Marxism, and many versions of scientific progress build their strength and motivation around this.

This approach inherently attacks the status quo by arguing for its inevitable destruction and replacement by a better world. The modern ideal of progress sees the starting point as one rife with injustice, stasis, poverty, and a failure to live up to the potential of human dignity. The belief in progress toward a more equal and just social order challenges existing historical understandings of what is possible and desirable for people held in place by the traditions and order of a society. Perversely this can produce a heartless politics that has little time for traditional or unique communities. While sometimes it can inspire vast patience since progress will happen whether people want it to or not and all setbacks are temporary, it can also arouse angry impatience at the stubbornness of those whom history is passing by.

The main alternative to this insistence upon inevitability is a theory that sees progress as possible but volunteeristic. It depends upon the efforts and care of humans. In Kant's view, the realization of man's potential for improvement is "a work of freedom rather than a manifestation of historical necessity."[19] The historian J. B. Bury in his classic *Idea of Progress* argues that a further implication is that "the process must be the necessary outcome of the psychical and social nature of man; it must not be at the mercy of any external will; otherwise there will be no guarantee of its continuance and its issue, and the idea of Progress would lapse into the idea of Providence."[20] But nothing is guaranteed. This view harnesses a strong but more cautious commitment, and a greater concern to build the foundations of progress, recognizing it can be taken away or destroyed. The idea of volunteeristic progress offers no real patience because its accomplishments are fragile ones. Such progress does not inspire unquestioning exuberance, but casts politics and commitment in a more cautious, realistic, and less revolutionary light.

Second, the modern ideology of progress, whether inevitable or volunteeristic, generates strong moral obligations. For the theories of inevitable progress the moral imperative is clear. People are obligated to join the march or at least not impede it. It can become, as it did in Marxism and in some triumphalist versions of neo-liberal capitalism, a massive form of historical utilitarianism. This utilitarianism seeks aggregate happiness and utility for its outcome. The costs involved in destroying individuals or communities in the way are minor given the immense economic, social, and moral benefits that true progress entails. The strong theories of progress possess a moral obligation based on the greater good.

The more volunteeristic variations of progress also come with their own moral obligations. These are less clear, but derive from the obligations to help respect and further the dignity and rights of each human being.[21] Progress, because it is not guaranteed and not a pure utilitarian equation, becomes more complex. This variation seriously entertains the costs to people, traditional societies, and ways of life. It creates a more open and nuanced discussion that acknowledges these costs without giving up the ideal that we are obligated to help further the welfare and dignity of all humans and that progress can happen, even if not guaranteed.

Whether inevitable or volunteeristic, utilitarian or pluralistic, both views influence the tenor and motivation of those committed to progress as well as the pace of movement and quality of engagement with those who defy progress with their own values.

The modern understanding of progress and its many variations emerge from a confluence of two streams of thought. First, it flows from the long and winding history of divine providence and God's will within Medieval and early modern Christianity. This strain of Christianity, even confronting the sinful nature of humanity and the world, believed that God cooperated with humans and the Church to seek the improvement of all humans over time.[22] Bury posits that the translation of this thought necessary for modern views of progress came from sixteenth century historian Jean Bodin's rejection of degeneration over time and the superiority of the past.[23] The second stream represents the torrent of thought and experience rolling from the western experience of modern science and secular reflection that has, to varying degrees, spread throughout the world for the last three centuries.

The idea that humans could continuously improve their lives through science and knowledge broadened expectations that humans could control nature, themselves, and the social order in ways undreamed of in the past. In manufacturing, building, engineering, and medicine, people began to believe that they could continuously improve the quality of what they built or achieved by applying the tenets of reason and science to their activity.[24] In medicine in the eighteenth and nineteenth centuries, great strides were made in understanding physiology and disease by studying the body and developing tools and theories that permitted doctors to understand the role of microbes and germs in human life. This application of knowledge enabled medicine to improve the quality of life for individuals whose illnesses previously meant in theological and traditional terms that they could not survive. Similarly, the theories of Adam Smith and others shed light on how products could be made faster and more cheaply by responding to comparative advantage and the specialization of labor. This made many "luxuries" available to wider ranges of people.

Scientific knowledge in its embryonic form in the sixteenth and seventeenth centuries depended upon the commitment to knowledge that could be supported by experiments and verified across a community of people. Science rejected as conjecture any metaphysical explanations that were tautological or depended upon causes that could not be seen or replicated.[25]

The advantages of the scientific method were many. First it democratized knowledge and enabled unassailable claims of tradition or theology to be challenged. It demanded explanations that did not depend upon the privileged knowledge of mystics, priests, nobles, or sages. Unlike most explanations invoking God's will, explanations invoking physical laws could be successfully replicated by priest, peasant, burgher, or scientist. Its power and truth resided in its method—independent of the authority structures of religion, tradition, or nobility. Moreover, science undermined rigid and privileged hierarchies by, in theory, exposing them to verification. Claims that a bloodline inculcated the nobility with superior virtues and wisdom were now open to empirical testing. Second, it accumulated over time by building upon the discoveries of others. It could be replicated and refuted or verified, and expanded or refined. It grew from conjecture to test, from error to revision, from theory to law. Third, such knowledge possessed clarity and certainty. The laws of physics would remain the same across time periods and cultures. This provided a kind of knowledge more durable and superior to traditional or religious explanations. Once the knowledge was discovered, it might be forgotten or forbidden, but its truth remained and it did not need to be reinvented.

The secularization of the idea of progress dramatically increased the range of public policy, not because progress enthusiasts lacked faith, but because of people's belief in their ability to solve previously intractable problems. The modern faith in public policy is built on the belief that human knowledge can be allied to power and problem-solving.[26] The confidence that reason, built upon scientific induction and deduction, could both understand the world and be used to change it, seeped into the consciousness of politics and policy in multiple ways. These involved several related issues over who controls knowledge, how knowledge is used, and which knowledge gets pursued.

First, controlling knowledge confers power and legitimacy, and progress based on modern science threatens and undermines traditional sources of authority. The insights of science, organization, and economics have combined to give the state greater leverage and influence over the lives of people and in some societies, trump the declining influence of tradition and religion.[27] Public policy literature has a long history of discussions over the role of advisors and the nature of the knowledge advisors should hand on to leaders and governments.[28] In one of the seminal documents on progress, *The New Atlantis*, Francis Bacon argues in the sixteenth century that scientists should rule because only they have the knowledge to produce the conditions to provide human happiness.[29] This conflicts with the claims of traditional elites who might emphasize the wisdom of individual experience or the insight and knowledge of divine revelation and the sacred texts or clerics of the tradition. If a society develops a strong body of knowledge devoted to politics and leadership the purveyors can themselves become a reinforcing caste, as in a mandarin order that trains leaders in the knowledge and virtues needed to make policy and rule.

Second, who controls the knowledge affects how the knowledge is used. The positive outcomes from applying new knowledge in medicine, engineering, and construction led to changes in sewage and water that transformed the health of urban populations in western Europe. Social welfare states were created along with massive industrialization. But the darker side of the progress equation emerged in the multiple arms races that occurred over three centuries as European armies developed increasingly sophisticated military weapons and strategies to match them. War-making became a bloodier and more dangerous activity as it pulled a wider population into its web of weapons production and destruction. Increasing knowledge and achievements enabled the emerging states of western Europe to amass great amounts of coercive and organizational power and created the foundation for the colonial empires that the continent would spawn.[30]

Third, public policy can have a large impact on what knowledge even gets pursued. Governments subsidize research as an engine of economic growth and security. Their investments direct knowledge and their laws can shape it. Eugenics, for example, promised great improvements in the human stock through selective breeding and elimination of the unfit, influencing several states to pass laws requiring "sterilization of the feeble-minded."[31] Public policy determines whether public funds are spent on missile defense research or cancer research. Within the health budget, policy decisions allocate dollars between breast cancer, HIV/AIDS, and malaria research. The beneficiaries of new knowledge in each of these areas will probably differ, and politics, as well as science, surround the decisions. As biologist Bernard Davis noted twenty years ago, "the increasing dependence of research on public funds [has] encouraged acceptance of the neo-Marxist view that science is primarily an instrument of the prevailing political system rather than a methodology for seeking universal, objective truths about nature."[32]

The modern prognoses of change and progress gain their energy from a universalistic ethic that has a moral dimension to recognize, respect, and extend progress to all human beings regardless of ancestry or gender. On the other hand, the universal claims of progress collide with diverse moral and cultural groups and their claims to protect or insulate themselves from "the production of knowledge that would undermine the foundations of public morality."[33] In his widely respected work, *History of the Idea of Progress,* Nisbet identified two propositions in the history of the idea of progress: knowledge and happiness, as achieved with the perfection of humans' moral and spiritual condition on earth. But since the Garden of Eden and Pandora's Box these themes have been argued to conflict. The great historian A. J. Toynbee argued that so close is the correlation between technological advance and moral decline that the appearance of the former may be used to forecast the latter.[34] Political battles over interpreting the Koran or the Bible, or what some see as our Faustian bargain with modern science in technologies such as human cloning and in vitro fertilization, reflect such rifts over legitimate knowledge and how to apply it to policy.

The Goals, Methods, and Organizations of Public Policy

The modern ideal of progress, the idea that the rational, human application of science and knowledge can improve lives, creates unprecedented promise and responsibility for policy makers. Most citizens, at least in the United States, believe that public policy should reflect a vision of a better future, and that great leaders and good policy can help to shape it. Policy debates begin with the presumption that public policy has a role in progress and that things can change for the better.

Public policy is a purposeful set of actions informed by social values. Policy conflicts about progress revolve around the question: which among the available but incompletely understood visions of the future will best lead to the betterment of the world? The answer, of course, depends on who people are, what they know, and how "the betterment of the world" is defined. Hence the success of public policy in promoting progress depends on our individual and collective ability to overcome at least four challenges. The first two are challenges in defining and measuring the goals of progress—are there any universal visions of progress to provide policy makers with an agenda? If not, what is progress relative to, and against whose base is progress defined? Deciding on which vision to pursue largely determines how the benefits and costs of progress will be measured and shared. Once defined, the remaining challenges are choosing the methods to implement the goals and the individuals and organizations responsible.

The Goals of Public Policy

Etymologically meaning to move forward from a place, the very notion of progress is imbedded in a goal-oriented context.[35] The goal-centered nature of public policy relies on the ideal of progress and the implications of seeking a progressive politics. Goals build upon and create the values and visions of the political actors in a society. They are contestable, and reaching a goal often means rejecting or overriding the goals of others—leaving behind a way of life or existing situation. Not surprisingly, most public policy involves ongoing negotiations over defining the goals, criteria, and metrics by which subsequent policy can be evaluated.[36]

Defining Progress

In many ways, as any good policy analyst knows, the most important moment for policy lies in the definition of the problem itself.[37] Crafting good public policy presumes that decision makers are working from common principles about what constitutes an improvement from the status quo. But the diversity of human populations makes it highly unlikely that people will agree upon criteria for progress that can be applied across time and places.

Fortunately, common principles of progress need not always encompass the entire world. For a community trying to determine whether or not to build a new sports field with evening lighting, for example, the relevant universe may be a neighborhood of 500 homes. For policy makers the universe includes those whose lives will be affected by their choices; in this case, those local residents who will be better or worse off from the vision of progress they follow. Increasingly, however, this may also include advocacy and NGOs bringing more global concerns to policy discussions such as whether the energy sources for the additional lighting will contribute to global warning or whether the field is built on land taken from "disenfranchised" people.

People may agree to a common goal, such as a safe place for children to play, but differ in how they rank policies that trade off certain principles. Libertarians may stress freedom; socialists, equality; community leaders, civil society; parents, security; and others, fairness. There will also be conflict over to whom those principles are accorded. Freedom for kids to play near their home late at night will conflict with the freedom of proximate residents from the resulting glare of lights, noise, and traffic. Equality of local amenities for all neighborhoods means unequal traffic and noise burdens for residents within those neighborhoods. In practice, principles are underdetermined even when people agree on them. When they collide, public policy decides those tradeoffs.

When principles or policies on what constitutes progress differ, politics focuses upon whose vision is to be pursued. For the almost sixty percent of the world's population living in states where democratic governments are elected by universal suffrage,[38] such policies are usually publicly debated and decided by some sort of majority rule in referenda or by elected or appointed officials who may or may not represent the majority (depending on the electoral system, voter turnout, etc.). In authoritarian or single party states, individuals or small groups may decide policy according to their vision of progress. In traditional states the whole point may be to roll back modern progress and return to a golden age or less corrupted time.

Even if a consensus on broad-based criteria for identifying progress can be temporarily secured, definitions of progress change over time. Historically, for example, progress has been defined as "domination over nature" exemplified most in the great modernizing dreams of Soviet and Chinese Marxism.[39] Since at least the 1970s, however, there has been an increasing appreciation of the limits to nature and more recent views of progress often cite the responsible stewardship of the earth's environmental resources.[40]

Universal, and enduring, definitions of what constitutes progress are usually elusive, even when many may believe progress is a good thing. If a common framework does not exist, much of policy making involves developing compromises among competing frames.[41] Since policies create winners and losers, the challenge for public policy is making the world a better place given "the fact of reasonable pluralism"[42] over what constitutes progress. Policies assign rights to individuals and groups—homeowners and parents—and over resources: playing fields, property, peace, and control of the national levers of power. By choosing a vision of progress and setting corresponding goals, policies choose for whom progress is pursued.

Relative Well-being and Equity

Progress is by definition relative. It has traditionally been defined relative to a point in time—how well off are we today compared to yesterday? But in addition to gauging their progress against a personal baseline, it is also clear that people define their well-being relative to others.[43] Policy makers and the media cite not just a "drop in violent crime" but a drop "relative to the national trend."[44] Research suggests that individuals tend to assess their own progress relative to next-door neighbors, friends or relatives across the country, or even strangers across the world. This raises the possibility, for example, of an American with crippling arthritis suddenly feeling worse off when Canada legalizes marijuana smoking for sufferers of debilitating diseases.[45] This relative dimension has become more important globally as information technologies have given the media unprecedented access—people across the world are increasingly aware of each other's lifestyles, creating rising expectations and sometimes backlashes against perceived incursions of dominant western images and values.

Because people view their well-being relative to others, as well as absolutely, policy makers must also be concerned with progress across space, that is, distributional issues and equity. The rising average income levels of many countries have often been heralded by many as progress and a proxy for advances in general welfare.[46] Closer measures reveal, however, that the gap between rich and poor has increased in the United States and elsewhere, as well as between rich and poor nations worldwide.[47] If every person's absolute level of wealth increased relative to their baseline, but the gains varied considerably among individuals, is this progress?[48] For individuals who have just reached subsistence levels, an absolute measure of greater wealth is probably meaningful. But for those who, despite absolute improvements, feel they are falling farther behind, the answer is not so clear.

Material wealth has been one of the most visible measures of progress because of the immense physical production capacities, huge new urban complexes, and great concentrations of capital created by the industrial revolution. But this material revolution also spawned working class movements demanding more protection and a share of the better life, exemplified by the great bourgeois revolutions of the eighteenth century and the growth of socialism and Marxism in the nineteenth century. The modern ideal of progress changed ideas of entitlement and expectations that the fruits of progress would be shared by all. The ongoing battles over globalization typified in demonstrations against the World Trade Organization suggest that these tensions over distribution have not been resolved. The importance of relative well-being implies that policy makers must address both increasing wealth and its distribution, since non-beneficiaries may feel worse off even if their absolute position has improved, or not changed.

Though most of the post-industrial revolution aspirations focussed upon material progress, beneath these changes lay a deeper set of claims. Modern ideas of progress suggest that the plight of *all* humans can be improved by the sustained application of human reason, science, and technology to their problems.[49] It also means that every person possesses a moral dignity that gives them claims to be recognized and respected by the society and state. These claims shatter the traditional and religious understandings of stable social orders with clearly defined roles and classes for different citizens and groups. They threaten traditional and authoritarian regimes which endeavor to insulate their societies from outside influences and resort to traditional, relativist, or post modern arguments to counter demands for progress across class, ethnic, gender, and religious boundaries.

Ideas of equality extended the agenda of public policy beyond the interests of the elite and the rich, to the interests and dignity of all citizens. Western progressive movements demanded the incorporation of property owners, not just hereditary nobles, then all able-bodied males, an end to slavery, and the enfranchisement of women. But this expansion is incomplete, and elsewhere has not occurred, or is occurring very slowly. In many countries, for example, women cannot vote or own property.[50] For a policy maker to consider progress across space requires making judgements across people, groups, and cultures. Is availability of the "morning-after" pill progress, and do women in countries without access feel worse off than before access became available to some? Is banning female genital cutting progress; legally recognizing same-sex marriages? Establishing new rights for groups may make traditionalists feel worse off as their dominance is threatened. Yet moral conceptions of progress play out not only as concerns about general welfare but also about rights and dignity. Post-modernists will argue that these questions cannot be answered and that even if individuals compare themselves to others, policy makers must practice cultural relativism. They claim progress cannot be assessed across groups or cultures—rather for each group, progress can only be assessed according to their own historical record (though the ethics of an individual group's behavior can be criticized).[51]

Measuring the Effects of Progress and Policy

Because public policies are driven by goals, they generate discussions over measurement. Measurement is essential for evaluating whether or not the desired goals have been met; it is essential for holding policy makers accountable to the public. But measures of progress, like all public policy goals, should be valid—that is, they should reflect what they are intended to measure. The search for validity is intimately tied to our ability to define progress and to define a common goal. Measures of progress should also be reliable—that is, repeated measurement should yield the same result.

Policies normally have visible products or results that can be identified and then interpreted by the political actors, such as changes in high school dropout rates or crime statistics. But even these seemingly straightforward measures are subject to criticisms: how was dropout defined, which high school populations were sampled, and over what time period? Unlike in the physical or biological sciences, data from the social sciences—"human interactions, behaviors, and aspirations—are not, and cannot, be standardized."[52] Even if the technical issues can be settled and valid and reliable indicators agreed upon, there is still room for debates over what outcomes can be attributed to particular policies, whether the results actually contribute towards the goals, and how the unanticipated consequences should be counted.[53] In this volume, for example, Zumeta and Brandon discuss measurement efforts in education. In evaluating the well-being of children, Brandon writes about confounding the three different measures of outcomes, features of the environment, and access to resources or policy interventions. Inkeles discusses how the metrics for a broad goal such as "progress" are even more controversial.[54]

Aggregate goals such as increasing the wealth or health of society facilitate measurement by reducing outcomes to clear but overly simplified indicators. This simplification loses information and may be potentially misleading. For instance, economic growth as measured by gross domestic product (GDP) is one of the most commonly cited proxies of progress.[55] As economist Kenneth Boulding explains, "Although it was recognized that it did not reflect the entirety of human needs, it was assumed that any alternative more comprehensive indicator would be sufficiently closely related so that changes in the one could be identified by studying changes in the other."[56] But using GDP is often criticized in this role because it excludes the value of leisure and non-market wage activities, such as parents staying at home to raise their children, and includes the value of divorce litigation and war; it does not accurately reflect the depletion or degradation of natural resources; and it ignores human rights and other non-pecuniary dimensions to the quality of life.[57] In other words, many, including Inkeless, Heilbroner, and Cullen and Bretherton in the chapters that follow, do not believe that GDP growth is a valid measure of progress.[58]

Few people would contest that more economic prosperity is preferred to less economic prosperity, but using GDP as a proxy for progress, for example, raises the issue of what is sacrificed when policies use invalid indicators. At its most benign, focussing on GDP may distort priorities from other goals such as poverty alleviation or inequality. More seriously, focussing on GDP may actually favor policies such as increased resource extraction that run counter to other goals of progress including environmental protection.[59] Further, using averages, for example, average GDP per capita, hides important information on the distribution of wealth and may suggest a country is doing "well" if average GDP is growing, even if the number of people in poverty has not declined.

Measuring human progress in the arts and humanities becomes even more difficult than measuring aggregate indicators of wealth or health, or most measures of changes in our physical quality of life. Quantity measures, sometimes reasonable indicators of material wealth, fare poorly in the arena of art, literature, or religion. They are seldom helpful for discussing ethics or morality or judging progress in social interactions. But quality measures, as in any domain, are more subjective. Most people would agree that more Picasso paintings were preferred to fewer Picasso paintings (except, of course, owners of Picasso paintings whose value was enhanced by their very scarcity). But fewer people would agree on whether Picasso's transition to "cubism" was progress.

Progress in art, as in other realms, has been measured by increases in freedom.[60] But even this criterion elicits differing views on whether the freedom for greater creative license is a valid measure of progress. The molecular biologist Gunther Stent argues that "The absence of recognizable canons reduces his act of creation to near-randomness for the perceiver. In other words, artistic evolution along the one-way street to freedom embodies an element of self-limitation."[61] Alternatively, Almond, Chodorow, and Pearce conclude that though "the idea of progress is applicable to the arts in limited ways.... There is, however, progress in the arts in the sense of the encouragement and fostering of artistic talent, in the display and accessibility of art objects to larger audiences, in the appreciation and interpretation of art objects, and in the enrichment of artistic techniques from the influences of science and technology."[62] Even if some core of critics could agree on a set of criteria to evaluate art, for example, over time, evaluating progress in these realms across cultures is highly controversial.

One classic solution to problems of validity has been to look at human happiness as a way to measure and evaluate progress.[63] Bury relates the ultimate goal of progress to happiness, "as the issue of the earth's great business, a condition of general happiness will ultimately be enjoyed."[64] Similarly for public policy, Charles Murray argues that "the purpose of government is to facilitate the pursuit of happiness of its citizens."[65] In this case a person's subjective well-being is measured—their personal assessment of their happiness or other similar attitude. In theory, this permits more transnational comparisons exempt from criticisms of not being culturally relative (unless of course, the culture does not value happiness).[66]

The irony of using happiness as a measure of progress is how poorly it tracks wealth—a traditional measure of progress—at higher levels of income. Inkeles concludes from an earlier study that "national populations had a culturally fixed tendency to report themselves as happy or unhappy, and a rise in the standard of living was not automatically reflected in an increase in the proportion who reported life satisfaction."[67] Further, it appears that for the more affluent, absolute gains in material well-being can actually bring decreasing returns in "happiness." Andrew Oswald finds that "in a developed nation, economic progress buys only a small amount of extra happiness."[68] Richard Easterlin reports that "There has been no improvement in average happiness in the United States over almost half a century—a period in which real GDP per capita more than doubled.... As incomes rise, the aspiration level does too, and the effect of this increase in aspirations is to vitiate the expected growth in happiness due to higher incomes."[69] Money can buy happiness, Easterlin seems to be saying, but only if the amounts get bigger and other people aren't getting more: "We feel rich if we have more than our neighbors, poor if we have less, and feeling relatively well-off is equated with being happy."[70] These findings reinforce the contention that in defining and measuring their goals policy makers must address both progress over time, and across space.

The Methods of Public Policy

Public policy involves discussions over the proper means to achieve goals. "The means and methods of past progress help shape policy for future progress."[71] The potential methods range widely from persuasion to incentives to coercion.[72] Debates over how to control population, for instance, might involve exhortations and advertising by government and social groups, incentives to have fewer children or penalties for having more, prohibitions on more than a specified number of children, or mandatory sterilization. The choice of means can be as important to the potential success or failure of the program as the actual decision to pursue goals.

The debate about means intricately connects to discussions over progress since the methods chosen might be seen as progressive or not. Coercion imposes high costs on people and the state but can be direct and targeted, while exhortation or incentives can often take much longer and are less certain. Creating institutions that possess huge concentrations of power and coercion to achieve progress can also reduce accountability and lead to tyrannies. At the same time, the means chosen impact the actual depth of change. If progress seeks behavioral outcomes, laws, sanctions, and incentives might be appropriate means. But if it seeks to renovate human nature and human's social, intellectual, and moral essence, far greater control over the means of production, media, education, religion, family, and social organizations might be required.

The wider and deeper the range of changes demanded and the more "corrupt" the society, the greater the need for a total destruction of the existing order before true progress can take place towards a new social order. Certain theories of progress may argue that it is necessary to use extraordinary methods to achieve these ends. Many movements seeking progress demand revolutions or an apocalypse that will cleanse society of corruption and create the foundations for a new order to rise from the ruins of the old. The higher the expectations for progress and total change, the more powerful the vision and motivation, the more tempting the argument for using revolutionary violence becomes.[73]

If a person argues that the free market generates the most progress because of its capacity to produce great wealth and economic innovation, then public policy may choose to enable free markets by minimizing regulation. On the other hand if social equity or environmental sustainability are central to progress, then this might imply tighter governmental regulations over market place activities either to distribute wealth, regulate wages and benefits, or control externalities. Yet even here there will be debate over the best instrument to achieve the goal—should the more direct government command and control instruments be used, or economic incentives such as permit trading or taxes.

Politics

Public policy involves direct and unabashed politics. Change challenges basic values, often inspiring intense reactions to policy innovations in the name of progress. Policy debates and political mobilization will revolve around the meaning of core values within the culture. Public policy often unleashes clashes among the various subcultures within a society if the values dominating policy lead to actions that threaten the practices and identities of these communities. Making public policy becomes a process fraught with political conflict, debate, dialogue, and cooperation.

Gaining support for a policy, however good the idea, noble the purpose, and well-grounded the knowledge, requires the support of coalitions. Political actors will oppose the policy for a wide variety of reasons and unless some level of collaboration or compromise can be reached, a successful policy will need a strong sustainable coalition. The coalition will be needed both to get the major legitimizing institutions to pass and promulgate the policy and to sustain the budgetary and resource levels and the political will to implement it over time.[74]

Coalition building is linked to the need to implement and make decisions across a wide variety of institutions. Creating public policy plays out at the highest level of policy making, at the midlevel of appointed and career officials, and at the street level where individuals must make cumulative decisions about actions to give reality to the policy.[75] This means that public policy never ends. There will be immense slippage, and simply passing a policy or law does not guarantee actions congruent with desired outcomes. It involves ongoing negotiations among all actors and across all sectors and levels of government and society, made more challenging by the specialization of modern political institutions and service delivery groups.

The Rhetoric of Policy Making and Progress

Making and sustaining public policy depends not only upon directing resources through institutions and coercion, but also upon rhetoric, rituals, and symbols that evoke the legitimacy and support of the population. At a fundamental level, debates about policy challenge and recreate a society's understanding of itself and its possibilities. These debates shape the meaning of memory as well as the vision and imagination about the future. Successful and sustained policy builds an abiding acceptance through aligning incentives and policy with the beliefs and values of the impacted populations.

Progress pervades the rhetorical battles in a very deep way. Proponents of progress use a language that immediately indicts the existing arrangements. To argue for "progress" insinuates that the baseline has failed in some way to address human needs and aspirations—it can and needs to get better. The rhetoric of progress throws defenders of the status quo on the defensive; they become conservatives, reactionaries, fundamentalists seeking to define and defend the good in the existing social order against false ideals of progress. Culture wars mark the defensive polarization of such political battles.[76] Counterclaims about subversion, violation, imperialism, and corruption emerge in response to incursions of economic, social, or moral practices demanded by new patterns of applying reason, knowledge, and power to expand the moral status and productive capacity of all people. This becomes especially virulent when indigenous ways of life confront external changes wrought by economic or political changes.[77]

The Organizations of Public Policy

Public policy comprises the means by which individuals or groups within a society collectively pursue their common good. Public policy does not reduce to the actions of government, in fact, governmental actions may hide the true intent and nature of a policy. Rather public policy embraces a coordinated pattern of actions across the society.[78] When policy works, it influences multiple decisions made by individuals such that their decisions and actions contribute to the goals sought.

Policies allocate valuable rights. Hence "public" policy conflicts migrate to the individuals and organizations of the society that possess the legitimacy and sanctioning power to make and implement policy. This explains why public policy tends to equate with government actions; governments usually possess the authorized stature, resources and coercive power to enact the policy.[79]

In most societies, however, government may be only one organization possessing public legitimacy and power to act in ways that influence public outcomes. In some traditional societies and failed states, only local warlords possess the power to implement actions even if they do not possess wide legitimacy. In single party states, the party may control the agenda and final content of goals, in others the military, in still others the clerical caste. The legitimizing authority will shape the amount of coercion, law, social or other institutional mechanisms employed to achieve policy goals as well as the means of funding the goals through taxation, spoils, extortion, donation, or profit.

The government role usually determines what residual role will be played by others. A government's decision not to act *de facto* constitutes a policy to permit other forces such as tribal, economic, social, or religious to dominate. Modern neo-liberalism, for instance, sees the engine of progress as residing in Schumpeter's "creative destruction" wrought by capitalism.[80] Its proposed laissez-faire response really means that the power and imperatives of markets will dominate the social and economic life of societies. Similarly, the acquiescence or silence of government in traditional societies means that traditional local patterns of power and domination will continue in place until disrupted by other influences.

The ideal of progress usually identifies certain organizations as inimical to progress and others as carriers of progress. Marxism diagnosed the liberal bourgeois state as an impediment to progress and social equality. Lenin added that only the communist party carried the knowledge and moral discipline necessary for society to progress.[81] The political battles in socialist revolutions turn around the lack of legitimacy of the state and the unique role of the party to dominate and rule. In a mirror image, political battles between modernizers and religious fundamentalist groups often hinge on claims to represent progress versus claims that such progress represents corruption or impurity and should be rejected. In a number of countries, such as Turkey under Attaturk, the military claims to represent progress and engages in ruthless politics with traditional and religious structures of authority and power. At the same time imperialism and colonialism often justify themselves on the basis of bringing progress to the conquered indigenous people. At various times Rome, China, the Ottomans, Great Britain, the United States, and the Soviet Union justified their hegemony over countries by the advantages of the "civilization" they brought. Behind all these claims to rule is the presumption that the new way of life constitutes a significant improvement over the traditional ways of the society. The rhetoric of progress gives it a self-justifying rationale.

Public policy requires artful leadership throughout the process and leaders themselves can be powerful forces of progressive change. Cullen and Bretherton argue in this volume that "leaders may command attention and motivate followers by charisma, by example, or by force." The legitimacy of leadership is always part of the battle over progress. Leaders will vie for being the true harbinger of progress or the defender of tradition. There will be ongoing concerns over how to develop an issue and get it on the agenda.[82] Often this involves not only the work of coalition building but gathering and disseminating knowledge and influencing the culture to support change. Leadership might also require linking the values of progress and change to the deeper value structure of the society and attending to the political skills of timing, recognizing opportunities, and building long-term acceptance.[83]

Conclusion

Progress is an historically explosive concept because it throws fundamental issues into stark relief. Progress precipitates intense arguments because by its very nature it challenges the existing distribution of culture, power, and authority. It intensifies the predictable conflicts that will occur over defining problems, coordinating across groups, battling over legitimacy, and determining who should carry and implement the banner of progress. This conflict is exemplified in contemporary battles across the globe. On one side cosmopolitan and modernizing elites influenced by ideologies such as liberalism, socialism, feminism, or environmentalism seek to change their societies. They face localized fundamentalisms backed by traditional or established elites that challenge the pretensions of universal claims to both further progress and of certain groups to act to further that progress.

The quest for, or belief in universal principles competes with relativistic claims that progress either does not exist or can only be discussed in terms of local cultures and languages on their own terms. The debates over progress are fueled by the potential of science and technology that make material and moral progress possible for all. Yet these very forces of knowledge and production may cause immense social and environmental problems. These problems can undo the very conditions of modern ideas of progress that hold all men and women as endowed with basic freedoms and with the rights to subsistence and control over their own lives.

These tensions occur in all domains. Progress in the material world, so evident in industrialized countries, competes with social dislocation, inequality, and environmental stewardship. Progress in relations with others strives to find basic rights for men and women against a backlash designed to petrify social orders. At the same time, wide claims of tolerance and mutual respect compete with the resurgence of ethnic conflict in the wake of failed states and an embryonic worldwide humanitarian and emergency relief system. Individuals struggle with their own perennial needs for identity, meaning, sacredness, engagement, and affiliation. The dignity of each person plays out in social and economic fields building on the moral and intellectual resources of both local societies and the increasing common pool of humanity. Here the freedom of human thought and action made possible by modern wealth and knowledge conflict with the dehumanization of specialization, mass production, and fundamentalisms. Individually each of these tensions are reflected in efforts to define, measure and promote or undermine progress. Modern policy makers must seek to reconcile these tensions if progress is to remain a tenable guide for global political and economic life.

Notes

1. Cited from Charles Murray, *In Pursuit of Happiness and Good Government* (New York: Simon and Schuster, 1988), 20.

2. *The Compact Edition of the Oxford English Dictionary*, vol. 2 (Oxford: Oxford University Press, 1971), s.v. "progress."

3. Erving Goffman, *Frame Analysis: An Essay on the Organization of Experience* (Boston: Northeastern University Press, 1986).

4. Carl L. Becker, *The Heavenly City of the Eighteenth Century Philosophers* (New Haven: Yale University Press, 1932), 8-11.

5. Most famously, perhaps, Machiavelli. See Robert Nisbet, *History of the Idea of Progress* (New York: Basic Books, 1980), 106.

6. J. Patrick Dobel, "The Corruption of the State," *American Political Science Review* 72, no. 3 (September 1978): 958-73.

7. W. Warren Wager, ed., *The Idea of Progress Since the Renaissance* (New York: John Wiley and Sons, 1969), 28-32.

8. Mortimer J. Adler and William Gorman, ed., *The Great Ideas: A Syntopicon of Great Books of the Western World*, vol. 2 (Chicago: William Benton, 1952), 441.

9. Thomas Hobbes, *Leviathan*, ed. C. B. MacPherson (Harmondsworth: Penguin Press, 1981), 13.

10. Despite his direct rejection of Christianity, the intractable nature he presumes resembles clearly the fallen nature of human beings. See, Hobbes, *Leviathan*.

11. Aristotle, *The Politics*, trans. Carnes Lord (Chicago: University of Chicago Press, 1984); Niccolo Machiavelli, *The Prince*, trans. George Bull (Harmondsworth: Penguin Press, 1961); Jean Jacques Rousseau, *The Social Contract*, trans. Maurice Cranston (Harmondsworth: Penguin, 1968). All emphasized the importance of the founding act and how the founders of a state imprint it with their virtue and laws.

12. Niccolo Machiavelli, *The Prince*, chap. XV-XXI; Thucydides, *The Complete Writings of Thucydides* (New York: Modern Library, 1934), chap. IX, XVII.

13. Matt Ridley, *The Red Queen: Sex and the Evolution of Human Nature* (New York: Penguin Books, 1993).

14. Ridley, *The Red Queen*; Jared Diamond, *Guns, Germs, and Steel: The Fates of Human Societies* (New York: W. W. Norton, 1997).

15. W. Warren Wagar, ed., *The Idea of Progress Since the Renaissance* (New York:

John Wiley and Sons, 1969), 24-26; G. Iggers, "The Idea of Progress in Historiography and Social Thought Since the Enlightenment," in *Progress and Its Discontents*, ed. Gabriel Almond, Marvin Chodorow, and Roy Harvey Pearce (Berkeley: University of California Press, 1982), 188-90; Charles Frankel, "The Idea of Progress," in *The Encyclopedia of Philosophy*, vol. 6, ed. Paul Edwards (New York: Macmillan, 1972), 483-87. Though definitions of evolutionary progress, for example, might stress net, not necessarily uniform and continuous, progress. Net progress "requires only that later members of the sequence be better *on the average* than earlier members." See Francisco Ayala, "The Evolutionary Concept of Progress" in *Progress and Its Discontents*, ed. Gabriel Almond, Marvin Chodorow, and Roy Harvey Pearce (Berkeley: University of California Press, 1982), 111.

16. Nisbet, *History*, 4.

17. For an in-depth discussion of Saint Augustine's *The City of God*, see Nisbet, *History*, chapter 2.

18. Adler and Gorman, *The Great Ideas*, 440.

19. Adler and Gorman, *The Great Ideas*, 440.

20. J. B. Bury, *The Idea of Progress; an Inquiry into Its Origins and Growth* (London: Macmillan, 1920), 5.

21. See, for example, Nisbet writing on Adam Smith, Thomas Malthus, and Henry George, or Keohane on Condorcet in Nisbet, *History*, 190, 218, 206, 36 (respectively).

22. Nisbet, *History*, chapter 1-5.

23. Bury, *The Idea of Progress*, 38.

24. G. Poggi, "The Modern State and the Idea of Progress," in *Progress and Its Discontents*, ed. Gabriel Almond, Marvin Chodorow, and Roy Harvey Pearce (Berkeley: University of California Press, 1982), 337-59; Iggers, "The Idea of Progress in Historiogaphy," 41-67.

25. Iggers, "The Idea of Progress in Historiogaphy," 150-53; Frankel, "The Idea of Progress," 483-87.

26. Poggi, "The Modern State," 346-48.

27. Poggi, "The Modern State," 337-60.

28. Herbert Goldhamer, *The Adviser* (New York: Elsevier, 1978); Aaron B. Widavsky, *Speaking Truth to Power: The Art and Craft of Policy Analysis* (Boston: Little, Brown, 1979).

29. Francis Bacon, *The New Atlantis* (Kila, Mont.: Kessinger, 1992).

30. Paul Kennedy, *The Rise and Fall of the Great Powers: Economic Change and Military Conflict from 1500 to 2000* (New York: Random House, 1987).

31. J. Edsall, "Progress in Our Understanding of Biology" in *Progress and Its Discontents*, ed. Gabriel Almond, Marvin Chodorow, and Roy Harvey Pearce (Berkeley: University of California Press, 1982), 151. See also, Arthur James Todd, *Theories of Social Progress* (New York: MacMillan Co., 1919), chap. XVII.

32. Bernard D. Davis, "Fear of Progress in Biology," " in *Progress and Its Discontents*, ed. Gabriel Almond, Marvin Chodorow, and Roy Harvey Pearce (Berkeley: University of California Press, 1982), 183.

33. Davis, "Fear of Progress in Biology," 184.

34. Nisbet, *History*, 6.

35. *The American Heritage Dictionary, Second College Edition* (Boston: Houghton Mifflin Company, 1985), s.v. "progress."

36. David L. Weimer and Aidean R. Vining, *Policy Analysis: Concepts and Practice*, 3d ed. (Upper Saddle River, N.J.: Prentice Hall, 1999), chapter 1-4.

37. Weimer and Vining, *Policy Analysis;* Edith Stokey and Richard Zeckhauser, *A Primer for Policy Analysis* (New York: W. W. Norton, 1978); Deborah Stone, *Policy Paradox: The Art of Political Decision Making* (New York: Norton, 1997).

38. Freedom House, "Democracy's Century: A Survey of Global Political Change in the 20th Century" *Freedom House,* 7 Dec. 1999, at www.freedomhouse.org/reports/century.html (accessed July 2001).

39. Judith Shapiro, *Mao's War Against Nature: Politics and the Environment in Revolutionary China* (Cambridge: Cambridge University Press, 2001). Also see Richard White "The Nature of Progress" and Leo Marx "Domination of Nature and the Redefinition of Progress," in *Progress: Fact or Illusion?*, ed. Leo Marx and Bruce Mazlish (Ann Arbor: University of Michigan Press, 1996).

40. Leo Marx points out that in 1783 in his Notes on Virginia, Thomas Jefferson foreshadowed a vision of progress resting on what we would now call environmental sustainability. See Marx, "Domination of Nature."

41. J. Patrick Dobel, *Compromise and Political Action: Political Morality in Liberal and Democratic Life* (Totowa, N.J.: Rowman & Littlefield, 1990).

42. John Rawls, *Justice as Fairness: A Restatement*, ed. Erin Kelly (Cambridge, Mass.: Harvard University Press, 2001), 3.

43. Richard A. Easterlin, *Growth Triumphant: The Twenty-first Century in Historical Perspective* (Ann Arbor: University of Michigan Press, 1996); Michael McBride, "Relative-income Effects on Subjective Well-being in the Cross-section," *Journal of Economic Behavior and Organization* 45, no. 3 (July 2001): 251-78.

44. Hector Castro and Phuong Cat Le, "Seattle's Violent Crime Rate Falls," *Seattle Post Intelligencer*, 26 January 2002, (B1).

45. Colin Nickerson, "Marijuana Use by Terminally Ill gets the Blessing of Canada," *The Boston Globe*, printed in the *Seattle Post-Intelligencer*, 31 July 2001, (A2).

46. See Hazel Henderson, "What's Next in the Great Debate about Measuring Wealth and Progress?" *Challenge* 39, no. 6 (Nov.-Dec. 1996): 50; and Clifford Cobb, Tedd Halstead, and Jonathon Howe, "If GDP is Up Why is America Down?," *Atlantic Monthly* 276, no. 4 (October 1995).

47. According to United Nations Human Development Programme, *Human Development Report 1999* (New York: Oxford University Press, 1999), 38-39, "an analysis of long-term trends in world income distribution (across countries) shows that the distance between the richest and poorest country was about 3 to 1 in 1820, 11 to 1 in 1913, 35 to 1 in 1950, 44 to 1 in 1973, and 72 to 1 in 1992. These trends mask the fact that many countries have caught up with the most advanced."

48. Of course, not every person's absolute well being has improved. For those individuals, however, it is easy to argue that material progress has not occurred.

49. See C. Leigh Anderson and David A. Hennes, "Introduction" in this volume for a discussion on equality and universality.

50. As Condorcet noted in the late eighteenth century "the forces of enlightenment are still in possession of no more than a very small portion of the globe." N. Keohane "The Enlightenment Idea of Progress Revisited," in *Progress and Its Discontents*, ed. Gabriel Almond, Marvin Chodorow, and Roy Harvey Pearce (Berkeley: University of California Press, 1982), 36.

51. Merrilee Salmon argues that "respect for other cultures and a commitment to studying them in the context of their own historical development need not prevent anthropologists from criticising the morality of some practices of those cultures. Cultural relativism does not entail ethical relativism." From Merrilee Salmon, "Ethical Considerations in Anthropology and Archaeology or Relativism and Justice For All," *Journal of Anthropological Research* 53, no. 1 (Spring 1997): 47-63.

52. Gabriel Almond, Marvin Chodorow, and Roy Harvey Pearce, ed., *Progress and its Discontents* (Berkeley: University of California Press, 1982), 12.

53. Richard I. Hofferbert, *The Study of Public Policy* (Indianapolis, Ind.: Bobbs-Merrill, 1974), 3-9.

54. See Alex Inkeles, "Two Steps Forward and One Step Back: An Assessment of Progress in the Twentieth Century," in chapter 2 of this volume for a fuller discussion of measurement issues.

55. The average annual increase in GNP per capita is billed as "the 2 percent answer to the American Dream." See, Council of Economic Advisors, *Economic Report of the President & The Annual Report of the Council of Economic Advisors* (Washington D.C.: United States Government Printing Office, 2000), 23. See also Henderson, "What's next;" Cobb, Halstead, and Howe, "If GDP Is Up;" and A.J. Oswald, "Happiness and Economic Performance," *The Economic Journal* 107, no. 445 (1997): 1815-32.

56. Kenneth Boulding, *Human Betterment* (Beverly Hills; Calif.: Sage Publications, 1985), 16.

57. See Henderson, "What's Next;" Cobb, Halstead, and Howe, "If GDP is Up;" Oswald "Happiness;" and M. W. Kusnic and J. Da Vanzo, *Accounting for Nonmarket Activities in the Distribution of Income: An Empirical Investigation* (Santa Monica: Rand, 1984) for critques of equating GNP growth with progress.

58. Some would argue that GDP is not even a good measure of economic performance. See Boulding, *Human Betterment*, chapter 1.

59. Cullen and Bretherton argue that "optimizing economic policy to maximize GNP growth will tend to maximize rather than minimize resource consumption." See, Alison Cullen and Christopher Bretherton, "Progressing toward Environmental Sustainability," 379, chapter 22 of this volume.

60. Nisbet argues that many great minds believed that the ultimate objective of progress was increased personal freedom. See Nisbet, *History*, chapter 6.

61. Richard John Neuhaus, "The Idea of Moral Progress," *First Things: The Journal of Religion and Public Life* 95 (August/September 1999): 21.

62. Almond, Chodorow, and Harvey Pearce, ed., *Progress and Its Discontents*, 12.

63. See McBride, "Relative-income," 253; Keohane "The Enlightenment Idea," 21-40; and Nisbet on John Stuart Mill, Joseph Priestley, and others, Nisbet, *History*, 201, 226.

64. Bury, *The Idea of Progress*, 5.

65. Murray, *In Pursuit of Happiness*, 27.

66. Comte, however, argued that it is impossible to compare happiness across states. See Bury, *The Idea of Progress*, 191.

67. See Inkeles, "Two Steps Forward," 27, chapter 2 in this volume for more discussion of this point.

68. Oswald, "Happiness," 1827.

69. Edward Cornish, "Happiness and Wealth," *The Futurist* 31, no. 5 (September/October 1997): 13.

70. Cornish, "Happiness and Wealth," 13.

71. Adler and Gorman, *The Great Ideas*, 439.

72. Charles F. Lindblom, *Politics and Markets: The World's Political Economic Systems* (New York: Basic Books, 1977).

73. Norman Cohn, *The Pursuit of the Millennium* (London: Secker & Warburg, 1957); Melvin Lasky, *Utopia and Revolution* (Chicago: University of Chicago Press, 1976).

74. Eugene Bardach, *The Implementation Game: What Happens After a Bill Becomes a Law* (Cambridge, Mass.: MIT Press, 1977).

75. Laurence E. Lynn, Jr., *Managing Public Policy* (Boston: Little Brown, 1987); Michael Lipsky, *Street-level Bureaucracy: Dilemmas of the Individual in Public Service* (New York: Russell Sage Foundation, 1980).

76. John Davison Hunter, *Culture Wars: The Struggle to Define America* (New York: Basic Books, 1991).

77. Thomas L. Friedman, *The Lexus and the Olive Tree* (New York: Farrar, Straus, Giroux, 1999).

78. James E. Anderson, *Public Policy Making*, 3d ed. (New York: Holt, Rinehart, and Winston, 1984), 3-5.

79. Anderson, *Public Policy Making*, 4-6.

80. Joseph Schumpeter, *Capitalism, Socialism, and Democracy* (New York: Harper and Row, 1976).

81. Karl Marx, *The Eighteenth Brumaire of Louis Bonaparte, with explanatory notes* (New York: International Publishers, 1963); Vladimir Ilitch Lenin, *What is to Be Done?*, trans. S. V. and Patricia Utechin (Oxford: Clarendon Press, 1963).

82. John W. Kingdon, *Agendas, Alternatives, and Public Policies* (New York: Longman, 1995).

83. J. Patrick Dobel, "Political Prudence and the Ethics of Leadership," *Public Administration Review* 58, no. 1 (January/February 1998): 74-81; William H. Riker, *The Art of Political Manipulation* (New Haven: Yale University Press, 1986).

Chapter 2

Two Steps Forward and One Step Back: An Assessment of Progress in the Twentieth Century

Alex Inkeles

Even a casual survey of the history of history tells us that no human condition will be recognized as progress across *all* communities and *all* times. The tearing of one's flesh, the starving of one's body, even self-immolation have in many times and places been seen by large numbers of people as constituting progress toward some goal such as granting salvation to the soul or as bestowing some other general and eternal state of well-being. Nevertheless, there seem to be some conditions that are valued as progress in almost all communities in virtually all times. Among these are increasing freedom from the scourge of such devastating infectious diseases as smallpox and diphtheria, and the enjoyment of better health generally; longer life; greater freedom from hunger and extreme heat or cold; and security in one's person and possessions. The list can be considerably expanded. Many, indeed, most of these benefits can be objectively measured. Those measures, *taken individually*, or even when taken as *a group of indicators,* can be used to make a strong case that the last century has been an era of extraordinary human progress.

However, anyone who performs such a statistical exercise, and reaches the aforementioned conclusion, must acknowledge the highly specific nature of the evidence she has drawn on, and recognize how limited this way of judging human progress is. Even staying within the framework of those who are oriented toward measurement, we find formidable challenges. The universe of conditions it would be relevant to consider is quite large, and we may wonder how adequate a sample of those relevant conditions has been drawn in the research results presented to us. And there are daunting uncertainties about how we should properly weight one or another indicator.

While some celebrate the widespread rise in life expectancy at birth, others ask us not to forget the tens of millions of soldiers who died on the battlefields of World War I and II, to say nothing of the millions of civilians who perished from bombing, starvation, and rampaging diseases which were concomitants of that fighting. R. J. Rummel went further to assess the extent of lethal violence against whole populations perpetrated not by other nations but rather by governments acting against their own citizens or subjects. He came to the startling conclusion that the number of individuals so dispatched *within* nations in the twentieth century far exceeded all the deaths resulting from all the wars *between* nations in that same span of time.[1] Beyond the stupefying impact of the sheer numbers involved, we must also confront the distinctive perversity, the palpable evil, of such monstrous campaigns of genocide as the Holocaust. All this helps us understand why Daniel Bell concluded that far from being the best of centuries, the twentieth was arguably the worst in human history.[2]

Bell's verdict on the twentieth century brings to the fore the issue of how to weight the numbers we can collect about the human condition. Is each year which modern sanitation and medicine *add* to the life of a child or an old man to be given the same weight as each year *lost* in the life of a young man who dies on the battlefield? In this case we may perhaps readily come to agree that it is fruitless to struggle over such distinctions, and that we should treat any year of life lost or gained as just one year of life. But we will not readily come to such agreement when deeply held values are involved, for example, when we are asked to weigh the years lost by a fetus whose future is decided by an abortion. For many this raises an issue that cannot be resolved by any arithmetic, no matter how cleverly devised, but rather must be settled on absolute moral grounds.

Uncertainty and ambiguity about the relevance for assessing progress of those social facts which can be readily measured is greatly magnified when we turn to qualities which are less objectively verifiable. We know that people want to live longer, and we can easily judge how far progress towards that goal is being achieved by looking at the statistics on life expectancy. But people also want those additional years to be more meaningful and rewarding. And these are subtle and elusive qualities not easily measured.

To inquire whether life is meaningful and rewarding causes us to focus on the individual, and on his or her level of satisfaction, rather than on social and political institutions. This approach has the great advantage that one can ask *a person* whether or not he is satisfied or pleased with one or another condition or arrangement, and on that basis make a judgment about progress. One cannot put the same question to *an institution*, which in this respect is inevitably dumb. To judge progress in the institutional realm one must apply an external standard based on some stated but almost inevitably much contested value. Probably one can get wide agreement that those institutional arrangements are preferable that provide order rather than chaos, consistency rather than arbitrariness, and transparency rather than obscurity. We might then say, the more institutions manifest or generate the qualities and conditions placed first in these pairs, the more they have progressed.

It is more difficult to win consensus for the proposition that it is progress to move from authoritarian to democratic political institutions, or to transform a socialist economy to one based on capitalist principles, or to shift from limited involvement of government in private life to a full blown welfare state. This is a complex realm in which almost every conclusion is challenged, and it cannot be dealt with adequately in a brief communication. Consequently, however interesting and important questions about the progress of institutions may be, I have here excluded them from consideration.

Objective Indicators and the Assessment of Progress

The indicators one might consider in judging whether or not a particular person or community is experiencing progress are numerous, and by carefully selecting one or another measure one might tilt the summary judgment more towards progress or away from it. One could, of course, strive for an exhaustive list of indicators, or try to devise some summary statistic of progress. But such efforts would face formidable problems and endless dispute as to what should or should not be included. And the problem of how to weight different properties is daunting. For example, if an ordinary year of life were given a base value of ten, what should be the weight of that year be if it was spent fighting a terrible disabling and disfiguring disease? Should it be scored a mere five or three or even a negative number? And by contrast if the year was spent in robust health entirely free of illness or disease how far should it be weighed above the average of ten? Should it be weighed at twelve points, or fifteen, or even given double the average weight? The resolution of these issues, if they could be resolved, would require major research staffed by philosophers as well as sociologists, and would demand years of their best joint effort. Limited as I am here both as to scope and space, I have selected a small set of indicators which I believe are important not only in my view but likely will be so in the opinion of most observers. But I also give voice to those who take a position contrary to what seems to be a general consensus, questioning both the logic of selecting the commonly selected indicators of progress and the validity of the numbers presented. As a representative of this perspective I give particular voice to the distinguished anthropologist, Professor Richard Shweder of the Committee on Human Development of the University of Chicago, who in the context of a conference focussed on issues similar to those we deal with characterized himself as "one of the heretics at this revival meeting."[3]

The Gift of Life

We do not need to reinvent the legend of Faust to know that the average person would give a great deal in exchange for our granting him an extra year of life beyond that which had been allocated by Nature or by God. How then should he respond if what we could offer was not one additional year but thirty or even forty years of additional life? Yet it is precisely such a gain in life expectancy that the average person born in England, France, Germany, and the United States in 1990 enjoyed in comparison with those born in the same countries 100 years before. Moreover, this benefit of extra life was not limited to these few favored countries. Instead, it was rather widely conferred on the populations of other nations within and outside of Europe. Indeed, Japan was a world leader, moving from a life expectancy of less than forty years in 1900 to over eighty by the end of the century.

In the less developed countries comparably dramatic gains in longevity generally came later in the century, and the absolute levels recorded did not equal that of the more developed countries. Nevertheless, almost all of the populations of the world's poor countries gained greatly in longevity during the twentieth century. In Latin America, for example, longevity rose from being below thirty in 1890 to well over sixty by 1990. And India, one of the world's poorest countries, almost tripled longevity over the course of the century, going from a life expectancy just above twenty to one just above sixty years.[4] Clearly this was not a case where the rich grew richer while the poor grew poorer. On the contrary, as the Indian case highlights, *the rate of improvement* in the least developed countries was greater than that in the more developed. Consequently, the relative advantage of the most advanced, being approximately 2:1 at the beginning of the century, had by its end shrunk almost to the point of equality with a ratio of approximately 7:6.

Even these gains, nearly universally interpreted as signs of human progress, do not escape a challenge from Professor Shweder. Measures of life expectancy, he points out, consider a child's fate only from the moment of birth, and thus do not consider the consequences of abortion as a "hazard of the womb." He asks us to consider "how different our life expectancy tables would be if we factored in the twenty to twenty-five percent abortion rates in the United States and Canada or the fifty percent abortion rates in Russia as compared to rates as low as two to ten percent in India, Tunisia, and some parts of the 'underdeveloped' world."

Professor Shweder likely underestimates the extent of abortion among populations living in the poorest condition. He also seems to underemphasize the fact that merely getting the chance to go full term does not in itself grant the fetus many years of life when infant and child mortality are high. Nevertheless, his challenge is substantial, and at the very least we should try to calculate life expectancy taking into account the years lost through abortion. But for a balanced judgment, we would also have to consider the limits on the quality of life both for those thus granted existence as well as the impact on all the rest of their compatriots obliged to share a world of limited resources with an ever, larger population. All this gives each of us an opportunity to work out our individual estimate of how far, on balance, the measured gains in life expectancy, with or without the record on abortion, constitute a clear instance of human progress.

In making that assessment one surely should consider not only the sheer number of years a person lives, but also the quality of life in the extra years that person has been granted. To that end I propose we look at two indicators for which we have reasonably good statistics, namely nutrition and disease.

Nutrition

Getting born is only the first step in winning the assurance of a chance to life. A life dogged by constant hunger is a life of misery. And beyond the pangs of hunger, undernourishment results in developmental disabilities like rickets, heightened vulnerability to all manner of infectious disease, and in the extreme case, to death.

Shortage of proper food comes in two forms, persistent and acute. The persistent form is expressed as malnutrition, the acute as famine. Famines have been a continuous accompaniment of human existence. It must surely have afflicted many scattered populations before recorded history. The Bible brings it to our attention as a feature of ancient times in the story of Joseph and his advice to the Pharaoh to store up grain against his vision of the lean years to come. Historically famines due to natural disasters such as drought and flood could not be overcome readily because surpluses that could be brought from elsewhere were scarce, and in any event the afflicted populations did not have the economic wherewithal to buy such surpluses, nor the means to transport them.

Such limits cannot excuse the famines of the nineteenth century. Only lack of social sensitivity and political will can explain the great Irish famine, which began in 1845. The record for the twentieth century is especially damaging to the case of those who might argue for the seamless progress of human kind. Famine claimed millions of live in China before the "Liberation" in 1949; in Communist Russia in the first years of the Revolution and then again in connection with the collectivization of agriculture; and in India, notably in the Great Bengal famine of 1943. The Second World War seemed to mark a turning point beyond which such massive famines would never again occur, but this optimistic view was dashed by the famines in Communist China following "The Great Leap Forward."

Nothing comparable to these disasters, indeed very little that might qualify as general famine on a large scale has occurred since that time. The passage of almost half a century without major famine may then mark a turning point in human progress, but given recent history this estimate must be recognized as highly tentative.

The record regarding the less dramatic but probably even more destructive incidence of undernourishment and malnutrition is equally mixed and permits only a tentative judgement of progress. In poor countries caloric intake is highly stratified. In India, for example, data for 1971-72 revealed that for those with the lowest per capita income the daily intake of calories was only a third of that ingested by those in the highest decile on the scale of income.[5] A much greater and more dramatic spread between those that have and those that have not is manifested when one makes comparisons *across nations,* and uses as a proxy for nutrition the percent of children under five years of age who are underweight. According to The World Bank data for the 1990 decade, the wealthier countries report at most 1 or 2 percent of those aged five or younger to be underweight for their age. By contrast, in low-income countries a staggering 36 percent suffer from this deficiency, and neither adding nor subtracting the two giants in this category, namely China and India, made any difference. The lower half of the middle income countries stood at an intermediate point, with some 14 percent of the under five children being underweight.[6]

Historical data on nutrition are spotty, especially for the new nations, so it is difficult to measure progress over time. The contrasts we have observed within and across countries suggest that over time, as national income rises, the proportion of malnourished children will fall. But the differences still existing at the end of the century are so great, it will surely take a long time before the grievous disparities between the most and the least economically advanced nations is substantially narrowed.

We seem here to face a paradox. Over the last century the gap in life expectancy separating the most and the least economically advanced nations was greatly reduced. By contrast, the differences in their ability to adequately nourish their populations persisted at very high levels. We can resolve the paradox by examining the history of advances in sanitation and public hygiene.

Advances in Sanitation and Medical Technology

Most contemporary citizens of urban communities automatically assume their life conditions to be superior to those of people living in the countryside. Marx spoke for many when he condemned "the idiocy of rural life." But the actual history of the late eighteenth and early nineteenth century tells a different story. Dickens is a better guide to the social reality of city life in that century span than was Marx. The early cities of the modern era provided a poorer prognosis for life than did the countryside, and as the first great cities of those times grew in size and density they equally grew in the misery of very large segments of their populations. Sickness and disease were rampant and epidemic, and the rates of morbidity and mortality—indicators we today celebrate as evidence of human progress—actually rose, rather than fell, from year to year. Cholera, dysentery, and diphtheria regularly carried off large numbers, especially among the young.

A new awareness of the link between sanitation and pervasive disease and excessive mortality developed after Edwin Chadwick published his landmark *Report on the Sanitary Conditions of the Labouring Population of Great Britain* in 1842. Under its influence governments took the first great countermeasures to halt these rampant diseases by building sewage systems to carry off the concentrated wastes of the rapidly expanding urban conglomerates. Probably equally important was the protection of the water supply, which was otherwise a universal carrier of a variety of deadly diseases.

Improvements in sanitation, great as their effects might be, were no help in controlling diseases such as smallpox and diphtheria. Reducing *their* impact depended on the development of vaccination. Among the first of the scourges to thus be brought under control was smallpox, which in the seventeenth and early eighteenth century disfigured multitudes and sent great numbers of all ages to the grave. It is a remarkable achievement that worldwide campaigns to inoculate people against this disease gave it the rare distinction of being the first to be made extinct as a result of the growth of knowledge and the enlargement of cooperative human effort. Less universal in effect, but still enormously successful, have been subsequent programs to inoculate against diphtheria, typhoid fever, and scarlet fever.

The extreme disadvantage suffered by the populations of poorer countries, which we have so often noted, is greatly reduced in the case of inoculation against the devastating diseases of childhood. By the end of the twentieth century even the low income countries reported rates of inoculation against measles and diphtheria of 80 and 82 percent, respectively. This put the poorer countries remarkably close to the performance of even the upper-middle income nations.[7]

Unfortunately, few of the other perils of early life in a very poor country can be deflected by such "magic bullets" as are provided by inoculation. The cumulative effect of these other liabilities causes the rates of mortality for those under the age of five to continue to be sharply differentiated as one moves across the range of national income per capita.[8] The contrast between the health experience of the more and less advantaged nations takes a different but not less striking form in the case of AIDS, the latest scourge of human kind, which is taking an exceptionally heavy toll on both young and old in that set of the world's poorest nations constituting Africa.

Making allowances for such continuing differences in access to good health, one can still claim that advances in sanitation and public health have meant marked progress for most of human kind by granting them the benefit of enjoying their extra years of life in a condition relatively free of the historically classic epidemic diseases.

Again Richard Shweder challenges what seems so obvious to so many. Accepting the risk of being called "neo-antiquarian" he makes the claim that the longer a population lives "the greater the frequency of chronic illness, the greater the likelihood of functional impairment, and hence the higher the aggregate amount of pain experienced by that population." He therefore questions whether a longer life "is unambiguously a better life."

There is good reason to argue that Professor Shweder is wrong both about the facts and the conclusion he draws from them. Of course, everyone must eventually die, and their death must have a cause such as cancer or heart failure. But the fact is that at least in the more advanced countries the vast majority of the elderly are not suffering the functional impairment, or the life of pain, Professor Shweder imagines them to be experiencing. Instead, more and more people live longer lives without debilitating disease. For example, in the United States, which by no means has the best record in the world, 84 percent of men over 65 years of age were free *of even one* of the standard set of nine physical limitations—such as being unable to climb stairs or to kneel—often assumed to be typical of the aged. Moreover, the proportion having one or more of the nine disabilities has been steadily falling, going down from 20 percent in 1982 to 16 percent in 1994. These objective facts encourage us to accept the validity of the more subjective reports indicating that 72 percent of all those over 65, men and women combined, consider themselves as in either good or excellent health.[9]

Moving on to More Qualitative Measures

If the space I have been allotted would permit, I could go on to list and document a large number of other ways in which the condition of people all over the world has changed in directions most would identify as constituting progress. Thus, in the physical world I could demonstrate the extent to which people have come to live in more durable structures more fully supplied with basic amenities. A foray into social indicators would permit me to document the vast increase in literacy and in the average number of years of schooling people attain. In still another realm, the worldwide diffusion of political rights, of participatory citizenship, and of democratic institutions would be recorded. And a case could be made for the ever-growing movement towards equality for those social groups, especially women, previously marginalized or even totally excluded from full participation in social and political life.

However, there is a significant audience which does not accept the conclusion that these numerous and diverse changes in the human condition suffice to prove that we are enjoying ever-wider and deeper *progress*. They question whether, within the longer life we have been granted, we enjoy more affection and love; whether we can count on being treated with respect, shielded from ridicule and degradation; whether we can savor a strong sense of community or must accept being isolated and alone; whether we feel more or less empowered; whether life brings more joys or more sorrow; or, whether we feel *in sum more or less satisfied and happy* than those who came before us, or even than we ourselves felt a decade ago. They may not go so far as to raise the biblical challenge of asking what does it avail a man to gain the world if he loses his soul, but that query captures the essence of their reservation. Such critics want evidence of increases in such qualities as courtesy, kindness, and loyalty, and they question the assumption that just because a person lives longer she lives "better."

At issue here are elusive qualities, not easily measured. Certainly the condition of the soul is something a social scientist must leave to a different kind of specialist. But other more qualitative assessments of peoples' lives have been attempted in surveys conducted by sociologists and political scientists, and they yield some interesting results which must be sobering and challenging to those who express what Shweder has rather scornfully labeled "triumphal progressivism."

On Measuring Happiness

As early as 1960, in a review of the studies of subjective well-being, I posed the question: "Does raising the income of all increase the happiness of all?"[10] The evidence then available indicated that national populations had a culturally fixed tendency to report themselves as happy or unhappy, and a rise in the standard of living was not automatically reflected in an increase in the proportion who reported life satisfaction. More recent work by Richard Easterlin seems to establish the point unequivocally. As nations become richer, their populations do not become, on average, happier. The most dramatic, but by no means unique, evidence for this proposition comes from Japan. Because of the "economic miracle" the country experienced, the average Japanese individual in 1987 enjoyed a real per capita income *five times as great* as that which had been available in 1957. Yet, as Easterlin shows, despite their experience of extraordinary improvements in consumption and living conditions, the typical Japanese individual reported himself or herself as no happier or more satisfied with life at the end of the period than they had at the beginning.[11]

As Easterlin notes, the explanation for this seeming paradox lies in the fact that in responding to questions about subjective well-being people are making a *relative* judgement, that is, each person compares herself with others in the same country. Even if, with the passage of time, she has come to have more income, the fact that others also now have more income leaves her, in effect, in the same relative position she was in before. There is, therefore, no reason for her to feel she is "better off." It is as if people everywhere were listening to the wisdom of Mark Twain, who suggested that to be happy we should "proportion our wants to our possessions, our ambitions to our capacities."

The picture might look different if people were asked to judge their condition against an absolute rather than a relative standard. Pursuit of that possibility, however, would keep us too long occupied with material welfare, and we must give some attention, before we close, to issues of progress in what is sometimes called the realm of the spirit.

On Sentiments, Human Relations, and Matters More Spiritual

In judging their condition people weigh heavily a large number of qualities and experiences. They want love and affection, intimacy, and support. They seek to avoid the loss of dignity and to maximize the signs of respect they are shown. If the times and their attendant social conditions assure individuals more of these and similar social goods, they will see this as progress, whereas a diminution in these goods will be seen as retrogressive.

In the more developed countries the period following the Second World War witnessed a veritable flood of popular and even academic accounts which purported to document the accelerating loss of these basic gratifications, a process often treated as the inevitable accompaniment of urban living, economic development, and the late stages of capitalism. One of the earliest works typical of this emergent trend was David Reisman's *The Lonely Crowd*, which became standard required reading in social science and humanities courses in colleges all across the United States. Virtually every year since has yielded best sellers telling the public that it suffers from ever increasing isolation, anxiety, psychological insecurity, aimlessness, boredom, and other comparable varieties of social malaise.

These diagnoses of the condition of modern men and women may well be correct. The problem they present to an even mildly skeptical observer is that these accounts are highly selective and the evidence markedly anecdotal. Part of the problem stems from the fact that the conditions being described are complex and elusive. Even more an obstacle to systematic measurement, the malaise of the modern man is claimed to be something not obviously apparent except on very close inspection of the inner life of the person. Nevertheless, we have available a considerable number of systematically measured indictors of the seemingly more subtle, elusive sentiments and feelings of the population concerning a wide range of issues. What emerges is a complex pattern with evidence of numerous gains that may, however, be offset by equally numerous losses. And whatever one's summary judgment, one can expect it to be hotly contested by someone whose claim to authority is at least as good as one's own.

In an early effort to resolve the issue I searched the roster of public opinion research for studies which tried to measure the more subtle and elusive qualities so often stressed in evaluations of life in modern societies. Because I required that the surveys be taken simultaneously in a variety of countries, and that within each country the social class structure was accounted for, I found few relevant studies. But the qualities measured in those studies were diverse and of a nature very relevant to our interest here.[12]

The outcome of my effort provided both good news and bad news for those who incline to the view that progress in national development is matched by progress in human development. Five of the eight qualities for which I found adequate data showed a pattern that we may interpret as a sign of progress. These were anti-authoritarianism, a sense of social efficacy, satisfaction with life, active participation in social and political life, and a sense of trust. All of these personal dispositions showed a tendency to increase in strength as one moved from the less economically to the more economically developed nations. However, three of the eight measures showed a decidedly contrary tendency. Benevolence, optimism, and faith in science were less often manifested by those living in the more economically advanced nations, a finding that gives support to the more negative assessment of economic development and societal modernization. Moreover, it seems certain that if I redid this study today, there would be a fourth item high on the list of negative assessments— namely the feeling that we are all, everywhere, doing terrible damage to our environment.

It seems clear from this experience that whether one finds evidence of progress in human values will depend greatly on the measures one selects as indicators of such progress. The point is well illustrated by the controversy generated by the most recent efforts to measure the sentiments and values expressed by the populations of nations at different stages of modern economic development.

Ronald Inglehart is a key protagonist in the debate. In a massive study including many countries he found evidence of a profound shift in values, with decreasing emphasis on what he called "materialist" values and a rising tide of sentiments he labeled "postmaterialism." Included in the former are concerns with maintaining public order and stressing strong armed forces. Among the qualities which define postmaterialism are the desire for a less impersonal society and having more say on the job. He found considerable evidence that the more developed a country is economically, the more its people held postmaterialist values. And within each country, in almost every nation, the younger generations coming on stream more often supported postmaterialist values. The long term consequence of this process, assuming it continues, is that over time more and more nations will come to be dominated by populations holding postmaterialist values.[13]

Of course, the spread of postmaterialist values cannot automatically be taken to mean humanity is progressing. Inglehart makes no such claim. Indeed, the word *progress* does not appear in the index to his book. But there are certainly many for whom the implications are clear. For them, it clearly is progress if more and more people are coming to give priority to the value of having more say on the job and of living in a less impersonal society. For others, however, the issue is not what interpretation to put on the facts, but rather what facts to consider. Inglehart's data identify the United States as one of the countries in which postmaterialist attitudes are most clearly evident among the youth, and most sharply increasing in popularity over time. But looking at a different source of data, Easterlin and Crimmins find that rather than becoming less materialistic America's youth are becoming *increasingly more materialistic*. They note, for example, that between 1976 and 1986 there was an increase of at least 10 percent in the proportion of American youth who aspired to having at least two automobiles, a high quality stereo system, and a substantial number of other consumer goods. Such aspirations hardly seem to support the idea that there is the rising tide sweeping the younger generation of Americans into a postmaterialist future.[14]

Commenting on the apparent contradiction in the findings presented by Inglehart and Easterlin, Professor Terry Clark proposes a resolution of their differences. He suggests they may both be right, but only in different realms. *In the private realm* young people want more material goods, as Easterlin and Crimmins note. Yet at the same time *in the public realm* where private goods are not at issue, they seek more attractive surroundings and more democracy in the work place, just as Inglehart noted.[15]

Clark's proposal may resolve an apparent conflict of fact, but it does not decide the question as to whether or not the facts indicate progress. Is it progress to have materialism rise in the private realm while communal values simultaneously gain in importance in the public realm, or would it be more progressive to have materialism fall while communalism rose? Or would some other combination of rising and falling on these two dimensions be a firmer indication of progress? Social science cannot provide the answer. It must depend on the values held by each individual and each community.

Notes

1. R. J. Rummel, *Death by Government* (New Brunswick: Transaction Publishers, 1994).

2. Daniel Bell, personal communication.

3. Richard Shweder, "Moral Maps, 'First World' Conceits and the New Evangelists," in *Culture Matters: How Values Shape Human Progress*, ed. Lawerence E. Harrison and Samuel P. Huntington (New York: Basic Books, 2000), 158-177.

4. Indian Council of Social Science Research, *Social Information of India: Trends and Structure* (Delhi: Hindustan Publishing Corporation, 1983), 170, 224, 242; World Bank, *World Development Indicators, 2000* (Washington D.C., World Bank, 2000), table 2.18.

5. Indian Council of Social Science Research, *Social Information*, 245.

6. World Bank, *World Development Indicators*, table 2.17.

7. World Bank, *World Development Indicators*, table 2.15.

8. World Bank, *World Development Indicators*, table 1.2.

9. Federal Interagency Forum on Aging-Related Statistics, *Older Americans 2000:*

Key Indicators of Well-being, (Washington D.C.: U.S. Census Bureau, 2000), appendix A, indicator 17 and 18.

10. Alex Inkeles, "Industrial Man: The Relation of the Status to Experience, Perception, and Value," *The American Journal of Sociology* 66, no. 1 (July 1960): 18.

11. Richard A. Easterlin, *Growth Triumphant: The Twenty-first Century in Historical Perspective* (Ann Arbor: The University of Michigan Press, 1996).

12. Alex Inkeles and Larry Diamond, "Personal Development and National Development: A Cross-National Perspective," in *The Quality of Life: Comparative Studies*, ed. Alexander Szalai and Frank M. Andrews (London: Sage Publications, 1980).

13. Ronald Inglehart, *Modernization and Postmodernization: Cultural, Economic, and Political Change in 43 Societies* (Princeton, N.J.: Princeton University Press, 1997).

14. Richard A. Easterlin and Eileen M. Crimmins, "American Youth Are Becoming More Materialistic," in *Citizen Politics in Post-Industrial Societies*, ed. Terry Nichols Clark and Michael Rempel (Boulder, Colo: Westview Press, 1997).

15. Terry Nichols Clark, "Is Materialism Rising in America?" *Society* 37, no. 6 (Sep/Oct 2000): 47-48.

Chapter 3

Making Progress in Implementation Scholarship: A Survey of the Literature

Janet W. Looney

> **implement**\-ment\ *vt* (1806) **1:** CARRY OUT. ACCOMPLISH: *esp:* to give practical effect to and ensure of actual fulfillment by concrete measures <plans not yet *~ed* due to lack of funds> **2:** to provide instruments or means of expression for—im-ple-men-ta-tion ...[1]

In the policy realm, implementation encompasses administrative decisions and actions taken to put legislatively defined goals into effect. Good implementation cannot in and of itself guarantee successful programs. Other factors, including policy based on good causal theory, sufficient authority, and adequate political, fiscal, and administrative support affect the outcome. Nevertheless, effective implementation is fundamental to an effective policy process.

A rich literature emerged in the 1970s as scholars began to view implementation as a potential stumbling block in the policy process. During the early years of this period, scholars focused on describing and identifying problems in the implementation process, largely through the development of case studies. By the late 1970s, several scholars emphasized the need for greater analytical and methodological rigor. A common analytical framework, or a "meta-theory" of implementation would allow analysts to more easily identify the elements of successful program performance. By the mid-1980s, several had grown frustrated with the difficulty of this methodological task. While no meta-theory of implementation has emerged, there have been solid conceptual advances in implementation studies as well as in closely related fields—such as public management studies, the study of policy design, and so on. The growing diversity of literature is arguably a sign of progress in the field.

This essay reviews the rapid evolution of scholarship in implementation studies over the past thirty years. The discussion raises questions about accountability and capacity under newer models of public management and implementation, and addresses lessons learned through evaluation of program implementation. The fundamental questions related to how a community will promote progress are much the same, at least in industrialized societies, across the world, although the resolution of these issues will vary by time and place.

Viewpoints on Implementation

System-Wide Versus Local Solutions

The tension between system-wide and local solutions has defined much of the literature on implementation for the past twenty-five years, and permeates policy makers' decisions as to how to most effectively promote policy goals. The "big government" model that has dominated American public administration for most of the twentieth century, often referred to as the "top-down" model, focuses on process, providing assurance of equity of benefit, consistency, and accountability.[2] Conversely, decentralized models of governance, including the transfer of program authority from the federal to state and local governments are often referred to as "bottom-up" models.

Authors of early literature on public administration and intergovernmental relations recognized the importance of implementation in the policy process. Martha Derthick, for example, wrote on the apparent non-compliance of state agencies that were supposed to be implementing federal housing programs.[3] Widespread consciousness of implementation as a "problem variable" in realizing progress can perhaps be identified most clearly with the 1973 publication of Jeffrey Pressman and Aaron Wildavsky's *Implementation: how great expectations in Washington are dashed in Oakland: or, why it's amazing that federal programs work at all, this being a saga of the Economic Development Administration as told by two sympathetic observers who seek to build morals on a foundation of ruined hopes. Implementation* addresses the failure of the federal Economic Development Administration to implement an inner-city employment program in Oakland, California. Pressman and Wildavsky identify significant points of vulnerability in local implementation of the federal program, including 1) the complexity of joint action; 2) inadequate causal theory; and 3) unrealistic expectations of the program. Overall, the study provided a pessimistic assessment of the likelihood that ambitious federal programs, in the American context of fragmented power, will realize their goals. The lessons? Keep program design simple. Take care to develop program designs suitable to the problem being addressed. Limit the number of decision points. Limit the number of contingencies that will be met in the process of program implementation. Most importantly, Pressman and Wildavsky emphasize implementation as a learning process.[4]

Often cited as the seminal work in the field, *Implementation* inspired the development of a number of case studies focused on describing and identifying implementation barriers. As the field matured and the number of case studies grew, scholars turned to the task of developing theoretical frameworks to explain implementation successes and failures. During this second phase of implementation research, two models came to dominate the field: top-down and bottom-up implementation. Other researchers strove to combine the two perspectives, or to at least match the appropriate model to program situations.[5]

System-Wide Approaches to Implementation: The Top-Down Model

The top-down model of implementation, also known as the planning-and-control model or the rational model, looks to the quality of policy planning and decision making at the top level to explain policy successes and failures. This model builds on classic public administration scholarship, with its focus on "Weberian notions of bureaucratic rationality," and judges the success of program implementation by the extent to which a policy is put into practice. The model assumes that policies articulate clear and consistent objectives, the administration is neutral, well-intentioned and well-informed, and that implementation is separate from the politics of policy formulation. The primary concern of top-down modelers is the degree to which policy outcomes match original policy design.[6]

Top-down models have been subject to criticism. Richard Elmore, who refers to the model as "forward mapping," observes that

> The most serious problem with forward mapping is its implicit and unquestioned assumption that policy makers control the organizational, political, and technological processes that affect implementation. The notion that policy makers exercise, or ought to exercise, some kind of direct control over policy implementation might be called the "noble lie" of conventional public administration and policy analysis.[7]

For example, the old Aid to Families with Dependent Children (AFDC) program[8] placed heavy emphasis on bureaucratic compliance with program regulations and ensuring the accuracy of cash eligibility determinations. Evelyn Brodkin suggests that caseworkers nevertheless exercised substantial discretion in their work through overzealous attention to paperwork, or biased service, "tangling [welfare recipients] in a Gordian know of verification requirements or, less often, reducing the tangle for those they favored."[9]

An Increasing Focus on Local Implementation: The Bottom-Up Model

The bottom-up model of implementation, also known as the mutual adaptation model, the process model, the interaction model, the political model, backward mapping, or the "implementation game" model highlights the adaptation of policies at the level of service delivery.[10] Backward mapping, as described by Elmore, assumes that the "closer one is to the source of the problem, the greater is one's ability to influence it; and the problem-solving ability of complex systems depends not on hierarchical control but on maximizing discretion at the point where the problem is most immediate."

Weatherley and Lipsky's study of street-level bureaucracy recognized that service deliverers exercise substantial discretion in setting work priorities. Weatherley and Lipsky conclude that successful policy implementation requires 1) careful training of local level personnel (i.e., development of their professional capacity); 2) leadership to assist in the establishment, expansion, and improvement of services at the local level; and, 3) further evaluation and analysis of coping behaviors of implementing officials and the development of a system of rewards and deterrence measures to guide behaviors that fulfill public objectives.[11]

Nakamura and Smallwood,[12] in reaction to top-down models, developed a systems overview that includes examination of elements and linkages. Implementation is only one part of the policy process, according to them, and cannot be examined as a separate phenomenon. The policy process involves a system of "functional environments," which includes policy formation, implementation, and evaluation. Each of these environments involves multiple players and fields connected by a variety of "communications and compliance linkages." The Nakamura and Smallwood model is typical of bottom-up strategies, which emphasize the dynamic character of policy formulation and implementation. The Weatherley and Lipsky study, though not explicitly prescribing bottom-up planning as a strategy for policy design, emphasizes the need for top-down planners to understand street-level behavior in order to plan well.

Bottom-up strategies formulate policy with extensive input from service deliverers and clients. Critics charge that this focus on the micro-level of implementation ignores macro-level analysis necessary for formulating adequate causal theory, as well as socio-economic factors indirectly influencing the policy problem. Similarly, opponents charge that bottom-up strategies merely make piecemeal efforts to address the symptoms rather than the underlying causes of policy problems.

Critics of bottom-up theory focus on the amount of control entrusted to local service deliverers. These critics do not deny that street-level bureaucrats exercise a great deal of discretion in implementing policy. However, they take issue with the idea that discretion and flexibility should provide the basis of policy design.[13] They argue that local level discretion and flexibility as a basis for policy design circumvents the democratic process and the accountability of central authorities for the policy design and implementation process. They maintain that the bottom-up model strips central decision makers of their ability to influence the implementation process through incentives and other tools. For example, Cullen and Bretherton note that voluntary (and often incentive based) pollution prevention programs emerged in the 1980s as a response to dissatisfaction with command and control environmental regulation. The voluntary programs have been criticized for their uncertain impact. Cullen and Bretherton argue that voluntary programs or market-based incentives (which align private sector economic interests with voluntary actions) may be most effective when balanced with specific government-mandated environmental targets and some level of command and control.[14]

Finding the Balance

By the late 1980s, social scientists were attempting to synthesize the two models by defining and measuring more precisely "where the optimum, that is, more realistically, reasonable level of planning is"[15] in order to anticipate implementation problems while still maintaining program flexibility.

Sabatier,[16] in a revision of his earlier focus on top-down models, which claims to combine the best features of top-down and bottom-up models of implementation recommends that policy makers first examine the policy problem or subsystem, and then the manner in which key players deal with the problem in order to discover the most appropriate planning and implementation strategies. He asserts that policy makers also need to examine the effects of socio-economic factors external to the immediate policy issue; the attempts of various players to realize their own objectives over time through manipulation of the legal mechanisms of a governmental program; the validity of causal assumptions driving programs and strategies; and, improved ability of key players to understand the problem and to implement policy (i.e., increasing the professionalism and experience of implementing officials).

To account for the role of learning based on experience and new information, Sabatier further recommends that analyses of implementation focus on changes over periods of a decade or more. According to Sabatier, this framework also provides a sound basis for gathering and evaluating data as social scientists attempt to build theoretical constructs of implementation.

Berman[17] provides a different approach to synthesizing top-down and bottom-up implementation models. Rather than attempting to combine the best elements of both models, Berman develops a "Contingency Theory" and undertakes to identify appropriate implementation models for various policy situations. According to Berman, "a fundamental truth of implementation: There is no universally best way to implement policy. Either programmed or adaptive implementation can be effective if applied to the appropriate policy situation, but a mismatch between approach and situation aggravates the very implementation problems these approaches seek to overcome."[18]

Berman recommends that policy makers further implementation strategy through "matching, mixing, and switching." According to Berman, implementation strategies should be chosen to match the scope of change required, the degree of technical certainty, the extent of agreement about the policy, the coordination present in the implementing system and the stability of the policy's environment. More than one implementation strategy may be appropriate for a given policy situation, and implementers should be flexible enough to "mix" or "switch" strategies.[19]

Several scholars propose contingency theories or models to explain levels of success in program implementation. For example, Peterson, Rabe, and Wong find that the effectiveness of federal programs is based on certain characteristics, including the extent to which 1) a policy focuses on redistribution of resources rather than developmental objectives (e.g., cash assistance rather than economic or community development); 2) local implementers of federal policy are immune to political pressures; and 3) local agencies are staffed by professionals who understand and identify with the goal of a policy. These distinctions predict the effectiveness of programs as illustrated below:

ADMINISTRATION	*DEVELOPMENTAL PROGRAMS*	*REDISTRIBUTIVE PROGRAMS*
Professional	Moderately effective	Increasingly effective
Politicized	Effective	Ineffective

Peterson, et al. do not develop general strategies to cope with various situations. Rather they find that, especially in the case of redistributive programs (for example, in the areas of health, education, and housing), there are a variety of professional and political realities confronting policy makers and service deliverers that require greater depth of knowledge and specialization.[20]

Richard Matland develops an "ambiguity-conflict" model as one way to synthesize top-down and bottom-up approaches. Matland points out that members of the top-down school tend to focus on relatively straightforward policies with clear goals, such as smallpox eradication; members of the bottom-up school tend to study policies that have greater ambiguity, such as a coalition-based community development program, or experimental implementation of a new program, like Headstart.

According to Matland, earlier theoretical work failed to identify the conditions necessary for program effectiveness. Drawing upon the work of organization theorists and scholars of decision making, Matland proposes a predictive model of the implementation process. He identifies four perspectives: 1) low levels of conflict and ambiguity (administrative implementation); 2) high conflict and low ambiguity (political implementation); 3) low conflict and high ambiguity (experimental implementation); and 4) high levels of conflict and ambiguity (symbolic implementation).[21] The model is intended to provide a guide for policy designers anticipating potential problems in implementation, and for researchers seeking to identify those elements most likely to influence policy outcomes.

Denise Scheberle, in her examination of environmental policy in the federal context, develops a contingency model based on "trust and the politics of implementation." Scheberle's analysis of five environmental programs centers on factors which facilitate or hinder environmental policy implementation, and the nature of working relationships between federal and state officials working in these programs. Scheberle identifies four types of working relationships: 1) high levels of trust, coupled with high levels of involvement, (a "pulling together," or synergistic relationship); 2) high levels of trust, coupled with low levels of involvement (a cooperative but lonely relationship); 3) coming apart with avoidance; and, 4) coming apart and contentious. Scheberle finds that agreement on the wisdom of a policy goal, avoidance of micro-management at the federal level, and greater receptivity to the legitimate national interest in running effective programs will help increase trust between federal and state implementing officials.[22]

Contingency models have helped to put more shape around the "implementation problem," bringing scholarship closer to the goal of defining and measuring more precisely the "reasonable level of planning"[23] between top-down and bottom-up approaches to implementation. Common themes running through these models include the importance of understanding individual and institutional behavior, the policy context, and the political dimensions of a policy intervention.

Devolution: The Newest Iteration of the Top-Down, Bottom-Up Debate

Implementation research occurs in a dynamic policy environment. The newest iteration of the top-down, bottom-up debate is being played out in the policy making arena with the "devolution" of many social and environmental programs from the federal to the state level, placing greater emphasis on the development of locally-based solutions. Devolution—also referred to as the "New Federalism," has been accompanied by a greater focus on program performance and outcomes. This results-oriented approach is intended to avoid the "one-size-fits-all" approach inherent in models that emphasize adherence to bureaucratic process, rather than successful outcomes. Outcome models encourage a "whatever it takes" approach to help clients reach an established program goal. Significantly, we are only beginning to understand the implications of more local, performance-based approaches to policy implementation. There are questions regarding the accountability of local bureaucrats to citizens—and questions regarding the capacity of local institutions and individuals to address complex program goals.

The New Federalism reflects a shift in approach from the "public administration" paradigm that has dominated American government for more than a century to a "new public management" paradigm. Robert Behn recounts that the public administration paradigm was designed to increase government accountability to its citizens and curtail the corruption permeating federal and local governments. Influenced in large part by Woodrow Wilson's 1887 essay, "The Study of Administration," the public administration paradigm emphasized adherence to bureaucratic procedures and the separation of implementation from the politics of public policy formulation (a top-down approach).[24] The public administration model was in many ways successful at increasing accountability—its desired outcome. But, as Behn notes, by the end of the twentieth century, "American government is plagued less by the problem of corruption than by the problem of performance."[25]

The "new public management" model assumes that front-line civil servants, who are closest to problems, are well placed to develop effective solutions. The new public management model (a bottom-up approach) is intended to empower civil servants to produce results, rather than merely to implement rules and regulations dictated at higher levels of government.[26] Proponents of the new public management paradigm reject the idea that there is "one best solution" to implementation. Instead, they emphasize multiple "best-practices," and the empowerment of civil servants to make their own decisions and to develop innovative solutions. The new public management model does not pretend to separate politics of the policy process and policy implementation, as did the public administration model. Instead, implementation success is measured in terms of the ability of civil servants to produce results and to meet targets set in legislation.

Evelyn Brodkin and others argue, however, that result-oriented models do not necessarily protect citizens from potential biases, abuses, or lack of capacity on the part of civil servants.[27] Behn raises questions regarding democratic accountability, asking, under the new public management, "*how* we will hold *whom* accountable for *what*?"[28] It is also somewhat more difficult, Behn notes, to establish clear lines of accountability for producing results under models that encourage partnerships with private and non-profit agencies and among public agencies[29] or, to ensure that the intentions of democratically elected officials are carried out at the delivery level.

Effective implementation under the new public management paradigm requires that organizations and individual civil servants have the capacity to develop effective solutions accountably, to use discretion wisely, to manage non-profit or privately contracted programs, or develop effective relationships with their counterparts in other agencies. Organizational capacity-building and individual professional development in the current environment are therefore key to effective implementation.

The Federalism Research Group led by the Rockefeller Institute of Government at State University of New York, Albany has created a network of field researchers in twenty-five states. Their multi-year State Capacity Study on the implementation of welfare, Medicaid, food stamps, and workforce development focuses on the management resources, capabilities, and problems of state governments and local governments in implementing these programs.[30] This ongoing research is paying special attention to how, in the context of the New Federalism, state and local implementation strategies are evolving to meet ongoing and new challenges.

The development of individual professional capacity requires organizational support. Research points to the importance of values and motivations of civil servants, and recognition of the pressures of their daily worklife; the development of appropriate incentives; the culture of the particular agency; opportunities for ongoing professional development; the availability of resources to meet program goals; and, the involvement of civil servants in the program design and implementation process.[31]

Finally, it is important to note trends toward increasing privatization of government as another type of devolution. Writing on privatization in 1989, Lester Salamon found increasing governmental expenditures through grants-in-aid, loans and loan guarantees, and contracting out as evidence of the privatization of government. Each of these "tools" of government, as Salamon calls them, has its own distinctive organization, procedures and skill requirements. Salamon suggests that there is a need for theory "that focuses not only on the distinction between the public and private sectors, but also takes account of the distinctive features of the various technologies that the public sector uses to carry out its purposes."[32] Literature on the various "tools" of privatization has grown significantly over the last twelve years.[33]

The Quest for a "Theory of Implementation"

There are still few systematic studies identifying the general conditions most likely to lead to successful program implementation, and several scholars have expressed their frustration with the field of implementation studies and lack of methodological rigor. Helen Ingram[34] claimed that the field had "yet to reach conceptual clarity" and proposed that a focus on the policy process might be more productive. Sabatier and Jenkins-Smith similarly recommended the study of "policy change and learning" as a more productive route.[35] In somewhat more dramatic fashion, Peter deLeon declared that the "study of policy implementation has reached an intellectual dead end." In an article with Nancy deLeon, he stated that "if there is no single overriding, generic theory of policy implementation, there is almost certainly little relief to be found in the empiricist's orientation of listing and testing of multiple variables in dozens of cases, in search of an optimal set of conditions."[36] Yet, effective implementation is still considered to be a crucial part of the policy process.

James Lester and Malcolm Goggin identify four different viewpoints on what should happen to the field itself. According to Lester and Goggin, "implementation scholars tend to take either a positive or a negative view about the utility of continuing research in this area and they either see a need to change our conceptual or methodological approaches or not to do so."[37] They characterize the four archetypes of implementation scholars as "reformers" (those who believe implementation research is important, but is in need of modification of conceptual and methodological approaches), "testers" (those who see no need for radical change in the field, and are more interested in testing existing frameworks "to identify the 'crucial variables' believed to affect policy implementation"), "skeptics" (those who would take a more radical approach to reconceptualizing the field, bringing in new frames of reference), and "terminators" (those who have dismissed the field as lacking in usefulness).[38] In these discussions, the scholarship of implementation is increasingly the object of study itself.

There has also been a proliferation of specialized research, addressing implementation in education, health, urban planning, environmental policy, and so on, each area deserving of its own in-depth review. Literature devoted to the more "generic" implementation processes can draw upon these findings, and vice versa. Based on levels of federal funding, support from private foundations for research in specific policy areas, as well as the large number of professional conferences bringing together academic and practitioner audiences in policy-specific areas, it is clear that there is great demand for this kind of research.

Despite the broad range of scholarly approaches to implementation, Lester and Goggin suggest that a "meta-theory" of implementation may still be developed. A meta-theory would provide a common analytical framework, provide the basis for an accumulation of research on implementation, and help to better explain and predict outcomes of a particular policy intervention. The diversity of approaches within the field, however, is testament to the complexity of the implementation process, and the difficulty, if not impossibility, of developing a meta-theory. We are unlikely to develop any simple formula as to how to best promote progress, just as the skeptics of the implementation field argue.

The difficulty of developing a meta-theory of implementation should not be viewed as a failure of scholarship. Rather, the diversity of scholarship in the field might be viewed as an indicator of progress—a mark of the richness and depth of the field. We might draw an analogy with progress in the natural sciences where, as author Scott Montgomery notes, the splintering of the field into many subdisciplines has enabled the deepening and expansion of knowledge.

The central tensions between top-down and bottom-up approaches to implementation are likely to persist over generations, and to be answered differently by successive generations according to values and changing conceptions of progress over time. Writing on "Progress and Public Policy" more than thirty years ago, Aaron Wildavsky noted that

> The clash between spontaneity and control, interaction and cogitation, lies at the heart of the idea of progress. Of course, no control can be total, and no reaction can be entirely spontaneous. Interaction is always bounded by constraints, and cogitation never quite gets it all. But what central controllers would call unfortunate unanticipated consequences, deviations from the blueprint of the future society, are the very staple of local social interaction. Only by knowing each situation as well as individuals do could all relationships be anticipated. The unexpected is the stuff of life that each person must communicate to the other precisely because no one else can possibly know. That is why it is so often observed that discoveries are made when the discoverer is not looking for them, at least not in the place they end up being found.[39]

Ultimately, advances in the scholarship of implementation are connected to its usefulness for policy makers and practitioners in the field. A better understanding of the relationship between implementation scholarship and practice is essential. Research that effectively walks the line between theory and practice, and informs everyday decisions can better promote progress in implementation practice itself.

Evaluating Program Implementation: Learning More about What Works

Research on program implementation has been augmented by increasingly sophisticated program evaluation methodologies and tools. We know more about what works and why than in the past, although we still have much to learn. Federal, state, and local government, foundations, and individual program managers have also placed increasing emphasis on ensuring that programs—particularly newer programs—are monitored closely for results, and when resources permit, adopt some kind of external review. While evaluation is closely linked to implementation, it is a distinct part of the policy process.

In the last decade, the increasing emphasis on performance and outcome-based measurement has provided a type of "quick and dirty" analysis, serving primarily as a tool for managers to track progress and make program adjustments when necessary. Focusing on just a few measurements, however, particularly when attached to funding incentives or legislative mandates, can shape or re-shape some program goals in ways that undermine other, more subtle program goals. For example, caseload reduction goals under welfare reform—the Personal Responsibility and Work Opportunity Reconciliation Act of 1996—potentially overshadow goals related to helping clients get living wage jobs and reach self-sufficiency.

Nor do these measures necessarily provide information on longer-term program impact.[40]

Research that focuses on meta-analysis of what has worked in various programs addressing similar target populations over time is less common. The challenges in conducting this type of research are formidable. Program goals, populations served, the type of data gathered, and other variables change over time. As a consequence, we lose the opportunity to learn more about the characteristics of successful programs. It is also exceedingly difficult to track clients after they have left a program—for reasons of privacy, mobility, and the expense of tracking—so in most cases, the long-term impact of program interventions is unknown.

Finally, determining what to assess, how to assess it, and how to report the results is extremely difficult.[41] Program evaluations are often plagued by the same problems that permeate efforts to better define and conceptualize the field of implementation studies—disciplinary specialization. The viewpoint of a particular discipline will necessarily shape the questions asked and answers derived, and may ignore important evidence that might be more apparent to other evaluators.

As Richard Nathan notes, "The data simply do not exist, nor can they ever be collected, which would tell us everything we want to know about every attitude, emotion, and form of behavior of every individual and relevant group in society in such a way that we could use these data to construct models and produce theories that would approach the predictive power of theories in the natural sciences."[42]

Conclusion

The tension between top-down and bottom-up models has defined much of the literature on implementation for the past twenty-five years. This tension permeates policy makers' decisions as to how to most effectively promote policy goals and thus to achieve progress, and remains key to understanding the challenges of implementation. Efforts to resolve this tension, or to find the balance between the two approaches, are likely to vary by culture and over time. The current generation has favored an approach of devolution and performance management, but has yet to resolve questions regarding accountability and capacity to deliver services. We know more about what works than we have in the past. Nevertheless, given the challenges of collecting data and conducting in-depth research, we are unlikely to ever develop truly predictive models for implementation. Progress will occur so long as we push beyond the boundaries of our current knowledge of "what works."

* Many thanks to Jacob Adams, Stephen Page, Jonathon Solovy, and William Zumeta for their input.

Notes

1. *Webster's Ninth New Collegiate Dictionary* (Springfield, Mass.: Merriam-Webster, 1986), s.v. "implement."

2. Marcia K. Meyers, Karin MacDonald, and Bonnie Glaser, "Discretion, Devolution and Equity: Public Bureaucracies and Community Based Organizations in the Implementation of Welfare Reform," paper presented at the 1996 Annual Meeting of the American Political Science Association, San Francisco, Calif., August 29 - September 1, 1996.

3. Martha Derthick, *New Towns in Town* (Washington, D.C.: The Urban Institute, 1972).

4. Jeffrey L. Pressman and Aaron Wildavsky, *Implementation*, 3d ed., (Berkely: University of California Press, 1984).

5. Richard Matland, "Synthesizing the Implementation Literature: The Ambiguity-Conflict Model of Policy Implementation," *Journal of Public Administration Research and Theory* 5, no. 2 (April 1995): 145-174. See also Paul Berman, "Thinking about Programmed and Adaptive Implementation: Matching Strategies to Situations," in *Why Policies Succeed or Fail,* ed. H. Ingram and D. Mann (Beverly Hills: Sage Publications, 1980), 205-227.

6. John Craig, "Comparative African Experiences in Implementing Educational Policies," World Bank discussion papers, Africa Technical Department Series, The International Bank for Reconstruction (Washington D.C.: World Bank, 1990), 21-22.

7. Richard F. Elmore, "Backward Mapping: Implementation Research and Policy Decisions," in *Studying Implementation,* ed. Walter Williams, et al. (Chatham, N.J.: Chatham House, 1982), 23. For a European viewpoint on bottom-up implementation, see, for example, Benny Hjern, "Implementation Research—The Link Gone Missing," *Journal of Public Policy* 2 , no. 1 (February 1982): 301-308; and Benny Hjern and Chris Hull, "Implementation Research as Empirical Constitutionalism," *European Journal of Political Research* 10, no. 2 (Special Issue, 1983): 105-15. Richard Elmore's approach to "backward mapping" provides a foundation for other work in the study of policy design. See, for example, Helen M. Ingram and Anne Schneider, "Improving Implementation through Framing Smarter Statues," *Journal of Public Policy* 10, no. 1 (January-March 1990): 67-88.

8. The Personal Responsibility and Work Opportunity Reconciliation Act of 1996 replaces AFDC with the Temporary Assistance for Needy Families (TANF) program. The TANF program places less emphasis on bureaucratic process, and greater emphasis on reduction of the client caseload, including exits from TANF due to employment. States are encouraged to find innovative approaches to meeting performance goals. Some would argue, however, that federal caseload reduction targets limit innovation, for example, discouraging programs that emphasize mid to long-term training for TANF recipients. Case workers have similar opportunities to exercise discretion in handling client eligibility determinations and in other paperwork as under AFDC.

9. Evelyn Z. Brodkin, "Inside the Welfare Contract: Discretion and Accountability in State Welfare Administration," *Social Service Review* 71, no. 1 (March 1997): 1-33.

10. Craig, "Comparative African Experiences."

11. Richard Weatherley and Michael Lipsky, "Street-Level Bureaucrats and Institutional Innovation: Implementing Special Education Reform," *Harvard Educational Re-*

view 47 no. 2 (May 1977): 171-197. See also Michael Lipsky, *Toward a Theory of Street-Level Bureaucracy* (Madison: University of Wisconsin, 1969).

12. Robert T. Nakamura and Frank Smallwood, *The Politics of Policy Implementation* (New York: St. Martins, 1980).

13. Stephen H. Linder and B. Guy Peters, "A Design Perspective on Policy Implementation: The Fallacies of Misplaced Prescription," *Policy Studies Review* 6, no. 3 (February 1987): 459-75. See also Daniel Mazmanian and Paul Sabatier, ed., *Effective Policy Implementation* (Lexington, Mass.: Lexington Books, 1981). Mazmanian and Sabatier argue that there are three general sets of factors affecting implementation, including tractability of a problem, ability of a statue to structure implementation and non statutory variables affecting implementation. They identify sixteen independent variables influencing goal compliance within this framework.

14. Allison Cullen and Chris Bretherton, "Progressing toward Environmental Sustainability," in chapter 22 of this volume.

15. Walter Williams "Implementing Public Programs," in *Handbook of Public Administration,* ed. J. L. Perry (San Francisco: Jossey-Bass, 1989), 248-58.

16. Paul A. Sabatier, "Top-Down and Bottom-Up Approaches to Implementation Research: A Critical Analysis and Suggested Synthesis," *Journal of Public Policy* 6, no. 1 (January-March 1986): 21-48.

17. Berman, "Thinking about Programmed and Adaptive Implementation."

18. Berman, "Thinking about Programmed and Adaptive Implementation," 206.

19. Berman, "Thinking about Programmed and Adaptive Implementation."

20. Paul E. Peterson, Barry G. Rabe, and Kenneth K. Wong, *When Federalism Works* (Washington, D.C.: Brookings Institution, 1986).

21. Matland, "Synthesizing the Implementation Literature," 159-79.

22. Denise Scheberle, *Federalism and Environmental Policy: Trust and the Politics of Implementation* (Washington, D.C.: Georgetown University Press. 1997).

23. Williams, "Implementing Public Programs."

24. Robert D. Behn, "The New Public-Management Paradigm and the Search for Democratic Accountability," *International Public Management Journal* 1, no. 2 (1998): 132.

25. Behn, "The New Public-Management," 133.

26. Behn, "The New Public-Management."

27. Brodkin, "Inside the Welfare Contract."

28. Behn, "The New Public-Management," 142.

29. Behn, "The New Public-Management," 142-48.

30. "Federalism Research Group," *Nelson A. Rockefeller Institute of Government* 2000, at www.rockinst.org/quick_tour/federalism/research_summary.html (accessed 4 March 2002).

31. For example, see research on school change, Michael Fullan and Andy Hargreaves, *What's Worth Fighting For? Working Together for Your School* (Toronto: Ontario Public School Teachers' Federation, 1992). See also Brodkin, "Inside the Welfare Contract."

32. Lester Salamon, *Beyond Privatization: The Tools of Government Action* (Washington D.C.: Urban Institute Press, 1989), 3-49.

33. A brief overview of this literature might include Peter J. May and Raymond J. Burby, "Making Sense Out of Regulatory Enforcement," *Law and Policy* 20 (1998): 157-82; Steven Rathgeb Smith and Michael Lipsky, *Non-profits for Hire: The Welfare State in the Age of Contracting* (Cambridge, Mass.: Harvard University Press, 1993); Meyers, et al., "Discretion, Devolution and Equity;" Lester M. Salamon, "The New Governance and the Tools of Public Action: An Introduction," *Fordham Urban Law Journal* 28, no. 5 (June 2001): 1611-74.

34. Helen M. Ingram, "Implementation: A Review and Suggested Framework," in *Public Administration: The State of the Art*, ed. Naomi Lynn and Aaron Wildavsky (Chatham, N.J.: Chatham House Publishers, 1990) cited in James P. Lester and Malcolm L. Goggin, "Back to the Future: The Rediscovery of Implementation Studies," *Policy Currents: Newsletter of the Public Policy Section American Political Science Association* 8, no. 3 (September 1998): 1-9.

35. Lester and Goggin, "Back to the Future," 1-9.

36. Peter deLeon and Linda deLeon, *A Democratic Approach to Policy Implementation*, paper presented at the Sixth Meeting of the National Public Management Research Conference, University of Indiana, Bloomington, October 18-20, 2001, 6.

37. Lester and Goggin, "Back to the Future."

38. Lester and Goggin, "Back to the Future."

39. Aaron Wildavsky, "Progress and Public Policy," in *Progress and Its Discontents*, ed. Gabriel A. Almond, Marvin Chodorow, and Roy Harvey Pearce (Berkeley: University of California Press, 1982), 361-74.

40. Brodkin, "Investigating Policy's 'Practical' Meaning," 6.

41. Dean Fink and Louise Stoll, "Educational Change: Easier Said than Done," in *International Handbook of Educational Change*, ed. Andy Hargreaves, Ann Lieberman, Michael Fullan and David Hopkins (Dondrecht: Kluwer Academic Publishers, 1998), 349-74.

42. Richard P. Nathan, *Social Science in Government: The Role of Policy Researchers* (Albany, N.Y. : Rockefeller Institute Press, 2000), 11.

Section II – The Domains of Progress

Part One

Progress in Ourselves

Part one addresses progress in ourselves—that is, in our "moral, aesthetic, and intellectual sensibilities." The chapters in this section explore the biological and social evolution of progress, the achievement of individual and social complexity, progress in religion, in literature, in our ability to make moral judgements at a pace commensurate with scientific or medical progress, in child and family well-being, and in providing access to education.

The section opens with Daly and Wilson's consideration of "whether the evolution of life on earth over geological time has entailed progress" and whether the evolution of humans provides grounds for progress in equality, justice, and human well-being. They answer yes to both questions.

According to Daly and Wilson, "if one defines 'progress' as *change in the direction of greater complexity*, which is probably the most popular meaning when one speaks of possible progress in evolution, there is abundant evidence that the Darwinian process has engendered it, albeit inconsistently." They also propose that an alternative definition of evolutionary progress "might be *growth of intelligence or understanding*." They claim there is ample evidence of such progress.

Daly and Wilson base their argument, in part, on the idea that the survival of complex organisms depends on the fitness prospects of their neighbors—on common cause and cooperative action. They also argue that "the Darwinian process entails within its own dynamics the seeds of cooperative and other-regarding sentiments, including empathy and love."

Daly and Wilson's parallel arguments for progress in the Darwinian process and in social realms provide the groundwork for defining a closer relation between the biomedical and social sciences. They posit that a more detailed description of our complex evolved psychological nature might help us to discover and implement better social policies as we are able to recognize two fundamental human forces. First, humans have a "deep-seated passion for social comparison" and are motivated to correct situations of inequitable access to resources through individual and collective action, including violence. Second, while humans may too easily divide between a "we" worthy of moral consideration and a "they" that is not, the in-group psychology can work for "indefinitely large coalitions."

Daly and Wilson see hope for the future despite the genocidal horrors of the twentieth century. Recent generations have enjoyed longer, more peaceful lives. "It is *because* the Darwinian process has consistently favored those individuals who looked out for their own interests and those of their relatives and allies, resisting theft and coercion," Daly and Wilson conclude, "that the human animal so resents injustice. And it is in that resentment that we see hope for an unrelenting pressure for social progress."

In chapter 5, Mihaly Czikszentmihalyi pursues the claim that the human ability to make moral judgements on the appropriate use of technology, or to anticipate potential negative consequences of technology, has not kept up with the rate and intricacies of technological change. According to Czikszentmihalyi, "If progress is to result in real forward movement, we need to make sure that the cultural instructions for how to use it catch up with technology."

In the past, religion created an ethos of social and political responsibility. While the content of religion is still vital, we need to find new ways to express human potentialities. "Genuine progress," Czikszentmihalyi says, "will have to take into account the evolution of mind and spirit."

Czikszentmihalyi proposes that such evolution is a process of increasing complexity. Complexity involves a balance between differentiation (refinement of specialized structures) and integration (alignment of different parts). Complex individuals are "uniquely individuated," with "desires, goals, and actions . . . in harmony with each other." Similarly, a complex institution "allows individual temperaments and skills to contribute to the well-being of the whole." Political entities allow "the fullest flowering of individual uniqueness compatible with the common weal."

A new definition of progress for the future, Czikszentmihalyi proposes, should include four elements: recognition of the limits of nature; responsible use of technology; recognition of complexity as the leading edge of evolution; and, commitment to implementing complexity in our own lives and in our institutions.

In chapter 6, Hubert Locke explores religion and progress in "Faith and the Future." Locke distinguishes between progress as a fact and as an idea. In the case of the former, Locke refers to the record of achievement and improvement *in* religions—for example, in their commitment to religious pluralism, toleration, and commitment to working for social change. In the case of the latter, Locke refers to progress *and* religion, or the question of whether religion has contributed to, or thwarted, the advancement of humankind. In both cases, he says, the evidence is mixed. However, Locke suggests that an examination of progress in religion requires that we look at religion's best moments, not its worst.

While some have debated the contribution of religion to progress, others have questioned "the very idea of change and improvement in human societies." Locke notes that while Judeo-Christian faiths teach the importance of compassion and justice, many religionists glorify the denunciation of privilege and power. Other religionists have found the idea that humans are advancing in a positive or desirable direction to be a questionable proposition.

Locke concludes that progress in the realm of ethics and education is more accurately described as a process of maturation, or in the arts, as occurring at decisive times, or turning points (Paul Tillich's "kairos"). We need not venture, he says, into the notion that there is such a thing as progress in the realm of human creativity.

In chapter 7, Charles Johnson turns to the question of whether we might find evidence of progress in such a subjective and culturally relative area as literature—and whether literature has contributed to progress. Johnson answers both questions in the affirmative. Quoting Ernest Hemingway's counsel to modern writers to "write what hasn't been written before or beat dead men at what they have done," Johnson notes that we can view evolution in literature through our ability to correct the "foul-ups and partial breakthroughs in past literary art." Johnson provides evidence of progress in several works of modern literature and its ability to give greater attention to the surface details of contemporary life, to enliven diverse voices and vernaculars and social manners, to better communicate human complexity, or, like Locke, to reveal small, epiphanic moments.

One can also judge progress in literature, Johnson notes, by its ability not only to "[sharpen] our perception" but to change it. As Johnson notes, "fiction at its best challenges the status quo. It forces us to question our social relations, prejudices, understanding of the world, ourselves, and the meaning of humanity." In changing our perception, fiction can impact policy: literature can anticipate technology; inspire social change or resistance to oppression; expose political systems; or fuel civil war. Johnson quotes Saul Bellow regarding the artist as the "spokesman for his community."

Johnson writes that it is also important for public policy to support artists—who often gain experience at their art at great expense. Public support for writers should come through public financial support of small presses that allow unknown and iconoclastic writers to publish their work. Organizations such as the National Endowment for the Arts are also critical to the survival of art—and to ensuring that art is not subject to the whims of the market alone.

In chapter 8, Albert Jonsen turns to the question of ethics and biomedical progress. Bioethics emerged in the twentieth century as a means of making systematic moral decisions in the realm of medical progress. Bioethicists address both clinical issues (such as sustaining life and allowing death) and issues of public policy (such as allocation of resources, research with human beings, and privacy of medical-genetic information).

The common feature of moral dilemmas associated with medical progress, Jonsen finds, is that each is an "undesirable and often unforeseen [consequence] ... of desirable and intended medical benefits." The most troubling of these consequences, according to Jonsen, is that as the quality of care increases, with its attendant costs, access to it seems to decrease; in the United States and in developing nations, a huge portion of the population does not have access to needed medical treatments or preventive measures. In recent years, new dilemmas have emerged with progress in genetic interventions. Progress in medicine may now include not only those who are sick, but also those who know they might become sick. Such information also gives rise to concerns about privacy and the use of genetic information.

While bioethicists tend to reside mostly in the scholarly world, the ethical issues with which they deal, such as respect for the individual and fairness in distributing the goods of a community, have shaped public policy debates. As Jonsen notes, public policy tends to adopt a utilitarian ethos focused on the greater good for the greater number, countered by respect for persons and fairness in the community. Bioethicists are committed to the task of balancing these moral ideas and helping to translate them into public policy and practice.

In chapter 9, Richard Brandon proposes that "societal progress . . . means steadily improving the well-being of all citizens, starting with the well-being of children, and reducing the disparities in levels of well-being among different groups of children and families." Brandon argues that child well-being must go beyond having children survive to having them thrive. This means that children grow up strong, literate, and competent to deal with the world around them; and are supported in their emotional and social well-being by their families and by the broader society. In the United States, Brandon suggests, meeting this goal will, in part, require public financing and universal access to high quality early care and learning. Developing nations must also allocate resources to early pre-primary learning, or face a growing disparity in chances for children as compared to those of children in industrialized nations that provide enriched early learning environments.

Brandon argues that measures of child well-being should consider their health, educational performance, economic security, and behavioral status. Measures of child well-being are also more appropriately stated in positive terms, rather than in terms of deficiencies. Brandon builds his case for public financing and universal access to early care and learning in the United States, noting that early childhood is the only stage in the life cycle for which the United States lacks a major public entitlement program that includes the broad middle class. "Yet," Brandon notes, "we expect parents of young children, who are usually at their earliest years in the labor force and therefore lowest earnings levels, to bear the full responsibility of early care and education." He concludes that continuing progress will require substantially greater investments in the care of young children.

In the final chapter of section one, William Zumeta surveys progress in education and in education policy. Zumeta follows Kenneth Boulding's definition of progress as "'human betterment' so as to encompass not only gains in the collective and material life but also in the realms of the self, ideas, and the natural world." The goal of public policy in education is to help a society achieve or improve upon standards of performance, including rates of educational participation and attainment, and quality and equity of access to education. Education, Zumeta claims, is "inextricably intertwined with progress defined as human betterment."

Zumeta examines the measurement of educational progress. These measures do not always tell us whether policies are efficient or effective, or whether there is a healthy connection between traditional cultural values and local needs in schools. However, more sophisticated measures of education, which tell more than reported years of schooling, are difficult to collect. The movement toward competency testing in education and the labor market, along with trends toward globalization in the labor market, may accelerate and improve upon international testing.

The conditions necessary for progress in education, according to Zumeta, include a social and legal framework for education (codified in laws and funding arrangements), the economic wherewithal for investment, a commitment to equity in educational opportunities, and a rational and broadly accepted process for allocating resources. Zumeta also notes that accountability in quality and in allocation of resources is central to progress in education and human betterment. He acknowledges, however, that "there is considerable controversy over the specifics of accountability measures but little doubt that schools and colleges will be called to account more explicitly than in the past." Finally, Zumeta notes that the conditions necessary for progress in education entail responsiveness to local needs, and innovation in "responding to new knowledge, social needs, and technological possibilities." While societies pursue these ends through different structural arrangements, Zumeta notes, there has been an increase in decentralized mechanisms for governance (including the growth of private education), and therefore greater local control.

Donor nations and international development agencies can play a useful role in linking aid to educational policies that promote equity; provide fiscal assistance for low-wealth countries; help to create efficiencies in education (focusing, for example, on performance-management or in maintenance of the capital infrastructure); ensure fiscal investments in education are both effective and efficient; and, help to smooth out the worst effects of low economic cycles. Policy makers can also help to stimulate exports and the growth of the private sector in an effort to create more jobs for educated individuals, and can help ensure broader investment in primary education (which Zumeta notes, tend to pay better dividends than do investments in higher education).

Progress in ourselves, as described by several of our authors, is much harder to define, measure, and promote than progress in the social or material and natural worlds. Yet, our ability to manage our technological progress depends upon our progress within this realm. Public policies supporting "human betterment" involve difficult decisions regarding the efficient, effective, and equitable allocation of resources, and moral questions regarding restraints on our use of resources or on establishing the boundaries of medical and human experimentation. Public policy can also help to support the expression of humanity through support for the arts and education, or can help to support individual and collective action toward social progress. In short, progress in ourselves requires a well-developed understanding of the human condition, its possibilities and limits.

Chapter 4

Progress and Evolution

Martin Daly and Margo Wilson

Like *progress* the word *evolution* refers to an historical process of cumulative change. Nevertheless, how these two concepts are related to one another, if at all, is a complex and controversial issue, primarily but not solely because of ambiguity about what would constitute a progressive trend, as opposed to retrogression or an absence of direction, in the context of the modification of life forms over generations.

In this essay, we address two distinct aspects of the relationship between progress and evolution. First, we consider whether the evolution of life on earth over geological time has entailed progress in any of several related senses. We suggest that it has, despite some arguments to the contrary. Secondly, we consider whether the proposition that the human animal is a product of Darwinian processes has any implications with respect to social progress in historical time. We suggest that it does, and that those implications provide some grounds for cautious optimism as regards the prospects for continuing gains in equality, justice, and human well-being.

Progress in the Evolutionary History of Life on Earth

For biologists, "evolution" refers to change in any attribute of a population, species, or higher taxon over generations: form or function, anatomy or biochemistry, central tendency or distribution. It is customary to distinguish at least four forces that affect the direction and tempo of evolution, namely

(1) selection: systematic differences in the reproduction and proliferation of types within a population as a result of their different properties;
(2) drift: consequential differences in the reproduction of types within a population as a result of "chance," i.e., *not* as a result of their different properties;
(3) mutation: random errors in the replication of genetic elements; and
(4) migration into and out of the population.

In the absence of the first force, selection, each of the other three tends to destroy order and to increase entropy or noise. Only selection is potentially progressive in the sense that it causes adaptive complexity to increase, as small improvements are selectively retained and build on one another.

Charles Darwin (1859), the first to appreciate that selection could explain complex adaptation in nature, was intimately acquainted with the practices of farmers and hobbyists who pursued specific goals like increased milk production or showier flowers by selective breeding of domesticated plants and animals, and he coined the term "natural selection" by explicit analogy with this "artificial" selection.[1] Of course, Darwin was well aware that "nature" is not an intentional agent and *has* no goals, and he painstakingly explained why intention is inessential for the emergence of functional "design." Basically, each small improvement that spreads to "fixation" (universality) in a population sets the stage for further improvements, so over many generations, the cumulative products of this automatic process of differential success can be attributes of increasing intricacy, such as the vertebrate eye and visual system, whose immediate functions (image analysis, in this case) subserve more distal functions of survival and, ultimately, reproduction.[2]

A major misconception in lay understandings of evolutionary biology is the notion that there is a unidimensional progression—the *scala naturae*—proceeding from earlier, simpler, "lower" animals to *Homo sapiens* at its summit. Evolutionists are essentially unanimous—and often very exercised—in their insistence that this popular view rests on a profound incomprehension of the evolutionary process. For one thing, the human animal is certainly *not* the most recent product of that process: yes, the hominid lineage has undergone some relatively rapid evolution in the last couple of million years, but so have other, unrelated lineages, and other groups have speciated in the millennia since anatomically modern humans first appeared. Moreover, and even more importantly, there is no satisfactory criterion for ranking species as "higher" or "lower." Most attempts to do so are transparently anthropocentric: corollaries of the premise that "we're number one" and that the rest of creation is relatively "advanced" to the degree that it resembles us. But even if one finds the intuitive grounds for placing human beings atop the *scala naturae* compelling, how could one then decide the relative positions of an orchid and a clam? Only arbitrarily.

Contemporary monkeys, fishes, algae, or bacteria are not our ancestors. They are our contemporaries, and they are every bit as much the current culmination of billions of years of evolution as is *Homo sapiens sapiens*. A much better model than the *scala naturae* is therefore that of a shrub whose terminal buds correspond to contemporary species. The shrub is constantly being pruned by extinctions, and its surface is constantly being reestablished and rearranged by fresh branchings.

That said, however, the inadequacy of the pre-Darwinian notion of a *scala naturae* provides no reason to conclude that the history of life on earth is devoid of tendencies that might reasonably be called "progressive." Life presumably began, after all, with some relatively simple process of chemical replication, and attained such milestones as cell walls, messenger RNA, specialized organs, and everything else that impresses us about the complexity of life, only as the cumulative consequences of the selective retention of superior mutants, those relatively rare accidental variants, proved to be better at survival and reproduction than their "normal" predecessors. Thus, if one defines "progress" as *change in the direction of greater complexity*, which is probably the most popular meaning when one speaks of possible progress in evolution, there is abundant evidence that the Darwinian process has engendered it, albeit inconsistently as discussed below.

An alternative definition of evolutionary progress might be *growth of intelligence or understanding*, and there is plenty of evidence for that, as well. The earliest life forms must necessarily have detected few aspects of the primordial soup in which they lived and shown little flexibility in their responses thereto. The origin of the cell, more than two billion years ago, entailed large gains in the capacity of living things to process information about environmental variables like pH, temperature, and light levels, and to respond contingently. So, of course, did the subsequent innovations of multicellularity and specialized organs at the organism/environment interface, and so, even more clearly, did the further innovations of nerve cells and networks whose basic functions are information processing and transmission. Finally, with respect to the narrower question of progress in the human lineage, the amount of brain tissue, especially the neocortex, clearly increased with some sustained directionality (albeit for reasons that are still the subject of speculation and controversy) over the course of hominid evolution, and there is no reason to doubt that cognitive capacity was increasing too.[3]

Another conception of progress, rather different from mere growth in either complexity or intelligence, has stronger moral overtones. This is the idea that progressive change is that which entails *expanding spheres of common cause and cooperative action*. This may sound like the sort of trend that could only be discerned in human history, but such tendencies are again apparent in organic evolution too. The several innovations in the evolution of multicellular organisms with specialized organ systems, for example, entailed new levels of shared fate. Autonomous single-celled organisms find themselves in a more or less purely competitive, zero-sum contest for shares of the ancestry of future populations, such that one's gain is another's loss, but the individual cells of an organism such as a person or an oak tree are in a very different situation: they are all in the same boat because they can advance their own prospects for Darwinian fitness (genetic posterity) only by advancing the fitness prospects of their neighbors.

Heart cells, liver cells, bone cells, etc., all work together for the common good—that is, the survival and reproduction of the whole organism of which they are parts—because this is how the genetic instructions underlying their development can be transmitted and hence preserved. Moreover, it now seems clear that the eukaryotic cell itself originated as a coalition (perhaps initially exploitative, but eventually cooperative) of previously autonomous organelles, and that chromosomes and nuclear genomes are likewise coalitions of previously independent replicators whose fates have become linked and whose actions have therefore evolved to be complementary.[4] The evolutionary elaboration of common cause and cooperative action is not bounded even by the limits of the individual organism, for although it is indeed true at one level that the individuals who comprise a population or species (or at least those individuals of a given sex) are engaged in a zero-sum contest over shares of future populations' ancestry, it is also true that various considerations, especially kinship, can have the effect of engendering a positive correlation between the expected fitnesses of two or more individuals, thus creating conditions conducive to the evolution of cooperation and other-regarding sentiments such as parental, fraternal, and romantic love.[5]

Change in the physical environment is aimless, and sometimes exhibits repeated reversals, such as the recurrent advance and retreat of polar ice caps over millennia. Insofar as evolution is a process of adaptation to such change, it is unlikely to exhibit any sort of sustained directionality. Other changes in the physical environment, such as that in the composition of the atmosphere as a result of life processes,[6] are more consistent in their direction over long periods of time, but even this consistency is not enough to impart a cumulative character to evolution of the sort that we might deem progressive. Rather, the principle considerations that afford the possibility of progressive trends in evolution do not depend on changes in the physical environment at all. They are, first, the "bootstrapping" effect implied by the fact that in the absence of foresight, adaptive designs arise only as minor improvements on last year's model, and second, the fact that evolution entails "arms races" as a result of the fact that the selective milieu does not consist solely of the physical environment but of a co-evolving biotic environment as well.

The bootstrapping effect is most dramatically illustrated by the ways in which major innovations in the history of life have repeatedly opened the way to an explosion of further invention. Dawkins (1989) argued that such events have repeatedly changed aspects of what the evolutionary process can do next and how, a history of expanding possibilities that he refers to as the "evolution of evolvability."[7] In a similar vein, Maynard Smith and Szathmáry (1995) identify and discuss a succession of "major evolutionary transitions" in the form or function of replicating entities, each of which changed the landscape of further possibility: the origins of metabolism, self-replication, a nucleic acid based genetic code, cell walls, cell nuclei, sexual reproduction, multicellular organisms, nervous systems, animal societies, and human language.[8]

As for what evolutionists call "arms races," a crucial consideration is that the environment of evolving species includes *other* evolving species with contrary interests. An improvement in the speed, agility, or immune system of one species constitutes a deterioration of the environment for other species that prey upon or parasitize it, and intensifies selective pressures on these predators and parasites to overcome the new defenses. In some cases, such as when alternative host genotypes are differentially vulnerable to a corresponding set of parasite genotypes, cyclical change in their respective frequencies over generations may result and the evolutionary arms race goes nowhere. Van Valen (1973) dubbed these "Red Queen" processes, after the Wonderland character who told Alice that "it takes all the running *you* can do, to stay in the same place," and this term has sometimes been applied to co-evolution generally.[9] However, co-evolutionary arms races that produce a true Red Queen cyclical stasis appear to be relatively rare. More typically, arms races engender some degree of sustained directional change, such as an increase in size or fleetness or complexity of information processing over many generations.

It is not just your predators, prey, and parasites that are potentially co-evolving antagonists. Competitors co-evolve, too, as do any interactants whose commonality of purpose is less than total. Thus, co-evolutionary arms races can occur not only between two interacting species, but within a single species as well. Partners in sexual reproduction constitute a prime example. Because a man and woman each supply half of a given child's genes, that child is equally a potential contributor to the fitness of both parents, and we might therefore expect that selection should have favored concordant ambitions in the couple. However, the fact that a particular male is keen to sire a female's children does not guarantee that he is the best choice from her perspective, and even after a deal has been struck and a child conceived, either party could still gain fitness at the other's expense by shirking. The upshot is that heterosexual transactions have evolved to be complex and nuanced, with each party concerned to advertise its own virtues, to verify the truth of the other's claims, and to enforce cooperative agreements. Mate choice is a powerful evolutionary force, as Darwin (1871) was the first to realize.[10] Indeed, a good case can be made that mate choice has been the principal architect of much of what we value in human nature, including artistic expression and our appreciation thereof.[11]

Despite these considerations, the notion of progress in evolution is anathema to at least a few biologists. Several complementary arguments against the idea have been advanced, especially by Gould (1989, 1996).[12] One fact that has been invoked as evidence against progressive trends in evolution is that many lineages neither exhibit sustained complexification over geological time nor are supplanted by those that do. Bacteria are apparently no more complex than they were when multi-cellular organisms first appeared on the scene, for example, and they still outnumber (perhaps even out*weigh*!) these latecomers. Well, in fact, we don't actually know whether modern bacteria are more complex than their ancient ancestors, but that's a mere quibble. The more serious flaw in this argument is in its logic, which could just as readily be used to prove that there has been no progress in evolutionary biology since Darwin's time, since those who are completely ignorant of the subject still outnumber the cognoscenti. The issue is not whether *everything* has been getting more complex, but whether there has been a sustained increase in *maximal* complexity, and at least on some time scales, there clearly has been. This consideration also undermines the force of another favorite argument against progress in evolution, namely that selection sometimes favors the *loss* of complex structures, as in the evolution of blind cave-dwelling animals and many internal parasites. Finally, Gould (1989) has made much of the role of happenstance ("contingency") in the extinction of species and higher taxa, arguing that if the small human population that existed 50 or 100,000 years ago had been unlucky enough to encounter any of various disasters, nothing exactly like ourselves would exist now or ever in the future.[13] This is uncontroversial (except perhaps among those who believe that this particular upright ape is the image of divinity and the point of the creation), but it has no obvious bearing, one way or the other, on the question of whether there is something about the processes by which species and biotic communities evolve that tends to engender increasing levels of complexity, or intelligence, or cooperation, or any other abstract "good."[14]

The evolutionary anthropologist Don Symons has said that in order to understand an argument, you have to know who is being argued *against*, and it is no secret who it is that opponents of the notion of progress in evolution have been most concerned to refute: "social Darwinists." This label refers to the adherents of a fringe political philosophy, a century ago, who maintained that because "survival of the fittest" is the engine of evolutionary improvement, it should be encouraged. Like Calvinists who justified inequity by arguing that advantage accrues to the deserving, social Darwinists maintained that the wealthy and privileged are superior and deserve their advantages. This doctrine found little if any support among evolutionary biologists and had little if any influence on them. Indeed, it never had a large following *anywhere*, but it did appeal (little wonder) to some rich men, such as the American industrialist J. P. Morgan. The fact that its advocates included a few such powerful men probably explains why social Darwinism has been the object of far more discussion than ever was warranted on the strength of its arguments or the size of its following. One modern consequence of this intellectual history is that distaste for the notion of progress in evolution continues to be fuelled by moral sentiment: if the evolution of life forms is given its direction by competition and weeding out the "unfit," then the whole process seems antithetical to progress in the sense of growth of the dominion of good and diminution of the dominion of evil. Moreover, many people, even highly educated ones, still imagine that Darwinism itself is a reactionary ideology rather than what it actually is: the foundation of modern biology.

Ironically, one must concede that there *is* a sort of logic to the revulsion that some people feel toward the blind, creative, Darwinian process. Evolution's arrow (if such a thing exists) does not point toward the abolition of pain and suffering. Evolution by selection *invented* pain and suffering as motivational devices that encourage fitness-promoting behavior. Neither does the evolutionary process tend to produce an ever-increasing stock of human happiness (other than as a byproduct of an ever-increasing stock of humans). Like suffering, pleasure is regulated and is *fleeting by design*, because chronic satisfaction would be counterproductive for an organism whose prospects for increasing its expected future fitness must ever entail striving after goals as yet unattained. Selection does not even favor mercy, or at least it does not do so routinely. Killing quickly and cleanly can evolve where predators who behave otherwise risk injury to themselves, but in the absence of such risks, many predators and parasites blithely devour their prey alive.

Every complex organism embodies a cornucopia of niches for parasites and pathogens, whose life processes degrade that complexity and often make the complex organism suffer as they do so. It was once popular to imagine that selection favors evolutionary trends away from exploitative and destructive parasitism and towards a more benign mutualism. Unfortunately, this soothing notion has little theoretical or empirical basis. The microbes that are favored by selection, for example, are simply those whose attributes are most effective at infecting their hosts, at replicating within their hosts, and above all, at getting themselves or their progeny transmitted to other suitable hosts before the present host is destroyed. At least one eminent evolutionary biologist, George Williams (1988), has seriously argued that we should look upon the blind, oblivious process of evolution by selection as not merely amoral, but evil.[15] In its defense, however, one can reply that as selection has built more complex life forms, it created the situation in which human values and the possibility (however slim) of trends that satisfy them came into existence, and that the Darwinian process entails within its own dynamics the seeds of cooperative and other-regarding sentiments, including empathy and love.

Implications of the Proposition That Human Nature Evolved under Selection

The evolutionary process has equipped organisms like ourselves with a highly complex suite of functional machinery: teeth and bones, hearts and livers, brains and immune systems, and much, much more. These distinct but functionally integrated components are dedicated to specific tasks, solving problems that our ancestors encountered regularly: mastication and digestion, nourishing tissues and removing their wastes, detecting and interpreting threats, distinguishing invading micro-organisms from self, and so on and on.

The biomedical view of human nature assumes the complex functionality of our anatomy, physiology, and biochemistry, and progress in biomedical science consists primarily of producing an ever-more elaborate description of our evolved human nature. Curiously, however, the social sciences have seldom seen their mission in the same terms, and the very notion that the human animal possesses a multifaceted psychological and social nature, which we might usefully strive to describe, is often attacked as reactionary. The supposed alternative to a "nativism" that attributes the structure and organization of our minds to human evolution is philosophical "empiricism," which Dennett (1995) defines as "the view that we furnish our minds with details that all come from the outside world, via experience" within each individual's lifespan.[16]

In the mid-twentieth century, an extreme version of empiricism called "behaviorism" was prominent in psychological science. With the admirable goal of ridding psychology of pseudo-explanatory *post hoc* mental constructs and "innate abilities," behaviorists aspired to explain the richness of human and nonhuman behavior in terms of a few simple "laws of learning," or even one. This ambition slowly collapsed under the weight of two broad classes of discoveries. One is that the human brain contains hundreds (perhaps thousands) of distinct anatomical structures and chemical subsystems, where different sorts of information are processed and different sets of genes are active, and which exhibit demonstrable continuity ("homology") with the structure and function of components of nonhuman brains. The other nail in the coffin of extreme versions of behaviorism was provided by a series of demonstrations showing that individual experience is not sufficiently informative to train an unstructured all-purpose learning device to do the many expert things that we do effortlessly, such as seeing and speaking and deciding that something novel is or is not potential food. As behaviorism came under attack in the 1960s and 1970s, the alternative view that people and other animals possess evolved mental mechanisms that direct their attention and their development was initially portrayed, even by critics of behaviorism, as a matter of "constraints" on learning ability. Selective readiness to associate nausea with tastes but not with sounds, to take one familiar example, sounds like a narrowing of what an "unconstrained" capacity for associative learning might achieve. However, increasing recognition of the limited capabilities of an unstructured brain has turned this conception on its head: the evolution of complex, domain-specific mental mechanisms is now considered *enabling*, not constraining.[17]

One might infer from this brief summary that the battle between nativism and empiricism is over, and nativism has won. A better conclusion, however, is that such nature-nurture disputes were grounded in a false opposition. "Environmentally induced" is not the antithesis of "evolved." Any complex evolved attribute of a multicellular organism develops in each individual with susceptibility to environmental variations, and much of that susceptibility is adaptive conditional response "designed" by selection to exploit the information value of those environmental variations. This is not to deny, however, that debates that are ostensibly about nature *versus* nurture sometimes concern issues of scientific substance. There is current controversy, for example, about whether certain aspects of probabilistic inference, linguistic competence, kin recognition, and the evaluation of potential mates are performed by mental devices that evolved for those specific tasks or should be understood as the products of more general problem-solving machinery, and although quarreling persists even about what counts as evidence, there are some tractable scientific questions here. It is in debates such as these that scientists may still be described as proponents of relatively empiricist or nativist positions.

Our reason for dwelling on this dimension is, of course, that it is widely presumed to be relevant to opinions about the possibility or likelihood of progress in human affairs. Empiricist views of human nature are commonly considered optimistic and politically progressive, while relatively nativist views are seen as pessimistic and reactionary, since empiricists since Locke supposedly believe that the world can be changed for the better, while nativists, with their Hobbesian, misanthropic belief in a "fixed" human nature, do not.

Despite the widespread acceptance of this view of the political implications of empiricism and nativism, there are good reasons to reject it. On the one hand, the history of biomedical science puts the lie to the idea that relatively nativistic views of human nature imply a doctrine of despair: progress in medical knowledge and practice has shown again and again that an increasingly rich description of our evolved physiological nature is essential for the design of increasingly effective and humane interventions. Why, then, should the pursuit of a more detailed description of our complex evolved *psychological* nature impede or discourage the discovery or implementation of better social policies? And on the other hand, the presumption that relatively empiricist views of human nature have a natural affinity with political and social progress is easily challenged. As many writers have noted, the arch-empiricist's view of human nature as a "blank slate" was a totalitarian's dream. A blank slate devoid of any sort of complex, evolved self-interest is anybody's manipulandum, and fair game to boot: you cannot violate people's interests by manipulating them to serve new, externally imposed objectives if their prior objectives were no more their own than the new ones. Thus, coercive "reprogramming" of dissidents is morally unproblematic under extreme empiricist worldviews, which have been embraced by some of the worst tyrants of recent history. At the very least, one must conclude that while anti-nativists may be "optimistic" as regards the malleability of human nature, the programmatic manifestations of that optimism are not unequivocally "progressive."

The proposition that human nature evolved under the influence of natural selection suggests that an extreme version of empiricism cannot be true. Fitness is relative, and selection favors those attributes, including attributes of the mind, that reproduce more successfully than rivals. This competitive aspect of selection implies that the social malleability of an evolved psyche cannot be limitless, because limitless malleability would mean limitless vulnerability to manipulation and exploitation. Conflicting interests are endemic in any sexually reproducing species, and this fact has assured that the human psyche has evolved defenses against being deceived and exploited, even while profiting from social life and information sharing.

The human animal has a deep-seated passion for social comparison and has not been selected to tolerate relative disadvantage gladly. Inequitable access to resources motivates people to change their situations by both individual and collective action, including violent action. Despotic tyranny seems to be inherently unstable in human history, while the rise of democratic power-sharing and impartial third-party justice in state-level societies has coincided with (and apparently caused) a decline in the private use of personal violence to levels previously unknown.[18] It is true, and frightening, that the evolved human mind readily divides others into a "we" that is worthy of moral consideration and compassion *versus* a "they" that is not,[19] but it is also true that this in-group psychology works for indefinitely large coalitions and that an historical trend toward greater inclusiveness of the "moral circle" is conspicuous and apparently still underway.[20] Alexander (1987) and others have argued persuasively that violent conflict between rival coalitions became a major selective force during hominid evolution, equipping us with cognitive and emotional capacities to form cooperative alliances unlimited by kinship or even personal acquaintanceship.[21] If this is true, then empathy and our capacity to extend its scope to an indefinitely large in-group are the ironic and hopeful consequences of a war-like past.

Despite the genocidal and other horrors of the twentieth century, recent generations have enjoyed longer life expectancies and a better chance of dying peacefully in bed than our ancestors ever had. There is obviously room for a good deal more progress in these matters, and importantly, there is also clamorous *demand* for such progress. The evolved human psyche does not accede to relative disadvantage uncomplainingly, and resorts to more dangerous tactics in its struggle to achieve equity, the more severe the disadvantage and the less there is to lose.[22] It is *because* the Darwinian process has consistently favored those individuals who looked out for their own interests and those of their relatives and allies, resisting theft and coercion, that the human animal so resents injustice. And it is in that resentment that we see hope for an unrelenting pressure for social progress.

Notes

1. C. Darwin, *On the Origin of Species by Means of Natural Selection* (London: Murray, 1859).

2. For a highly readable, book-length elaboration of the basic idea that Darwinian selection is the creative force in evolution, see R. Dawkins, *The Blind Watchmaker* (Harlow: Longman, 1986).

3. T. W. Deacon, *The Symbolic Species: the Co-evolution of Language and the Brain* (New York: Norton, 1997).

4. L. Margulis, *Symbiosis in Cell Evolution* (New York: Freeman, 1993).

5. See, for example, S. A. Frank, *Foundations of Social Evolution* (Princeton: Princeton University Press, 1998).

6. J. F. Kasting, "Earth's Early Atmosphere," *Science* 259 (February 1993): 920-26.

7. R. Dawkins, "The evolution of evolvability," in *Artificial Life*, ed. C. Langton (Santa Fe: Addison Wesley, 1989).

8. J. Maynard Smith and E. Szathmáry, *The Major Transitions in Evolution* (Oxford: Oxford University Press, 1995).

9. L. Van Valen, "A New Evolutionary Law," *Evolutionary Theory* 1 (1973): 1-30.

10. C. Darwin, *The Descent of Man and Selection in Relation to Sex* (London: Murray, 1871).

11. See G. F. Miller, *The Mating Mind: How Sexual Choice Shaped the Evolution of Human Nature* (New York: Doubleday, 2000).

12. S. J. Gould, *Wonderful Life: the Burgess Shale and the Nature of History* (New York: Norton, 1989); S. J. Gould, *Full House* (New York: Harmony Books, 1996).

13. Gould, *Wonderful Life.*

14. For more extensive discussion and refutation of these arguments against progress in evolution, see R. Wright, *Nonzero: the Logic of Human Destiny* (New York: Pantheon, 2000).

15. G. C. Williams, "Huxley's *Evolution and Ethics* in sociobiological perspective," *Zygon* 23 (1988): 383-407.

16. D. C. Dennett, *Darwin's Dangerous Idea: Evolution and the Meanings of Life* (New York: Touchstone, 1995).

17. For a fuller account of the history reviewed in this paragraph, see S. Pinker, *How the Mind Works* (New York: Norton, 1997).

18. M. Daly and M. Wilson, *Homicide* (Hawthorne, N.Y.: Aldine de Gruyter, 1988).

19. H. J. Tajfel, *Social Identity and Intergroup Relations* (Cambridge: Cambridge University Press, 1982).

20. P. Singer, *The Expanding Circle: Ethics and Sociobiology* (Oxford: Clarendon, 1981).

21. R. D. Alexander, *The Evolution of Moral Systems* (Hawthorne, N.Y.: Aldine de Gruyter, 1987).

22. M. Daly and M. Wilson, "Risk-taking, Intrasexual Competition, and Homicide," *Nebraska Symposium on Motivation* 48 (2000) : 1-35.

Chapter 5

The Meaning of Progress in the New Millennium

Mihaly Csikszentmihalyi

Progress means literally a forward movement, and its usual connotations refer to the human ability to create technologies for controlling natural processes at the service of our species' well-being. At present, technology itself is subordinated to the so-called free market, so that every new invention, including ways to change our bodies and our genes, has to obey the logic of the highest bidder. The implicit meaning of progress is a way of life where unimpeded exchange leads to ever-increasing production and consumption of material commodities.

It is clear, however, that progress in this limited sense is a double-edged sword. Almost all technological advances bring with them unintended consequences that may take many years to reveal their full costs. From dams that increase the salinity of croplands thereby turning them into deserts to waste problems that pollute the land; from the hole in the ozone layer to global warming—these potentially tragic developments of the last century must be reckoned in the ledgers of technology against its many wonderful accomplishments.

It is not a question of blaming technology for such ills, nor the individuals who implement it. The blame rests on the differential rates of reproduction of technological "memes"—customs, laws, religious prohibitions—in relation to memes that tell us what the consequences of using technology are, and how to make it all work in our long-term favor—which must include the well-being of the planetary eco-system on which our survival depends. That there should be such a difference in the evolution of what we may loosely call technology and morality is not surprising. After all, the fruits of science have multiplied so vigorously in the past hundred years we cannot honestly foresee their effects. And being ignorant of them, we prefer to assume that they will be benign. In past civilizations, the rate of technological change was slow enough for people to observe the feedback to their actions, and develop memes to limit the negative effects of the novelties they invented.[1] We don't have that luxury.

If progress is to result in real forward movement, we need to make sure that the cultural instructions for how to use it catch up with technology. Genetic instructions program us to take as much as we can from the environment without much concern for consequences. This was a viable survival strategy as long as the most any person could take were a few deer and edible roots. Anthropologists have noted that for most of human history hunter-gatherers were not in a position to create material surplus, or to accumulate property, because they had to be always on the move in search of food.[2] There was little difference among individuals in terms of access to resources, and no way for one person to exploit the labor of another. With the advent of agriculture about ten thousand years ago, this situation changed. As surplus grain began to be stored, resources could be accumulated resulting in large disparities in wealth and power.[3] Slavery and serfdom were made possible—as well as cities living off the agricultural surplus, and large nations and empires.

By the time the great religious systems were developed two to three thousand years ago, it was becoming clear that restraints on greed were necessary. The old restraints based on scarcity did not work well in the suddenly wealthy civilizations based on clear-cutting forests and irrigating plains. The new religions tried to develop a global sense of responsibility that matched the expanded social and political environment in which people lived. The Zoroastrians prescribed that each evening a person should ask forgiveness for the water, the fire, and the meat he or she consumed.[4] Christianity attempted to control rampant greed by including gluttony, covetousness, and envy among the seven deadly sins. Similar restraints were built into the other religious systems, from Buddhism to Islam, from Taoism to Confucianism. Obviously these restraints were far from effective, since they had to work against the contrary instructions of our genetic program. Nevertheless, at slow rates of technological change they acted as a brake on unrestrained greed.

Parallel to the religious systems that tried to bring about a moral climate that would act as a social control on the expanding powers of consumption and destruction, civil society attempted to develop laws and regulations to counteract runaway indulgence. Ancient history is full of examples, from the rigorous asceticism of Sparta where no tool more delicate than an ax or a saw was permitted in the building of houses and furniture, to the laws of republican Rome enacted in 215 B.C. which ruled what kind of clothes citizens could wear and what food they could eat. Such sumptuary laws which were enacted all over Europe and Asia fell into disuse only in the twentieth century, as consumption became increasingly recognized as the engine that drove the economy. By mid-century, the political philosopher Hannah Arendt could write that "consumption is no longer restricted to the necessities but, on the contrary, mainly concentrates on the superfluities of life ... harbors the grave danger that eventually no object of the world will be safe from consumption and annihilation through consumption."[5]

Now that the main place of worship left standing in the developed world is the shrine of Adam Smith's Invisible Hand, it is useful to reflect on what important role the great world religions have played in the past. They have diligently poured grains of sand into the sleek machinery of naked self-interest, retarding its relentless progress. In so doing they have precariously preserved valuable components of human experience that otherwise may have been annihilated by the calculus of comfort and greed—such as love, self-discipline, and spiritual values.

But the age of the great religions is past. Although in many parts of the world they still keep a strong hold on the minds and the conduct of the faithful, the reasons they offer for why we should or should not do certain things are getting increasingly out of sync with the rest of the worldview, which is based on the growing evidence of the senses interpreted by reason. So while much of the moral content of religions is still vital, the symbolic forms in which it is couched no longer compels belief. We must find new ways to express the leading edge of human potentialities before the primitive genetic programs, wielding the sophisticated powers of technology, reduce our options to the dismal logic of greed. Genuine progress will have to take into account the evolution of mind and spirit.

The default option is to sit back and wait for natural selection to do its job, slowly weeding out genes for wanton wastefulness and excessive selfishness. According to some readings of the evolutionary record, it is possible to discern a movement in the direction of greater self-restraint. Robert Wright sees human destiny evolving towards increasingly non-zero-sum relationships and institutions based on win-win rather than win-lose strategies.[6] Peter Singer believes that one positive trend in history has been the "expanding circle" of other individuals whose well-being is seen as necessary to complement one's own.[7] The problem with waiting for evolution to do its shtick is that it may be too late. If our ability to consume and destroy keep growing at their present pace, we need to develop memes that are robust enough to contain them.

The first step in this direction is to face up squarely to the peculiar limitations of the human organism. We have to recognize how much of our needs and emotions are built into our nervous system, and how difficult it is to control them.[8] Most religions have expressed this condition with notions such as "original sin." From a contemporary point of view "sins" such as anger, gluttony, lechery, and sloth refer to the natural tendency of any living organism to gain as much as possible with the least expenditure of energy—a tendency that has to be restrained for individuals to coexist harmoniously in an environment where anger is magnified by lethal weapons, hunger can be indulged to excess, and so on. But unless we clearly understand how much a part of us such "sins" are, we are likely to be misled into self-delusion.

At the same time, we have to recognize that with the advent of self-reflective consciousness—the ability to reflect on the internal states of the mind—human beings have stepped out from the ranks of creation. Humans have lost the innocence enjoyed by the other animals who simply follow instinct and chance. We have began to interfere with the machinery of life—through farming, mining, nuclear and genetic engineering, we are rapidly changing the balance of biological and molecular patterns on the planet. It is becoming clear that these interferences will have lethal results unless we assume responsibility for the future of the planet, or at least for those parts of it that are affected by our actions.

But how shall these actions be directed? The mythical accounts of past religions will have to be replaced by an understanding of evolution as a process of increasing complexity which is now partly in our hands, either to enhance or to deny.[9] This process is made of two components: *Differentiation*, or the increasing refinements of specialized structures and functions, and *integration*, or the increasingly harmonious alignment of the differentiated parts. These trends have progressed at the level of atoms, molecules, individual organisms—as well as the level of consciousness, knowledge, and social institutions. Our minds recoil at the notion of stifling sameness, of boring routine, as well as at the notion of chaos and unpredictability. Between these two extremes—in the order at the edge of chaos—lies the evolution of complexity.[10] Supporting it with our actions is the challenge presented by the powers our consciousness has acquired.

At the personal level, this involves allowing one's individuality to be fully realized, while creating strong ties with other people, ideas, and institutions. Neither mediocrity and complacency on the one hand, nor single-minded specialization on the other, lead to complexity. Conformity and self-seeking are equally inimical to it. A complex person is one whose consciousness is uniquely individuated, yet whose desires, goals, and actions are in harmony with each other.[11]

The same parameters apply to institutions. Any group is complex to the extent that it allows individual temperaments and skills to contribute to the well-being of the whole. As Durkheim[12] and many since him have noted, there is no necessary conflict between individuality and belonging to a group; indeed the division of labor that sociability makes possible is the prerequisite for the blossoming of individual differences. A complex family, for instance, is one where each member is expected and encouraged to develop his or her unique qualities and interests, yet where every member knows that the others are as committed to his or her goals as they are to theirs.[13]

At the level of larger groups the same principle prevails: The great political concepts of *liberty* and *equality* refer to the two components of complexity that must both be present for a wholesome society. Capitalist nations tend to compromise complexity by favoring freedom and neglecting equality. During this past century the Socialist experiment has shown the dangers of neglecting freedom in favor of equality. The constant challenge for political entities is to preserve the dialectic of complexity by allowing the fullest flowering of individual uniqueness compatible with the common weal.

To follow this direction means that we will have to learn ways to control those aspects of technology and the free market that militate against differentiation and integration. Currently most scientists and economists adopt a deterministic attitude towards their fields. They claim that the march of progress cannot be stopped, or at least should not be interfered with. Genetic engineering, nanotechnologies, globalization "are here to stay" and we better resign ourselves to the inevitable. Thus choice and freedom become subordinated to the memes—the artifacts and institutions—that we have created. Unless we regain control, we are destined to be enslaved by the stuff of our dreams.

The alternative is to dedicate ourselves consciously to the pursuit of a good life. A good life that develops individuality to its fullest, while encouraging the integration of the person with increasingly wider communities, including that of the planet, and beyond that, with the overarching cosmos. We have to realize what social scientists are finally pointing out, echoing what stoics and epicureans, Christians and Buddhists have pointed out long ago: that material goods do not make us happy; that the most meaningful life is one where we develop our potentialities at the service of a goal that is greater than our own self-interest.[14]

We will have to learn to distinguish between two kinds of experiences that nowadays we often confuse: pleasure and enjoyment. Pleasure is what we feel when innate needs are satisfied: sex, food, rest, and the titillation of bored senses produce it. Pleasure is an important component of life, but it does not result in complexity—it simply returns the organism to a balanced, homeostatic state. Enjoyment, on the other hand, is the experience that leads to growth. It is what we feel after physical exercise, when we master a skill, when playing music or an interesting game. It is what keeps creative persons struggling against heavy odds, and what leads children to learning. Enjoyment occurs when a person's skills are engaged in confronting challenges that are not easy to meet, thus stretching one's capacities to new levels.[15]

In general, when a society achieves a certain level of comfort and affluence, the tendency is to devote most of one's energies to the pursuit of pleasure. This is understandable, since pleasure is easier to achieve and easier to experience. It is certainly happening now in the so-called first world, where people spend most of their free time numbing their minds with drink, drugs, and primitive forms of entertainment disguised in fancy production values. While the market keeps offering ever-more opportunities for pleasure, the chances of experiencing enjoyment—especially for young people—become more scarce. A society dedicated to pleasure may survive if it is lucky, but it will not contribute much to further evolution.

Fortunately, not all the signs pointing to the future are dire. Many organizations are striving to realize some or all the precepts that lead to greater complexity. From volunteers who help the ill and destitute to environmental organizations concerned with saving plant and animal species, from churches to groups working with inner city youth, millions of men and women are taking on the responsibility to keep complexity from disintegrating, and to advance it. What they lack is a single vision, a compelling reason that does not depend on religious tradition that while native to some, must be alien to others. The dream of early Christianity was to build a catholic, that is universal, ecumenical church. Will the third millennium realize this dream in a new guise, basing it on what we know now of the past, and what we wish for the future? One thing seems certain: If we do not start along this path, either we destroy the world on which we depend, or the robots we are inventing and endowing with intelligence at the exponential rate specified by Moore's law, will push us aside as too dangerous for our own good, and take over.

Where to begin? One obvious move would be to bring together the various groups that are already tackling separate parts of the problem, and begin to see if a common vision can be attained. Currently we do not lack separate interest groups, NGOs, grass-root movements dedicated to important and good causes. Thus differentiation is not lacking. But it is often frustrating to see the lack of integration among these often parallel, overlapping attempts to solve our problems. A global understanding of evolution may provide a unifying agenda that would lift the level of complexity of our response to a new level. It would be an enormously powerful force on behalf of a better future.

Another direction is through education. Again, our ways to educate children are overly differentiated without being meaningfully integrated. The result is tunnel-vision specialization at best, and at worst frustrating confusion. From the earliest time, children should be exposed to a knowledge of their own nature. The basic injunction of the Delphic oracle, "know thyself," should apply to every child, not just to graybeard philosophers. Next, before tackling separate scholastic subjects, it would help for children to be exposed to an understanding of how their actions impact other people and the environment. Before being given the tools of technological power, young men and women need to learn the responsibility that such power requires. Instead of a value-free presentation of disjointed facts, young people should then learn what makes life beautiful and meaningful. And before being given the task of changing the world, they should be expected to demonstrate that they can lead enjoyable, meaningful, and useful lives themselves.

Rapid change is also going to make heavy demands on our political ingenuity. Public policies will have to be implemented soon to cope with the possibilities opened up by genetic engineering. In many ways, this is the technology most emblematic of our predicament. If it is true that we now have the means to change our bodies and our brains, what choices shall we make? Will our species have the maturity to use this knowledge to eliminate diseases and handicaps, or will we use it to increase differentiation by making those who can afford it more healthy, handsome, and smart? On the threshold of interfering massively with natural selection, it is especially vital that we dedicate ourselves to supporting the central feature of the evolutionary process—the increase of complexity.

Whether we like it or not, the globalization made possible by advances in communication and transportation will force us to confront public policy issues on a global scale. The gap between nations in the quality of material life and resource consumption cannot be sustained indefinitely. It could be argued that Karl Marx's prediction about the inevitability of class conflict was proven wrong because he assumed that nations would continue to operate as closed economic systems. What multinationals have done is to export the proletariat to the Third World; but Marx may still have the last laugh unless we find ways to integrate their well-being with ours.

In the long run perhaps the most important task is to provide institutional support for alternatives to material consumption. It has been said that if the rest of the world were to use energy and resources at the rate the United States and Europe are doing, we would need four additional planets—which we obviously don't have access to at present.[16] The future of our world depends on the decisions that billions of Chinese and Indians will be making in the next decades. Clearly, if they have the option, they will all opt for cars and refrigerators. At what point are we going to take responsibility for this clear and present danger? When will we find the political nerve to make the massive investments in renewable energy and alternative transportation that are needed if we are to survive?

But true alternatives to consumption also include a revival of interest and support for non-material goods—for the social, aesthetic, spiritual aspects of life. There is compelling evidence that beyond a rather low threshold of material well-being, the quality of life is improved more by political freedom, the number of friends, a stable marriage, a set of transcendent beliefs, than it is by additional affluence. The United States has contributed much to spreading technology and a material lifestyle to the rest of the world, but beyond jazz, blue jeans, movies and rather compromised messages about democracy, it has done little to strengthen memes that contribute more to the quality of life than increased consumption of detergents and bubble gum does.

Public policy in European countries at least supports the arts and culture more than the United States does—admittedly such support is often more a pork barrel for unemployed artists and intellectuals than the reflection of a genuine, principled attempt to provide alternatives to an excessive reliance on material consumption. But much more is needed. In the Renaissance, the bankers of Florence understood that they needed to invest their money in the arts and humanities if they wanted to develop an alternative symbolic system to the one the Church owned a monopoly on. So they supported artists and architects that expressed the joyful freedom of the human spirit—even when their works were destined for churches and monasteries. It could be argued that they succeeded only too well, substituting *carpe diem* for a concern with eternity. But the point is that without support for a symbolic expression of the evolutionary path towards complexity, an expression that appeals to the spirit and the sense of beauty, we are left with no alternatives to the lifestyle extolled by soft drink commercials on television.

It would be sensible if all of this could be done gradually and spontaneously. If we are to use past history as a guide, however, it is more likely that those who could implement change are already too comfortable and complacent with their lifestyle, while those who suffer are impotent to bring change about. In the past, great revolutions of the human spirit usually came from the periphery of power, from marginal individuals and groups. Jesus and the Buddha, Luther and Lenin developed their universal visions from the provinces, or from exile. So it is possible that the revolution that will shape our future is not going to be created by the kind of people who read these pages, but by some third world or inner city person, probably well-versed in science—perhaps a woman—whose need for personal meaning is so strong and the ability to express a viable alternative so compelling as to convince us of its rightness.

Whether the new vision will appear gradually or in a flash, and whether it will be shaped by traditional leaders or revolutionaries, it seems clear that without a new definition of progress our species risks forfeiting its chances for further evolution. To summarize, the goal that should sustain us in the future is likely to include, first, a recognition and acknowledgement of our nature and its limitations. Second, an acceptance of the responsibilities brought about by self-reflective consciousness and the command over technology it provided—including responsibility for the planet, and for its future. Third, a recognition of complexity as the leading edge of evolution. Fourth, the goal would include a commitment to implementing complexity in our personal lives as well as institutions. Policies that support the evolutionary trend in families, education, access to resources, and responsibility for the environment will have to be implemented on a global scale. The balance between striving for pleasure and enjoyment would have to be restored. And finally, a new covenant that enriches the spirit and fulfills our need for beauty needs to be forged, a covenant that reaffirms our place in the unfolding of creation. Of course none of this is going to be easy. Progress may not be pleasant, but knowing that it leads towards a meaningful goal will make it enjoyable.

Notes

1. R. Dawkins, *The Selfish Gene* (Oxford: Oxford University, 1976); S. Blackmore, *The Meme Machine* (Oxford, U.K.: Oxford University, 1999).

2. M. Sahlins, *Stone-Age Economics* (Chicago: Aldine, 1972).

3. K. Wittfogel, *Oriental Despotism* (New Haven, Conn.: Yale University Press, 1957).

4. F. Massimini and A. Delle Fave, "Religion and Cultural Evolution," *Zygon: Journal of Science and Religion* 16, no. 1 (1991): 27-48.

5. H. Arendt, *The Human Condition* (Chicago: The University of Chicago Press, 1958).

6. R. Wright, *NonZero: The Logic of Human Destiny* (New York: Pantheon Books, 2000).

7. P. Singer, *The Expanding Circle: Ethics and Sociobiology* (New York: Farrar, Straus and Giroux, 1981).

8. S. Pinker, *How the Mind Works* (New York: W.W. Norton, 1997).

9. M. Csikszentmihalyi, *The Evolving Self* (New York: Harper Collins, 1993).

10. S. A. Kaufman, *The Origins of Order: Self-organization and Selection in Evolution* (New York: Oxford University Press, 1993).

11. M. Csikszentmihalyi and K. Rathunde, "The Development of the Person: An experiential Perspective on the Ontogenesis of Psychological Complexity," in *Handbook of Child Psychology*, vol. 1, ed. W. Damon and R. Lerner (New York: Wiley, 1987), 635-685.

12. E. Durkheim, *The Division of Labor in Society* (New York: The Free Press, 1893/1947).

13. K. Rathunde, "The context of optimal experience: An exploratory model of the Family," *New Ideas in Psychology* 7 (1989): 91-97.

14. M. Csikszentmihalyi, "If We Are So Rich, Why Aren't We Happy," *American Psychologist* 54, no. 3 (1999): 10, 821-27; D. Myers, *The American Paradox: Spiritual Hunger in an Age of Plenty* (New Haven, Conn.: Yale University Press, 2000).

Chapter 6

Faith and the Future: Religion and the Problem of Progress in the New Millennium

Hubert Locke

In the summer of 1893, the city of Chicago played host to the World's Columbian Exposition, celebrating (a year late) the four hundredth anniversary of Columbus' voyage to America. Some two years in planning, the Chicago World's Fair—as it was popularly known—followed on the heels of the Paris Exhibition of 1889, at which the Eiffel Tower had been the principal attraction. The Chicago Fair was the fifteenth international extravaganza of its kind and the second to be held in the United States. There had been some dispute as to whether Chicago was an appropriate site for a world fair—several other cities, including New York, St. Louis, and the nation's capital, vied for the honor but a three-year lobbying effort paid off when the U.S. Congress decided Chicago should be the site and authorized the Treasury to mint $2.5 million Columbian half-dollars to aid in the financing of the enterprise.[1]

On the eve of the twentieth century, Chicago was rapidly becoming a veritable symbol of American progress, having leaped ahead of other midwestern cities as the agricultural and railroad center of the country, "supplying the nation with its meat and telling it what to pay for wheat and corn."[2] The Fair took for its theme "A Century of Progress" and celebrated the triumphs of the new technologies of the era—Westinghouse electric lighting, Krupp armaments, the gigantic

Yerkes telescope, and other marvels in mining, transportation, construction, and communications. Never before, exulted the popular historian Hubert Howe Bancroft, had "such an opportunity been presented of comparing the relative progress of manufacturing industries among European, American, and Asiatic nations, together with their inventive genius, whether in the direction of labor-saving devices or of improvements in quality and design."[3] In the eyes of many, the World's Columbian Exposition came to be seen as "the consummate symbol of America's pride in its brief past and confidence in its limitless future."[4]

The note of progress was sounded throughout the Fair's proceedings. At its formal dedication, the Fair's director-general proclaimed, "In a presence so vast on an occasion so pre-eminent in the progress of universal affairs, I am moved by emotions that can sweep a human heart but once in a life." Seven months later, at the Fair's opening, its director-general announced, "It is our hope that this great exposition may inaugurate a new era of moral and material progress, and our fervent aspiration that the association of the nations here may secure not only warmer and stronger friendships, but lasting peace throughout the world."[5] In his welcome address to the opening session of the Parliament on World Religions its chair, Chicago judge Charles C. Bonney, stated, "This day the sun of a new era of religious peace and progress rises over the world, dispelling the dark clouds of sectarian strife."[6]

The Parliament on World's Religions was one of the several intellectual attractions at the Fair and, in one observer's estimate, "the most phenomenal fact of the Columbian Exposition."[7] It met for seventeen days and its participants heard 216 papers delivered by religious scholars from around the world. Throngs of several thousand people listened to internationally prominent religious speakers in evening sessions that were so popular they had to be repeated twice to accommodate the crowds. With Buddhist, Hindu, Taoist, Shintoist, Jain, Muslim, and Zoroastrian delegates joining American Protestant, Catholic, and Jewish participants, the Parliament was a spiritual reflection of the demographic realities of the Fair's host city and, as America approached the zenith of its immigrant era, those of the nation itself. But many of its American attendees hoped that the Parliament also might be a harbinger of the religious unity that could come to characterize the world community.

In spite of the American enthusiasm for its promise and possibilities, the Parliament did not result in any major breakthroughs in rapprochement between the world's major religious faiths. In retrospect, it can be seen as reflecting the tension that presents itself whenever the twin themes of religion and progress are under scrutiny. On one hand, there is the issue of progress *in* religion: to utilize Arthur Lovejoy's definition of progress it can be asked whether there has been any sequence of stages of development in (religion's) past and present in which the latter stages—with perhaps occasional retardations and regressions—are superior to the earlier.[8] The opposing question—that of progress *and* religion—is of equal and, for many, perhaps greater importance. If, as Robert Nisbet suggests, the idea of progress holds that humankind "has advanced in the past—from some aboriginal condition of primitiveness, barbarism, or even nullity—is now advancing, and will continue to advance through the foreseeable future," it can be asked whether religion has contributed to or thwarted that advancement. [9]

A. Progress in Religion

In considering the question of progress in religion, it is useful to keep in mind a distinction between progress as a fact and progress as an idea.

When men [sic] examine the fact of progress, they look to the past and find there evidence for or against the assertion that a change for the better has taken place in this or that respect. Two things are involved: a study of the changes which have occurred and the judgment—based on some standard of appraisal—that the changes have been for the better. But when men [sic] entertain the idea of progress, they turn from the past and present and look to the future. They regard the past merely as a basis for prophecy, and the present as an occasion for making plans to fulfill their prophecies or hopes. The fact of progress belongs to the record of achievement; the idea of progress sets a goal to be achieved.[10]

The Parliament on World Religions was enamored with progress as an idea. Its participants imagined that "a new era of human unity was dawning"[11] and they fervently wished that new dawn not only to be informed by and infused with a spirit of religious pluralism and toleration but also a renewed commitment to working for social change. With the oratorical flourish that was typical of the era, its chair, the minister of Chicago's prestigious First Presbyterian Church, asserted:

> We are met as religious men [sic], believing even in this capital of material wonders, in the presence of an Exposition which displays the unparalleled marvels of steam and electricity, that there is a spiritual root to all progress.... [But] since this is a world of sin and sorrow, as well as speculation, our attention is ... to be given to those greatest practical themes which press upon good men everywhere. How can we make this suffering and needy world less a home of grief and strife and far more a commonwealth of love, a kingdom of heaven?[12]

For its organizers, the Parliament itself was a sign—perhaps the principal signal—of progress in religion. The very fact that sixty religious leaders representing what, at the time, were considered the world's ten major religions would meet in solemn assembly to "present to the world ... the substantial unity of many religions in the good deeds of the religious life" was, in itself, a remarkably progressive feat.[13] For those who attended, however, the agreement to avoid proselytizing, discrimination, and controversy and, instead, to celebrate the "brotherhood of religions" represented a significant advance on the front of religious harmony and progress.

Not content to merely celebrate religious unity, American speakers at the

Parliament waded into the principal social issues of the era. Following a paper by Richard T. Ely, professor at the University of Wisconsin and one of the forerunners in the field of sociology, on "Christianity as a Social Force" Julia Ward Howe, the redoubtable suffragette and author of "The Battle Hymn of the Republic" spoke passionately on women's rights—"surely nothing is religion," she declared, "which puts one sex above another."[14] And a Black Unitarian laywoman, Fannie Barrier Williams spoke eloquently to the "Condition of the American Negro." "In nothing," she stated, "do the American people so contradict the spirit of their institutions, the high sentiments of their civilization, and the maxims of their religion as they do in denying to our men and women the full rights to life, liberty, and the pursuit of happiness."[15]

While it is tempting to dismiss seventeen days of speech-making as extended rhetorical exercises, it is important to observe that, on the eve of the twentieth century, there was a widespread conviction among the three major faiths in America that conditions in this country could be materially improved for those people who existed at the margins of the nation's social and economic growth and development. The conscience of many American Protestants, sharpened by the battles over slavery, blossomed in the post Civil-War period into the Social Gospel Movement, an endeavor infused with the notion that the Kingdom of God—as a vision of the ideal society—could and should be realized in America. This movement had its fainter but no less fervent counterpart in Roman Catholic circles, marked by the efforts of Cardinals Gibbons of Baltimore and Ireland, of St. Paul, Bishop John Spaulding of Peoria, and later by the creation of the National Catholic Welfare Conference. Joining with their counterparts in the American Jewish community, Christian clergy addressed issues of child labor, a minimum wage, health and safety standards in industry, the right of workers to organize and bargain with their employees on a wide range of labor issues, and an array of other social and economic matters that became part of the religious agenda for social justice.

As a sign of progress in religion, the Parliament can be assessed, a century later, in the light of the numerous events of the past one hundred years that represent substantial advances in ecumenical and interfaith relations which the Parliament can be said either to have helped inaugurate or to which it lent symbolic support. With the Christian world, ecumenism has become the order of the day; mergers and consolidation of denominational groups and, in a larger context, the amalgamation of their relief and development programs have become normative in religious circles, and long before mergers became the rage in the world of business and industry. Interfaith efforts, reaching across the boundaries of the major world faiths have also given rise to significant international efforts—the International Association for Religious Freedom, the World Congress of Faiths, the World Conference on Religion and Peace, the Global Forum. If the question is progress in religion and that progress is measured against past history, only the most unregenerate sectarians and those who are skeptical of the religious enterprise under any and all circumstances will fail to be impressed by these developments.

Skeptics will insist, whenever the matter of progress in religion is under discussion, that some explanation be given for such contemporary phenomena as the conflict in Northern Ireland, the religious intolerance of various fundamentalist movements which appear in all the world's major religions, and other episodic excesses committed in the name of religion. It does not ease the burden of the question to point out that ideological excess and right-wing sentiments are not unique to religion and that far more conflicts occur in the modern world for ethnic and economic reasons than for religious ones. Religion should no more be judged by its aberrations than the ideals of democracy assessed by a tally of the actions of petty tyrants who steal elections.

Discussions of religion are usually enhanced, in fact, by adhering to the distinction made by Gordon Allport in the introduction to his classic little study, *The Individual and His Religion*. "My reason," Allport writes, "for not dwelling more fully than I do upon the function religion plays in infantile and neurotic personalities is that I am seeking to trace the full course of religious development in the normally mature and productive personality. I am dealing with the psychology, not with the psychopathology, of religion."[16] There are, regrettably, more than enough examples of the pathological in the record of the world's religions; progress in religion requires that we examine its best moments, not its worst experiences.

B. Progress and Religion

While the question of progress in religion encourages an examination of the ideas of compassion, justice, and equality as religious goals and the extent to which religion in its various forms has moved toward the attainment of those virtues, the issue of progress and religion obliges us to look at the latter as a fact of history and to ask whether and to what extent religion has contributed to or thwarted human progress. Perhaps no issue has been the subject of greater scrutiny than this.

It is useful to begin with a reminder that the idea of progress is, in large measure, an idea of the Enlightenment, that period in Western history which saw the humanistic spirit of the Renaissance combine with the scientific revolution of the seventeenth and eighteenth centuries to mark the beginning of the modern era. The Enlightenment ushered in an era of immense optimism in the West; it was a period in which "the dependence upon supernatural powers, the submission to authority...were widely overcome and men [sic] faced life with a new confidence in themselves, with a new recognition of human power and achievement, with a new appreciation of present values." The Marquis de Condorcet, one of the supreme optimists of the era, reflected the "new age" thinking of the times; in his *The Progress of the Human Mind*, the Marquis proclaimed that the period was ripe for the inauguration of the "tenth epoque":

> How consoling for the philosopher ... is this view of the human race, emanci-

pated from its shackles, released from the empire of fate and from that of the enemies of its progress, advancing with a firm and sure step along the path of truth, virtue, and happiness! It is the contemplation of this prospect that rewards him for all his efforts.

The Enlightenment also ushered in a period of intense debate—one that has continued into the present—as to whether, in the grand march of progress, religion has been an aid or a hindrance. Most Enlightenment thinkers, especially in the eighteenth century, saw their age as having been freed from the dominance of religious ideas and doctrines; they deemed the advances in science to be positive proof that the repressive influences of religion had been curbed, if not subdued.

In the nineteenth century, Karl Marx joined with those who saw religion as standing in the way of every stride toward genuine human progress. "Religion," Marx argued, "is only the illusory sun which revolves round man as long as he does not revolve round himself.... The abolition of religion as the illusory happiness of the people is required for their real happiness." Consequently, the proletarian revolution which he envisioned would see not only the abolition of private property but the transcending of religion as one of the attendant evils of a capitalistic system.[17]

The twentieth century, however, saw a different answer emerge in the debate. A decade after the Chicago Fair and its Parliament, Max Weber published *The Protestant Ethic and the Spirit of Capitalism*, a work which argued—as its title implies—that while the "material conditions for capitalism were present at many times and in many places ... it only came into existence in the West" and because of ideas advanced by Martin Luther during the Protestant Reformation. Weber's argument was expanded and modified by the British social historian, R. H. Tawney[18] who found the teachings of John Calvin rather than Luther to be determinative. Curiously, Marx and Weber shared the conviction that Christianity, in general, and Protestantism, in particular, were particularly well-suited to a society "based upon the production of commodities" although, unlike Weber, Marx did not consider this to be a positive contribution.

The Weber-Tawney thesis, as it is known, has its fair share of critics but, to the extent that one considers capitalist societies to be centers and sources of scientific and technological advancement, it remains one of the seminal arguments that link religious ideas with human progress in the modern world. The argument has been applied, in fact, to the rise of tolerance in matters of belief; increasingly, in the seventeenth century, it became "obvious that persecution was incompatible with prosperity, since it was the non-conformists who were in the forefront of economic progress."[19]

For Marx and, to a lesser degree for Weber, the question of religion and progress was a metaphysical, rather than an empirical, question. In spite of his attempts to link his analysis of religion with social conditions "in the real world," Marx could barely conceal his contempt for what he terms "the Furies of private interest" of which he considers "the English Established Church [which] will more readily pardon an attack on thirty-eight of its thirty-nine Articles than on one thirty-ninth of its income" to be a principal example.[20] From an empirical perspective, this essential weakness in the conventional arguments about religion and progress continues to mark most current discussions. For better or worse, the issue—when it is addressed by observers of the religious enterprise—continues to be examined and discussed as an abstract and speculative consideration, rather than as a documentable proposition.

Among religionists in the Western world, a different problem maintains. In religious circles, there has always been a deep-seated unease about the very idea of change and improvement in human societies. There is, in the sacred texts of the Judeo-Christian faiths, a long-standing ambivalence about the possibility of improvement in the human condition. At one level, adherents are admonished to do works of compassion and justice that will ameliorate the circumstances of those who are less fortunate, with specific references to the poor, orphans, prisoners, and the disabled. Examples abound of religious figures whose spiritual stature derives from their denunciations of the structures and processes of privilege and power. But at another level, there is cynicism—and in several instances, Divine cautions—about thinking that mortals have the capacity to bring about improvement in the world. From the fabled story of the Tower of Babel to the pessimism of the writer of the Book of Ecclesiastes for whom everything that happens on the earth is aimless, fruitless, and transitory, there is a thread of uncertainty about the prospect for change and advancement, especially in the human condition.

Beneath this ambivalence and uncertainty lies a conviction that was blasphemous to the optimists of the Enlightenment era and one that continues to be troublesome for those who see progress as either a law or the hope of human history. Optimism about the possibilities of human progress requires optimism about humans and their possibilities—a belief that humankind is "slowly advancing ... in a definite and desirable direction"[21] and it is this proposition that a significant body of religious thought has found questionable.

Religious pessimism about progress is by no means a universal sentiment in the Judeo-Christian tradition. The Parliament on World Religions, to make a final reference to that signal event, was an exuberant expression of religious optimism on the eve of the twentieth century. But the twentieth century itself proved to be an era in which assertions about human betterment were strained to the maximum in credibility.

The First World War, fought ostensibly to "end all wars," turned out to be more massive in its human destructiveness than anyone could possibly imagine. A decade later, the collapse of the economies of the West and the resultant hardships endured by countless millions gave further pause to those for whom progress meant an inexorable change for the better.

The historian of religion, Martin Marty, provides a crisp summary of the idea of progress in twentieth century theology in an essay which notes that "[b]elief in progress and, better, theological interpretations of progress turn out to be episodic. They go into eclipse or fall out of fashion but then remain in the stream as a latent virus, ready to reactivate themselves."[22] Of the theologians whose work he sketches, no one, perhaps, has had more to say about progress and its limits than Reinhold Niebuhr, named by *Life* magazine in 1990 as one of the one hundred most important Americans of the twentieth century.

Throughout his career, Niebuhr found himself continually amazed by the seeming unlimited reaches of human pride and its capacity for self-deception. In one brief, sardonic commentary on the nineteenth and twentieth centuries, Niebuhr states:

> Contemporary experience represents a *Nemesis* which is justly proportioned in its swiftness and enormity to the degree of *Hybris* which has expressed itself in modern life. In one century modern man had claimed to have achieved the dizzying heights of the mastery both of the natural process and historical destiny. In the following century he is hopelessly enmeshed in an historical fate, threatening mutual destruction, from which he seems incapable of extricating himself. A word of Scripture fits the situation perfectly: 'He that sitteth in the heavens shall laugh: the Lord shall have them in derision.'[23]

The continuing debate within the world's one remaining "superpower" regarding nuclear treaties and missile defense only serves to heighten the acuity of Niebuhr's observation.

While his was not an absolute denial of human progress, Niebuhr's view was that of a chastened cynic. "On the one hand," he wrote in his famed Gifford lectures,

> the extension of all forms of knowledge, the elaboration of mechanical and social techniques, the corresponding development of human powers and historical potencies and the consequent increase of the extent and complexity of the human community have indubitably proved that life is subject to growth in its collective and total, as well as in its individual, forms. On the other hand the course of history, particularly in the past two centuries, has proven the earlier identification of growth and progress to be false. We have, or ought to have, learned, particularly from the tragedies of contemporary history, that each new development of life, whether in individual or social terms, presents us with new possibilities of realizing the good in history; that we have obligations corresponding to these new possibilities; but that we also face new hazards on each new level and that that the new level of historic achievement offers us no emancipation from contradictions and ambiguities to which all life in history is subject. We have learned, in other words, that history is not its own redeemer.[24]

Such a sharply critical view of human progress rooted in a fundamentally critical view of human nature has made Niebuhr, in Marty's view, "especially nettling to those secular thinkers who wanted to revive faith in progress."[25] Niebuhr begins with a "doctrine," in religious terms, that sees human beings as creating for themselves their own greatest difficulty: "man," he writes in the opening of his Gifford Lectures, "has always been his own most vexing problem." And it is humankind's unbridled belief in itself—the unrestrained optimism that marks the human character—which also mars it. Niebuhr quotes the Victorian poet Swinburne as a supreme example of this self-adulation: "The seal of his knowledge is sure, the truth and his spirit are wed;... Glory to Man in the highest! for man is the master of things." It is precisely this—in Niebuhr's view—unseemly arrogance, especially when placed against the realities of history (Niebuhr delivered the second series of his Gifford Lectures a month after the Nazis invaded Poland) that, from a religious perspective, makes it impossible for Niebuhr to take the idea of human progress seriously.

What many regard as a more temperate perspective is found in the views of Paul Tillich. Possibly the most widely read and revered theologian of the twentieth century whose writings attracted avid interest from scholars and intellectuals who otherwise showed scant interest in religious thought, Tillich was especially appreciated for his capacity to translate theology into language that spoke to the human condition—that addressed the concerns and anxieties of a modern age. Nowhere was he more skilled in this endeavor than in his acute observations and insights on the problem of progress.

In a lecture on "The Decline and Validity of the Idea of Progress" delivered at Ohio University shortly before his death in 1965, Tillich described the distinction between progress as a concept and an idea. The former, he suggested, is an abstraction "based on the description of a group of facts, of objects of observation which may well be verified or falsified." The latter—progress as an idea—"is an interpretation of existence as a whole.... Progress as an idea is a symbol for an attitude toward our existence....What is extracted from a special realm of facts has become an expression of a general attitude toward life."

Tillich then notes the religious background of the idea of progress. In echoes of Max Weber, Tillich finds the Judeo-Christian belief in a God who "will establish his heavenly rule over all the world" and that of a progressive realization of the kingdom of God on earth to be formative for the idea of progress and unique to the religious traditions of the West, including Islam. He then turns to the "secular elaboration of the idea of progress" among whose achievements is the freeing of humans from the dependence on fate that characterized the ancient and medieval world. It was this sentiment that produced the Renaissance utopian writings and the social reality that was seen in the great extensions of the time—"the colonial extension of Europe in all directions; space extension, which has remained an element in the idea of progress up to the space exploration [of] today; and technical extension—continuous progress in controlling nature and putting it into the service of man." But there was another element of great importance in the idea of progress, namely the vision of nature as a progressive process from the atom to the molecule to the cell, to the developed organism, and finally to man. This is evolution, progress in largeness of elements united in one being, with centeredness and, therefore, power being in the individual. And this line, then, was drawn beyond nature through humanity, from primitive to civilized man, to us as representatives of the age of reason in which the potentialities of creation have come to their fulfillment.

By the nineteenth century, then, progress had become not only "a conscious doctrine but an unconscious dogma" which Tillich—with Niebuhr—sees as fatally undercut by the events of the twentieth century. "Today," he concludes, "we need a new inquiry into the validity and the limits of the idea of progress"—an understanding of history in which the idea of progress is replaced by two other concepts. First, rather than the idea of a single, continuous line of progress, Tillich suggests that progress in the ethical realm be seen as a process of maturation or "of coming to maturity"—what he calls in another context "deeper understanding of man's essential nature in individual and social relations." The second replacement concept he terms the concept of *kairos* or the "decisive moment." In ethics and education we can speak of maturation rather than progress as a more accurate and meaningful description of the growth that takes, or ought to take, place. In the arts, we can learn to appreciate "great moments, decisive times, turning points" without venturing the indefensible notion that there can be something called progress in this realm of human creativity.

Conclusion

When the idea of progress is viewed from a religious perspective, at least two matters are clear. The first—and most obvious—is that a distinction is maintained between assessments of advancement, growth, and development in the scientific and technological realms in contrast with the realm of human behavior. It is equally clear that this distinction has to do with more than differences in the modes of mastery or the records of achievement and failure in the two areas. It is a distinction not merely of actuality (i.e., scientific and technological triumphs in contrast with social and political calamities) but of possibility—the latter is incapable of attaining the former. Fundamentally, in the religious worldview, progress is seen as a matter of capacity or potentiality; however reluctantly religion has had to concede the point, it acknowledges that the possibilities of mastery of the natural universe are likely limitless. But religion views the mastery of ourselves as far more problematic. Especially suspect are the optimistic assumptions of the nineteenth century that advancements in human knowledge would produce improvements in human conducts. These have proven to be ephemeral and, in the view of Niebuhr and others, deceptive.

At the same time, religion maintains its own inclination toward ideas of change and improvement in human conduct and behavior. There is a continual challenge or demand that individuals live lives of higher and nobler purpose, accompanied by a set of moral norms that indicate what "higher" and "nobler" mean. It is this predisposition toward change and its desirability in the face of doubt and despair about its possibilities that produces religion's ambivalence regarding the idea of progress.

The primary, if not the sole, question that many wish to ask whenever the theme of religion and progress is posed is whether religion has been a help or a hindrance to the manifold efforts to improve the human condition. Those who view religion with a priori disdain consider the answer to this question as self-evident and rush to recite every horror of the past in which religion has had a role as evidence. It is quite easy to become fixated on the catastrophes of history, past and present—the Crusades, the Holocaust, the religious battles of India, Nigeria and Northern Ireland—and find that the blame for such inhuman episodes lies squarely with religion and the religious impulse.

A more charitable and, for most minds, accurate reading of the record however would suggest that throughout history religion has served as an indispensable measuring rod, wherever the idea of progress is taken seriously. The idea of progress implies movement and change; it necessitates some vision or desired objective toward which individuals and human society are thought to be advancing or toward which human advancement is deemed worthwhile, if the idea is to have any value.

Religion has provided, down through the ages, a vision of that toward which individuals and societies ought to move. In the sacred writings of every religion there is a set of ideals regarding the relationship of human creatures to nature, to one another, and to a Higher Realm that serves, in religion's better moments, to inspire women and men toward acts of justice and compassion in the world. It is this goals-setting function of religion that gives it an essential place at the table, whenever concerns about human progress are under consideration.

Notes

1. David F. Burg, *Chicago's White City of 1893* (Lexington: The University Press of Kentucky, 1976), xii, 42, 86.

2. J.C. Furnas, *The Americans, A Social History of the United States, 1587-1914* (New York, G.P. Putnam's Sons, 1969), 762.

3. Burg, *Chicago's White City*, 202.

4. Harvey Cox, *Fire from Heaven, The Rise of Pentecostal Spirituality and the Reshaping of Religion in the Twenty-First Century* (Reading, Mass.: Addison Wesley Publishing Company, 1995), 22.

5. Burg, *Chicago's White City*, 102, 110.

6. Richard H. Seager, *The Dawn of Religious Pluralism* (LaSallee, Ill.: Open Court Publishing Company, 1993) 21.

7. Seager, *The Dawn*, 5.

8. Arthur Lovejoy, *The Great Chain of Being: A Study of the History of an Idea* (New York: Harper, 1960), 1.

9. Robert Nisbet, *History of the Idea of Progress* (New York: Basic Books, 1980), 4.

10. Robert Maynard Hutchins, ed., *Great Books of the Western World*, vol. 3 (Chicago: Encyclopaedia Britannica, 1952), 438.

11. Seager, *The Dawn,* xvii.

12. Seager, *The Dawn*, 26, 28.

13. The Archbishop of Canterbury declined an invitation to participate, noting that to accept would constitute tacit admission of the equality of all religions whereas Christianity was the only one true faith—and by implication Anglicanism its one true expression, see Burg, *Chicago's White City*, 264-65.

14. Seager, *The Dawn*, 77.

15. Seager, *The Dawn*, 149.

16. Gordon W. Allport, *The Individual and His Religion* (New York: The Macmillan Company, 1950), viii.

17. James C. Livingston, *Modern Christian Thought: From the Enlightenment to Vatican II* (New York: The Macmillan Company, 1971), 189-92.

18. R. H. Tawney, *Religion and the Rise of Capitalism, a Historical Study [1926]* (Glouchester, Mass.: P. Smith, 1962).

19. J. Bronowski and Bruce Mazlish, *The Western Intellectual Tradition, From Leonardo to Hegel* (New York: Harper and Brothers, 1960), 96.

20. Robert Maynard Hutchins, ed., *Great Books of the Western World*, vol. 50 (Chicago: Encyclopaedia Britannica, 1952), 7.

21. J.B. Bury, *The Idea of Progress: An Inquiry into Its Origin and Growth [1932]* (New York: Dover, 1955).

22. Martin Marty, "The Idea of Progress in Twentieth-Century Theology," in *Progress and Its Discontents*, ed. Almond, Chodorow, and Pearce (Berkeley: University of California Press, 1979), 485.

23. Psalm 2:4; Reinhold Niebuhr, *Faith and History* (New York: Scribner's, 1949), 8.

24. Reinhold Niebuhr, *The Nature and Destiny of Man* (New York: Scribner's, 1941), 205-6.

25. Marty, "The Idea of Progress," 488.

Chapter 7

Progress in Literature

Charles Johnson

What a writer in our time has to do is write what hasn't been written before or beat dead men at what they have done.

—Ernest Hemingway

At the dawn of the twenty-first century we are now so accustomed to reading every week about astonishing advances in such fields as medicine and technology that evidence for "progress" in the sciences, theoretical and applied, is inescapable. Consider for a moment just a few of the scientific endeavors of the last twelve months: two independent teams of astronomers at four institutions announced the discovery of the first multi-planet system around a normal star (Upsilon Andromedae) other than our own; in August, November, and January, NASA's spacecraft Galileo, launched in 1989, made its closest-ever flybys of Jupiter's moons—Thebe, Almalthea, and Metis—transmitting back images and information from 386 million miles away; research teams in Europe and the United States reported the successful decoding of DNA for a complete plant chromosome, while scientists at the University of Washington's Department of Molecular Biotechnology announced they had mapped roughly 85 percent of the genetic code for rice; in Tokyo, scientist Makoto Asashima and his research team grew frog ears and eyes in a laboratory, using the animal's embryo cells; New York's Dobelle Institute, a medical device company, premiered in January, 2000 a device that enabled a sixty-two year old blind man to read large letters and move around objects courtesy of a tiny camera—an artificial eye—wired directly to his brain; PPL Therapeutics in Edinburgh, Scotland, the company that cloned Dolly the sheep, followed that groundbreaking event by cloning five piglets.

Few would doubt that one essential feature of life in the twenty-first century—perhaps *the* dominant, dizzying and often Faustian characteristic—is exponential growth and inexorable change in man's ability to quantify, manipulate, and diagram life's material dimensions—from measuring the climate on Mars to charting human DNA in the Genome Project. Science triumphs by painstaking methods developed over two millennia: the apodictic rigor of mathematics, a correspondence theory of truth, predictability, precise measurements calculated in nanoseconds (the oscillations of the cesium atom), intersubjective observations capable of being confirmed by researchers all over the globe, regardless of their cultural backgrounds, and a demand for (ever-increasing) empirical evidence that renders the conclusions and products of but a few months ago obsolete and current knowledge provisional.

But what of literature? Can the term *progress* be applied to a field which, traditionally in the West since the time of Plato, falls into the category of the subjective, the culturally (and racially) relative, the unquantifiable, and is everywhere dominated by unpredictable emotional responses, shifting opinions, the vagaries of "taste" and personal preference? The apparent absurdity (and I will argue it is *only* apparent) of speaking about "progress" in the arts can be best illustrated by asking, hypothetically, if one artistic work ever disproves, replaces, refutes, or refines another as, say, Copernicus's heliocentric science proved to be less cumbersome and complicated than Ptolemy's geocentrism and Kant's analysis of consciousness proved to be a more convincing account than the earlier one presented by David Hume? If, for example, Richard Wright's *Native Son* was rendered obsolete twelve years later by Ralph Ellison's *Invisible Man,* or if a canvass by Jackson Pollock "disproves" one by Pablo Picasso? The criteria we apply to the sciences seem to fail the instant they are applied to the arts. Yet we would err, and we would do wrong, if we concluded that "progress" is not evident in the evolution of literary practice.

To illustrate this point we need look no farther than the relatively recent history of the English novel, which as a distinctive narrative art is dated by many, if not most, critics to 1739 when Samuel Richardson published his "novel of character," *Pamela.* (Some critics, we should note, argue instead for Daniel DeFoe's "novel of incident" *Robinson Crusoe* in 1719 and *Moll Flanders* in 1722.) Storytelling—in the forms of the epic, drama, and the lyric—is, of course, an activity as old as humankind. But in *An Outline of the Novel* (1965) Richard M. Eastman persuasively argues that prose narratives premiered in continental literature as late medieval romances, tales of knights and their adventures (the term for the novel in most European languages is "roman," indicating its ancestry in "romance"). By the early Renaissance, popular narratives presented short, prose tales of common life (Boccaccio) in common language, and came to be known by the Italian word novella or "little new thing," from which comes our English word, novel. Among the "proto-novels" before the eighteenth century, Eastman identifies Malory's *Morte d'Arthur* (1485), and Cervantes' *Don Quixote* (1605-1615), and to these important predecessors we can add picaresque fiction (the episodic tales of rogues or "picaros").

Those earlier works, Eastman explains, developed narrative strategies later useful for the singular design of the novel as we know it, but its essential architecture could not properly emerge until after three cultural transformations had taken place. (1) The epistemological revolution fathered by Descartes, Bacon, and Locke, whose works presented a new, inductive science privileging no longer the deductive methods of medieval schoolmen but instead an individual consciousness that experienced and confirmed "reality" through the senses, a development that stimulated in the 1600s and 1700s the unique European passion for recording individual experience at a specific time and place, for biographies, autobiographies, letters, and the field of journalism itself. (2) The Protestant Reformation, which in the 1500s encouraged universal literacy by emphasizing each individual Christian's direct relationship to God and the importance of reading the Bible. (3) The end of feudalism, which saw the rise of an energetic, bourgeoisie class that supported the publishing trade and hungered for a new literature capable of portraying its struggles (not those of an aristocracy) and revealing the geography of the natural world this class was eager to explore.

No form satisfied those challenges quite as well as the novel, a long narrative that drew its defining characteristics from DeFoe's journalistic attention to the surface detail of contemporary life; from Henry Fielding's sense of Aristotelian unity, his familiarity with Restoration drama, and his sensitivity to diverse voices and vernaculars and social manners in *Tom Jones;* and from Laurence Stern's realization of the possibilities for small, epiphanic moments or events disclosing a character to his depths in *Tristram Shanty.*

Based on this eighteenth century archetype, the novel was able to undergo infinite variations on its basic paradigm, expanding its range of subjects (*all* phenomenal experience was its subject), absorbing countless other forms such as the epic, romance, and allegory, and creating for itself sub-genres. (As experimental novelist Ishmael Reed once remarked, "A novel can be the 6 'o clock news," a point proven earlier in the 1930s when John Dos Passos sprinkled documentary-like "newsreels" throughout his epic U.S.A. trilogy.) By the late nineteenth century, which saw in Europe the emergence of the philosophies of positivism and naturalism, the novel's "realistic" foundations permitted even greater efforts to achieve a more "scientific" rendering of human affairs (think of Flaubert's *Madame Bovary)*, efforts that were informed by the new fields of psychology and sociology. As it exists today, the novel's *eidos*—or essence—necessarily includes the presence, to a lesser or greater degree, of the character, plot, and structural features established by its eighteenth century practitioners, the naturalistic refinements it experienced in the nineteenth, and a "psychological realism" that emerged in the early twentieth. Its fundamental, capacious design has not significantly changed in three centuries. However, we should not see this as a rigid *formula*. To better understand this distinction between *form* and *formula* it would be helpful if we looked at the history of a related form: the modern short story.

As mentioned previously, storytelling is ancient, with written examples reaching back to the Egyptian's "The Tales of the Magicians," which possibly date from 4,000 B.C. The *tale* was attractive, as a form, to writers as diverse as Geoffrey Chaucer, Nathaniel Hawthorne, and Washington Irving; within its long tradition we find other forms of short prose—the sketch, apologue, parable, anecdote, vignette, and fable, to name but a few. In May of 1842, in *Graham's Magazine,* Edgar Allan Poe published a review of Hawthorne's *Twice-Told Tales* entitled, "On the Aim and Technique of the Short Story," and in that brilliant essay—as well as in his own work—defined the modern short story as a form distinct from the novel, novella, and other kinds of short prose. Poe asserted that the short prose narrative should require "from a half-hour to one or two hours" to read. Furthermore, he insisted that its writer

> having conceived, with deliberate care, a certain unique or single effect to be wrought out, he then invents such incidents—he then combines such events as may best aid him in establishing this preconceived effect. If his very initial sentence tend not to the outbringing of this effect, then he has failed in his first step. In the whole composition there should be no word written, of which the tendency, direct or indirect, is not to the one pre-established design.

Clearly, the novel cannot be read in two hours or convey but a single emotional effect. Poe stressed the importance of "invention, creation, imagination, and originality." To his demand that every word reinforce that overall effect, Poe added in another essay, "The Philosophy of Composition" (1846), that "It is only with the denouement constantly in view that we can give a plot its indispensable air of consequence, of causation, by making the incidents, and especially the tone at all points, tend to the development of the intention." And in yet a third essay on Hawthorne, published in 1847, Poe condemns his use of allegory, saying "If allegory ever established a fact, it is by dint of overturning a fiction." What emerged from the theory and practice of this nineteenth century genius, who has been credited with inventing the modern short story, was a craft that judged all examples of this form's success by its "unity of effect."

Others built upon Poe's insights, among them critic Brander Matthews who, in his essay "The Philosophy of the Short-Story" (1901), attempted to give an even more precise definition: "the Short-story fulfills the three false unities of French classic drama: it shows one action, in one place, on one day. A short-story deals with a single character, a single event, a single emotion, or the series of emotions called forth by a single situation." From Poe's attempt to define a *form* the short story quickly crystallized (some would say "ossified") into a *formula* that enjoyed enormous popularity with the public and popular magazine editors at the turn of the century. Readers hungered for this quickly digested new fiction; hundreds of "how-to" books for writers in the early 1900s were based upon it. Indeed, it's influence can be seen most clearly in O. Henry's fiction, specifically his story of a classic reversal, "Gift of the Magi." It is present in the work of black America's first renowned short story writer, Charles Chesnutt (read "The Wife of His Youth"), in "The Monkey's Paw," and in many of Rod Serling's scripts for the "Twilight Zone." In other words, so influential and powerful was this *form*-become-*formula* that for many twentieth century readers it limned the contours of what a short story must be, and even today in novels, short stories, motion pictures, television episodes and comic books instances of it provide the entertainment values of suspense, surprise, and intensity.

Inevitably, a backlash against the rigidity and predictability of this design had to occur. In his studies on American literature, *The Symbolic Meaning,* D. H. Lawrence was at times savage in his criticism of the way Poe's "philosophy of composition" mechanized the form of the story to such an extent that life's mystery, spontaneity, and vitality were lost (these were crucial aesthetic aspects that defined Lawrence's own brilliant contribution to the novel and short story). In "Edgar Allan Poe," Lawrence decided that, "Poe is hardly an artist. He is rather a supreme scientist.... He is not sensual, he is sensational. The difference between these two is a difference between growth and decay.... As an artist Poe is unfailingly in bad taste—always bad taste. He seeks a sensation from every phrase or object and the effect is vulgar."

For Lawrence, "A tale is a concatenation of scientific cause and effect. But in a story the movement depends on the sudden appearance of spontaneous emotion or gesture, causeless, arising out of the living self." Most of those who rebelled in theory and practice damned the early twentieth century magazine editors for demanding that short fiction fit such an "artificial mold." "The very technique of the short story is pathological," Herbert Ellsworth Cory stated in a 1917 article in *Dial,* "and tintillates our nerves in our pathological moments. The short story is the blood kinsman of the quick-lunch, the vaudeville, and the joy-ride." Two years earlier, Henry Seidel Canby bemoaned in *Atlantic Monthly* that

> Once started, the narrative must move, move, move furiously, each action and every speech pointing directly toward the unknown climax. A pause is a confession of weakness.... Then the climax, which must neatly, quickly, and definitely end the action for all time, either by a solution you have been urged to hope for by the wily author in every preceding paragraph, or in a way which is logically correct but never, never suspected.

For Canby, and many others, this "formula is rigid, not plastic as life is plastic. It fails to grasp innumerable stories which break the surface of American life day by day and disappear uncaught. Stories of quiet, homely life, events significant for themselves that never reach a burning climax, situations that end in irony, or doubt, or aspiration, it mars in the telling."

These judgments were shared by such fine storytellers as Sherwood Anderson: "As for the plot short stories of the magazines," he wrote in 1924, "those bastard children of De Maupassant, Poe and O. Henry—it was certain there were no plot short stories ever lived in any life I had known anything about." In his own fiction in *Winesburg, Ohio,* Anderson rejected the earlier emphasis on plot-driven storytelling and focused on what he called a form that more organically "grew out of the materials of the tale and the tellers reaction to them."

Put simply, the early nineteenth century efforts to define the short story, which placed it on its feet as a distinct form, led quickly to senility, and that in turn produced an outcry for reform, specifically for greater artistic freedom by the 1920s. This revolt against formalism was, of course, pervasive in all the arts after World War I—in poetry's free verse movement, the paintings of Picasso, and the sculpture of Eric Gill. The Victorian era—and its vision of life—had ended. Just as a new science was beginning, signaled by the gathering of twenty-nine physicists to work on quantum mechanics in Brussels, Belgium in 1927 (nine of the twenty-nine, among them Albert Einstein, later received Nobel Prizes for their contributions to quantum theory), so too were literary artists redefining their practice to create a distinctly twentieth century literature.

Through the use of stream-of consciousness techniques, James Joyce achieved a representation of subjective states of consciousness unequaled before or after *Ulysseus* or *Finnegan's Wake.* Ernest Hemingway's devotion to craft produced a major style of writing, one so widely imitated that his influence is everywhere evident in the novelists of the 1950s, in all genres and sub-genres, and clearly impacted the diction and word economy of so-called minimalist storytellers (Raymond Carver) in the 1980s.

I agree with critic Alfred Kazin that Hemingway's subjects are emotionally adolescent (bullfights, hunting, and other violent activities), that he "brought a major art to a minor vision of life," but Hemingway's declaration of the writer's ambition shows he deeply understood how an individual artistic performance can significantly enhance culture: "Write what hasn't been written before or beat dead men at what they have done" helps us see that in at least one sense we can view the evolution of literature the same way we view the progress of science. At any given moment, physicists here and abroad are laboring to answer *objective* questions handed down by Einstein, Bohr, and others—tracking down sub-atomic entities, for example, or patching up cracks in Unified Field Theory; it's a competitive race of sorts, as James D. Watson points out in *The Double Helix.* Similarly, the history of literary practice creates objective aesthetic possibilities, artistic works demanded historically by the foul-ups and partial breakthroughs in past literary art, novels and stories that fill in the blanks and potholes created by the oversights, and omissions of those writers who preceded us. No, these are not your average "commercial" novels or mere entertainments, only great books that advance literary practice. As the old saying goes, good fiction sharpens our perception; great fiction *changes* it.

In the realm of American literature at any time there are always subjects, unexplored, that cry out for dramatization—for example, until 1998 no novel philosophically treated the life of Martin Luther King Jr. until my own *Dreamer* appeared; and I would submit that today's literary fiction has yet to broach either the complexity and meaning of the scientific discoveries I briefly catalogued at the beginning of this essay, or the remarkable multi-cultural texture of the American social world in the late 1990s.

"Or beat dead men at what they have done." Again, Hemingway illuminates how each significant advance in writing need not involve a new subject. Rather, it is quite enough if that work completes or expands upon an earlier, flawed performance, or deepens its investigations as Ellison's many-splendored *Invisible Man* opens the subject of black American life in the 1940s to greater imaginative realms than Wright achieved in *Native Son.* Now, don't get me wrong: Ellison's book does not "refute" Wright's novel. Both works are masterpieces—one of naturalism, the other of surrealism and sumptuous stylistic synthesis. But, yes, *Invisible Man,* in its multi-leveled philosophical explorations, embodied a far greater vision and wider deployment of *techne* than *Native Son*, the work of Ellison's mentor.

Can we speak of literary "progress" in other ways? I believe we can. When Western audiences became better informed about the world through the mediums of radio and newscasts and later television, fiction put aside its nineteenth century burden of *reportage*. While there are readers today who apparently enjoy this (I know of one professor at Boston University who argued one night over dinner that what makes Melville's *Moby Dick* a great novel is the fact that one can learn about whaling from it), contemporary writers can leave travelogue material to the travel-writers, concentrating instead on creating economical, poetic descriptive passages in which each and every image reinforces character, atmosphere, tone, and event. We can also say that characterization in twentieth century fiction advances beyond much of what appeared in nineteenth century literature, where too often characters were defined one-dimensionally by a single, dominant emotion or trait (nobility, envy, love) and thereby left much to be desired in terms of human complexity, as in Harriet Beecher Stowe's *Uncle Tom's Cabin.* Except in mass-market pulp writing, what author Fred Pfeil once called "industrial fiction, " or in B-movies, melodrama has disappeared—at least where serious, literary fiction is concerned.

Also left behind with the nineteenth century are *sentimentality* and *purple prose*. Oh yes, Harlequin romances, so popular today, are steeped in both, and their readers consume (or so I've been told by one writer for this sub-genre) three such novels a day on average; they are popular largely with women readers who want the same love story told over and over, with variations only in setting and time. But this, obviously, is not art. For the finest literary fiction of the twentieth century is, if nothing else, so acutely aware of language performance—consider the work of

Nabokov, Djuna Barnes in *Nightwood*, or William Gass's novels—that this cliché-larded, mawkish sentence from Mary J. Holmes' justifiably forgotten novel *Madeline* (1881) could never appear on the pages of a serious fiction in 2000 C.E.: "He bent down over her now, for her face was hidden in her hands, all sense of sight shut out, all sense of hearing, too, save the words he was pouring into her ear—words which burned their way into her heart, making it throb for a single moment with gratified pride, and then grow heavy as lead as she knew how impossible it was for her to pay the debt in the way which he wanted."

Progress, indeed.

Except for the enduring masterpieces of earlier times, contemporary writing in general is *better* in respect to craft—and on the level of the sentence—than garden-variety prose fiction of the last century. In their forms, the novel and short story are creatively freer, and this liberation can be traced not only to the innovators of the 1920s but also to the so-called imaginative writers of the "New Fiction" (and "magical realism") that emerged in the 1970s, authors such as John Gardner, Robert Coover, and John Barth who deserve credit for developing fresh strategies for solving the problems of viewpoint, opening our fiction to exciting new (and sometimes old) ontologies, and for unsealing a door to "fabulation" closed since the nineteenth century by the hard-core naturalists. Inside that room of fictional possibilities they found a tale and yarn-telling tradition still close to the roots of oral storytelling, where one could discover philosophical insights in fairy tales, folklore, and myths: stories about fantastic creatures—golems and grendels—we are not likely to bump into at the corner supermarket, but in the New Fiction we could. For in the universe of the mind (and the college-based New Fiction writers were interested in nothing if not mind, perception, epistemology), Frankenstein's monster and J. F. K., quarks and Pegasus, Rip Van Winkle, and Chairman Mao all existed side by side as phenomenal objects for consciousness, none more "real" than another in our dreams or between the covers of a book. It is a fiction conscious of itself as fiction, and conscious of storytelling's four millennium-old traditions. Indeed, in a post-Wittgenstein and Heideggear period, in a post-modern culture aware of a subatomic world of protons and electrons in constant motion unknown to the ninteenth century, some of the New Fiction's authors presented "reality" itself as a cultural construct, an interpretation of experience, a *fiction* based on the ensorceling power of language alone.

To these changes we must add one final instance of progress that is of enormous importance. Since the 1970s, writers of color—who for centuries were marginalized or simply ignored—have irreversibly transformed the social world as it is portrayed in American fiction. Moreover, their stories depicting black, Asian, native American, and Hispanic experiences and history have broadened as well as deepened the way we perceive ourselves and this nation's past. In the hands of bestselling and award-winning writers such as Richard Wright, Ralph Ellison, Maxine Hong Kingston, Oscar Hijuelos, Toni Morrison, Amy Tan, Ha Jin, Leslie Silko, and Jhumpa Lahiri, the novel and short story *opened* for late twentieth century readers onto lives, events, and non-white views of the world that qualified and refined the fictional practice of former times by making readers conscious—sometimes painfully so—of the racial and cultural Others whose presence in America and the world is as essential and worthy of study as the lives of northern Europeans.

Many have claimed that literature is dangerous. They are right to fear its power. The list of novels banned from high school English classes in the twentieth century reads like a roster of the most lauded modern and contemporary fiction. The reason for this, I believe, is twofold. First, because fiction at its best challenges the status quo. It forces us to question our social relations, prejudices, understanding of the world, ourselves, and the meaning of humanity. It can be scientifically prescient, anticipating the impact of technology—and even specific inventions—on our lives, an event that happens frequently in first-rate science fiction. It can fuel civil war, as Stowe's *Uncle Tom's Cabin* did in the nineteenth century; expose political systems, as George Orwell did with *1984* and *Animal Farm;* lead to reforms in the way patients are treated in mental institutions, which occurred after Ken Kesey published *One Flew Over the Cuckoo's Nest;* and inspire resistance to oppression, as Winston Churchill discovered when he read "If We Must Die," a poem by Harlem Renaissance writer Claude McKay, over the airwaves during the Nazi bombing of London.

Secondly, literature is dangerous *ontologically* because reading is the most radical and liberating of all enterprises. (Thus, novels are banned, and in the antebellum South it was illegal to teach slaves how to read.) Open any novel. What is there? Black marks—signs—on white paper. First they are silent. They are lifeless, lacking signification until the consciousness of the reader imbues them with meaning, allowing a fictitious character like Huckleberry Finn, say, to emerge hugely from the monotonous rows of ebony type. Once this magical act takes place in the mind of the reader, an entire world appears redivivus, in his consciousness: "a vivid and continuous dream," as John Gardner once called it, one that so ensorcells us that we forget the room we're sitting in or fail to hear the telephone ring. In other words, the world experienced within any book is *transcendent*. It exists for consciousness alone (Huckleberry Finn exists *only* as a mental construct, like a mathematical entity). But, as Jean-Paul Sartre describes so well in his classic work, *What Is Literature?*, the rare experience found in books is the "conjoint effort of author and reader." It is dialectical. While the writer composes his "world" in words, his (or her) work requires an attentive reader who will "put himself from the very beginning and almost without a guide at the height of this silence" of signs. Reading, Sartre tells us, is *directed creation*. A contract of sorts: "To write is to make an appeal to the reader that he lead into objective existence the revelation which I have undertaken by means of language." Do you get it? I hope so. For each book *requires* that a reader exercise his orbific freedom for the "world" and theater of meaning embodied on its pages to *be*. As readers, we invest the cold signs on the pages of *Native Son* with our *own* emotions, *our* understanding of poverty, oppression, and fear; then, in what is almost an act of thaumaturgy, the powerful figures and tropes Wright has created reward us richly by returning our subjective feelings to us transformed, refined, and alchemized by language into a new vision with the capacity to change our lives forever.

This magic rests in your hands, as readers. It is a power to co-create and travel through numerous imaginative and intellectual realms that one can invoke at any time, anywhere. A power that serves democracy itself. If film is a communal experience, as so many have claimed, then reading is the triumph of the individual consciousness and human freedom.

Yet that freedom we experience in literature is frequently won at a great expense by fiction's creators. Non-white writers, and the innovators who advanced the novel and story as disciplines, often had to publish outside the "mainstream" of American literature at the beginning of their careers. Many black authors found acceptance for their creations only in black publications before placing their work with white publishing companies. It is well known that in the 1920s, a revolutionary period for Western literature, many authors found their break with the status quo forced them into self-publishing. Or some received recognition first in Europe before their art was lauded at home. Closer to our own time, "experimental" writers originally rejected by New York publishers—Ronald Sukenick, Jonathan Baumbach, Russell Banks, and Clarence Major—founded the Fiction Collective, a publishing cooperative controlled by writers themselves, to insure that their unusual and daring ways of telling stories reached the public. It is a fact that American culture at any time has been dominated by commercial fiction, which seldom, if ever, innovates in the ways Hemingway called for. Thus, in order for their works to see the light of day, our artists of vision have relied upon small presses and numerous literary journals, most of which are too poor to pay contributors or reward them well. Yet it is there that many of tomorrow's most important authors are publishing their stories and novel excerpts.

If we hope to see the continued formal and thematic growth of American literature in this century, it is incumbent upon the public to financially support those small presses and "little magazines" that allow unknown and iconclastic writers to break into print. For twenty years I have insisted upon this with my own writing students, graduate and undergraduate. Each term I ask them to subscribe to a literary journal of distinction they would like their work to appear in, to *read* that publication for a year, and by doing so support other artists in their community. This is but a small gesture we all, as individual citizens concerned about literary art, can perform.

But more than small gestures are required. Since the late 1960s, the National Endowment for the Arts (NEA) has each year given individual fellowships to American writers, invariably young creators of talent, whose selection is made by a panel of accomplished writers who review thousands of submissions. The grants, I believe, are now at $20,000 each. They buy crucial writing time for "emerging" talents, who must maintain fatiguing "day jobs" in order to support their art. Unfortunately, the NEA has in recent years been a lightning rod for controversy, specifically for projects it funded in the areas of performance and plastic arts, not literature, that offended the values of conservative Americans. Time and again their elected officials in the House of Representatives have called for the abolition of supporting the arts through the national treasury. The market, they argue, should determine what art succeeds and what art fails—the public, in other words, should be allowed to support a performance or simply walk away.

This argument is not without merit, but its proponents fail to recognize that if the public—the market—at any moment is chosen as the sole arbiter of which artistic works will be supported, ephemeral fashions and social whims will replace critical standards. By this standard, we would have lost long ago groundbreaking novels and stories that were misunderstood in their time, or were decades ahead of their time, but now are canonized. Any nation that genuinely cares about the health of its cultural life must politically support those in Congress devoted to funding the NEA, which in addition to issuing grants to individual writers also funds a wide range of literary journals that could not survive without its annual support.

All art entertains; but all entertainment is not art. Any nation that understands the difference between these two—art as escapist fare and art as enduring cultural artifact—will support literature's efflorescence, even as it must fund research and development in the sciences. And, lastly, it must see the wisdom in Nobel laurate Saul Bellow's observation in his 1970s essay "Culture Now":

> This society, like decadent Rome, is an amusement society. That is the grim fact. Art cannot and should not compete with amusement. It has business at the heart of humanity. The artist, as Collingwood tells us, must be a prophet, 'not in the sense that he foretells things to come, but that he tells the audience, at the risk of their displeasure, the secrets of their own hearts.' That is why he exists. He is a spokesman for his community. This account of the artist's business is old, much older than Collingwood, very old, but in modern times this truth, which we all feel, is seldom expressed.... No community altogether knows its own heart; and by failing in this knowledge a community deceives itself on the one subject concerning which ignorance means death.... The remedy is art itself. Art is the community's medicine for the worst disease of the mind, the corruption of consciousness."

Notes

1. Material on the evolution of the novel is taken from Richard M. Eastman, *A Guide to The Novel* (San Francisco,: Chandler Publishing Company, 1965).

2. This discussion of the short story's evolution is drawn from Eugene Current-Garcia and Walton R. Patrick, ed., *What Is the Short Story?* (Glenview, Ill.: Scott, Foresman and Company, 1974).

Chapter 8

Paradoxical Progress: Medical Advances and Moral Anxiety

Albert R. Jonsen

The National Institutes of Health (NIH), America's powerful engine of scientific advances in medicine, was 100 years old in 1987. From a one room laboratory on Staten Island, it spread not only to an expansive campus in Bethesda, Maryland but to thousands of laboratories and clinics where NIH funded researchers study the mechanisms of disease and the means to sustain and restore health, spending (in that year) one and a half billion American tax dollars in so doing. On the 100th anniversary, Public Broadcasting produced a television series entitled, "The Health Century." The preface to the series' companion book opened with a biblical reference: "At the point of death, Hezekiah, King of Judah, turned his face to the wall and prayed to God to grant him fifteen more years." The author goes on to say, "We are modern Hezekiahs … the practical means of extending our life span and granting ourselves years free from chronic disease lie now before us as a result of the advances in research and therapy of the Health Century.…We have a good chance of getting Hezekiah's fifteen years and many more. This book tells the story of that progress."[1]

Unquestionably, the one hundred years chronicled in "The Health Century" manifested medical progress probably greater than during the twenty-five centuries since Greece's Hippocratic physicians made the first great mark in western medical history. Yet that medical progress, bestowing benefits unseen in the past, also generated moral perplexities never before encountered. King Hezekiah did indeed get his fifteen years but he lived those added years under a dire prediction by the prophet Isaiah, "Behold, the days are coming when all that is in your house ... shall be carried to Babylon; nothing will be left and your sons will be eunuchs in the palace of the King of Babylon, says the Lord." Hezekiah responds with a resigned wish, "So be it, if there will be peace and security in my days."[2] Life extended is a mixed blessing, bestowing good and evil. King Hezikiah's delight at the extension of his life must have been tempered by his dismay at the events that would mar his added years. All reflective humans are aware of the mix of blessings and curses that life contains. Yet few humans charge themselves with a deliberate attempt to understand how the blessings and curses are related to each other and to untangle them or mitigate their impact to the extent possible. During the second half of the twentieth century, medical progress generated just such a genre of persons called bioethicists, and a new species of moral philosophy called bioethics. This essay recapitulates the paradox of medical progress and the creation of bioethics.

The essence of the paradox is neatly expressed in a history of American medicine, published ten years before "The Health Century" was produced. Its authors, both distinguished physicians who had played a part in the centuries' progress, wrote, "A nagging residual question that can only be answered by future experience is whether medical care of the highest quality made possible by a century of extraordinary progress in medical science can be delivered to the entire population at a level of funding, whether by taxation or insurance, that the public can afford and will tolerate."[3] The application of the biological sciences to the diagnosis and treatment of disease, that has moved with relentless pace through the Health Century, not only gave physicians concepts, tools, medicines, and techniques to understand and counter injury and disease more effectively than ever before, it also created vast structures of institutions, systems, and policies within which the doctor would work. The healing hand now holds instruments that can be used only by trained teams, within medical centers, financed by insurance and government subsidies, watched by administrative and legal eyes. The instruments themselves and what they do is devised by many scientists and technicians, made in precision plants and marketed by multi-national firms, attentive to profits and to patents. Medical advances can be listed as the introduction of individual items, quinine for fever, digitalis for heart failure, ether for anesthesia, but the individual items on the long list of the last century's medical history bring along with them expansion and rearrangement of the world and work of caring for the sick. Health care today is as much pharmaceutical companies and insurance companies and government agencies as it is doctors and nurses.

Progress in science is often more palpable than progress in other cultural realms. Ideas, such as freedom, work their way into many minds under diverse guises, and emerge in social movements that generate ambiguous results. Artistic innovation, such as cubism or rock music, seem to move backwards as much as forward. But a scientific advance opens mysterious nature to understanding and very often produces a means of manipulating it for human purposes. The abstractions of Einstein's mind translated into a new physics and quantum mechanics, which exploded into the human world as nuclear power. In the biomedical sciences, physiological hypotheses are tested under empirical conditions and, if verified, become the stimuli for diagnostic and therapeutic interventions that, in turn, touch human life at its most vulnerable. Biomedical progress seems to show itself, from laboratory to clinic, as an unambiguous human good. Indeed, the public often proclaims the instances of this progress as "miracles."

One example of such a medical miracle was the introduction of chronic hemodialysis for irreversible and fatal kidney disease. In 1960, Dr. Belding Scribner of the University of Washington invented a small plastic loop that could be sutured permanently into the forearm of a patient suffering from end-stage kidney disease. The loop allowed the patient to be connected several times a week to a machine, an "artificial kidney" that would cleanse the patient's blood of the metabolic toxins that, if allowed to accumulate, would quickly cause death. By this small invention, a universally fatal condition was transformed into a chronic condition that persons could not only live with but even return to relatively normal life. A medical miracle replayed the biblical miracle: it granted Hezekiah's fifteen years and more to those at the point of death.

Biblical miracles, however, are not the consequences of a century of preparation. God's miracles come out of the blue. Dr. Scribner's miracle was the culmination of years of research and experimentation into renal disease. Although the second century C.E. physician, Galen, clearly demonstrated that the kidneys manufactured urine, the exact nature of their function was obscure until the first half of the nineteenth century. Scientists such as the British physicians Richard Bright and William Bowman and the German physiologist Carl Ludwig elucidated the anatomical structure of the kidneys and proposed theories about the physiological processes whereby they filtered, reabsorbed, and eliminated products of metabolism. Only in 1917 did Arthur Cushny's "modern theory" initiate an understanding of the exquisite talents of the paired organs in maintaining homeostasis, eliminating toxins, regulating metabolism, and controlling blood pressure. In the physiology laboratories of the early twentieth century, the humble kidney became a wondrous organ. Yet its wonders could be understood in straightforward biochemical terms. Dr. Cushny wrote of his "modern theory" that "it reduces the kidney to a machine instead of postulating for it the capacity of a highly trained analytic chemist."[4] The elegant simplicity of the modern theory stimulated intense research into the actual complexities of kidney function and revealed for the first time the pathologies that caused renal failure. Indeed, the analogy with a machine was realized by John Abel, an American colleague of Cushny's, who made what he called an "artificial kidney" that could wash certain substances out of the blood of dogs by passing it through an external bath

Abel predicted in 1913 that one day his machine could be used to treat humans in acute renal failure. He predicted rightly but many problems obstructed the application to humans: a more efficient permeable membrane to filter the multiple components of blood was needed, a more powerful anticoagulant to prevent clotting as blood passed through the machine was required (Able used groundup leeches!), an even more refined science of renal metabolism was desirable. Their prediction was realized in the 1940s, when Dutch physician Willem Kolff applied a version of their device and saved the lives of several persons in acute renal failure. Patients whose kidneys had been injured by poisons, by low blood flow, or by trauma, but remained essentially viable, could be seen through their crisis by dialysis. Yet, again, obstacles prevented the chronic use of artificial kidney, particularly, the necessity for multiple surgical procedures to connect and disconnect patients to the machine. Patients whose kidneys were destroyed by the chronic inflammation of the glomeruli, organs essential to its filtering work, would die soon after diagnosis. Patients on their way to that final state could be treated, with little effect, with a low protein diet. Dr. Scribner's invention of the arteriovenous cannulae and shunt allowed these patients to be hooked to the machine again and again and, for the first time in history, patients with irreversible kidney failure had a reprieve from death (kidney transplantation had begun in the 1950s but organs were scarce and, once transplanted, often failed: dialysis provided the reliable alternative and backup for transplantation).

The miracle had its own maladies. Within two years of its successful use for a handful of patients in Seattle, dialysis came to the attention of the broader public. *Life* magazine writer Shana Alexander visited Scribner's program and wrote the longest article ever to appear in *Life*, "They decide who lives, who dies. Medical miracle puts moral burden on small committee."[5] "They" was a group of persons, mostly non-medical, who had accepted the task of choosing, out of the many persons with end-stage renal disease, those very few who could be admitted to the treatment. They were invited to serve on this "small committee" by the King County Medical Society, which was attempting to resolve, in some reasonable way, the first paradox created by this new treatment. The paradox was essentially that cited above: a new treatment appears that is effective but costly and difficult to administer: not all in need can receive it. Faced with this paradox, the Seattle doctors imposed upon the small committee the moral burden of choosing life or death. The choice was forced, not only because the new treatment was costly beyond the reach of most patients, but also because its effective use depended on trained personnel in short supply and on precision machines slow to be produced. Dialysis, in its beginnings, had to be performed in organized medical settings by dedicated, highly skilled nurses and physicians. Successful treatment did not come to an end: once a patient was maintained, he or she remained a patient for years, utilizing available resources until they died or the program was expanded. The choice of who should be admitted into the program was an agonizing one, filled with doubts and marred by unconscious prejudice. It became the main scene of Alexander's dramatic article and, thereby, opened a vigorous public debate in the

United States.

Dr. Scribner confessed his astonishment. "We simply could not understand," he said, "why everyone was more interested in the existence and operation of the lay selection committee than in the fact that in two years we had taken a disease and converted it from a 100 percent fatal prognosis to a two year survival. Nor were any of us prepared for the very severe storm of criticism that was to be forthcoming."[6] From the medical point of view, chronic hemodialysis represented genuine progress: a disease with a 100 percent fatal prognosis was subjugated. But its subjugation, which meant good life for those who would otherwise have quickly died, aroused serious questions. Those questions were aired in the medical and scholarly literature: was the lay committee an abdication of medical responsibility? Were its members, mere mortals, usurping divine authority? Were their judgments marred by class preferences, racial, and sexual prejudice? What qualities of any person win them the right to live? How should a scarce medical resource be fairly allocated? The questions also echoed in legislative halls: should the government pay for dialysis? If for dialysis, why not for other lifesaving treatments? Should payments be limited in amount and duration? The scholarly debates issued many suggestions for more equitable methods of selection than by committee: utilitarian criteria that favored the most productive members of society were proposed; random selection by lottery to avoid bias was urged. But the legislative debates resolved these arguments. In 1972 Congress amended the Social Security Act to provided for federal funding of renal dialysis and transplantation, thus making the procedures less costly and more widely available. The acute crisis of individual selection was alleviated, not by ethical analysis but by budgetary allocation. Still, the ethical arguments pushed the problem into the arena of public policy.[7]

The ethical analysis had elucidated the problem and sharpened it to the point where a clear perception of what moral values were at stake came into focus. Concepts of fairness, equity, rights, and utility were explored and the arguments for various resolutions propounded and criticized. The Congressmen who voted for Section 2991 had not read all or any of this ethical analysis: they were moved by the pleas of patients and even by the sight of one of them being dialyzed during a Senate hearing. Still, the problem posed by the allocation of medical resources had seeped into public understanding. It was an issue now on the public agenda and would emerge again and again in the ensuing years. During the late 1980s, the growing awareness of the inflating costs of medical care stimulated a debate over the rationing of health care resources in general. In the face of a general reluctance to deprive persons of needed medical care in a nation as wealthy as the United States, many proposals for the restructuring of the delivery system, the financing system, and the political structures of health care were argued, culminating in the ill-fated Clinton Health Plan in 1992. Within these debates the same questions initiated in the dialysis debate were raised again and again, without satisfactory resolution. In one experiment only did the debates issue in a genuine policy reform that reflected the ethical dimensions: the state of Oregon encouraged widespread public debate about priorities in health care and, after several years of consideration, established a list of health services that would have priority in claims on public funding. Although cost of services played a role in the creation of this list, other, more properly ethical considerations, such as the seriousness of the health need, the efficacy of the services and the equity of distribution were emphasized. Despite the success of the Oregon experiment (which continues to be utilized with significant public and professional satisfaction), the on-going debates about health care remain a confused tangle of economic, political and ethical considerations. Yet again, the value of the persistent voice about ethics is to keep these questions in the mix of considerations and prevent the debates from turning only on the economic and political. Many bioethicists have written perceptive commentary on justice in health care that have provided a vocabulary and forms of argument for this major public debate.[8]

In the wake of the dialysis controversy, a small group of scholars began to attend to the ethical problems raised by the new medicine. By 1970, the word "bioethics" had been coined and appropriated for a novel sort of moral philosophy that explored these issues in depth and fostered their discussion in public and policy settings. Gradually, professors of bioethics were appointed, largely in schools of medicine, and a literature appeared in medical, legal, philosophical, and theological journals. Bioethics was defined, in the *Encyclopedia of Bioethics* (1978) as "the systematic study of human conduct in the area of the life sciences and health care, insofar as this conduct is examined in the light of moral values and principles." The editor explained the "intense and widespread interest in bioethics" by noting that "Although many bioethical issues have been discussed since ancient times, the introduction of modern biomedical technologies, especially since the 1950s, has intensified some age-old questions and has given rise to perplexing new problems—the prolongation of life, euthanasia, prenatal diagnosis and abortion, human experimentation, genetic interventions and reproductive technologies, behavior control and psychosurgery, the definition of death, the right to privacy, allocation of scarce health resources and dilemmas in the maintenance of environmental health."[9]

Bioethics is, for the most part, a reflection on the moral problems raised by medical progress. Each of the questions noted above has its own dimensions but they share a common feature: they are the undesirable and often unforeseen consequences (or better, concomitants) of desirable and intended medical benefits. Ironically, this awareness of mixed benefits is not itself the product of modern medical progress. It is a familiar notion in medicine, reaching as far back as the earliest ethical admonition to the practitioners of ancient Greece: "Be of benefit and do no harm," they were advised. This maxim recognizes that almost all invasions of the human body to heal may also cause harm. The prospect of healing and the seriousness of the disease must justify any attendant dangers. Physicians throughout history have been acutely aware that their helping work could be dangerous to their patients.[10]

The modern meaning of the venerable maxim encompasses much more than the harm to the patient (although that should never be forgotten). It envisions the risks, harms, dangers, and distortions that may affect society, or groups within society, as the result of medical progress. The allocation problem raised by dialysis was one of the early examples of this social harm attendant on a medical advance. We have faced many other examples. A phenomenal flow of effective antibiotics for a wide range of infectious diseases has gradually caused the recrudescence of many resistant organisms, making the medications useless for many formally treatable diseases. Transplantation of major organs has become so successful that there are not anywhere near the number of organs needed by patients. Skills at evaluating the effectiveness of treatment have become sharpened, suggesting that many common treatments lack scientific evidence of their utility, but at the same time hesitating to question long-established treatments, lest patients be deprived of necessary care. Also, all scientific progress in medicine must be tried for the first time in humans. Human experimentation, almost by definition, must subject some persons to the risk of harm in order that others might benefit. By far the most troubling of the unwanted consequences is that mentioned in the opening of this essay: as quality of care increases, access to it seems to decrease, leaving many without any care at all. In the United States, where the quality of care is acknowledged to be higher than anywhere in the world, a huge portion of the population are unable to obtain needed medical help, much less preventive measures. Throughout the developing nations, vast populations reach out futilely for the benefits of contemporary scientific medicine and public health.

Dialysis was our opening example: it represents one of the first genuine life-sustaining technologies, but its efficacy rested on the accumulation of a century of classic physiology and pathophysiology, as well as contemporary materials science and production. The classical biomedical sciences were shaped in the nineteenth century: biochemistry, cellular pathology, and endocrinology. Medical science has moved far from those classical concepts. It is now centered in molecular biology and seeks the origins of health and disease in subunits of the cell that had been closed to scientific investigation until only half a century ago. The Human Genome Project, which is but one segment of the vast revolution in biomedical science, utilizes the concepts and methods of molecular biology for a particular task: to discover the exact points in the molecular structure of deoxyribonucleic acid (DNA) that produce the biochemical products that make the physical organism grow and function and, by default, malfunction. This Project, opened at the beginning of the 1990s, brings investigators from around the world to the task. It has been essentially completed in the year 2000, several years before its expected conclusion (although much work remains in designating the precise sites and complex interrelationships of genes). The knowledge derived from the mapping and sequencing of human DNA has enormous potential. It will not only reveal the structure, function, and malfunction of the organism, it will also suggest ways to remedy malfunction, sometimes at the root of genetic mutations, sometimes by targeted drug and gene therapies. It will also reveal the interconnection of physical, psychic, and behavioral characteristics and shed light on the ancient problem of whether we are what we are by nature or nurture. It will cast human nature in a new light.

All this is unquestionably progress. It moves from vague hints about cellular structure available to scientists of the 1900s to the revolutionary thesis, announced by Watson and Crick in 1953 that DNA molecules were wound into a double helical form, to the elaborate computerized methods of analyzing millions of segments of DNA and linking those segments with the production of various proteins, and eventually cellular and organic structure and function. If progress is measured by increasing precision and comprehensiveness of ideas and by the ability to turn these ideas into verifiable data that ranges over a wider and wider range of phenomena, molecular biology of the twentieth century represents progress. That progress has only begun to move toward realization in clinical medicine. The first steps, taken in the last two decades, have been in the diagnostic direction. It is possible to designate certain diseases as predominately genetic in origin, that is, caused by specific mutations in the DNA of the sufferer. Many of these diseases were already known as genetic, in the sense that it was evident that they were passed down within kinships. Now, however, scientists can locate exact points in chromosomal structure where changes and breaks have taken place and are passed on by the classical rules of genetics.

However, a striking difference between this sort of diagnosis and the diagnostic procedures of traditional medicine now appears. In traditional medicine, physicians noted signs and symptoms that suggested some organic malfunction and, by a process of reasoning and testing, attempted to identify the causality of that malfunction as closely as possible and then, if possible, remedy it. Genetic diagnosis is quite different. It does not need signs and symptoms. It needs nothing more than a family history (and sometimes not even that). The person who is studied may not be ill at all. The result of the study is a prediction of the future: you have the mutation associated with, say, breast cancer. The prediction is itself subject to many vagaries, for it is based on probabilities that, given certain conditions (many of them unknown) the person will eventually experience the disease. Only in rare cases does a genetic diagnosis promise a certain future. Genetic diagnosis also differs from traditional medicine in that no treatment of the genetic disorder itself is available: we cannot yet fix broken genes. The diagnostician may only say, "there is such and such a probability that you will develop this condition at some time in the future. When it, appears it can be treated or not—depending on the state of the medical art." Few preventive measures for predicted genetic disease now exist, with the exception of advising carriers not to reproduce or to abort affected fetuses.

Here, then, is the negative side of the benefits of the Human Genome Project. The list of the diseases associated with genetic mutations grows almost daily. As medical science and skills become more capable of applying the knowledge derived from that Project to persons, more persons will learn that they bear in themselves the seeds of one, or many, unpleasant, even lethal conditions. Yet they will not now feel ill, nor may they ever. They will also know that they can pass those seeds of disease onto their progeny. Philosophers since Socrates have extolled the aphorism, know thyself, but we may now ask whether we would wish to know our genetic futures. The medical world, which has been populated by healers and the sick, will now also encompass those who are not sick but know that they might be, anxious to follow each hint that suggests that their predicted disease is starting to show itself, eager for information about therapeutic advances, and needing information about reproductive choices. They are neither patients nor not patients but rather unpatients, like the undead of the old horror movies, neither out of this world nor of it. This again is a form of the paradox stated earlier: here, however, quality medical science may be available, in the form of genetic information, but persons cannot avail themselves of treatment, not because it costs too much, but because it does not exist.

At the same time, many other parties may be avid to gain that same information. Person's health prospects are important in deciding to employ, to insure, to elect, to marry, and for many other purposes. Persons may present their best face but those who look at it may know that, behind the smile, is a propensity to cardiovascular disease, or alcoholism, or schizophrenia, or Alzheimer's disease. The fine points of probability may be less important to those interested parties than to the individual with the genetic condition. The careful formulation about probability of eventual disease may be simplified into, "He has a propensity to paranoia." Banks of information can be amassed about the health prospects of an individual, drawn from a single vial of blood. The problems posed by leaking confidentiality loom over genetic medicine far more ominously than over traditional medicine. Those problems are the adverse affects of progress.

Certainly, medicine's progress is not alone in facing the paradoxes of benefit and harm. Every innovation enters the world as an infant whose future may open out in many directions, some of them unfortunate, even tragic. The metaphysicians of progress who proclaimed that time moved the world and the human race inevitably toward a more perfect state of being often explained the horrors of life as necessary means to the end, as Voltaire's Dr. Pangloss optimistically asserted that the suffering that he and Candide had experienced were necessary to bring them to the best of all possible worlds. But those metaphysicians, children of the Enlightenment, began to doubt this doctrine when the War to End All Wars initiated a century of radically ambiguous progress. The paradigm of that progress is, perhaps, the harnessing of nuclear power. Everywhere we are aware of the adverse effects of innovation: our strangled freeways are a vivid reminder. However, nowhere outside of medicine has the ambiguity of progress created a systematic reflection on the moral consequences of progress. Bioethics is just that: a discipline that attends to the genuine achievements of medical science, not simply as miracle, but as mixed miracle. Bioethicists propose that we must not merely admire the miracles and deplore their adverse effects. We must take responsibility for these double effects, consistently attempting to maximize the benefits and minimize the harms. They propose that these efforts must affect clinical practice, institutional structures, and public policy. Bioethics is the study of the moral ambiguity of medical progress.

The discipline of bioethics derived from beginnings in the classical disciplines about ethics, moral philosophy, and moral theology. However, as a discipline, bioethics has emerged from the speculative world of its parental disciplines and reached toward the practical world of clinical decisions (about sustaining life and allowing death) and of public policy (about allocation of resources, research with human beings, and privacy of medical-genetic information). Its practitioners write extensively about these subjects and often participate in the public forums that influence policy. Yet they remain scholars rather than policy makers, more comfortable at articulating the dimensions of problems than formulating real-world systems and structures to resolve them. At the same time, their articulation of the issues that can properly be called ethical, such as respect for the individual and fairness in distributing the goods of a community, has shaped the debates and the policies. The tendency of public policy to adopt, in a clandestine manner, a utilitarian ethos, the greater good of the greater number, has been consistently countered by another ethos, deeply embedded in the western cultural tradition, of respect for persons and fairness in the community. It is not always easy to translate these moral ideals into practice and public policy but the discipline of bioethics, as it has developed, is dedicated to the task.

Notes

1. Edward Shorter, *The Health Century* (New York: Doubleday, 1987), xiii.
2. II Kings 20:16
3. James Bordley and Harvey A. McGehee, *Two Centuries of American Medicine 1776-1976* (Philadelphia: W.B. Saunders Company, 1976), viii.
4. Arthur Cushny, *The Secretion of Urine* (London: Longmans, Green and Co., 1917) in *Selected Readings in the History of Physiology*, ed. John Fulton (Springfield, Ill.: Thomas, 1966), 367.
5. Shana Alexander, "They Decide Who Lives, Who Dies: Medical Miracle Puts Moral Burden on Small Committee" *Life* 53 (November 1962): 102-25.
6. Quoted in Reneé Fox and Judith Swazey, *The Courage to Fail: A Social View of Organ Transplanation and Dialysis* (Chicago: University of Chicago Press, 1974), 241.
7. Albert Jonsen, *The Birth of Bioethics* (New York: Oxford University Press, 1998), 7.
8. Norman Daniels, *Just Health Care*, (Cambridge: Cambridge University Press, 1985); E. Haavi Morreim, *Balancing Act: The New Medical Ethics of Medicine's New Economics* (Dordrecht, Boston: Kulwer Academic publishers, 1991).

9. Warren Reich ed., *Encyclopedia of Bioethics* (New York: The Free Press, 1978), xix.

10. Albert Jonsen, *A Short History of Medical Ethics* (New York: Oxford University Press, 2000).

Chapter 9

Young Children: The First Step in Progress

Richard N. Brandon

Human progress occurs over generations, and each generation begins with the birth of children. To me, societal progress therefore means steadily improving the well-being of all citizens, starting with the well-being of children, and reducing the disparities in levels of well-being among different groups of children and families.

Many features of how well children are cared for in their early years determine how well they will succeed in the rest of their lives. In this chapter I suggest that children whose early lives are characterized by economic sufficiency, good nutrition, and health care; nurturing by parents and other adults; stable family arrangements and safe communities will experience higher levels of well-being for the rest of their lives. An adequate concept and measurements of child well-being must go beyond having children survive, to having them thrive. In the United States, I argue, this will require public financing of universal access to high quality early care and learning. For less developed nations, failing to allocate resources to early pre-primary learning will increase the growing disparity between their level of human capital and their children's chances of success, and that of industrialized nations providing highly enriched early learning environments.

Measuring the Well-being of Children and Families

Despite the central role of child development in achieving progress, there is not a widely accepted set of measures of child well-being that serve the needs of policy makers.

International reviews of the well-being of children tend to include—and often confound—three different types of measures. *Child outcomes or conditions* are the metrics by which we determine how well-off children actually are as a result of the various environmental factors, resources, and policies that affect them. *Features of the environments* (physical and social) in which children live affect their outcomes or conditions. *Access to resources or policy interventions* may support young children, either by directly improving their outcomes or by improving their physical and social environments in a way that leads to better outcomes.

Outcomes or conditions of children—their health, educational performance, economic security, emotional, and behavioral status—are the true measures of how well we are succeeding in nurturing children. Environmental situations, whether they are toxic water supplies or toxic family relations, indicate risks for poor outcomes, but do not necessarily indicate that any particular child will lag in development. The environment should be monitored as a guide to directing resources, but should not be confounded with outcomes. The resources or policy interventions directed to children and their environments can reduce environmental risks and promote positive outcomes, but are not themselves outcomes. In far too many cases, resource allocations may be insufficient or ineffective at improving outcomes—unless we distinguish the two, we will not be able to keep refining policies and selecting the best interventions. Providing access to primary school is necessary, but not sufficient, to achieve the outcome of strong child learning. It must be accompanied by early learning opportunities and the creation of sufficiently safe and stimulating environments in which learning can occur.

The United Nations Children's Fund (UNICEF) review, *The State of The World's Children, 2000*, illustrates the problem. It contains a wide range of interesting measures, but does not distinguish among outcomes, environments, and access to resources or policy interventions. I have sorted the UNICEF indicators into categories to demonstrate the differences:

•*Demographic characteristics*: total population; annual births; growth; birth and death rates; fertility.

•*Outcomes or conditions of children and women*: mortality (infant, under five); life expectancy; adult literacy; low birth weight; malnourishment; female/male comparisons for life expectancy; literacy; maternal mortality rate.

•*Features of the environments (physical, social, and economic) in which they live*: GNP per capita; distribution of income; rate of breastfeeding; access to safe water; adequate sanitation; number of radio and television sets; GNP growth and inflation rates; population below one dollar per day.

•*Access to resources or policy interventions which support young children*: immunization rate; financing of vaccines by government; primary and secondary school enrollment and attendance rates; allocation of government expenditures to health, education, or defense; debt services; births attended by a health professional.

Several things are striking about this large set of indicators. First, few indicators speak to actual outcomes or conditions. Those that do focus on the most minimal aspects of survival. Second, there is little measurement of the social relationships affecting children: the rates of positive versus dangerous interactions within or among families, communities, tribes, regions, and nations. This lack may be due not to misunderstanding the importance of social relationships, but to the difficulty of measuring them in a consistent manner, and the failure of governmental bodies to invest in such measurement. Finally, because there has not been a clear conceptual linkage among outcomes, environment, and access to resources, the list of policies and resources used is too narrow to address the range of concerns about outcomes or conditions of children. For example, there are no environmental or policy resource indicators that would link to malnutrition. While poverty is a key environmental risk factor, there are no measures of investment in economic development, or allocation of resources to improving the lot of the poor. For a set of indicators to be effective policy tools, there must be a direct mapping of environmental conditions to the specific outcomes they affect, and of resources and policy interventions onto the environmental factors and outcomes they can improve.

I believe that to determine the level of progress toward meeting the needs of young children, measures should: (1) move beyond having children survive to having them thrive—not just avoiding early death, disease, and malnutrition, but growing strong, literate, and competent to deal with the world around them; (2) consider not just physical well-being, but also emotional and social well-being; (3) move from a momentary, cross-sectional look at well-being, to a dynamic construct, where it is expected that well-being will be improving over time, individually, and for the society; and (4) move beyond assigning a purely parental or family responsibility for children, to accepting societal responsibility, which implies reducing the disparity in levels of well-being among different socio-economic groups, and measuring civic commitment to the needs of children.

Moving Beyond Having Children Survive, to Having Them Thrive

International comparisons such as those in the UNICEF report mostly focus on surviving the vulnerable first years of life. Thus, UNICEF uses the under age five mortality rate as its primary indicator. The differences among groups of countries in table 1 show how important this is.[1] When we see how many children in the poorest countries are dying (about one in six) or barely surviving, it is understandable why there is a focus on such a minimal criterion. But compelling as it is to increase the survival rates, it is also necessary to consider what it would take to allow the 83 percent of children in the poorest countries who survive early childhood to thrive.

	1960	1998	Average Annual Percent Reduction, 1998-1960	Ratio, Least Developed/Developing to Industrialized[29]	
				1960	1998
Least Developed Countries	282	167	1.5	7.6	27.8
Developing Countries	216	95	2.5	5.8	15.8
Industrialized Countries	37	6	4.7		
United States		8			
World	193	86	2.4		

Table 1
Under-Five Mortality Rate[28]
[Number of children dying between birth and exactly five years of age, per 1,000 live births]

The data in table 1 suggests several conclusions. First, that there has been tremendous progress in the survival of young children, with the mortality rate dropping by more than half in the last forty years. Second, that there continues to be vast discrepancies. In the least developed countries, there has been the lowest percent reduction and the rate remains alarmingly high, with one in six babies born dying by age five. The industrialized countries have enjoyed the greatest percent decrease, even starting from the lowest base level. In industrialized countries, the under-five mortality rate has been dropping at three times the annual rate of reduction in the least developed countries, and the ratio between the poorest and richest countries has grown by a factor of almost four over the last forty years, from 7.6 in 1960 to 27.8 in 1998.[2] By a narrow definition focused on levels, there has been progress, since in all groups of nations the under-five mortality rate is declining. But by a definition which includes the reduction of disparities, progress has been negative.

Table 2 shows that while the industrialized countries consider the effects of malnutrition too rare to measure, malnutrition remains a major issue for poorer countries. There, from one-third to one-half of all young children are underweight or stunted, and one-eighth are severely underweight, or evidencing moderate to severe wasting.

Is it reasonable to consider more ambitious "thriving" policies for children in countries where survival remains an issue? Examining the disparities in other measures suggests that it is. In the least developed countries, only two-thirds (68 percent) of children are enrolled in primary school, compared to nearly 100 percent in the industrialized and developing nations.[3]

	Percent children 0-5 suffering from ... (most recent year, 1990-98)			
	Underweight moderate, severe	**Underweight, severe**	**Wasting, moderate, severe**	**Stunting, moderate, severe**
Least Developed Countries	40	13	12	47
Developing Countries	31	12	11	39
Industrialized Countries	n/a	n/a	n/a	n/a
World	30	11	11	37

Table 2
***Malnutrition of Young Children*[30]**

Does it make sense to focus on pre-school activities before making primary school available to all children? Affluent nations provide many of their children enriched learning environments at ages zero to six, which give them a better chance of success in school and adult years. It is now widely recognized that children learn from birth, and that the "pre-school" years constitute a vital first step in a continuous process of learning and development.[4] When that is recognized, education policies and measures should begin with early learning, and less developed countries should be promoting pre-school and primary school access in tandem. If we consider only survival strategies for children in the poorest countries, then as individuals and societies they will have an educational disadvantage that compounds their health disadvantages. Thus, adopting a proper definition of well-being, as the outcome of "learning" rather than as the resource of "being in school," can lead to a more effective set of policies.

Consider Not Just Physical Well-being, but Also Emotional and Social Well-being

Ten years ago, I offered the following definition:[5]

> Child/family well-being is the situation where:
> First, every child and family in a community [national, state, local] has adequate physical health; safety in the home, school, streets, and workplace; satisfactory emotional status and happiness; adequate educational capacity; adequate occupational capacity; a satisfactory economic standard of living; a community of

> residence able to nurture the ability of families and individuals to obtain the above goals. Second, there is an ability to sustain these attributes of well-being over time, to resist pressures which threaten well-being, and to seek and utilize assistance when any dimension of well-being becomes unsatisfactory. Third, that the general public is knowledgeable and aware of the potential for improvement in various dimensions of well-being, and adopts such improvement as a societal goal. Communities should foster the capacity of individuals and families to achieve their highest potential levels of function, rather than promoting satisfaction with minimum levels. Finally, that population sub-groups with lower [and inadequate] levels of well-being are improving relative to the better-off sub-groups.

Summarizing the deliberations of a recent international work group, Andrews and Ben Arieh (1999) suggested a definition which includes dimensions of social connectedness, civic life skills, personal life skills, safety and physical status, and children's subculture.[6] This improves earlier definitions by combining the individual attributes of children with their relationships to family, community, and culture.

It should be noted that as we move to this kind of richer, multi-dimensional definition of well-being, measurement problems become more difficult. Measuring whether a child is thriving requires asking what degree of physical health or educational attainment is "adequate," what type of emotional state or economic standard of living is "satisfactory" at the particular time. Moreover, the answers to these questions cannot be answered uniformly and independent of local conditions. Measuring "social connectedness" in any one culture is a challenging enterprise, requiring observations of a wide range of behavior spread over time and geography, involving many individuals whose relationships cannot necessarily be pre-determined and specified. Measuring these interactions comparably across cultures, within and among nations, is a daunting task. How would one calibrate the forms of address, discipline, and encouragement used between neighborhood adults and children in Japan, Somalia, Italy, and Sweden? The more such measures are customized to reflect a single culture, the more complex the measurement task, and the more difficult to compare measures across societies. Yet the normal simplifications—measuring the family structure, the number of parents, or other adults a child lives with—miss the real nature of the interactions which will have greatest influence on a child's well-being.

Move from a Momentary, Cross-sectional Look at Well-being to a Dynamic Construct

Child well-being is not a static, momentary event. Rather, child development is a process that unfolds over time and affects children in a cumulative fashion.[7] We must consider a child's ability to withstand external stresses and changes, and maintain or improve their well-being. While the dire conditions of the poorest, sickest, and starving children are appalling, merely eliminating them does not assure progress to well-being in a changing world. Rather, children, families, and communities must have the resources to steadily improve their well-being, and to withstand periodic threats caused by economic cycles, famines, epidemics, wars, and other disruptions.

For example, adequate immunization improves the ability to avoid certain major diseases, but it would take some measure of nutritional reserves and strength of the immune system to indicate how well a child would maintain health as circumstances evolve. Similarly, to measure economic thriving, we should measure whether parents have the job skills, contacts, and transportation necessary to maintain employment at decent wages as economies change, locally and globally, not just how many children live in poverty.

There are both individual and communal aspects to dynamic progress. At the communal level, we must ask whether child well-being serves as an active goal, with policies always seeking improvements for the population at large and reductions in disparities. This is particularly important when measuring well-being in industrialized societies, where survival is rarely an issue. Here, poverty has both absolute and relative aspects. There are absolute levels of economic resources required to provide food, shelter, housing, transportation, and health care needs. However, if certain children or families are continually living at a minimum survival level, while others are experiencing growing affluence and the educational and occupational advantages that affluence can buy, then the relative well-being of those at the minimum survival level is declining. Thus, a communal, dynamic concept of progress requires that the community endorse and implement policies that reduce discrepancies in child well-being over time.

Moving Beyond Parental or Family Responsibility for Children to Societal Responsibility

A major feature of progress, I believe, is considering children as valued individuals with their own rights to well-being, and recognition that the entire community and society have a stake in the well-being of children. This latter recognition is critical in the United States, where our political culture of limited powers of government require a demonstration that there is a "market failure" before government is expected to intervene. It is presumed that parents will care for their children unless it can be shown that they consistently fail to meet their needs, and that there are structural features in the economy that inhibit them from doing so.

The United States has accepted societal responsibility in some areas, notably public education and protection from abuse or neglect. We know that most families cannot afford to provide for their children's education personally or by paying privately for schooling. We believe that there is a community value to a well-educated citizenry and levy taxes on the entire community, not just parents, to pay for elementary and secondary public education. We do the same with higher education, but only provide access for about half the population. We know that some parents will abuse or neglect their children, and recognize the need for public agencies to intervene and protect children from parental maltreatment, and pay for prevention, foster care, and prosecution. Over the last forty years, we have recognized that not every family can afford to purchase health insurance, nor will every employer provide this as a benefit to employees. We have gradually increased public financing of health care, from covering only the poorest to assisting moderate income households.

In the area of Early Care and Education (ECE), the United States is only beginning to think in terms of community value and responsibility. Federal welfare policy has shifted in the last decade, requiring low income mothers of young children to work outside the home, but has not yet come to grips with the societal responsibility toward young children implicit in that requirement.

The Status of Early Care and Education Policy in the United States[8]

The system of paid ECE that has evolved in the United States embodies a perverse equation: care costs too little to achieve high quality, but it costs too much to be affordable for many parents. The average cost of full time care for one child is almost twenty percent of average take home pay.[9] Yet the seven to eight dollar per hour average pay of early childhood teachers is too low to attract or retain college graduates or individuals with special training.[10] Most other big ticket necessities that families cannot reasonably afford to pay (housing, medical bills, college tuition) have a mechanism to spread cost or risk over a long period of time (such as social security, a home mortgage, college loan) or over a broad population (K-12 education paid for by the entire community, a health insurance beneficiary pool). Table 3 below shows that the public financial commitment to early education is less than one twentieth the size of that made to elementary and secondary education, where societal responsibility is well accepted. On a per population basis, it is less than one tenth.

	ECE (FY1999)		Elementary/Secondary Public Education (FY1997-98)	
	$ Billions	**% GDP**	**$ Billions**	**% GDP**
Federal	11	0.11	22	0.25
State and Local	4	0.04	303	3.45
National	15	0.16	325	3.71

Table 3
U.S Public Spending for Education,
Early (Age 0-5) and Elementary/Secondary (age 6-18)[31]

Two-thirds of American children under the age of six now have no non-employed parent.[11] Thus, a significant portion of early nurturing is provided by other adults. We know that the quality of early nurturing has significant impacts on children's physical, emotional, cognitive, and social development.[12] But there is concern that the quality of much non-parental care is too low to achieve optimum child development.[13] We also know that low income children cared for in high quality ECE arrangements achieve higher levels of development than those in low quality arrangements, either in or out of their homes.[14] Many reasons have been cited for this low quality, including poor training and compensation of teachers, inadequate regulatory controls, and lack of public and parental understanding of or ability to afford quality care. We must therefore consider the entire ECE system, including all the elements that produce high quality care with an emphasis on providing sufficient financing to address the many facets of quality improvement, while achieving affordability for all families who desire care.[15]

In recent years, the policy debate about financial support for child care has been focused on its role in facilitating low income mothers' labor force participation.[16] This has led to a substantial increase in federal and state funding for subsidies to low income parents. However, it has also resulted in many states buying the greatest quantity of care for the lowest cost. Paying little attention to the quality of care reflects a tendency in U.S. social welfare policy in which benefits designated for the poor are given at minimum levels without regard to adequacy.[17] Wolfe elegantly lays out the economic arguments for treating ECE as a merit good,[18] while Heckman argues that there is a greater societal rate of return from investing in ECE than in higher education.[19]

Public Policy Conflicts Among Different Aspects of Child-Family Well-being

Blau argues that there is an inherent trade off between child care subsidy policies that improve work incentives for parents and those that provide developmental nurturing for children.[20] The large scale entrance of mothers of young children into the paid work force in the United States has been caused by a combination of expanding work opportunities for women, more reliable family planning methods, the necessity of having two working adults to maintain a desired living standard, and a recent policy of requiring low income mothers to work outside the home. The share of U.S. mothers with young children working increased from 19 percent in 1960 to 57 percent in 1987.[21] While industrialized nations in Europe have moved faster and farther in opening social and economic opportunities for women, they have also recognized the value of parents staying home to care for infants, and have instituted a variety of paid family leave policies available to either parent. As noted by Ruhm and Teague, this was a two-step process.[22] Following World War II, European nations used maternal leave requirements—often mandatory—to return mothers to the home and remove them from the workforce. In a second wave, paid leave has been accompanied by job security and antidiscrimination provisions assuring the long-term labor force participation of mothers.

Ironically, failure to provide for paid family leave in the United States, while requiring low income mothers to work, has exacerbated the need for paid early care and education. A somewhat higher percentage of affluent mothers stay home to care for their young children, and a higher percent of low income mothers put their children in care. However, the more affluent parents tend to use more stable, developmentally stimulating, and expensive care, while low income families tend to rely more on relatives and other informal care arrangements.[23] The arrangements used by more affluent parents have better educated teachers with training in child development, who provide more stimulating activities and use better equipment and materials.[24]

The United States is the only Western industrialized nation that does not provide publicly funded support to assure that young children have adequate nutrition, health care, and early care and education.[25] And within U.S. social policy, early childhood is the only stage in the life cycle for which we lack a major public entitlement program that encompasses the broad middle class. For children six to eighteen, we have public schools funded for all. For high school graduates, we have public assistance for higher education, ranging from publicly financed colleges and universities, to grant and subsidized loan programs which reach a large share of the population desiring higher education. For working age adults, we have unemployment insurance and tax subsidies for home ownership, pensions, and health insurance. For retirees, we have publicly financed income support (social security and tax-preferred private pension and savings plans) and health care (Medicare, Medicaid, and military) systems. Yet we expect parents of young children, who are usually at their earliest years in the labor force and therefore lowest earnings levels, to bear the full responsibility of early care and education. The resulting poor conditions of care and economic stresses on families are a serious impediment to making progress in the well-being of children in the United States.

Lessons from Other Social Benefits

The structure of social benefits affects the quality of services provided. As part of exploring universal financing for ECE, I examined various near-universal U.S. social benefit programs to consider what lessons might be applied to ECE financing.[26]

The U.S. social benefits that maintain public support for quality services are those assisting middle income and affluent individuals, not just the poor.[27] Examples include retirement benefits (Social Security, Medicare, IRAs, and 401(k)s; highways; K-12 and higher education financing; and home ownership subsidies (tax deductibility of mortgages and federally charted corporations assuring mortgage funds). This suggests that if early care and education in the United States is to be transformed to meet children's developmental needs it must be financed not solely as assistance to low income families, but as a near universal social benefit in which middle income and affluent households have a stake.

There were several other elements common to these programs which could be considered in the design of a universal financing system for ECE, including

A mixture of public and private revenue sources and incentives. Both mandatory public revenue and expenditure components, to which every individual or corporation must contribute, and voluntary benefits provided by private entities, such as employers, with tax incentives that encourage participation by employers and employees.

A complex system of multiple financing mechanisms available to different individuals or households with benefits often related to income. These include tax preferences for individuals or corporations, tax preferred savings accounts, grants or vouchers, subsidized or market rate loans, secondary market credit mechanisms, and subsidies to providers of services.

A segmentation of covered populations or types of service. Varying levels of coverage or benefits are experienced by different income, age, or other population groups, leaving few benefits truly universal and allowing inequalities among income groups to continue. Universality in the United States is usually achieved in increments, rather than in a single, equitable measure.

Including the costs of paying for infrastructure (training, facilities, quality assurance, research, and development) in beneficiary payments, making them less visible and less vulnerable to budget cuts.

A mixture of service providers. Public, private non-profit, and private for-profit entities receive revenues from different sources and make differing services available to individuals. Attaching financial assistance to the individual or household, rather than to a specific provider, enhances consumer choice. The American predilection for parental choice in education and in the nurturing of young children makes progress toward universality more likely to come from providing financial access to a diverse set of providers than from instituting a single state or national service system.

A major public agency responsible for administering some or all benefits and revenues, and for tracking who is/not served. It serves as a locus of information gathering and dissemination, analysis and advocacy for the services or benefits provided. There are counterpart federal, state, and local agencies.

Spreading risk beyond individual families in many ways. Risk is spread over a geographic community, defined by state or local jurisdiction, for elementary/secondary and higher education. Costs are spread over time for retirement savings and home mortgages and over defined groups of current and potential users in health insurance and transportation approaches.

Conclusion: Investing Early in Progress

Continuing progress will require devoting substantially increased resources to the care of young children. As poor nations develop economically, they are likely to find a greater share of parents and relatives working. At that point, the quality of paid care for young children, and the balance between parental leave and child care policies are likely to become important issues. We must also consider international equity issues regarding early education. Economically advanced nations are making a concerted effort to maximize the early cognitive, social, and emotional development of their children, giving them a step up on the ladder to educational and economic success. If poorer nations allocate resources only to providing access to elementary school, then children in the poorest nations will enter school with an extra disadvantage.

In the United States, physical survival is assured for virtually all young children. However, the poor quality of non-parental care on which the majority of our young children depend inhibits the likelihood that they will achieve the many aspects of well-being set forth. The dimensions of a reasonable set of public policy solutions are starting to emerge. Minimizing cost while setting compensation scales to attract and retain trained, competent ECE teachers and while reaching a variety of vulnerable populations implies that we are likely to require a complex system that combines revenues from multiple sources and targets different benefits to different groups. As we consider the specific features of such a universal financing system, we will encounter major trade-offs between coverage and cost, and between cost and quality. The best balance of policies is also likely to change over time, as we hopefully progress from a fragmented, under-funded system to a more mature, well-funded system. Whether our local, state, and national communities are willing to invest the funding indicated by these analyses will be a measure of how far we have progressed in our understanding that early childhood is the first step in progress to the future. Appropriate measures of child well-being will be required to hold us accountable by measuring whether this progress is achieved.

Notes

1. For this section, I am not considering the full range of child survival indicators, which would include environmental health and safety, security from violence, and adequate supervision.

2. Some of this may be due to high rates of HIV/AIDS in sub-Saharan Africa and South Asia, highlighting the disparity in both treatment drugs and resources allocated to prevention.

3. UNICEF, *The State of the World's Children 2002* (New York: United Nations, 2000).

4. J. P. Shonkoff and D. A. Phillips, *From Neurons to Neighborhoods: The Science of*

Early Child Development (Washington, D.C.: National Academy Press, 2000).

5. R. Brandon, "Social Accountability: A Conceptual Framework for Measuring Child/Family Well-being," working paper (Seattle, Wash.: Human Services Policy Center, 1992).

6. I have rephrased their statements for brevity and consistency with statements as measurable outcomes. See A. B. Andrews and A. Ben-Arieh, "Measuring and Monitoring Children's Well-being across the World" *Social Work* 44, no. 2 (1999): 105-15.

7. J. Shonkoff, D. A. Phillips and B. Keilty, *Early Childhood Intervention: Views From the Field*, report of a workshop (Washington D.C.: National Academy Press, 2000).

8. This section draws on materials from: R. N. Brandon, S. L. Kagan, and J. M. Joesch, "Design Choices: Universal Financing for Early Care and Education," HSPC Policy Brief prepared as part of the Financing Universal Early Care and Education For America's Children Project, University of Washington, Seattle, 2000.

9. R. Brandon and D. Smith, *Access to Quality Early Childhood Care and Education* (Seattle, Wash.: Human Services Policy Center, 1996).

10. U.S. Bureau of Labor Statistics, "1998 National Occupational Employment and Wage Estimates," *U.S. Department of Labor* 1999, at www.bls.gov/oes/1998/oesnat98.htm (accessed Oct. 2001).

11. Annie E. Casey Foundation, *Kids Count Data Book* (Baltimore: Annie E. Casey Foundation, 2000).

12. D. Vandell and B. Wolfe, *Child Care Quality: Does It Matter and Does It Need to be Improved?* prepared for the U.S. Department of Health and Human Services, Office of the Assistant Secretary for Planning and Evaluation, Washington D.C., May 2002; Shonkoff, Phillips and Keilty, *Early Childhood Intervention*; C. D. Hayes, J. L. Palmer, and M. J. Zaslow, ed., *Who Cares for America's Children?* (Washington, D.C.: National Academy Press, National Research Council, 1990); National Institute of Child Health and Human Development (NICHD) Early Child Care Research Network, "Child Care and Mother-Child Interaction in the First 3 Years of Life," *Developmental Psychology* 35, no. 6 (1999): 1399-1443; C. T. Ramey, et al., "Early Learning Later Success: The Carolina Abecedarian Project," (Chapel Hill, N.C.: Frank Porter Graham Child Development Center, 1999).

13. Vandell and Wolfe, *Child Care Quality*; D. Gomby, et al., "Long-Term Outcomes of Early Childhood Programs: Analysis and Recommendations," *The Future of Children* 5, no. 3 (Winter 1995): 6-24; Cost, Quality, and Outcomes Team, *Cost, Quality, and Child Outcomes in Child Care Centers,* executive summary (Denver, Colo.: 1995).

14. NICHD, "Child Care."

15. S. L. Kagan and N. E. Cohen, *Not By Chance: Creating an Early Care and Education System for America's Children* (New Haven, Conn.: Yale University, The Bush Center in Child Development and Social Policy, 1997).

16. R. Brandon, "Public Attitudes About Early Care and Education," in *Effective Language for Discussing Early Childhood Education and Policy* (Washington, D.C.: Benton Foundation and University of Washington Human Services Policy Center, 1998): 20-30.

17. D. T. Ellwood, *Poor Support: Poverty in the American Family* (New York: Basic Books, 1988).

18. Vandell and Wolfe, *Childcare Quality.*

19. J. J. Heckman and L. Lochner, "Rethinking Education and Training Policy: Understanding the Sources of Skill Formation in a Modern Economy," in *Securing the Future: Investing in Children from Birth to College*, ed. Sheldon Danziger and Jane Waldfogel (New York: Russell Sage Foundation, 2000).

20. D. M. Blau, *Child Care Subsidy Programs*, working paper 7806 (Cambridge, Mass.: National Bureau of Economic Research, 2000).

21. Arleen Leibowitz, Jacob Klerman, and Linda Waite, *Women's Employment During Pregnancy and Following Birth* (Washington D.C.: Bureau of Labor Statistics, 1992).

22. C. J. Ruhm and J. L. Teague, *Parental Leave Policies in Europe and North America*, working paper 5065 (Cambridge, Mass.: National Bureau of Economic Research, 1995).

23. E. Puhn Pungello and B. Kurtz-Costes, "Why and How Working Women Choose Child Care: A Review with a Focus on Infancy," *Developmental Review* 19, no. 1 (March 1999): 31-96.

24. S. Helburne, et al., *Cost, Quality and Child Outcomes in Child Care Centers*, Technical Report (Denver: University of Colorado at Denver, Dept of Economics, 1995).

25. S. B. Kamerman, "Child and Family Benefits in Eastern and Central Europe and in the West—Learning From the Transition," *Environmental Planning* C 11, no. 2 (1993): 199-211.

26. I am co-directing a project that is developing a simulation model to estimate the costs and impacts of alternative approaches to broad-scale financing of ECE in the United States.

27. H. Heclo, "The Political Foundations of Antipoverty Policy," in *Fighting Poverty: What Works and What Doesn't*, ed. Sheldon H. Danziger and Daniel H. Weinberg (Cambridge, Mass.: Harvard University Press, 1986).

28. UNICEF, *The State of the World's Children 2002* (New York: United Nations, 2000).

29. Author's calculation from UNICEF data; annual reduction rates calculated by UNICEF.

30. UNICEF, *The State*.

31. Author's calculations. Data for ECE from Blau, *Child Care*; data for K-12 from National Center for Educational Statistics, "Statistics in Brief: Revenues for Public Elementary and Secondary Education: School Year 1997-98," NCES 2000-348 (Washington, D.C.: NCES, 2000); GDP data from Council of Economic Advisors, *Economic Report of the President, 2000* (Washington D.C.: U.S. Government Printing Office, 2000).

Chapter 10

Progress and Education: Supporting the Realization of Human Aspirations

William Zumeta

Our progress as a nation can be no swifter than our progress in education.

John F. Kennedy[1]

Clearly, education has an important place in a volume devoted to thinking about human progress. Indeed it is hard to conceive of such progress independent of education. Economists tell us that education, more than ever before, is the key to economic and technological progress[2] which many would argue underlies other forms of progress. Conversely, progress also seems to lead to greater emphasis on learning—witness the great civilizations of the ancients: China, Egypt, Greece, Persia. In modern times, we also find that states and individuals tend to invest more in education as their wealth grows.[3] This is not surprising for wealth makes little sense as an end in itself. Civilization is usually defined in substantial measure in terms of appreciation and cultivation of the finer things that are strongly linked to an educated populace: art, music, and literature, as well as technological prowess and advanced material comforts. These represent forms of achievement of the unique potential of the human species. Substantial attention to artistic and cultural pursuits by a society implies enough wealth (economic capacity) to afford to devote human and other resources to the production and consumption of cultural objects and activities. Similarly, technological progress requires sufficient economic surplus beyond immediate consumption needs to invest in innovative efforts. This leads back to the role of economics and thus to education's investment role in helping produce a societal surplus for investment in these ends. In short, progress and education are inextricably linked.[4]

In this chapter I will attempt to illuminate some of the reasons why education is so crucial to human and societal progress today and will consider significant measurement issues (and cite trends in some key measures), focusing on some of the difficulties and limitations associated with the prevailing conceptualizations embodied in widely-used measures of progress in education. I will also seek to explain and illustrate how certain pathologies may develop and sustain themselves in educational systems in the name of progress. I will then turn to the examination of the conditions necessary for sustaining progress in education. The chapter concludes with a brief summation of its key points.

Progress and Education

In *Social Process and Human Progress*, Clarence Case suggests that progress means "change for the better... in the common or collective life ... or, most briefly and exactly, social betterment."[5] I would broaden this definition somewhat, following Kenneth Boulding (1985), to say "human betterment" so as to encompass not only gains in the collective and material life but also in the realms of the self, ideas, and the natural world.[6] This broad conception of progress connects to the idea in policy studies that the goal of collective action, or public policy, is to help a society achieve or improve according to some standard of performance, either by remedying felt problems or taking advantage of opportunities.[7]

A major area of policy involvement for governments everywhere is education. This is because education has important elements of what economists call a "public good," that is, some of its benefits accrue to society as a whole rather than strictly to the individuals participating. Such a circumstance would lead to underinvestment in education from a societal point of view—because individuals would be unmotivated to invest beyond the level justified by expected benefits to themselves—unless public policy and finance were to take on some part of the burden. Among the most important of the "social spillover" benefits of a more educated populace that justify public investment are improved labor force capacity to innovate and adapt to change, including the adaptations necessary for technological change and economic growth; gains in tolerance or acceptance of others different from oneself; creation of larger markets for artistic and cultural productions; and improved capacity to understand complex systems and relationships such as those between human societies and the natural world.[8] Each of these types of effects relates to the prospects for human progress in the realms delineated in this volume's framework for conceptualizing progress. These types of social benefits, together with the crucial importance of education for individuals'—and groups'—chances for full participation in the modern economy and society and full appreciation of life,[9] justify the key role that public policies play in education throughout the world. Indeed, education and progress are so inextricably connected that important dimensions of progress in education, and thus by extension human progress, can be usefully measured by conceptually simple devices such as educational participation and diploma completion rates.

It should be mentioned here that the social spillover character of education does not mean that public policies chosen for it will necessarily be effective or efficient in pursuing the sought-after benefits. Policies may purchase too much of one type of education and too little of another (by education level or field), or they may pursue learning inefficiently (e.g., too many buildings but not enough for maintenance, materials or trained teachers; reluctance to take advantage of new, potentially more efficient technologies). Policies may also simply be unfair: they may provide more or more valuable educational opportunities to some groups than to others. Another problem is that social spillovers from education in terms of building national values and coherence may be exploited to the point of what many value systems would call abuse, where education becomes largely a tool of political or ideological indoctrination, sometimes for nefarious ends.

Finally, it is important to note that, although public sector (governmental or quasi-governmental) operation of schools, training institutions, colleges, and universities is the norm, the above points regarding the need for public policies about education and its funding do not imply that educational institutions must be run by the state. Many, probably most, countries have some form of privately-operated schools alongside the usually larger public school system,[10] and a smaller but growing number have substantial private postsecondary, or "tertiary," sectors.[11] At the tertiary level, the private sector may serve as the main expansion valve in periods where social demand is growing rapidly but the state cannot or will not respond with commensurate expansion of the public sector.[12] The public purposes of such private sectors may be officially recognized in the form of state subsidies.[13]

Measurement of Progress in Education

For reasons suggested, simple measures of forward movement in education, such as participation and diploma/degree completion rates by age, have considerable value. Diploma/degree, or simply schooling level, completion measures are usually categorized by primary or secondary completion, sometimes further subdivided by lower and upper secondary school. At the tertiary level, diplomas may be categorized as vocational/technical, baccalaureate, graduate or master's level, and doctoral level. Enrollment as a proportion of the relevant age group is important as an indicator of opportunities available but diploma or degree completion should in theory be more meaningful because it signifies a discrete level of accomplishment that is usually widely recognized by the economy and society (notably in the labor market). In practice, due to differences in diploma standards and meaning, especially in the developing world, most large-scale, cross-national comparisons emphasize enrollment-to-population ratios, by schooling level.[14] Gross enrollment-to-school-age population ratios are sometimes adjusted for estimates of grade-repeaters and dropouts to produce net enrollment ratios, but these are rough estimates at best. Gross enrollment and school-age population figures are subject to incomplete census data and other anomalies (such as gross enrollment ratios greater than 100 percent) in many countries.[15]

Regarding trends over time in these indicators, according to the World Bank:

> Developing countries have made enormous progress in expanding access to schooling, enrolling more children than ever before. Between 1960 and 1992 the share of 6- to 11-year-olds enrolled rose from less than half to 77 percent, although recently the rate of growth has slowed considerably. In the same period the share of 12- to 17-year-olds in school more than doubled (from 21 percent to 47 percent), and for 18- to 23-year-olds it more than tripled.[16]

Over the more recent period from 1980 to 1996, *World Development Indicators*[17] shows substantial gains in gross enrollment ratios (net enrollment ratio data were not widely available for 1980) in all world regions except Sub-Saharan Africa for the primary education ratio and Europe and Central Asia for the secondary ratio.[18] Covering a still more recent period, the United Nations Development Program's (UNDP) 1999 *Human Development Report* indicates a gain over 1990 to 1997 in the aggregate gross primary/secondary enrollment ratio from 74 percent to 81 percent.[19] Although some individual countries lag, these gains are interpreted by both sources as representing notable progress.[20]

A key measure of educational progress is the basic literacy rate of the population since literacy is a crucial threshold for being able to use one's education or effectively pursue more education or training. Ideally this is a competency-based measure but, in fact, it is often simply inferred from completion of a school grade level that should imply literacy. *World Development Indicators* focuses attention on the fraction of the age cohort reaching grade five as a fair indicator of students' acquisition of the "basic literacy and numeracy skills that would enable them to continue learning."[21] Although most countries with data available for 1980 and 1996 show gains in this indirect literacy indicator over the period, the fact remains that in developing countries "only two-thirds of the children who start primary school are still there five years later."[22] The evidence suggests that low quality and unattractive (unsafe, unsanitary, etc.) schools play a substantial role in discouraging both students and parents from sustaining the costs—including costs of time away from household or market labor—of attendance.[23] Poor connections between traditional cultural values and local needs and the emphases of schools also play a deterrent role in some instances.[24]

Adult literacy rates are also pertinent. To compute national rates of adult literacy, the UNDP *Human Development Report (HDR)* (and its accompanying Human Development Index) utilizes a definition based on "the percentage of people aged 15 and above who can, with understanding, both read and write a short simple statement on their everyday life."[25] Still, in practice, adult literacy is often estimated from self-reports and years of schooling completed.[26] Using its definition, *HDR* reports that the aggregate adult literacy rate rose from 64 percent to 76 percent from 1990 to 1997,[27] a very considerable pace of increase. The World Bank, following the lead of United Nations Educational, Scientific and Cultural Organization (UNESCO), focuses on a narrower age range, fifteen to twenty-four, that is thought to "better capture the ability of recent participants in the formal education system."[28] From this, it derives a youth *il*literacy rate. Over the years 1980 to 1997, this rate is estimated to have fallen (i.e., improved) by about one-third worldwide. Even the lowest income group of countries saw gains of a similar magnitude, although the overall youth illiteracy rate remained at an estimated 23 percent for males and 41 percent for females in 1997.[29]

Increasingly, these participation and attainment measures are also examined by gender, ethnicity, geographic area within nations, and student socioeconomic origin. Such comparisons are useful for they provide an indication of equity in the social allocation of educational opportunities. Regions that are historically more developed or politically favored typically show higher education rates than less favored areas. More generally, rural regions tend to have lower educational participation and attainment rates than urban regions,[30] but broad regional aggregates may mask significant differences disfavoring the urban core of major cities in both developed and developing countries. One factor working against rural areas, of course, is the simple economic logic of locating major educational institutions at the upper secondary and tertiary levels where the most people are close by. But political factors, including ethnic and class biases, play an important role in location decisions that in turn affect participation.[31] They also play a prominent role in decisions regarding provision of the additional resources that are usually needed to aid students from disadvantaged backgrounds in moving toward equality in educational attainment, as distinct from simply participation.

Gender differences in educational participation and attainment has been of increased interest and policy attention in recent years. In many countries, girls and women still show substantially lower participation and attainment rates than boys and men.[32] These differences of course are born of deep-seated and widespread cultural notions about the role of women in the home as opposed to the labor market and leadership positions in society. Yet, studies in recent years have provided solid evidence that investments in the education of girls and women pay large returns in reduced infant mortality and better general family nutrition and health, improved child-rearing practices including the education of children, and utilization of more environmentally sustainable farming practices, in addition to adding to their society's reservoir of "human capital" for the economy.[33]

These "hard" benefits are in addition to what many would argue is a clear moral imperative simply to provide equitable treatment for each sex. Policies of many donor nations and international development agencies now reflect a recognition that investment in equalizing the educational opportunities and attainments of females serves many critical social goals. Some of the influence of this thinking dates from the 1990 World Conference on Education For All, held in Jomtien, Thailand. This conference led both to more intensive research on the issue and to a commitment to pursue gender equality in primary and secondary enrollments that has been enshrined in subsequent international organization policy statements and programs.[34] For example, the United Nations Development Program's Human Development Indicators project, initiated in 1990, now includes a Gender Development Index and a Gender Empowerment Measure, designed to shed light on and measure progress in gender inequalities in education and other areas.[35]

Trend data show some signs of progress on this front. The proportion of girls enrolled in school has increased in the majority of countries in recent years. "Girls' enrollments have caught up with boys' in most high income, Latin American and Caribbean, and Eastern European countries. But they lag behind in South Asia and the Middle East" [and Sub-Saharan Africa], and the regional aggregates mask some large disparities across countries.[36] Girls tend to drop out of school more than boys. Thus an average six-year-old girl in a low or middle income country can, based on current attendance rates, expect to attend school for just 7.7 years or about 1.5 years less than her male counterpart.[37] The largest gender gap persists in South Asia while the gap is closing in the other regions. Still, there remains a long way to go in a number of countries where girls simply are not culturally valued as highly as boys for complex and deeply-rooted reasons. These basic cultural biases, which exist to some extent in all cultures, work to tug girls away from advanced schooling and to blunt policy efforts to eliminate gender gaps.[38]

Another useful measure of progress is public (as well as total social) expenditure on education and trends in this. Although expenditures represent "inputs" of resources and policy makers today are increasingly concerned about "outputs" and "outcomes" from the application of resources, it is nevertheless useful to measure the level of effort nations are making in absolute terms and relative to national product. While growing expenditures are not a sufficient condition for better results in education—i.e., greater participation and achievement and attainment levels—progress is unlikely in the face of stagnant or declining spending.

Overall, recent trends are somewhat encouraging. Between 1980 and 1996, *World Development Indicators* reports that the median share of GNP devoted to education worldwide increased from 4.0 percent to 4.8 percent, with gains in this value occurring in most of the world's regions.[39] [40] Low and middle income countries as a group showed a gain in the education share of GNP from 3.5 percent to 4.3 percent. (Data on low income countries alone were not reported for 1996.)

Still, primary pupil-teacher ratios varied widely, from fifty-six to one in low income countries to eighteen to one in the wealthiest group. The education level of these teachers varies greatly as well and in a similar direction.

Difficulties and Limitations of the Standard Measures of Educational Progress

In addition to important inequities that can be hidden by aggregate measures, the measurement of progress in education is beset by a number of conceptual and practical difficulties. Most basic perhaps is difficulty in identifying the appropriate units of education to measure. The meaning of a year of formal schooling can vary widely even across developed countries,[41] much less in less-developed countries with sometimes rudimentary education systems in some areas and poor recordkeeping. Simply counting reported years of schooling to which students have been exposed seems seriously inadequate and a poor basis for benchmarking progress. Of course, finding better measures that are practical to collect is more easily said than done.

Ideally, one would like to see standard measures of quality in education that could be applied across countries and consistently over time. Measures such as teacher-to-student ratios, qualifications of teachers, quality of facilities, and total expenditures per student are of some use when the data are comparable, but are strictly input-based. As is increasingly recognized, they fail to provide a dependable link to educational results (outcomes), although gross differences in some of them have been shown to be related to outcomes.[42] Many analysts now argue that dropout or completion rates are a useful proxy for quality as other quality indicators seem to be strongly related to students' persistence in school.[43] [44] Literacy rates imply an assessment of a key competency that is a legitimate educational outcome. To the extent these assessments are made accurately (and ideally not by merely assuming that *x* years of schooling implies literacy), literacy rates are an important step in the right direction in terms of measurement and increased rates imply significant educational progress for a nation or group. More generally, the movement toward competency testing in education and the labor market—which has been given a boost in recent years by the development of Internet-based courses—together with the trend toward globalization of labor markets suggests that in the fairly near term we will see an acceleration of movement toward comparable assessments of what an individual's educational exposure (from whatever source) has produced.

International testing regimes, such as the Third International Mathematics and Science Study (TIMSS),[45] can also provide some comparable basis for assessing the relative quality of schooling in different countries, but there are large problems and issues regarding the coverage of these tests, student sampling procedures, cultural bias issues in testing, comparability of questions in different languages, and comparability of student incentives to perform. Moreover, only a few dozen countries at most participate in the testing regimes. So, we are far from a foolproof international mechanism for comparing national systems in terms of quality of educational results. This presents a fundamental caveat in interpretation of the meaning of assessments of progress in education based on participation and years of schooling attained.

A broader limitation is that systems for reporting education participation and attainment are almost entirely limited to the formal schooling system. Yet, meaningful, useful education also occurs outside formal school settings, in training institutions outside the official educational system (some of which is counted though not always comparably), in on-the-job training which is sometimes very informal, and in education-related programs offered by cultural institutions, youth programs, religious organizations, and other "non-educational" entities. In less-developed societies, informal community-based activities can play an important educational role that might be facilitated by explicit policies if better understood.

Educational institutions and systems are supposed to produce more than educated people. Colleges and universities in particular produce research results that increase knowledge and eventually improve human welfare, technical assistance to the broader society on many kinds of problems, artistic and cultural contributions to community life, and, in some contexts, an important contribution to social capacity for self-reflection, criticism, and innovation.[46] Outside the realm of impacts on scientific knowledge and industrial products and the like, these contributions are not very well or comparably counted so progress is difficult to assess. This can cause problems for policy making for there is a tendency in that process to pay most attention to what can be reliably measured. But, although it is tempting, simply adding more students to institutions that are trying to balance all these functions optimally can have undesirable consequences for their non-teaching capacities, not to mention unfortunate implications for educational quality.[47]

An implicit assumption in the discussion to this point is that, when it comes to education, more is better. In short, subject to the caveats just covered, progress is effectively measured by higher levels of educational participation and attainment in a society. Even this generalization has its limitations. First, it is possible for the social spillover aspect of education in regard to socialization to be distorted so that it becomes a pathological politicization. Although of course one observer's pathological politicization may be another's notion of appropriate building of a cohesive national ethos, the possibility remains for the use of the schools for naked political indoctrination and the attempt to stamp out critical thinking on many matters. At its worst, the schools can be used as a kind of permanent campaign platform for the regime or ideology in power. By most lights, more of this form of "education" is rarely for the better.[48]

Another problem is the tendency of many educational systems to produce imbalances in their products resulting in persistent overinvestment in some parts of the system (often in universities and graduates in certain fields) simultaneous with endemic underinvestment in other fields and in primary and secondary education, especially to underserved groups. In a now classic work first published in 1975, British sociologist Ronald Dore made the case that "late-developing" societies were prone to what he called the "diploma disease."[49] Owing in large part to their European colonial roots, societies developing relatively late and in a more planned way seemed to emphasize excessively university and other upper levels of study in general subjects (European languages and literature, social sciences, theoretical studies in mathematics and science) at the expense of widespread primary education and practical and technologically-oriented subjects arguably more relevant to the needs of the country. Of course, there are fewer well-tried models of the latter types of studies to draw from and they tend to be more expensive. Also flowing generally from European colonial models, the late-developers' systems tended to select students for higher levels of education and ultimately for modern sector employment—usually dominated by public and quasi-public employment since commercial and industrial sectors were very small—on the basis of national examinations emphasizing memorization and "book learning" rather than critical reflection, application, and problem-solving.

Dore noted, based on several intensive case studies reported in the book[50] and observations from elsewhere, that over time as school and examination success were highly rewarded in the somewhat artificial labor markets, a powerful "social demand" for schooling tended to develop. This placed political pressures on governments to expand school capacity, although not in a direction very productive for development. As the numbers of graduates at any given education level grew, they outstripped the demand for workers by modern sector employers, leading to both credential inflation and "educated unemployment."[51] This situation represents a waste of resources, is likely to hurt quality, and even creates potential for political instability. In spite of the poor returns from education under Dore's scenario, social demand for it nonetheless seemed to grow. The emphasis on test-cramming increased as people sought desperately to ensure at least an opportunity for modern sector employment and its status and economic benefits for themselves or their children.[52] Of course, Dore lamented the misdirection of educational effort and human resources and the weak (or nil) contribution to development his scenario implied.

A recent volume commemorates and seeks to appraise Dore's thesis in light of developments in recent decades.[53] In short, although not all factors in development have worked out as Dore assumed they would and many countries have avoided the "diploma disease" fate, his insights about this particular pathology have proven profound and influential. As was suggested near the beginning of this chapter, investments in education by themselves do not guarantee any salutary outcome unless they are accompanied by complementary investments and policies, including efforts to stimulate exports or other sources of private sector growth.[54] Moreover, investments in quality of education are in many respects a necessary complement to those in increased capacity (quantity).[55] And, many studies have now shown that general investments in broad diffusion of primary education pay better dividends than those concentrated in expanding the upper reaches of the education system.[56] Dore's thesis is consistent with all of these findings.

Conditions Necessary for Progress in Education

Several conditions critical to progress in education can be identified. In the absence of these, progress is likely to be short-lived, stunted, or in one way or another unstable.

Social and Legal Commitment to and Framework for Education

This is the most basic commitment. Some societies may simply be more committed to education, or at least education for the modern world, than others.[57] Where a strong commitment exists, it is usually codified in constitutions, laws, and funding arrangements. For example, several U.S. state constitutions provide that education is, in the words of the Washington State constitution, the "paramount duty" of the state, and a few states specify funding formulas that seek to guarantee a sufficient level of funding for schools and even colleges.[58] Such arrangements may possibly ameliorate the worst of cyclical declines in funding, but how efficacious they are in ensuring more than minimal adequacy is open to question. Nonetheless, it is probably worthwhile to specify in law where responsibility for education lies within a nation's governmental structure and it cannot hurt to say that it is important. Further, the legal structure can usefully specify a commitment to academic freedom of educational institutions and their staffs, although the form of this will inevitably be subject to differing polities' norms.

Economic Wherewithal to Invest

If human progress is linked to educational investments, then clearly resources available to invest in education are a fundamental necessity. This is not much of a problem for prosperous nations as evidence shows that education expenditures tend to rise faster than GDP.[59] But low wealth nations are caught in the basic conundrum of development: lacking wealth, it is difficult to increase investments necessary to create future wealth. External donor aid can help here and so can efficiencies in the use of available resources. Indeed, donors can seek to leverage their support by insisting on the utilization of well-understood efficiency measures within a framework of flexible, performance-oriented management.[60] Such measures include restrictions on overbuilding, provision of adequate resources for maintenance of capital infrastructure and for supplies and materials, emphasis on adequate teacher training, and focus on broad diffusion of primary and literacy education (and girls' education) rather than on ostensibly more prestigious university programs.

Donors may also be able to aid in smoothing out the worst effects of economic cycles in developing nations which can devastate school budgets. Indeed, this latter problem is not limited to the developing world—economic downturns can seriously disrupt progress toward education goals in developed countries as well, putting at risk drives to improve academic achievement and equalize schooling resources available to different groups or locales. Hence, it is important that substantial gains be achieved during periods of prosperity when such goals are more economically and politically sustainable.

Commitment to Equity in Educational Opportunity

Some commitment to equity in the allocation of educational opportunities is essential by definition if progress is defined broadly as human betterment (not just betterment for elites) because education is so fundamental to individual and societal welfare and aspirations in today's world. But commitment to equity may also serve instrumental purposes related to progress. Recent research by Lopez, Thomas, and Wang (1998) shows that equity in the distribution of education was positively associated with per capita economic growth for a sample of "middle income" Asian and Latin American countries over 1970-1994. As already noted, measures to promote gender equity have demonstrably broad benefits for societies, both economically and socially. Substantial movement toward equity more generally may also help support social comity and a broader sense of stake in a nation's social, political, and economic system. This in turn can improve the climate for investment in education and other areas and thus fuel economic growth. Healthy growth potentially frees still more resources for investment and facilitates further efforts promoting equity. In this way, commitment to educational equity can be seen as linked to progress in several dimensions. Donor organizations can thus assist here by linking their aid to educational policies that promote equity.

Legitimate, Informed Processes for Allocating Educational Resources

If education is to receive sustained public support, a nation needs rational and broadly acceptable processes for the allocation of resources to and within the enterprise. Some reasonable balance must be struck among needs for allocations to be perceived as fair, responsive to both local and larger needs, and tolerably efficient and affordable. These desiderata imply a balance of political and professional inputs into decision making processes and also that the arrangements for all this will inevitably vary from country to country. For example, traditions in some countries support substantial public subsidies to private schools and colleges which many desire for themselves or their children, while other nations have no such history.[61] Nations also make very different decisions about local versus national control over academic standards and even curricula. These differences mean that approaches to interpreting and determining equity and efficiency in allocations will vary, but there is a universal need to pay attention to these core values if the public is to retain confidence in the educational system and be willing to make continuing investments in it. Effective national leadership can be crucial here in guiding perceptions about the fairness and rationality of decision making processes as well as the reality.

Accountability Mechanisms

Closely related to the previous point is the notion that educational systems and processes, like other major functions in modern public and private sectors, need to be transparently accountable. Traditional financial accountability is part of this (and not to be taken lightly in much of the world), but increasingly accountability now also relates more broadly to whether institutions are producing desired results with the resources they absorb.[62] Thus, governmental authorities—and also other stakeholders like parents and employers—want to see evidence that students are learning, completing their courses of study at reasonable rates and in good time, and finding appropriate places in the labor market.[63] There is considerable controversy over the specifics of accountability measures but little doubt that schools and colleges will be called to account more explicitly than in the past. International donors are among the leaders in this movement.[64] On the whole the accountability thrust should work to the advantage of education, both in better assuring that precious resources used—not least the years of youth—produce socially desired results, and in ensuring that crucial stakeholder support is sustained.

Scope for Innovation and Social Responsiveness

If education is to continue to serve human betterment, it needs to be responsive to a variety of needs in societies (e.g., it should be locally responsive) and also to be innovative in responding to new knowledge, social needs, and technological possibilities. While different societies will inevitably pursue these ends via different structural arrangements, it is noteworthy that interest has increased in more decentralized mechanisms for governing in many education systems, including growth in private sectors of education.[65] Decentralization can increase academic autonomy and at least the potential for innovation and rapid responsiveness. Even some of the most centralized of education systems, those of several of the former communist nations of eastern Europe, have recently developed private education sectors, particularly at the postsecondary level.[66]

In the United States, long known for its locally controlled school systems and weak central authority, two somewhat conflicting tendencies are at work. On the one hand, there are strong pressures to find ways to permit parents of elementary and secondary students to choose and influence the schools their children attend, via plans ranging from increased public school choice through public "charter" schools with substantial autonomy from the local school board[67] to voucher plans in which families can take the public subsidy provided for their children and select any (non-religious) school of their choosing.[68] At the same time, the federal government has sought to take a leadership role in increasing educational standards in schools and this has led to considerable resistance as being inconsistent with long-standing traditions of local control. The federal government has sought to work in partnership with states in this effort, but states too have met resistance from the local level. One of the weaknesses of a highly decentralized system is that it inevitably produces uneven performance, even variable standards, and has difficulty improving these in a consistent way.

At the tertiary level, U.S. higher education has been marked by both an unusual degree of state, and even local (*viz.*, community colleges), control and by an unusually diverse and vital private higher education sector.[69] This system is also uneven across states and localities but is, overall, widely praised for its broadly accessible and locally responsive community colleges, its many high-quality state universities, and its stunningly diverse private sector, crowned by the likes of Harvard, MIT, and Stanford, that are unmatched in academic stature in the world. These private colleges and universities receive critical government support indirectly in the form of tax preferences, student financial aid, and research grants. Significantly, the private institutions have provided models for public college and university governance, in particular the lay governing board, that have helped to ensure reasonable academic autonomy for these creatures of the state.[70] The American model of higher education has been widely envied elsewhere in the world and elements of it have been imitated or adapted. There is considerable interest today in particular in the decentralized elements of this model: locally-based community colleges and autonomous private institutions whose students receive government help but who must compete with each other and with public colleges to enroll them. These elements have potential for improving academic standards, efficiency, and responsiveness to local and other societal needs, as they have in the United States.[71]

Conclusion

This chapter has sought to conceptualize what progress in relation to education means and to explore issues in the measurement of progress and the policy framework necessary to support and sustain it. Education was held to be inextricably intertwined with progress defined as human betterment. Considerable gains over recent decades in education participation and attainment in much of the world were documented. While there is a long way to go in some regions and in areas such as quality and equality of access to educational opportunities, experience and systematic research have begun pointing the way toward more efficient and equitable practices and policies. Together with gains in the proportion of their wealth that nations have been willing to allocate to education and technological developments that can help conquer distance and cost problems, these trends give promise that education can continue to make its key contribution to the betterment of the human condition.

Notes

1. John F. Kennedy, "Special Message to the Congress on Education," February 20, 1961.

2. Ray Marshall and Marc Tucker, *Thinking For a Living: Education and the Wealth of Nations* (New York: Basic Books, 1992); Eric A. Hanushek, "Interpreting Recent Research on Schooling in Developing Countries," *The World Bank Research Observer* 10 no. 2 (August 1995): 227-254; Ramón López, Vinod Thomas and Yan Wang, "Addressing the Education Puzzle: The Distribution of Education and Economic Reform," *World Bank Series: Working Papers—Education, Child Labor, Returns to Schooling*, 1998, at www.worldbank.org/html/dec/Publications/Workpapers/wps2000series/wps2031/wps2031.pdf (accessed 21 Aug. 2000).

3. Elchanan Cohn and Terry G. Geske, *The Economics of Education,* 3rd edition (Oxford, U.K.: Pergamon Press, 1990).

4. This is not to say that investments in education *necessarily* produce economic or cultural gains. Comparative research has shown that education investments must be well-targeted and complemented by investments and policies in other areas to be efficacious, see López, Thomas, and Wang, *Addressing*. As will be made clear, there is no dearth of cases where apparent gains in the education of the populace have not been accompanied by gains in other development indices, see Ronald Dore, *The Diploma Disease: Education, Qualification and Development* (Berkeley, Calif.: The University of California Press, 1975); Ronald Dore, "The Argument of the Diploma Disease: A Summary," *Assessment in Education: Principles, Policy & Practice* 4, no. 1 (January 1997): 23-32; Shuanglin Lin, "Education and Economic Development: Evidence from China," *Comparative Economic Studies* 39, no. 3-4 (1998): 66-87; Toshio Toyoda, "Kenya 1975-1995: An Introductory Note on Educational Expansion," *Assessment in Education: Principles, Policy & Practice* 4, no. 1 (January 1997): 87–90; various sources cited in López, Thomas, and Wang, *Addressing*. It is hard to imagine much economic or cultural progress in the absence of advances in education however.

5. Clarence Case, *Social Process and Human Progress* (New York: Harcourt, 1931), 3.

6. Kenneth Boulding, *Human Betterment* (Beverly Hills, Calif.: Sage, 1985).

7. Eugene Bardach, *A Practical Guide for Policy Analysis: The Eightfold Path to More Effective Problem Solving* (New York: Chatham House/Seven Bridges Press, 2000);

David L. Weimer and Aidan R. Vining, *Policy Analysis: Concepts and Practice,* Third edition (Upper Saddle River, N.J.: Prentice-Hall, 1999).

8. On the social spillover benefits from education, see Cohn and Geske, *The Economics*, chapter 3. The list is long although not universally agreed upon, see Milton Friedman, *Capitalism and Freedom* (Chicago: University of Chicago Press, 1960).

9. On the robust, and evidently growing, relationship between education and individual earnings, see Kevin M. Murphy, W. Craig Riddell, and Paul M. Romer, "Wages, Skills, and Technology in the United States and Canada," in *General Purpose Technologies and Economic Growth*, ed. Elhanen Helpman (Cambridge, Mass.: MIT Press, 1998). Since education is so crucial to individual well-being, public policy has an important role in ensuring that access to it is fairly distributed.

10. Some nations employ more or less joint public-private arrangements for operating schools, often in cooperation with a dominant religious group, such as the Catholic Church in parts of Europe, Latin America, and Canada. See World Bank, *World Development Report 1997* for an example from Bolivia.

11. Daniel C. Levy, *Higher Education and the State in Latin America* (Chicago: University of Chicago Press, 1986); Burton Bollag, "Private Colleges Reshape Higher Education in Eastern Europe and Former Soviet States," *The Chronicle of Higher Education* (June 1999): A43-A44; Andrea Useem, "In East Africa, New Private Colleges Fill a Growing Gap between Supply and Demand," *The Chronicle of Higher Education* (September 1999): A65-A66.

12. Burton R. Clark, *The Higher Education System: Academic Organization in Cross-National Perspective* (Berkeley, Calif.: University of California Press, 1983); Brian Cooksey and Sibylle Riedmiller, "Tanzanian Education in the Nineties: Beyond the Diploma Disease," *Assessment in Education: Principles, Policy & Practice* 4, no. 1 (January 1997): 121-35.

13. Roger L. Geiger, *Private Sectors in Higher Education: Structure, Function, and Change in Eight Countries* (Ann Arbor: University of Michigan Press, 1986); William Zumeta, "State Policies and Private Higher Education: Policies, Correlates, and Linkages," *Journal of Higher Education* 63 (July/August 1992): 363-417.

14. See, for example, United Nations Development Program, *Human Development Report 1999* (New York: Oxford University Press, 1999); and World Bank, *World Development Indicators 1999* (Washington D.C.: World Bank, 1999) which are cited extensively in this section.

15. World Bank, *World Development Indicators 1999*, 81.

16. World Bank, *Education Strategy Paper* (Washington D.C.: World Bank, 1998) cited in World Bank, *World Development Indicators 1999*, 36.

17. This is a periodic publication of the World Bank in collaboration with many other international organizations, World Bank *World Development Indicators 1999*, xii-xxi.

18. World Bank, *World Development Indicators 1999*, 80.

19. United Nations Development Program, *Human Development Report 1999*, 22.

20. See the next section for a discussion of the limits of enrollment measures alone.

21. World Bank, *World Development Indicators 1999*, 85.

22. World Bank, *World Development Indicators 1998*, cited in World Bank, *World Development Indicators 1999*, 36.

23. Hanushek, "Interpreting," 227-54; World Bank, *World Development Indicators 1999*, 36-37.

24. Yumi Lee and Peter Ninnes, "A Multilevel Global and Cultural Critique of the 'Diploma Disease,'" *Comparative Education Review* 39, no. 2 (1995): 169-77; Cooksey and Riedmiller, *Tanzanian Education.*

25. United Nations Development Program, *Human Development Report*, 225

26. World Bank, *World Development Indicators 1999*, 85.

27. United Nations Development Program, *Human Development Report*, 22.

28. World Bank, *World Development Indicators 1999*, 85.

29. World Bank, *World Development Indicators 1999*, 82-85.

30. Lin, "Education and Economic Development;" Ole Therkildsen, "Local Government and Households in Primary Education in Tanzania: Some Lessons for Reform," Research Working Paper 98.6 (Copenhagen: Centre for Development Research, 1998).

31. World Bank, *World Development Report: Workers in an Integrating World* (New York: Oxford University Press, 1995b): chapter 6.

32. Even in advanced countries, women generally lag behind men in achievement of advanced degrees and degrees in scientific and technological fields. See Allen R. Sanderson, Bernard Dugoni, Thomas Hoffer, and Lance Seffa, *Doctorate Recipients from United States Universities: Summary Report 1998* (Chicago: National Opinion Research Center at the University of Chicago, 1999).

33. World Resources Institute, *World Resources, 1994-95* (New York: Oxford University Press, 1994): 52-57; World Bank, *World Development Indicators 1999*, 23, 89.

34. World Bank, *World Development Indicators 1999*, 35-39.

35. United Nations Development Program, *Human Development Report*, 127.

36. World Bank, *World Development Indicators 1999*, 89.

37. World Bank, *World Development Indicators 1999*, 37.

38. The World Bank outlines proven strategies for increasing girls' enrollment and persistence—improved quality and relevance of education, safer schools closer to home, more female teachers, enforcement of labor market equity policies—but also notes that "the environment in which education decisions are made leads to underinvestment in girls' schooling and to a persistent gender gap." See World Bank, *World Development Indicators 1999*, 36-38.

39. World Bank, *World Development Indicators 1999*, 94-97.

40. The only clear exception was the Latin America and Caribbean region which showed a slight decrease over the period. Europe and Central Asia did not have comparable data for the two years, but the 1996 figure was the highest of any region at 5.4 percent. The lowest 1996 value was for East Asia and the Pacific region at 2.7 percent, up from 2.1 percent in 1980. See World Bank, *World Development Indicators 1999*, 76. Yet, as the World Bank points out, despite low education spending East Asia has higher enrollment rates than the Middle East and African regions which spend much more as a percentage of GNP. See World Bank *Priorities and Strategies for Education: A World Bank Re-*

view (New York: Oxford University Press, 1995a).

41. For example, the typical U.S. public school year is around 180 days of class attendance while the typical number of days in the school year in Japan is 240 days, not counting the time spent by many students who attend "cram schools" after hours. See Marcia L. Johnson and Jeffrey R. Johnson, *Daily Life in Japanese High Schools* (Bloomington, Ind.: ERIC Clearinghouse for Social Studies/Social Science Education, ED 406301, 1996). Even within the United States the variation in the educational meaning of a year of schooling in an elite private or public school and a year in a struggling school in the urban core or a remote rural area is vast. A crude measure is the difference across states in annual expenditures per pupil, which ranged from almost $10,000 down to less than $4,000 in the public education sector alone in 1994 to 1995. See U.S. Department of Education, National Center for Educational Statistics, *Digest of Education Statistics*, NCES 98-015 (Washington D.C.: National Center for Education Statistics, 1998): 170.

42. Hanushek, "Interpreting."

43. Hanushek, "Interpreting;" World Bank, Departments of Policy Research and Poverty & Social Policy, "Investing in Education," *Poverty Lines*, No. 2 (April 1996); World Bank, *World Development Indicators 1999*, 35-39, 85).

44. The World Bank cites evidence that "In Egypt, bringing the quality of all schools up to the level of the best would reduce the annual dropout rate by two-thirds, from 9.3 percent to 3.2 percent." See World Bank, "Investing in Education." Hanushek argues that the conventional view that education quantity and quality must be traded off in the allocation of resources is substantially misguided. Instead, since quality instruction, facilities, etc. are necessary to induce students to persist and achieve enough to receive real value from their education, investments in quantity *per se* (or broad access to low quality education) will not be efficacious absent adequate quality. On the other hand, well-targeted efforts to improve quality should enhance participation and persistence, hence quantity of education received. See Hanushek, "Interpreting," 236-39.

45. World Bank, *World Development Indicators 1999*, 39.

46. Some of these contributions can also be provided by secondary schools, particularly in communities where no tertiary education institution exists.

47. Burton R. Clark, *Academic Power in Italy: Bureaucracy and Oligarchy in a National University System* (Chicago: University of Chicago Press, 1977).

48. For several illustrations of excesses in nations torn by ethnic conflict, see Stephen P. Heyneman, "From the Party/State to Multiethnic Democracy: Education and Social Cohesion in Europe and Central Asia," *Educational Evaluation and Policy Analysis* 22, no. 2 (Summer 2000): 173-91.

49. Dore, *The Diploma.*

50. In order of recency of development these cases were Kenya, Sri Lanka, Japan, and England.

51. In the 1990s the World Bank reports, "In Africa, for instance, spending per student in higher education is about 44 times that per student in primary education, and the share of higher education in total public spending is now higher than in any other region of the world. Yet one-half of Africa's primary-school-age children are not enrolled in

school, and the universities in the region are often of low quality." See World Bank, *Priorities and Strategies for Education*, 3.

52. Some analysts have termed this "paper qualification syndrome." See Cooksey and Riedmiller, *Tanzanian.*

53. Angela W. Little, "The Diploma Disease Twenty Years On," special issue of *Assessment in Education: Principles, Policy & Practice* 4, no.1 (January 1997).

54. Lin, "Education and Economic Development;" López, Thomas, and Wang, *Addressing.*

55. Hanushek, "Interpreting;" Robert Barro and John Wha Lee, "International Measures of Schooling Years and Schooling Quality," *The American Economic Review* 86, no. 2 (1996): 218-23.

56. World Bank, *Priorities and Strategies for Education*; López, Thomas, and Wang, *Addressing.*

57. See, for example, Dore, *The Diploma* on Sri Lanka; Lin, "Education and Economic Development" on pre-Mao China.

58. California's Proposition 98 formula for funding elementary/secondary schools and community colleges as a guaranteed share of the state budget is an example.

59. Economists term this positive income elasticity of demand for education. See Cohn and Geske, *The Economics of Education.*

60. World Bank, *Priorities and Strategies for Education.*

61. Geiger, *Private Sectors.*

62. Note that in education the costs associated with students' time are at least as important as direct resource costs, see Cohn and Geske, *The Economics.* This is very tangibly so in the developing world where school-age children can be employed to assist significantly in earning their family's livelihood.

63. William Zumeta, "Public Policy and Higher Education Accountability: Lessons from the Past and Present for the New Millennium," in *Affordability, Access, and Accountability: The States and Public Higher Education*, ed. Donald E. Heller (Baltimore: Johns Hopkins University Press, 2001).

64. World Bank, *Priorities and Strategies for Education.*

65. Hanushek, "Interpreting;" Paul T. Hill, Lawrence C. Pierce, and James W. Guthrie, *Reinventing Public Education: How Contracting Can Transform America's Schools* (Chicago: University of Chicago Press, 1997); Alberto Z. Calderón, "Voucher Programs for Secondary Schools: The Colombian Experience," Human Capital Development Working Paper 66 (Washington D.C.: World Bank, 1996).

66. Burton Bollag, "Private Colleges Reshape Higher Education in Eastern Europe and Former Soviet States," *The Chronicle of Higher Education* (June 11, 1999): A43-A44.

67. But note that most of these models also require accountability from these schools. See Hill, Pierce, and Guthrie, *Reineventing.*

68. The restriction on using public funds at religious schools is a product of U.S. history codified in its constitution. Many other nations trying such schemes would not exclude religious schools. See, for example, World Bank, *World Development Report 1997*,

(New York: Oxford University Press, 1997): 89.

69. William Zumeta, "How Did They Do It? The Surprising Enrollment Success of Private, Nonprofit Higher Education from 1980 to 1995," paper presented at the Association for the Study of Higher Education annual conference, San Antonio, TX., November 19, 1999.

70. B. Clark, *The Higher Education System*; Clark Kerr, *The Great Transformation in American Higher Education, 1960-1980* (Albany: State University of New York Press, 1991).

71. See also World Bank, *Priorities and Strategies for Education*, on the social value of private sectors at the upper educational levels.

Part Two

Progress in Our Relations with Others

Part two considers "progress in our relations with others." The chapters explore our ability to solve collective-action problems, promote the progress of cultures, prevent ethnopolitical warfare and massacres, curtail destruction in "contentious politics" while supporting free expression and participation in public life, support international development, and promote free press and democratic governance.

This section begins with Elinor Ostrom's exploration of "Achieving Progress in Solving Collective-Action Problems." Ostrom argues that "progress in the next millennium will occur by our recognition of limits to human capabilities, to disciplinary boundaries, and to overly simple policy solutions." Progress, according to Ostrom, occurs when "difficult problems are solved in ways that do not generate still further costs for those not involved."

According to Ostrom, policy analysts attempting to solve problems of collective action are overly influenced by "a narrow, short-term economic view of human rationality combining an all-powerful computation capacity, on the one hand, with no capability to adapt and stick to moral norms of trustworthiness, reciprocity, and fair contributions to the provision of collective benefits, on the other." Ostrom believes that humans can overcome cognitive limitations through effective heuristics—that is, general trial and error problem-solving. She also notes that extensive experimental research has shown that a substantial proportion of the population in most modern societies are capable of trustworthy behavior.

The development of a "broader theory of rationality," according to Ostrom, requires a cross-disciplinary approach. Ostrom notes that economists, social psychologists, evolutionary psychologists, sociologists, anthropologists, and political scientists share an interest in understanding behavior and its role in public policy. She also notes that social scientists need to pay more attention to evolutionary theory developed in biology and ecology as a strong theoretical tool for understanding human behavior that recognizes self-interest as well as reciprocity and trust.

The problem of "overly simple policy solutions," Ostrom suggests, might be overcome through systems of polycentric governance. As Ostrom describes, "Polycentric systems are themselves complex, adaptive systems without one central authority dominating all of the others. Due to the redundance and rapidity of this trial-and-error learning process, a polycentric system has a higher probability (than either a fully decentralized or a fully centralized system) to avoid major disasters and eventually to discover rules that work relatively well." Thus a society can make up for "what it lacks in individual decision making skills by allowing deviant trials and by promoting the inexpensive circulation of information."

In chapter 12, Richard Zerbe raises the provocative and challenging question, "Is There Cultural Progress?" Zerbe defines cultural progress as "the growth in the ability of a culture to support individuals in developing more empathic, mature, and intimate relationship with other beings. *Culture* is simply the body of learning that is passed on within a group." Placing his analysis of cultural progress within a framework of modern psychology, Zerbe argues we can think of cultural progress in terms of "maturity," recognizing it on the same basis we recognize more and less mature individuals.

While Zerbe argues against cultural relativism—that is, the idea that one culture cannot be seen as being superior to another—he maintains that maturity involves the ability to maintain cultural diversity within a cooperative unity. Zerbe notes that "what I call culture is largely a reflection of cooperation among humans. As this cooperation has become richer, so has culture; and this growth in richness is cultural progress."

Cooperation, according to Zerbe, "can take two forms. One is rooted in self-regard, the other in empathy." As Zerbe notes, the stronger the sense of empathy, the greater the possibilities for cooperation. Zerbe notes that "Cooperative empathy requires the ability of one class or group or country to extend opportunity and justice to another."

Another important component of the mature society, according to Zerbe, is its respect for the individual. Zerbe finds that more mature cultures tend toward democratic rule and recognizing the ethical right of all groups and individuals to be heard. Another aspect of maturity in cultures is found in compassion toward weaker members.

Zerbe identifies seven general rules for policy development that are consistent with cultural maturity. First among these is the rule of appropriateness—that is, policies or programs that are appropriate to the cultural maturity of the parties at which they are aimed. Second is the rule of law, which is subject to the rule for appropriateness, where laws are seen as fair and consistent with attempts to equalize life's chances. The third rule promotes policy intervention when necessary to promote the rule of law and empathic understanding. The fourth rule is the granting of status to members of society for mature actions. Zerbe identifies quality parenting as worthy of greater status in a mature culture. The fifth rule promotes child rearing and education in order to create the "optimal expected environment" for children. The sixth rule recognizes universal human rights, or support for basic rights that are consistent with empathy and subject to the rule of appropriateness. Finally, the seventh rule recognizes the importance of the environment—that is, of extending empathy to creatures, and perhaps to ecosystems.

Zerbe concludes that "Just as there are more mature individuals, so also are there more mature cultures. The more mature culture is evidenced by the extent of its enfranchisement by the ability of its members to cooperate and to empathize with others by the extent to which the cultural institutions encourage values of empathy."

In chapter 13, Daniel Chirot explores ethnopolitical warfare and massacres in the twentieth century. Progress in this area, according to Chirot, might be defined simply as "less ethnic conflict and violence." According to this definition we have not made progress in the twentieth century. Chirot notes, however, that the record is not entirely bleak. The American civil rights movement (where dozens, rather than hundreds, thousands or millions were killed), the peaceful end to Apartheid in South Africa, the existence of relatively harmonious ethnic relations in Malaysia (a country on the verge of ethnic massacre in 1960), and other examples may point the way toward greater progress in the future.

Chirot notes that there is a "sharp divide" between "modernists," who believe that the more advanced a civilization, the more likely it is to commit ethnopolitical atrocities, and those who characterize such violence as "barbaric reversions to primitivism." Modernists see violence of the twentieth century as being a "different and worse phenomenon" based on the "bureaucratic rationalization of modern states," and the "'scientific' notion that societies can be engineered." On the other side of the debate is the claim that we are not so far from our past. This debate matters because, as Chirot notes, if the modernists are right, "social change is heading in a fundamentally wrong direction and mass killings based on ethnicity, nationalism, class, or some other politically defined category are only bound to increase." In this view, the idea that public policy can help to remedy social ills is fundamentally flawed. Those who disagree with the modernists, however, would see "any sign of progress ... as a foretaste of a better future." Chirot concludes that human motives for violence have not changed, but that the rise of the modern nation state has increased the scope and frequency of genocides.

Chirot believes that there are limits to progress in the area of ethnic conflict. We can, however, point to a few lessons regarding what conditions alleviate such conflicts. First, individualizing others and resisting tribalization (that is, treating whole groups as individual enemies) will point to the immorality of genocidal revenge. A second vital point—perhaps the most important lesson according to Chirot, is to recognize the danger of "full justice," which makes compromise difficult. Third, Chirot says, it is important to embrace doubt and impurity: "One of the main causes of genocidal acts in the twentieth century" he says, "has been ideological certitude."

As Chirot notes, while we may know more about how to avoid violent ethnic progress, "until the lessons of the past century are more widely absorbed, the trend toward retribalization and the commitment of so many to absolutist, communal myths of solidarity and purity will continue to produce numerous ethnopolitical and ethnoreligious conflicts and wars. Progress is possible, but so far there has not been nearly enough, and what there has been could easily be reversed."

In chapter 14, Charles Tilly turns to the issue of "progress in contentious politics." Contentious politics, according to Tilly, include "all episodic, public, collective making of claims that, if realized, would bear on the interests of some political actor. Contentious politics thus defined runs from demonstrations to wars, from political rallies to massacres." Progress in contentious politics might be measured as "movement away from destruction and toward participation."

According to Tilly, "students of contentious politics" are still sorting out the causes of destruction or of increased participation. However, some progress has been made in developing measurement conventions, such as "battle deaths per year as a criterion of war's intensity." Tilly offers his own insights regarding progress in contentious politics, as well as policy implications following from his conclusions. These include the need for: "1) policing of domestic claim making; 2) impeding international trade in contraband; 3) intervention against state-incited mass killing; 4) slowing national self-determination." These policy initiatives have been "repeatedly implemented with some success (reforms of policing) to hardly even contemplated in the contemporary world (denial of claims to national self-determination)."

In chapter 15, San Ng and Marc Lindenberg discuss the emerging "Rights-Based Approach" (RBA) of the international development non-governmental (NGO) sector. Rooted in concepts of human rights, the RBA, they argue, offers several advantages over traditional international development models, which have emphasized economic growth to the exclusion of social development. The RBA draws upon the existing international legal framework on human rights, provides a basis upon which NGOs can hold governments accountable, offers a coherent structure for the work of multiple NGOs and government agencies, and moves development from an approach of charity to one of empowerment at the individual and community level.

While the RBA is gaining popularity as a concept in the development field, relatively few northern-based NGOs are explicitly using the RBA as an approach to programming at this point. The RBA involves new ways of thinking, and because the RBA acknowledges the complexity of economic and social development, it also involves higher levels of complexity in NGO planning, policy development, programming, organizational management, and external relations. While the RBA is too new to formally evaluate its effectiveness in the field, Ng and Lindenberg conclude that it holds great promise as a basis for more effective approaches to international development.

Part two concludes with Margaret Gordon's chapter on "Free Press, Profit Margins, and Democratic Governance: Is There A Fatal Flaw?" Gordon notes the central function of the press in democracy: "Some 225 years ago, the framers of the United States Constitution ... believed that a press which was free to investigate, monitor, and criticize (or praise) government activity was yet another valuable check on that power. Freedom from pre-publication censorship (no 'prior restraint') was essential to the press's 'watchdog' function, and it is for that reason that freedom of the press was included in the First Amendment to the Constitution." The early press was also expected to educate citizens about current events. The U.S. press developed under these precepts has served as a model for emerging democracies.

Yet, Gordon notes, according to international press rankings, the United States ranks lower than eleven other nations in terms of its "free flow of information." "The United States media rankings were lowered by its scores on 'economic influence on the content of its journalism,' indicating there was restricted flow of information." Gordon argues that in the current model, journalists focus more on what they believe will sell than what they believe citizens "need to know."

Quality journalism, according to Gordon, would provide the news "citizens need in order to be educated about current events and issues, make thoughtful civic decisions, engage in civic dialogues and action, and generally exercise their responsibilities as citizens." Gordon observes that increasing numbers of journalists have left the profession with the sense that the drive for profit has undermined the purpose of the free press and their professional values.

Citing examples of recent civic journalism projects, Gordon sees reason to be optimistic. For example, in the late 1980s, Knight-Ridder, Inc., a major U.S. newspaper chain, experimented with election coverage that placed less emphasis upon "the 'horse-race' nature of politics (who's ahead, who's winning)." The Pew Center for Civic Journalism was established in 1993 to encourage media experiments with the goal of increasing citizen involvement in civic life. The National Public Radio (NPR) has also experimented with new ways of covering elections, and has encouraged and facilitated partnerships between NPR affiliates and their local newspapers.

Gordon notes there has been no systematic effort to track the impacts of these projects, although there is some evidence of increased civic participation in some communities. The projects have also given some journalists pause, as they argue that it is unprofessional for news media to be involved in community action. Some argue that media involvement in community action might be construed as creating the news. Others argue that the projects were "simply 'old-fashioned good journalism.'"

Gordon, however, believes that if civic journalism were to expand to include the largest markets, and to deepen to incorporate daily news coverage, the impacts of the "new journalism" could be profound, and "could ultimately lead to a widely-held belief that *reasonable* profit levels closer to U.S. averages are sufficient, and that to risk losing quality journalism for extraordinary, short-term profits is too dangerous in a democracy."

In each of the chapters of this section, our authors have provided clear definitions, broad indicators, and general policy prescriptions for progress in their particular area of expertise. The issues they consider range from the most basic issues of life and death to higher-level concerns regarding choice and freedom of expression. Each of our authors offers a fairly mixed assessment of prospects for progress, or even for what we may view as progress. Public policy may help us to improve our situation, but will not in and of itself guarantee that the path will be smooth or will take us in the right direction.

Chapter 11

Achieving Progress in Solving Collective-Action Problems

Elinor Ostrom

> Why have so many social scientists idealized our human knowledge and abilities in ways aspiring to the characteristics of some Supreme Being, rather than reflecting our more real limitations?
>
> Gerd Gigerenzer, *Simple Heuristics that Make Us Smart*[1]

> All societies, political or academic, must choose among alternatives; These choices can be good, or bad. The worst choice may be looking for 'answers' before there is consensus, or at least a debate, on what the real questions should be.
>
> Michael C. Munger, "Five Questions: An Integrated Research Agenda for Public Choice"[2]

The Challenge of a New Millennium

The beginning of a new millennium challenges all scientists to examine the progress we have made and how progress into the future can be sustained, if not even accelerated. This is a noble purpose and I appreciate being asked to share my own thinking about these issues with such a distinguished group of colleagues. During the past millennium we have certainly made extraordinary progress in our understanding of the physical world. Since the Darwinian breakthrough in the 1860s and the neo-Darwinian synthesis of the early twentieth century, our understanding of the biological world has also expanded considerably. The rough decoding of the human genome during this past year marks an especially important breakthrough made possible by both conceptual and technological advances.

In this paper, I will argue that progress in the next millennium will occur by our recognition of limits to human capabilities, to disciplinary boundaries, and to overly simple policy solutions. Some of the most difficult problems we face are those that are called "collective-action problems." All collective-action problems involve the need for individuals to invest their efforts to achieve a common good. The common good may range in scale from the provision of local schools in a small neighborhood to providing peace and security and reducing the threat of global warming at a global level. At whatever scale is involved, some groups of individuals will jointly benefit from the provision of a collective benefit. Those who will benefit the most, however, are those who do not contribute at all to the provision of the joint benefit and free ride on the efforts of others. If all free ride, of course, no benefit at all is provided. Collective-action problems pervade all forms of social organizations from within the family, to the organization of production activities within a firm, to the provision of public goods and the management of common-pool resources at local, regional, national, and global scales. Progress occurs when these difficult problems are solved in ways that do not generate still further costs for those not involved.

During the past century, policy analysts trying to solve collective-action problems have been strongly influenced by a narrow, short-term economic view of human rationality combining an all-powerful computation capacity, on the one hand, with no capability to adapt and stick to moral norms of trustworthiness, reciprocity, and fair contributions to the provision of collective benefits, on the other. To achieve public goods, it is thought that national governments must devise policies that change incentives so it becomes in the self-interest of all individuals to contribute to collective action. Public officials, and their expert policy advisors, are also thought to be endowed with strong cognitive capabilities that help them generate the full array of policy alternatives. Further, they are posited to be motivated to select the policy that maximizes public welfare (something that self-interested citizens supposedly will not do). Many of the policies proposed during the past century have involved extremely simple remedies to complex problems such as the massive consolidation of local governments (supposedly to solve urban problems) and the uniform regulation of natural resources for large jurisdictions (supposedly to solve environmental problems).

Extensive experimental research has shown that a substantial proportion of the population in most modern societies has somehow overcome the limitations of extreme, short-term self-interest to develop reputations for trustworthy behavior and to adopt norms of reciprocity. A norm of reciprocity is the shared value that one should contribute to joint efforts when one expects others to do so or simply to help others who help you. It is captured to some extent by the saying, "I will scratch your back if you will scratch mine." Extensive research has also provided substantial evidence that humans do not possess the cognitive capabilities assigned to them in most policy analyses, but that they frequently overcome their cognitive limitations by adopting effective heuristics. In other words, instead of doing a full analysis of each decision that individuals face, they use "rules of thumb" developed as a result of trial-and-error learning. Some of these rules of thumb work well when there are many opportunities to learn from experience. Unfortunately, however, public policies related to urban services in metropolitan areas and the management of natural resources, as discussed below, were adopted on a widespread basis before learning could occur from initial experiments. Gaining better models of human behavior is thus a major research imperative shared by all the social sciences.

Instead of trying to find single, optimal policies all at once for complex problems, we need to learn how to provide broad arenas in which individuals, who have more information at hand about local ecological and cultural conditions than officials located at a distant national capital, can adopt a variety of policies—each of which needs to be viewed as a policy experiment. Some of these experiments face a chance of failing, and local units are not immune from ignorance, corruption, or shortsightedness any more than regional, national, or international regimes. For social learning to occur, overlapping arenas as well as highly parallel structures (multiple units of government operating at the same level) are needed so that information about successful innovation can be more rapidly diffused. Thus, as discussed in some detail below, polycentric systems—those organized at multiple scales with considerable autonomy and diversity at each scale—are more likely to continue progress in the next millennium by more effective organization for contestation and learning. Earlier trends in the twentieth century to reduce the autonomy of small- to medium-sized units of government are slowly being reversed by recent efforts to achieve higher levels of devolution. But simply asking local and state governments to carry out one national policy may not provide as many opportunities for trial-and-error learning to occur as may be needed to deal effectively with more complex policy issues. The faster that economies and societies change, the greater the need for higher levels of innovation and experimentation. It is hard to experiment if one is doing so for an entire nation at a time! Encouraging many small- to medium-sized units of government, whose jurisdictions relate to relatively local problems that vary from one place to another, to experiment is a more effective way of learning from innovation as contrasted to turning difficult and complex problems over to one set of policy analysts charged with designing optimal solutions.

Recognizing Limits

Human Limits and How We Overcome Them

The pathbreaking work of Mancur Olson[3] (1965) on *The Logic of Collective Action* and the use of game theory for the analysis of collective-action problems[4] have greatly improved the analytical capacity of social scientists. By replacing the naive assumptions of earlier group theorists that individuals will always pursue common ends, these modes of analysis force analysts to recognize the essential tensions involved in an immense range of social interactions. In contrast to the type of interaction that can successfully be organized within the context of a competitive market, markets tend to fail to provide optimal levels of collective goods of diverse scales and types.[5]

Using the same model of individual behavior used to analyze outcomes of provision, production, and consumption processes of private goods to examine collective-action problems was an essential first step toward providing a firmer foundation for all types of public policy. This provided a clear and unambiguous foundation for making specific predictions in a variety of settings. The empirical support for these predictions within a competitive market setting gave the enterprise an initial strong impetus.

Homo economicus has, however, turned out to be a special analytical tool rather than the general model of human behavior that many thought would be the case. Models of complete rationality have been highly successful in predicting marginal behavior in competitive situations in which selection pressures screen out those who do not maximize external values, such as profits in a competitive market[6] or the probability of electoral success in party competition.[7] Thin models of rational choice have been unsuccessful in explaining or predicting behavior in one-shot or finitely repeated social dilemmas in which the theoretical prediction is that no one will cooperate. Substantial evidence from experiments demonstrates that cooperation levels for most one-shot or finitely repeated social dilemmas far exceed the predicted levels.[8] Field research also shows that individuals systematically engage in collective action to provide local public goods or manage common-pool resources without an external authority to offer inducements or impose sanctions.[9]

By now there is a huge literature generated by experimental researchers from economics, social psychology, sociology, and political science that has produced an impressive array of "facts." At least seven general findings have been replicated so frequently that they can be considered as core findings for all future work dependent upon developing a coherent model of human behavior.[10] These are:

1. In a one-shot or the first round of a finitely repeated, linear public good game,

subjects contribute between 40 and 60 percent of their endowments to provide a joint benefit.[11]

2. After the first round, contribution levels tend to decay downward, but remain well above zero. A repeated finding is that over seventy percent of subjects contribute nothing in the announced last round of a finitely repeated sequence.[12]

3. Those who believe others will cooperate in providing a public good are more likely to cooperate themselves.[13] A rational individual (as modeled in noncooperative game theory) in a public good game, however, should not in any way be affected by a belief regarding the contribution levels of others. The dominant strategy is a zero contribution no matter what others do.

4. Learning the game better tends to lead to more cooperation. Isaac, Walker, and Williams (1994) repeated the same public good game for ten rounds, forty rounds, and sixty rounds with experienced subjects who were specifically told the end period of each design.[14] The rate of decay was found to be inversely related to the number of decision rounds. In other words, subjects learn how to cooperate at a moderate level for ever-longer periods of time.

5. Face-to-face communication in public good and common-pool resource games produces substantial increases in cooperation that are sustained across all periods including the last period of a finite series.[15] The positive effect of communication is not predicted because the verbal agreements in these experiments are not enforced. Since subjects could use the opportunity for cheap talk to talk others into cooperating while planning to defect themselves, the predicted equilibrium outcome does not change for a finitely repeated dilemma where subjects are allowed to communicate but no third party enforces their agreements. Subjects used the opportunity to discuss the optimal joint strategy, to extract promises from one another, and to give verbal tongue-lashings when aggregate contributions fell below promised levels.[16]

6. Subjects will expend personal resources to punish others who make below-average contributions to a collective benefit if an experiment provides this opportunity.[17] Using the model of Homo economicus, no one would be predicted to spend anything to punish others, particularly in the last round of a finitely repeated game.

7. The rate of contribution to a public good is affected by various contextual factors including the framing of the situation and the rules used for assigning participants, increasing competition among them, allowing communication, authorizing sanctioning mechanisms, or allocating benefits.

These facts are hard to explain using standard economic theory or noncooperative game theory, which assume that all individuals who face the same objective situation will behave in the same way by calculating the strategy that maximizes their objective payoff given the expected behavior of others. These well-substantiated facts from the experimental laboratory, plus the well-known facts of individual contributions to collective-action in field settings, force one to adopt a more classical view of human behavior.

An important change that a more general model of human behavior requires is the acceptance of the existence of multiple types of players. Elsewhere,[18] I have posited the existence of at least three types of actors involved in diverse collective-action problems: (1) conditional cooperators who are willing to initiate cooperative action when they expect others to reciprocate and are willing to repeatedly cooperate so long as a sufficient proportion of those with whom they are interacting also cooperate;[19] (2) willing punishers who are willing, if given the opportunity, to pay a personal cost to punish others who they presume are free riders; and (3) rational egoists who focus only on expected material payoffs in any situation they face.[20]

The first four findings listed above are explained by an assumption that a substantial portion of participants are conditional cooperators at least in the United States, Germany, Israel, Switzerland, Japan, and other urbanized and commercially advanced countries where these experiments have been run.[21] Of course, the presence of substantial numbers of rational egoists is also necessary to explain these findings. The fifth and sixth findings depend on the presence of willing punishers. The seventh finding calls out for a general effort to provide strong theory linking various contextual variables to the willingness of participants to contribute to the provision of public goods.

A different set of experiments and related empirical work has challenged the other strong assumption of Homo economicus models—that of the full calculation of all possible alternatives. When the environment of a repeated decision situation severely constrains the number of options to be considered, as in an open, competitive-market setting, this assumption is not so unrealistic. "Complete information" in such a setting is of the prices of different goods and transportation costs—all of which can be obtained within a few minutes.

Many other situations confronting humans involve complex settings where the time it would take to process all-known, action-outcome linkages would be so long as to make any consideration of a full analysis unreasonable by either the individuals directly involved or the policy makers they select. For even moderately complex problems, humans use a variety of modes to reduce the costs of search and analysis.[22] While some heuristics lead to biased outcomes,[23] others turn out to be accurate and rapid in uncertain situations.[24] Much of the high performance of thin, rational choice models in explaining competitive market behavior is the result of the institutional setting of the market rather than the internal decision mechanisms of the participants. As Alchian (1950) long ago explained, a competitive market selects for strategies that perform well in it. Thus, survivors are more likely to follow optimal strategies than nonsurvivors, but they may have used any of a wide diversity of heuristics in arriving at these optimal strategies.

Thus, substantial evidence should lead us to change the model of human behavior that we use in modern policy analysis to a behavioral theory of rational choice that assumes that individuals strive to do as well as they can, but that individuals are fallible. One way of doing as well as one can in a wide variety of collective-action situations is to learn how to be a trustworthy contributor to joint effort and how to recognize who else is trustworthy and likely to contribute—and, how to be wary of the opportunistic ones. Another way of doing as well as they can is to learn practical heuristics—decision procedures at both an individual and a group level—that enable them to do much better than random decisions and eventually to learn how to approach optimal strategies by experimentation and by watching those who are successful and learning from their activities.

In the resource management field, many people have developed effective ways of managing local habitats by adopting rules of thumb as to when the resource could be used, what technology was appropriate, and what positive actions should be undertaken. These heuristic methods were embedded in religious rituals, songs, and poems that were the means of transferring these "do's" and "don'ts" from one generation to another. Stephen Lansing and James Kremer (1993), for example, learned the basic rule structure of Balinese Water Temple Networks, which had evolved over centuries, and re-created them in a computer simulation that also included the known rainfall and temperature patterns of the region.[25] The simulated Water Temple Networks consistently generated higher yields than the simulated plans proposed by engineers hired by the Asian Development Bank to modernize these irrigation works.

Using a broader theory of rationality leads to quite different types of questions than those asked by "command and control" policy analysts. Instead of asking "What will rational individuals do?" or "What is the best policy that a central government should follow?," one asks: "How can individuals organize themselves so as to create conditions more likely to encourage reciprocity or the willingness to contribute to joint efforts so long as others do?," "How do different kinds of institutions support or undermine norms of reciprocity?," "How can individuals and organizations engage in trial-and-error explorations without major disasters?," "How do individuals and organizations learn most effectively from each other's experiences?," and "What can be learned from organizations that have coped successfully with collective-action problems over very long periods of time (e.g., several centuries!)?"

The finding from many field studies throughout the world, for example, that monitoring and graduated sanctions are close to universal in all long-lasting common-pool resource institutions, is important. This finding tells us that reciprocity alone is unlikely to enable individuals to solve collective-action problems related to common-pool resource problems over time.[26] On the other hand, the sanctions are graduated rather than initially severe. The economic theory of crime, used as a foundation for most contemporary policies related to monitoring and punishment,[27] is based on a strict expected valuation theory that is incapable of being used to explain the graduated nature of the sanctions.

If people can learn reciprocity and use it as the fundamental norm for organizing their lives, and if they agree to a set of rules contingent upon others following those rules, then graduated sanctions are a way of informing those who have made an error or faced a temptation derived from a personal emergency, that indeed others are watching. It also tells them that if someone else were to break the agreed-upon rule, the likelihood is that they would be observed. Given this information function of monitoring and graduated sanctions, individuals are more secure in continuing to follow a positive form of reciprocity.[28]

Disciplinary Limits and How We Need to Overcome Them

Developing a broader theory of rationality useful for policy analysis immediately requires input from multiple disciplines. Many economists are struggling with exactly these issues—particularly those who have seen the lack of empirical support for so many predictions.[29] Social psychologists,[30] evolutionary psychologists,[31] sociologists and anthropologists,[32] and political scientists[33] are all concerned about building a better foundation for both understanding behavior as a necessary step before trying to improve public policy. And social scientists need to pay considerably more attention to the work of biologists and ecologists as evolutionary theory is providing a strong underlying theoretical apparatus to help in the construction of a theory of human behavior that posits human tendencies toward both egoistic pursuits while recognizing the importance of reciprocity and trust.[34]

Scholars who have long been interested in diverse public policies have often found themselves somewhat limited by their own disciplinary boundaries within contemporary universities. Cynics sometimes state it this way: "The world has problems, but universities have departments."[35] The incentives to stay within the confines of the way a discipline asks questions—particularly for younger scholars—are powerful and frequently counterproductive for the achievement of knowledge needed to analyze policy questions. Even the efforts of senior scholars can be criticized by those who worry about an escape from a tight disciplinary focus.[36] As Brewer himself envisioned the nature of policy analysis, it involves asking the following types of questions:

- What goal values are sought and by whom?
- What trends affect the realization of these values? Or, where did the problem originate?
- What factors are responsible for the trends? Or, what are the driving or influencing conditions?
- What is the probable course of future events and developments—especially if interventions are not made?
- What can be done to change that course to realize or achieve more of the desired goals, and for whom?[37]

These questions are not the primary domain of *any* single discipline. When honest scholars have tried to examine these types of questions from their own disciplinary lenses, they have acknowledged the limits of their own view and thus the importance of involving other disciplines in their explanation.

For example, Robert Ellickson first attempted as a lawyer to understand the structure of rules and norms that affected how farmers in Shasta County, California, related to one another in regard to a wide variety of everyday problems—including who was responsible for fencing in (or out) the cattle that farmers were pasturing on their own land. The farmers had hardly used lawyers or the courts to establish local rules regarding constraining externalities. Ellickson found that the legal theories taught in law school, and even by many of the interdisciplinary approaches that combined law with one of the social sciences (e.g., law and economics; law and society), were insufficient. In light of his experience, Ellickson argued that to develop even a rudimentary theory of social order, theorists would need to understand the behavior of multiple "controllers" (e.g., individuals who watched over events of importance to a community, from neighbors through various organizational and governmental forms of regulation). "In other words, a general theory of social control requires subtheories of human nature, of market transactions, of social interactions, of organizations, and of governments. For starters a theorist thus needs a command of psychology, economics, sociology, organization theory, and political science."[38] Progress in policy analysis can be enhanced by following Ellickson's advice.

The Limits (or Failure) of Simple Policy Solutions

Another recurrent theme in American academia is to criticize the number of governments that exist in the United States and the competition that exists among them. During the 1960s and 1970s, for example, the "Metropolitan Reform" movement was the dominant way of thinking about urban governance. The cause of many problems was posited to be the presence of many units of government that were seen as redundant and inefficient. In addition, multiple units of government were viewed as competitive and providing a means whereby the rich could escape without contributing to the provision of public services needed by the poor and disadvantaged members of central cities.[39] Policy analysts repetitively recommended simple, top-down, command-and-control solutions in the belief that those doing analysis of policy problems for large territories would achieve close to optimal policy solutions for difficult problems.

In the field of education, beliefs that large numbers of schools were inefficient and that massive consolidation would lead to increased efficiency as well as equity led to the reduction of school districts in a long series of massive campaigns against considerable citizen opposition during three-quarters of this century. In 1932, almost 130,000 school districts existed in the United States. This number was halved by 1952 and quartered by 1962, and halved once again by the early 1970s. The massive consolidation of school districts has slowed down during the past several decades. Today we have around fifteen thousand school districts in the United States for a population that has almost doubled since the campaign to consolidate schools was initiated.[40] During the heat of this policy reform, research was almost nonexistent on the effect of school size, number of schools in a region, and related issues. It was such a simple solution to what was perceived by academics and public officials as an obvious problem that both were willing to push hard for this reform.

Since the 1970s, considerable research on the effects of these variables on school performance has provided contrary evidence to the implicit theory used by policy makers to support the school consolidation movement. A recent study for the National Bureau of Economic Research, for example, finds that having a larger number of schools in a metropolitan area is associated with higher average student performance (as measured by students' educational attainment, local wages, and test scores) while also being characterized by lower per-pupil spending.[41] Now, after years of trying to increase size and reduce the number of schools, policy makers are reconsidering the consequences of past reforms and recommending charter schools, voucher systems, and many other reforms to create more responsive schools through a variety of structural reforms.[42] Similarly, empirical studies of the effect of the size and number of urban public service providers also found that small size and multiplicity did not have the adverse consequences frequently attributed to them and that improvements (rather than reductions) in performance were frequently associated with the presence of a multiplicity of units of government.[43] Hawkins and Ihrke (1999), for example, have conducted a recent survey of more than seventy empirical studies of fragmentation showing that over two-thirds of the empirical research do not support the policies recommended by the metropolitan reform movement.[44]

A second set of simple policies gone amuck relates to the presumed necessity of nationalizing ownership and management of common-pool resources such as forests, rivers and lakes, irrigation systems, grazing areas, and inshore fisheries, and imposing one set of policies for an entire nation. Common-pool resources are characterized by difficulties of excluding beneficiaries and subtractability of use.[45] In the conventional theory, appropriators are frequently assumed to be homogeneous in terms of their assets, skills, discount rates, and cultural views. They are also assumed to be short-term, profit-maximizing actors who possess complete information. In the conventional theory, *anyone* can enter the resource and take resource units. Appropriators only gain property rights to what they harvest, which they then sell in an open competitive market. The open-access condition is a theoretical given. Given these assumptions, the logical conclusion is that common-pool resources will be overused and eventually destroyed.

Many textbooks on environmental policy present this conventional theory of an open-access common-pool resource as the *only* theory needed for making effective policies.[46] Massive deforestation in tropical countries and the collapse of multiple ocean fisheries are cited by many policy analysts and public officials as sufficient evidence to confirm the general validity of the theory. Garrett Hardin's (1968) dramatic article in *Science* convinced others that the conventional theory captures the core of the problem.[47] The metaphor of resource users helplessly trapped in a relentless tragedy has been used by scholars and policy makers to rationalize central government control of forests, inshore fisheries, and many other common-pool resources. Thus, reform proposals that stressed the essential role of the state as the source of rules and their enforcement have seemed to have a firm academic foundation.

Recent research has found that many appropriators have organized themselves so as to regulate the use of common-pool resources, and some have sustained resources and their own organizations for very long periods of time.[48] Further, national governmental agencies are frequently found to be unsuccessful in their efforts to design effective and uniform sets of rules to regulate important common-pool resources across a broad domain. Many developing countries nationalized all land and water resources during the 1950s and 1960s. The institutional arrangements that local users had devised to limit entry and use lost their legal standing, but the national governments lacked funds and personnel to monitor these resources effectively. Thus, common-pool resources were converted to a *de jure* government property regime but reverted to a *de facto* open-access regime.[49]

The incentives of the collective-action problem that users faced were accentuated because now users were implicitly told that they would not receive the benefits of adopting a long-term view in their use of the resource. When resources that were previously controlled by local participants have been nationalized, state control has usually proved to be less effective and efficient than control by those directly affected, if not disastrous in its consequences.[50] The substantial increase in the rates of deforestation following adoption of policies to nationalize forests that had earlier been governed by local user-groups has been well documented for Thailand,[51] Africa,[52] Nepal,[53] and India.[54] Similar increases in uncontrolled over-harvesting have occurred in regard to inshore fisheries taken over by state or national agencies from local control by the inshore fishers themselves.[55] These policies have confused resources that are genuinely large-scale in extent with resources that exist throughout a nation but are not highly interconnected and vary substantially in the structure of their ecological systems from place to place.

Both sets of policy reforms—centralizing urban governance and the governance of common-pool resources—have been based on an overly simplified view of the nature of social order. Policy makers tend to distrust local citizens to create effective forms of governance. And, consequently, they assume that a multiplicity of self-organized regimes (some formal, some informal) are by their very nature disorderly and ineffective. Order is presumed to result from central direction. Unfortunately, this perspective is viewed as self-evident. It is hard to make progress against self-evident truths! These common-sense assumptions, however, lead to proposals to improve the operation of political systems that have had the opposite effect. By removing decisions about the ways to innovate, adapt, and coordinate efforts from those who are directly affected, these policy reforms have created institutions that are less able to respond to the problems for which they were created.

Creating Arenas for Experimentation and Learning

Thus, underlying much policy analysis of the last years has been a presumption that the responsibility for designing institutional rules to overcome various kinds of collective-action problems—including common-pool resource problems—should be assumed by large-scale and centralized governments.[56] Policy analysts have had great faith in their own capacity to analyze theoretical models of typical problems and have come forward with a set of institutional fixes that will lead those involved in a collective-action problem to take actions generating higher, rather than lower, outcomes. In doing so, policy analysts tend to think of citizens or users as motivated by narrow, self-interested preferences and of themselves as motivated by a general public interest. Both assumptions are exaggerated. The evidence referred to above is consistent with a broader theory of a boundedly rational, learning, and potentially norm-using individual.[57] The evidence gathered from studies of the behavior of policy analysts and government officials is consistent with a presumption that officials are similar to citizens in regard to their internal motivation. Officials may be placed in institutional settings, however, that bring substantial temptations for personal gain and even illegal payoffs without much chance for others to learn about behavior. Officials may also be isolated from the people and locations they are supposed to represent and not have much knowledge about time and place information. Officials in one jurisdiction (or one department within a larger jurisdiction) may put the interest of their own unit ahead of achieving objectives requiring full participation of all units. Thus, finding ways of solving collective-action problems exists within the public sector as well as in the private sector.

A better foundation for public policy is to assume that neither citizens nor their officials may be able to analyze all situations fully, but given a conducive, macro-political regime, they may make efforts to solve complex problems through trial-and-error testing out of different rules for solving various collective-action problems. Recent recognition of the need for demonstration projects and learning general guidelines or "best practices" from the more successful policies are consistent with this effort. To learn from policy experiments does require some long-term continuity of both leadership and citizenry. Our capacity to learn from policy experiments may thus be threatened by the increased mobility of public officials and citizens.

Colleagues at the Workshop in Political Theory and Policy Analysis have been studying the kinds of rules that users of common-pool resources in many parts of the world have adopted.[58] Studying these rule systems leads to a recognition of the complexity of situations that individuals face and the consequent complexity of the rule systems they devise. Herein, I can only provide a short glimpse of that complexity; I hope, however, to convey its extent. Let us turn first to the type of rules used to regulate common-pool resources in the field—the boundary rules that define who is eligible to use a common-pool resource—that users in the field have crafted. A key problem of all common-pool problems is that of excluding free riders (e.g., finding ways to require contributions or exclude noncontributors). If one is to exclude free riders, a commitment is necessary that one set of users is authorized to use a resource and others are not. Empirical studies of boundary rules used in field settings have identified twenty-seven different types of boundary rules developed by resource users to be used alone or in combination.[59] While many of these rules are not known to external authorities, they are considered legitimate prescriptions by local users. A second essential set of rules relates to harvesting and other activities in which individuals participate. Empirical studies have identified over one hundred types of rules that specify when, where, how, and how much of the products of a commons may be appropriated by someone who is authorized to do so. The number of rules related to incentives and sanctions, to information conditions, and to procedural requirements that could be used to regulate activities related to a common-pool resource is also very large. Since rules are used in combination with one another, the potential configuration of rules that could be used to commit participants to follow strategies that improve the efficiency, equity, and sustainability of common-pool resources approaches infinity.

Given the immense size of the potential rule space involved in determining a set of rules to govern a common-pool resource (or any other form of collective good), searching the space in a full analysis process is obviously not a tractable problem. All the game theorists in the world working at the same time on a single problem could not generate the full set of rule combinations that could be considered for the regulation of a single groundwater basin, fishery, or forest. One way to try to gain tractability in contemporary policy analysis has been to simplify the problem drastically and identify a limited set of rules that can be considered, hoping that one has identified the essential core of the problem and its solution.

Consequently, instead of assuming that the choice of institutional rules to improve the performance of human systems that utilize common-pool resources—or other local collective goods for that matter—is a process of designing optimal rules, we need to understand the policy design process as involving an effort to tinker with a large number of component parts.[60] Those who tinker with any tools—including rules—try to find combinations that work together more effectively than other combinations. Policy changes are experiments based on more or less informed expectations about potential outcomes and the distribution of these outcomes for participants across time and space.[61] Whenever individuals agree to add a rule, change a rule, or adopt someone else's proposed rule set, they are conducting a policy experiment. Further, the complexity of the ever-changing biophysical world combined with the complexity of rule systems means that any proposed rule change faces a nontrivial probability of error.

When only a single governing authority makes decisions about rules for an entire region, policy makers have to experiment simultaneously with *all* of the collective-action problems of a particular type within a jurisdiction with each policy change. And, once a change has been made and implemented, further changes will not be made rapidly. The process of experimentation will usually be slow. Information about results may be contradictory and difficult to interpret. Thus, an experiment that is based on erroneous data about one key structural variable or one false assumption about how actors will react can lead to a very large disaster.[62] In any design process where substantial probability of error exists, having multiple teams of designers has repeatedly been shown to have considerable advantage.[63] The important point is: If the systems are relatively separable, allocating responsibility to multiple units for experimenting with rules will not avoid failure, but will drastically reduce the probability of immense failures for an entire region. The users of each common-pool resource can experiment with a variety of rule changes in their own systems, retaining those that work relatively well, and searching for others that will work better. Since the rules are used by only a relatively small group, they can be changed more rapidly, if they are shown not to work well, since direct feedback provides relatively accurate information about those rules that are less effective.

Due to the disillusion of many analysts with the performance of highly centralized systems in the management of natural resources, frequent proposals have recently been made to support radical decentralization of centralized regimes.[64] One form of decentralization is to radically move decision making down to a horizontal layer of governments that is composed entirely of local bodies, each of which govern a smaller-scale resource system. From one simple solution—centralizing everything—policy analysts are flipping to another simple solution—radical decentralization. Such a form has advantages and disadvantages in regard to the governance of common-pool resources. Many of these can be applied to urban public services as well.[65]

Advantages and Disadvantages of Fully Decentralized Systems

Among the advantages of assigning the authority to regulate smaller-scale and separable common-pool resources to the users are:[66]

- *Local knowledge.* Appropriators who have lived and appropriated from a resource system over a long period of time have developed relatively accurate mental models of how the biophysical system itself operates, since the very success of their appropriation efforts depends on such knowledge. They also know others living in the area well and what norms of behavior are considered appropriate by the community.

- *Inclusion of trustworthy participants.* Appropriators can devise rules that increase the probability that others are trustworthy and will use reciprocity. This lowers the cost of relying entirely on formal sanctions and paying for extensive guarding.
- *Reliance on disaggregated knowledge.* Feedback about how the resource system responds to changes in actions of appropriators is generated in a disaggregated way. Fishers are quite aware, for example, when the size and species distribution of their catch changes over time. Irrigators learn whether a particular allocation system is efficient by comparing the net yield they obtain under one set of rules versus others.
- *Better adapted rules.* Given the above, appropriators are more likely to craft rules that are better adapted to each common-pool resource than any general system of rules.
- *Lower enforcement costs.* Since local appropriators have to bear the cost of monitoring, they are apt to craft rules that make infractions highly obvious so that monitoring costs are lower. Further, by creating rules that are seen as legitimate, rule conformance will tend to be higher.
- *Redundancy.* The probability of failure for an entire region is greatly reduced by the establishment of parallel systems of rule making, interpretation, and enforcement.

There are, of course, limits to all ways of organizing the governance of common-pool resources. Among the limits of a fully decentralized system are:

- *Some appropriators will not organize.* While the evidence from the field is that many local appropriators do invest considerable time and energy into their own regulatory efforts, other groups of appropriators do not do so. There appear to be many reasons for why some groups do not organize, including the presence of low-cost alternative sources of income and thus a reduced dependency on the resource, conflict among appropriators along multiple dimensions, lack of leadership, and fear of having their efforts overturned by outside authorities. Tragically, some of the most needy groups may be those least likely to self-organize.[67]
- *Some self-organized efforts will fail.* Given the complexity of the task involved in designing rules, some groups will select combinations of rules that generate failure instead of success. They may be unable to adapt rapidly enough to avoid the collapse of a resource system.
- *Local tyrannies.* Not all self-organized resource governance systems will be organized democratically or rely on the input of most appropriators. Some will be dominated by a local leader or a power elite who only change rules that will be of advantage to them. This problem is accentuated in locations where the cost of exit is particularly high and reduced where appropriators can leave.

- *Stagnation.* Where local ecological systems are characterized by considerable variance, experimentation can produce severe and unexpected results leading appropriators to cling to systems that have worked relatively well in the past, and stop innovating long before they have developed rules likely to lead to better outcomes.
- *Inappropriate discrimination.* It is always necessary to exclude some individuals from using a resource who do not have a legal right to use a resource and are not contributing to the sustainability of that resource. However, exclusion can be based on inappropriate grounds or on ascribed characteristics that have nothing to do with legal rights or the trustworthiness of individuals to follow a set of agreed-upon rules.
- *Limited access to scientific information.* While time and place information may be extensively developed and used, local groups may not have access to scientific knowledge concerning the type of resource system involved.
- *Conflict among appropriators.* Without access to an external set of conflict-resolution mechanisms, conflict within and across common-pool resource systems can escalate and provoke physical violence. Two or more groups may claim the same territory and may continue to make raids on one another over a very long period of time.
- *Inability to cope with larger-scale common-pool resources.* Without access to some larger-scale jurisdiction, local appropriators may have substantial difficulties regulating only a part of a larger-scale, common-pool resource. They may not be able to exclude others who refuse to abide by the rules that a local group would prefer to use. Given this, local appropriators have no incentives to restrict their own use.

Thus, while there are advantages of creating fully parallel local regimes, radical decentralization is not really a viable policy. It is based on a theory of governance that poses a discrete choice between organizing resource regimes strictly at a local level or organizing them from the center. It is also based on a naive theory of community.[68] There is a better way.

The Advantages of Polycentricity

Many of the capabilities of parallel adaptive systems can be retained in a polycentric governance system. By polycentric, I mean a system where citizens are able to organize not just one but multiple governing authorities at differing scales.[69] Each unit may exercise considerable independence to make and enforce rules within a circumscribed scope of authority for a specified geographical area. In a polycentric system, some units are general-purpose governments while others may be highly specialized. Self-organized resource governance systems, in such a system, may be special districts, private associations, or parts of a local government. These are nested in several levels of general-purpose governments that also provide civil equity as well as criminal courts. All federal systems, such as the United States, are polycentric to some extent. Policies that systematically reduce the autonomy and number of local governments, as has happened in the United States over the last century, threaten the vitality and capacity of these systems to perform most effectively.

In a polycentric system, the users of each common-pool resource or each locality would have some authority to make at least some of the rules related to how that particular resource will be utilized. Thus, they would achieve many of the advantages of utilizing local knowledge as well as the redundancy and rapidity of a trial-and-error learning process. One of the important lessons of extensive research is that there is no single blueprint for an effective organization to solve similar problems—let alone substantially different ones. Enabling citizens and their officials to create collective-action organizations in the public and/or private sphere at multiple levels takes considerable time and effort and will rarely approach either a fully centralized or a fully decentralized system.

On the other hand, problems associated with local tyrannies and inappropriate discrimination can be addressed in larger, general-purpose governmental units that are responsible for protecting the rights of all citizens and for the oversight of appropriate exercises of authority within smaller units of government. It is also possible to make a more effective blend of scientific information with local knowledge where major universities and research stations are located in larger units, but have a responsibility to relate recent scientific findings to multiple smaller units within their region. Because polycentric systems have overlapping units, information about what has worked well in one setting can be transmitted to others who may try it in their own settings. Associations of local, resource governance units can be encouraged to speed up the exchange of information about relevant local conditions and about policy experiments that have proved particularly successful. These are particularly important institutions that have not been studied sufficiently during the past decades. Councils of government, associations of city managers, city clerks, and irrigation district officials, and many informal ways enable people interested in similar problems to get together to discuss what they are doing, what experiments have failed, and what seems to be working well. These private associations can make an immense difference in the speed and accuracy of learning from public-sector experimentation. Individuals who are embedded in multiple "games" simultaneously behave differently than those able to isolate themselves from public scrutiny, open information exchange, and multiple ways of reorganizing clusters of units into larger or smaller teams to accomplish some specific objectives.

Besides the advantages of rapid experimentation and learning in a policy system, when failure occurs at whatever level, there are "redundant" systems that can step in. When small systems fail, there are larger systems to call upon—and vice versa. One should expect failures at all levels at different periods of time (and hope that all levels do not fail at the same time!). It was the federal courts that took on the important task of eliminating formal laws that facilitated racial segregation in the 1950s. On the other hand, it was a local grand jury that brought the initial charges in the Watergate scandal that finally brought down the Nixon presidency. Both large and small-scale governments can fail to perform effectively or efficiently due to simple error or malfeasance. By having redundancy in a system, the probability of both levels of government failing at the same time is far less than the probability of either failing independently.

Polycentric systems are themselves complex, adaptive systems without one central authority dominating all of the others. Due to the redundance and rapidity of this trial-and-error learning process, a polycentric system has a higher probability (than either a fully decentralized or a fully centralized system) to avoid major disasters and eventually to discover rules that work relatively well. Because polycentric systems have overlapping organizations, information about what has worked well in one setting can be transmitted to others who may try it out in their settings. Thus, polycentric governance systems are similar in some important ways to genetic algorithms that have been shown to search large and complexly interrelated performance systems for those rules that increase system performance.[70] There is no guarantee that such systems will find the combination of rules at diverse levels that is optimal for any particular environment. In fact, one should expect that all governance systems will operate at less than optimal levels, given the immense difficulty of fine-tuning any complex, multi-tiered system.

Making Progress through Experimentation and Learning

Thus, instead of a focus on the design of highly centralized governments so they can manage and control all similar collective-action problems in a large territory, progress is more likely (but never guaranteed) with the design of much more complex and adaptive institutions. It is essential that we recognize the limits of all individuals—citizens and public officials alike. Economic progress has been made by moving away from mercantile economic systems where there were limited numbers of firms. Part of this progress is the result of competitive pressures to design new innovations that better meet the preferences of buyers. The market as an institution can be thought of as a mechanism to simulate new innovations and select those that improve efficiency over time.[71]

Many problems exist, however, for which market mechanisms fail and collective-action problems are among the most pervasive of these problems. For too long we have been burdened by an oversimplified dichotomy of the market or the state.[72] Creating highly centralized regimes to solve many local collective-action problems has repeatedly been shown to fail to produce desired outcomes. There is another way. That way establishes multiple regimes at multiple scales within a very general constitutional system. Thus a "society in pursuit of quality decision making can make up for what it lacks in individual decision making skills by allowing deviant trials and by promoting the inexpensive circulation of information."[73]

To make progress in the next millennium requires a major reorientation of how policy analysis is conceptualized, taught, and practiced. Newly developing theories of complex, adaptive systems[74] and studies of the evolution of systems of order[75] need to be foundational reading rather than traditional theories of the state. Taking the work of de Tocqueville seriously (who was among the first external observers of the American federal system to understand how it worked), and of the theory of federal systems, is also important.[76] Finding ways of creating new arenas that provide opportunities for peaceful contestation and for the exchange of information about the results of past experiences is a more urgent task than creating neat organizational charts and increasing the powers of centralized regimes.

With this approach, policy analysis opens up a world of possibilities. Instead of claiming to have the skill of finding the optimal solution, we have to live with the concept of multiple equilibria that vary from extremely destructive to very productive. The core problem we face is how to discover ways of encouraging innovation and new strategies without destroying extant structures of order too rapidly. Thus, those of us involved in the study of policy analysis need to teach a variety of new topics—institutional design and the evolution of social orders—and rekindle old topics that focused on the role of citizens in sustaining the vigor and openness of a democratic system.

Notes

1. Gerd Gigerenzer, Peter M. Todd, and the ABC Research Group, *Simple Heuristics that Make Us Smart* (Oxford: Oxford University Press, 1999), 33.

2. Michael C. Munger, "Five Questions: An Integrated Research Agenda for Public Choice," *Public Choice* 103 (2000): 1-12.

3. Mancur Olson, *The Logic of Collective Action: Public Goods and the Theory of Groups* (Cambridge, Mass: Harvard University Press, 1965).

4. Russell Hardin, *Collective Action* (Baltimore: Johns Hopkins University Press, 1982); Michael Taylor, *Anarchy and Cooperation* (New York: Cambridge University Press, 1982); Michael Taylor, *The Possibility of Cooperation* (New York: Cambridge University Press, 1987).

5. This does not mean, however, that private entrepreneurs are not able to provide some kinds of collective goods through their own efforts. Michael R. Montgomery and Richard Bean, "Market Failure, Government Failure, and the Private Supply of Public Goods: The Case of Climate-Controlled Walkway Networks," *Public Choice* 99, no. 3-4 (1999): 403-37 undertook a fascinating empirical study of government and private sector

provision of climate-controlled walkways in fifty-five large city cores in North America. They found that the owners of commercial buildings who would benefit from such walkways in the skies were able to overcome collective-action problems in many cities by devising their own rules of how these should be paid for. In fact, they found that government policies in some cities were a detriment to the provision of these public goods.

6. Armen A. Alchian, "Uncertainty, Evolution, and Economic Theory," *Journal of Political Economy* 58 (1950): 211-22; Vernon L. Smith, "Rational Choice: The Contrast Between Economics and Psychology," *Journal of Political Economy* 99 (1991): 877-97; Charles R. Plott, "The Application of Laboratory Experimental Methods to Public Choice," in *Collective Decision Making: Applications from Public Choice Theory*, ed. Clifford S. Russell (Baltimore: Johns Hopkins University Press, 1979): 137-60.

7. Debra Satz and John Ferejohn, "Rational Choice and Social Theory," *The Journal of Philosophy* 91, no. 2 (February 1994): 71-82.

8. Elinor Ostrom, "A Behavioral Approach to the Rational Choice Theory of Collective Action," *American Political Science Review* 92, no. 1 (March 1998): 1-22.

9. Elinor Ostrom, Roy Gardner, and James Walker, *Rules, Games, and Common-Pool Resources* (Ann Arbor: University of Michigan Press, 1994).

10. Elinor Ostrom, "Collective Action and the Evolution of Social Norms," *Journal of Economic Perspectives* 14, no. 3 (Summer 2000): 137-58.

11. Douglas D. Davis and Charles A. Holt, *Experimental Economics* (Princeton, N.J.: Princeton University Press, 1993); John Ledyard, "Public Goods: A Survey of Experimental Research," in *The Handbook of Experimental Economics*, ed. J. Kagel and Alvin Roth (Princeton, N.J.: Princeton University Press, 1995), 111-94.

12. For a meta analysis, see Ernst Fehr and Klaus M. Schmidt, "A Theory of Fairness, Competition, and Cooperation," *Quarterly Journal of Economics* 114, no. 3 (August 1999): 817-68.

13. John M. Orbell, Alphons van de Kragt, and Robyn M. Dawes, "Covenants without the Sword: The Role of Promises in Social Dilemma Circumstances," in *Social Norms and Economic Institutions,* ed. Kenneth J. Koford and Jeffrey B. Miller (Ann Arbor: University of Michigan Press, 1991), 117-34.

14. Mark R. Isaac, James Walker, and Arlington W. Williams, "Group Size and the Voluntary Provision of Public Goods: Experimental Evidence Utilizing Large Groups," *Journal of Public Economics* 54, no.1 (May 1994): 1-36.

15. David Sally, "Conversation and Cooperation in Social Dilemmas: A Meta-Analysis of Experiments from 1958 to 1992," *Rationality and Society* 7, no. 1 (January 1995): 58-92; Elinor Ostrom and James Walker, "Neither Markets Nor States: Linking Transformation Processes in Collective Action Arenas," in *Perspectives on Public Choice: A Handbook*, ed. Dennis C. Mueller (Cambridge: Cambridge University Press, 1997), 35-72.

16. Face-to-face bargaining also has a very efficacious effect on two-person bargaining situations even with asymmetric information when contrasted to written communication. See Kathleen L. Valley, J. Moag, and Max H. Bazerman, "A Matter of Trust: Effects of Communication on the Efficiency and Distribution of Outcomes," *Journal of Economic Behavior and Organization* 34, no. 2 (1998): 211-38.

17. Elinor Ostrom, James Walker, and Roy Gardner, "Covenants with and without a Sword: Self-Governance Is Possible," *American Political Science Review* 86, no. 2 (June 1992): 404-17.

18. E. Ostrom, "Collective Action."

19. A modified form of Tit for Tat, see Robert Axelrod, *The Evolution of Cooperation* (New York: Basic Books, 1984); Robert Axelrod, "An Evolutionary Approach to Norms," *American Political Science Review* 80, no. 4 (December 1986): 1095-111.

20. For formal models of the evolution of different types of players characterized by differences in their preferences regarding cooperation, see the work of Werner Güth and Hartmut Kliemt, "The Indirect Evolutionary Approach: Bridging the Gap Between Rationality and Adaptation," *Rationality and Society* 10, no. 3 (August 1998): 377-99; Werner Güth, Hartmut Kliemt, and Bezalel Peleg, "Co-Evolution of Preferences and Information in Simple Games of Trust," discussion paper 72 (Berlin: Humboldt University, Economics Faculty, 1998); and Joel M. Guttman, "Self-Enforcing Agreements and the Evolution of Preferences for Reciprocity," working paper (Ramat-Gan, Israel: Bar-Ilan University, Department of Economics, 1999).

21. In a very large study of indigenous, rural groups around the world, there are only two groups—the Machiguenga in the Peruvian Amazon and the Mapuche in Chile—who do not tend to offer around half of the initial "pie" allocated to them in an ultimatum game and who do not tend to turn down offers of below twenty percent. Joseph Henrich and Natalie Smith, "Culture Matters in Bargaining and Cooperation: Cross-Cultural Evidence from Peru, Chile, and the U.S.," working paper, (Ann Arbor: University of Michigan Business School, 2000) provides a very interesting overview of the behavior of these two groups and how they differ from others in more commercial-oriented societies.

22. Mark Pingle and Richard H. Day, "Modes of Economizing Behavior: Experimental Evidence," *Journal of Economic Behavior and Organization* 29 no. 2 (March 1996): 191-210; Daniel Kaheman, "Experimental Economics: A Psychological Perspective." In *Bounded Rational Behavior in Experimental Games and Markets*, ed. Reinhard Tietz, Wolf Abers, and Reinhard Selten (Berlin: Springer-Verlag, 1988): 11-18.

23. Colin F. Camerer, "Progress in Behavior Game Theory." *Journal of Economic Perspectives* 11, no. 4 (Fall 1997): 167-88.

24. Gigerenzer, et al., *Simple Heuristics*, 33.

25. Stephen J. Lansing and James N. Kremer, "Emergent Properties of Balinese Water Temple Nerworks: Coadaption on a Rugged Fitness Landscape," *American Anthropologist* 95, no. 1 (1993): 97-114.

26. Elinor Ostrom, *Governing the Commons: The Evolution of Institutions for Collective Action* (New York: Cambridge University Press, 1990).

27. Gary S. Becker, "Crime and Punishment: An Economic Approach." *Journal of Political Economy* 76 (1968): 169-217.

28. Elinor Ostrom, "Reformulating the Commons," in *Protecting the Commons: A Framework for Resource Management in the Americas*, ed. Joanna Burger, Elinor Ostrom, Richard Norgaard, David Policansky, and Bernard Goldstein (Washington D.C.: Island Press, 2001).

29. Camerer, "Progress," 167; Reinhard Selten, "Bounded Rationality," *Journal of Institutional and Theoretical Economics* 146, no. 4 (December 1990): 649-58; Reinhard Selten, "Evolution, Learning, and Economic Behavior," *Games and Economic Behavior* 3, no. 1 (February 1991): 3-24; Fehr and Schmidt, "A Theory of Fairness," 817; Bruno S. Frey, *Not Just for the Money: An Economic Theory of Personal Motivation* (Cheltenham, England: Edward Elgar, 1997).

30. David M. Messick, "Alternative Logics for Decision Making in Social Settings," *Journal of Economic Behavior and Organization* 39, no. 1 (May 1999): 11-28.

31. Leda Cosmides and John Tooby, "Cognitive Adaptations for Social Exchange," in *The Adapted Mind: Evolutionary Psychology and the Generation of Culture,* ed. Jerome H. Barkow, Leda Cosmides, and John Tooby, (New York: Oxford University Press, 1992): 163-228.

32. Peter Kollock, "Social Dilemmas: The Anatomy of Cooperation," *Annual Review of Sociology* 24 (1998): 183-214; Christopher Boehm, *Hierarchy in the Forest: The Evolution of Egalitarian Behavior* (Harvard: Harvard University Press, 1999).

33. Axelrod, *The Evolution of Cooperation*; Robert Axelrod and Michael D. Cohen, *Harnessing Complexity: Organizational Implications of a Scientific Frontier* (New York: The Free Press, 2000); Herbert A. Simon, *Models of Bounded Rationality: Empirically Grounded Economic Reason* (Cambridge: MIT Press, 1997).

34. Frans de Waal, *Good Natured: The Origins of Right and Wrong in Humans and Other Animals* (Cambridge: Harvard University Press, 1996); Bobbi S. Low, *Why Sex Matters: A Darwinian Look at Human Behavior* (Princeton, N.J.: Princeton University Press, 2000); Robert Trivers, "The Evolution of Reciprocal Altruism," *Quarterly Review of Biology* 46 (1971): 35-57.

35. Garry D. Brewer, "The Challenges of Interdisciplinarity," *Policy Sciences* 32, no. 4 (1999): 328.

36. As president of my own disciplinary association—the American Political Science Association—I visited all of the regional meetings of political scientists during the 1996–1997 academic year. When asked about my current work, I described our research on the structure and consequences of forestry institutions using field methods and remotely sensed images (to measure the impact of local institutions on the environment). I was asked more than once whether the use of Geographic Information Systems and remotely sensed images were "really political science?" Imagine the impact of that question on a young scholar!

37. Brewer, "The Challenges," 328.

38. Robert C. Ellickson, "A Critique of Economic and Sociological Theories of Social Control," *Journal of Legal Studies* 26 (January 1987): 67-99.

39. See Amos Hawley and Basil G. Zimmer, *The Metropolitan Community: Its People and Government* (Beverly Hills, Calif.: Sage, 1970); David Rusk, *Cities without Suburbs* (Washington, D.C.: Woodrow Wilson Center Press, 1993); and literature summarized in Ross G. Stephens and Nelson Wikstrom, *Metropolitan Government and Governance: Theoretical Perspectives, Empirical Analysis, and the Future* (Oxford: Oxford University Press, 1999).

40. Vincent Ostrom, Robert Bish, and Elinor Ostrom, *Local Government in the United States* (San Francisco: ICS Press, 1988).

41. Caroline Hoxby "Does Competition Among Public Schools Benefit Students and Taxpayers?," working paper 4979 (Cambridge: National Bureau of Economic Research, 1994); see also Lant Pritchett and Deon Filmer, "What Education Production Functions Really Show: A Positive Theory of Education Expenditures," *Economics of Education Review* 18, no. 2 (June 1999): 223-39.

42 For a review of recent books on these reforms, see Howard Gardner, "Vouchers or Charters or *What*," *The New York Review of Books* 47, no. 16 (October 19, 2000): 44-49.

43. For an overview, see Micheal McGinnis, *Polycentricity and Local Public Economies: Readings from the Workshop in Political Theory and Policy Analysis* (Ann Arbor: University of Michigan Press, 1999b).

44. Brett W. Hawkins and Doublas M. Ihrke, "Reexamining the Suburban Exploitation Thesis in American Metropolitan Areas," *Publius* 29, no. 3 (1999): 109-21.

45. E. Ostrom, Gardner, and Walker, *Rules, Games.*

46. But, see Jean-Marie Baland and Jean-Philippe Platteau, *Halting Degradation of Natural Resources: Is There a Role for Rural Communities?* (Oxford: Clarendon Press, 1996).

47. Garrett Hardin, "The Tragedy of the Commons," *Science* 162 (1968): 1243-48.

48. Bonnie J. McCay and James M. Acheson, *The Question of the Commons: The Culture and Ecology of Communal Resources* (Tucson: University of Arizona Press, 1987); Fikret Berkes, *Common Property Resources: Ecology and Community-Based Sustainable Development* (London: Belhaven, 1989); E. Ostrom, *Governing the Commons*; William Blomquist, *Dividing the Waters: Governing Groundwater in Southern California* (San Francisco: ICS Press, 1992); Daniel W. Bromley, David Feeny, Margaret McKean, Pauline Peters, Jere Gilles, Ronald Oakerson, C. Ford Runge, and James Thomson, *Making the Commons Work: Theory, Practice, and Policy (*San Francisco: ICS Press, 1992); Shui Yan Tang, *Institutions and Collective Action: Self Governance in Irrigation* (San Francisco: ICS Press, 1992); among many others.

49. J. E. M. Arnold, "Devolution of Control of Common Pool Resources to Local Communities: Experiences in Forestry." Paper presented at the meeting of the UNU/WIDER Project on Land Reform Revisited: Access to Land, Rural Poverty, and Public Action, Santiago, Chile, April 16-18, 1998.

50. Donald Curtis, *Beyond Government: Organizations for Common Benefit* (London: Macmillan, 1991); Theodore Panayotou and Peter S. Ashton, *Not by Timber Alone: Economics and Ecology for Sustaining Tropical Forests* (Washington, D.C.: Island Press, 1992); William Ascher, *Communities and Sustainable Forestry in Developing Countries* (San Francisco: ICS Press, 1995).

51. David H. Feeny, "Agricultural Expansion and Forest Depletion in Thailand, 1900-1975," in *World Deforestation in the Twentieth Century*, ed. John F. Richards and Richard P. Tucker (Durham, N.C.: Duke University Press, 1988), 112-43.

52. Gill Shepherd, *Managing Africa's Tropical Dry Forests: A Review of Indigenous Methods* (London: Overseas Development Institute, 1992); James T. Thomson, "Ecologi-

cal Deterioration: Local-Level Rule-Making and Enforcement Problems in Niger," in *Desertification: Environmental Degradation in and around Arid Lands*, ed. Michael H. Glantz (Boulder, Colo.: Westview Press, 1977), 57-79; James T. Thomson, David Feeny, and Ronald J. Oakerson, "Institutional Dynamics: The Evolution and Dissolution of Common-Property Resource Management" in *Making the Commons Work: Theory, Practice, and Policy*, ed. Daniel W. Bromley, et al. (San Francisco: ICS Press, 1992), 129-60.

53. J. E. M. Arnold and J. Gabriel Campbell, "Collective Management of Hill Forests in Nepal: The Community Forestry Development Project," In *Proceedings of the Conference on Common Property Resource Management,* National Research Council, (Washington, D.C.: National Academy Press, 1986): 425-54.

54. Madhav Gadgil and Prema Iyer, "On the Diversification of Common-Property Resource Use by Indian Society," in *Common Property Resources: Ecology and Community-Based Sustainable Development*, ed. Fikret Berkes (London: Belhaven Press, 1989), 240-72; Narpat S. Jodha, "Depletion of Common Property Resources in India: Micro-level Evidence," in *Rural Development and Population: Institutions and Policy*, ed. G. McNicoll and M. Cain (Oxford: Oxford University Press, 1990), 261-83; Narpat S. Jodha, "Property Rights and Development," in *Rights to Nature*, ed. Susan S. Hanna, Carl Folke, and Karl-Göran Mäler (Washington D.C.: Island Press, 1996).

55. John C. Cordell and Margaret A. McKean, "Sea Tenure in Bahia, Brazil," in *Making the Commons Work: Theory, Practice, and Policy*, ed. Daniel W. Bromley, et al. (San Francisco: ICS Press, 1992), 183-205; Wilfrido D. Cruz, "Overfishing and Conflict in a Traditional Fishery: San Miguel Bay, Philippines," in *Proceedings of the Conference on Common,* 1986; Partha Dasgupta, *The Control of Resources* (Cambridge: Harvard University Press, 1982); Robert Higgs, "Legally Induced Technical Regress in the Washington Salmon Fishery," in *Empirical Studies in Institutional Change*, ed. Lee J. Alston, Thráinn Eggertsson, and Douglass C. North (New York: Cambridge University Press, 1996), 247-79; Evelyn Pinkerton, *Co-operative Management of Local Fisheries: New Directions for Improved Management and Community Development* (Vancouver: University of British Columbia Press, 1989).

56. For different views, however, see Herbert A. Simon, *Models of Bounded Rationality: Empirically Grounded Economic Reason* (Cambridge: MIT Press, 1997); Martin Landau, "Redundancy, Rationality, and the Problem of Duplication and Overlap," *Public Administration Review* 29, no. 4 (July-August 1969): 346-58; Vincent Ostrom, *The Political Theory of a Compound Republic: Designing the American Experiment*, 2nd revised edition (San Francisco: ICS Press, 1987); Vincent Ostrom, *The Meaning of Democracy and the Vulnerability of Democracies: A Response to Tocqueville's Challenge* (Ann Arbor: University of Michigan, 1997); Jonathon Bendor and Dilip Mookherjee, "Institutional Structure and the Logic of Ongoing Collective Action," *American Political Science Review* 81, no.1 (March 1987): 129-54.

57. E. Ostrom, "A Behavioral Approach," 1-22.

58. The methodology is decribed in Elinor Ostrom, "Coping with Tragedies of the Commons," *Annual Review of Political Science* 2, (1999): 493-535.

59. E. Ostrom, "Coping with Tragedies," 493; E. Ostrom, Gardner, and Walker, *Rules,*

Games.

60. Francois Jacob, "Evolution and Tinkering," *Science* 196 no. 4295 (1977): 1161-66.

61. Donald T. Campbell, "Reforms as Experiments," *American Psychologist* 24, no. 4 (1969): 409-29; Donald T. Campbell, "On the Conflicts between Biological and Social Evolution and between Psychology and Moral Tradition," *American Psychologist* 30, no. 11 (1975): 1103-26.

62. James Wilson, Bobbi Low, Robert Costanza, and Elinor Ostrom, "Scale Misperceptions and the Spatial Dynamics of a Social-Ecological System," *Ecological Economics* 31, no. 2 (November 1999): 243-57.

63. Landau, "Redundancy, Rationality;" Martin Landau, "Federalism, Redundancy, and System Reliability," *Publius* 3, no. 2 (1973): 173-96; Jonathan Bendor, *Parallel Systems: Redundancy in Government* (Berkeley: University of California Press, 1985).

64. For an overview of the relevant literature, see Arun Agrawal, Charla Britt, and Keshav Kanel, *Decentralization in Nepal: A Comparative Analysis,* a report on the Participatory District Development Program (Oakland, Calif.: ICS Press, 1999); Arun Agrawal and Jesse Ribot, "Accountability in Decentralization: A Framework with South Asian and West African Cases," *Journal of Developing Areas* 33, no. 4 (Summer 1999): 473-502.

65. McGinnis, *Polycentricity.*

66. E. Ostrom, "Coping with Tragedies," 493.

67. (Brett, private correspondence)

68. Arun Agrawal and Clark Gibson, "Community in Natural Resource Conservation," *World Development* 27, no. 4 (1999): 629-49.

69. Vincent Ostrom, Charles M. Tiebout, and Robert Warren, "The Organization of Government in Metropolitan Areas: A Theoretical Inquiry," *American Political Science Review* 55, no. 4 (December 1961): 831-42; Michael McGinnis, *Polycentric Governance and Development: Readings from the Workshop in Political Theory and Policy Analysis* (Ann Arbor: University of Michigan Press, 1999a); Michael McGinnis, *Polycentric Games and Institutions: Readings from the Workshop in Political Theory* (Ann Arbor: University of Michigan Press, 2000).

70. John H. Holland, *Hidden Order: How Adaptation Builds Complexity* (Reading, Mass.: Addison-Wesley, 1995).

71. It is important to note, however, that there is no guarantee that any evolutionary process will discover the optimal structure for solving a particular problem. The dynamics of evolutionary processes are sensitive both to the initial starting positions and to strategic moves of key actors early in the process.

72. Jonathon Bendor and Dilip Mookherjee, "Institutional Structure and the Logic of Ongoing Collective Action," *American Political Science Review* 81, no. 1 (March): 144 conclude that: "We believe that this focusing on the polar pair of completely decentralized and completely centralized solutions has led us to overlook an important class of organizational forms: nested structures that combine strategies of conditional cooperation at local levels and strategies of selective incentives at the global level."

73. Pingle and Day, "Modes of Economizing Behavior," 206.

74. Holland, *Hidden Order*; Axelrod and Cohen, *Harnessing Complexity.*

75. Christopher Boehm, *Hierarchy in the Forest: The Evolution of Egalitarian Behavior* (Harvard: Harvard University Press, 1999); Robert Boyd and Peter J. Richerson, *Culture and the Evolutionary Press* (Chicago: University of Chicago Press, 1985).

76. V. Ostrom, *The Meaning of Democracy.*

Chapter 12

Is There Cultural Progress?

Richard O. Zerbe, Jr.

The greatest changes in human history occur not in the mechanical gadgets which men use or in the institutionalized arrangements by which they live, but in their attitudes and in the values they accept.

James H. Bossard and Eleanor Stoker Boll,
The Sociology of Child Development[1]

1.0 Introduction

1.1 Two Examples of Cultural Clashes

In the year 167 B.C. Judas Maccabeus led a band of Jews in defending Jewish culture and religion against its Hellenization. Antiochus, the Seleucid king, led the Hellenization culture revolution. The Seleucids, among the successors to the empire of Alexander the Great, found that uniformity of culture and standardization of its procedures made governing more simple. Within the Hellenistic religious culture there was always room for one more god, so there was no objection to letting the Jews keep their god. But for the Jews, there was only one God, and religion was the Way of Life that had nothing in common with the empty rituals of the Greeks. When Antiochus set a statue of Zeus in the Jewish Temple at Jerusalem, a line had been crossed. For the Jews this was the "Abomination of

Desolation on the altar of holocausts." Thus it was that Judas Maccabeus (the Hammer), with troops outnumbered by more than two to one, fell upon and routed the Greeks. The following year Judas' army defeated a Greek force more than six times the size of the Jewish army. The Jews made a new altar for the Temple and held an eight day celebration, which has become the Feast of Hanukkah.[2]

In 1519, Hernan Cortes began the conquest of Aztecs at the high central plateau of Mexico. In 1531, Francisco Pizzaro set out on a similar conquest of Peru. The conquerors sought wealth, power, the greater glory of the crown, and the spread of Catholicism. The moral justification for the brutal subjugation of a brutal (Aztec) people was religious: "From the start the monarchy believed it had a moral and Christian mission in the New World."[3] The Church worked for three centuries at the "civilization" of native Americans. They took Indians from their tribes and villages, taught them Christianity, and returned them to villages to proselytize. The Church attempted to make itself the protector of the Indian subjects and to develop their rights.

1.2 The Plan of this Essay

Cultural conflict raises the issue of whether or not all cultures are of equal worth so that there is no basis for choosing among them. The example of Antiochus raises the issue of the advantages of cultural uniformity and standardization as compared to those of cultural diversity. These are issues relevant to public policy.

This essay considers briefly four questions: (1) is there such a thing as cultural progress? (I argue that there is such a thing, and that we think of cultural progress in terms of "maturity," akin to the concepts of maturity developed in psychology); (2) how might we define it or know it when we see it? (It can be recognized on the same basis as we recognize more and less mature individuals); (3) how can cultural diversity within a cooperative unit be maintained? (I argue that maturity involves the greater ability to hold in a productive tension positions that may seem contradictory at first glance); (4) what policies and programs can promote cultural progress? (I provide several examples.) I propose here to provide a framework for thinking about these issues.

In considering these questions, I propose to apply psychological concepts of individual maturity to cultures as an approach to gauging progress. I argue that cultural development, as with individual development, reflects different levels of maturity. I suggest the possibility that attributes of cultural and individual maturity have evolutionary survival value, for cultures as well as individuals. Our most cherished values of justice, for example, may point towards end points of an evolutionary process.

2.0 Is There Such a Thing as Cultural Progress?

Cultural progress, if addressed at all, is usually framed in terms of results such as those noted earlier in the century by Maurice Parmelle:

> Certainly in more recent times we can find reason for hope in cultural progress. We need not go back more than a century and a half in the most advanced countries of Western culture to find a good deal of abuse of animals and human beings—the extensive existence of slavery, market cruelties in the treatment of criminals, the brutal beating of small children, little interest in the poor except on the basis of personal almsgiving, incredible horrors in the treatment of feebleminded and insane. In the years since then, the condition of one after another of these groups has been transformed: the treatment of the sick, the insane, and various physically and mentally defective and sick persons has been humanized; there has been widespread amelioration in the condition of criminals; a large amount of social legislation has been passed to improve working conditions; slavery has been abolished; women have been placed more nearly on an equality with men; societies for the prevention of cruelty to animals have flourished; and extensive philanthropic movements have been directed toward the relief of distress and the reduction of poverty.[4]

But against this sort of recitation can be set a list of twentieth century atrocities. To evaluate the possibilities of progress we need a more basic understanding of what it might be and where it might come from.

Definitions: *Cultural progress* is the growth in the ability of a culture to support individuals in developing more empathic, mature, and intimate relationships with other beings. *Culture* is simply the body of learning that is passed on within a group. This definition encompasses technology but is not confined to it.

This definition of cultural progress is consistent with the way we speak of progress in other areas. We speak of progress in peace, in spreading wealth more broadly, and in technology. Differences in culture can lead to differences in the rate of technological innovation, and to differences in how values such as equality are defined, so that we can speak of cultural progress in the same sense we speak of progress in other areas. These developments that we call progress are themselves part and parcel of culture so that culture is more than just an instrument of progress; it must also be an object of it.

This definition of culture is consistent with the classic definition of the anthropologist Edward Tylor. For Tylor, culture consists of language, customs, institutions, codes, tools, techniques, concepts, beliefs, etc.[5] The cultural commentator, Jacques Barzun, notes that anthropologists ended up "defining culture among primitive people as everything they did: the way they ate, their canoes, their marriage customs—nothing was left out. When that idea is applied to history, you find that the arts, social customs, government, religion, and so forth all became part of cultural history."[6]

2.1 The Existing View

Modern cultural anthropologists appear to believe that the concepts of cultural progress are anathemas. This cultural relativism is itself the result of a sort of psychic trauma within the profession. Cultural relativism serves to eliminate assertions of cultural superiority as a justification for attacking unjust impositions of one culture on another.[7] Such impositions have a bad history. So it is easy to understand the appeal of cultural relativism.[8] Concepts of cultural superiority have been used to justify the most egregious behavior. The conquistadors used this argument—especially as it pertained to the superiority of the Catholic religion—to enslave native tribes. Southern slaveholders used their belief in the superiority of Christianity to justify slavery. The Nazis, after all, believed not only in their racial but in their cultural superiority. The colonizations by Western Europeans were rationalized by religious arrogance and noteworthy for their insensitivity to native religious practices and customs. The Marxist values of equality were perverted to eliminate or displace millions of relatively well to do farmers (Kulaks). Cultural or value superiority has in fact been used to justify the most appalling treatment of others. Cultural relativism arose to combat this sort of arrogance. A cultural relativist felt she could say, you cannot justify treating the natives as if they are inferior; their culture is as good as yours.

In 1918, an essay in the *American Anthropologist* attacked the idea of cultural evolution (by which they meant cultural progress) as "the most inane, sterile, and pernicious theory ever conceived in the history of science."[9] By 1939 another anthropologist was able to report that cultural "evolutionism can muster hardly a single proponent."[10] One sort of music is not superior to another; one sort of art is not to be compared unfavorably with another sort. Nor should one set of values be set superior to another set. To even entertain the notion, as I do here, that some cultures are more mature than others, is a violation of our own quasi-norm of cultural relativism.

The anthropological literature offers us even today little in the way of a concept of cultural progress. Joseph Campbell (1983) seems to have captured the prevailing anthropologists view in his contention that all religions are cyclical, mythical, and ahistorical.[11] This view, associated with Eastern philosophy, stands in contrast to the view, arising from the Jewish and Greek cultures especially, that one may read human history from a teleological perspective, that, in short, there is historical progress.

For some time it has been politically incorrect to speak of the possibility of cultural progress. The notion of progress suggests the notion of cultural maturity and cultural maturity is a forbidden concept. Our own culture is said to have a self contradictory "dogma of otherness,"[12] a belief that all cultures are of equal merit—that there should be no cultural dogmas.[13] This attitude is part of a more general postmodernism in which "there are no clear lines of advance and ... when people accept futility and the absurd as normal."[14] The postmodern culture is simply decadent in Barzun's terms.[15]

The important exception to the prevailing view was the attempt by Lewis Henry Morgan in 1877, and Morgan's approach became taboo in his own profession.[16] Morgan's concept of development is mainly technological and partly institutional so that it does not reflect the values approach I offer here. Morgan's stages of institutions have some correspondence to stages of psychological development. Morgan sees the development of the family and of the concept of individual property as reflecting individual development.

One might consider cultural relativism as simply the view that all cultures are the most appropriate adaptation to the environment given the circumstances—so each culture might be seen as simply appropriate to its challenges. In this sense, no culture is superior to another, just different. This is similar to the psychoanalytic view that individual development comes from adaptations to external and internal circumstance. The psychoanalytic view, however, is that these short term, perhaps necessary adaptations, may be inferior from a longer term perspective.

We can accept the view that each culture is often an appropriate adaptation to its circumstances without giving up a notion of cultural maturity or superiority. By considering cultural maturity we can consider ways in which it can be achieved just as the analyst considers ways in which an individual may better gain greater maturity.

2.2 The Internal Contradiction of Cultural Relativism

Although cultural relativism arose out of attempts to eliminate unjust judgments of cultural inferiority, it is the wrong tool to condemn unjust treatment; it is logically inconsistent. In its extreme form it says that all cultures are equally valuable. In this form it has no standing to condemn the acts of a brutal culture, as it cannot say a culture is brutal or unjust, or it can say that it is brutal but cannot say that brutality is bad. Cultural relativism has no answer to the imperialist defense that exploitation of others is just a part of its culture if all cultures are of equal worth. Talbott (2000) asks, suppose you came across a sixteenth century conquistador threatening to kill any native who did not convert to Catholicism. You attempt to preach tolerance. But the conquistador replies that you are attempting to subvert his culture, which has no such norm of tolerance. A culture that fully acted upon a belief in cultural relativism would be eliminated by more aggressive cultures. Moreover, cultural relativism carries a cost—abdication of cultural responsibility for others and an inability to act to improve culture. Yet just as clearly cultural absolutism leads to the very sorts of unethical behavior that cultural relativism was created to condemn. There is another, better ground than cultural relativism or absolutism for condemning colonial exploitation. I will suggest that concepts of individual development and the idea of empathy can be adapted to do this work.

3.0 Toward a Theory of Cultural Progress and Maturity

3.1 The Plan

The ability to cooperate is a vehicle of progress.[17] This vehicle is enhanced by cultural maturity, a concept that can be understood in the context of psychological maturity. I suggest how cooperation can be productive. Then I suggest that cooperation can be a product of natural selection. Finally, I note psychological components to cooperation that help to define cultural maturity.

The term I emphasize in characterizing the development of a moral sense is empathy. Empathy is not just an impulse toward doing good. It requires rather an understanding of others and a sense of what they need. It is an ability to put oneself in others' places. Such empathy is not simply charity nor just attempting to do good but something more complex—the empathic understanding of what the individual needs to support his or her journey to a mature personality. The analogy is to the good parent who knows what the child needs. My focus will be on the growth in the ability to empathize as a measure of levels of maturation in both individuals and in cultures. The stronger the sense of empathy with the other player, the more likely one is to cooperate. Imagine, for example, that you are playing with someone you care about deeply. My assertion is that you would be more likely to cooperate. The ability to care for others grows with maturity so that cooperation is also more likely with maturity.

3.2 Cooperation

Cooperative ability captures important parts of individual development as growth in empathy. What I call culture is largely a reflection of cooperation among humans.[18] As this cooperation has become richer, so has culture; and this growth in richness is cultural progress. Cooperation grows not only in complexity but spatially. The social advantage of cooperation is that it increases the size of the social pie, whether we measure this by technological, artistic, or social measures.

Cooperation can take two forms. One is rooted in self-regard, the other in empathy. First, parties can cooperate for mutual advantage. This sort of cooperation involves the ability to solve collective action problems among those in similar positions and requires a culture of cooperation and a sort of prescient self-regard. Societies are continually faced with problems which require social cooperation to solve and for which a failure of cooperation leads to loss of opportunity. These problems are called collective action problems. A common form of such problems is known as the prisoners' dilemma (PD). In a PD problem, a player can either defect or cooperate. If a player defects he receives the highest available reward in the single game if the other player (in this context the sucker) cooperates. If the player cooperates (is the sucker) and the other player defects, he receives the lowest possible reward. If both players cooperate, however, both receive substantial rewards. If both defect they each do better than if they were the sucker but not as well as in cooperation. These sorts of PD games or collective action problems are common in social issues. They arise because the non-cooperator will do better than the cooperator even though the cooperative solution is better for the group as a whole. That is, the cooperative solution is socially superior to the non-cooperative solution even though the cooperator does less well than the non-cooperator.

Where, for example, there is unrestricted access to a valuable asset, problems of the commons arise. The problem arises from the fact that the asset will not be used in a way that maximizes its total value. These difficulties arise in many fisheries or in air or water pollution or in a too great growth in population.

The most important collective action problems perhaps are those of political agreement such as developing constitutions and rules of conduct. Interest group politics can represent a norm that leads to political breakdown and the non-cooperative solution. Because the non-cooperator does better than the cooperator, there needs to be some incentive for cooperation. The more efficient incentive is probably furnished by culture. There are certain features of culture that are known to promote cooperation.[19] It is well known that you are more likely to cooperate if the PD game is a repeated one.[20] This is because successful non-cooperation, which occurs when one party cooperates and the other does not, is less likely in repeated games. People are less likely to be a sucker repeatedly than a sucker once. This result also obviously requires some ability to think ahead, another signal of mental maturity. What if you are playing a repeated game with someone you are certain will defect. What is a mature strategy? Not always to cooperate. A sucker is not self-actualized. Rather, what if you cooperate on the first round and thereafter do what the other person did in the previous round. This tit for tat strategy, which opens the door to cooperation, is remarkably successful against other strategies.[21] But, it also has the potential to teach cooperation since the defector will not do as well as a cooperator if many others play tit for tat. But it only works well if there are other potential cooperators. In a sufficiently primitive society where few think ahead, an individual who pursues cooperation is unlikely to fare well even if the game is repeated. This sort of cooperation can arise from simple self-regard. An example in which culture allowed self-regard to solve a prisoner's dilemma type of collective action problem is provided by the example of the California gold miners in 1949.[22]

The second form of cooperation is more subtle. It occurs when at least one party is able to empathize with those in quite different positions. This second form of cooperation, which I shall call empathic cooperation, concerns society's ability to provide individuals with the cultural milieu that is most supportive of their individual development as defined in terms of psychoanalytic thinking. These two ideas of cooperation are my defining measures of cultural progress.[23]

Cooperation is easier under certain conditions. For example, group homogeneity, as evidenced by common culture, promotes cooperation. Zerbe and Anderson (2001), for example, show that while conditions in the California gold fields promoted cooperation, intra-ethnic cooperation was much easier to achieve than inter-ethnic cooperation. Without some substantial level of maturity then inter-ethnic cooperation may be impossible, as it requires the ability to understand or empathize with those that are substantially different.

Cooperation can extend beyond self-regard. This second form of cooperation requires a willingness to reach sympathetically and empathetically to the disenfranchised so as to move towards a society in which each person has an equal chance at life's prospects. To move towards an ideal environment for individual development requires something more than prescient self-regard—it requires co-operative empathy, which is part of what I am defining as cultural maturity. Cultural maturity imagines not just simple cooperation but a cultural ideal that gives the individual the best chance of realizing his or her maximum potential. As Erikson notes, society should be "so constituted as to meet and invite this succession of potentialities for interaction and the proper sequence of their enfolding."[24]

In the development of the Jewish culture, Cahill[25] sees a tit for tat mentality operating until the time of David. David's sins are worse than Saul's, but David is better treated by God, for David discovers forgiveness and redemption. This is not surprising as David's internal discovery of the sense of self is apparent, and a sense of self is necessary to cooperate. With the exception of the Psalms, the sense of "I" is absent from ancient literature and is not discovered again until the humanistic literature of the early modern period, such as with *The Autobiography of Benvenuto Cellini*.[26]

Cooperative empathy requires the ability of one class or group or country to extend opportunity and justice to another. This ability is akin to the notions advanced by Rawls (1971) who asks us to form basic rules by imagining what our choice would be in an initial or original position.[27] This position is one in which the rule chooser does not know, among other things, what position she will occupy in the society until after the rule is chosen. That is, the person could be anyone; this procedure envisions complete empathy.[28]

3.3 Cultural Progress and Natural Selection[29]

The critic will say that my adoption of empathy as a vehicle of cultural progress is a mere value judgment. Of course this is true, though it may be an appealing value judgment. But it may be more. It may be that empathy and its associated ability to cooperate are themselves a product of evolutionary forces with survival value.

The evolutionary biologist Richard Dawkins invented the term meme to stand for the cultural evolution analog of the gene in biological evolution.[30] [31] A meme or set of memes can be ideas, technologies, religious or political philosophies, or any other components of culture. The critical similarities they share with genes are 1) they are passed on through time and across cultures, 2) they exhibit variation through time and space, and 3) some memes are better than others at propagating themselves. These are unusual concepts to apply to ideas and cultures, but it is clear that if there is any hope of progress or sense in human cultural history there must be some sort of genealogy of cultures. Cultures and societies do not spring up anew from amorphous bands of people. And some ideas are clearly better at being spread than others. For example, a philosophy that requires its adherents to commit suicide in silence is less likely to grow and gain new believers than one that requires its adherents to teach. The classic example is that of the Shakers who, believing sex to be wrong, died out.[32] Therefore ideas can be thought of as competing in a cultural landscape just as genes compete in a biological landscape. But for the purposes of this paper a cultural version of biological descent with modification is not enough. I suggest that the features of cultural maturity I have identified give cultures a competitive advantage, giving them an overall tendency to become more common.

The sociologist Rodney Stark (1996) analyzed and modeled the early growth of Christianity in the context of the Roman Empire. He found that, regardless of metaphysics or miracles, many features of the new religion gave it an advantage in the sense of evolutionary fitness—the ability to propagate itself more effectively than its competitors. These advantages led to an increase in the numbers of Christians in the Empire relative to pagans, leading to the domination of Europe by the Catholic Church in the Middle Ages. This type of competitive advantage does not necessarily imply conflict, conquest, or subjugation, merely a superior ability to reproduce.

Early Christianity showed a feature of cultural maturity of progress in the enhanced status and respect women and female children held in the church relative to pagan attitudes. In Greco-Roman society females were treated with little respect for their humanity.[33] Female children were routinely disposed of, with even large Roman families seldom raising more than one daughter. Women and marriage were held in low regard, and many Roman men remained single, ignored their wives, and avoided having children. Abortion was incredibly common considering the crude methods of the time, which frequently killed both fetus and mother. As a result of these attitudes and practices, the core areas of the Roman Empire were facing severe population shortages by the Christian era.

By contrast, the earliest Christians found the Roman practices immoral and reprehensible. Abortion and infanticide were considered murder, a significant expansion of empathy and compassion. Wives were treated more fairly, with rights to love, attention, and fidelity from their husbands. Family life and procreation was stressed as godly, in opposition to the immorality and casual promiscuity of the Romans. Therefore, not only were more women attracted to the new religion because of their higher status, but their average fertility was improved by the practices of Christianity. The new religion was able to grow and eventually dominate Europe by a combination of conversion and reproduction superior to paganism, as a direct result of improved cultural maturity.

Twice in the early years of the Christian era the Roman Empire was swept by epidemics, and the responses of the people demonstrated the improved cultural maturity of the Christian religion. In the late second century a massive plague killed as much as one-third of the population, including the Emperor Marcus Aurelius, and a similar epidemic also caused massive mortality about a hundred years later. The established religion and philosophies of the Roman Empire were unable to provide their followers with solace or guidance against these disasters, resulting in panic, despair, and abandonment of the sick and dying. Stark quotes Dionysius, bishop of Alexandria, writing that "At the first onset of disease they [the pagans] pushed the sufferers away and fled from their dearest, throwing them into the roads before they were dead. . . ."[34] By contrast, the Christian community found in their religion both metaphysical justification for suffering and the comfort of an afterlife. Even more important from the viewpoint of cultural progress, the Christian ideals of love for their fellow men as an expression of love for God motivated care of the sick and dying of both Christian and pagan communities. While modern treatments for the diseases were of course unavailable, simple nursing care was probably effective in reducing death rates. Thus the compassion and empathy of the Christians would have led to an increase in the relative proportions of Christians, through improved survival and a powerful incentive and example for potential converts.

Much the same process may have operated in the cities of the Roman Empire in normal times. Stark (1996) demonstrated that Christianity was a largely urban movement in the early Empire. The cities of the period were incredibly crowded, filthy, and disease ridden, with death rates so high that they could only persist with constant immigration from the countryside: "Given limited water and means of sanitation, and the incredible density of humans and animals, most people in Greco-Roman cities must have lived in filth beyond imagining."[35] In the face of disease, natural disasters, war, and the constant population flux Christianity provided both mental and physical comfort.

As Stark writes:

> To cities filled with the homeless and impoverished, Christianity offered charity as well as hope. To cities filled with newcomers and strangers, Christianity offered an immediate basis for attachments. To cities filled with orphans and widows, Christianity provided a new and expanded sense of family. To cities torn by violent ethnic strife, Christianity offered a new basis for social solidarity. To cities faced with epidemics, fires and earthquakes, Christianity offered effective nursing services.[36]

As with epidemics, these factors gave Christianity improved survival, fertility, and success in propagation.[37] Cultures evolve and are subject to the rules of natural selection. But they evolve much more rapidly than species. The century suggests that ethical superiority gives survival value to a culture and possibility, according to Ernst Mayr (1997), to generic survival of impulses towards caring. The increasing progress of democratic rule and of enfranchisement suggests at least the cultural survivability of cooperation.

3.4 Maturity and the Individual Stages of Development

Just as some individuals can be seen as more mature so can some cultures. Modern psychological thinking inclines towards the view that there are a number of mental states that are variously elicited by environment and that the "optimally expected environment" can elicit more mature behavior.

Psychoanalytic and psychological thinkers have several, more or less detailed and more or less congruent, stages of individual human personality development. These theories include those from the psychoanalytic literature, for example, Sigmund Freud (1971), Erik Erikson (1963, 1964), Melanie Klein (1948) Carl Rogers (1989), and Daniel Stern (1985), and those from the psychological literature which include Jean Piaget (1985), Abraham Maslow (1982), and Lawrence Kohlberg (1983).[38]

The psychoanalytic writers stress the development of a sense of self which allows the ability to empathize with others.[39] As the sense of self develops, one's empathy is able to extend ahead to future generations, and with this development there is also a growth of creativity and productivity.[40]

The psychological writers more directly address moral development. Maslow's (1982) highest stage of development is that of self-actualization. Characteristics of self-actualized persons include: clear, efficient perceptions of reality; acceptance of self, others, and nature; spontaneity, simplicity and naturalness; problem centering (having something outside they "must" do as a mission); detachment and need for privacy; autonomy, independence of culture and environment and will; continued freshness of relations; ... ethical discrimination between means and ends, and between good and evil; philosophical, unhostile sense of humor; creativeness; transcendence of any particular culture; resisting cultural molding.[41]

Within the psychological literature there are serious attempts to derive moral stages rooted in both sense and sensibility, in reason and emotion, and in psychological experiment and human response to instances of situational ethics. The sort of questions considered are, for example, will an individual who is asked as part of the classic experiment to administer electric shock to another, agree to do it, under what conditions, and what are the differences in behavior among individuals.

Some, such as Kohlberg (1983), focus on stages of moral development derived by experiment and reason. Others[42] stress the role of the emotions and empathy in determining morality. Kohlberg develops a hierarchy of justice reasoning based on a cognitive approach to morality. For Piaget and Kohlberg justice is determined by judgment, and for Kohlberg the stages of moral development have to do with increasing moral adequacy defined in a cognitive sense. This approach, if viewed from philosophy, might be termed the approach of reason or Kantian. The approach from sensibility, such as Gilligan's, might be termed an approach from Hume. It does not seem too bold to say that both reason and sensibility are proper contributors to this exercise and that an approach from psychology grounded in psychological experiment as well as in reason and sensibility has particular appeal.

3.5 The Common Ground of Psychoanalytic and Psychological Stages

All of the psychoanalytic and psychological proponents of developmental stages have in common a sort of sense of progress or, perhaps I should say, of maturation. They also have a picture of appropriateness, which is to say that treatment of an individual should be geared to the individual's level of maturity and intellectual capacity. The needs of one stage of development are not necessarily the needs of another. The caretaker who brings a baby its toy may wisely not bring a toy to the child who is able to get it for him or her self.

Development theories have in common a picture of normal human development that takes place when conditions are reasonable. They all show as healthy development the development of basic trust, the growth in the sense of self, of empathy with others, of a realistic or increasingly accurate picture of the world, and an increasing ability to self-regulate. The process of maturity involves a process by which one goes from a sense of merger with the world in which the self is the center of all, but essentially helpless, to a state in which one more and more clearly differentiates oneself from others. We know from our own experience that interaction with an adult person who considers only him or her self results in a different and less satisfying experience than interaction with a more mature person who evidences empathy.

True empathy arises from growth of the sense of self. If the sense of self is insufficiently developed, one cannot afford to empathize with others without risking some loss of a sense of self.[43] The growth of sense of self comes at a cost. It is associated with a more realistic view of the world and thus a loss of grandiosity. One moves from feeling one is the center of the world to realizing one is a very small part of it. Among the benefits of this gain are that of accuracy, of a realistic view of one's place in the world and the universe, and of what one can actually do or effect. But this is realistically and necessarily a small place.

The individual copes with this by gaining increasing powers of self-regulation, inner resources, and resiliency. Thus in normal development the individual arrives at a realistic sense of his or her place but with the resources to make the most effective use of actual abilities. In gaining a firmer sense of self, a heightened sense of differentiation, the individual paradoxically gains a greater sense of empathy with others. In becoming separate, and in gaining a more accurate picture of the world, the individual is better able to see others as separate and as they are. Thus the common ground of psychological stages consists of at least the following elements as characteristics of human maturity: sense of self; empathy; realistic view of world;[44] the development of a moral or ethical self; an ability to self regulate; and an ability to plan ahead. This is why, in a religious sense, the Jews were culturally more mature than the Seleucid kingdom—their religion showed a greater sense of self-differentiation.

A cultural analog to the development of the individual sense of self may be found in the story of Abraham. To create or discover one God from many gods is an expression of individuality and responsibility. Our god(s) is a reflection of our self-image as Genesis in a sense notes. To see one god is to see one separate individual. This in turn encouraged the development of individual responsibility and of a moral code.[45] Appreciation of a single creator could only arise from those who appreciated themselves. The great achievement of Jewish culture is the early development of a moral code. Jewish culture created a moral universe superimposed on the physical one.[46] Moreover the nature of this ethical and moral universe evolves with Jewish culture from the harsh and temperamental patriarchal God of the Torah to the broader empathic concern with social justice of Isaiah and of Jesus.[47]

According to Cahill, it was from the Jewish culture that the very idea of progress developed. As Cahill[48] says, "The story the Hebrew Bible has to tell is the story of an evolving consciousness, a consciousness that went through many stages of development and that, like all living things, sometimes grew slowly and at other times in great spurts." Time was not cyclical in Jewish culture but has a beginning and an end: "No people have ever insisted more firmly than the Jews that history has a purpose and humanity a destiny."[49]

The suggestion is that from the increased sense of self, combined with a sense of destiny, grew a moral code. The development of this moral universe by the Jews not only helped the survival of their culture but offered (imperfect) protection against the cultural development of narcissistic rage and adoption of the paranoid-schizoid position.[50] As Cahill[51] says, "The story of Jewish identity across the millennia against impossible odds is a unique miracle of cultural survival."

This development of a sense of self is associated with the development of a more realistic view of the world and of empathy for others. As the baby does not see itself as separate from the world or its mother, so the early society saw itself as the center and the measure of all things. In the early Christian view, the earth was the center of the universe and man was the center of earth: "The Lord God created man to have dominion over the fish of the sea, and over the fowl of the air, and over the cattle, and over all the earth and over every creeping thing that creepeth upon the earth." Wilderness and nature were forces to be subdued and tamed. Only man had reason; only man had a soul. The historian of science, Lynn White, sees our ecological problems as deriving from Christian attitudes towards man's relation to nature, which lead us to think of ourselves as "superior" to nature, contemptuous of it, and willing to use it for our slightest whim.[52] Thus the Copernican revolution was as profoundly a moral or cultural revolution as a scientific one, for it allowed the development of a more realistic sense of self. To accept that the earth is not the center of the universe suggests that man might not be the measure of all things.

Failure to develop optimally can result in pathologies for cultures as well as for individuals. In modern psychoanalytic theory the concept of narcissistic injury has been found to be a common reaction to the failure of empathy at early stages.[53] Narcissistic injury is characterized by a inability to empathize with others, by a sort of self-righteousness that is also tied into misunderstanding of one's place in the world and a search for the omnipotent other with a concomitant failure to find it.[54]

World War II, for example, can be seen as an outgrowth of the primitive personality of Adolph Hitler combined with narcissistic rage by the German people, in response to the twin evils of the depression and the treaty of Versailles.[55] Groups may fail to develop a mature culture because they are badly treated.[56] Groups that treat each other badly can trigger a regression towards the primitive that results in a cycle of violence and cultural stagnation. Apparently being badly treated can create psychic trauma that carries on from generation to generation so that the culture is stuck in part at a more primitive stage. One might explain the current experience in Yugoslavia in such terms. That is, the long standing animosities of Yugoslavia can be seen as the result of a sort of long standing psychic trauma as can the current experience in Northern Ireland and the Middle East—i.e., Israelis and Palestinians. Similarly, the easily invoked narcissistic rage that August Wilson shows among black males in ghetto conditions in King Hedley II can be partly understood from this perspective.[57]

The typical individual response to a threat to identity is a regression to a more primitive stage. So also for a culture the threat to its identity will trigger a regression to a more primitive state. The move toward fundamentalism in religion, a current worldwide phenomenon, is seen by Karen Armstrong (2000) not only as an expression of a need for more spiritual values in political life, but as a reaction to threat to religion engendered by rapid modernity and secularism which in many cases is expressed as a contempt for religious values. This fear is largely justified. In Egypt, for example, Nasser, as part of his attempt to build a secular state, imprisoned under harsh conditions about thirty thousand members of the Muslim Brotherhood mostly for nothing stronger than passing out leaflets or attending a meeting. In Iran, the Shah ordered soldiers to fire on an orderly crowd, killing hundreds protesting only for freedom to wear religious dress.[58] Even in the United States, fundamentalism became doctrinaire (the omnipotent other) and self-righteous after the humiliation of fundamentalists with the Scopes trial.[59]

My core suggestion is that we recognize that for culture, as for individuals, there are various levels of maturity so that one culture, or some aspect of a culture, can be said to represent a more mature stage than another, and that things can go wrong in the development of both individuals and cultures. Cultural trauma, for example, can occur so that corrosive hatred becomes endemic.

3.6 Cultural Maturity

The characteristics of a more mature culture may be inferred from those of a mature individual. At base the notion here is that culture is rooted in attitudes and values.[60] A more mature culture will be one with a more widespread political and economic enfranchisement since such an enfranchisement reflects empathy and an ethical sense. Thus for the West we might characterize the increasing enfranchisement of the electorate and of unpropertied men, women, and blacks as progress.

A more mature culture will be one that respects the rule of just laws. I will say that the more mature the culture the less coercion required to achieve adherence to just laws. Indeed, the greater the agreement achieved through culture, the less the need for adjudication. A culture that achieves adherence to law primarily through coercion is not one that shows respect for the law. Mature adherence to a rule of law requires both an understanding and appreciation of its role in solving a collective action problem but it also requires laws that are regarded as fair. Experience suggests that this sort of adherence is difficult to obtain, and in large or diverse societies may require substantial historical time.

For example, the concept of law as a collective culture expression of what is right or fair for society developed slowly in Britain. Magna Carta was more significant for what it came to be than for what it was in 1215.[61] What it became was a touchstone for just rather than tyrannical authority and for the concept that justice arose from a consideration of interests broadly defined which could only be determined by widespread empowerment. The doctrine represented by Magna Carta was constantly invoked as part of the process of creating a rule of law. It gained authority beyond its original provisions as a principle representing the fair settlement of a collective action problem. In the United States, Alexander Hamilton defended John Peter Zenger's right to publish freely, by reference to Magna Carta, even though the document itself is mute with respect to free speech.[62]

The situation has been different in Russia: "Communism itself can be seen as a vision of progress rooted in the Jewish-Christian tradition, modeled on biblical faith and demanding of their adherents that they always hold in their hearts a belief in the future. . . ."[63] But it lacked a sense of individual self, and a concomitant respect for the individual, so there was no appreciation of individual self-determination, no sense as that which grew out of the "Israelite vision of individuals, subjects of value because they are images of God each with a unique and personal destiny. . . ."[64] The most disturbing and, from the historical point of view, important characteristic of the Lenin terror was not the quantity of the victims, but the absence of legal principle on which they were selected. Within a few months of seizing power, Lenin had abandoned the notion of individual guilt, and with it the whole Judeo-Christian ethic of personal responsibility."[65] Lenin abandoned what was already a weak rule of law. The difficulties in introducing a rule of law into Russia remain to this day.

A more mature culture will tend more toward democratic rule as such rule recognizes the ethical right of all groups and individuals to be heard and the danger of the arrogance of power. Thus we might characterize in this regard at least, the culture of Britain, the United States, and Europe as more mature than regimes with less broad voting enfranchisement and less regard for the rule of law.

A mature culture will exhibit compassion toward its weaker members, as this is an expression of empathy rooted in a sense of self. Cultures with a stronger tradition of familial care than the United States might be regarded as more mature in this regard. In part the environmental movement can be read as a growth in empathy and therefore as a gain in cultural maturity.[66]

4.0 The Modern Challenge: Diversity within Cooperation

Individual and cultural maturity require not only a sense of separateness of identity and uniqueness but also the ability to cooperate with others. Merger with others is not maturity; it is an infant state. Humans need both individual identity and a deliberately sought sharing of experiences about the same events and things.

The ability to maintain cultural diversity within unity is a difficult step. Quebec threatens to separate from the rest of Canada. Some Basques wish to separate from Spain. The French worry about maintaining their culture in the context of European union and the importation of music and movies and supermarkets from the United States. To maintain diversity within unity is only possible with a sufficiently strong sense of self whose identity is unthreatened by the level of tolerance or empathy required to accept important differences. Nor can cooperation among diverse groups be accomplished without the development of basic trust, the first stage in Erikson's human development categories. Basic trust is established among diversity by the development of laws or customs (norms) that are seen as fair. As Daniel Moynihan has observed, the deepest and most persuasive source of human conflict is in ethnic rivalry.[67] None of this is to deny the role of other forces, e.g. economic class, as causes for underlying ethnic conflict. Beyond ethnicity, every group has diversity (disabilities, gender, sexual preferences, etc.), so that diversity is a matter of degree. The question of what sorts of diversity are more tolerable is not addressed, but the assertion I make is that the ability to tolerate differences is partially cultural and is related to cultural maturity.[68]

Man's early experience seems to have been tribal and ethnically homogenous within groups but highly conflictual between groups.[69] The usual response of members of separate tribes in Papua New Guinea has been to attempt to kill one another unless they could establish a connection to some common ancestor.[70] The suggestion is that the sort of ethnic/religious conflicts in Eastern Europe or the continuing effects of American slavery can be ameliorated by a growth in cultural maturity.

The accomplishments of the United States, Britain, Canada, and Switzerland, for example, in maintaining diversity within unity have been remarkable and also rare. This idea of cooperation within differences, of diversity within unity, is at the heart of Herman Daly's (1999) distinction between globalization and internationalization.[71] Globalization is a merger, a move toward one world; internationalization, which Daly favors, is for cooperation among separate entities. Thus, internationalization would support cooperation among countries with, for example, respect to international trade and environmental policies; globalization would support one world government.[72]

5.0 What Policies Promote Culture Progress?

5.1 Implications of the Theory

What are the implications of this discussion for public policy and progress? Although this essay considers abstract and general issues of culture, it nevertheless points to types of policies consistent with cultural maturity, which involves a consideration of others. Policy considerations in a mature culture will involve rules and polices that are appropriate for those to whom they are directed and that promote the general welfare. Such rules would include those that help some without harming others (a Pareto test), that satisfy benefit cost tests subject to distributional constraints,[73] and that extend life opportunities to those who would otherwise be without them. But to fully characterize such rules or policies would overburden this essay. Rather, I will suggest some general policy directions as follows:

Appropriateness: *The general rule is to adopt policy or programs that are appropriate to the cultural maturity of the parties at which it is aimed.*

The view here is of culture as representing different stages of maturation. It allows us, for example, to say that the institutions most appropriate for one level of cultural maturity may not be the best for another. It points towards incremental movements. The wholesale adoption of the United States' legal apparatus by another country without a tradition of a rule of law would not produce good results.[74] For a more mature culture to insist on imposing democratic rule may reflect a failure of empathy if the culture is not ready for it. When technologically more developed cultures meet with less developed ones, "things fall apart."

The question of whether or not economic and or political union is a good thing depends on their degree of tolerance for differences, which in turn depends on their maturity and ability to empathize with each other. The dismemberment of the USSR may then have been predictable, as has been also the ability of the European nations to slowly grow toward economic union.

The Rule of Law: *Subject to the rule for appropriateness, the general rule is to encourage development of a rule of (just) law.*

The rule of law is shorthand for rules that are seen as fair in the sense that they would likely be chosen from an initial position. A rule of law is consistent with attempts to equalize life's chances. So I will say that actions and policies that promote the rule of law are more mature to those that tend to destroy it. History shows us that that the attainment of a rule of law is no easy task.

On a single recent Monday on the front page of *The Wall Street Journal*[75] we have the following examples of legal breakdown:

> Russia—Police pounced early in the morning, armed with guns, a saw, and orders from the Committee for Emergency Situation, a municipal crisis unit responsible for order in time of war, natural disaster and other calamitous events.... Their target: Bathhouse and Laundry Complex No. 4.... Stripped bare, the issue is this: Can the cold hand of free-market economics keep people clean? The local government says no. Accusing Mr. Vanin (the owner) of overpricing and underinvesting, it has tried to nationalize his bathhouse.

> Chinese police detained a woman who described in a Wall Street Journal front page account last week how her mother was beaten to death in police custody for refusing to abandon faith in the banned spiritual discipline Falun Gong.

> An Iran clerical court shut down at least three reformist newspapers in a crackdown that appears to have the backing of Ayatollah Khamenei, Iran's supreme leader. On Saturday, a reporter investigating the 1998 killings of five dissidents was arrested.

These accounts may be contrasted with the following on the same page of the Wall Street Journal:

> A Bosnian Serb was arrested Friday in the U. S. patrolled sector of Bosnia and taken to The Hague for a war-crimes trial. Dragan Nikolic, the first person indicted by the U. N. tribunal, is accused of killing, raping and torturing Muslims at a prison camp he ran.

This latter action by the United Nations as promoting the rule of law better meets the empathic test than the other actions mentioned.

Intervention: *The general rule is that the promotion of the rule of law and empathic understanding may justify the intervention of one culture into the rule of another.*

The view of cultural development as representing stages in maturity provides a justification for intervention when one culture invades another. In the 1990s there was ethnic-based breakdown among groups in Yugoslavia triggered by the psychic trauma of past ethnic conflicts and by the individual pathology of Slobodan Milosevic. In the late 1990s, the United States and the United Nations intervened in an attempt to stop "ethnic cleansing." Viewed in this light, the U.S. and UN intervention in Yugoslavia might be seen as representing action by a more mature culture.

The British, in granting independence to India and in making the partition into India and Pakistan, may have wished in some rather vague sense to do the right thing. But the British, as well as some of the Indian elite such as Nehru, were proceeding from a position of arrogance, a failure of empathy. There was no appreciation and little understanding for the actual people or groups involved and the realities of power. Thus, there was an abdication of responsibility. "The princes were abandoned. The minority sects and clans were simply forgotten. The untouchables were ignored. All the real difficulties ... were left to resolve themselves."[76] The recent role of the United States in Sierra Leone may be of a similar immature quality—not because intervention was a bad idea but because it may have been made without an empathic understanding of the country's needs. An empathic understanding of another's needs involves an ability to "walk in the other's shoes," and thus to better craft an intervention that will work.

Status: *The general rule is that the form of status tells us something about the nature of the culture.*

I suggest that the structure of status within a culture may be an indicator of its cultural maturity. Status is a reward that a culture confers on its members for valued acts or positions. A more mature culture will grant status to its members for mature actions. A culture creates incentives, rewards, and punishments for the behavior of its members. One important incentive created by culture is that of status. Now imagine two neighbors that compete for status by buying more and more prestigious cars which, aside from status, neither particularly wants. They gain no status relative to each other and use resources that end up as a waste since neither wants the larger cars. Instead imagine now that status comes primarily from the quality of parenting that each person provides his or her children. Competition for status will increase the well-being of others in a manner that is more productive than the competition for more prestigious cars.

Open source software is software that includes the source code so that a programmer can look at it and change it to fix bugs or to improve it. Typically programmers send their contribution to a keeper of the code who decides whether to keep the change as part of the code. Linus Torvalds, the creator of Linux, screens code patches for the core part of Linux.[77] Thousands of top-notch programmers contribute freely to the development of open source software. Why? Well, the contributors to open source code gain status. "If you do good work, you become a big shot. Your name is forever associated with the code you have contributed, and because the code is open, everyone can see just what you have accomplished."[78]

In addition, showing that you are a good programmer can contribute to your career. Mr. Torvalds was a graduate student in Finland when he invented Linux and now is a highly paid executive in Silicon Valley. So here status works to encourage contributions to a public good. This form of status, unlike the competition for the bigger car, contributes positively to the society. Such incentives are a feature of the more progressive economy. *An implication is that cultural inculcation of notions of status can contribute to the production of public goods.*

Child Rearing and Education: *The general fair rule is to support policies that promote the "optimal expected environment" for children. The best opportunity to extend life opportunities to others is when the others are children.*

Although the theory of an optimal child environment is reasonably well worked out ("the optimal expected environment"), knowledge runs ahead of policy here. By both benefit cost and by equity tests, the provision of effective care for children at risk is justified and is an indication of cultural maturity. Such programs can increase benefits for the larger society as well as for the disadvantaged individuals. For example, the Perry Preschool, a precursor to Head Start and other well run Head Start programs, was found to boost short run I.Q., long run achievement, the likelihood of high school graduation, employment, and reduce crime and welfare participation.[79] The Perry Preschool Program created cost savings to government alone sufficient to justify the program from a benefit cost perspective.[80] The fact is that the number of possible improvements to the educational system exceeds the space to survey them. Cuba is much reviled in this country and its defects have prevented us from considering the possibility that any aspect of their society, including their educational system, may have valuable lessons for us.

Universal Human Rights: *The general rule is to support those basic rights that would be approved by people in an original position as these are consistent with empathy, subject to the rule of appropriateness.*

The original or initial position is defined as one in which the decision maker does not know what his or her own place will be in society with respect to any variable—sex, age, etc.—which may define how the decision is received. Professor Talbott has developed a justification for certain basic universal human rights. These rights include "baseline rights" which protect individuals from such types of death as murder or death by starvation or from exposure, mayhem, torture, serious physical or sexual assault and imprisonment, or the threat of a high probability of any of these harms. They include "equity rights" which come into play when there are significant inequalities in life prospects for its citizens. Equity rights require that "inequalities not be too inequitable." Included in equity rights are (1) anti-discrimination rights and (2) rights to decent life prospects.

Of course some people's rights are other people's duties. This justification for the sort of universal human rights suggested by Talbott is consistent with the concept of cultural maturity presented here. In particular, the justification is that certain rules are desirable because they help everyone by, for example, solving a collective action problem. Thus a rule that gives basic protection to human life is desirable and justifiable because everyone benefits from it as compared to anarchy that would exist without the rule. I shall point out that a moral justification lies also in the choices of members of society that are empathic with each other.

Environmental Policy*: The general rule is that empathy may extend to creatures other than humans and perhaps, arguably, to ecosystems.*

The expansion of environmental values within the United States and internationally has been amazing, fueled by changes in income, education, and sentiment.[81] The change in attitudes has been accompanied by the creation of a more substantial body of environmental and natural resource law. The history of this change has been well documented.[82] In general these changes appear consistent with cultural progress as defined here in the sense that a greater appreciation of environment involves, among other things, greater empathy with other creatures.

New attitudes and new policy and law are being formed in a cauldron of alternate change and retrenchment. One example is the treatment of moral sentiments by those affected only indirectly by environmental change. Traditionally, third parties, those who do not, for example, directly use the environmental amenity, do not have legal standing to bring suit. This contrasts with those with economic damage who do have standing. The inclusion of moral sentiments may be on the horizon.[83] The inclusion of such sentiments, showing the regard for others, is consistent with the concept of cultural maturity presented here.

6.0. Conclusion

Just as there are more mature individuals, so also are there more mature cultures. The more mature culture is evidenced by the extent of its enfranchisement by the ability of it members to cooperate and to empathize with others by the extent to which the cultural institutions encourage values of empathy. Cultures grow and die and they evolve. It may be that cultures that promote the ability to empathize are more likely to survive and that consequently what we see as virtue may be necessity.

The forces of Hellenization under Antiochus failed the empathy test of cultural maturity. They failed to respect the desirable elements of the Jewish culture and what made it unique. This appreciation might have achieved diversity within unity. The superiority of the Spanish with respects to the Indian tribes was purely, or at least primarily, technological. No other form of cultural superiority was much in evidence.

Recently the eminent economist D. Gale Johnson (2000) noted that during the last two centuries, and especially in the twentieth century, there has been an enormous increase in knowledge and a growth of communicating that knowledge that has been transformed into technology and ways of utilizing resources more efficiently. This increase in knowledge has resulted from both an increase in population itself and from the increase in the percentage of the population devoted to the creation of new knowledge. Not long ago farmers accounted for eighty percent of the world's labor force and at the turn of the century for about fifty percent of the labor force in the United States. Now the farm labor force in the United States is a tiny fraction. The recent rapid growth of productivity has increased real per capital incomes. During the 1980s alone, the *increase* in the world's output exceeded by a factor of ten the total world output in 1820.

Moreover, the majority of the poor people of the world have shared in the improvements in well being made possible by the advancement of knowledge. Infant mortality, life expectancy, and per capita food supplies have increased all over the world.[84]

A culture progresses when it develops the empathy and understanding that allow it to structure incentives so as to reward behavior that promotes social and individual maturity—something closer to the "optimal expected environment." In our own society a good step would be to undertake action that increases the status associated with providing quality childcare.

* I would like to dedicate this essay to Robert Janes and to the late Ivri Kumin. I thank Leigh Anderson, Robert Janes, Janet Looney, Michael Mason, Sally Parks, David Spain, Louis Wolcher, Heidi Wolf, and Diane Zerbe for helpful comments. Although the essay has benefited from all of their comments, I bear responsibility for its contents.

Notes

1. James H. Bossard and Eleanor Stoker Boll, *The Sociology of Child Development* (New York: Harper & Row, 1966), 516.

2. Thomas Cahill, *Desire of the Everlasting Hills* (New York: Doubleday, 1999), 33-39.

3. J. M. Roberts, *History of the World* (New York: Oxford University Press, 1993), 511.

4. Bossard and Boll, *The Sociology*, 534, citing Maurice Parmelee, *Poverty and Social Progress* (New York: The Macmillan Company, 1916), chapter 17.

5. Edward Burnett Tylor, *Primitive Culture; Researches into the Development of Mythology, Philosophy, Religion, Art, and Custom*, 2 vols. (London: J. Murray, 1871), 1.

6. Edward Rothstein, "A Sojourner in the Past Retraces His Steps," *New York Times*, 15 April 2000, (A15).

7. There are more sophisticated versions of cultural relativism that are not addressed here. If my picture of it is a caricature, it is nevertheless a useful one. The cultural relativist holds that it is inappropriate to judge members of one culture by the norms of another. Rather, members of each culture should be judged by the norms of their own culture. See

William Talbott, "Are There Universal Human Rights?" working paper (Seattle, Wash.: Philosophy Department, University of Washington, 2000), 19. For useful references see Michael Cole and Sylvia Scribner, *Culture and Thought* (New York: John Wiley & Sons, 1974); Leslie A. White, *The Development of Civilization to the Fall of Rome* (New York: McGraw-Hill Book Company, Inc., 1959); Leslie A. White, *The Concept of Cultural Systems* (New York: Columbia University Press, 1975).

8. Louis Wolcher points out that cultural relativism also may be seen as arising from Nietzsche's picture of a world as a constant flux of unknowable and unsayable Becoming. Will to power creates the illusion of Being and cultures arise then as the expressions of conflicts of wills to power.

9. Robert Wright, *Nonzero: The Logic of Human Destiny* (New York: Pantheon Books, 2000), 15.

10. Wright, *Nonzero*, 15.

11. Joseph Campbell, *Historical Atlas of World Mythology*, A. van der Marck Editions (San Francisco: distributed by Harper Row, 1983).

12. David Brin, *Otherness* (New York: Bantam Books, 1994), 90.

13. Brin, *Otherness*, 90; Talbott, "Are There Universal?" 19.

14. Rothstein, *A Sojourner*, quoting Barzun.

15. Jacques Barzun, *From Dawn to Decadence* (New York: Harper Collins, 2000), 11.

16. Lewis H. Morgan, *Ancient Society* (New York: Henry Holt, 1877).

17. This is not to deny that one may cooperate to achieve bad ends or ends that conflict with the goals of others.

18. Cooperation is analyzed by the sociologist Marcel Mauss, *The Gift* (New York: W. W. Norton, 1967) in terms of gift exchange, which he finds has profound social significance.

19. The ability to plan ahead appears to be a product of culture including education.

20. Robert Axlerod, *The Evolution of Cooperation* (New York: Basic Books, 1984).

21. Axlerod, *The Evolution*.

22. Richard O. Zerbe, Jr. and Leigh Anderson, "Culture Fairness in the Development of Institutions in the California Gold Fields," *The Journal of Economic History* 61, no.1 (2001): 114-143.

23. With respect to cooperation, the very development of the human brain, the answer to why our brain is relatively large, has been explained in terms of the benefits from social cooperation and the mental complexity needed to handle it. See Robert Wright, *The Moral Animal: Why We Are the Way We Are* (New York: Vintage Books, 1995).

24. Erik H. Erikson, *Childhood and Society* (New York: Norton, 1963), 271.

25. Thomas Cahill, *Gifts of the Jews* (New York: Doubleday, 1998), 198.

26. Cahill, *Gifts*, 199.

27. John Rawls, *A Theory of Justice* (Cambridge: Belknap Press, 1971).

28. Recently, Richard O. Zerbe Jr., *Efficiency in Law and Economics* (Cheltenham, U.K.: Edward Elgar, 2001). I have suggested how the definition of economic efficiency can be logically extended to include moral sentiments.

29. My student Michael Mason helpfully provided me with most of this section.

30. Richard Dawkins, *The Extended Phenotype: The Gene as the Unit of Selection* (Oxford; San Francisco: Freeman, 1982); Richard Dawkins, *The Extended Phenotype: The Long Reach of the Gene* (Oxford; New York: Oxford University Press, 1999).

31. Genes themselves can also cooperate, see Mark Ridley, *The Cooperative Gene* (New York: Simon and Schuster, 2001).

32. A. N. Wilson, *Tolstoy* (New York: Norton, 1998), 375-6.

33. Rodney Stark, *The Rise of Christianity: a Sociologist Reconsiders History* (Princeton, N.J.: Princeton University Press, 1996).

34. Stark, *The Rise*, 83.

35. Stark, *The Rise*, 153.

36. Stark, *The Rise*, 161.

37. Later, in the fifteenth century, the decadence of the church combined with increasing nationalism lead to a theological revolution.

38. Sigmund Freud, *Abstracts of the Standard Edition of the Complete Psychological Works of Sigmund Freud*, ed. Carrie Lee Rothgeb (Rockville, MD.: National Institute of Mental Health, 1971); Erik Erikson, *Childhood*; Erik Erikson, *Insight and Responsibility* (New York: Norton, 1964); Melanie Klein, *Contributions to psycho-analysis, 1921-1945* (London: Hogarth Press, 1948); Carl R. Rogers, *A Carl Rogers reader*, ed. Howard Kirschenbaum and Valerie Land Henderson (Boston: Houghton Mifflin, 1989); and Daniel N. Stern, *The Interpersonal World of the Infant: A View From Psychoanalysis and Developmental Psychology* (New York: Basic Books, 1985); and those from the psychological literature which include Jean Piaget *The Child's Conception of the World* (Savage, MD.: Littlefield Adams Quality Paperbacks, 1985); Abraham Maslow (Harold), *Toward a Psychology of Being* (New York: Van Nostrand Reinhold, 1982); and Lawrence Kohlberg, Charles Levine, and Alexandra Hewer, *Moral Stages: A Current Formulation and a Response to Critics* (New York: Little, Brown and Company, 1983).

39. Failure at this stage leads to an over-involvement with self, to an exaggeration of self-centeredness, in short to selfishness. This is a failure to be able to fully enjoy and appreciate the other. Erikson characterizes the final stage by noting that to complete this stage is to love others in a non-narcissistic mode, to possess some sense of an orderly world and, I would say especially, to have a spiritual sense of the world and of its life.

40. The development of empathy can be seen through the lens of Melanie Klein's model. Specifically in the Klein model the development of empathy involves a move from the more primitive paranoid-schizoid position with fragmented psyche with the associated pain of persecutory anxiety when danger seems to threaten the self, to the depressive position. In the depressive position, one has developed the capacity for empathic resonance with others and anxiety is felt on behalf of others so that regret and the wish to make reparation are products of this stage. (Sally Parks helped with my understanding of the Kleinian model.)

41. Charles R. Potkay and Bem P. Allen, *Personality: Theory, Research, and Applications* (Monterey, Calif.: Brooks/Cole Publishing Company, 1986), table 7.1.

42. Carole Gilligan, *In a Different Voice: Psychological theory and Women's Devel-*

opment (Cambridge: Harvard University Press, 1982).

43. An interpretation of the relevance of the crucifixion of Jesus by Gil Bailie, *Violence Unveiled: Humanity at the Crossroads* (New York: Crossroad, 1995), is that the crucifixion opened the way for empathy with the victim in contrast to the earlier view of the victim as vulnerable and weak and therefore contemptible, who could be readily disposed of with impunity. This interpretation links with Klein's discussion of the movement from the paranoid-schizoid to the depressive position.

44. By realistic view of the world, I mean a view that allows accurate prediction and description.

45. Paul Johnson, *A History of the Jews* (New York: Harper & Row, 1987).

46. Paul Johnson says that the Jews "discovered" a moral universe, but I have used the word "created." See Johnson, *A History*, 1.

47. Johnson, *A History*, 8-79.

48. Cahill, *Desire*, 246.

49. Johnson, *A History*, 2.

50. For a depiction of the use of a moral code to organize and to uphold one's dignity under oppressive circumstances, see Walter Mosley, *Always Outnumbered, Always Outgunned* (New York: Norton, 1997). It seems clear that the adoption of an ethical outlook can promote group survival. Less clear is whether genes that promote ethical behavior increase individual survival. For a suggestion that this could be the case, see Ernst Mayr, *This Is Biology* (Cambridge, Mass.: Harvard University Press, 1997).

51. Cahill, *Desire*, 246.

52. John Passmore, *Man's Responsibility for Nature* (New York: Charles Scribner's Sons, 1974), 4.

53. Heinz Kohut, *The Analysis of the Self; A Systematic Approach to the Psychoanalytic Treatment of Narcissistic Personality Disorders* (New York: International Universities Press, 1971).

54. A similar concept is differentiation between the "paranoid-schizoid" position and the "depressive" position. See Klein, *Contributions.*

55. John Maynard Keynes, *The Economic Consequences of the Peace* (New York: Harcourt, Brace and Howe, 1920).

56. There is of course an interaction between individual and cultural development. Culture can affect the individual for better or worse and culture in turn is influenced by individuals. Individual failures of development can result in social failures. A way to look at the origins of World War I is through the thwarted personality development of Kaiser Wilhelm II. Wilhelm was born with a defective arm. His hand and arm were "miniaturized, feeble and almost useless" according to Robert K. Massie, *Dreadnought: Britian, Germany and the Coming of the Great War* (New York: Random House, 1991), 26. His mother, Vicky, daughter of Queen Victoria of England, was obsessed with the damaged arm. He was made to feel his inferiority keenly and, through his mother, to feel the inferiority of Germany to England. A typical psychological reaction to this sort of attack is the development of a sense of grandiosity. So in his mother's eyes, Wilhelm "is always surprised when he is thought unkind or rude … fancies that his opinions are quite infallible

and that his conduct is always perfect—and cannot stand the smallest (critical) remark though he criticizes and abuses his elders and his relations" according to Massie, *Dreadnought*, 41, quoting a letter from Vicky to Queen Victoria. This individual rose to power in an atmosphere of Prussian antagonism to England. The deadly interaction between the Kaiser's personality and the prevailing imperialistic rivalries led eventually to war.

57. August Wilson sees himself as speaking mainly to positive elements in African American culture, but he is too consummate an artist to be able to ignore those less desirable elements that have arisen from unjust treatment. August Wilson, "American Histories: Chasing Dreams and Nightmares; Sailing the Stream of Black Culture," *New York Times*, 23 April 2000, (C1).

58. Karen Armstrong, *The Battle for God* (New York: Knopf, 2000).

59. Armstrong, *The Battle.*

60. Bossard and Boll, *The Sociology*, 516.

61. James Q. Wilson, "The History and Future of Democracy," lecture at the Reagan Presidential Library, Pepperdine University School of Public Policy, 15 November 1999.

62. Wilson,"The History."

63. Cahill, *Gifts of the Jews*, 249.

64. Cahill, *Gifts of the Jews*, 249.

65. Johnson, *A History*, 68.

66. Support for this view can be gained from a perusal of such books as are edited by Susan S. Hanna, Carl Folke, and Karl-Gorom Maler, ed., *Rights to Nature* (Washington D.C.: Island Press, 1996); Marian Chertow and Daniel Estry, ed., *Thinking Ecologically: the Next Generation of Environmental Policy* (New Haven: Yale University Press, 1997); and the books by Roderick Frazier Nash, *The Rights of Nature* (Madison: University of Wisconsin Press, 1989); and Zygmunt Plater, Robert Abrams, William Goldfarb, and Robert Graham, *Environmental Law and Policy* (St. Paul: West Group, 1998).

67. Wilson, "The History;" see also Zerbe and Anderson, "Culture Fairness."

68. The ability to tolerate diversity is also useful in ameliorating the tendencies toward a winner take all society.

69. Jared Diamond, *Guns, Germs, and Steel* (New York: Norton, 1997).

70. Diamond, *Guns*, 271-72.

71. Herman Daly, *Ecological Economics and the Ecology of Economics: Essays in Criticism* (Cheltenham, U.K.: E. Elgar, 1999).

72. It is true, however, that in the modern world we have developed powerful engines of cooperation, the corporation, governmental institutions, the WTO, and the like. Yet many feel we have lost some more basic sense of community, e.g., Slavenka Drakulic, *Café Europa: Life after Communism* (New York: Penguin Books, 1996), 9, 45.

73. Richard O. Zerbe, Jr., "An Integration of Equity and Efficiency," *Washington Law Review* 73 no. 2 (1998): 349-361; Zerbe, *Efficiency.*

74. We would say, for example, that Macbeth is greater or more mature, or more interesting in its complexity as literature than Peter Rabbit. But we would not say that Macbeth is better literature for a three year old. Peter Rabbit is more age appropriate for a

three year old.

75. *Wall Street Journal*, 24 April 2000, (A1).

76. Johnson, *A History*, 473-74.

77. Virginia Postrel, "The Arrival of Open-source Software Arouses Researchers' Curiosity on What Motivates Programmers to Work Free," *New York Times*, 20 April 2000, (C2).

78. Postrel, "The Arrival," quoting Eric Raymond.

79. L. A. Karoly, et al., *Investing in Our Children: What We Know and Don't Know About the Costs and Benefits of Early Childhood Interventions*, MR-898-TWWF, (Santa Monica: RAND, 1998).

80. A recent report of the organization Save the Children ranked 106 countries in terms of the well being of mothers. The report compares countries on the basis of a mother's access to medical care, maternal mortality rates, access to contraceptive devices and to family planning, literacy, and participation in government. The organization cited a clear link between the well-being of mothers and that of their children. The United States placed fifth. Lawrence L. Knutson, "Study rates best, worst countries for mothers," *The Seattle Times*, 10 May 2000, (A14).

81. Nash, *The Rights of Nature*; Timothy M. Swanson, *The International Regulation of Extinction*, (London: Macmillan Press LTD, 1994); Plater, et al., *Environmental Law*.

82. Plater, et al., *Environmental Law*.

83. Richard O. Zerbe, Jr., "A Place to Stand in Environmental Law and Economics," forthcoming in *Research in Law and Economics* (New York: Elsevier, 2002).

84. D. Gale Johnson, "Population, Food, and Knowledge" *American Economic Review* 90, no. 1 (:2000) 13.

Chapter 13

Ethnopolitical Warfare and Massacres: Is There Progress?

Daniel Chirot

In the 1990s and early 2000s murderous ethnic wars in Yugoslavia, the Caucasus, the Middle East, and many parts of Africa have been in our headlines, but such events are not new. They have been present in the Middle East and much of Africa for decades. Even some rich parts of Western Europe, Northern Ireland (where Protestants and Catholics view each other as ethnicities with different ancestries) and Spain, have witnessed significant killings caused by ethnic conflict. There are continuing ethnoreligious wars in Burma, Sri Lanka, India, and Indonesia. And there are dozens of potential other ethnic wars in such disparate places as Fiji, Guyana, and Algeria. In the first half of the twentieth century there were many episodes of horrendous ethnic cleansing and genocides ranging from the near extermination of the Herero by German colonial troops in Southwest Africa in 1904-1905, to the genocide of Armenians by the Ottoman Empire in 1915, and of course the Nazi genocide of Jews, Gypsies, and Slavs during World War II.[1]

Given this grim history, can we pretend there has been progress in managing ethnic conflict in the past hundred years, or would this be little more than a pious lie? Progress may be defined simply. If there is less ethnic conflict and violence, that is progress. By that measure, there was no progress in the twentieth century; however, that does not resolve the question because, in fact, the record is not entirely bleak. For every terrible situation that either has led to mass killings or retains the potential to do so, there are others where there have been great improvements in the twentieth century. The United States, for example, is far more peaceful and equitable than it was 100 years ago. There was a civil rights revolution from the 1950s to the 1980s in which only dozens were killed, not hundreds, thousands, or millions. Of course, this required the imposition, by force, of civil rights laws backed by the Federal Government against a recalcitrant South, so that white Southerners could see that the costs of resistance far outweighed the costs of compromise.[2]

There have been other good outcomes. South Africa did not have a genocidal war to the finish; whites and blacks compromised and whites handed political power to the blacks, though there, also, both sides were faced by endless, costly war and growing bloodshed, so that it began to appear as if compromise might be cheaper than continuing confrontation. Malaysia, which was on the verge of an ethnic massacre and cleansing in 1969, is now peaceful and ethnic relations are relatively harmonious. Many ethnic hostilities in such countries as Thailand, or between Czechs and Slovaks, between Russians and Balts, between Catalonians and Spaniards, between Turks and Bulgars in Bulgaria, between Hungarians and Romanians in Transylvania, and between French and English speaking Canadians have either been resolved or are being contained and remain peaceful. Some African countries such as mainland Tanzania have had no ethnic warfare despite the presence of many different ethnolinguistic groups. All over the world there are positive as well as negative cases which show that ethnic differences may exist, and even cause severe violence, but without degenerating into massacres, ethnic cleansings, and all out war.[3] Are there lessons to be drawn from such cases that point the way toward greater progress in the future?

Are Genocides and Ethnic Cleansings Anachronisms or Modern?

There is a sharp divide between those who believe that the more advanced a civilization, the more likely it is to commit such atrocities and those who, on the contrary, view such acts as barbaric reversions to primitivism. A widely cited "modernist" perspective was offered by the Polish-English sociologist Zygmunt Bauman. For him the Nazi Holocaust rested on two pillars. One was the bureaucratic rationalization of modern states without which neither Hitler nor Stalin would have been able to kill so many millions.[4]

The second base of the Holocaust and of the communist mass murder of many categories of people was, according to Bauman, the very modern, "scientific" notion that societies can be engineered. For the Nazis, a perfectly engineered society was racially pure, and genocide was based on ethnicity.[5] For the communists the perfectly engineered society was purified of antagonistic classes, which presumably did not lead to ethnic murder, though in the end, whole categories of people were still condemned on the basis of ascribed membership in certain classes. Indeed, an argument can be made that the roots of Leninism and Stalinism are "perhaps not found in Marx at all, but in a deviant version of Darwinism, applied to social questions with the same catastrophic result that occur when such ideas are applied to racial issues."[6] In any case, by the late 1930s, even Stalin, who had previously rejected the primacy of biology over social behavior, was changing his attitude. During World War II and afterward, Stalinist policies of ethnic cleansing were systematically applied in many parts of the Soviet Union on the basis of ethnic origin. This reached its height with the anti-Semitic campaign in Stalin's last years which were probably preparing for the mass deportation of Jews to Siberia, something stopped only by Stalin's death in 1953.[7] Hannah Arendt, still the most cited of the theoreticians of totalitarianism's crimes, believed that fundamentally the alienation of modern life was responsible for the crimes of both Stalin and Hitlerism.[8] This is also a "modernist" view, and the theme of her *Eichmann in Jerusalem*[9] is that bureaucratic conformity was the instrument through which such things could happen. Arendt was well aware of how bloody the past was, but nevertheless believed that what had happened under totalitarian regimes in the twentieth century was a different and worse phenomenon.

The modernist perspective is rejected by those who remind us that the past was not so different. There were the massacres of whole peoples by Europeans during colonization,[10] the devastating Mongol wars in thirteenth century Persia, Russia, and China in which many millions were directly slaughtered or died because of policies that deliberately destroyed agriculture,[11] and the genocidal massacres in the ancient world such as those perpetrated by Alexander the Great.[12] Thousands of other documented historical examples can be found in every part of the world that has had states.

Some anthropologists claim that ecological stress in Stone Age, pre-state horticultural societies led to periodic genocidal wars between neighboring villages and tribes,[13] though this view is contested by many who think that such warfare was provoked by the arrival of Western influence.[14] The argument in anthropology reproduces the venerable philosophical dispute between followers of Hobbes and Rousseau about "the state of nature."

If the "modernists" are right, social change is heading in a fundamentally wrong direction and mass killings based on ethnicity, nationalism, class, or some other politically defined category are only bound to increase. The modern notion that we can remedy social ills by carefully planned public policy means that we are bound to fall again into the trap of adopting simplistic ideologies that will lead to new totalitarian nightmares. Those who do not conform, whether on religious or ideological grounds, or because they are of an ethnic group that does not fit, will again be persecuted, expelled, and often killed. If, on the contrary, those who think the opposite, that such killings are an anachronism, are correct, then any sign of progress should be viewed as a foretaste of a better future. That is the attitude of the Carnegie Commission's Report, *Preventing Deadly Conflict*, which states: "We humans do not have the luxury any longer of indulging our prejudices and ethnocentrism. They are anachronisms of our ancient past."[15] In other words, we can adopt wise policies that will free human societies from such horrors once and for all.

Faced by such opposite interpretations, how can we evaluate the chances for progress in resolving ethnic and related conflicts in the future?

The Causes of Genocides, Massacres, and Ethnic Cleansings

A useful approach is to look at the causes of all politically motivated massacres, and to see which kinds of causes are more or less likely to occur in a contemporary, modern context. Then we can try to judge whether progress in curbing ethnic war has occurred, or is even possible. Five kinds of causes can be distinguished.

Convenience: A Rational Calculus

One of the most common is simply convenience. For example, William the Conqueror found it impossible to bring Yorkshire under control, and feared that if he did not, his hold on newly conquered England would be fatally compromised. So in 1069 he ordered a genocidal policy to destroy and clear out the population of Yorkshire, reasoning correctly that this would deprive its lords of support for continuing their rebellion. The strategy worked so well that as late as 1086, after Yorkshire had been subdued and resettled by migrants from other parts of England, its population density was still only one fifth that of neighboring parts of England.[16] A more recent example occurred in mid-nineteenth century Russia. In 1860, after almost a century of inconclusive warfare against the Muslim Circassians in the northwestern Caucasus, the Russian Empire decided they could not be subdued. They were considered "savages" and "bandits," which means that the usual tactic of co-opting their chiefs, turning them into Russian nobles, and transforming the other locals into dependent peasants was not working. The Circassians inhabited a poor and difficult mountainous region with few riches, but the area was strategically important as it controlled a part of the Black Sea coast and access to the Ottoman Empire. The Tsar's army went on a four year campaign to starve, burn, kill, and expel the remaining Circassians. Of about two million, half died, about 120,000 to 150,000 resettled elsewhere in Russia, some 700,000 fled to the Ottoman Empire, and fewer than 200,000 survived in their original homeland. Some observers drew an explicit analogy with the way in which contemporary Americans were treating their native populations.[17] Indeed, many of the most genocidal episodes in America's wars against Native Americans were motivated by precisely this, a rational calculus that the natives were too much trouble and had to be eliminated so that the white settlers could enjoy the economic benefits of untroubled occupation of the land.

This was the utilitarian calculus which prompted Slobodan Milosevic to try to clear Kosovo of Albanians. Serbian nationalists had an emotional attachment to Kosovo, the province had valuable mineral resources, displaced Serbs needed land, and the Albanians were in the way to the satisfaction of all these objectives.[18]

To Teach Them a Lesson or Serve as a Warning

There have been countless massacres that had no overall genocidal intent, but were localized and tactical. David Morgan likens Chingiz Khan's annihilation of certain cities to President Harry Truman's decision to wipe out Hiroshima and Nagasaki: "The apparent rationale was that if the population of one city was subjected to a frightful massacre, the next city would be more likely to surrender without resistance, thus avoiding unnecessary Mongol [or American] casualties."[19] Of course, every man, woman, and child caught in these massacres was a target, not just military forces or assets, but that was accepted as inevitable by the Americans in 1945. Chingiz probably did not lose much sleep over such actions, either.

As in massacres of "convenience," such "lessons" may take on genocidal proportions if the perpetrators have an overwhelming military advantage that allows them to kill large numbers without suffering significant casualties themselves.

Revenge, Justice, and Honor

"Teaching them a lesson" easily slides into a search for revenge, which easily comes to be viewed as a matter of honor and justice. Julius Caesar, when he had to, engaged in such massive killings in Gaul to bring "treacherous" tribes under control and salvage his "honor" wounded by their refusal to submit.[20] All Caesar wanted was to be able to control Gaul and extract its resources, but he was particularly angered by the "treachery" of those who insisted on resisting when it was obvious that their cause was hopeless.

In 1904 the Herero in the German colony of Southwest Africa rebelled against their cruel and abusive German masters, and defeated the small German military force in the colony. This was a poor colony that the Germans were trying to sell because it was so unprofitable, but when the news reached Berlin, Kaiser Wilhelm II was infuriated and decided that German honor needed revenge. An army of 10,000 was sent out with the Kaiser's orders to crush the revolt by "fair means or foul." At the next census taken in the colony, in 1911, there were 15,000 Herero left out of the original population of about 80,000, and another 5,000 had managed to break out and make it to adjoining British colonies.[21] Here, economic practicality had almost nothing to do with what was the twentieth century's first genocide.

The Rape of Nanjing in 1937-1938 by the Japanese army was motivated largely by a desire for revenge because the Chinese had had the temerity to fight bitterly against the invading Japanese, and also to "teach them a lesson." On orders of the high command, tens of thousands of women were raped and up to three hundred thousand Chinese were systematically tortured, beheaded, mutilated, and otherwise murdered.[22]

Fear

Nothing stimulates the genocidal impulse as quickly as fear. A social group of any size that feels its very existence is at stake unless an aggressor or potential aggressor is eliminated will not hesitate to commit massacres in order to save itself. There are countless stories of combatants killing innocent civilians because they identify all of them as potentially murderous enemies. Fear, however, can be much more complex than that experienced in a confused battle. It can be a gnawing, long term apprehension that an enemy group will, if it ever gets the power to do so, eliminate "us."[23] This explains the extreme examples of cruel murder that soil the histories of virtually every ruling royal or imperial family in pre-modern history. As members of families fought for power, even surviving babies or small children who might lay a claim to the throne were dangerous because they could serve as rallying points for opponents to the monarch. The Armenian genocide was unleashed by the fear of the Ottoman government that Armenians were going to try to create an independent state in Eastern Anatolia allied to Russia, and expel the region's Muslim population.[24] This was a particularly modern genocide because until the idea of nationalism and the need to create culturally homogeneous nation-states made its way into the Ottoman Empire from Western Europe, relations between Armenians and the Empire had been quite good.[25]

Without going into details about Yugoslavia it is easy to see that there was competition over resources and rising fear that if the members of the opposing group were not eliminated through murder and expulsion, then they would commit murders and expulsions. There were massacres during World War II, and in the early 1990s there was reasonable fear that new ones were about to be committed, so preventive action was called for.[26] There were voices calling for moderation and understanding, as well as extremists demanding revenge and drastic solutions to eliminate the danger once and for all. The extremists won, in large part because there had been enough of a recent history of violent conflict to make such fears entirely plausible. The case of Yugoslavia is particularly important as an example of how a seemingly benign public policy can cause harm, something which has not been fully appreciated by most journalistic commentators. At the peak of communism's strength under Tito, deliberate policies were instituted to reduce inequality between the disparate regions of Yugoslavia. This exacerbated competition between the regions, and therefore between the ethnic groups that dominated each one. Even as official policy downplayed historical ethnic animosities and tried to bury the resentments left over from the killings during World War II, government policy was setting ethnic groups against each other as it tried to tax the rich regions to help the poor ones. Once the economy began to stagnate and Tito's autocratic rule weakened, even before his death, ethnic tensions steadily increased. Finally, the sharp economic decline of Yugslavia in the 1980s combined with the collapse of communist rule opened the final struggle between the regions and ethnic groups that led to the catastrophe of the 1990s.[27]

Fear of Pollution

Perhaps the most virulent kind of massacre is caused by a fear of pollution. In the sixteenth century wars of religion in France some 750,000 people were killed. The very term "massacre" comes from these wars.[28] Of all the motives, the urge to purify Catholicism of the stain of heresy was at the heart of the worst episodes.[29] As Mark Greengrass has phrased it in summarizing much of the literature on these wars, "Hence the particularly gruesome cruelty meted out towards Protestants, the perverted mutilation of their bodies after their death. This was not sadism as we might understand it. Rather, the heretics were nonhumans, diabolic agents, and their pursuants were God's secret, avenging angels."[30]

In 1965 in Indonesia at least one half million and perhaps up to one million supposed communists were killed, mostly by civilians backed by the army.[31] In East Java, where some of the worst excesses took place, the massacre frequently took on a ritualistic aspect far removed from the ostensibly modern political struggle occurring between communists and anti-communists. Not only were whole families destroyed, but torture and mutilation were common: "Heads, sexual organs, and limbs were displayed along the side of the main road outside Pasuruan. Canals were choked with bodies." Muslim youth groups were the most active and brutal killers as they slaughtered those accused of being communists and anti-Muslims.[32] This was not an ethnic massacre (though in some cities Chinese were particularly targeted), but in practice, the distinction between ethnic and religious warfare is small, and the definition of the enemy as being virtually non-human is what happens in the most severe ethnic conflicts.

That combination of historical vengeance and wish to rid the land of religiously polluting people is very clearly evident in Biblical episodes of genocide, particularly in the injunction to kill all of the Amalekites:

> And Samuel said to Saul ... 'Now go a smite Amalek, and utterly destroy all that they have; do not spare them but kill both man and woman, infant and suckling, ox and sheep, camel and ass.'[33]

Saul's failure to wipe out all the Amalekites and his rather reasonable granting of permission to his men to keep the valuable animals of the Amalekites then becomes one of the main reasons for his downfall because he has not wiped out the offending pollution.[34]

The fear of pollution is most acute when there is a sense that failure to ritually cleanse the social and natural order will result in catastrophe, or when terrible events have occurred and societies search for explanations which they find in their past failure to observe ritual purity. That is when a kind of fanatical fury, a mixture of panic, rage, and a wish for vengeance occur, whether in Indonesia in 1965, in France during the sixteenth century religious wars, or in Biblical tales.

It was the merit of the psychologist Walter Langer's classified wartime study of Adolf Hitler's mentality (later published in 1972) to point out the many mentions in Hitler's writings of the fear of disease, of pollution, of corruption, and of degeneracy—all of them ascribed to racial mixing and particularly to the Jewish disease.[35] Hitler himself was perfectly clear on this. He wrote in *Mein Kampf*:

> Blood mixture and the resultant drop in racial level is the sole cause of the dying out of old cultures; for men do not perish as a result of lost wars, but by the loss of that force of resistance which is contained only in pure blood.[36]

What is New: The Nation as Family, Village, and Clan

We do not know if the Israelites really did kill all the Amalekites, or how many of them there were, but where there are historical records, as with the Romans, Normans, Mongols, or other imperial killers, attempts to actually exterminate every last member of a hostile tribe or nation were quite rare. Once the power of an enemy had been decisively broken, any commoners (but sometimes not family members of leaders) could expect to be left alone.

Even with the mass slaughters of natives by Europeans in the Americas or Australia, once native populations were reduced to complete impotence and could no longer fight back in any way, usually the remnants were left to live in their miserably reduced circumstances.

There were two major types of exception in the past. One consisted of families or clans of potential leaders, royal rivals, whose survival could threaten a ruler and his own children. Then, hunting down the last of the survivors could be critically important. Empires such as the Ottoman, Byzantine, and Chinese, suffered many times from civil wars between imperial relatives, but so did many lesser kingdoms and principalities. This was reason enough to kill children and women as well as adult men, or imprison and exile them, if necessary, to insure future security. A particularly bloody example was the massacre of tens of thousands of Confucian officials and their entire families of the Chinese emperor Jianwen when he was overthrown by his uncle, the emperor Yongle, in 1402.[37]

A second type of exception was in wars where the vanquished enemy was in one constrained place, and could therefore be subjected to immediate and complete extermination for any of the five kinds of reasons that could lead to massacres. Thus, occasionally, we know that vanquished villages, tribes, or conquered cities could be wiped out entirely, or partly killed with the rest being enslaved and dispersed. This was common enough, but rarely if ever led to sustained hunts for every last survivor. If any happened to escape, unless they were members of a particularly dangerous leading family, they were left alone. This was true in all the pre-modern examples cited above.

The same can be said for ethnic and religious cleansings. In the past, these were rarely if ever very thorough, even in one of the most extreme pre-modern cases, the Spanish expulsion of Jews in 1492. Many Jews converted, and some who left subsequently returned. Despite the persecution of converted Jews, *conversos*, those killed hardly numbered more than a few thousand. Converted Jews (and Muslims) in Spain were gradually integrated into the population, and there was never a concerted attempt to exterminate all of them or totally rid Spain of their descendants.[38] Suggesting a comparison of this case with what happened in Europe in the twentieth century, as Benzion Netanyahu[39] does, is therefore not justified. There were common elements, but the modern totality of the Nazi program was absent in Spain.

The "modernists," therefore, have a strong case. The sheer scope of modern genocides, and even more tellingly, of the much more frequent cases of ethnic cleansings as empires have fallen apart and been replaced by nations that tried to homogenize themselves, are new phenomena.[40] The differences, however, are not in the all too human motives that have provoked such events in the past and the present. *What has changed is the kind of social unit subjected to such treatment.*

The rise of the modern nation-state in which legitimacy is conferred on the state by the adherence of its people to the idea of their nation is what is new. None of the great empires of the past claimed to be exclusively mono-ethnic or in any sense mono-cultural. None would have become very big if such a claim had been taken seriously. This, along with the lack of technical means explains the sloppiness of and incompleteness of most past genocidal episodes and ethnic cleansings.

This is not the place to review once more the vast literature on the rise of nationalism. Suffice it to say that virtually all contemporary specialists of this subject believe that modern nationalism has made demands on its people for greater cultural homogeneity, either through conversion to a common language and set of values (as in the United States), or more often, through acceptance of ethnic or religious (or both) homogeneity. The notion that a cultural group has some right to rule itself became standard in Western Europe as a consequence of the French Revolution and the spread of English and French Enlightenment principles.[41] That the Western Europeans violated these principles in their own imperial ventures contributed greatly to the spread of the same principles and to anti-imperialist nationalisms, as well as to the general moral rejection of colonialism in the second half of the twentieth century.[42] It is a principle which has in no sense weakened and which continues to create problems for those trying to bring peace to many troubled, culturally heterogeneous political entities from the Balkans to Russia, to much of Africa, Central Asia, South Asia, and Southeast Asia.[43]

This transformation has meant that the modern nation has become the village, the clan, the tribe, the small city-state with which most people identified in the past. Liah Greenfeld[44] has claimed forcefully that becoming modern means becoming a member of a larger nation, no longer just a member of a village, region, or religion. The nation for most people today is the chief focus of political identity, and those who, for one reason or another, do not believe that the state they live in legitimately represents their group strive to leave or create their own nation-state.

It is important to stress the logic of the modern nation. If there are any cultural differences between identifiable ethnic or religious groups, or between regions, it is certain that there will be some felt inequalities. These may have to do with prestige, with remembrance of past historical slights, with different amounts of political power or wealth, with different customs, or any combination of these. All large agrarian and post-agrarian societies of more than a few thousand people, and certainly of more than 100,000 have inequalities, and in a modern nation when groups are forced to interact and compete for control of state power and resources, the potential for conflict always exists. Mono-cultural nationalism that includes everyone within the state's borders is the only sure way of avoiding ethnic conflict, because it is impossible to predict when a previously unmobilized group will discover its identity and a set of grievances. Sometimes those who protest do so because they are richer than other ethnic groups, such as the Croats and Slovenes in Yugoslavia who resented being taxed to promote equality; and sometimes they are poorer and demand more resources, such as the Albanians of Macedonia. Sometimes they are neither richer nor poorer, but have cultural grievances, as do the French Canadians, or the Spanish Basques.[45]

This means that any group within the state's borders that does not accept the state's legitimacy on cultural grounds threatens the state's very integrity, because it questions the right of the ruling nation to control that state. Even if a particularly defined cultural group with grievances wants to be loyal, suspicion that it is not, or that it threatens the nation's legitimacy opens it up to the possibility of persecution. We should not be surprised by this. Threatening neighbors, villages, families, clans, or tribes have always elicited violent defensive reactions, and once war is engaged, the motives of revenge and justice, as well as fear of defeat come into play. When fear that the very identity of the group is in mortal danger is ritualized and rationalized as fear of pollution, the way is open for the most cruel kinds of ethnic conflict.

In small scale, pre-state societies, whole groups of adjoining villages or clans could become involved in such struggles for survival, and commit terrible acts on each other from time to time. Everyone was involved as the whole population was mobilized for the struggle. In agrarian states, whether small kingdoms or large empires, during most of the time only small minorities, elites, were involved in such desperate political struggles. Royal families killed each other with great regularity, and rebellious provinces or tribes within the polity were subject to massive retribution. But most of the time, few of the peasant masses were mobilized for war, or were directly involved in the political struggles that occupied the elites. The modern nation, in a sense, has retribalized populations. Again, everyone is supposed to be a citizen and may be mobilized in one way or another for war; and everyone is supposed to feel the same kind of loyalty previously reserved only for direct kin or neighbors. That means that warfare between nations and within a state for control of that state by different ethnic or religious groups involves, once again, everyone. We can easily grasp this phenomenon if we are looking at feuding families, but in fact, the nation transforms us into vast families. The kinship may be factually fictitious, but the sentiment is real. The importance of the nation as a moral family has been heightened by the nature of modern warfare that directly involves everyone, not just elites and their soldiers. So it was in the past when neighboring villages, clans, and tribes fought each other, and so it is once more, but on a far larger scale.

One sees this kind of reasoning in Rwanda, where, in 1994, the Hutu political elite reasoned that if they did not wipe out every last Tutsi (as wells as Hutu members of the opposition) their political power would be broken, and their very existence mortally threatened. Though the transformation of Tutsis and Hutus into rival ethnicities was a twentieth century invention propagated largely by the Belgians during their period of colonial rule, by the time of independence in the 1960s it was an unfortunate reality, and by 1994 had already led to long series of bloody conflicts. What finally set off the genocide itself was an internationally brokered agreement for power sharing that would have destroyed the Hutu elite's access to the few resources available in this badly overcrowded, poverty stricken country. As these Hutu leaders saw it, as long as there were still Tutsi alive they would make claims and receive international legitimacy as a minority ethnic group, but if none were left, they could make no such claims.[46]

In a society where everyone can be mobilized, where legitimacy rests on mass support, even if there are no free elections, those opposed to the system, or suspected of being hostile to the regime, are a mortal danger by the very fact that they survive, even if they seem momentarily weak.

In that sense, the modernist view that there is something new about some of the genocides and ethnic cleansings of the twentieth century is right. The conditions that produce such nightmares have in no sense gone away, so it is likely that there will be more of them in the twenty-first century. The extreme cases may be only a small minority of all ethnic conflicts in the world, as they were in the twentieth century, but they will continue to shock us.

The Limits of Progress

Given the fact that the modernist view has merit, and that neither nationalism nor ethnic self-awareness are on the decline, even in Western Europe and the United States, is there any promise of progress in managing ethnic tensions? The short answer is a clear no. Perhaps some contemporary democratic regimes are ashamed to kill merely for the sake of convenience or simply to "teach them a lesson," and there are international conventions against genocides and ethnic cleansings.[47] But outlawing genocide in 1948 did not prevent massive killings and deportations of whole populations in the many cases where it occurred subsequently. Only military defeat broke the backs of genocidal regimes in Cambodia, Rwanda, Uganda, and Serbia. In other terrible cases, as in the Soviet Union and China, only the death of the leaders, Stalin and Mao, reduced the level of killings and mass deportations, some (but not the majority) of which were ethnic.[48] When fear is present, especially the kind of panic that leads a nation to believe that its very existence is threatened, the potential for ethnic war, cleansing, and even mass killing rises quickly. If that fear is reinforced by a religious or other ideologically based sense that the danger has to be cleansed out of existence, genocidal behavior becomes quite likely.

Secure and prosperous democracies in today's world usually seem able to settle their own internal ethnic tensions peacefully, while very occasionally intervening to stop ethnic wars in less fortunate parts of the world; but it would be naïve to suppose that this indicates a long-term trend for the better. What would happen if these secure nations became involved in internal or external wars that threatened their own basic survival?

Conditions that Lessen the Probability of Violence: Some Policy Implications

On the other hand, the future need not be as bleak as the recent past. By looking at cases where ethnic conflicts have been settled, we can point to a few clear lessons to be drawn, and we can develop a better understanding of what conditions alleviate such conflicts.

Individualizing the Others and Resisting Tribalization

Mass killing of an enemy group, especially for the sake of convenience or "to teach them a lesson," requires viewing that group as a whole, not as differentiated individuals. When applied to ethnically, religiously, or nationally defined groups, this means considering them as indivisible families with a common worldview and common interests. All Jews, for example, or Tutsis, Armenians, and Irish Catholics have to be seen as alike. Such views may be held also by those who dominate the targeted group, so that any deviation from the group is seen as treachery. The individual is seen by both outsiders and insiders as subordinated to, and defined by the group, and that group is hereditarily determined.

Some modern Western societies over the past two to three centuries have steadily developed an unusual way of thinking about the role of individuals. In this historically novel approach individual rights, responsibilities, and interests predominate over group attributes. Whereas in most societies and at most times individuals have been defined primarily as members of their family, clan, village, or tribe, the glorification of individualism in some Western societies has produced a new view of our place in society. We are no longer defined as mere appendages to a community and its leaders. Once this becomes widely accepted, treating a whole group as an indivisible enemy becomes more difficult. Genocidal revenge becomes more than impractical, it becomes immoral.[49]

It is quite clear that the capacity to individualize is not a new invention. Intermarriage, for example, created the possibility of viewing other, potentially enemy groups as being something more than just hostile collectivities, as some individuals in it were kin. Today the systematic extension of our capacity to individualize far more than ever before is the surest antidote to the dangers posed by the opposing tendency to retribalize society.

Whether or not the twenty-first century witnesses even bloodier ethnic and nationalist wars and killings than the twentieth will depend on whether individualization or retribalization become the dominant trend. Wherever ethnicity becomes the main basis for political allegiance, and strict group loyalty is demanded, as some ethnic entrepreneurs, even in the United States demand, then retribalization will create a fertile ground for increasing ethnic conflict. And if that happens, the rest of the world will stand little chance of avoiding a growing number of ethnopolitical wars.

It is important to point out that detribalization is possible even in non-Western, economically impoverished societies, though that is difficult. In mainland Tanzania, for example, Julius Nyerere successfully created a sense of Tanzanian nationalism in which individuals were not assigned positions on the basis of their ethnicity, in which ethnic politics were forbidden, and in which local tribal cultures (that is, multiculturalism) were relegated to marginality and increasingly eschewed by the political elite. Instead, a new African culture based on Swahili and Tanzanian identity were created, and in this region beset by ethnic wars, there have been none in mainland Tanzania. Nyerere was helped by the fact that there were so many different linguistic groups in his county, with none having anything close to a dominant plurality; but he was hurt by the catastrophic nature of his economic policies which kept his country poor, and so, presumably, more open to internal conflict.[50]

The Tanzanian case is a good reminder that determined public policy that fights tribalization can have an effect.

Remembering that Full Justice Makes Compromise Difficult

Perhaps the most important lesson about successful cases of ethnic conflict resolution is that demands for justice need to be tempered. Demanding that whole groups, whites in South Africa, for example, be punished for the indignities, suffering, and killings of the apartheid era, would make compromise impossible. It is not group punishment alone that needs to be abandoned. One of the most overlooked lessons of the Truth and Reconciliation Commission has been that it is best to forego most cases of individual justice seeking as well. To go very far in prosecuting the many guilty whites would have frightened the entire white population and made their flight, or earlier, their resistance to the bitter end almost inevitable.[51]

Who can imagine that compromise between Catholics and Protestants in Northern Ireland[52] could ever occur if "justice" for all the evil done were really pursued? And after the breakdown of the Oslo "Peace Process" in 2000, what can the impassioned cries for "justice" on both sides really accomplish other than to provoke an eventual war to the death between Israelis and Palestinians.

It is counterintuitive at best, and morally distasteful for many of us to admit that seeking too much justice may make settlement of disputes impossible, yet in case after case, that should be obvious. This even applies to the most egregious cases. Would Germany and Japan have evolved into stable, peaceful democracies if all those guilty of the heinous crimes millions of their soldiers and administrators committed during World War II had been punished? Was it not better, in the long run, to punish a symbolic handful, and leave rancorous arguments about guilt to later generations, long after stability and civility had been restored?

In Praise of Doubt and Impurity

One of the main causes of genocidal acts in the twentieth century has been ideological certitude. Hitler was certain that he understood "racial science" and that its findings compelled him to eliminate all those who might pollute the Aryan Germans. This meant that Jews, Gypsies, and eventually the Slavs as well as the feebleminded and homosexuals were slated for destruction. Stalin was certain that he understood "Marxist economic science," and this obliged him to destroy those classes that stood in the way of the construction of socialism. For both Stalin and Hitler there was no doubt.[53]

Historians and philosophers of science understand that such certitude is antithetical to modern science, and more akin to the religious certitude we associate with fanaticism. Modern science is much more modest. There are no final answers, and every finding must be tested.

Psychologists who developed the notion of "authoritarian personalities" fifty years ago noted that a belief in perfect order correlated with authoritarianism.[54] So does the worship of perfect cleanliness and purity.

Those who are aware of the limitations of knowledge, who tolerate the ambiguities of life, and who strive for improvement while rejecting the possibility of perfection are far less likely to think of conflict in absolutist or collective terms.

They are also less likely to panic at the thought of ritually polluting contact with the forbidden.

In short, it is possible to point to types of organization, behavior, and ideology that mitigate the retribalization of the modern world. It is particularly in societies that try to adhere to Enlightenment ideals of free exchange, democracy, and individualism that the strongest resistance can still be found to accepting a world of warring tribes. It is because those Western societies that have upheld Enlightenment ideals have remained the strongest and most prosperous in the world that the idea of genocide is currently unacceptable in the international arena, even if enforcement of international law has proved to be very limited. This should never be interpreted to mean that non-Western societies are somehow incapable of learning and applying some of the same lessons, as both Tanzania and South Africa demonstrate. But the task is a difficult one, and demands leaders who renounce the use of tribal politics and who can overcome those of their opponents who use ethnic and religious resentment to promote themselves.

Given the seeming growth in various kinds of religious fundamentalism, from Christian versions in the United States, to Jewish ones in Israel, to Hindu ones in India, and most of all to various Muslim ones in the Islamic world, the compulsion to cleanse society of pollution will grow. As religion and ethnicity are highly correlated in most of the world, such a trend is most alarming.[55] Without vigilance and a clear awareness of how nurturing grievances based on cultural particularisms of all kinds create a climate of increasing conflict, even prosperous Western societies can fall, once again, into severe ethnopolitical conflict.

Our experiences in the twentieth century have made us more knowledgeable about how to avoid bloody ethnic conflict. In that sense there has been progress. But experience and knowledge only indirectly shape ideology. Until the lessons of the past century are more widely absorbed, the trend toward retribalization and the commitment of so many to absolutist, communal myths of solidarity and purity will continue to produce numerous ethnopolitical and ethnoreligious conflicts and wars. Progress is possible, but so far there has not been nearly enough, and what there has been could easily be reversed.

Postscript: The Implications of Recent International Conciliation Efforts

In the rich capitalist democracies, mostly in Western Europe and the United States, there is a growing sentiment that international intervention should be used to stop ethnic conflicts. This was the basis of what has become a massive and open-ended involvement by the United Nations, NATO, the European Union, and the United States in Yugoslavia's affairs. In the end, however, massive American force and the quasi-occupations of Bosnia and Kosovo have not moved either place closer to ethnic harmony. At best, foreign troops have been able to freeze conflict, though in Macedonia, they have trouble doing even that. What foreign intervention by a powerful nation can do, if it is applied firmly enough, is to defeat one of the parties in a conflict. Serbia was crushed by American bombing in 1999, and stopped from ethnically cleansing Kosovo of its Albanian majority. Serbia was earlier defeated by NATO bombing and by a Croatian army armed and trained by the Americans in 1995, and that stopped the killing in Bosnia.[56]

The United States, Belgium, or France could have intervened in Rwanda in 1994 and stopped the genocide there, but chose not to. The truth of the matter is that UN intervention is ineffective unless it is massively backed by the Western powers, and practically, that means the United States; but most of the world is not prepared to accept the re-imposition of colonial rule by Europeans or Americans, and the Western powers, including the United States, are less and less willing to suffer the casualties and expenses such intervention requires. Furthermore, when large and locally powerful states are involved in ethnic conflicts, as when Russia massacres Chechens, China represses Tibetans, or Nigeria sinks into ever more serious ethnoreligious bloodshed, the very idea of international intervention is exposed for what it is—something that might occasionally (but very rarely) be used in imposing order on little states, but never could be in large ones.

Australian intervention in East Timor probably stopped the massacre of the local population by Indonesian backed militias, or at least slowed it down, but that could only happen after Indonesia had fallen into internal chaos as a result of the Asian economic crisis of 1997.[57]

There is nothing wrong with the idea of international intervention as such. However bumbling and ineffective it has shown itself to be in solving long-term problems, it can, if applied with enough force, stop genocide and ethnic cleansing. But we must be realistic and recognize what this involves: costly intervention by rich Western powers, condemnation by irate non-Western nations, and endless frustration in places where quick military victory is impossible.

It is better to promote internal policies that might lead to conciliation and the lessening of ethnic tensions than to get involved in military intervention because the former is cheaper and at least holds out the promise of long-term solutions. The European Union's insistence that East European states behave properly toward their minorities, for example, has produced more benevolent policies in those states that want to join Europe and gain economic aid. Where there is no great fear on the part of either minorities or majorities that they risk serious harm by being tolerant and accommodating, foreign pressure can have some effect if it holds out a promise of real benefits; however, where economic decline, fear, and a violent recent history are combined, as in Yugoslavia, Western pressure has been far less effective, and as we have seen, a thin, artificial veneer of toleration can only be secured by direct military occupation.[58]

Promoting policies that will produce greater ethnic peace and getting policy makers to implement them is difficult. Even in cases where there has been very intensive American involvement in peace talks for long periods of time, for example in Northern Ireland and the Israeli-Palestinian peace talks, the results have been shaky at best, and perhaps disastrous at worst, as in the fiasco at Camp David in 2000 that led to a renewed Israeli-Palestinian war. We should not be too sanguine about finding better solutions in cases that are more removed from the direct concern of the United States or Europe. The struggle to make progress is going to be a very long one, and we are still at the beginning, not far ahead of where we were at the start of the twentieth century. We know what works to lessen ethnic conflict, but we do not know how to make certain that the right policies are applied when leaders, ruling ideologies, or popular opinion reject such solutions.

Notes

1. Donald L. Horowitz, *Ethnic Groups in Conflict* (Berkeley: University of California Press, 1985); Donald L. Horowitz, *The Deadly Ethnic Riot* (Berkeley: University of California Press, 2001); David A. Lake and Donald Rothchild, *The International Spread of Ethnic Conflict* (Princeton: Princeton University Press, 1998).

2. John S. Reed, "Why Has There Been No Race War in the American South," in *Ethnopolitical Warfare: Causes, Consequences, and Possible Solutions*, ed. Daniel Chirot and E. P. Seligman (Washington D.C.: American Psychological Association Press, 2001), 275-85.

3. Daniel Chirot, "Introduction," in *Ethnopolitical Warfare: Causes, Consequences, and Possible Solutions,* ed. Daniel Chirot and E. P. Seligman (Washington D.C.: American Psychological Association Press, 2001), 3-26.

4. Zygmunt Bauman, *Modernity and the Holocaust* (Ithaca: Cornell University Press, 1989), 90.

5. Bauman, *Modernity*, 66-72.

6. Stéphane Courtois, et al., *The Black Book of Communism: Crimes, Terror, Repression* (Cambridge: Harvard University Press, 1999), 752-53.

7. Amir Weiner, *Making Sense of War: The Second World War and the Fate of the Bolshevik Revolution* (Princeton: Princeton University Press, 2001), 138-54, 191-99, 203, 274; Adam B. Ulam, *Stalin: The Man and His Era* (New York: Viking, 1977), 684, 730-31.

8. Hannah Arendt, *The Origins of Totalitarianism* (New York: Harcourt, Brace, 1951).

9. Hannah Arendt, *Eichmann in Jerusalem: A Report on the Banality of Evil* (New York: Viking, 1963).

10. Russell Thornton, *American Indian Holocaust and Survival: A Population History since 1492* (Norman, Okla.: Oklahoma University Press, 1987); Robert Hughes, *The Fatal Shore* (New York: Vintage, 1988), 414-24.

11. David Morgan, *The Mongols* (Oxford: Basil Blackwell, 1986), 69-83.

12. A.B. Bosworth, *Alexander and the East: The Tragedy of Triumph* (Oxford: Oxford University Press, 1996).

13. Paul Shankman, "Culture Contact, Cultural Ecology, and Dani Warfare," *MAN*

26, no. 2 (June 1991): 299-321.

14. Jeffrey P. Blick, "Genocidal Warfare in Tribal Societies as a Result of European Induced Culture Conflict," *MAN* 28, no. 4 (December 1988): 654-70.

15. Carnegie Commission, *Preventing Deadly Conflict* (New York: Carnegie Corporation, 1997), xii.

16. William E. Kapelle, *The Norman Conquest of the North: The Region and Its Transformation, 1000-1135* (Chapel Hill: University of North Carolina Press, 1979), 118-90.

17. Stephen D. Shenfield, "The Circassians: A Forgotten Genocide?" in *The Massacre in History,* ed. Mark Levene and Penny Roberts (New York, Oxford: Berghahn Books, 1999): 149-62.

18. Julie Mertus, *Kosovo: How Myths and Truths Started a War* (Berkeley: University of California Press, 1999); Misha Glenny, *The Balkans: Nationalism, War and the Great Powers, 1804-1999* (New York: Viking, 2000), 652-59.

19. Morgan, *Mongols*, 93.

20. Jacques Harmand, *Vercingétorix* (Paris: Fayard, 1984), 92-93.

21. Horst Drechsler, *"Let Us Die Fighting": The Struggle of the Herero and Nama against German Imperialism (1884-1915)* (London: Zed Books, 1980).

22. Iris Chang, *The Rape of Nanking: The Forgotten Holocaust of World War II* (New York: Penguin, 1997); Timothy Brook ed., *Documents on the Rape of Nanking* (Ann Arbor: University of Michigan Press, 1999); Joshua A. Fogel, *The Nanjing Massacre in History and Historiography* (Berkeley: University of California Press, 2000).

23. Robert H. Bates, J. P. Rui de Figueiredo, and Barry Weingast, "The Politics of Interpretation: Rationality, Culture, and Transition," *Politics and Society* 26, no. 2 (June 1998): 221-256.

24. Fikret Adanir, "Armenian Deportations and Massacres in 1915." in *Ethnopolitical Warfare: Causes, Consequences, and Possible Solutions*, ed. Daniel Chirot and Martin E. P. Seligman (Washington D.C.: American Psychological Association Press, 2001), 71-82.

25. Ronald G. Suny, "Empire and Nation: Armenians, Turks, and the end of the Ottoman Empire," *Armenian Forum* 1, no. 2 (1998): 17-51.

26. Anthony Oberschall, "From Ethnic Cooperation to Violence and War in Yugoslavia," in *Ethnopolitical Warfare: Causes, Consequences, and Possible Solutions,* ed. Daniel Chirot and Martin E. P. Seligman (Washington D.C.: American Psychological Association Press, 2001), 119-50; Horowitz, *The Deadly Ethnic Riot*, 548.

27. Ivo Banac, *The National Question in Yugoslavia: Origins, History, Politics* (Ithaca: Cornell University Press, 1984); Aleska Djilas, *The Contested Country: Yugoslav Unity and Communist Revolution 1919-1953* (Cambridge: Harvard University Press, 1991); Tim Judah, *The Serbs: History, Myth and the Destruction of Yugoslavia* (New Haven: Yale University Press, 1997); Susan Woodward, *Balkan Tragedy: Chaos and Dissolution After the Cold War* (Washington, D.C.: Brookings Institution, 1995); Marcus Tanner, *Croatia: A Nation Forged in War* (New Haven: Yale University Press, 1997).

28. Mark Greengrass, "Hidden Transcripts: Secret Histories and Personal Testimonies of Religious Violence in the French Wars of Religion," in *The Massacre in History*, ed. Mark Levene and Penny Roberts (New York and Oxford: Berghahn Books, 1999): 70.

29. Natalie Z. Davis, "The Rites of Violence," in *Society and Culture in Early Modern France,* ed. Natalie Z. Davis (Stanford: Stanford University Press, 1975): 6; Denis Crouzet, *Les Guerriers de Dieu: La Violence au Temps des Troubles de Religion (vers 1525—vers 1610)* (Seyssel: Champ Vallon, 1990).

30. Greengrass, "Hidden Transcripts," 72.

31. Harold Crouch, *The Army and Politics in Indonesia* (Ithaca: Cornell University Press, 1978), 97-157.

32. Robert W. Hefner, *The Political Economy of Mountain Java: An Interpretive History* (Berkeley: University of California Press, 1990): 210.

33. *The Holy Bible*, Revised Standard Version, (New York: Thomas Nelson & Sons, 1952): I Sam. 15: 1-3.

34. *The Holy Bible,* Revised Standard Version, (New York: Thomas Nelson & Sons, 1952): 1 Sam. 15: 23.

35. Walter C. Langer, *The Mind of Adolf Hitler* (New York: Basic Books, 1972).

36. Adolf Hitler, *Mein Kampf,* Translated by Ralph Manheim (Boston: Houghton Mifflin, 1971), 296.

37. Hok-lam Chan, "The Chien-wen, Yung-lo, Hung-his, and Hsüan-te Reigns," in *The Cambridge History of China, Volume 7: the Ming Dynasty, 1368-1644*, ed. Frederick W. Mote and Denis Twitchett, Part I (Cambridge: Cambridge University Press, 1981) 201-202.

38. Henry Kamen, *The Spanish Inquisition: A Historical Revision* (New Haven: Yale University Press, 1997), 283-304.

39. Benzion Netanyahu, *The Origins of the Inquisition in Fifteenth Century Spain* (New York: Random House, 1995).

40. Karen Barkey, "Thinking about the Consequences of the End of Empire," in *After Empire: Multiethnic Societies and Nation-Building*, ed. Karen Barkey and Mark Von Hagen (Boulder, Colo.: Westview, 1997), 103; Rogers Brubaker, "Aftermaths of Empire and the Unmixing of Peoples," in *After Empire: Multiethnic Societies and Nation-Building*, ed. Karen Barkey and Mark Von Hagen (Boulder, Colo.: Westview, 1997), 155-80.

41. Ernst Gellner, *Nations and Nationalism* (Ithaca: Cornell University Press, 1983); Elie Kedourie, *Nationalism* (London: Hutchinson, 1960).

42. Eric J. Hobsbawm, *Nations and Nationalism Since 1780: Programme, Myth, Reality* (Cambridge: Cambridge University Press, 1990).

43. Walker Connor, *Ethnonationalism: The Quest for Understanding* (Princeton: Princeton University Press, 1994), 196-209.

44. Liah Greenfeld, *Nationalism: Five Roads to Modernity* (Cambridge: Harvard University Press, 1992).

45. Misha Glenny, *The Fall of Yugoslavia: The Third Balkan War,* (New York: Penguin, 1993); Juan Diez Medrano, *Divided Nations: Class, Politics, and Nationalism in the Basque Country and Catalonia* (Ithaca: Cornell University Press, 1995); Robert Bothwell, *Canada and Quebec: One Country, Two Histories* (Vancouver: University of British Columbia Press, 1995).

46. Gérard Prunier *The Rwanda Crisis: History of a Genocide* (New York: Columbia University Press, 1997).

47. Helen Fein, "Genocide: A Sociological Perspective," *Current Sociology* 38, no. 1 (Spring 1990): 1; Michael Freeman, "Genocide, Civilization and Modernity," *The British Journal of Sociology* 46, no. 2 (June 1995): 209; Leo Kuper, *Genocide* (New Haven: Yale University Press, 1981), 210-14; Ruti Teitel, "Judgment at the Hague," *East European Constitutional Review* 5, no. 4 (Fall 1996): 81.

48. Daniel Chirot, *Modern Tyrants: The Power and Prevalence of Evil in Our Age* (Princeton: Princeton University Press, 1996); Prunier, *The Rwanda Crisis.*

49. Daniel Chirot, "Modernism without Liberalism: The Ideological Roots of Modern Tyranny," *Contention* 13, (Fall 1995): 147-58.

50. Aili Mari Tripp and Crawford Young, "The Accommodation of Cultural Diversity in Tanzania," in *Ethnopolitical Warfare: Causes, Consequences, and Possible Solutions*, ed. Daniel Chirot and Martin E. P. Seligman (Washington D.C.: American Psychological Association Press, 2001), 259-74.

51. Brandon Hamber, "Who Pays for Peace? Implications of the Negotiated Settlements in Post-Apartheid South Africa," in *Ethnopolitical Warfare: Causes, Consequences, and Possible Solutions*, ed. Daniel Chirot and Martin E. P. Seligman (Washington D.C.: American Psychological Association Press, 2001), 235-58; Alex Boraine, *A Country Unmasked: Inside South Africa's Truth and Reconciliation Commission* (New York: Oxford University Press, 2001).

52. Tony Gallagher, "The Northern Ireland Conflict: Prospects and Possibilities," in *Ethnopolitical Warfare: Causes, Consequences, and Possible Solutions*, ed. Daniel Chirot and Martin E. P. Seligman (Washington D.C.: American Psychological Association Press, 2001), 205-14.

53. Chirot, *Modern*, 20-23.

54. T.W. Adorno, E. Frenkel-Brunswick, D. J. Levinson, and R. Sanford, *The Authoritarian Personality* (New York: Harper, 1950).

55. Bassam Tibi, *The Challenge of Fundamentalism: Political Islam and the New World Disorder* (Berkeley: University of California Press, 1998); Mark Juergensmeyer, *Terror in the Mind of God: The Global Rise of Religious Violence* (Berkeley: University of California Press, 2000).

56. Glenny, *The Balkans*, 652-62.

57. Andrew MacIntyre, "Political Institutions and the Economic Crisis in Thailand and Indonesia," in *The Politics of the Asian Economic Crisis*, ed. T. J. Pempel (Ithaca: Cornell University Press, 1999), 154-61; Paul Gorjao, "The End of a Cycle: Australian and Portuguese Foreign Policies and the Fate of East Timor" *Contemporary Southeast Asia* 23, no. 1 (April 2001): 101-23.

58. Andrew G. Janos, *East Central Europe in the Modern World* (Stanford: Stanford University Press, 2000), 366-72, 390-98.

Chapter 14

Progress and Contentious Politics

Charles Tilly

Progress in contentious politics is a matter of life and death. Contentious politics includes all episodic, public, collective making of claims that, if realized, would bear on the interests of some political actor. Contentious politics thus defined runs from demonstrations to wars, from political rallies to massacres. Because some such events center on violence and most of them run some risk of damage to persons and property, we might reasonably consider decline in death rates from contentious politics to constitute one element of progress.

Is the world progressing? In crude but vivid vital statistics, the world death rate for large-scale war ran around 90 per million population per year during the eighteenth century, 150 per million during the nineteenth century, somewhere above 400 per million during the twentieth. In absolute terms, and perhaps per capita as well, the sixty years beginning in 1940 brought more deaths from genocide (government-directed or government-authorized killing of populations identified by race, ethnicity and/or religion) and politicide (wholesale killing of populations identified by political affiliation) than any comparable period in human history. If death rates from political violence measure progress, over the world as a whole the last few centuries have produced the opposite: regress.

Inhabitants of capitalist democracies might forgivably think otherwise. To varying degrees, governments in those countries have seized unprecedented control over concentrated means of violence, thus reducing the scope of armed bands, warlords, and mercenaries within their domestic politics. Armed police patrol their territories, disarming weapon-wielding civilians who get in their way. Their governments usually rely on specialized non-military police for crowd control rather than sending in regular military forces. By and large, their mass meetings, demonstrations, election campaigns, legislative sessions, and other forms of public politics proceed with little or no killing, wounding, and destruction of property—a remarkable contrast with their own pasts and with much of the contemporary world.

To be sure, Basque separatists still harass Spain's Guardia Civil, Northern Ireland remains a powder keg, while from time to time the United States generates ghetto rebellions, violent demonstrations, and standoffs with militias. On the whole, nevertheless, during the last century capitalist democracies have created a remarkable concentration of coercive means and action in the hands of governmental agents. The concentration of coercive means has not produced a decline in the violence of contentious politics, but a shift of that violence to increasingly lethal wars, both civil and international, especially wars conducted outside the home territories of capitalist democracies. For all the security such a transformation affords the daily lives of civilians in capitalist democracies, it is not obvious that exchanging domestic for international violence constitutes progress. The more civilians of other countries die in international conflicts, the bleaker the balance.

Away from capitalist democracies, in any case, recent decades have brought even grimmer news. Countries outside that charmed circle range between those in which concentration of coercive means has occurred in the company of domestic authoritarianism, on one side, and those in which violence has infested domestic politics, on the other. The two extremes separate the relative peace of tyranny from the turbulence of genocide, politicide, banditry, and civil war. Myanmar (with military rulers leaving almost no space for domestic contention) and the Congo Republic (with contending armies and profiteers despoiling the country) mark the two poles. Some unlucky countries stretch from pole to pole; Afghanistan, for instance, has recently assumed that awkward posture, with Taliban-controlled areas enduring tight repression, other territories beset by warlords, and clandestine flows of arms, drugs, or other illicit goods supporting all sides. Throughout the range between the poles, expanded trade in arms, mercenaries, drugs, diamonds, and other contraband has raised the stakes of violent conflict as it has increased the resources available to specialists in violence. Nowhere along that continuum can we speak of progress in contentious politics. In sheer levels of political violence, the world has actually regressed since 1940.

That regression has some surprising features. If World War II revealed the depravity to which war-making powers could descend, during the postwar recovery many observers and policy makers thought the victorious allies could lead the world as a whole toward peace, prosperity, and various forms of democracy. That only happened in a few places. Immense India did develop a precarious, shambling, incomplete sort of democracy. Smaller former European colonies such as

Jamaica and Malta likewise created fractious versions of democracy. After strong initial tutelage, defeated powers (notably Germany, Italy, and Japan) became significant capitalist democracies. A few other areas enjoying privileged access to western markets and military protection (especially South Korea and Taiwan) eventually experienced significant industrialization and discarded authoritarian rulers. After a great surge of violence in domestic politics, South Africa overturned its Apartheid regime and took significant steps toward racial equality. Such post-socialist countries as Slovenia, Hungary, and Estonia now show some signs of moving toward capitalist democracy.

Elsewhere, the picture was chilling. Democratization and economic growth occurred at best unevenly and uncertainly across Latin America. Over much of Asia, Africa, Oceania, and Eastern Europe the postwar period brought strife-filled disaster, and no democratization at all. What is more, apparently atavistic forms of solidarity—especially ethnic, lineage, religious, linguistic, and racial solidarity—became more prominent bases of political mobilization instead of giving way to divisions by class industry and citizenship. Steeped in enlightenment ideas about the eventual triumph of instrumental rationality, both social scientists and statesmen found the political resurgence of ethnicity, kinship, religion, language, and race baffling. People proved even more willing to kill each other on behalf of ostensibly outmoded solidarities than on behalf of political ideals or class. As a consequence, much of the world regressed toward more extensive and lethal political violence.

Regression did not result from lack of contact between capitalist democracies and the rest of the world. The experiences of capitalist democracies and other countries have been influencing each other powerfully for several centuries. Decolonization by no means ended that mutual embrace. Net flows of arms and mercenaries, for example, run from richer to poorer countries, while drugs, diamonds, and other contraband, on balance, flow from poorer to richer. During the last half-century, western powers (capitalist or otherwise) have usually favored domestic authoritarianism over civil war, and have intervened accordingly with military, economic, and political support for authoritarian regimes.

Although the Soviet Union's collapse ended its intense competition with the United States for loyalties of geopolitically significant poorer states, the great power practice of propping up autocrats to check their opposition or their neighbors has by no means disappeared. Finally, the readiness of great powers to recognize distinctive nationality as a basis of political independence has encouraged political entrepreneurs throughout the world to organize nationalist campaigns on the basis of ethnicity, language, and religion, if not explicitly of race. By these means, the contentious politics of rich countries and poor shape each other.

People commonly use words such as conflict, strife, struggle, protest, disturbance, upheaval, revolt, and resistance to describe large tracts of contentious politics' domain. The heavier term *contentious politics* helps single out those forms of public conflict in which governments and political actors figure as claimants, objects of claims, or third parties to claims. Contentious politics *excludes* routine bureaucratic activities, string-pulling, favor-giving, information-gathering, tax-collection, military service, and similar non-episodic, non-public, and non-collective political activities except in so far as they give rise to episodic, public, and collective making of claims. Contentious politics *includes* demonstrating, rallying, striking, marching, meeting, warring, sabotaging, staging coups, organizing revolutions, and similar claim making, just so long as it involves episodic, public, and collective interaction.

What might constitute progress in contentious politics? We can follow Amartya Sen in treating capability as a person's freedom to choose among possible modes of living. As compared to the narrow range of well-being indexed by per capita income or per capita market production, capability rests on health, life expectancy, material resources, social constraints, and social opportunities. Let us accordingly consider progress to consist of durable changes that bring net increases in the capabilities of all human beings summed over their lifetimes. At constant capabilities, increasing life expectancies therefore constitute progress. At constant life expectancy, increasing capabilities constitute progress.

All other things equal, a durable net decline in per capita killing, wounding, and property destruction over the course of contentious claim making therefore qualifies as progress. Beyond that point, however, paradox looms. A ready intuition treats declines in both contention and violence as progress. Conflict, after all, sounds like a bad thing. But participation in peaceable public claim making brings significant benefits to participants and to their polities. It advances their capabilities. Relatively broad and equal participation generally spreads political knowledge, increases citizen sensitivity to governmental malfeasance, provides voice for grievances, favors effective production of public goods, and facilitates innovation without deep disruption of governmental services. On balance we should therefore welcome increases in per capita levels of contention, provided that contention gives voice to broad segments of the population and generates low levels of violence.

Figure 1 schematizes the situation, as seen from the perspective of an individual polity. Progress, it declares, consists of movement away from destruction and toward participation. An increase in the share of the world's population living within low-destruction, high-participation polities constitutes progress. Moves away from authoritarianism, tyranny, or civil war and toward democracy qualify as progressive.

Crucial questions arise at precisely this point:

- If the external involvement of governments in wars—international and civil—increases as destruction declines within domestic politics, does progress occur?
- If governments achieve pacification of domestic politics by means of incarceration, selective execution, and other forms of repression that reduce per capita destruction, does that qualify as progress?

• What if we expand the meaning of violence and destruction beyond physical damage to psychic damage, injustice, regimentation, and/or degradation of life's quality?

No quick formulas will resolve these age-old problems of political philosophy. But my own provisional replies run as follows:

• Although any measurement of progress refers to some arena and therefore varies from one arena to another, from a global viewpoint when war-driven destruction increases faster than the destructiveness of domestic politics declines, the world regresses.
• Above some minimum of organized protection endorsed by the bulk of the population and not directed against well defined minorities, pacification by means of repression counts against, not for, progress.
• Expanding the meaning of destruction from physical damage will increase the proportion of all human experience taking place in the upper half of figure 1 and will enormously complicate the actual measurement of destruction, but it will not change the fundamental character of the problem.

Students of contentious politics are still attempting to discover what causes decreases in destruction and increases in participation. The vast amount of recent work on these subjects has produced some measurement conventions, for example, battle deaths per year as a criterion of war's intensity. It has installed some prevalent distinctions, for example, between contention in domestic and international arenas. It has finally, generated a wide array of controversial but at least partly documented hypotheses, for example, that pairs of democracies are significantly less likely to war against each other than are other pairings of regimes. Between those who say a glass is half empty and those who declare it half full, half-empty critics can easily point to disagreement on almost every major proposition in the field, while half-full advocates can point to the great body of substantive knowledge that has accumulated concerning particular polities and varieties of contention. Contentious politics is, appropriately, a field in ferment.

Because explanations of change in destruction and participation remain uncertain, I have little choice but to offer my own best conjectures. They emerge from years of work on contentious politics in different parts of the world, past and present. Yet they remain conjectures. They run as follows:

1. Destruction rises with the extent to which organizations specializing in deployment of coercive means—armies, police forces, coordinated banditry, pirate confederations, mercenary enterprises, and the like—increase in size, geographic scope, resources, and coherence.
2. Destruction also rises with the extent to which leaders of such organizations evade civilian control.

3. In the case of government-incited killing of civilians, destruction increases to the extent that its organization also offers opportunities for private vengeance and incentives to predation.
4. Participation rises with the extent to which public politics achieves insulation from prevalent categorical inequalities in the population at large, notably including divisions by gender, race, ethnicity, religion, and class.
5. Participation rises with the extent to which public politics integrates networks of trust—those webs of social relations to which people commit long-term, high-risk enterprises such as procreation, cohabitation, child care, old age security, long-distance trade, and learning of profitable skills.
6. Participation rises with the extent to which public politics itself incorporates institutions and practices supporting a) broad, equal rights, and obligations, b) binding consultation concerning changes in governmental personnel, resources, and policies, and c) protection of citizens, especially members of minorities, from arbitrary action by governmental agents.

Although the sixth stipulation flirts with tautology, the six principles combine into a crude theory of political processes promoting pacification and democratization. They imply, for example, that little pacification or democratization will occur without subordination of military organizations to civilian control and diversion of military effort into non-destructive pursuits. They also imply that inequality as such does not generate destruction or threaten democracy, but its translation into public politics does both. They imply, finally, that pacification and democratization are only likely to occur through external shock (e.g., defeat in war) or internal struggle (e.g., revolution). I claim only that these are plausible conjectures in the present state of knowledge, that they are empirically verifiable, that they differ significantly from common arguments reducing destruction and participation to effects of dominant cultures or widely shared psychological conditions, and that if true they have significant implications for public policy.

Let us follow up some of the more obvious policy implications, in order from relatively feasible at a local or national scale to inevitably depending on international cooperation: 1) policing of domestic claim making; 2) impeding international trade in contraband; 3) intervention against state-incited mass killing; 4) slowing national self-determination. Unsurprisingly, these policy initiatives run from repeatedly implemented with some success (reforms of policing) to hardly even contemplated in the contemporary world (denial of claims to national self-determination).

Policing of Domestic Claim Making. Within local and national limits, reforms of policing can both reduce destruction and promote participation. Removal of regular military formations, of paramilitary forces, and of temporarily deputized civilians from control of assemblies and public spaces in favor of civilian controlled police forces establishes a significant first step. Beyond that step, police training in non-violent crowd control and negotiation with claim-makers promotes peaceful contention. It does so partly by distinguishing sharply between tolerated and forbidden forms of claim making, partly by providing protection of claim-makers from their opponents, and partly by making encounters between claimants and authorities more predictable. This policy not only generalizes existing models but also appeals to widely held political standards.

Inhibition of Contraband. The flow of arms and mercenaries in one direction meets the flow of drugs, gems, and other contraband in the other direction. Their confluence supports dealers, smugglers, rebels, and other opponents of governmental control. To cut either flow would reduce sustenance for rogue military forces and local groups of rebels. Since capitalist democracies export a significant share of the arms and mercenaries while importing an even more significant share of the contraband, their effective limitation of supply and demand as well as effective control of export and import would reduce destruction. That reduction of destruction would, in turn, promote political participation in countries currently ravaged by contraband-fed wars. This policy confronts serious opposition and subversion from interested parties, but would at least command widespread public support.

Intervention against State-Incited Killing. Unilateral action by a single government—even the powerful U.S. government—has little chance of effectiveness in this arena. But with international cooperation a three-stage policy is, in principle, possible. The first stage is active discouragement of categorically exclusionary practices in national politics, such as restriction of citizenship, voting, office-holding, employment, and office-holding to certified members of a particular ethnic group; standard diplomatic, financial, and organizational interventions apply. The second stage is to form a rapid intervention force (no doubt based on international organizations and perhaps authorized by prior treaties among participating governments) specialized in protecting potential victims from their killers. The third stage is to provide policing that inhibits secondary opportunism in the form of vengeance, looting, rape, and dispossession. Any such policies face significant resistance in the name of national sovereignty. Yet international organizations—NATO, the United Nations, the European Union, the International Monetary Fund, and others—breach sovereignty daily on behalf of various transnational interests.

Checking National Self-Determination. Such a policy, if implemented, would reduce destruction and promote participation both because it would inhibit increasingly brutal struggles for recognition as authentic representatives of suppressed nationalities and because it would reduce justification of attacks on minorities that deny the priority of titular nationalities. Any policy under this heading would have to include three components. First would come slowing the ratification of claims to national independence or regional autonomy on the basis of distinctive culture and long-time occupation of territory. Second, establishment of models and rewards for creation of representative systems that avoid matching of territory, culture, and government while guaranteeing rights to members of cultural minorities. Third, monitoring political participation—including participation in contentious politics—to discourage exclusion and repression on the basis of categorical membership. These policies, too, would face objections in the name of national sovereignty, resistance on the part of co-ethnics and co-religionists in adjacent territories, and short-run mobilizations led by nationalist activists. Over the longer run, however, they would contribute substantially to diminution of destruction and promotion of participation.

These proposed policies follow from my earlier conjectures concerning causes of change in destruction and participation. To the extent that my conjectures err, of course, the policies lose value. Nevertheless, two robust, urgent conclusions follow. First, progress in contentious politics matters enormously for human welfare. Second, improving the reliability of explanations for destruction and participation is no mere matter of scholarly curiosity. It has immense bearing on human life and death.

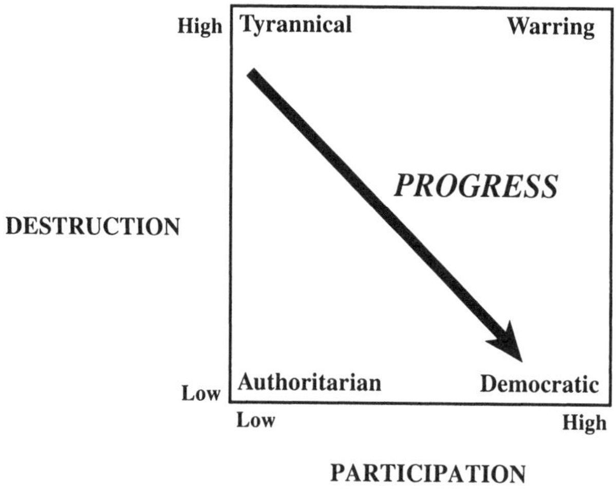

Figure 1: Progress in Contentious Politics

Chapter 15

NGOs, Development, and Human Rights: A Story of Progress and Policy

San C. Ng and Marc Lindenberg

> When we think of progress in the U.S. or Europe we don't realize what most people in the developing world today would say progress means to them. Most of us would look at how much money we have in the bank or how much we earn, social prestige or how many times our name appears in the paper, what kind of neighborhood we live in or maybe our academic credentials.
> In the developing world people tell me that progress for them and their families would be having a place to live, feeling safe and secure in their homes and communities, having enough to eat, sufficient firewood to cook supper and the ability to get clean water from an unpolluted stream. We need to support their views of progress in the new millennium.
> Jimmy Carter[1]

Introduction

The words *progress* and *development* seemingly go hand-in-hand. Despite the fact that the goal of poverty alleviation has dominated development policies for the past fifty years, the painful reality of global poverty and inequity persists. Today, 1.2 billion people, or a fifth of the world's population, are living on less than a dollar a day, while the wealth of the three richest men in the world is greater than the combined Gross National Product (GNP) of the least developed countries.[2] These and other gloomy numbers seem to suggest that development efforts have failed.[3] Some critics even suggest that development efforts have led to regression in poor countries. Yet there are many debates as to what really constitutes progress in development. Defenders of development[4] claim that the poor would be worse off without these efforts, that the benefits of development are inadequately or incompletely measured.

President Carter's view of progress, presented at the beginning of this chapter, is based on John Rawls' notion that social welfare increases when we increase the welfare of the worst off.[5] Consistent with Carter and most development practitioners, in this chapter we view progress as greater effectiveness in efforts to improve the lives of the worst off.[6] While governments and aid agencies have delivered mainstream development activities since the 1960s, the number of international non-governmental organizations (NGOs) has grown exponentially since the 1970s. During this time, professionals in both sectors have attempted to translate goals for poverty alleviation into policies that work. International development NGOs' disillusionment with governmental approaches to poverty alleviation have grappled with a variety of alternative approaches to tackling global poverty. In the last five years, a few international development NGOs have turned to the existing international framework on human rights as an alternative to current development approaches. Proponents of what is now termed the Rights-Based Approach (RBA) claim the RBA represents a new paradigm in poverty alleviation.

Using the RBA as a focal point, this chapter examines the evolution of international development NGO approaches to poverty alleviation. After defining the role of NGOs within the international development system, we then examine the evolution of theories and practices adopted in NGO work and conclude that while there has been progress, the search for better approaches to poverty alleviation continues. Next, we set out the evolution of the human rights concepts, and the RBA as an alternative approach to international development. We optimistically conclude that the RBA framework can increase the effectiveness of development policy.

Recent History of the NGO Sector

The public, private, and civil society sectors fulfill different, though overlapping, functions in society.[7] The public sector protects, secures, and regulates the lives and actions of citizens, and manages how the society functions and progresses. The private sector creates opportunities for citizens to earn a livelihood and to create and accumulate wealth. The civil society sector encourages the pursuit of individual interests, promotes grassroots development, and otherwise fills in gaps in areas that the other two sectors do not address. NGOs are formal organizations within the civil society sector and differ from the public and private sectors in that they are voluntary and independent. While governments and governmental aid agencies have dominated the field of international development assistance over the past forty years, the civil society and private sectors are playing increasingly important roles. Increasing overlap of activities between and among the three sectors is leading to new forms of partnerships.[8]

The three-sector system involves the flow of resources, usually from developed countries to development agencies (including NGOs) which then implement poverty alleviation activities in developing countries. NGOs are but an actor within this system. Figure 1 maps the flow of aid within each sector of society as well as the relationships between them. The relationship of the three sectors is complicated by segregation between the North and South, and at national and local levels. At the same time, this relationship fosters partnerships and leads to the development of innovative approaches.

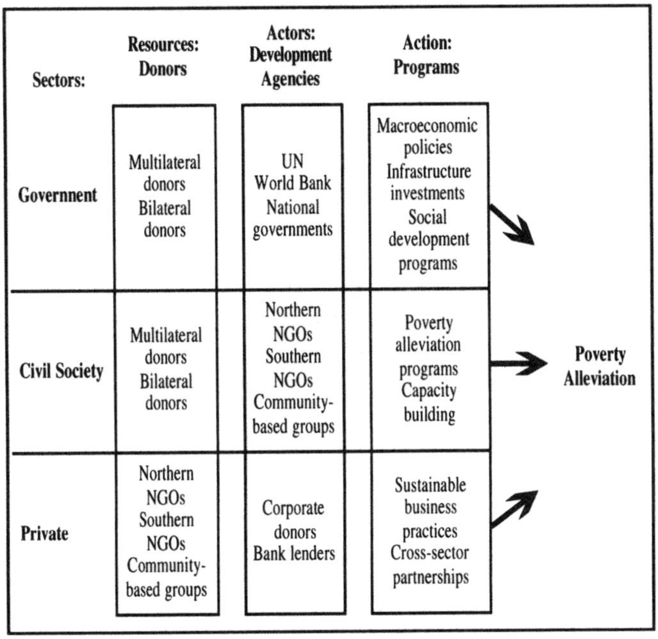
Sectors:
Resources: Donors
Actors: Development Agencies
Action: Programs
Governnent
Multilateral donors Bilateral donors
UN World Bank National governments
Macroeconomic policies Infrastructure investments Social development programs
Civil Society
Multilateral donors Bilateral donors
Northern NGOs Southern NGOs Community-based groups
Poverty alleviation programs Capacity building
Poverty Alleviation
Private
Northern NGOs Southern NGOs Community-based groups
Corporate donors Bank lenders
Sustainable business practices Cross-sector partnerships

Figure 1

Within the international aid system, NGOs vary by size, function, and geographical location. Northern international relief and development NGOs, the focus of this chapter, refer to those organizations whose headquarters are registered and located in a northern country in addition to having country or program offices in developing countries. Their functions range from short-term natural and humanitarian disaster relief to mid-term rehabilitation and long-term development programs. Activities, which may include direct service delivery, support programs, capacity building, and advocacy, and are usually implemented through multi-sectoral operations.[9]

Although the concept of development assistance is relatively new, the concept of caring for the wounded and protecting humanity is not. While there were virtually no formal international humanitarian organizations prior to the nineteenth century, individuals and religious organizations have championed for humanity and engaged in humanitarian work throughout the centuries. Advancement in the technology of warfare in the nineteenth century brought the plight of the war-wounded to the forefront of humanitarian concerns. Early international efforts[10] included those of women like Florence Nightingale who directly aided British soldiers during the Crimean War in 1854. The Young Men's Christian Association (YMCA) was one of the first organizations to advocate for extending care to all in need regardless of geographic boundaries. One of the biggest international achievements came in 1863 when a group of government representatives from fourteen nations met in Geneva and created the International Committee of the Red Cross (ICRC).[11] This organization provided care and provided for the basic needs of the war-wounded. The ICRC inspired the development of national Red Cross societies, as well as other humanitarian organizations across the world.

By the early twentieth century, NGOs were slowly increasing in number and were expanding their missions. One of the oldest northern NGOs, Save the Children,[12] was founded in 1919, following the horrific events of the First World War, with the goal of promoting children's rights. Several NGOs, such as Oxfam[13] and CARE,[14] were formed during and after the Second World War to provide famine and humanitarian relief in Europe. With the emphasis on economic restructuring and development after the war, a global nonprofit/NGO sector emerged in the 1960s to fill in the gaps left by governments and corporations. Although government institutions and their mainstream economic growth programs dominated the early development scene, NGO growth took off in the 1970s and accelerated in the 1980s and 1990s.[15] In this process, NGOs became major players in international development.

This evolution of NGOs is the pivot of progress as we have defined it. These organizations define an industry whose fundamental mission is to better lives. Moreover, growth of the NGO sector has made it easier to channel resources from private and individual donors to those in need. The flexibility, commitment, and broad-based participation in the NGO sector also give it a comparative advantage in the business of international development.

This progress of NGOs has not occurred without challenge. In the 1990s, the NGO sector experienced growing pains and a period of soul searching.[16] Accelerating globalization had brought about complex challenges,[17] including new and perplexing forms of poverty, weaker global institutions, declining capacity of national governments to provide services, new pressures for efficiency and accountability, as well as greater competition for funding. NGOs, in addition to addressing these challenges, have attempted to increase their effectiveness by adopting more holistic approaches.

History of Development Approaches

This section looks at the evolution of major development theories, the impact of this evolution on NGO practice, and current approaches to more "integrated" development.

The growth model emerged as the mainstream model of development in the 1960s and 1970s and, to a certain extent, persists today. This model propagated a relatively simple approach to development, based on the belief that the benefits of a country's economic growth would naturally trickle down from the rich to the poor. The growth model has its roots in the industrialization of European countries in the 1700s and the economic theories that followed to explain that phenomena.[18] While earlier income from the predominantly agricultural societies was too little to amount to what would be called "development," the emergence of capitalist systems, and subsequent industrialization allowed countries to acquire unprecedented material wealth. For the first time in history, a link was made between economic growth and development. Many economic theories postulated that economic progress was the natural and only path to development.

In the same tradition, growth, or modernization theories, which emerged after the Second World War, linked development to economic growth. These theories went one step further and advocated development as a transition from the "traditional" (or undeveloped) to the "modern" (or developed) society, the latter being modeled after the developmental processes of European countries. Poverty was simply seen as the lack of economic growth at the national level. Health, longevity, literacy, and other social development would occur as a result of increased resource flows from the developed to the developing world. Early NGO policy attempted to promote economic and material welfare by fulfilling basic needs and providing opportunities to increase income through direct service provision and investing in community infrastructure.

A longstanding alternative to the economic growth theory is based in socialist thought and places an overriding concern on equity and power distribution. Traditional socialist theories, which emerged with the growth of capitalist systems, did not question the assumption that capitalism (i.e., economic growth) can lead to development. However, in the 1960s and 1970s, socialist theorists began to question this assumption.[19] Dependency theorists viewed industrialization as a process that led the already oppressed developing world into greater dependence on the developed world through the invasion of global corporations, leading to even lower levels of development.[20] These thinkers defined poverty as powerlessness in society and a lack of control over resources. Thus, development was viewed as an internally driven process with the goal of increasing capacity of marginalized groups, and ownership of the development process at the grassroots level. There was, however, little guidance about how this might translate into policy, although NGOs experimented loosely with programs on education and training.

By the 1980s, many academics and practitioners were becoming disillusioned with the mainstream approach as well as alternative socialist, or dependency theories. Not only were development strategies under the two approaches proving to be ineffective, but world conditions appeared to be worsening. The inability of developing countries to pay their debts to public and private banking institutions, deepening poverty, a widening gap between rich and poor, and a rise in civil wars led to a period of disenchantment with past theory and policy. Academics and practitioners questioned the assumption that growth was equal to development, as the negative environmental effects of industrialization became more apparent. Moreover, the collapse of communism led to skepticism toward socialist alternatives. This crisis of confidence in development theories created an opportunity to re-examine the old approaches[21] and provided NGOs with incentive to try alternative approaches to poverty alleviation.

In the 1990s, NGOs encouraged innovative approaches to relieving pervasive poverty. For example, the growth-premised concept of "human development,"[22] while still focusing on macro-level growth, expanded to include the promotion of social goals such as literacy, longevity, reducing child mortality, and gender equality. Efforts usually included programs that provided direct assistance to the poor on several levels. At the same time, alternative development models emerged, all motivated by the aim of empowering development.[23] NGOs adopted a people-centered, participatory, and local approach to development. The concept of "sustainable" development also took root. In practice, this translated into programs that were aimed at reducing impacts to the environment.

The first three rows of table 1 show how these dominant theories have had different implications for NGO policies. As explored, these policies are based on different theories that are premised upon different assumptions, they set different goals and advocate different strategies. While dichotomies are often established in theory, it has been argued that the lines between these theories are blurring.[24] Many claim that the growth paradigm ended its reign in the 1990s, and was replaced by a more integrated approach to poverty alleviation. Lending validity to this argument, an evaluation of developing countries concluded that high performers of human development made use of integrated approaches, including both macro-level policies and grassroots level action, over a period of years to achieve success.[25] According to this evaluation, high performing countries commonly had a stable and proactive government (regardless of regime type) that pushed for outward economic growth at a macro-level and invested simultaneously on the grassroots level in health, education, and infrastructure. They also promoted a higher level of civil and political rights. NGOs today use integrated frameworks—with a mix of approaches unique to each organization.

Tradition	Approach	Assumptions	Analytic Lens	Main Goal	NGO Strategies
Mainstream	Growth	Development is modeled after the path of the industrialized world	Modern rich vs. Traditional poor	Economic efficiency and productivity	Poverty reduction by fulfilling basic needs, promoting modern technology, and increasing income via multi-sectoral programs
Alternative	Empowerment	Development is possible only after power is more equitably distributed	Powerful vs. Exploited	End domination	Grassroots development by local participation, capacity building of oppressed groups, and promotion of civil society through collective action
Alternative	Environment	Development is possible without growth or industrialization	Over-consumers vs. Under-consumers	Sustainability	Sustainable development by reducing impacts of economic growth and industrialization
Integrated	Rights	Development is that which allows individuals to be free from poverty and suffering	Duty-bearer vs. Right-holder	Enhance-ment of capabilities	Development programs rooted in human rights principles, encouraging state to fulfill duties, use of international legal process, and advocacy

Table 1

Development theories have evolved from simple ideas about poverty alleviation into more sophisticated and holistic approaches. Goals for poverty alleviation are now viewed in wider contexts that involve a blend of factors, such as material well-being, social justice, sustainability, and human rights. More integrated modern approaches take into account the specific conditions of each country, including previous development experiences. There is also greater attention to Southern voices, and to placing people at the center. Policies and solutions are increasingly focused and relevant to those in need. However, the quest for more effective approaches continues.

Evolution of the Idea of Human Rights

The Rights-Based Approach (RBA) in Concept

Since the mid-1990s, interest has been growing in a new approach to development premised on the concept of human rights. This approach became known as the Rights-Based Approach, or RBA. While there are varying views of the RBA, one starting point is the "capability" approach suggested by Amartya Sen. Sen defines poverty as the deprivation of freedoms, including economic, social, and other freedoms, which can prevent an individual from living the life he or she values.[26] Development is seen as the enhancement of these capabilities. The concept of human rights and the international legal framework that has evolved in the past fifty years can be both a lens to identify the absence of certain capabilities as well as a tool to enhance them. The last row of table 1 compares the RBA's theoretical and practical differences with the other approaches described in the previous section.

Proponents of the RBA claim that this creates a new paradigm in development because, unlike other approaches that are premised on charity or welfarism, the RBA utilizes the empowering concepts of freedoms, rights, and human dignity. Moreover, a distinctive feature and additional advantage of the RBA is that the legal framework is already established within the international system (in particular that of economic, social, and cultural rights) and serves as a very practical tool that can enhance NGO work. Furthermore, because these rights encompass material well-being, social equity, and other freedoms, the RBA is comprehensive enough to embrace past approaches to development.

The concept of human rights arguably has its roots in the major religions across the world that promoted the concept of universal respect for others. Ancient traditions in Hinduism, Judaism, Buddhism, Confucianism, Christianity, and Islam all affirmed the moral worth and dignity of the individual and also proposed ways to think beyond oneself to serve, or help, others. Scholars also grappled with the difficult question of human relationships and social responsibility. These early religious doctrines and scholarly philosophies focused on universal responsibilities rather than rights. The concept of "natural law" introduced by classical

Greek philosophers around 4 B.C. suggested that these ideas of responsibilities and duties were derived from the law of nature, or based on God, that governed all human beings.[27]

Although "natural law" formed the foundation of human rights, it took major societal transformations and intellectual vigor to arrive at the concept of rights as we know it. The decline of feudalism and the rise of capitalism in the 1700s contributed to a longing for political and economic freedom. This led to the view that all human beings are born with a set of universal, or "natural rights," based on the theory of "natural law." At the same time, the European Renaissance and Enlightenment prompted an intellectual movement that resisted religious bondage and headed toward rationality. The concept of "natural rights" left its religious roots, and was redefined as the intrinsic nature of being human. By the early 1800s, the language was changed from "natural" rights to "human" rights.[28]

Until the mid-eighteenth century, the idea of human rights was primarily theoretical. Human rights was perhaps first applied in practice by leaders of the American and French revolutions in the eighteenth century who championed the idea of freedom to be included in the language of rights. In the nineteenth century, the anti-slavery movement became the first collective human rights movement in history. Other human rights causes included the plight of oppressed indigenous peoples, women's rights, and equity for workers. By the twentieth century, rights had a place in both theory and application. At the end of the Second World War, the horrors of genocide prompted an institutionalization of human rights on a scale never achieved before.

In 1948, human rights were recognized at the international level for the first time with the United Nations General Assembly's adoption of the Universal Declaration on Human Rights. This non-binding document contained general provisions on a relatively full range of internationally recognized rights[29] that fell into two categories—one civil and political, and the other economic, social and cultural. Because ideologies of democracy seemingly supported civil and political rights, whereas social and economic rights were supported by Communism, the Cold War created a political dichotomy between these two categories of rights. This resulted in 1966 in two separate international treaties, or Covenants, for each set of rights.[30] The Covenants provide details about the previously recognized rights as well as fundamental procedural arrangements. Since then, the Covenants, together with the Universal Declaration, have been seen as the authority on international standards of human rights that governments should promote. (See box 1 for examples of some major rights in these instruments.[31]) These documents also spearheaded an evolving legal framework that has shaped human rights work within an international legal system. The encoding of these rights into the Declaration and treaties encouraged further growth and institutionalization of rights from the 1970s to the present. Adopted international treaties included those against torture[32] and discrimination against women[33] and children.[34] Human rights have become an integral part of international relations in the last half of the twentieth century, and continue to evolve.

Box 1: Examples of Major Human Rights

Civil and Political Rights
- Right to life, liberty, and security of person
- Right to freedom of movement
- Right to work
- Right to freedom from slavery, torture, and cruel, inhuman, or degrading treatment
- Right to a fair trial, the presumption of innocence and the prohibition against the application of ex-post facto laws and penalties
- Right to privacy
- Right to freedom of speech, religion, and assembly
- Right to participate in the political process

Economic, Social and Cultural Rights
- Right to food and housing
- Right to highest attainable standard of physical and mental health
- Right to an adequate standard of living
- Right to education and access to information
- Right to social security, to work, and protection against unemployment
- Right to enjoy just and favorable conditions of work
- Right to form trade unions and to strike
- Right to participate freely in the cultural life of the community
- Right to protection of the family

In the last forty years NGO activity has increased in the realm of human rights. Northern human rights NGOs, such as Amnesty International and Human Rights Watch, have been created to curb international violations of human rights, in particular civil and political rights. These organizations rely on the power of publicity and political pressure. They have played a prominent role in human rights advocacy by participating in United Nations meetings, lobbying to persuade governments to sign human rights treaties, and advocating for civil and political rights.[35] While the notion of economic, social, and cultural rights runs parallel to development agendas targeting poverty, neither human rights nor development NGOs have actively promoted these rights. The end of the Cold War led to a theoretical reintegration of the two sets of rights and an awareness of the potential of economic, social, and cultural rights in development work. Human rights NGOs such as Amnesty International and Human Rights Watch have questioned how they should also address economic, social, and cultural rights. At the same time, development NGOs are broadening their approach to include a broader set of rights.

The increasing focus on human rights throughout the last fifty years has resulted in institutionalizing standards and creating a system of accountability. Not only does this support human rights work, but it also provides the foundation to an alternative approach to poverty alleviation.

Progress at an Intersection: NGOs, Development, and Rights

International development NGOs now represent a vital and still evolving sector. International development NGOs are continuously seeking more effective solutions based on their mission to better lives. Development theories based on human rights have given rise to a variety of focused and relevant policies as alternatives to mainstream development. Figure 2 represents a summary of this argument.

Policy and the Rights-Based Approach

In this section, we look at how the RBA is currently being translated into policy by NGOs, in particular northern international NGOs, and how that policy affects management and implementation. Using the practitioner's view of progress—that social welfare increased when we increase the welfare of the worst off—we evaluate the RBA as a tool in helping to shape practical goals and increasing NGO effectiveness toward poverty alleviation.

The RBA is not only visionary but also practical. While the RBA is based on a concept of human rights, it also has an institutional basis in the legal framework of human rights. The international legal system makes the RBA a practical and powerful tool. Adopting the RBA into development policy, however, does not necessarily translate into the political pressure of lobbying and publicity typically employed by human rights NGOs addressing civil and political rights. Rather, the RBA is used as an analytical tool for understanding poverty, analyzing individual situations, setting goals for, and designing, implementing, monitoring, and evaluating programs.[36] The RBA requires NGOs to re-examine their missions, articulate their work in human rights terms, embrace the tradition of solidarity in human rights, use the existing international legal framework (in particular on social and economic rights), and focus on human rights education on all levels. The approach is multi-disciplinary, people-centered, participatory, and impact and sustainability-focused. RBA activities span a wide range among the NGOs and can include advocacy efforts, campaigns, violation reporting, negotiations with governments, direct and indirect human rights projects, peace-building efforts, capacity building of oppressed groups, and education.

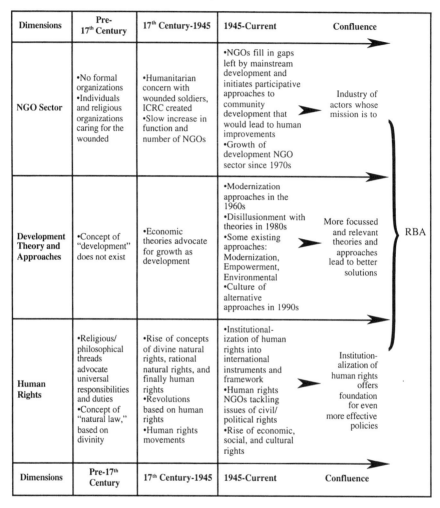

Dimensions	Pre-17th Century	17th Century-1945	1945-Current	Confluence	
NGO Sector	•No formal organizations •Individuals and religious organizations caring for the wounded	•Humanitarian concern with wounded soldiers, ICRC created •Slow increase in function and number of NGOs	•NGOs fill in gaps left by mainstream development and initiates participative approaches to community development that would lead to human improvements •Growth of development NGO sector since 1970s	Industry of actors whose mission is to	
Development Theory and Approaches	•Concept of "development" does not exist	•Economic theories advocate for growth as development	•Modernization approaches in the 1960s •Disillusionment with theories in 1980s •Some existing approaches: Modernization, Empowerment, Environmental •Culture of alternative approaches in 1990s	More focussed and relevant theories and approaches lead to better solutions	RBA
Human Rights	•Religious/ philosophical threads advocate universal responsibilities and duties •Concept of "natural law," based on divinity	•Rise of concepts of divine natural rights, rational natural rights, and finally human rights •Revolutions based on human rights •Human rights movements	•Institutionalization of human rights into international instruments and framework •Human rights NGOs tackling issues of civil/ political rights •Rise of economic, social, and cultural rights	Institutionalization of human rights offers foundation for even more effective policies	
Dimensions	**Pre-17th Century**	**17th Century-1945**	**1945-Current**	**Confluence**	

Figure 2: Evolution of NGOs, Development, and Rights

NGO Responses

There are varying responses to the RBA.[37] Among the northern international NGOs, Oxfam, CARE, and Save the Children are explicitly adopting the RBA and finding ways to incorporate the concept into their work. Oxfam finds the RBA is consistent with its view of poverty as social exclusion and framed five of its program goals in human rights language. Using rights as a centerpiece of its program and advocacy activities, Oxfam has launched full-scale and pilot projects in the field. CARE's rights-based approach emerged from its foundation of community-based approaches, such as its post-Second World War focus on food security and its subsequent emphasis on household livelihood security (HLS). These approaches put the community and family at the core of activities. CARE is finding ways to use the rights framework to increase its effectiveness by going beyond fulfilling needs to analyzing the root causes of poverty, and uses the RBA as an enhancement of its existing HLS approach. Save the Children (Save) perceives rights as being at the core of its original goals of protecting and promoting children's rights.

While Oxfam, CARE, and Save are explicitly experimenting with the RBA, other organizations utilize it implicitly. For example, Mercy Corps[38] views the RBA as consistent with its founding human rights principles, although it is still in the strategic process of fitting the RBA into its wider framework of civil society. International Medical Corps (IMC)[39] has not employed the RBA as a formal framework but sees human rights, especially in the realm of humanitarian law, as very relevant since IMC works in volatile situations where the violation of human rights is blatant.

Faith-based organizations such as World Vision[40] and World Concern[41] take a slightly different stance. World Concern views the existing legal framework as a practical tool that is one step closer to the theological concept of human dignity upon which much of its work is premised. Thus, it prefers to view rights from the angle of "ethics" and uses the notion of human rights only if it is a useful tool for specific projects. World Vision's leaders argue that the RBA still does not address the deeper theological layer that faith-based organizations address. Instead of "rights," World Vision programs promote "justice." The RBA is seen as a tool that can be appropriately used for projects that fall within this framework. Figure 3 summarizes these responses.

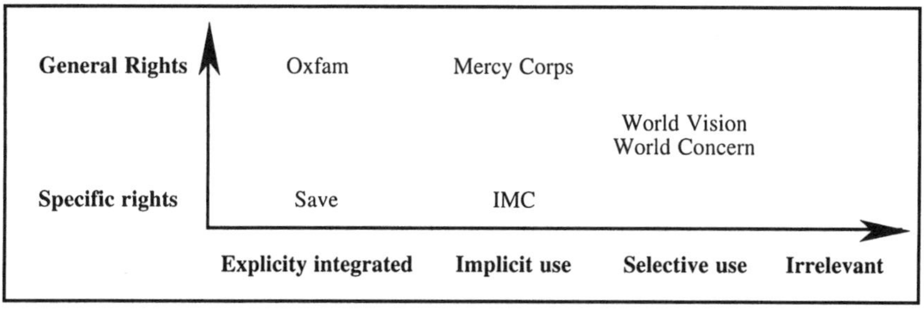

Figure 3: Some NGO Responses to the RBA

NGO Policy and Implementation

Although the RBA is gaining popularity as a concept in the development field, relatively few northern development NGOs are explicitly employing the RBA as an approach to programming. Those that have explicitly adopted a rights angle are still in the experimentation stage. Not only is the RBA a complicated concept that involves new ways of thinking, but its employment introduces new complexities to an NGO's policy, programming, organizational management, and external relations. Table 2 portrays a comparison of how the RBA is being implemented in CARE, Oxfam, and Save.

Dimensions	CARE	Oxfam	Save
Policy	The RBA is an enhancement of CARE's HLS approach so that underlying causes can be analyzed	Rights is the centerpiece of programming and advocacy activities; Five aims linking poverty to rights	The UN Convention on the Rights of the Child grounds SAVE to its roots and is the basis of its child programming; focus on four rights
Programming	Case studies and field-based pilot projects	Full scale and pilot projects across eight regional directions, managed by regional teams	Advocacy and research activities intensified; increased levels of programming to include national and global
Organization	Human Rights Coordinator; Reference group formed	Eight virtual teams formed based on regional directions	Advocacy and research teams
External	Strategic alliances formed	Joint projects with other NGOs	Partnerships with multinational corporations

Table 2: Implementation of the RBA in NGOs—Some Examples

Once an organization has decided to base policy on the RBA, it works to fit the concepts of the RBA into its existing framework of programming and reexamine its own mission. The organization then articulates its priorities in terms of rights. CARE, for example, has chosen to use the RBA as a tool to analyze the causes of poverty within its existing HLS framework, prioritizing the rights as livelihood, education, health, safety, security, and equity. Oxfam, on the other hand, has centered its development efforts around rights, and communicates its five aims (sustainable livelihood, health and education, life and security, advocacy, and equity) in the language of rights. As part of its rights-based approach, Save utilizes the United Nations Convention on the Rights of the Child as the basis for its child-focused programming, concentrating on the survival, development, protection, and participation of children.

Implementation may involve full-scale projects as well as pilot projects. An example of a full-scale project is Oxfam's West Africa education project, which promotes girls' rights to education by linking direct funding and capacity building programs to advocacy efforts on a regional and global level. Without the RBA, the same project might merely focus on providing schooling to girls locally without the upward link to the regional and global levels, or it might act as a high-level advocacy project without a link to the field. CARE country offices have begun to analyze deeper causes of poverty through pilot projects so that service delivery can be enhanced by more effective policies targeted at advocacy, increasing government accountability, and positively influencing cultural norms. Organizations may also add new elements to existing programs. For example, Save now emphasizes advocacy and research on rights in addition to its basic programming; Oxfam has intensified efforts in campaigning and advocacy; and CARE is in the process of incorporating the RBA into its sectoral work. Overall, the tone of implementation is one of experimentation and learning from the bottom-up.

The challenge of internal management is tremendous and each organization takes a unique route. Oxfam, for example, formulated directions for each of its eight regions and created regional teams that involve both management and field staff from all programming sectors. In contrast, CARE started by employing a human rights coordinator based in Africa and creating an RBA reference group involving twenty field and headquarters' staff to stimulate organizational learning. Organizations also need to formulate strategies to manage the change process.

An organization's external environment is also impacted. The RBA typically encourages new partnerships on all levels, such as with human rights NGOs or governments. CARE, for example, has formed strategic alliances with human rights NGOs in the field, Oxfam has partnered with other development NGOs working on similar issues, while Save has started partnering with multinational companies. Aside from new partners, organizations are faced with managing existing stakeholders so that the RBA can be legitimately used in the organization's work. Examples of stakeholders include the organization's board, donors, existing partners, program beneficiaries, and even the general public.

Challenges and Process Improvement

The RBA brings about many challenges for organizations. First, although the RBA can help in the development of comprehensive, integrated programming, it is also a complex concept. Organizations need to grapple with the legitimacy of the concept of rights, its role as an ends or means of development, and fitting the RBA smoothly into their organizational structure. Second, the legalistic language of international laws, complicated institutional structures, and the lack of enforcement mechanisms causes organizations to question the effectiveness of the RBA concept. In addition, organizational change in incorporating the RBA necessarily brings about internal management challenges. In large, with decentralized organizations with complicated structures, such as CARE, Oxfam, and Save, organizational change involves building staff buy-in on all levels, managing with flexibility without compromising a unified mission, communicating effectively, employing skilled staff, and garnering enough resources to make the changes. Tensions will inevitably arise in external relationships with stakeholders, partners, and the general public in a period of change. Oxfam, CARE, and Save are investing considerable resources in building support from their boards and donors and are carefully managing their relationships with human rights organizations, states, and the public.

In spite of challenges, these international development NGOs generally agree that the RBA affords many advantages. Moreover, many of these challenges can be mitigated through process improvement, including involving stakeholders throughout the organization, allowing flexibility in field offices for experimentation, and promoting a learning culture supported by ongoing research and program evaluation. Emphasis upon bottom-up change allows the RBA to be tweaked so that it best fits any situation, resulting in effective programming.

The RBA as Progress?

Despite the array of challenges, NGOs generally view the RBA as a useful and timely tool for policy formation. For NGOs, the value added by the RBA comes in its philosophical grounding as well as its practicality. Because rights are tied to the concept of freedom and dignity, the RBA is perceived as more empowering than approaches of welfarism or charity that have dominated development efforts in the past. Since the RBA is so comprehensive, it can accommodate other approaches to development as well, and is thus flexible enough to fit within an organization's existing framework. The human rights tradition of solidarity mitigates the natural competitiveness between NGOs. It also encourages close partnerships that can increase these organizations' collective impact. Furthermore, the RBA's emphasis on organizational learning fosters positive changes within organizations by introducing radical new ways of learning and managing.

Aside from its philosophical appeal, the RBA is also a practical tool. As an analytical tool, it allows NGOs to examine the systemic causes of poverty, thus employing resources more effectively. Its comprehensive nature helps to link programs within an organization. The existing international legal framework on human rights brings a common language to development agencies, promoting a coherent approach to their work as well as closer relationships. It also allows NGOs an avenue to increase government accountability. Unlike other approaches, the RBA enhances legitimacy and accountability on all levels through the use of international laws and judicial systems. For example, it can legitimize NGO efforts in politically charged situations by demanding that governments fulfill their obligations to citizens. While the RBA is too new to be formally evaluated in the field, the approach holds great promise as a foundation for more effective approaches to development.

Conclusion

This chapter has adopted the development practitioner's notion of progress, which is based on John Rawls' view that social welfare increases when the welfare of the worst off is increased. Practitioners set practical goals and search for viable approaches, with the aim of increasing effectiveness in poverty alleviation. The evolution of NGOs has given rise to an industry dedicated to bettering lives. Ideas and theories have become more sophisticated, contributing to better practice in the field. In addition, the values promoted by human rights concepts have matured through the formation of a legal framework and system, offering potential for increased competency in poverty alleviation. Progress in these dimensions brings forth the promise of more effective solutions in the form of the RBA.

In the realm of public policy, the RBA is seen as another step forward because it helps NGOs shape and re-shape their policies for poverty alleviation work with the hope of increased effectiveness. Despite differing NGO responses, challenges in implementation, and the difficulty in evaluating impact, the RBA can add value to institutions based on both its philosophy and practicality. The RBA's inherent value is in helping policy makers look at poverty differently, learn in different ways, use challenges to increase their effectiveness, and improve the lives of the worst off. This, perhaps, is the best tool we have for promoting progress in development today.

Notes

1. Jimmy Carter, lecture of the Progress Project speaker series, Seattle, Wash., January 2000.

2. William Pfaff, "The Development Numbers Say Economic Globalism Has Failed," *International Herald Tribune,* 4 July 2000, at www.iht.com/IHT/WP/00/index.html (accessed 15 Oct. 2001).

3. Pfaf, "Development Numbers."

4. See for example, Michel Camdessus, "After-crisis Thoughts on Poverty Alleviation and Peace for Development," speech presented at the 1999 Substantive Session of the UN Economic and Social Council, Geneva, 5 July 1999.

5. See John Rawls, *A Theory of Justice* (Cambridge, Mass.: Belknap Press of Harvard University Press, 1971).

6. See for example the view by Kofi A. Annan, Donald J. Johnston, Horst Koeler, and James D. Wolfenson, "foreword" *2000 A Better World for All, Progress towards the International Development Goals* 2000, at www.paris21.org/betterworld (accessed 7 Oct. 2001).

7. Alan Fowler, *Striking a Balance, A Guide to Enhancing the Effectiveness of Non-Governmental Organizations in International Development* (London: Earthscan, 1998), 20-39.

8. In general, the government sector tends to be small compared to the business sector in the northern countries, while the reverse is true for developing countries.

9. Marc Lindenberg and Coralie Bryant, *Going Global: Transforming Relief and Development NGOs* (Bloomfield, Conn.: Kumarian Press, 2001), 5-8.

10. Paul Gordon Lauren, *The Evolution of International Human Rights* (Philadelphia: University of Pennsylvania Press, 1998), 57-62.

11. While not an NGO in the strictest sense since it was created under a government treaty, it nevertheless has been involved in a wide range of humanitarian activities.

12. See Save the Children's homepage, www.savechildren.net/.

13. See Oxfam International's homepage, www.oxfam.org/.

14. See CARE's homepage, www.care.org/.

15. Lindenberg and Bryant, *Going Global,* 3-5.

16. Janet Salm, "Coping with Globalization: A profile of the northern NGO sector," *Nonprofit and Voluntary Sector Quarterly* 28, no. 4 supplement (1999): 101-2.

17. Marc Lindenberg and Patrick J. Dobel, "The Challenges of Globalization for Northern Relief and Development NGOs," *Nonprofit and Voluntary Sector Quarterly* 28, no. 4 supplement (1999): 2-24.

18. Jorge Larrain, *Theories of Development* (Cambridge, U.K.: Polity Press, 1989) 18-28

19. Larrain, *Theories*, 85-107.

20. Larrain, *Theories*, 111-33.

21. See David Booth, "Development Research: From Impasse to a New Agenda" in *Beyond the Impasse: New Directions in Development Theory*, ed. F. Schuurman (London: Zed Books, 1993), 49-76.

22. For example, The Word Bank in its 1990 *World Development Report* propagated that development meant encouraging economic growth on the one hand, and the provision of basic social services on the other. The United Nations Development Program (UNDP) in the *Human Development Report 1990* introduced a new index to measure progress in development that went beyond GDP to include human development factors like longevity and literacy.

23. See for example, David Korten, *Getting to the 21st Century: Voluntary Action and the Global Agenda* (West Hartford: Kumarian Press, 1990), 33-90.

24. See for example, Donovan Storey, "Human Development Strategies and Human Development Reports on the Pacific: A Viable Alternative or Just Another Development?" paper presented at the Second Biennial Aotearoa/New Zealand International Development Studies Network (DEVNET) conference, Victoria University of Wellington, 17-19 November 2000.

25. Marc Lindenberg, *The Human Development Race* (San Francisco: ICS Press, 1993), 47-86, 181-90.

26. Jean Dreze and Amartya Sen, *India: Economic Development and Social Opportunity* (Delhi: Oxford India Paperbaks, 1998), 11; also see Armartya Sen, *Development as Freedom* (New York: Knopf, 2000).

27. Lauren, *The Evolution*, 4-13.

28. Lauren, *The Evolution*, 13-20.

29. Lauren, *The Evolution*, 205-33.

30. The International Covenant on Civil and Political Rights (ICCPR) and the International Covenant on Economic Social and Cultural Rights (ICESCR) both adopted 16 Dec. 1966, GA Res 2200 (XXI).

31. Adapted from Appendix 1, Box 3 of Australian International Development Assistance Bureau (AIDAB) "AIDAB Programs Operations Guide" in *The Rights Way to Development: A Human Rights Approach to Development Assistance* (Sydney: Breakout Printing, 1995), 134.

32. Convention against Torture and Other Cruel, Inhuman and Degrading Treatment or Punishment, adopted 10 Dec. 1984, GA Res 39/46.

33. Convention on the Elimination of All Forms of Discrimination against Women, adopted 18 Dec. 1979, GA Res. 34/180.

34. Convention of the Rights of the Child, adopted 20 Nov. 1989, GA Res 44/25.

35. See Morten E. Winston, "Assessing the Effectiveness of International Human Rights NGOs: Amnesty International," in *NGOs and Human Rights*, ed. Claude E. Welch, Jr., (Philadelphia: University of Pennsylvania Press, 2001), 25-54; also see Widney Brown, "Human Rights Watch: An Overview," in *NGOs and Human Rights*, ed. Claude. E. Welch, Jr. (Philadelphia: University of Pennsylvania Press, 2001), 72-84.

36. See Human Rights Council, "Manual for a Human Rights Approach to Development Assistance,"*The Rights Way to Development Manual,* 1998, at www.members .ozemail.com.au/~hrca/The_Rights_Way_to_Development_Manual.htm (accessed 7 Oct. 2001).

37. Representatives of NGOs mentioned under this section attended the 3rd NGO Leaders Conference in Oxford, U.K. from 2-4 July 2001. See www.depts.washington.edu/ ngoconf/. The contents of this section are based in part on the discussions during the conference.

38. See Mercy Corps' homepage, www.mercycorps.org/.

39. See International Medical Corps' homepage, www.imc-la.com/.

40. See World Vision's homepage, www.worldvision.org/.

41. See World Concern's homepage, www.worldconcern.org/.

Chapter 16

Free Press, Profit Margins, and Democratic Governance: Is There a Fatal Flaw?

Margaret T. Gordon

He who pays the piper calls the tune.

Introduction

Nations and organizations contemplating development loans or other monetary aid to democratizing governments find it noteworthy—and a clear sign of progress—when such nations establish a free press. In a number of instances, the U.S. press has been a model for emerging democracies, and it is not unusual for them to send their journalists to American journalism programs in colleges, universities, and special institutes for training.[1] Once enrolled, they learn the basic tenets of American journalism—objective, accurate, balanced, multi-source reporting; the separation of opinion from news; the "watchdog" function of the press as it scrutinizes public officials and monitors the creation and implementation of public policy; coverage of elections in a democracy; and the role of advertising in America's free press.

Some 225 years ago, the framers of the United States Constitution deliberately balanced political power within the new government so that none of the three branches (executive, legislative, and judicial) could dominate the others, and they believed that a press which was free to investigate, monitor, and criticize (or praise) government activity was yet another valuable check on that power. Freedom from pre-publication censorship (no "prior restraint") was essential to the press's "watchdog" function, and it is for that reason that freedom of the press was included in the First Amendment to the Constitution. In fact, this element was so important to Thomas Jefferson, one of the primary architects of the Constitution and our nation's third president, that he declared that if forced to choose, he would prefer to live in a nation with newspapers but without government than in one with a government but without newspapers.

In addition to its watchdog function, this early press was expected to educate people about the news of the day. In Jefferson's time and now, the news media set the parameters for what the public can know. Journalists have access to more information than most of the rest of us, and we count on them to sift, filter, and review it and to summarize for us what is most important. We tend not to know about what they don't tell us.

"Free Flow" or "Restricted Flow" of Information

Given the history and acknowledged role of the news media in our society, many Americans think of the United States as having a strong free press, perhaps the freest in the world. Therefore, it may surprise many people to learn that eleven other nations[2] were rated recently as having greater press freedom.[3] In this instance, "freedom" was defined as the degree to which each country's government permitted the "free flow of information."[4] The authors were careful to distinguish between press freedom and press responsibility, noting that a press that is irresponsible diminishes its own credibility in the perception of the public, and that is reflected in the degree of freedom in the flow of information.

The Freedom House[5] twenty-second annual report examines for each of 186 countries their "press laws and administration, the degree of political and economic influence on the content of journalism, and the actual cases of press-freedom violations."[6] The U.S. media rankings were lowered by its scores on "economic influence on the content of its journalism," indicating there was restricted flow of information. While the overall ranking of twelfth in a field of 186 nations indicates substantial press freedom in the United States and a general worthiness of emulation (especially when compared with the vast majority of nations) the relatively lower U.S. scores for economic influence on content parallel the concerns of many critics of the American media in recent years.[7]

The critics caution that the pressures media executives feel to produce profits in line with corporate and market analysts' expectations have caused them to adopt news gathering, decision making, and production processes too market driven for a healthy democracy. In this essay, I argue that the trends in the *business practices* of the news media are related to a sense of alienation and rampant cynicism among members of the public toward *both* the news media and government at federal and local levels. Citizen trust, tempered with healthy skepticism, is important—if not essential—for compliance with the laws of the land, participation in the military, willingness to pay taxes, participation in the electoral processes, and general interest in and support of government policies. Therefore, the deep levels of distrust reported in recent years[8] need to be addressed.

I also will argue that the situation has worsened enough in recent years that increasing numbers of journalists, too, have become disillusioned and left the profession, saying they are no longer proud to be part of it.[9] It is not that they do not understand or have sympathy with the fact that in America most news media are private businesses and need to make money to survive. Rather, it is their sense that the drive for profits has become so extreme that it leads to decisions that undermine the purposes of a free press and professional values. More than a few journalists express feeling the presence of a sort of inexorable force insisting on profits often significantly larger than the average for American businesses, regardless of other unexpected mediating factors such as costs of covering wars and skyrocketing prices of newsprint.

While perhaps less organized or overt than that of a government-controlled press, this ubiquitous profit pressure has strong "chilling" effects on the daily work journalists try to do. Instead of focusing on the public good or what citizens need to know, they find themselves focusing more and more on what they believe will sell. They feel the effects of the truism, "He who pays the piper calls the tune." For some reason, there does not seem to be the belief within the news media that news about government—especially its day-to-day activities including its achievements and successes—can be made interesting and relevant enough that it will sell. Nor does there seem to be a sense of obligation to find ways to *make* such news interesting and relevant.

Potential Danger for Our Democracy

Therefore, I conclude that there may be a fatal flaw in the theory that a system of privately owned news media, even one with First Amendment freedom to report and publish, can and will provide the public with the information necessary for responsible citizenship. If that is the case, I conclude further that the democratic process as we know it in the United States is in danger.

Put another way, I argue that despite what others might see as signs of progress—the vast arrays of information on the Internet, the information revolution, continuous reporting 24 hours a day 7 days a week, and the increased numbers of cable television channels and specialty magazines—the "progress" of our mainstream news media is limited or even negative because the overall purposes and goals for a free press in a democracy are being undermined. The fact that many nations are seeking to emulate the editorial practices of our news media causes concern about outcomes for democracy in those nations, too, especially if they are emulating our media's business and advertising practices as well as our reporting methods.

Although I believe there is a sense of urgency about these issues, I do not see the picture as completely bleak; there are some bright spots on the horizon. There have been a number of efforts during the past decade inside and outside the news media that are working to counter some of these trends. Several have had some success, especially in small to medium-sized markets, in reconnecting with the citizenry and rekindling public interest in civic participation. I describe some of these efforts—variously named public journalism, civic journalism, community journalism, and advocacy journalism—and discuss their implications.

Central to these discussions is the concept of "quality journalism." I define quality journalism as "news citizens need in order to be educated about current events and issues, make thoughtful civic decisions, engage in civic dialogues and action, and generally exercise their responsibilities as citizens." To the extent the news media are producing quality journalism, I conclude they are making progress, and to the extent the journalism is less than "quality," or turning people away from government and citizenship, I conclude there is no progress and may be retrenchment.

Progress and the American News Media

Since at least the first recorded history there have been messengers bearing news of the times. The veracity of the news bearers, their reception, and the modes and circumstances of delivery have been important to the impacts and perceptions of the actual new information. Leaders throughout the ages and around the world have understood the adage that "information is power," and have tried to control it. The information-rich have usually had political, economic, social, and power advantages over the information poor.

Although the invention of the printing press during the Middle Ages was heralded by some as a catalyst for learning for all, dissemination of information was still limited primarily to the privileged, those who could read and afford publications. Printed matter then often focused on religious or political issues. Later, the English settlers who came to the United States of America brought with them the notion that in order to participate in their own governance and make informed decisions, citizens needed to be educated about the issues of the day. Newsletters, brochures, and tracts disseminated to voters (originally only the white male landowners) were thought to provide the best vehicle for achieving that civic education.

In early America, such newsletters were still the mouthpieces of political parties and religious institutions, but by the early to mid-1800s developments were underway which would begin to change the situation forever by including the masses. Following the lead of London newspapers, Benjamin Day, owner and editor of the *New York Sun* broadened the sale of his newspapers to the common people by adding to the more staid political news some sensational stories "appealing to the baser appetites" of the "common man." And then he sold the papers daily and for only a penny. His plan, or what we today would call his "marketing strategy" for making his newspaper into a "mass medium" was to reveal very slowly the details of sensational (usually crime) stories so that people would buy the papers day after day in order to keep up with the lurid facts. At the same time, of course, they would be exposed to current political issues and politicians. Day hired a court reporter and began to entertain the masses with stories of a lascivious murder-rape case involving a prostitute and a gentleman.

Sensationalized crime news has remained a constant ingredient in the formula that modern-day editors and producers use in designing newspapers and broadcast news shows in the hope they will attract and keep readers and viewers. The phrase "if it bleeds, it leads" is well known among modern-day journalists, and it captures their attitudes towards the public. Their beliefs are reflected in the content of most of the nightly local TV news shows, and on many of the nation's front pages. On average, crime news comprises approximately twenty percent of stories.[10] Violent crimes, especially rapes, are over-represented in comparison with their actual occurrence and can lead to exaggerated fears and concerns about personal safety.[11]

Over time, the sensationalized approach to covering crime news has been broadened to include sensationalized and personalized stories about celebrities, first from the entertainment field and then politics. Walter Winchell was especially influential in this part of U.S. journalism history as he publicized the exploits of the rich and famous, drawing the attention of more and more "common" men, and women.

In most of the first half of the twentieth century, newspapers were a source of profits and influence for their owners who usually were long-term residents of the communities where the papers circulated. Publisher-owners were involved in those communities and their editorial support was sought by those standing for election, and paid attention to by readers. With the advent of television and more and more sophisticated advertising and marketing, many media outlets became so profitable that some editors and owners as well as non-journalist entrepreneurs became interested in owning them purely as investments. Newspaper owners bought other newspapers, creating chains of newspapers, and some bought radio and television stations as well. Non-journalist owners often lived long distances away, and too often had little interest in the politics or well-being of the communities where their media outlets were.

Selling News on the Stock Market

A critical juncture, in retrospect, appears to have been reached when the national Gannett Company newspaper chain, led by Allen Neuharth "went public" in 1967[12] and began to sell its shares on the U.S. stock market. Former *Chicago Tribune* editor, James Squires, states, "Neuharth knew he was peddling a vastly different kind of business, one based on newspaper monopolies in small towns poised on the brink of industrial growth. So he presented the newspaper business in general and Gannett in particular on Wall Street in a way it had never been presented anywhere to anyone before; he billed it as a 'dependable profit machine' in good times or bad." [13] His strategy was to use the small, monopolistic papers to "show big profits by consistent natural growth in good times and—when times were hard—by cutting newsprint and raising advertising and circulation prices to the limit of market resistance."[14] The strategy worked, and over time Gannett media managers began to feel beholden to stockholders and market analysts whose predictions about profits affect the price of stock. One stock analyst quoted by Squires said, "Gannett's management lives, breathes, and sleeps profits and would trade profits over Pulitzer Prizes any day."[15] (This view is directly counter to that of professional journalism training and values.) Gannett editors routinely were given target profit levels that they were expected to reach, and often those levels were significantly higher than the national average profit levels for American businesses. It was (and is) not unheard of for publishers and editors in their chain to be expected to post profits in the thirty to forty percent range;[16] the targets and outcomes tend to be secret and are difficult to decipher from earnings reports. (Some Gannett journalists believe they were pressured for profits in order to support the development and first several years of *USA Today*, another creature of Neuharth.)

Such high levels of profits do not come from newspaper circulation figures or viewer ratings per se, but from the rates advertisers are willing to pay for space in the papers or time on air. [17] The advertising rates that can be charged are determined by estimates of the numbers of papers sold, the number of listeners, and the number of viewers advertisers can expect to reach. Television managers make decisions to keep or jettison shows on the basis of fractions of points of "audience share" as reported by the Nielsen rating services.

If advertising revenues are not sufficient, in order to meet the target profit levels, media managers have been forced to cut expenses. Frequently that has meant reducing newsroom staff, and in other ways disinvesting in the news-gathering and reporting processes. In recent decades, newspapers and television networks have dramatically reduced their numbers of news bureaus in Washington, D.C., and foreign capitals. Many news operations now depend on the ubiquitous Cable News Network (CNN) and the remaining wire services for their foreign news, and often for national news—leading to homogeneous reports and a lack of exposure to alternative points of view. Newspapers and broadcast news shows contain more wire service stories than in the past, fewer stories are written by local journalists, and there is less and less support for "enterprise journalism" or "investigative" pieces or anything beyond the most basic local news coverage.

Local News Loses Out

Local government coverage has been a major victim of these trends. Mayors complain that only the bad news and conflicts are reported as the old city hall beat is deserted.[18] This means that citizens get little or no local government news, and have little understanding of its agencies, processes, or accomplishments.

At the same time news media ownership has been consolidating into large general conglomerates involving entertainment (e.g., Disney and Warner Brothers Studios) and non-media corporations (e.g., General Electric). The competition for audience attention has increased dramatically. Media groups have responded by "narrow casting" and creating new, slick periodicals to reflect every conceivable interest. Cable television has multiplied the number of available channels, to the point that many stations are desperate for footage lest they show little but repeats. VCRs make it possible for people to watch shows whenever they desire, destroying the old conception of a mass audience. Such "time-shifting," along with channel surfing and zapping of commercials, complicates attempts to measure effects. Add to these factors the availability of news on the Internet—not to mention all the other types of information—and it is no wonder that getting the audience's attention is a major concern of both content providers, advertisers, and researchers trying to measure effects. Just as the media are trying harder and harder to capture the attention of the public to deliver to their advertisers, and are publishing more and more personalized, sensationalized, and conflict-filled news to do so, more Americans are working more jobs for longer hours. Many people say it is increasingly difficult to keep up with the information related to their work and personal interests, let alone the array of political, social, and economic issues that affect their civic responsibilities.

One result of these combined trends is that newspaper readership has declined dramatically, and with it the number of daily newspapers. When they don't get the readership, they don't get the advertising revenues and profits the owners want, and they fold. Similarly, network television viewing has also declined (though cable channel viewing is up) and media managers desperately shift to new program lineups hoping to recapture enough viewers to keep their ad rates high.

A second result is that despite the increase in the sheer *amount* of information the news media are pushing out daily, it is relatively rare that there are in-depth portrayals of the activities or impacts of government actions at federal, state, or local levels. Consequently, busy people, not aware of the information they are missing, are only vaguely informed and therefore sometimes indifferent to the pleas for understanding or support from officials. This situation also makes it possible for some political actors to take advantage of the public's ignorance. The consequences may be compounded when politicians make decisions and take action based on polls of uninformed citizens.

A third outcome is that politicians and public officials, as well as leaders of non-profit organizations, are put in the position of having to hire media experts to communicate with the public[19] and to stage "psuedo events"[20] to get media attention. Those without the resources to hire media experts to relate to the media and thereby to the public, simply lose out.

Journalists' Concerns Grow

In the fall of 1998, nearly 250 U.S. journalists, owners, managers, and practitioners in the old and new media, scholars, critics, and citizens—young and old—converged at the University of Washington to discuss the prospects for "Quality[21] Journalism in the 21st Century: The Challenges of Money, Medium, and Message." The conference was one of several co-sponsored around the United States by the Washington, D.C.-based Committee of Concerned Journalists.[22] In this instance, the local partners were *The Seattle Times* and the University of Washington Graduate School of Public Affairs.

The sensibilities of conference delegates were heightened by a shared sense they were in the midst of dramatic changes being experienced by a wide array of media industries—going together though a sea change with important but as yet not understood consequences for our society. There was recognition and discussion among the attendees of a dizzying blur of intertwined and paradoxical trends, for example:

- increasing globalization and Americanization of media markets, but signs of "push back" competition from some nations, e.g., India;
- labor unions fought for increased compensation packages, and also about threats to professionalism of reporters;
- growing awareness of the complexity and importance of recognizing and targeting a wider range of ethnic groups both as markets and for inclusion as employees in news rooms;
- "Moore's Law" of computing (computers will get twice as fast and half as expensive every eighteen months) and resulting problems for how to deal with the related expenses of hardware, software, and training;
- the convergence of communications platforms with concomitant needs for multimedia journalists;
- the awareness of a "digital divide" separating the information haves and have-nots, and increased outreach investment through their Web presence;
- growth of interactive and many-to-many communications, even in an industry based on one-way communications;
- twenty-four hour, seven day news cycles with pressures to keep up with the competition, but less time than ever to research, digest, and analyze consequences;
- simultaneous counter trends of increased consolidation of ownership (and some say "voices") and fragmentation of outlets within each;
- increased competition for the attention of media consumers as they work more;

• the simultaneous "commodification" of more and more "news products" designed to sell better and the decline of news quality; and
• the blurring of information, entertainment, and advertising.

The patterns and trends discussed that day appear to have intensified and become more entrenched. Once we reach the other side of this sea change—if we ever do—will we have made progress, and how will we know? Will the American news media be doing a better job of providing the public with the information people need to be responsible, participating citizens? There was general agreement that day that the answer to that question depends on the ability and willingness of journalists and interested others to identify and set quality standards, and to create and use safeguards related to the information needs of a thriving democracy. Many delegates seemed to believe that much of the public is no longer interested in quality news, that meeting high journalistic standards is expensive and may be a meaningless gesture that would lessen profits, and that lowered profits would result in owners taking their capital elsewhere to invest. Conferees opined that they feel let down, and compelled to choose between "going along" and accepting definitions of news as "that which sells" and changing careers. They also saw the public as sitting back, turning off, and turning away. Among some of the delegates there was talk about how they as journalists could provoke the public into demanding the quality news it needs and deserves.

What Do the Public and the Journalists Really Want?

So what information *does* the public actually want from the news media? Over and over again, people say in response to polls and in focus groups that they need and want thoughtful, multifaceted discussions of issues facing the nation and their communities; accounts of the experience, values, and qualifications of candidates; straightforward, unbiased, accurate reports of the deliberations and actions of politicians and public officials; and evidence of balance and fairness in reporting. Instead, they say, they are being barraged with sensationalized stories about the personal lives of celebrities or politicians, stories of conflict, crime, and corruption. Ordinary folk say that much of the relevant news about our political and policy making processes is either absent altogether or covered in a way that seems spun out of control.[23]

But simultaneously, journalists say their marketing departments insist the public actually does want more of the violent, bizarre, gossipy, sensationalized information. The supermarket tabloids do sell, they point out. The success of the sensational has meant that even the "prestige" outlets are occasionally shaping news into sensationalized "infotainment" messages designed to entertain without necessarily informing or edifying. The Internet exacerbates the problem by enhancing the speed with which news—accurate or not—circles the globe, making it ever more difficult to make corrections or alter impressions.

Journalists, politicians, and citizens either have ignored the evidence of what was happening to the news business for too long, or they have felt helpless to do anything about it.

For their part, some journalists say they are ashamed of their profession; many are deeply cynical; and most seem simply resigned to the profit-centered realities of today's media world. They know that the media have lost credibility[24] with the public, and they blame profit pressures. A Pew Research Center report published in 1999 states: "To reporters and editors, the reasons for journalism's problems are clear—growing financial and business pressures. At local and national levels, majorities of working journalists say that increased bottom-line pressure is hurting the quality of coverage." While increased concern about financial pressures is evident among both print and broadcast journalists, it has grown most among those working in television: 53 percent of national television journalists say that profit pressures are hurting the quality of coverage and not just changing the way work is done.

Other findings in the report indicate that journalists value their "watchdog" role more than the public does; 87 percent of the journalists think that watchful criticism is worthwhile because it keeps politicians from doing things that should not be done, while only 58 percent of the public agrees. Half the journalists and media executives themselves say that in reporting on the personal and ethical behavior of public figures, news organizations go too far and often drive the controversies rather than merely reporting the facts. Even more of the public, nearly three-fourths, say such reporting perpetuates scandal, and *actually gets in the way of the nation solving its problems.*

Images of Governments

Images of Local Government

One would hope that the news portrayals of local government are more positive, but the scant research evidence about images of local governments in the news suggests a slightly different but equally discouraging picture. In the case of city and county governments, there is simply a general *dearth* of news about them. In a 1998 study of the portrayals of eight U.S. cities in their daily newspapers, stories about city or county activities comprised only 13.5 percent of the local stories[25] and furthermore, locally-based stories were less than a third of all the stories that appeared. Mayors in these local communities were virtually invisible in the local press; fewer than 2 percent of the stories cited mayors as sources of information in the stories or included any comments about their positions on issues or actions in the cities. It would have been impossible for residents in these communities to gain a comprehensive view of their leaders' plans or their local government's activities—let alone achievements—if the major daily newspapers were their only sources.

As a whole, the newspapers studied also portrayed their own cities as fairly inhospitable places. Readers were likely to find an emphasis on crime and other problems in the community, highlighted by sensationalistic headlines. Stories about local and distant crime constituted 17.3 percent of all the local stories and another 7.1 percent focused on local courts.

Given the evidence, it is not unreasonable to suggest that there is a relationship between the negative images of government in the media and public's distrust of government. If members of the public are exposed daily to negative images and/or to little or no information about government activities or successes, it should not be surprising that they have negative attitudes towards government and feel it has done little worthy of support.

Primetime Images of Government

Are these sentiments and concerns overblown? Are the impacts of news mediated by the non-news aspects of the media, the dramatic television, and the softer side of newspapers? Unfortunately, there is not much relief to be found there. In fact, script writers for dramatic television appear to have taken their cues from the news, emphasizing crime, conflict, and corruption.

The Partnership for Trust in Government, a project of the Ford Foundation and the Washington, D.C.-based Council for Excellence in Government, released a report in 1999 of a study of images of government shown in prime time television. Their report, "Images of Government in TV Entertainment," discusses images appearing in TV entertainment (not news). The images of government and government workers were overwhelmingly negative.

Examining more than forty years of prime-time programming, the study reported that depictions of government officials and government systems have grown increasingly negative since 1955. It said television has created an image of civil servants and public officials as politicians and bureaucrats who serve their own interests or special interests rather than the public interest, and casts government institutions in an even worse light than the individuals who staff them.

Among the specific findings are:

- Since 1975, three out of every four TV episodes involving the U.S. political or legal systems have shown them as corrupt.
- Public officials as portrayed on television committed crimes twice as often as characters in other occupations.
- Not a single episode in 1990s prime time television showed government serving the public.
- Mayors are portrayed as confused and clueless; the post carrier is shown stock-

> piling mail in a storage room; and a secret government agency is plotting to kill off citizens with biological weapons. The helpful civil servant and the concerned public official are rare exceptions.[26]

Public opinion research conducted for the Council for Excellence in Government by the Yankelovitch Partners immediately following the publication of the Council's report in 1999 revealed that fifty-five percent of television viewers *and sixty-six percent of young Americans* agreed that prime time dramatic television *accurately* depicted government officials, public servants, and the public service.

These frightening findings have important consequences for current and future attitudes of Americans, and their willingness to trust and support government agencies and activities with their dollars and their commitment. The cultural environment produced by such prime time portrayals is likely to discourage bright, qualified, young people from wanting to serve the public, especially as government employees. It seems a long time since our nation's youth were inspired by press coverage of President John F. Kennedy exhorting them to "ask not what the country can do" for them, but what they "can do for the country."

Governments' Portrayals of Themselves

What about how governments portray themselves? Do they do a better job than the news and entertainment media of portraying their achievements to their communities? While elected politicians and those campaigning for office in the United States for some time have had communications advisors with various titles—press officers, information officers, public relations officers, handlers, spin meisters—it is a somewhat newer phenomenon for public agencies, especially at the local level, to have staff whose primary job it is to deal with the press and to develop strategies that will affect the public's image(s) of them. However, in recent years, managing press relations has become an increasingly important part of a successful public administrator's portfolio. Further, it seems media management becomes more important and more time consuming as leaders progress up the organizational and/or political hierarchy(ies).

Can media managers control or even influence the press? Can they set the political agenda? Several American scholars[27] have studied the extent to which the press sets the political agenda (as opposed to the politicians or the public). By comparing the public's views of the *importance* of several issues with the *amount* of space or air time devoted by the media to those issues, the researchers find that the amount of coverage devoted to an issue by the media subtly *teaches* the public how important the issue is. That is, the issues that come to be defined in the minds of citizens as "most important" are those to which the media have allocated the most space or air time.

It stands to reason that those agencies and organizations that can afford to hire skilled media strategists are likely to be more successful at getting their plans, goals, and ideas across to the public through the media than those that can't afford such assistance. Since many public agencies, especially at the state and local levels, cannot hire such expertise, it is difficult for them to combat the negative images rampant in the media today.

Recognizing this difficulty, some journalists and advocates have set out to assist non-profits through what they call media advocacy designed to teach these organizations how to get the media attention they want and need to survive.[28]

Even if the agencies have to forego skilled media advisors and operatives, can't they still get out the basic facts that could illustrate their accomplishments? One responsibility the federal agencies have had for some time is that of providing the public—and the media—with basic statistical information about the population, the economy, foreign trade, crime, and a number of other topics. However, despite America's overall relative wealth, even the federal agencies responsible for collecting and analyzing statistics are finding it difficult to obtain support for research that they believe is needed for sound policy making. Walter Williams, in his book, *Honest Numbers and Democracy,*[29] reports that highly ranked, seasoned policy analysts and "think tank researchers" are concerned about the data that are no longer being collected, and the pressures to cut corners in order to meet reduced budgets for this kind of work. The pressures to reduce costs result in important questions going unanswered, or even unasked.

Budgets for federally sponsored university-based research on such topics as the U.S. Census, and the need to update various indices which affect both the stock markets and corporate planning have also been cut. Less information is available to the media from these agencies, and therefore less is being reported. Further, measurements are taken less frequently. Thus, it is common for citizens to be uninformed or misinformed about such figures as the amount our country spends on foreign aid. Recent data show that most Americans think our federal government spends too much on foreign aid, estimating the figure at about 15 percent and saying a better amount to spend would be about 5 percent. The fact is the United States spends closer to 1 percent. Such discrepancies in knowledge make policy making with respect to foreign aid and garnering public support for it very difficult indeed.

A widely circulated recent report[30] from a committee on Public Trust and Civic Engagement chaired by Paul Volker for the National Academy of Public Administration, urges public agencies—despite the difficulties— to be much more pro-active in informing both the media and the public about their accomplishments, the difficulties they confront, and the steps they take to assure that their processes are transparent and accountable.

Repairing the Disconnect: Listening to Citizens

Fearing the consequences of the long-term declines in readership and viewership discussed above, some far sighted media leaders began a few years ago to devise new approaches to news coverage designed to be more inclusive of all segments of their communities. (Of course, it was hoped this also would help them regain readers.) In the late 1980s, James K. Batten, then chair and chief executive officer of Knight-Ridder, Inc. (another major U.S. newspaper chain), "began talking about how the media needed to change, to begin once again reconnecting to citizens,[being] a vital building block in revitalizing citizenship—while maintaining its ability to tell hard truths."[31] At a corporate meeting in 1989, Batten suggested that future election coverage should begin by engaging citizens in discussions about the types of election news they wanted, and the roles they wanted the newspapers to play. He referred to it as "public journalism."[32]

Initially, a few newspapers in the chain[33] experimented with changing the nature of their election coverage so that it de-emphasized the "horse-race" nature of politics (who's ahead, who's winning) and the personalities involved. Instead they emphasized issues, policy alternatives, and qualifications of those running for office to deal with the issues identified. They commissioned focus groups and random sample telephone polls to find out what citizens thought were the most important issues facing their communities. They interviewed candidates about their positions on those issues, and they organized debates and forums so that citizens could see and hear candidates expressing and debating their views and ideas for solutions to perceived problems. In general, the journalists were pleased with the initial results.

In 1993, the Pew Charitable Trusts in Philadelphia became interested in the role of the media in civic participation and, as part of a new program, it established the Pew Center for Civic Journalism in Washington, D.C., with funding for ten years. The Pew Center was designed to facilitate projects of media outlets willing to experiment with *journalism that had as its goal an increase in the involvement of citizens in the civic life* of their communities and the nation. Currently a separate board of Pew Center directors reviews proposals and awards modest funding—usually for out-of-pocket costs (for newsrooms in newspapers, radio, and television stations)—for special projects that they define as "civic journalism." A number of the initial Pew Center's projects also were focused on election coverage, involved telephone polling and/or focus groups, and had as a goal increases in voter turnout.

As these activities were getting underway in 1994, representatives of National Public Radio approached some affiliates about ways to change the nature of that fall's election coverage, and they began encouraging and facilitating partnerships between affiliates and their local newspapers with respect to local election coverage. Most of their experiments were conducted in small to medium-sized markets, with most media remaining on the sidelines watching to see what the changes and impacts would be.

What were the impacts? Unfortunately, there was little systematic evidence collected during these early experiments that would allow sound conclusions to be drawn about the causes or effects of changes made. It is clear that by 1995-96, after a couple of cycles of changed reportage, in some Knight-Ridder communities voter turnout improved, and in some communities media declines were slowed or stopped. In still other locales, there seemed to be little impact that could be attributed to the new forms of journalism.[34]

Another consequence was that a number of journalists in communities with experimental coverage began to oppose the idea of public/civic journalism, arguing that it was unprofessional and inappropriate to ask readers how *they* wanted to see political campaigns covered, or for news media to become involved in any form of community action that could be construed as media involvement in *creating* the news. Others insisted the new coverage wasn't new at all, but was simply "old-fashioned good journalism."

To better illustrate the nature of civic/public journalism, what follows is an abbreviated description of the activities of one such project, the Front Porch Forum, conducted by four media partners in the Puget Sound region of the state of Washington.

The Front Porch Forum: A Civic Journalism Partnership in the Puget Sound Region

Sometime in 1995, representatives of National Public Radio (NPR) approached two public radio stations in the Puget Sound region of Washington (KUOW in Seattle and KPLU in Tacoma) and the region's largest daily newspaper (*The Seattle Times*) about collaborating on a joint civic/public journalism project that would precede the 1996 elections. "The timing was right" according to representatives of *The Times* who said such a project fit into their plans because they had already decided the traditional, horse-race style of coverage was no longer appropriate.

Each of the participating media outlets assigned reporters to participate in the project; some were skeptical. Most had heard of this "new" form of journalism, and depending on their training and experience held varying views. The group met irregularly, and eventually hired a local pollster to conduct a poll about what citizens believed to be the major problems facing the area. The reporters subsequently engaged local candidates about the issues identified by the survey, and focused on a small number of races that they covered in great depth.

The media partnership "cross publicized" the resulting radio and newspaper stories under the logo, "Front Porch Forum" which was accompanied by a small graphic suggesting a conversation among neighbors on a front porch. The journalists made no attempt to assess any impacts of the new style of coverage, but they reported receiving more calls and letters than usual in an election period. Informal questions and comments led them to believe the Front Porch Forum articles had attracted some followers as a "place" where community issues were discussed, but readers and listeners seemed not to be aware that it was a frequent feature, or that it was a new form of journalism. The journalists were interested enough in where the project might lead them that they applied to the Pew Center for a second grant for a non-election year project to be focused on the pros and cons of "growth" in the region.

The second Forum illustrated some significant differences between traditional journalism and civic journalism—especially cooperation among local competing media outlets; sharing of resources within the group; extensive use of social science methods; long-term timeframes sustained over several months; susceptibility to changes in personnel or resources; the relative lack of attention to measurement of impacts; the ways in which the new form of journalism resonated with the journalists' professional values; and the importance of having a neutral, paid, quarter-time coordinator for the project.[35] This last component was also found to be invaluable in other projects around the country involving two or more media outlets.

The Forum group was called together regularly (approximately every two weeks) by the coordinator,[36] who also prepared the agenda, provided refreshments, took notes, and distributed minutes the day following the meetings. At her initiative, the agenda always included the following statement of the group's mission:

> The mission of the Front Porch Forum is to strengthen our community through news coverage that focuses on citizens' concerns, encourages civic participation, improves public deliberation, and reconnects reporters, citizens, and candidates to community life.
> Objective 1: Find out what citizens treasure most about the Puget Sound region and what they consider the greatest threats to those treasures.
> Objective 2: Find out what citizens need to know before they can consider solutions to the threats they identify. Provide that information.
> Objective 3: Once that information is provided and digested by citizens, find out what solutions they favor—not just public policy, but individual lifestyle choices. In other words, find out what changes people are willing to make in their own lives to help solve the problems they've identified.
> Objective 4: Attempt to inject citizens' concerns, decisions, and choices into civic dialogue and decision making WITHOUT crossing the threshold into advocacy journalism.
> Objective 5: Use all this to produce compelling journalism.

Group meetings consisted of sharing information, brainstorming story ideas best suited to the different media formats, gathering ideas for cross-promotions including having a newspaper reporter with a "good radio voice" prepare three-minute radio spots in addition to his newspaper reports, and planning another "civic component" for involving citizens in the process.

The Forum's ultimate choice for a civic component was a "mock trial," set in the year 2020, and charging the region's leaders and citizens with failing in 1997 to make the tough decisions required to protect the region's quality of life. Expert witnesses were called to report on the actions they "had taken in 1997" [actually were currently taking] to deal with the issues. "Jurors" were 100 citizens selected from among the people polled in the random telephone survey who agreed to participate in the trial on two successive Saturdays; each was paid $100 from the Pew Center grant funds.

Following presentation of evidence on the first Saturday, the jurors debated the issues and, using hand-held voting machines, voted iteratively on their conclusions. They found the leaders *and themselves* "guilty." The "judge" "sentenced" them to discuss potential solutions and propose policy options for solving the problems.

Observing journalists expressed surprise at the high quality of debate and conversation, and excitement at the quality of material the process gave them for their stories. One said, "This is what [being a journalist] is supposed to be like," and another commented, "I think we can give them a higher quality of journalism than we have been." Another journalist, noting that some of the groups' policy proposals specified regulations already in place, blamed the journalists themselves for the fact the citizens didn't know the options already had been implemented.

About two weeks later, the journalists produced a coordinated, cross-promoted "roll out" of newspaper, radio, and television pieces all identified as part of the Front Porch Forum. Each outlet reported getting significantly more feedback from citizens than for other stories or projects. Members of the team were contacted by local political leaders wanting to "work with the Front Porch Forum" to involve citizens in solutions to some of the problems discussed, as well as on other issues. Citizens wrote and called with suggestions for other Forum topics saying, for example, "the Front Porch Forum ought to take on public education next." The journalists also invited several members of the "jury" to propose their policy options to candidates for local office, and to ask questions of the candidates in a debate format. A month later, most of the jurors said they had voted in the recent local election, had talked with others about the issues in the mock trial, felt more involved in civic issues, and many said they would participate in future events.

A third Front Porch Forum project on leadership faltered, cut off by an extended strike at *The Seattle Times*. It remains to be seen if there will be any long term effects on the journalists who participated in the civic journalism projects, on the media outlets, or on the public's images of the media or government. It is clear, however, that while the project was active, the journalists frequently indicated how much they valued working together, and how much the collaborations and interactions with citizens restored their faith in the profession and the public.

What's Next? Integration into Newsrooms or the Death of a Movement?

In addition to the Front Porch Forum project, there are many other experiments and innovations taking place across the nation. Attitudes and definitions of the new journalism have changed and morphed. The increased use of computers and database analysis has given rise to new types of reporting, including reports of analyses of information from government websites, population statistics, and crime statistics. Computer mapping and "civic mapping" techniques have generated new types of data as well as new ideas for stories. For example, "civic mapping," and "TCC" (total community coverage) tools have helped journalists find under-represented "voices" in their communities—most often minorities and immigrants. There is widespread use of formal and informal focus groups. "Study circles," task forces, and discussion groups have been created to find solutions to problems identified and discussed in local media.

Unfortunately, most of the media outlets that have undertaken the kinds of projects described here have not taken the next step and engaged in the careful, expensive, long-term research necessary to argue scientifically and persuasively that their projects have had measurable impacts. Nonetheless, many put forth informal "evidence" that the projects have "moved the needle," or made a difference in some way.

For example:
• In some communities voter turnout was higher following election coverage that involved citizens, focuses on issues and policies, and avoided the "horse-race" reporting;
• Ratings for a television station did not decline (as reporters and producers feared) during the week the station featured an intensive review of race relations in the community;
• Letters to the editor increased, calls increased, or "hits" to the websites increased during and after project publications;
• Projects have won awards from national professional associations and local civic organizations;
• In some instances there have been circulation or ratings gains, or increases in donations (to public stations); and
• Citizen groups have organized and taken action following publication of special projects describing serious local problems.

Many of the journalists who believe this new form of journalism is having an impact in their communities have become committed to it, and, interestingly, many of them are expressing renewed satisfaction with their work and their profession.[37]

The Pew Center holds several conferences and workshops each year where civic/public journalists share their new techniques and outcomes with one another. They encourage others to try the techniques in their own settings. Common themes frequently include issues raised above, i.e., whether civic journalism is anything new, or simply "good" journalism; whether the projects "cross over the line," the invisible but important line between reporting the news and creating it; and whether the projects "moved the needle."

What was more unusual, especially in the first couple of years, is that the meetings also had a "movement" aura, common in gatherings of like-minded people who may feel defensive in other settings about what they are doing. In this case, one quite frequently heard religious words, such as "converted" [to civic journalism], "the gospel" of civic journalism, "passion," "believers" and "committed." Most participants seemed to feel as if they were among friends, and didn't have to be defensive about the form of journalism they are practicing. Others had been sent to the meetings or workshops to observe, to learn about this new approach, consider its usefulness, and get ideas for whether or not it would "work" at their own media outlets. Often their skepticism was evident; sometimes they were persuaded to try it.

Qualitatively Different Conceptualizations

In May of 1999, Jan Schaffer, the then new Executive Director of the Pew Center for Civic Journalism in Washington, D.C., opened one of the Pew Center conference/workshops in San Francisco with the following statement: "Five years ago the Pew Center decided to test the hypothesis that if we journalists did our job differently, citizens would behave differently. We did and they did. The answer is 'yes.'"

Entitled "Community Journalism Summit," the meeting spotlighted several projects around the country that were designed to increase the inclusiveness of citizens, often as sources, in the news gathering processes. They were calling their efforts "community journalism." Noteworthy is that the conceptualizations and orientations of these projects were *categorically different* from pre-1990s journalism taught in professional colleges and universities or on-the-job in newsrooms. They were also different from public/civic/community journalism as originally conceived, but they had evolved directly from experiences with it. They showed that in the process of doing this kind of journalism they had become more like social scientists as they deftly employed a broad range of social science techniques and created new concepts.

Brief examples of the new conceptualizations include the following:

• In San Francisco, citizen complaints about the positioning of a new freeway led to the local media discovering that the target area had changed demographically over a five to ten year period from a primarily black neighborhood with many of the residents living in public housing projects to an area of recent, often struggling Asian immigrants who were living together in a variety of crowded conditions. There were significant language barriers that disrupted the provision of public services, and planned policies were not responsive to the new population. The project brought the journalists and then the public up to date.

• News organizations in several cities were using TCC (total community coverage) techniques developed by the Robert Maynard Institute to be more inclusive in their coverage by considering the "fault lines" of race, class, gender, generation, and geography (location). Reporters analyze all stories in terms of these demographic factors and consider sources "on the fault lines," or that "cross the fault lines."

• Another group of news media organizations is learning how to do "community mapping" in order to find "third places" where they can find perspectives of ordinary citizens rather than relying primarily on official sources. Third places are gathering spots such as neighborhood pubs, restaurants, churches, and other organizations.

• In Portland, Oregon, the leader of the crime and justice team[38] on the *Oregonian* was given two months to interview, consult, reflect, plan, and implement a new way "from the ground up" to cover crime in the community.

• In Portland, Maine, an in-depth multi-media focus on the financial and social costs of alcoholism in the state resulted ultimately in "study circles" and concerted action to address the problems causing and generated by the disease. The paper also broke new ground when it launched the series by devoting the entire front page as well as several inside pages to this single subject.

• In Colorado Springs, Colorado, the editor became an expert on "framing," originally a term confined to academic journals and books to categorize types of news. "Game frames" referred to sports imagery and news stories with winners and losers, such as politics. "Policy frames" refer to issues with public policy consequences of concern to the public. Staff assess how the various "frames" reporters use in developing their stories result in bias or slant the news.

• In Spokane, Washington, the editor of *The Spokesman-Review* sees civic journalism as a broad umbrella under which he can carry on experiments in newsgathering and reporting. A current project is focused on causes of crime. The largest state prison is located nearby, and townspeople are concerned that many former inmates choose to reside there. Reporters are studying key moments in the lives of young people that led to criminal behavior, types of treatment/counseling, changes in behavior, and the effects of imprisonment for felons from different types of families, races, schools, urban/rural origins, and exposure levels to violence in the media.

The discussions among the journalists in San Francisco as well as at the Front Porch Forum suggest that while the projects may have "moved the needle" on important issues in some communities, *perhaps the most important effects of the new journalism are on the journalists themselves.* Perhaps in the long run, the journalists efforts to reconnect with citizens and encourage them to engage in the civic life of their communities has simultaneously reawakened the *journalists' commitment to their own professional values.* Many say they believe it allows them to be the thoughtful, creative professionals they went into journalism to be. The journalists doing this listening/reconnecting work often seem to be more excited, less cynical, less likely to feel they are "selling out" to commercial interests, and more likely to feel creative and positive about their communities.[39] The quality journalism they are producing seems to benefit them as well as their readers, listeners, and viewers.

Will Better Informed Citizens Participate More? Trust the Media and Government More?

Will these new ways of conceptualizing journalistic work by recommitted journalists lead to better informed citizens who are more likely to participate and have greater trust in media and in government? Participants in the experiments hope that citizens will see the positive effects of their own involvement, and that they will feel more responsibility than in the past to demand quality journalism.

If the changes in the cultures of newsrooms discussed here continue to broaden so that they include the largest markets and to deepen so that they regularly incorporate daily news coverage—not just special projects—the impacts could increase geometrically, and they could be profound. They could actualize the expectations of those who protected the free press in the U.S. Constitution and in the First Amendment. They could reduce the often touted cynicism and negative bias of journalists since they find quality journalism to be personally and professionally challenging and satisfying. This new journalism also could ultimately lead to a widely-held belief that *reasonable* profit levels closer to U.S. averages are sufficient, and that to risk losing quality journalism for extraordinary, short-term profits is too dangerous in a democracy.

Then I would not think there was a "fatal flaw" in the American free press-democracy connection.

Then I would be less concerned about other new democracies emulating our free press. Then I would feel there had been progress.

Notes

1. For example, the Center for Foreign Journalists in Reston, Virginia, created in 1986 by Thomas Winship, former editor of the *Boston Globe*.

2. Australia, Austria, the Bahamas, Belgium, Denmark, Iceland, Jamaica, Nauru, New Zealand, Sweden, and Switzerland.

3. Freedom House, "Country Ratings, Press Freedom Worldwide," Twenty-Second Annual Report (New York: Freedom House, 1 January 2000).

4. Freedom House, "Country Ratings," 9.

5. Eleanor Roosevelt, wife of the former Democratic President of the United States, and Wendell L. Willkie, Roosevelt's Republican presidential opponent, were among the founders of Freedom House established in 1941 to "defend, secure, and expand the borders of freedom." It promotes human rights, democratic governance, free market economics, rule of law, free news media, and American leadership in international affairs.

6. Freedom House, "Press Freedom Survey," Twenty-Second Annual Report (New York: Freedom House, 1 January 2000), 4.

7. James Fallows, *Breaking the News: How the Media Undermine American Democracy* (New York: Pantheon, 1996); James Squires, *Read All About It: The Corporate Takeover of America's Newspapers* (New York: Times Books, 1993); and Robert McChesney, *Rich Media, Poor Democracy: Communication Politics in Dubious Times* (Urbana: University of Illinois Press, 1999).

8. For example, Susan Tolchin, *The Angry American: How Voter Rage is Changing the Nation* (New York: Westview Press, 1996); Joseph S. Nye, Jr., Philip D. Zelikow, and David C. King, *Why People Don't Trust Government* (Cambridge: Harvard University Press, 1997); Pew Research Center for the People and the Press, *Deconstructing Distrust: How Americans View Government* (Washington, D.C.: Pew Research Center for the People and the Press, 1998).

9. The recent case of Jay Harris resigning from his position as publisher of the San Jose *Mercury News* has given new life to these discussions among journalists. (See, for example, issues of the *American Journalism Review* and the *Columbia Journalism Review* for spring and summer 2001.) Harris is widely respected as an investigative journalist, professor at the Medill School of Journalism at Northwestern University, and long-time executive in the Knight-Ridder newspaper chain.

10. Margaret T. Gordon, Linda Heath, and Robert LeBailley, "What Newspapers Tell Us (And Don't Tell Us) about Rape," *Newspaper Research Journal* 2, no. 4 (July, 1981): 48-55.

11. Margaret T. Gordon and Stephanie Riger, *The Female Fear: The Social Costs of Rape* (New York: Free Press, 1989).

12. Squires, *Read All About It*, 21.

13. Squires, *Read All About It*, 21.

14. Squires, *Read All About It*, 22.

15. Squires, *Read All About It*, 56.

16. Squires, *Read All About It*, 126.

17. Ad rates are set several times annually for newspapers based on figures from the Audit Bureau of Circulation, and for TV based on audience share during "sweeps weeks."

18. Claudette Artwick and Margaret T. Gordon, "Daily Newspapers and the Portrayal of U.S. Cities," *Newspaper Research Journal* 19, no.1 (Winter 1998): 54-63.

19. Oscar Gandy, *Beyond Agenda Setting: Information Subsidies and Public Policy* (Norwood, N.J.: Ablex, 1982).

20. These are created to get media attention, and have become so commonplace they compete with one another. For example, press conferences, anniversary and commemoration events, and planned photo opportunities such as a Congressman walking through a blighted neighborhood in order to attract press attention to a bill he or she plans to introduce.

21. One of the purposes of the conference was to debate definitions of quality journalism and the resources and values necessary to produce it.

22. Local co-sponsors included *The Seattle Times* and the University of Washington Graduate School of Public Affairs (renamed in 1999 the Daniel J. Evans School of Public Affairs). The conference was held September 25, 1998, at the University of Washington. See Concerned Journalists Web site for other conferences and proceedings: www.journalism.org/ccj/index.html

23. See, for example, The Times Mirror Center for The People and The Press, *The New Political Landscape: The People, The Press and Politics*, (Washington, D.C.: The Times Mirror Center for The People and The Press, 1994); and The Pew Research Center for the People and the Press, *RetroPolitics* (Washington, D.C.: The Pew Research Center for the People and the Press, 1999).

24. See American Society of Newspaper Editors "Why Newspaper Credibility Has Been Dropping," (Reston, Va.: American Society of Newspaper Editors, 1999).

25. American Society of Newspaper Editors, "Why Newspaper Credibility;" Artwick and Gordon, "Daily Newspapers."

26. In the two years since the publication of that report, and perhaps partially because of it, the popular award winning show West Wing may have begun to dispel some of the negative images of public servants in viewers' minds.

27. See David Protess and Maxwell McCombs, ed., *Agenda Setting* (Hillsdale, N.J.: Lawrence Erlbaum Associates, 1991).

28. See, for example, The Benton Foundation, *Media Advocacy: Strategic Communications for Nonprofits* (Washington D.C.: Benton Foundation, 1991); and Jason Salzman, *Making the News: A Guide for Nonprofits and Activists* (Boulder, Colo.: Westview Press, 1998).

29. Walter Williams, *Honest Numbers and Democracy* (Washington, D.C.: Georgetown University Press, 1998).

30. National Academy of Public Administrators; panel on Civic Trust and Citizen Repsonsibility, chaired by Paul Volker, *A Government to Trust and Respect: Rebuilding Citizen-Government Relations for the 21st Century* (Washington D.C.: National Academy of Public Administrators, 1999).

31. Pew Center for Civic Journalism, "James K. Batten Awards," ter.org/batten/" at www.pewcenter.org/batten/ (accessed12 April 2001).

32. See also Davis Merritt, *Public Journalism and Public Life: Why Telling the News Is Not Enough* (Hillsdale, N.J.: Erlbaum, 1995), 80-81; Jay Rosen, *Getting the Connections Right: Public Journalism and the Troubles in the Press* (New York: Twentieth Century Fund, 1996); and Edmund Lambeth, Philip Meyer, and Esther Thorson, ed., *Assessing Public Journalism* (Columbia and London: University of Missouri Press, 1998).

33. The *Wichita Eagle* in 1990, and the *Charlotte Observer* in 1992.

34. E. Lambeth, P. Meyer, and E. Thorson, *Assessing Public Journalism* (Columbine, Mo. and London: University of Missouri Press, 1998).

35. For two years I was a participant-observer in the meetings of the media partnership, and attended all of the activities described. All meetings were taped. The tapes and my notes, along with the media publications were reviewed and analyzed for this paper.

36. Marion Woyvodich, a former journalist who had become disillusioned with the field and who was working for an organization named Good News, Good Deeds and attending graduate school preparing for a new career.

37. Using snowball sampling techniques for three months, I have been able to identify and catalogue over 120 such projects, many of which involve two or more media outlets. Many of the journalists have reported these sentiments at conferences or in personal conversations.

38. In the past, this group would have been referred to as police beat reporters.

39. See also Jan Schaffer, "The Media and Civic Engagement," speech to the Northern California Grantmakers Conference, San Francisco, Calif., June 22, 1999, at www.pewcenter.org/doingcj/speeches/s_grantmakers.html (accessed June 5, 2000)

Part Three

Progress in Our Material and Natural World

Part three explores progress in relation to our material and natural world. The chapters explore progress in the natural sciences, feminist views of progress in technology, progress in innovative credit and technology programs for the poor, the uses of information technology, our economic systems, and sustainable development.

This section opens with Scott Montgomery's chapter on "Progress and the Natural Sciences" exploring the "nature of scientific progress and views of it in society" in historical terms and in terms of its character and impact in research and the public sphere. Tracing the history of science, Montgomery notes that the character of scientific work has changed deeply—from the past-time of the gentleman scholar, to "a highly professional, expert style of knowledge that focused itself in ever smaller domains."

According to Montgomery, the creation of new fields has been the hallmark of progress in the sciences over the past 150 years. While increasing specialization is viewed as problematic, encouraging "arcane forms of discourse," it has also allowed the deepening and expansion of knowledge in the sciences. Although, as Montgomery notes, the concept of scientific progress has been placed in some doubt since the social conflicts of the 1960s and 1970s, this skepticism has not led to a general loss of faith in the sciences.

"Since well before the Second World War," according to Mongtomery, "major industrialized nations have sought to take some degree of command over the science within their borders, to influence its evolution and exploit its knowledge-base on a national (and often nationalist) basis.... This move toward (and basic rationale for) official science policy originated from perceptions of the increasing power of technical knowledge, both in a material and economic sense. Major goals of such a policy have been: 1) to fund (or not to fund) research on the basis of government priorities; 2) to regulate other areas of research that appear 'risk-prone,' either in a physical or symbolic (political) sense; 3) to advance the commercialization of new knowledge; 4) to strengthen research by supporting science education; and 5) to apportion benefits from research among investigators, universities, industry, and government itself."

"The truth is" he says, "that advances in science, particularly during the past century, have been very mixed and, often enough, unpredictable in their consequences, and this lack of predictability is to be expected.... There is no simple formula for understanding, predicting, or even controlling the direction of progress in natural science as a supra-national phenomenon of mind, nor is there ever likely to be—despite centuries of attempts by individuals, groups, and governments to do so."

In chapter 18, Robert Heilbroner's essay, "Progress: An Economist's View," explores the discipline of economics and its role in both helping to understand and to promote progress. Heilbroner defines progress as "improvement, betterment, advancement," a concept which also incorporates the idea of progress as a process of maturation and development. Progress, Heilbroner notes, is also bound with choice, and should be understood as being multi-dimensional—with advance often accompanied by retrogression. Heilbroner notes that "Progress makes us realize that social changes are not all the same, and that those which have progressive properties are in a quite different class from those which do not."

While the discipline of economics, Heilbroner believes, offers some advantages in choosing among alternative social policies and measuring their impact, such measures are limited by their exclusion of "negative externalities." Moreover, Heilbroner finds that while economics is thought to be the most scientific of the social disciplines, it is not a "true" science. Disciplines such as chemistry, physics, or astronomy "owe their high degree of explanatory trustworthiness to the absence, among the 'behaviors' they study, of anything resembling a key element in the behavior of human, and perhaps animal society: choice."

Heilbroner asks, "What use, then, might economics serve toward the design or successful pursuit of progressive change?" Socialism, Heilbroner finds, was gravely damaged by the communist experience of the twentieth century. Moreover, socialism has lacked a "convincing blueprint" as to its structure, boundaries, and relationship to market systems. Heilbroner concludes that "capitalism has the capability of developing in more than one socio-political direction, some of which seem to offer a substantial degree of progress. That is no guarantee ... but its possibility serves as an incentive for strengthening the bi-sectoral structure and deepening the socialized outlook from which the potentiality of progress may become an actuality."

In chapter 19, Ruth Schwartz Cowan discusses women's relationship to progress in the twentieth century. Cowan notes that many feminist scholars of her generation began their careers with a deep ambivalence about progress. While early feminist social scientists, according to Cowan, "recognized that they could vote and that their grandmothers could not; they understood that they were better educated than any previous generation of women; they recognized that they were markedly less likely to die in childbirth. Nonetheless, in their political outrage and their ambivalence about progress they seemed determined to read the past as one long slippery slope, heading ever *downward* from a feminine—if not also a feminist—utopia."

Cowan recounts that her early scholarly work reflected an anti-progressivist sentiment, similar to many of her peers. However, her own ideology changed as the result of two experiences. First, in her scholarly work, Cowan started with the assumption that women's lives had been better before the industrial revolution, and that the idea of progress was "a myth told by men to make women's oppression invisible." But, through her investigations Cowan eventually concluded that this view reflected a level of privilege, that the greater your distance from poverty, the more likely you are to think that life had been better in the past.

In her personal life Cowan relates her experience with a physician who, she realized later, had saved her life, but had behaved like a misogynist in her encounter with him. The lesson to be derived from this experience, Cowan says, is "that the idea of progress needs to be made as complex, subtle, and nuanced as life itself is. The same event can look both good and bad to two different beholders; indeed, it can look both good and bad to *the same* beholder; indeed, it can *be* both good and bad, both progressive and retrogressive, at the same time."

Cowan concludes that for nearly 200 years, democratic politics and economic affluence have increased choices, and increased freedom in the form of increased choices is progress—and that perhaps progress is "our most important product."

In chapter 20, Andrew Gordon and Tom Martin explore the broader implications of information technology for progress in both the industrialized and developing worlds. They briefly chronicle the history of progress in communications technology—from moveable type and the printing press, to computers and the Internet. But, they note that "nothing prepared observers for the blinding speed with which the Internet became widely available once it caught on."

Gordon and Martin provide several examples of ways in which the Internet has been used to enrich education, medicine, and international relief efforts, to maintain cultural connections and disseminate information that might not otherwise reach mainstream media, and to alleviate poverty. They also note the profound disadvantages created by new technologies: information overload, the cultural invasion of the Internet (with over 70 percent of its current content in English), the speed with which "disinformation" can be spread, the repression of information in authoritarian regimes, and accelerated resource exploitation and environmental degradation facilitated by improved information technology.

Gordon and Martin define progress as being subjective and "inevitably tied to one's identity and priorities." The tools of information technology, they note, "are ultimately only as useful as the justice and purposefulness with which they are used." While information technologies may help raise awareness of fundamental issues of justice and equality, then can also be used to hide, exploit, or bury information.

The development of the Internet and information technologies, Gordon and Martin argue, should not be left to market forces alone, because investments are made on the basis of potential profit. Therefore, intervention by governmental and non-governmental organizations, and policies that promote research, development, and dissemination of technologies that will benefit the poor are essential. Gordon and Martin also advocate for a more inclusive decision making process and new methods of analysis for the development and use of various information technologies. Given limited public and philanthropic dollars devoted to development, there are real trade-offs involved investing in information technology. Those most affected need to be included in the decision making process, as standards and regulations for information technology are part of the social code that defines progress.

In chapter 21, Muhammad Yunus tells the story of the founding of the Grameen Bank. Yunus recounts that he wanted to learn more about the poor people of Jobra, adjacent to where he taught economics at Chittagong University in Bangladesh. Bangladesh was in the midst of a terrible famine in 1974 when he first started to spend time in the community. As he found that people around the campus suffered for lack of very small amounts of money (sometimes less than a dollar), he decided to make loans out of his own pocket. The loans helped so much he decided to go to a bank to arrange the loans. The bank would only make the loans after Yunus had offered himself as a guarantor, but loans were repaid easily, and formed the basis of research toward the establishment of banking services for the rural poor. With the help of a central bank, he expanded the project to some neighboring villages between 1976 and 1979, and by 1983, established the Grameen Bank as an independent bank. The principle of the Grameen Bank is that "the less you have the higher the priority you get in receiving loans from Grameen."

Grameen's current ambitions are to create access to information technology (IT) and white-collar service employment for the world's poorest. The poor, Yunus notes, have tremendous motivation to learn and adapt. What has been needed is an organized effort to promote the interests of the poor in developing countries. There is now a family of companies around the Grameen Bank, several of them related to IT and communications, working on the perennial question of poverty alleviation through the newest technologies of cell phones and the Internet.

In the final chapter, Alison Cullen and Christopher Bretherton turn to the issue of environmental sustainability. They note that concerns regarding rapid population growth, exploitation of natural resources, and environmental degradation have lead to "growing consensus that the primary goal of environmental progress must be *environmental sustainability*—stabilizing the local and global impact of humanity on the natural world."

Cullen and Bretherton believe that environmental progress will require gathering effective information and educating the public, changes in individual and collective values, and changes in the options and requirements for action.

Any single approach to environmental sustainability, according to Cullen and Bretherton, is unlikely to prove completely effective. Rather, they advocate for integrating a broad range of approaches, including regulatory approaches to industry and land use, technological innovation, economic development that incorporates incentives for environmental sustainability, advocacy from non-governmental organizations, green metrics, risk management for environmental sustainability, and a focus on population growth.

Cullen and Bretherton are optimistic. They note that "Recent years have brought some progress, especially in addressing localized issues. Many environmental disasters have been averted or reversed, such as severe contamination of air, water, and soil, or near-extinction of some species. In many cases, these changes have resulted from an increased awareness of the gravity of the situation." Cullen and Bretherton also see evidence of evolving human value structures. While fundamental changes in values will occur at different rates within different populations, they conclude, "we believe that society will indeed progress toward environmentally sustainable decision making. Such change must be seeded on a local scale and supported at every level as it grows."

Progress in our material and natural world is often thought to be more easily defined, measured, and promoted through public policy than is progress in ourselves or in relation to others, but our authors offer only qualified support for this view. The predictive capacity of social sciences is limited. Nor is it possible to control our ability to promote progress in the natural sciences. Progress in the material and natural world has much to do with perceptions and values, as does progress in ourselves and our relations with others. Despite these limitations, however, we might still expect to harness our understanding of the material and natural world, and the tools of public policy to promote progress and sustainability.

Chapter 17

Progress and the Natural Sciences: Issues and Perspectives

Scott L. Montgomery

Introduction

An essay on the topic of science and progress, if not confined to certain shores, is likely to suffer the fate of the man who tried to swallow the ocean in order to collect beautiful shells. The topic is not merely large but expansive, fluid. As a result, I have chosen to discuss here several themes, at first in historical terms, dealing with the nature of scientific progress and views of it in society, then to focus on a specific aspect of this progress (specialization of knowledge) in terms of its present character and effects both in the research sector and the larger public sphere. My intent is to provide background and perspective, to pose issues more than attempt their solution. The latter, I believe, must be left to history itself.

This being said, we might begin with Herbert Spencer. "Progress," he wrote in 1850, "is not an accident, but a necessity … a part of nature … and thus of science."[1] Spencer was giving voice to a faith that remained largely unshaken in Western society for over two centuries, from the Enlightenment down to the outer edges of the twentieth century. He represents a high point in this faith, an example of inspired excess. His attempt to found a Darwinian theory of human society, and thus to claim a kind of ultimate explanatory power for scientific ideas, was less reductive or revolutionary in outlook than it was conventional in hope—science, jewel in the crown of intellectual advance, would one day provide answers to all human problems.

However we may shake our collective head over such thinking today, or celebrate in scholarly form the various oppositions to it over time, such faith in the benefits of scientific progress has been a decided historical force for much of the modern era—and it remains so today, though in qualified fashion. What have been its fundamental elements? Epistemologically, science was (and largely is) understood to be the bringer of a more solid and unassailable truth, a brand of understanding that advanced inevitably through new discoveries, new facts and theories, rigorous and rational methods, improved instruments, great geniuses of an exalted, even eccentric order—with no prospect of an end. Socially, meanwhile, science was felt, until quite recently, to be the inevitable "engine of human progress," the source of new technologies, provider of wonders and economic well-being, the basis for insights into human nature whose application would inevitably improve life and impress a more "natural" order on society. Politically and ideologically, too, scientific advance was viewed by many leaders as a source of certainty and power—a means to more precisely define and rank the human subject, to underwrite the "rational" (if unequal) distribution of opportunity and privilege, while simultaneously offering patriotic capital and, to be sure, material force in the form of military technology. Even beyond all this, in a more general cultural, even emotional sense, there was—and to some degree, there very much still is—the sensibility that, in a world so often wounded by regressive cycles of war, injustice, and misery, natural science continues to move forward in a very real, undaunted, and demonstrable fashion, to generate the "new," and to draw some portion of the imperfect present toward the possibility of a better future.

Without doubt, scientific advance has borne many burdens of utopian assumption. For too long, the aims of inquiry and of society in general were conflated in an ultimately unstable image of "progress." There was thus fated to be a fall. Even the great monuments of advances past—Copernicus, Galileo, Newton, Darwin, Einstein—and the potent discoveries of recent vintage (quantum physics, DNA structure, plate tectonics, etc.), could not sustain the idea that science was beyond accountability to the rest of society. In some sense, modern democracy was doomed to catch up with science, as it delivered ever-greater powers of creation and destruction in to the hands of the twentieth century. This fall came only very recently, however, in the wake of the social conflicts arising during the 1960s and early 1970s (though it had started, even within the scientific community, before this). Revelation of science's sometime ideological connections, the physical risks associated with certain areas of research, and the resistance of many scientists to public scrutiny, all helped bring an end to the unqualified "science for a better tomorrow" belief system.

There was, too, the changing nature of technical research itself in the post World War II period. The full blossoming of a "big science" enterprise, heavily reliant on public funding, was bound, sooner or later, to bring a good deal of research squarely into the political arena and make it directly answerable, in some part, to public concerns. Controversies over nuclear power, medical malpractice, environmental pollution, military weaponry, genetic testing, cloning, and other topics have also clarified that, like it or not, science is deeply embedded with ethical, sociopolitical, and therefore policy questions. Indeed, since the 1960s and 1970s, the discourse of "risk and benefit" has come to surround a great deal of research. Science today is viewed as both a Promethean fire and a Pandora's box, a source of knowledge that can both benefit and imperil humanity. Nor is natural science the model for all forms of knowledge. On the contrary, it is itself the subject of new fields of critical inquiry—historical, sociological, linguistic, anthropological. Even the hallowed "scientific method" (as a single, universal process) has been deeply questioned, admitted to be, at best, an ideal.[2] In short, many of the former grand narratives of modern science have been cast into question, even abandoned.

Progress and Science: Views from the Bridge

Where, then, does this leave the larger concept of "scientific progress?" In something of a quandary, to be sure. But not entirely. Western society continues to treat scientific research as one of its most important, future-seeking enterprises, worthy of admiration, earning of support. Certainly, there have been important controversies, as noted above. But opposition to natural science *per se* among the public has tended to be concentrated in a few specific groups. The apparent resurgence of Creationism and religious or other rejections of science are, in broad terms, local phenomena. Despite the attention these movements have received, there has been nothing to hint at a wholesale loss of faith in scientific work. On the contrary, there is evidence to suggest that attitudes among the general public remain extremely favorable—and have actually increased in appreciation during the 1990s.[3] In the meantime, Darwin and Einstein have yet to be supplanted by William Jennings Bryan or Nostradamus. Neither have the so-called science wars of the 1990s, fought by academics over the status of technical knowledge as truth,[4] had any real impact on public attitudes, let alone on research itself. There has been, in fact, no real "legitimation crisis"[5] for science—at least among investigators, the public-at-large, policy makers, corporations, world governments, educational institutions, universities, private foundations, publishers, and industry. On the contrary, during the last thirty years, and particularly with the advent of the "information revolution," scientific work has moved even more to the center of knowledge creation and distribution in the contemporary world. Recent rumors regarding a coming end to science, meanwhile, seem (as Mark Twain might say) greatly exaggerated.[6]

Western culture very much retains support for the continued progress and also the fundamental outlook of science—call it the "mirror theory of nature."[7] This theory proposes an extra-human physical reality available for accurate representation and (often) manipulation, and it has lost little or nothing of its original force. Styles of theorizing in natural science may indeed have evolved away from older ideas of fixed order. Certainly there is now, as never before, an openness to such notions as chaos, catastrophe, disjunction, violent, and sudden change in general. But among scientists, these ideas are part and parcel of progress today—they are pursued and experienced as improvement. They have quite measurably advanced predictive and explanatory powers, and, as such, have provided reasons to *intensify*, not relinquish, loyalty to the "mirror theory."

The idea of progress for natural science today might therefore focus on factors philosophical, sociological, political, and economic. But at some point, any such idea would become effete and irrelevant if it ignored the content of science itself. It is here, after all, where demonstrable forms of advancement are most present and pressing. It is in the area of technical knowledge, too, where society places many of its abiding hopes, its deepest investments of belief. Understandings about the material universe—old, new, and forthcoming—have been the capital of science, and a currency for society, during most of the late modern era.

Scientific Progress: Some Examples

What, then, is the nature of progress in scientific knowledge? This is a question that has occupied scholars for centuries. Early histories of scientific progress tended to be a roll call of great men (rarely women) and great discoveries. For better or worse, such histories remain very common today, being the correlative to the great names and touchstone works—the "classics," in other words—of the humanities.

What might be included among these "classics" of science? While there is unlikely to be any final consensus in this area, whether among historians or scientists, enough agreement does exist for what appear the most fundamental discoveries—findings and ideas without which the contemporary era in science would be unthinkable—for a brief (albeit sketchy and insufficient) list to be made.[8]

In physics, for example, it is generally felt that the modern period opened with Galileo and Newton, both of whom applied systematic experimental methods and higher level mathematics to problems of motion and matter. These two men, along with Nicolas Copernicus and Johannes Kepler, are also credited with the first great modern achievements in discovery and theory regarding astronomy—with the first scientific use of the telescope (Galileo), with establishing the heliocentric solar system (Copernicus, Galileo, Kepler), the basic laws of planetary movement (Kepler, Newton), and the principles (including gravity) that govern them (Newton). In particular, by the end of the eighteenth century, the advent of telescopic observation and Newtonian concepts effectively sundered the histories of astronomy and physics into different eras. After Newton came powerful innovations in the nineteenth century, especially from the study of electro-magnetic phenomena, the introduction of field theory (Michael Faraday, James Clerk Maxwell), and early concepts of heat, energy, and atomic structure (Hermann von Helmholtz, J. J. Thompson). With Einstein and relativity theory, another crucial shift occurred, putting in place new ideas that replaced the Newtonian model. Finally, the twentieth century has seen the problematizing of matter itself by the quantum revolution, led by such thinkers as Paul Dirac and Erwin Schrödinger, and extended more recently by Richard Feynman and Murray Gellmann.

Chemistry, meanwhile, also saw the beginnings of a more modern view in the late seventeenth century. Robert Boyle did much to foster appreciation for rigor and ingenuity in experimentation, and for publication of one's work (alchemy had long been involved in secrecy). A century later, Antoine Lavoisier brought chemical thought to a new level through his explanation of combustion, his analysis of the nature of chemical reactions generally, and his nomenclature for chemical substances. Between 1800 and 1900, chemical science gained enormous new powers and insights through such concepts as atomic theory (Robert Dalton) and thermodynamics (Carnot), as well as the construction of the periodic table (begun by Dmitri Mendeleev), the discovery of radioactivity by Henri Becquerel and the Curies, and the uncovering of methods for the transmutation of elements (Ernst Rutherford).

Biology, on the other hand, did not become a field, by name or specific domain, until relatively late. Instead, the study of life, like that of the Earth, was included within "natural history," a vast and rambling category of observation in search of some form of unifying theory. This descriptive stage reached a culmination in the system of Karl von Linné (Linneaus), who provided a nomenclatural scheme able to both name and classify any organism on Earth. However, the first great concept that gave what might be called a modern meaning to biological forms and their history was surely the theory of evolution by natural selection, Darwin's magnificent contribution. This was followed by a second conceptual advance only a half-century later, that of genetic inheritance (and the existence of the gene), begun by Gregor Mendel and pursued by many others in the first decades of the twentieth century. The gene itself, however, remained fairly mysterious and difficult to analyze until James Watson and Francis Crick unraveled the structure of its central agent, DNA, a feat which, within a few decades, made the next important revolution possible—that of molecular biology—in whose midst we very much find ourselves today.

Medical science is considered to have begun its modern period much earlier than these other disciplines, as far back as the Renaissance. At this time, the first accurate, detailed treatises on human anatomy appeared, above all in the work of Andreas Vesalius, whose *De humani corporis fabrica* (1543) provided an epochal atlas of the human body, setting standards that lasted down to the twentieth century. During the following two centuries, other innovations of great import were William Harvey's discovery of blood circulation (late seventeenth century) and Edward Jenner's development of a vaccine for smallpox (late eighteenth century). But it was not until Louis Pasteur's work in the 1870s and 1880s that a concept of disease and treatment based on rigorous, duplicable laboratory work resulted. This was the germ theory, derived from the discovery of microorganisms, a theory that led both to systematic vaccination and to the integration of antiseptic methods in all aspects of medical practice. Pasteur's work was deepened and expanded by Robert Koch and Adolf von Behring, who identified the natural resistance to disease that organisms possessed, based on complex molecules von Behring termed antibodies, and who therefore effectively discovered the human immune system. Subsequent to these innovations, the principal revolution in medicine of the twentieth and twenty-first centuries has come about due to the advent of molecular biology, which has helped re-conceptualize disease (e.g., in terms of communicational process) and is today generating new forms of therapy.

Finally, like biology and medicine, the geological sciences did not appear on the scene of modern science until quite late. Crucial ideas about the origin and nature of strata were proposed early on by Nicolas Steno in the seventeenth century, but it wasn't until the end of the eighteenth century that the concept of a dynamic Earth, subject to changes wrought by both internal and external processes acting over very long periods of time, came to be proposed. In the period between 1790 and 1835, this premise was put forward by James Hutton and confirmed and expanded by Charles Lyell, who established the first major unifying theory of geological science—the theory of Uniformitarianism, which stated that earth features take shape and are revised at a constant rate, to the same basic forces, such that observing those forces acting today will provide the key to the past. Since Lyell, geoscience has grown and deepened enormously in sophistication, but has benefited from only one other major conceptual revolution, that of Plate Tectonics, inaugurated in the late 1960s, and finally confirmed and accepted in the 1970s and 1980s.

Such a brief and breathless flyover of modern scientific advance, despite its "textbook" quality, has a particular purpose here. A large part of such progress has not brought with it, in a glittering wake, any specific improvements in human welfare, practically speaking, nor a more rational distribution of opportunity, privilege, health, wealth, and happiness. Thermodynamics and the germ theory may well have given us new machines and medicines, but relativity theory and plate tectonics have done little, in any direct way, to fulfill the Enlightenment dream of a more orderly, sane, and ideal society. Nor has scientific progress, inevitably and necessarily, resulted in technological breakthroughs: on the contrary, technology and engineering have often pursued their own course of innovation, which scientists in their turn have adopted with fertile result (the telescope, photography, and the computer revolution are excellent examples). We know, too, that the effects of scientific innovation have not always been positive or neutral (indeed, neutrality in this context is impossible, given the social meanings attributed to science), but have led to dangers of both local and universal aspect (as in nuclear weaponry). Indeed, some of the very "positives" once attributed to science—enhancing national prestige and military superiority—are now felt by many to be potential "negatives." The truth is that advances in science, particularly during the past century, have been very mixed and, often enough, unpredictable in their consequences, and this lack of predictability is to be expected. At base, progress in natural science increases the span of human power, and this power has many possible dimensions, even those that extend beyond the simple dichotomy of Promethean fires and Pandoran boxes. There is no simple formula for understanding, predicting, or even controlling the direction of progress in natural science as a supra-national phenomenon of mind, nor is there ever likely to be—despite centuries of attempts by individuals, groups, and governments to do so.

The Changing Character of Science

Whatever else might be said, science itself continues to move forward in no less profound a manner than in the past. The decoding of the human genome; the finding of new subatomic particles; exploration of planetary surfaces; chaos theory: these are just a few of the myriad advances that continue to be made.

What of the actual character of scientific work, then? This has changed, deeply. Up until the early part of the nineteenth century, for example, science in the West was largely the province of the gentleman-scholar. By contemporary standards it was casual, performed by men of means and education who could afford to pursue experimentation or field work without the need for mundane compensation. By the middle of the 1800s, however, this species of scientist was rapidly becoming vestigial. From a broad gathering of local societies, individuals, and private laboratories, European science had entered a new and aggressive phase of modernization, being rapidly transformed into an expanding series of professional disciplines, increasingly institutionalized into academic programs, underwritten by direct governmental and commercial support, and characterized by specialist terminologies that increasingly removed the relevant knowledge from the public sphere.

Many influences conspired to make this happen. Intellectually, fields such as chemistry and physics had reached a level of experimental sophistication whereby they became too demanding for part-time, gentlemanly work. At the same time, the sciences had grown considerably in number of practitioners during the eighteenth century, with the result that scientific societies were becoming centers of ritualized interaction, exchange, status-seeking, public lecturing, and other professionalizing activities. Governments during the Enlightenment had begun to realize and encourage the material advantages to be derived from scientific work, and this became especially visible in France under Napolean, who used engineers abundantly in all facets of his urban building campaigns and his military efforts.

Indeed, Napolean's victories over Prussia, in particular, were viewed as a result of rational, scientific planning. In the wake of its humiliation, Prussia moved aggressively to establish a university system with scientific training as a priority, to bolster technical work in many areas, including the funding of laboratories and the employing of scientists in helping expand the early stages of industrial revolution. England, too, now in the midst of its own industrial advance, saw much value in putting scientists and engineers to work for furthering economic and military strength.

Above all, the tone was soon set by German scientists, such as Justus Liebig and Hermann von Helmholz.[9] Great strides were made, particularly after 1850, by applying rigorous experimental and quantitative methods to the study of matter, force, and life. In the last fifty years of the nineteenth century, discoveries like those of microorganisms, electromagnetism, conservation of energy, molecular and atomic structure, antisepsis, x-rays, and a dozen other phenomena, more than proved the power and value of the new science. Whereas the research of 1800 was not so very different in kind from that of 1700, the scientific enterprise of 1900 was an entity of a wholly new and different order—vast, professional, deeply integrated into academic and industrial endeavor, highly dependent on technology, and ever more highly specialized.

Specialization: Origins and Role since 1800

Indeed, the creation of new fields is rightly viewed to be one of *the* defining aspects of scientific progress over the past 150 years. Specialization has been, among other things, the mark of success and fertility. From the beginning, it revealed that, in order to expand and deepen, natural science had to diversify and concentrate. It involved the pursuit of new subject areas (minerals, weather, engines, energy). It was inspired by greater precision and the demand for smaller levels of analytical scale (study of crystals, bacteria, molecular action). It thrived on improved laboratory technology (refracting telescopes, purification apparati, electricity, photography), and was nurtured by the application of higher level mathematics (physical chemistry, field theory, mathematical, and atomic physics). Finally, it was urged, in turn, by the public's faith and fascination in certain specific areas (paleontology, evolution) and the demand that scientists apply their prowess toward the solution of particular problems in society, such as the nature of disease (pathology), the origins of contagion (microbiology), and mental and emotional conditions (neurology, psychology), among others.

In 1800, scientific work was still referred to as "natural philosophy." By 1875, this term was either dead or in disgrace—*Naturphilosophie* had given way entirely to *Naturwissenschaft*. And *Wissenschaft* meant a highly professional, expert style of knowledge that focused itself in ever smaller domains. The larger fields of physics, chemistry, biology, and geology therefore did not long remain unified unto themselves. Instead, they diversified into a range of subfields: physics, for example, containing by 1880 the separate disciplines of optics, acoustics, mechanics, statics, atomic physics, studies of electromagnetism and heat, and solar physics. In geology, meanwhile, the new disciplines of mineralogy and paleontology were well known even by 1860, but soon after came geochemistry, geophysics, structural geology, sedimentology, geomorphology, and petrology. By the turn of the century, "chemistry" and "biology" too had become, for all practical purposes, umbrella terms for an array of specialties ranging from spectroscopy on the one hand to bacteriology and plant pathology on the other.

This general historical process has only increased to the present, for the same reasons (plus some others). Many of the single subfields of 1900 are now themselves huge realms of separated investigation: geophysics, for instance, now comprises over a dozen specialties like geomagnetism, geochronology, seismology, geodynamics, deep earth studies, plate kinematics, and so on, each of which contains its own many subareas of expertise. In paleontology, there are now disciplines focusing on a single genus of extinct animal (trilobite studies) or on a certain family of dinosaur (Cretaceous sauropods). Similarly, it is now possible in the life sciences to specialize on particular aspects of a single fauna (the dance behavior of a single species of bee); or, in physics, on a small group of particles; or, in astronomy on one type of star or a moon of Saturn.

The phenomenon of sub-sub-sub (etc.) specialties is well-recognized today among scientists, and is entirely accepted as a requirement for research. Calling oneself a "gravitational wave physicist" or an "authority on the eighteenth simian chromosome" is fully expected. One indication of its advance is the enormous proliferation of journals during the past 100 years,[10] a reality that reflects in large part new research in emerging fields (founding a specialty journal being an acknowledged requirement for legitimacy). Another sign of specialization's advance might be seen in academic departments over this same period. One notes immediately, for example, that in the more advanced research universities "geology" and "biology" have been replaced during the past several decades by the titles "geological sciences" and "biological" or "life" sciences, thus highlighting the growing multiplicity of disciplines—and, in effect, celebrating it.

Effects and Concerns

Increasing specialization—a hallmark of scientific progress—has been often viewed as problematical.[11] Development of professional specialties has meant the creation of knowledge increasingly embodied in arcane forms of discourse, produced and certified by those only with designated training and credentials, yet still possessing near-universal powers of truth. Progress in science has thus brought with it certain questions regarding access and control, particularly in democracies.

It is often lamented, as well, that expert specialties produce a broken world of mind. Each specialty, it is felt, labors to become a unique domain, to shield itself off from other research areas, and to eventually produce further subspecialties of its own, thereby building a local empire while also sundering the larger province of scientific knowledge into myriad gleaming shards. Such diagnoses often bemoan both the personal and social effects of this, for example: "The language of the *same* suffices us.... We lock ourselves into our own social, professional cell, and this sequestration has a neurotic value: it permits us to adapt ourselves as best we can to the fragmentation of our society."[12] This is a view shared by some historians of science as well, particularly those who (dare we say?) specialize in the eighteenth and nineteenth centuries. These scholars have interpreted a common intellectual culture during these periods, based on overriding notions about the natural world—above all, those of a religious and semi-religious nature (natural theology, for instance)—which helped to unite in some part scientists, those in the arts, and the public.[13] This shared context was presumably weakened by the advent of secular research, and then destroyed by the elevation of expert knowledge. Specialization thus stands accused for the death of cultural and epistemological unities. Progress in science has forced us to pay the price of lost communality in both intellectual and civic arenas.

Yet the most pragmatic criticism has concerned public understanding and access—the growing distance between knowledges of power (in this case natural science) and the ordinary citizen. This is a perception commonly aimed at the twentieth century above all, and bears a good deal of obvious truth. Scientific advance has indeed brought with it a widening gap between what any individual researcher knows (is trained to know) and what can be easily understood by others—including scientists in different fields. Again, both social and personal effects arise from this. Problems of authority are one such effect: because of its real-world power and influence in many cases, scientific knowledge must be shared with the rest of society (especially in a democracy), yet, because they are held as "experts" of the highest type, scientists are often the subjects of considerable deference. Controversies of the 1960s and 1970s revealed how specialist knowledge helped to underwrite claims that only scientists were qualified to direct, manage, and police their work. Such claims have since been debunked, especially with the advent of biotechnology (scientists are not necessarily experts in the social, ethical, and policy questions related to their work). Yet many researchers continue to feel the opposite—that the lay public and political leadership are unable to grasp the subtleties needed to make truly informed judgments in any particular case. Lacking technical knowledge, the non-scientist is thought to also lack both proper appreciation and a power of discrimination, particularly with regard to research priorities. Thus, in some degree at least, specialization does encourage a set of multi-tiered barriers between the scientist and the general populace—a situation that appears to have no easy solution and that may well constitute a central element in the larger circumstance of contemporary science.[14]

This suggests another effect: the rise of the mediator, i.e., the mass media. Non-scientists have increasingly come to rely on the media for acquiring the knowledge and the general sensibility to help guide decision making in key areas, for example, those concerning human cloning, stem cell research, nuclear energy, and so forth. In capitalist societies, however, the media must sell knowledge, not merely provide it, and thus they define a source with agendas of its own (truth, per se, being only one of these). What the public receives, by way of information on a "hot topic" such as cloning ("hotness" being itself a result of selective coverage), represents a complex, shifting tug-of-war between the interests of scientists and those of journalists and editors. Often missing in this equation is the fact that a great deal of contemporary science remains contingent, i.e., "science-in-the-making."[15] Its final status, as knowledge, has not been determined; thus, much of its presumed future consequences (Will we have babies made to order? Mass produced clones of entrepreneurs, saints, and great leaders whose DNA has been rescued from the moulder of centuries?) is speculation of the purest and least helpful kind.

Perspectives

Appealing as they may be, the arguments of cultural loss and inaccessibility need to be put in better historical perspective. The notion of a former "common cultural context" for all areas of intellectual endeavor, though not entirely a myth, does exaggerate the case more than a little. Up until the early eighteenth century, a broad-based intellectual tradition did exist in Europe, but was shared by those literate in the Latin language, a very minor part of the larger population. Moreover, this was hardly a context without strife or factionalism: one might recall, for evidence, the heated "Battle of the Books" (*Querelle des Ancients et Modernes* in France) that took place beginning at the end of the seventeenth century, in which one of the primary conflicts involved the choice of loyalty to a future-looking "modern" science or to the "eternal truths" of the "ancients."[16] A later rehearsal of this combat, meanwhile, took place in the wake of Darwin's *Origin of Species*, reaching a crescendo in the well-publicized debates between T. H. Huxley and Mathew Arnold in the 1870s and 1880s (the "two cultures" debate—scientific versus literary culture—has a more venerable history than often allowed). From the Renaissance onward, the West has been replete with varied battles for the mind. Nearly every case of an Euler, using algebra as a proof of God's existence, was countered by a Laplace, claiming he "had no need of such a hypothesis."

What, then, of the idea that specialization has shattered scientific knowledge itself into a glitter of unconnected domains? This notion ignores a very important element in the character of recent research. Disciplines in science are not hermetic precincts, but are more akin to living structures within a great body, in constant nutritive contact with each other, exchanging materials along porous edges. Increasing specialization, that is, has led to an increasing amount of cross-fertilization as well as divergence. One obvious form of this has come from the ability to examine phenomena in many fields at smaller and smaller levels of scale, so that understanding once the province of molecular chemistry and atomic physics becomes immediately relevant—nay, necessary, and fertilizing—to certain areas in biology, botany, zoology, and medicine. The early historical signs of this, in fact, can be found in such cross-over fields as biochemistry, geophysics, and physical chemistry, all of which had their origins (and their titles coined) in the late nineteenth century. Today, meanwhile, the process of commingling has advanced to create disciplines that bridge as many as three or more formerly separate areas: biopaleogeography (the distribution of life forms in ages past), psychoneuroimmunology (the influences of emotional and neurological states on the human immune system), planetary geochemistry (substances and chemical processes occurring on other worlds), and so on. Such crossbreeding is very much a core part of scientific advance, an outcome of specialization itself.

This type of commingling, it should be stressed, defines a major part of contemporary science. Often termed "transdisciplinary research," it comprises a mode of advance that has brought creative thought and result to every field. In some cases, it has resulted from the process noted above, that of investigation going to increasingly smaller levels of scale. But it has also gained momentum from other influences. Certainly the integration of computer technology into every aspect of science is a source. This has provided both new powers to create and analyze technical data and also to model natural systems. But interdisciplinary work has other sources as well, resulting from new territories of investigation, even literal ones—for example, the exploration of other planets and their moons, each of which is now attracting to its surface, interior, and history the entire range of sciences developed for comprehending the Earth. Were forms of life to be discovered there, then a similar descent of the biological sciences would inevitably occur as well.

Does all this mean that science is headed towards unity after all? The answer must be no. What is called transdisciplinary research involves sharing of knowledge, terminology, instrumentation, and methodology (as well as funding resources), but on a selective basis. A majority of specialty sub-fields continue to function with a significant degree of relative independence: formalizing a new area of research continues to mean establishing a degree of socio-intellectual separation (founding specialty journals, regular conferences, unique labs, and so forth). Overall, science is no more headed for final unity than complete intellectual diaspora. Nor does it seem likely that any single field, like sub-atomic physics, will reach out to encompass all others: a theory of elementary particles and fields would have little power to explain early hominid evolution in East Africa or the effects of continental collusion in India. Specialization, in other words, has also meant that there is no longer any fixed, single definition of the material world, one scale of reality into which all others can be collapsed. Visions of a "final theory" of any kind, though occasionally invoked today,[17] seem more like atavisms than predictions. Similarly, the notion that some form of "consilience" will occur among *all* branches of human knowledge, under the banner of science, seems little more than historical nostalgia.[18]

Issues of Communication

What, then, of the issues concerning inaccessibility? These are real, to be sure, but not unprecedented. Secret, difficult, or elite forms of knowledge are hardly a modern phenomenon. Learning related to the natural world, in particular, has been sufficiently complex to be abstruse for a great majority of people since ancient times. Mysteries and various rituals surrounded mathematics and alchemy in Egyptian, Greek, and Roman culture; astronomical knowledge, especially in the wake of Hipparchus and Ptolemy, was densely mathematical and challenging even to high-level scholars for over a millennium. Certainly, many of the great works of early modern science were themselves far beyond the grasp of the average person—how large an audience might we suppose existed for Newton's *Principia Mathematica* or the published results of Ohm, Gauss, and Faraday? Indeed, literacy itself was reserved for the very few during most of history.

It is precisely the unprecedented expansion in schooling and the growth of a literate public that has helped create the issue of inaccessibility. It is an issue, in other words, entirely commensurate with the founding of modern democracies and near-universal education. It becomes pressing not merely because of the clear power scientific knowledge commands, but because of the fundamental democratic principle that the public constitutes the source of socio-political authority and legitimacy and must therefore have available to it whatever understanding is needed to make intelligent decisions (in totalitarian regimes, the question of public access never arises). This, then, seems to lead readily to the problem (as many would have it) of what is called "scientific literacy." Today, true enough, *all* areas of scientific research have essentially become arcane. Questions of communication are therefore very important, for practical reasons. Continued progress in science depends to a significant degree on public support—in other words, on what the public understands about science (or believes it understands) and what areas it feels are worth pursuing in an era when government funding is neither infinite nor automatic (no "endless frontier" any longer).

Calls for improved scientific literacy, in fact, have come from several groups—scientists themselves, educators, and a loose collection of commentators, critics, and officials concerned about the presumably low level of scientific understanding among the general populace. These groups have different agendas, to be sure, but they tend to share a single model of the science-to-public transfer, aptly termed "the deficit model."[19] The model posits a lay (or student) mind that is relatively passive, vacant, and needy, with the scientist as both the provider and arbiter of knowledge to be given. In other words, there remains a strong tendency to defer to scientists with regard to educating the public, a reality that is very often true in the realm of science journalism as well. Because of this, in part, one also sees a tendency in discussions of the need for such literacy to revert to old moralisms about the advantages of science, those even reminiscent of Spencer's time.[20]

The "problem" of scientific literacy is therefore difficult on both epistemological and sociopolitical levels. It is an issue, as we have said, that has emerged from the fact that most of the dominant centers of scientific progress today exist in democratic societies (North America, Europe, and Japan, in particular). It is an issue, moreover, that may have no easy solution, or no solution at all in the sense of building stable bridges. The most basic definition of such literacy, after all—having good command of the key concepts and basic principles of science—is probably not even true of many researchers. This depends, of course, on the very notion of "key concepts" and "basic principles," another obvious area for considerable disagreement. The type and level of technical knowledge hoped for by most scientists and policy makers may not really be possible—and would not be the answer in any case to the dilemma posed by the advance of expert knowledge.

In fact, there has never been anything approaching a high level of "scientific literacy" among the public, either in the United States or Europe. During the 1800s, a certain portion of scientific thought was well within reach of educated people—geology, evolution, zoology, botany, observational astronomy; these were all subjects of considerable interest and descriptive content. But there remained huge areas of scientific work in the fields of physics, mathematics, experimental chemistry, theoretical astronomy, and cell theory, that were highly complex and rapidly evolving. What the average citizen of 1880 knew about heat, energy, and chemical structure paled in comparison to what she or he might have understood about natural selection. Today, too, a reasonable grasp of "key" chemical and physical concepts seems unlikely to grant one ready access to understanding quantum phase coherence in Bose-Einstein condensates.

Both the possibility and ultimate role of "scientific literacy" are therefore unclear, and are likely to remain so. Much of the focus on this issue, after all, has come from scientists, particularly those who perceive a vulnerability to loss of support and appreciation, who perceive in various trends (rise to political power of fundamentalist religious groups, more selective funding of research, postmodern studies of science) a fall in the status of science generally.[21] While this may be untrue in most respects, the perception within the technical community is very real that future financial support is not assured, but must be continually justified. In such a context, "scientific literacy" is in some part an attempt to spread the responsibility for approval more widely.

Certainly, *some* knowledge, whether this comes from education or from the popular media, seems required for people to comprehend the paths of progress today, as well as their potential effects and the issues they raise. There are many contemporary examples here: human cloning, stem cell research, planetary exploration, atmospheric chemistry (global warming), to name but a few. No vote need be taken on behalf of scientific illiteracy. It will remain a central problem for the future history of scientific progress to find ways that make the public feel involved, without either overly selling or damning the knowledge at hand. How much knowledge is required may well be as much a political and personal question as an instructional one. The "deficit model" ultimately does a disservice to science itself. For politicians and corporate sponsors, deciding whether a certain brand of research should be continued or stopped has depended far less on scientific issues than on political and economic ones. This is unlikely to change, no matter how scientifically literate an elected official may be. Science may sometimes be politics by other means, but politics is not science.

The Future: What Role Policy?

Since well before the Second World War, major industrialized nations have sought to take some degree of command over the science within their borders, to influence its evolution and exploit its knowledge-base on a national (and often nationalist) basis. In large part, this move toward (and basic rationale for) official science policy originated from perceptions of the increasing power of technical knowledge, both in a material and economic sense. Major goals of such policy have been: 1) to fund (or not to fund) research on the basis of government priorities; 2) to regulate other areas of research that appear "risk-prone," either in a physical or symbolic (political) sense; 3) to advance the commercialization of new knowledge; 4) to strengthen research by supporting science education; and 5) to apportion benefits from research among investigators, universities, industry, and government itself. These forms of involvement have been effected through an ever-evolving and widening array of institutional structures, ranging from direct funding to in-house research, setting up interdisciplinary research centers to supporting university-industry cooperation.

All of these forms of involvement are likely to remain very much in place—even to intensify—particularly if government financing of science continues to remain at high levels. While such levels have decreased in recent years—for example, funding of academic research decreased by twelve percent from 1989 to 1998 —the United States government still accounts for over sixty percent of total research and development support in domestic universities.[22] Moreover, one should note that this decreased support was more than compensated by increased funding on the part of industry, which benefited enormously from the economic boom of the 1990s. With the downturn of the economy in 2001, it seems safe to predict that such industrial support will decline, at least in the short-term. Furthermore, in the wake of the terrorist attacks of September 11 that year, it seems probable that significant increases in defense spending (which includes certain areas of scientific research) will occur, raising the overall level of federal support to pre-

2000 levels.

Such events, in fact, make it clear that government priorities—therefore political, economic, and military realities—have no small importance in affecting the direction of research today. Science policy, and indeed science policy analysis, are very much part of the current and future landscape. Whatever the benefits and drawbacks of this situation, however, the complexity of the relevant landscape, the changing degree of independence granted many federal agencies—as well as the inherent conflict between long term research goals and short-term political aims—have acted to prevent any consistent visions of an appropriate national research enterprise from taking effect.[23] In the United States, to take one example, the National Science Foundation began with a mission to favor basic (versus applied) research above all else, in contrast to certain other funding agencies (such as the National Institutes of Health), but was eventually forced by Congress to broaden its focus and include projects with practical applications, a change the agency has accepted but still resists in subtle ways.[24] On the other hand, the past four decades have seen a change in overall funding priorities for specific areas of science by the government, from engineering and the physical sciences in the 1950s and 1960s to the medical and biological sciences in the 1980s and 1990s—reflecting a complicated mix of influences, e.g., a shift from a focus on Cold War anxieties to public health concerns (especially diseases such as cancer, heart disease, and AIDS), the promises offered by the biotechnology revolution, the increasing reliance of medical research on expensive technologies, and so forth. Today, there are distinct tendencies toward what has been termed "academic pork barrel."[25] Yet, in the end, it must be remembered that science policy, as an instrument of government, has considerable but still limited power to guide an enterprise that greatly exceeds any national boundaries and that, within a country like the United States, is deeply integrated into corporate enterprise, now in the throes of globalization.

Issues of communication, meanwhile, are part of the context that demands a role for public policy in decisions about the future of government-funded science. Indeed, these issues are even clearer today than in the past, due to the unprecedented power of the Internet to distribute knowledge in nearly every form instantly and continually. What does the public need to know? In the United States, and to a large extent in much of Europe, this question has been left in the lap of the mass media and "scientific literacy," whose difficulties we have already seen, and is largely deferred to the scientific and educational communities. Indeed, based on recent reports and studies, government appears more directly concerned with public *attitudes* towards science than public levels of understanding—in short, with sensibilities that have political implications.[26] This lack of initiative in the area of communication therefore seems to be an important lacuna for science policy in general. Indeed, taking steps to directly further such communication would appear an excellent, even necessary way to increase public awareness of those areas of research that government has chosen to support, presumably for public benefit.

It seems clear, in any case, that a strong and practical science policy would have to attempt more in this area than an understanding of basic scientific principles, however defined. The nature of recent controversies in the research community—for example, the cold fusion media debacle, issues of scientific fraud, and the ongoing debates over intellectual property rights for the human genome—make it abundantly obvious that people also need to know something about how science works today. This means not only what institutions comprise it and how they are involved in the process of research, but what type of knowledge they produce and how this knowledge comes to be solidified, distributed, and shared.

An essential point, by any standard, is that the great majority of new science remains contingent, i.e., "science-in-the-making."[27] This means it is not yet fully confirmed or rejected, but incomplete *as knowledge*. It may be exciting, enormously prospective, even revolutionary (though what term is more hand-worn than this?)—but it is not yet entirely reliable and thus cannot be discussed in the same manner as past certainties or on the basis of claims by one or two "interested" researchers. Indeed, it is this very conditional quality (not a simple public relations impulse) that encourages scientists so often to speak about what their work "might lead to," what future "breakthroughs" await, and the like. Much of this discourse, however, remains reliant on the old idea of scientific progress as a matter of accumulating discoveries and impending "revolutions," and ignores the reality of how new understanding emerges from a complex, unregulated, and non-standardized process of analysis, debate, re-trial, controversy, sharing, and selection. A possible role for science communication policy would be to emphasize these aspects of contingency to the public and to information outlets, thereby providing much needed context for related debates in the media and elsewhere. As it is, the public continues to be fed images of scientific progress as a pendulum swing between Prometheus and Pandora. We remain trapped, that is, within a simplistic toss between "benefits" and "risks," wonder and anxiety, improvement and peril.

Intelligent discussions—not to say, decisions—about the possible effects of new research should be urged to go beyond this sort of helpless polarity. As it is, such thinking does little to involve the public in considerations of a higher order, for example: Who should benefit most directly from scientific progress—Government? The economy? Researchers? Industry? The public itself? Science policy can have a larger role in helping answer such questions (which are especially exigent today, given the new abilities of biotechnology to manipulate life in many forms) by seeking to draw a wider range of voices into the relevant debate. As it is, a low level of understanding of science helps keep much of the public at a distance, leaving most decisive power in the hands of government officials. Likewise, the notion that science races ahead, clean and firm, leaving muddy ethical questions in its wake is a common view that appears counterproductive: too often ethical questions related to research are posed in a "brave new world" scenario, ignoring historical precedent and presuming that investigators, by nature, are always ready to be the victims of their own enthusiasm for more knowledge (and money). The public, in short, deserves to know how science works as a real-world enterprise—not as an ideal process of disembodied mind and not as an extract of media clichés.

In the end, there can be little doubt that natural science will continue to advance apace. Historical, epistemological, institutional, and financial momenta in this direction are simply too vast to suffer reverse. Moreover, science is far too international an enterprise to be permanently constrained by changes any single nation may try to impose. Any promising new area of investigation (e.g., stem-cell research), if restricted in one country, will likely move ahead in others before too long. Certainly there may be exceptions—human cloning, for instance, could continue to be a topic of strong regulatory caution in a majority of developed nations. But again, there are limits to what science policy can control in the private sector (some international companies have already stated an interest in moving forward with cloning experiments).

If we accept natural science as a vast body of learning, always in progress and therefore deeply involved in social, political, and cultural realities, we have made a significant advance over our predecessors. We can understand, more than ever, that science does not belong only to scientists or their patrons. And if we are all to be carried forward, in some manner, by advances to come in this great intellectual enterprise, surely the most extensive in the history of humankind, then let us also comprehend something about the choices involved. The most basic choice of all, that of continued progress, has already been made.

Notes

1. Herbert Spencer, *Social Statics; or the Conditions Essential to Human Happiness, Specified, and the First of Them Developed*, revised edition (New York: D. Appleton, 1882): 42.

2. It is not only historians and sociologists of science who have cast doubt on the idea of a "scientific method." See, for example, the writings of Peter Medawar, Nobel Laureate in medicine, especially his two books *The Limits of Science* (New York: Harper & Row, 1984) and *The Threat and the Glory: Reflections on Science and Scientists* (New York: Harper Collins, 1990), the latter of which collects a number of his early papers, including "Is the Scientific Paper a Fraud" (first published in 1963).

3. Figures cited in the 1998 *Science and Engineering Indicators* suggest that, for the United States, interest in science and technology has risen from 61 percent in 1979 to 70 percent in 1997. The oldest running indicator of public attitudes, meanwhile, begun just before the launch of Sputnik, concerns the question of whether science provides benefit or harm to the world. In this case, people answered 88 percent in favor of a beneficial science

in 1957 and 87 percent in 1997. See, National Science Board, *Science and Engineering Indicators*, NSB 9-1 (Arlington, VA.: National Science Foundation, 1998), 7-5, 7-13.

4. The term "science wars" has been coined in reference to an ongoing debate centered on the question of whether (or to what degree) science is socially constructed knowledge, i.e., reflects human concerns and relationships, or whether it relates directly to an external, physical world of matter and process. The debate gained significant heat during the late 1990s, when a small group of scientists went public with the view that the constructivist position—and, by implication, many sociocultural studies of science—were essentially an "assault on truth." Recent attempts to mediate a truce and find some source for common ground have been mildly successful. For a good overview of the related controversy, including "position papers" by some of the protagonists on both sides, see J. A. Labinger and H. Collins, ed., *The One Culture? A Conversation about Science* (Chicago: University of Chicago Press, 2001).

5. The term is that of the social theorist Jürgen Habermas, see his *Legitimation Crisis*, transl. by Thomas McCarthy (Boston: Beacon Press, 1975).

6. J. Horgan, *The End of Science: Facing the Limits of Knowledge in the Twilight of the Scientific Age* (Reading, Mass.: Helix Books, 1996). Such predictions actually form a tradition, dating back several centuries. One of the most ardent proclamations was made by d'Alembert in the 1750s, while assembling the great *Encyclopedie*. For a review of this and other episodes in the "end of science" tradition, see Simon Schaffer, "Utopia Unlimited: On the End of Science," *Strategies* 4, no. 5 (1991): 151-181.

7. The phrase belongs to the well-known work by Richard Rorty, *Philosophy and the Mirror of Nature* (Princeton, N.J.: Princeton University Press, 1979).

8. For an excellent survey of recent thinking in this area by historians of science, see the indispensable reference, *Companion to the History of Modern Science*, edited by R. C. Olby, G. N. Cantor, J. R. R. Christie, and M. J. S. Hodge (London: Routledge, 1990), especially section IIA, "Turning Points."

9. See, for example, D. Cahan, ed., *Hermann von Helmholtz and the Foundations of Nineteenth-Century Science* (Berkeley: University of California Press, 1993). Some discussion of this topic, in overview fashion, can also be found in S. Montgomery, *The Scientific Voice* (New York: Guilford, 1996), especially pages 364-368.

10. Derek J. de Solla Price, *Little Science, Big Science* (New York: Columbia University Press, 1963). According to the data of Price (1963), the number of scientific journals increased from approximately 8,500 in the year 1900 to 80,000 by 1950. Current figures vary, but estimate on the order of 120,000 or more printed journals, a figure that does not include the increasing number of online serials in science.

11. Two recent discussions along these lines can be found in E. O. Wilson, *Consilience* (New York: Random House, 1999) and, with specific reference to university research and teaching, J. H. Roberts and J. Turner, *The Sacred and the Secular University* (Princeton, N.J.: Princeton University Press, 2000).

12. Roland Barthes, "The Division of Languages," translated by R. Howard in *The Rustle of Language* (New York: Farrar, Straus, Giroux, 1985), 116.

13. See, for example, R. M. Young, *Darwin's Metaphor: Nature's Place in Victorian*

Culture (Cambridge: Cambridge University Press, 1985).

14. In this respect, it seems worth noting that scientific advance has also brought with it the evolution of a new "mediating species"—the science writer. Science writing indeed seems a necessary, even inevitable, development with an obvious political dimension (if we take the idea of an "informed populace" seriously). Yet, this form of communication is not merely a source or mediator of knowledge. As pointed out recently, science journalism is a creator of social reality that must constantly choose between two masters, i.e., whether to remain as true as possible to scientific complexity or to translate such complexity into forms more familiar to the lay reader. This often makes the science writer/journalist less of a mediator per se than a new producer and agenda maker, whose work is added into the already complex mix and can sometimes stand at odds both with the scientific community and other interested parties. An excellent work on the place, power, and pitfalls of science journalism is offered by D. Nelkin, *Selling Science: How the Press Covers Science and Technology*, revised edition (San Francisco: W. H. Freeman, 1995).

15. J. Gregory and S. Miller, *Science in Public: Communication, Culture, and Credibility* (New York: Plenum, 1998).

16. See, for example, R. F. Jones, *Ancients and Moderns* (Berkeley: University of California Press, 1967), a particularly good source on the debate in England, noteworthy for the many quotations it offers from contemporary seventeenth century sources.

17. Such final theories—which, in a sense, share bread with the idea of an "end to science"—are most often invoked with regard to subatomic physics and cosmology. See, for instance, S. Weinberg, *Dreams of a Final Theory* (New York: Pantheon, 1992).

18. Such is the thesis of E. O. Wilson's *Consilience: The Unity of Knowledge* (New York: Vintage, 1998). Despite its adulatory reviews in the popular press, the book is viewed by most historians of science as "majestic" not in its leaning but in its naivete regarding historical realities (socio-economic, institutional, and political, for instance) involved in the pursuit of knowledge today.

19. J. Gregory and S. Miller, "Caught in the Crossfire: The Public's Role in the Science Wars," in J. A. Labinger and H. Collins, ed., *The One Culture? A Conversation about Science* (Chicago: University of Chicago Press, 2001): 61-72.

20. This is apparent in many evangelical declarations, especially those given by scientists. Here is an example, from the book *Science for All Americans* by F. James Rutherford and Andrew Ahlgren, a position paper published specifically for the American Association for the Advancement of Science: Science, energetically pursued, can provide humanity with knowledge of the biophysical environment and of social behavior that it needs to develop effective solutions to its global problems.... Scientific habits of mind can help people in every walk of life to deal sensibly with problems that often involve evidence, quantitative considerations, logical arguments, and uncertainty; without the ability to think critically and independently, citizens are easy prey to dogmatists, flimflam artists, and purveyors of simple solutions to complex problems. Scientific literacy is thus promoted on the basis of moral protections, even more than democratic participation or awareness. See Andrew Ahlgren and F. James Rutherford, *Science for All Americans* (Washington D.C.: AAAS Press, 1996), vi.

21. Two recent books reflective of such anxiety are P. R. Gross and N. Levitt, *Higher Superstition: The Academic Left and Its Quarrels with Science* (Baltimore: Johns Hopkins University Press, 1994) and P. R. Gross, N. Levitt, and M. W. Lewis, ed., *The Flight from Science and Reason* (New York: New York Academy of Sciences, 1996).

22. National Science Board, *Science and Engineering Indicators.*

23. A good discussion of science policy, placed in the context of socio-historical studies of science, is given by A. Webster, *Science, Technology, and Society* (New Brunswick, N.J.: Rutgers University Press, 1991).

24. T. Appel, *Shaping Biology: The National Science Foundation and American Biological Research, 1945-1975* (Baltimore: Johns Hopkins University Press, 2000).

25. J. D. Savage, *Funding Science in America: Congress, Universities, and the Politics of the Academic Pork Barrel* (Cambridge: Cambridge University Press, 1999).

26. In this regard, note the following paragraph, which closes the chapter on public science information in the 1998 National Science Board, *Science and Engineering Indicators*, 7-21:Overall, the American public appears to continue to expect science and technology to improve the quality of life, and the scientific community is accorded a higher level of trust and confidence than other major societal institutions. Nonetheless, the concerns regarding several specific technologies indicate that the public has not given the scientific community a blank check. The public wants to know what is happening, and *the scientific community needs to communicate its work ever more clearly and effective.* (italics added)

27. Gregory and Miller, *Science in Public.*

Chapter 18

Progress: An Economist's View

Robert Heilbroner

I

Progress is a daunting term, clear enough when we ask whether Mary has made any progress with her homework; hopelessly vague when we are asked whether the United States has made any progress during the last ten, or twenty, or perhaps 200 years: "It all depends," we answer, "on what you mean by progress." But progress is too rich an idea to be wasted on sequences of shallow change. Progress is a word that wets the imagination, encourages critical analysis, helps us find our way through today's indeterminate setting. What more could an impatient economist want?

What does one mean by progress in a study such as this? To me the word suggests improvement, betterment, advancement—meanings that point in the general direction of change that has brought subjectively welcome and objectively demonstrable alterations in "life"—another term of vast complexity. These are not once-for-all changes or strokes of good fortune, but the outcome of deep-rooted processes, that is, changes that I would describe as maturational—the gradual strengthening of understanding, and the incremental increase of moral and/or intellectual capabilities, whether of an individual or a group.

For all its ambiguities and difficulties, I think few would deny that some conception of progress is an indispensable starting point for all social policy, and indeed, for much social understanding. What use might economics serve toward the design or successful pursuit of progressive change? The question requires that we take another look at economics itself as a body of social explication. We must also address the question of whether capitalism or socialism is capable of giving rise to a progressive society. What follows is an attempt to make explicit the strengths and weaknesses of the powerful model of analysis called economics as an engine of social change.

II

The discipline of economics has earned its reputation for penetrative analysis because it enjoys two advantages denied its fellow disciplines such as political analysis, anthropology, sociology, and of course history itself. The first such advantage is that economics deals largely—although, as we shall see, not exclusively—with social activities that can be reduced to a single measuring unit—money. Thus economics allows us to compute the value of the vast array of activities that collectively give us our yearly Gross Domestic Product (GDP), worth nine trillion, five hundred and seven billion, nine hundred-odd million dollars in the month in which I wrote this piece. There is no conceptual equivalent to this marvelously concrete "economy" in the "polity" with which political analysis deals or the "society" to which sociology devotes its attention.

The second comparative advantage of economic analysis follows from the first. Its "numericity"—everywhere visible in impressive equational or graphic form—becomes a key element in the widespread view of economics as the closest any study of society can come to being a true science. In a world in which science is by far the most admired and envied scholarly endeavor, this bestows on economics a unique prestige. Needless to say, its views with respect to progress, therefore, enjoy a natural precedence among the counsels and judgments of social studies of all kinds.

I have, I must confess, a certain skepticism in the general view of economics as a uniquely reliable guide with respect to the key term of this paper. I am indeed interested in presenting its limitations, but I must make clear at the outset that for all the problems to which we shall directly turn, there is no doubt that progress, however described, must depend heavily on economics to achieve whatever measurable—please note the adjective—goals or paths it may propose. Economics is therefore a unique source of strength with regard to many social endeavors—a distinction that may not always be decisive with respect to the moral or other nonnumerated aspects of progress, but which can indeed play a strategic role in choosing among alternative social policies, or determining whether any given program is within reach.

Thus I am far from dismissing the importance of this most measure-related discipline of social analysis, but for that very reason I must now turn to the caveats that pertain to economics along with its capabilities. The first of these concerns the reliability of its measuring capability. Here I shall begin by quoting from an excellent article in the *Atlantic Monthly:*

> The nation's central measure of well being works like a calculating machine that adds but cannot subtract. It treats everything that happens in the market as a gain for humanity, while ignoring everything that happens outside the realms of monetized exchange, regardless of its importance to well being. By the curious standards of the GDP, an earthquake or a hurricane ... add to GDP because they cause money to change hands. It is as if a business kept a balance sheet by adding up all "transactions" without distinguishing between income and expense, or between assets and liabilities.[1]

As the quote implies, a second difficulty in using economic indicators to measure well-being is that this very focus turns a blind eye on the varying and even negative effects of some kinds of productive activity. Here we can refer to no less an authority than Adam Smith. Statistical calculation was not yet born in Smith's time, but the *Wealth of Nations*, published in 1776, expressly puts market activity high on its criteria for a good society. Yet, in the very first chapter of *Wealth*, Smith provides a disturbing caveat as he describes the extent to which the division of labor, which he places high among the sources of economic betterment, can also become a source of social deterioration—that is, negative progress. He illustrates this effect by discussing first how pins, instead of being wrought one at a time, can be made by a succession of tasks in which "one man draws out the wire, another straits it, a third cuts it ..." with the consequence that production per worker jumps from perhaps twenty pins per day (or as few as one) to over four thousand.[2]

Yet, for all his enthusiasm regarding the productive possibilities of the division of labor, toward the end of his book Smith adds this caveat:

> The understandings of the greater part of men are necessarily formed by their ordinary employments. The man whose whole life is spent in performing a few simple operations of which the effects, too, are, perhaps, always the same, or very nearly the same, has no occasion to exert his understanding.... He naturally loses, therefore, the habit of such exertion, and generally becomes as stupid ... as it is possible for a human creature to become.[3]

Here we confront a problem known to modern economists as "negative externalities"—unwelcome by-products that arise as side effects of otherwise useful activities. These need not be so socially harmful as that described by Smith—today's economists, for example, are more likely to stress diffuse externalities such as the smog generated by a factory—but these negative effects are not subtracted from the value of the factory's output. On a small, localized scale such oversights can no doubt be ignored in calculating a measure of national well-being, but when pollution reaches citywide extent, its negative contribution can no longer be overlooked. To enlarge the problem further, until recently it was believed by most researchers that the gradual process of global warming, caused by side effects of man-made combustion, could impose very serious costs on many parts of the world, including our own. Recent estimates have brightened this prospect, at least for more "polar" nations such as Canada, Russia, and the United States, certainly a finding of much cheer. Nonetheless, the advent of global warming itself, whether for better or worse, makes clear that whereas progress remains in our hands, as has always been the case, today so does retrogression, not just from such obviously destructive acts as warfare, but as a side effect of the hitherto wholly benign effort to improve our economic condition.

Next, I turn to the question of the "scientificity" of economics. Here two important qualifications must be raised. First, the true sciences, like chemistry, physics, or astronomy, owe their high degree of explanatory trustworthiness to the absence, among the "behaviors" they study, of anything resembling a key element in the behavior of human, and perhaps animal society: choice. Thus the very basis on which the high regard for scientific explanation rests is missing from the behavior of social "atoms," economic actors not the least.

At this point I shall not go further into the array of meanings that can be attached to progress, but will focus on one that is without question central to it. This is the attribution of choice and volition to the process of deciding on whatever course we identify as progressive. To put it differently, we could never accept as a progressive policy one that was forced upon us by the blind workings of nature. Progress is inescapably bound up with volition, expectation, judgment and other such psychological elements. To pursue a course because it is unavoidable may be the wisest choice—any other leading to grave consequences—but it cannot be described as "progressive" if, as I shall maintain, that key word is inseparable from an exercise of free determination.

Social reasoning, in other words, does not have the underlying certitude of scientific theorizing: there is no chemistry-like relationship on which we can depend in designing a system of law or allocation of incomes. The causal sequences on which rest the successes of science-based undertakings are not, alas, available for the attainment of social ends. Given that the predictability of science is a product of the absence of "choice" in the movements of its particles and forces, perhaps we can reconcile ourselves to our less-than-scientific state of being.

III

What use, then, might economics serve toward the design or successful pursuit of progressive change? The question requires that we take another look at economics itself as a body of social explication.

Economics, as we know it, did not exist for more than perhaps the last two or three percent of the time span between the appearance of Homo sapiens in Europe, circa fifty thousand B.C., down to the present. During the greater initial part of that immense span, the only form of social organization to which production and distribution were entrusted was that of tribal hunting and gathering groups, following procedures governed by age-old tradition. Nothing recognizable to us as an economic incentive—certainly nothing like a system of generalized buying and selling—played a role in guiding what we would call economic life over these millennia. This is not to say that production and distribution were without internal discipline. Rather, that discipline was provided by the imperatives of relations of kinship or the dictates of age-old tradition—both of which served as agencies of social continuance, not improvement.

Indeed, no change-oriented organization of daily life was to appear until the displacement of hunting and gathering by a new form of social organization which makes its appearance around the fifth millenium B.C. Now, in the valleys of the Nile and the Tigris and Euphrates, we see for the first time a pattern of societal organization marked by inequality, not commonality, of status; and by centralized rule that not only oversees the provisioning of society but carries on ambitious military adventures requiring armies of soldiers and builds extraordinary constructions necessitating armies of workers.

Was this extraordinary social transformation "progress?" We know that the answer depends on what we mean by the word. Nobelist Amartya Sen is right in his oft-repeated assertion that freedom is the necessary condition for all progressive change;[4] this stunning redesign of society might well be considered one of retrogression, considering its dependence on command from above and obedience below—the latter, to no small extent, that of slavery. Yet, who can compare the pyramids of Egypt with the huts of hunting and gathering peoples, and declare that this transformation represented social decline, not advance? Perhaps progress itself might be understood as inherently multi-dimensional—advance at one level often accompanied by retrogression at another.

IV

When do economic considerations begin to appear as the order-bestowing core of society, and more than that, its most powerful engine of social change? The answer lies in the gradual appearance of that complex order called capitalism, already in place in Adam Smith's England, whose modern-day beneficiaries or victims are ourselves. It is conventional to describe the essential elements of a capitalist system as comprising three distinct social arrangements. The first of these is, of course, the market system, in which the determination of both production and distribution moves away from the commands of emperors, the orders of feudal lords, and the disciplines of guilds, to the determinations of individuals or small organizations answerable to no directional force save whatever would hopefully serve their private interests. To this very day the term "market system" is often used to designate a capitalist order, without using that word which has negative overtones for some. And to this same day the manner in which generalized competition imposes both an overall discipline as strict as that of command systems, combined with a general incentive for the development of new techniques and products, constitutes the single most important teaching of the discipline of economics, more or less invented, although not so named, by the same redoubtable Adam Smith.

It was not yet clear to Smith, however, that the extraordinary role of the market was not the only defining property of what he called a "society of perfect liberty." In fact, it would not be until almost a century later that Karl Marx would identify another property of at least equal importance. He called it the "laws of motion" of capital, pointing to an internal dynamic of capital accumulation brought about by the competitive pressures and social structure of a capitalist society.

By the term "capital" Marx referred to a process rather than a static object. Before capitalism, a sum of wealth, however denominated, was treasured for itself, and rarely spent save for the acquisition of objects of prestige. But in a capitalist setting, wealth was no longer seen as an end in itself, but as the first of a series of steps that could bring about its increase. Thus a hoard of money became the starting point for a sequence of transactions that would display the dynamic potential of money-as-capital.

Typically, the first of these transactions was the exchange of money for a commodity whose use would yield its owner a profit. Here the most desired candidate was the commodity "labor power"—that is, a day's or week's or year's work from a laborer, by which all kinds of material commodities could be transformed into saleable form. Insofar as labor power itself was available in a highly stratified social order for less than its full value, this opened the way for a powerful process of capital expansion, as stationary wealth was transformed into a dynamic circuit of purchases of labor power and profitable sales of its product. Thus capital was sought not for itself but as the starting point for the creation of more capital—a process that would ideally go on indefinitely. In this way, self-generated "growth"—to use a modern term—becomes a hallmark of capitalism, at least as important for its historical impact as the internal dynamics of its competitive market setting, possibly more important from a progress-related perspective.

There remains a third identificatory property of the capitalist system that does not become widely recognized or appreciated until the twentieth century. This is the horizontal division of capitalism into two separate but interacting "sectors"—one private, consisting of the ever-changing activities of the market system; the other public, comprised of the agencies and actions by which government, mainly at a national level, seeks to guide the course of the private sector—intervening, for example, to forestall monopoly, or seeking to encourage private investment by lowering the interest rate.

This public-private interaction has become a highly contentious aspect of modern capitalism, generally viewed with unease by conservatives and with positive potential by liberals. What is essential for our purposes is that the two-sector form is today a universal feature of all capitalisms. I make this point because it calls to our attention that the structure of capitalism is not beyond modification, a consideration of potential importance in considering the possibilities for economic progress in our time.

This brings me to consider the last universal element of capitalism—an element which, unlike the three previously noted, is not unique to a capitalist order but comes to it from earlier social orders. Here I speak of the presence within all capitalisms of specific national cultures—sociopolitical outlooks of the kind we associate with the golden and not-so-golden ages of ancient Greece and Rome. In the case of contemporary capitalisms these cultures range from the socially conscious views and policies found in the Scandinavian group, Holland, and to a lesser extent Germany and perhaps Canada, to the socially unconscious views we associate with England and the United States. It is interesting to note that we can find such a range of social views as far back as the strong welfare policies of Bismarckian Germany and the strict laissez-faire conservatism of then contemporary England.

The spectrum continues to our day: in the mid 1990s, for example, transfer payments, largely for welfare purposes, came to over 20 percent of GDP in Germany and Northern Europe, compared with 16 percent in England and 13 percent in the United States.[5]

V

But what of socialism? Here I can be brief. Taken in its entirety, the experience of the communist world has gravely damaged socialism as a model for progress. What has lacked is a convincing blueprint, never mind real-life experience, as to the socio-political base on which a radically new socialist structure would be built. Is it to contain a market system? If so, how will boundaries be drawn between the reach of the market and that of the planning system that has always been considered the all-important economic core of socialism? And what of the bounds of government? If there is to be no market network, are there to be no boundaries to its reach? In that case, how is a socialist state to avoid the socio-political repression that has been its curse? It is this last consideration that removes China, for all its dramatic economic growth, and Russia, despite its liberalization under Kruschev and perhaps Putin, from serving as progressive models, at least for the Western world in our time.

It follows that throwing the word socialism into the ring of history without giving it institutional concreteness is not much better than trusting to the inspiration of its stirring but inadequate literature of hope. I shall therefore say no more about this question.

VI

The word progress lies unspoken behind the imagined trajectories of both socialism and capitalism. Progress would seem to suggest, I think, economic growth. Assuredly, growth suggests qualitative as well as quantitative improvement. But I think no one would suggest an arithmetic parallelism: GDP in the United States today may be twice what it was only ten years ago, but I know of no one who would claim that "life" is therefore twice as good. Progress denotes qualitative as well as quantitative change. Unfortunately, economics has no means of identifying, much less measuring, the difference.

Progress makes us realize that social changes are not all the same, and that those which have progressive properties are in a quite different class from those which do not. Is capitalism capable of giving rise to a progressive society? The great economists themselves have been of different minds with respect to the matter: Smith not aware of such a problem; Ricardo pessimistic; John Stuart Mill optimistic; Marshall cautious but hopeful; Marx of course optimistic for socialism which implied the disappearance of capitalism; Keynes pragmatic; Schumpeter gloomy; and too many economists, especially in this country, uninterested.

There are, indeed, structural reasons to doubt that capitalism would be a likely candidate for a progressive society. The market system has no maturational effect in its disciplinary or invigorating pressures—indeed, quite the opposite when one considers the role of the market in giving legitimacy to that assault on public trust called advertising. So too, capital expansion is a highly effective means for the development of technology or managerial efficiency, but hardly for the humanization of working life. Thus it seems difficult to perceive the dynamics of capitalism as deserving the designation of Progressive, spelled with a capital letter.

But is there another side to the matter? Could it lie in two attributes of capitalism of which we have already taken note—the first being its bi-sectoral structure, the second its spectrum of national cultures? The first gives us an economic system in which government is accorded a role of potentially great progressive importance, insofar as the public sector can—I do not say always will—serve as a counterweight to the private sector. There has been no such division of power in any prior social formation, so its appearance in capitalism has the potential of leading to an unprecedented widening of outlooks. Note that I say "potential." When we consider whether capitalism could harbor progressive tendencies we must recognize that nations with capitalist structures have ranged in their political cultures from the socialized—not socialist—nations of northern Europe to that of our own country, birthplace of the New Deal and still residence of the Ku Klux Klan.

Thus I see capitalism as a still indeterminate socioeconomic formation capable of moving to the Left as well as to the Right. This is, of course, a wishful point of view—but I ask whether it is possible to speak of the evolutionary capabilities of one's own society without a degree of personal identification in one's prognosis. Capitalism has the capability of developing in more than one socio-political direction, some of which seem to offer a substantial degree of progress. That is no guarantee of enjoying those benefits with respect to our own country, but its possibility serves as an incentive for strengthening the bi-sectoral structure and deepening the socialized outlook from which the potentiality of progress may become an actuality.

Notes

1. Clifford Cobb, Tedd Halstead, and Jonathon Howe, "If GDP Is Up Why Is America Down?," *Atlantic Monthly* 276, no. 4 (October 1995): 59.

2. Adam Smith, *Wealth of Nations*, Modern Library Edition (1776), 4-5.

3. Smith, *Wealth of Nations*, 734.

4. See title of Sen's most recent book: Amartya Sen, *Development as Freedom* (New York: Knopf, 2000).

5. See Angus Maddison, "The Nature and Functioning of European Capitalism: A Historical and Comparative Perspective," *BNL Quarterly Review 203* (December 1997): 464.

Chapter 19

Perhaps Progress Really Is Our Most Important Product: A Feminist Contemplates the Twentieth Century

Ruth Schwartz Cowan

Many Americans who came to maturity in the years just after the end of World War II have a love-hate relationship with the idea of progress.

Their parents—many of them immigrants or the children of immigrants—seem to have been convinced, not only that progress is good, but that they had seen its goodness, with their own eyes, in their own lifetimes. Whether they knew it or not, these Americans were heirs of the Enlightenment. They believed that progress was connected to education and knowledge—particularly scientific knowledge. They understood *progress* to mean *improvement*, particularly *improvement* in such indicators of well-being and comfort as life-expectancy and home ownership, per capita income and infant mortality. Well, yes, they knew that the Depression had happened, but by the post-war years they seemed to think that it had been just a blip in an almost inevitable march toward better health (think of antibiotics) and better jobs (from blue collar to white) and a better standard of living (from the tenements to the suburbs). At the very least, many post-war American adults—native-born Americans as well as immigrants and children of immigrants—believed that the United States was a better place to be living than the places from which they or their parents or their grandparents had escaped: they understood their lives to be far better in, say, 1957 than theirs, or *their* parents' had been in 1937, 1927, or 1917.[1]

However, the people who came to maturity during the Cold War, the children of the 1950s and 1960s, had a very different lived experience, an experience that contributed to their ambivalent feelings about the idea of progress. Yes, on the one hand, they learned in school that to be a big P *P*rogressive reformer was a very good thing; Progressive reformers had welcomed the immigrants with settlement houses, and worked for better regulation of tenements and factories and improved the quality of food and drugs. But, no, on the other hand, small p *pro*gressive reformers, reformers of the Stalin, Castro, and Mao variety, were not at all good people, and neither were their American sympathizers. Apparently, only some kinds of political progress were truly to be admired, but how these young people were to differentiate between the good and the bad (aside from the size of the p) was never made particularly clear.[2]

Worse yet, while the teachers and the media were extolling the virtues of science and technology, and while the best and brightest yearned to be either physicists or surgeons—the air raid sirens often sounded. While the cold war young were learning the wonders of the atom and the no-longer secrets of the universe, they were also learning to huddle under their desks, heads on knees, hands over heads. They trembled with the fear that *this time* the sirens would not stop wailing and that the no longer secret world would come to an ignoble end *precisely because of what the scientists and engineers had wrought*. In the postwar years, young people were taught, yes, to admire science as one of the hallmarks of civilization and to admire scientists for contributing to a host of improvements. But they also saw the photographs of the mushroom cloud and the devastated cities and the blasted bodies and the piles of bones outside the gas chambers—and they wondered whether there wasn't some other secret about science and technology which their teachers weren't talking about, or didn't really understand, some secret which suggested that, no, these two human enterprises weren't quite so civilized and progressive after all.[3]

I am a member of the first of those postwar generations (I was born in 1941) and two of my clearest, most visceral childhood memories give substance to the sources of our generational ambivalence. In the first memory I am sitting in my elementary school auditorium (wearing the special middy-blouse and taffeta tie that was required on assembly days) singing the United Nations anthem in hearty unison: "United Nations on the march, with flags unfurled; together fight for victory—a free, new world!" In my nine or ten year old brain *freedom* was connected to *peace* which was connected to the *UN* which was connected to *the future*, a bright future, and this was also connected with science and education and medicine; hadn't those united nations created UNESCO and UNICEF to make sure that it all came to pass for the children of the world?

In the second memory, I am also nine or ten years old, sitting in my elementary school classroom (at one of those one piece desks with an inkwell and a book shelf below the seat) peering at the atomic bomb radius map which hung next to the framed print of George Washington (there was probably a bomb shelter directional sign in the classroom also, but I don't remember it nearly as well as the radius map). I'm a parent now myself, and a teacher, and I still shudder at the thought of what could possibly have inspired school administrators to hang those maps in classrooms. I lived in New York City; the map was a line drawing of the city on which a series of concentric circles—targets—had been superimposed. The map was supposed to tell us what the level of destruction would be in different sections of the city if an atomic bomb fell on Times Square, the center of the target. In my memory I am staring at the map, trying to locate my father's office in one of those concentric circles—and then I am getting slightly hysterical as I realize that he is sitting at a desk in the innermost circle, the one destined for *complete and utter destruction.*

Taken together, these two memories suggest to me that, like many members of the Cold War generations, I felt progress in my bones only half the time, or perhaps it would be better to say, in only half of my bones. There was the good war, and the defeat of the bad guys, on the one hand—and then these strange new wars, in Korea and Vietnam, on the other. There was the lesson about the good Progressives on the one hand and the bad progressives on the other. There was the wonder of science and there was its destructive power, the benefits of penicillin and the polio vaccine coupled to the terrors of the bomb. Progress did not seem to be such a terribly good idea, or, better, it seemed both terrible and good at the same time. Even as a teenager I remember being cynical about the motto the General Electric Company had adopted for its advertisements: *Progress is our most important product.* A good sales pitch for my parents, perhaps: for me a source of ironic mirth.

Small wonder that when my generation came to maturity as scholars and intellectuals, we found ways to debunk both the Progressives and the scientists. In our revisionist reading, the Progressives turned out to be not such good people after all: eugenicists, nativists, and racists.[4] We discovered, in going back to the documents of the time, that the men and women who created the settlement houses really didn't much like the traditional cultures of the people whose housing and working conditions they tried so hard to remedy. We argued that the people the Progressives worked hardest to help were themselves and their friends: creating new professions (like social work) and new forms of employment (like civil service) for members of the white, Protestant aristocracy.

We criticized the scientists also. Those of us who became historians, sociologists, and philosophers of science discovered that scientists, once thought to be almost infallible, were in historical fact, just as biased and politicized as every other professional group; in sociological fact just as beholden to special interests and funding sources and professional networks. Specialists in science and technology studies argued that there were many possible truths and many good ways to build a better mousetrap. What was "best" or "true" to one group of scientists or engineers was *not* "best" or "true" to another; and what led one group to dominate the other was neither universal truth nor universal efficiency, but rather power, or social, politics.[5]

In short, intellectuals and scholars of the generations that came to maturity during the Cold War had considerable doubts about progress. In optimistic moments they noticed that affluence was more widespread (at least in the developed world) than ever before in history, but in dour moments, they suspected that affluence was a trap, set by those in power to keep those out of power from revolting. When in a positive mood they wrote books about how the idea of progress had inspired the American and French liberal revolutions; when feeling less than positive they wrote books about the idea of progress as a myth perpetrated by some people in order to gain hegemony over others. They argued amongst themselves about what *if anything* could be said to have improved in the 20th century—or since the since the Renaissance, or even since the pure democracies of the ancient Greeks: well, yes, people are living longer—but what good is it to live longer in a degraded environment, or in an alienated community, or in a debilitated family? Because of their historical situation, because of their lived experience, they grew up ambivalent about progress—and carried this ambivalence with them into their adult, public lives.[6]

The generation that was ambivalent about progress also happened to be the generation that powered the second wave of feminism and the new academic discipline called women's studies. During the late 1960s and early 1970s, as feminist scholars and activists became aware of the multiple, intersecting, omnipresent structures of sexism, they had cause to wonder how anyone could ever have believed that ours was *the best of all possible worlds.* At that time, feminist historians told us that women had had neither a Renaissance nor an Enlightenment.[7] Feminist social scientists concluded that both liberal democracy and the industrial revolution had actually increased women's oppression—despite a few appearances to the contrary.[8] Many of these feminist social scientists were also socialists; by the end of the 1970s, they found themselves forced to conclude that however progressive (with regard to gender) nineteenth century socialists had been *in theory,* many (perhaps all) twentieth century socialist regimes *in reality* had turned out also to be oppressive for women.[9] Socialism was as bad as capitalism; class politics, many feminists concluded, had, in the course of history, upstaged gender politics every time. If there had been progress, they were convinced, women certainly had not benefited from it: quite the reverse.

The founders of women's studies recognized that they could vote and that their grandmothers could not; they understood that they were better educated than any previous generation of women; they recognized that they were markedly less likely to die in childbirth. Nonetheless, in their political outrage and their ambivalence about progress they seemed determined to read the past as one long slippery slope, heading ever *downward* from a feminine—if not also a feminist—utopia: how else to explain the attraction of so many theories about long lost matriarchies or gynocracies?[10] The evidentiary grounds were slim, but the ideological convictions were heartfelt: if equality of any sort had once existed in human history then it was easier for this second wave of twentieth century feminist scholars and activists to believe that equality could be re-built in their own lifetimes.

Women's health activists conveyed the same *dys*progressive message. Was the Pill an improvement over the diaphragm? Absolutely not; the Pill, they said, caused blood clots and cancer. Was anesthesia a step forward in maternity care? Absolutely not; medicated childbirth, they argued, was a patriarchal plot to wrest caregiving from midwives and give physicians additional control over women's bodies.[11] Baby formulas, some argued, were invented to give doctors ever more control over women's daily lives and manufacturers ever-more ability to turn women—who had once been independent producers of all their children needed—into consumers.[12] And who was responsible for making abortion illegal? The physicians, of course (aided and abetted by the lawyers)—all male. In the golden age *before* the doctors professionalized, or so the argument ran, abortion had been legal (at least until quickening) and women had known just which natural abortifacients to administer at just which appropriate moment in a pregnancy.[13] No matter which aspect of health care was examined in those early, heady, days of women's studies and the women's health movement, some scholar or activist could be found to dash icy cold water on the widespread belief that modern medicine had improved women's lot; even antibiotics, voluntary sterilization, and childhood vaccinations had their feminist critics.[14]

As a member of that postwar generation I initially began my forays into both feminism and women's studies with the same crypto-conspiratorial, anti-progressivist ambivalence so many of my peers professed. Two experiences—one scholarly, the other personal—helped me to understand the error of my ideology.

In the early 1970s I began a research project focused on the history of household technology (washing machines, dishwashers, gas ranges, and the like) and its impact on housework.[15] I had been trained as an historian of science, had developed an interest in the relations between technological change and social change, and had decided that I wanted to focus my research on some aspect of women's history. Household technology and housewives seemed a natural fit, especially as, at that time in my life, I was, myself, knee deep in ambivalence about *my own* housework.

I began my research with an assumption which turned out to be false, namely that housework history would be populated by a fair number of feminine Luddites. I thought I was going to find an abundance of records of women who had resisted adopting new household technologies. I made this false assumption for two reasons: first because I thought that women would *naturally* find machine-powered work to be emotionally alienating; and second, because I thought that women, whose housework was their pride, joy, and craft, would not want to be de-skilled by machines. Following the lead of some of my colleagues in women's history (and also in labor history), I just assumed that industrialization—which had been bad news for women working in factories, would also turn out to be bad news for women working in their own homes. To put the matter another way, I assumed that women in the past would feel as I did in the present: that women's lives had been easier, better before the industrial revolution and that, as a consequence, the idea of progress was a trap, a ruse, a myth told by men to make women's oppression invisible.

So I started a file labeled "Resistors." One research year followed another research year; many of my files began to bulge—but not the one labeled "Resistors." In the end, after almost a decade of research, I had located only two examples of women who had resisted modernizing their homes. Both women were rich; both women employed several servants; both women were widows. One woman, in the 1920s, had refused to buy a refrigerator—because her cook was developing a romantic relationship with the iceman. The other woman had refused both to electrify her mansion *and* to give up her horse-drawn carriage, saying that she was perfectly comfortable living the same way her parents had. Aside from these two ladies, every other woman of whom I could find a record had welcomed modern conveniences into her home; indeed, many had gone to considerable lengths to obtain the devices that I thought they should have been spurning.

There were three possible ways to understand my slender folder; either my assumptions were wrong, or millions of women had been victims of "false consciousness," or the records of feminine Luddism had been suppressed. For a variety of reasons not worth exploring right now, I reluctantly concluded that I couldn't possibly be smarter than millions of my forebears and that the patriarchy couldn't possibly have managed to censor so many anonymous lives. The vast majority of American women seemed to have *wanted* vacuum cleaners and central heating, running water, and electric lights. And *kept wanting them*, year in and year out, generation after generation. American women must have expected change for the better, *progress,* when they invested in household technology, and they must have gotten what they expected, because they certainly voted with their feet (and their pocketbooks) to keep the appliance manufacturers and utility companies and supermarkets in business. That last point—that women got something that they appreciated, some improvement in their lives from their household technologies—is the crucial point that connects my research experience to the idea of progress; I will return to it shortly.

But first I need to recount a personal experience that surprised me in a similar way. In the winter of 1979 I suffered a miscarriage in the third month of a pregnancy. I began to bleed heavily late one evening; my husband rushed me to the emergency room of a nearby hospital. I had lost a lot of blood and was quite lightheaded. I was also crying, uncontrollably. The nurses in the delivery room wanted to start an IV drip (with oxytocin, I later figured out, to get my uterus to contract and, thereby, stop the bleeding) but they were having a lot of trouble either finding a vein or getting the needle in. So they called a physician, a gynecologist who was covering for my own physician that evening. When he arrived he solved the problem in short order—all the while speaking rudely to me and the nurses; he couldn't seem to get a sentence out without an expletive in it, and some of the expletives were references to me and my body and my emotional distress.

When I had calmed down, a day or two later, I was furious. In 1979 the women's health movement was just getting up a head of steam. Here was a living, breathing, cursing example of an obnoxious, condescending physician, a stereotypically patriarchal gynecologist. I wrote a letter of protest to my local medical board; I sent a copy to my own physician, and told him that I would switch to another practice unless he promised that the offending physician would no longer be his weekend cover. I complained to any and all who would listen; I identified the guilty party to all my friends and neighbors.

A year or two later, I was doing some research on the history of childbirth for a course that I was developing. While doing the research I kept noticing the expression "excessive bleeding" in reference to pregnant women who died in the months before giving birth. Suddenly I realized that those women were miscarrying—just as I had done—and that they, like me, had continued to bleed. With a dull, very dull, thud I was then forced to recognize that the obnoxious, condescending physician, the epitome of all that was wrong with patriarchal medicine, had probably saved my life. Had he not gotten that needle into one of my veins, had oxytocin not been available in the emergency room of that hospital, I might well have bled to death as so many, many of my forebears had.

My own research and my own experiences had now presented me with two counter-arguments to my ambivalence about progress. The first counter-argument arose from the history of household technology, what might be called the advanced frontier of progress. Apparently, the average American woman had gotten something she appreciated, some improvement in her life, from new household technologies. The second counter-argument arose from the history of women's health. Apparently, that history had been *dys*progressive (increasing the number and power of patriarchal, condescending physicians) and *pro*gressive (increasing women's life spans and improving their health) *at the same time*. A little sadder, but considerably wiser, I now viewed my youthful ambivalence about progress as a mistake born partly of a failure to be sufficiently conscious of class and partly of a failure to be sufficiently cognizant of life's complexities.

Class first. The lesson that I derive from the fact that the only two female Luddites I could find lived in mansions, surrounded by servants is this: only the wealthy (or those who want to appear wealthy) can nourish anti-progressivist nostalgia. Class and wealth are not, of course, perfectly synonymous, but I have found, over the years that I have been studying housework, that *with regard to attitudes about housework* they might just as well be. The class in which a person is raised, almost always determines that person's attitude toward housework, no matter how that person's economic status may (or may not) change in adult life. And attitudes about housework are very tightly connected to attitudes about progress, especially when progress is defined, as it so often is, as improvements in well-being and comfort; it is the technologies with which housework is done—dishwashers and washing-machines, telephones and paper diapers, automobiles and refrigerators—that we generally refer to when we talk about progress, that we assume have contributed to our well-being and comfort.

The lady who wouldn't electrify her house didn't have to clean her oil lamps herself; neither was she doing her laundry or—for that matter—worrying about whether she'd be able to afford her servant's wages five years down the road. The other lady, the one who wouldn't buy an automatic refrigerator because she didn't want to interrupt the relationship her cook was having with the iceman, bought one soon enough, it turned out, when she realized that without her husband's income she was going to have to fire the cook.

On the other side of the economic divide, the generations of poor women who carried water and scrubbed shirts and wrung out sodden linens with their own hands, did not complain about being de-skilled when they switched to automatic washing machines. Neither did they seem to notice (what home economists quickly documented) that they were spending more time doing their laundry by machine than they had spent doing it by hand. What they noticed instead was how much more productive their laundry work was: more clean dresses for their daughters to wear to school; more clean shirts for their husbands to wear to work; more possibilities for the family to join, or appear to join, the middle class.

So who was it that thought progress was an illusion, a myth? The middle and upper middle class children of parents who had once been poor, or the middle and upper middle class people who had never been poor as children: the people, in short, who had never known how it felt to heat tubs of water on a pot-bellied stove. The people just like me, who had washers and dryers in the basement—and sent their cleaning out to be done by a commercial service. The people who had the time to make the choice to occasionally wash out their dainty underclothes by hand; the people who had the income to be able to afford dainty underclothes in the first place. Only we were capable of wishing that the hands of the clock could be turned back to a "rosy" time when families peeled apples by the kitchen hearth, thick soups were kept bubbling on the back of the wood burning stove, and mothers focused their entire attention on the needs of their kids and spouses.

Nostalgia, *anti-progressive* nostalgia, erases the details of the labor that preceded and produced each of those mental images. The people who actually performed the labor are not prone to the same amnesia. Another way of putting this lesson that I have learned from studying the history of housework carefully is that appreciation for the extent of progress is not so much in the eyes of the beholder, as it is in the class of the worker—or the class of the worker's childhood. The richer you are, or your parents were, the greater your distance in time from poverty, the less back breaking labor you have to perform yourself, the more likely you are to think that life was better in the past than it is in the present.

When we take class and wealth into account, when we carefully ask who did the work, and how hard the work was, and what toll it took on body and soul, and what results the work produced, we have to conclude that technological change has made life better for most American women in the last one hundred years. Yes, the housework may take roughly the same amount of time as it used to—but the work is less taxing to muscle, heart, and bone. Yes, women still put in three times as many hours as men do in the work that maintains and sustains family life—but the work enables them to produce a standard of living for their families that was only available to the very rich in fairly recent times past. Progress may not have landed us in the very best of all *possible* worlds, but it has certainly landed the average American woman in a world far better (by objective measures) than any that came before.

Complexity second. The lesson that I derive from the fact that a modern physician can save women's lives while simultaneously behaving like a misogynist is that the idea of progress needs to be made as complex, subtle, and nuanced as life itself is. The same event can look both good and bad to two different beholders; indeed, it can look both good and bad to *the same* beholder; indeed, it can *be* both good and bad, both progressive and retrogressive, at the same time.

This is a lesson that it took feminist scholars and activists, particularly those involved in the women's health movement, a very long time to learn. To give just one example: feminist historians have done a 180 degree turn around in their assessment of Margaret Sanger since the 1970s. A major (some would say *the* major) birth control activist during the first half of the twentieth century, Margaret Sanger was reviled by the second wave of feminist historians.[16] They argued that Sanger had started out as a socialist and feminist activist, but that she had sold out, in the 1920s and 1930s, first to the capitalists (her first husband had been a socialist architect; her second was a wealthy businessman), then to the physicians (when she encouraged the passage of legislation allowing physicians to prescribe birth control devices to their patients), and, finally, to the eugenicists (when she argued that diffusion of legal birth control would improve "racial quality").

Twenty years later, however, as the result, partly of new research in the Sanger papers, but more significantly, of a new sophistication about the complexities of social reality, feminist historians have come to a very different set of conclusions; first that Sanger had sold *herself* into her second marriage in order to finance the birth control movement; second, that her alliance with physicians had not only been strategically necessary but also strategically successful; and, third, that in Sanger's day socialists were just as likely to approve of eugenics as conservatives were.[17] Margaret Sanger wasn't perfect, but no one is. She now goes down in history as a feminist reformer after all.

As with the history of the birth control movement, so also with many aspects of women's health care: mature reflection suggests that neither change nor its consequences is ever simple. Yes, the Pill has side effects—but it is more effective, and more completely under a woman's power, than any other form of pregnancy planning. Yes, hormone replacement therapy appears to increase the risk that a woman may develop breast cancer—but it also seems to decrease the risk that she will die of heart disease, or be crippled by osteoporosis, or suffer from senile dementia. Yes, childbirth has moved out of the household and into the hospital and women have lost the company of friends and relatives in the process—but maternal and infant mortality have also declined precipitously. Yes, for every two steps forward there has been one step back—but that's life. The available evidence indicates that, after mature reflection, most women decide that they do not want to retrace those two steps backward just to recapture what has been lost: they will give up the conviviality of home birth for the safety of hospital birth, the risk of side effects for the freedom of a sexual life without fear of pregnancy, the risk of breast cancer for the chance to be more active and alert.

Which brings me to a final set of thoughts about the idea and reality of progress, women's progress in particular. Perhaps, for all these years, we have been misdefining, or misunderstanding, the nature of progress. Perhaps what people mean—or ought to mean—when they talk about progress is not improvements in comfort and well-being, but rather increases in the number and range of choices. By that standard, progress has certainly occurred. The average American woman today has more choices than her mother, her grandmother, or her great-grandmother did (unless her mother, her grandmother, or her great-grandmother was much richer than she is—and in some cases, even then). She can choose, with virtually no obstacles, to continue her education past high school. She can choose, with many fewer obstacles to her choice, from a wide variety of jobs and careers. She can choose to marry or not to marry, with considerably less threat to her economic future. She has greater control than ever before possible about the timing and number of her pregnancies. She can choose to continue working while her children are small, because the choice is not going to imperil (as it once surely would have) the health of her child.

Such choices are not easy to make—indeed some are profoundly difficult—but I now see progress as consisting in the fact that they are makeable. Social conservatives, of course, will disagree with me. They generally yearn for a time when life was "simpler"—by which, in the case of gender role choices, they seem to mean a time, the past, when women had fewer choices because more of those choices were made either by men or by fate. On what have come to be called "life-style" issues, conservatives often favor policies that will reduce women's access to choices: they wish to make abortion illegal again, for example; they also oppose paid leaves for childbirth or childcare. Social progressives, contrarily, rejoice in the fact that the increased number of choices, however difficult, means increased autonomy, and increased freedom for women. They regard the abortion decision as a difficult and unfortunate one, but still want to protect a woman's right and ability to make it. Similarly, they recognize that paid parental leave may be expensive, but they regard the expense as one which a free society ought to be shouldering happily, because it is an expense which widens the range of choices citizens can make.

Many social and political forces have combined to produce the increased freedom and autonomy that women have enjoyed in the developed world in the last century. Great political leaders have been crucial, leaders who were sometimes inspired by the ideas of liberalism and other times the ideas of socialism. Affluence has also been essential, affluence which has partly resulted from governmental policy, partly from the behavior of markets, and partly from the great ideas and the personal drive of the men and women who have invented and developed new technologies—including medical and reproductive technologies—and new businesses.

Looking back over the long-term historical record, it seems that there are only two circumstances under which a freedom, once granted, has been taken away for long periods of time. The first circumstance is long-term economic collapse; the second is sheer force exercised by authoritarian rulers. For the better part of the past two hundred years democratic politics and economic affluence have been marching hand-in-hand to increase the autonomy and the freedom of millions of people, including millions of women. Perfect freedom, no; no such thing exists. But increased freedom in the form of increased choices, yes. That is indeed progress. And it is a wonder to me that more feminists aren't spending more of their time applauding and supporting both the democratic politics and the economic affluence that have made it possible.

Notes

1. This analysis derives from Neil M. Cowan and Ruth Schwartz Cowan, *Our Parent's Lives: Jewish Assimilation and Everyday Life* (New Brunswick: Rutgers University Press, 1996) but I believe it applies equally well to other immigrant groups of the early twentieth century and to the native born children and grandchildren of people who immigrated in the second half of the nineteenth century. See, Jeffrey Hart, *When the Going Was Good: American Life in the Fifties* (Westport, Conn.: Arlington House, 1982).

2. See, Lisle Abbot Rose, *The Cold War Comes to Main Street: America in the 1950s* (Lawrence: University of Kansas Press, 1996).

3. Many historians have explored the culture of the Cold War generations. I particularly recommend, Spencer Weart, *Nuclear Fear: A History of Images* (Cambridge: Harvard University Press, 1988); Paul S. Boyer, *Fallout: A Historian Reflects on America's Half-century Encounter with Nuclear Weapons* (Columbus: Ohio State University Press, 1998); Elaine Tyler May, *Homeward Bound: American Families in the Cold War Era* (New York: Basic Books, 1988); and Donald Katz, *Home Fires: An Intimate Portrait of One Middle Class Family in Postwar America* (New York: Harper Collins, 1992).

4. This analysis, the "dark side" of the Progressives, can be sampled in Paul Boyer, *Urban Masses and Moral Order in American, 1820-1920* (Cambridge: Harvard University Press, 1978); and Mark Haller, *Eugenics: Hereditarian Attitudes in American Thought*

(New Brunswick: Rutgers University Press, 1963).

5. The first shot over the bow of what later came to be called "the science wars" was Thomas Kuhn, *The Structure of Scientific Revolutions* (Chicago: University of Chicago Press, 1963). Kuhn, who was born in the 1920s, became distressed in the 1970s and 1980s about how younger scholars interpreted his work. For analyses of what later came to be called "the science wars" see: Steve Fuller, *Philosophy, Rhetoric and the End of Knowledge: The Coming of Science and Technology Studies* (Madison: University of Wisconsin Press, 1993); Steve Fuller, *Thomas Kuhn: A Philosophical History for Our Times* (Chicago: University of Chicago Press, 2000); Steven Brush, "Should History of Science Be Rated X?" *Science,* 183 (1975) 1164-83; and Paul Gross and Norman Levitt, *Higher Superstition: The Academic Left and Its Quarrels with Science* (Baltimore: Johns Hopkins University Press, 1994).

6. At the university in which I teach, a very popular professor created a course about fifteen years ago, called *Progress and Its Discontents.* For the first several years, many faculty—people who were then in middle age—volunteered to teach it. The course was recently dropped from the curriculum; younger faculty have no interest in the topic.

7. See, Joan Kelly-Gadol, "Did Women Have a Renaissance?" and Abby R. Kleinman, "Women in the Age of Light," in *Becoming Visible*, ed. Renata Bridenthal and Claudia Koonz (Boston: Houghton Mifflin, 1976), 137-64, 217-35.

8 . Many of these social scientific works can be sampled in Maggie Humm, ed., *Feminisms: A Reader* (London: Harvester Wheatsheaf, 1992) or June Sochen, ed., *The New Feminism in Twentieth-Century America* (Lexington, Mass.: D.C. Heath, 1971).

9. See, for example, Sheila Rowbotham, *Woman's Consciousness, Man's World* (Harmondsworth: Penguin, 1973); and Gerda Lerner, *The Creation of Patriarchy* (New York: Oxford University Press, 1986).

10. For a discussion and rebuttal of some of these theories, see Bonnie S. Anderson and Judith P. Zinsser, *A History of Their Own: Women in Europe from Prehistory to the Present*, vol. 1 (New York: Harper & Row, 1988), 3-24.

11. The classic text here is, Boston Women's Health Book Collective, *Our Bodies: Ourselves* (New York: Simon and Schuster, 1973) as well as the early volumes of the periodical, *Women & Health,* which began publication in 1976.

12. See, Rima Apple, *Mothers and Medicine: A Social History of Infant Feeding, 1890-1950* (Madison: University of Wisconsin Press, 1987).

13. This notion has its origin in James Mohr, *Abortion in America: The Origins and Evolution of National Policy* (New York: Oxford University Press, 1978), although it has been abstracted from its evidentiary base and popularized beyond recognition in many places.

14. See, for example, Ann Oakley, *The Captured Womb: A History of Antenatal Care in Britain* (Oxford: Blackwell, 1984); or Gena Corea, *The Hidden Malpractise: How American Medicine Mistreats Women as Patients and Professionals* (New York: Morrow, 1977).

15. The results of this research were reported in my book, *More Work for Mother: The Ironies of Household Technology from the Open Hearth to the Microwave* (New York:

Basic Books, 1983).

16. The classic work denigrating Sanger and her influence, is Linda Gordon, *Woman's Body, Woman's Right: A Social History of Birth Control in America* (New York: Grossman, 1976).

17. See both Ellen Chesler, *Woman of Valor: Margaret Sanger and the Birth Control Movement in America* (New York: Simon & Schuster, 1992); and Carole McCann, *Birth Control Politics in the United States, 1916-1945* (Ithaca: Cornell University Press, 1994).

Chapter 20

Information Technology and Progress

Andrew C. Gordon and Tom Martin

Introduction

There is often much to be learned from everyday events gone awry, even slightly awry. Fissures are revealed and opportunities emerge to learn little discussed truths about the thin veneer coating of our social system. A personal experience a few years ago was enlightening in these ways about society and technology.

We had stopped for a quick hamburger at a McDonald's restaurant—symbol of successful American capitalism—and were surprised at the length of each of the five service lines. There were at least six people in each line, and the disquiet in the restaurant was palpable. Naturally, we headed toward the shortest line.

The customer in front of us turned around to complain that everything had ground to a halt "because the computer was down." It took us awhile to absorb the weight of that simple statement: something as straightforward as ordering a hamburger had become nearly impossible because "the computer was down."

The customers soon learned that the workers that day knew very little about how much individual food items cost because they didn't have to: the "cash register" in front of them was really a computer terminal. When the computer was working, all the order-takers had to do was push the button displaying a picture of what was ordered—say a "Big Mac"—and the order was entered and signaled to the cooks. They didn't need to add or multiply because if, for example, someone wanted two Big Macs, the employee simply had to press the "2" button after pressing the "Big Mac" button. The computer transmitted the order to the cooks and performed the required math. They also need not ever have learned how to make change. If customers handed order-takers a ten-dollar bill and they typed "10" into their terminals, the correct change was immediately displayed for them. Without this computerized assistance, we all learned (to their clear embarrassment) how little these employees knew about the details of their job—or even about basic math. (Our line was quicker, it turned out, only because the order taker was carrying her calculator from school.)

For the McDonald's corporation, which experiences an annual staff turnover well over 200 percent and more,[1] the computer terminals reduce errors and provide instantaneous signals not only to the cooks but also, through complex computer networking, to corporate headquarters about the relative popularity of each product in each restaurant. This computerized solution enables the corporation and franchises to hire people at almost any skill level and ensure smooth operation.

At the same time, this apparently efficient management tool also reduces the few opportunities afforded to McDonald's employees to learn about the fast-food business, or even to practice rudimentary math and language skills.

This story is particularly relevant to our paper because it introduces a number of themes worth further exploration, including how ubiquitous computer use has become, how heavily we have come to rely on these technologies, and whose interests are best served as computers are increasingly deployed.

Everyone can agree that computers provide a clear sign of technological progress in creating and disseminating information, and that the speed of that progress has accelerated in recent years. What is also clear is that the associated benefits of technological change—at almost every step of the way—have accrued first and most to the already advantaged, the well educated, the visionary, the powerful. The extent to which the less advantaged and the truly disadvantaged have benefited has depended on the existence, determination, and skill of people who work to minimize social and economic disparities. Despite panglossian claims to the contrary, the age of the computer and the Internet follows the same pattern.

This paper outlines a brief history of transforming communication technologies. It also describes many instances in which the newest technologies have been used to take steps toward human progress by minimizing disparities, and other instances where new technologies have had unintended consequences or have been subverted by a few wishing to create chaos for others.

From Moveable Type and the Printing Press to Computers and the Internet

In discussing a broad topic like human progress, a long-term perspective is often necessary. We need to reserve our judgments until society has had enough time to absorb the effects of a transformational development. To keep matters in perspective, it might be useful to chart a partial history of the major communications advancements throughout human history.

c. 100,000 to 50,000 B.C.—The voice boxes and brains of our pre-human ancestors developed to a point sufficient for language to emerge
c. 50,000 B.C.—The first evidence of abstract visual representation, in the form of cave paintings
c. 3,000 B.C.—The first writing systems emerged in Mesopotamia
c. 1,700 B.C.—The first known printing device created on Crete (lost before it amounted to much)
c. 800 A.D.—Block printing, using movable type, developed in China (similar to the Cretan idea, but this time it stuck)
c. 1455 A.D.—Johannes Gutenberg invents the printing press
c. 1830 A.D.—The telegraph is invented
c. 1850 A.D.—Mass circulating newspapers appear

From the advent of speech onward, new tools of communication have helped to advance the survival and status of those who have mastered or controlled them. The first human beings to develop language probably gained a tactical advantage over other humans (or protohumans) in the search for food, or in battles between rival groups.

The Guttenberg printing press, incorporating moveable type, is among the technological breakthroughs most often remarked on, the importance of which may be attributed to the ways in which this mid-fifteenth century device ended the scarcity of books and therefore the monopoly on written knowledge and literacy possessed by society's elites, particularly royalty and the Church. But few envisioned the profound impact the printing press would have in enabling such a wide distribution of knowledge and thereby upending long established social hierarchies.

Often with technological advances only a handful of people grasp what is truly distinctive about a new technology, and those few frequently reap the early advantages. For example, the electric telegraph is an information technology that some understood far better than others when it was first introduced. Its development in the 1830s and 1840s on both sides of the Atlantic, and the ways in which it facilitated the expansion of the railroad, profoundly altered the course of human communication.

On a trip across the Atlantic from Europe to the United States in 1832, in pursuit of his career as a painter, Samuel Morse entered into a conversation about electromagnets when a knowledgeable fellow passenger declared that electricity can pass instantaneously through wires of any length. Morse is reported to have said, "If the presence of electricity can be made visible in any desired part of the circuit, I see no reason why intelligence might not be instantaneously transmitted by electricity to any distance."[2]

In this comment, Morse seized on telegraphy's most significant departure from the past—one which forever changed the way information was spread: it was the first technology in the history of communication where the *message arrived before the messenger*. The implications of this breakthrough were far-reaching. Before the electronic telegraph[3] and the advent of the railroad (an "older" but still fledgling technology), for example, many economies were locally bounded, with tight coordination only required among those people who were quite near one another in space. Before the telegraph, Wisconsin had thirty-nine time zones, and Michigan had twenty-seven.[4] But with the arrival of the railroad, there had to be a more generally agreed upon time when the train was going to come and go, and the telegraph, bearing "news" arriving nearly instantaneously from throughout the country, led to more commonly shared understandings of what *was* news, of what was important to know, and therefore promoted a homogenization of social perceptions across the nation.[5]

The reach of the telegraph likewise tended to diminish the importance of local events. Before the widespread availability of the telegraph, newspapers were typically dominated by local events (weddings, funerals, advertisements, etc.) and otherwise dated reports of news from elsewhere. But with telegraphy came news syndicates (the Associated Press was formed in New York in 1848, for example) and instantaneous bulletins of crucial news from distant places. With this immediate, far-flung access, some have argued, came the diminished importance of "the very centrality of [local] community." As Griffity has written about the changes the telegraph brought to Willem Allen White's *Emporia Gazette* in Kansas in the 1920s,

> Emporians could no longer gain the impression from reading their local newspaper that Emporia—or their own lives—mattered much in the scheme of things.... [They] may also have been aware of a concomitant waning of a sense of the legitimacy of their day-to-day lives. For, rather than focusing on local events, the paper dramatized far-away people and places. Instead of recording the life passage of their neighbors, it reported the abnormality of strangers.[6]

Because of the expense of the infrastructure, the telegraph was at first beyond the reach of ordinary people, except as an occasional indulgence for a particularly important message. Telephones, too, were largely the playthings of the rich when they were first introduced. But people soon realized the increasing value of telephones if they were in the hands of many people, and telephonic communication quickly became a medium, unlike the telegraph, by which ordinary citizens could send and receive their own messages, and promote their own causes. One of the most important features distinguishing the telephone, once well established, was that it no longer required a "telegraph operator"—an intermediary at each end to enable individual connections—a form of "disintermediation" that becomes even more profound with the Internet.

Technical Progress: Smaller, Faster, Cheaper

Computerization is but another major step in the history of developments in information technology. While people typically speak of advances in computers, it is more accurate to speak of advances in microprocessors. The "computers" most people refer to, even the smallest, are actually relatively enormous devices surrounding a much smaller microprocessor (often referred to as the CPU, or Central Processing Unit) which interprets strings of ones and zeros (bits, or binary digits). The rest of what is typically called the "computer" is a constellation of ancillary devices for information storage and for getting information into the CPU and out into other formats.

The first electronic computers were invented during the 1940s[7] and were of great importance to the war effort. Large, slow, unreliable, energy hogs[8] which required huge investments in maintenance and personnel, they utilized vacuum tubes to distinguish the functional equivalent of ones and zeros. Transistors—far smaller and more reliable semiconductor-based devices also capable of binary (on, off) signals—were invented at Bell Labs in 1947, and enabled the development of computing as we know it today. Enormous multiples in the power of microprocessors, even while they have become increasingly miniaturized, have contributed to their ubiquity.

In 1965, Gordon Moore observed that the number of transistors per square inch on integrated circuits had doubled every year, and predicted that this would continue for the foreseeable future. The estimate, now widely known as Moore's Law,[9] was revised to anticipate a doubling of computing power every eighteen months rather than every twelve, a still enormous pace that has continued to this day.

As self-evident as the general utility of computers may seem to us now, it was hardly transparent to the initial developers. In 1943, Thomas Watson, widely respected head of IBM (then a calculator manufacturer) declared, "I think there is a world market for maybe five computers." In *Popular Mechanics* magazine of 1949 a forecast predicted, "Computers in the future may weigh no more than 15 tons." And as recently as 1977, Ken Olson, the esteemed founder of Digital Equipment Corporation (DEC), is quoted as saying that "There is no reason anyone would want a computer in their home."

In a commentary on their attempt to interest the computer industry in his and Steve Wozniak's first Apple personal computer, Steve Jobs has reflected, "We went to Atari and said, 'Hey, we've got this amazing thing, even built with some of your parts, and what do you think about funding us? Or we'll give it to you. We just want to do it. Pay our salary, we'll come work for you.' And they said, 'No.' So then we went to Hewlett-Packard, and they said, 'Hey, we don't need you, you haven't got through college yet.'"[10]

The conceptions of these highly competent corporate giants were limited to "computers" similar in size, expense, and range of use to which then-current devices were put. But as before in the history of technology, breakthroughs in functionality came from people who were able to see well beyond current use.[11] Thus, for example, while the initial computers were used for numerical analysis, some people envisioned their value for text processing. When most people perceived that the kinds of information computers could deal with were limited to numbers (and then letters), a few others realized that binary digits were subject to no such inherent limitation, and could be used to represent many other "data types" including pictures, colors, sounds, and so on, with increasing fidelity as newer devices developed to rapidly process ever-more complex strings of bits.

Nor is there any reason to believe that we are even approaching the end of a chain of developments. Current technical projects include extensions of "data types" to smell and touch, and of miniaturization to the atomic and molecular level. (The emerging field of nanotechnology focuses on the design of molecular electronic circuits.) Recently developed micro-micro computer chips, capable of solving 400 million equations in a fifth of a second, will soon make it possible to speak into any telephone and have one's words translated instantaneously into another language. Such technological innovations, for good or ill, could conceivably lead to content that can be obtained through visual and voice cues, thereby allowing people to gain information while bypassing the intermediate step of achieving literacy.

But as one wag has observed, none of this "progress" ensures attention to every detail: "If cars experienced the same technological progress as computers, they would get 400 miles per gallon, have 40,000 horsepower, cost under $500, and blow up at least once per week killing all occupants."[12]

The Internet

As rapidly as the integrated circuit and the personal computer were disseminated, nothing prepared observers for the blinding speed with which the Internet became widely available once it caught on. What we know now as the Internet began as a United States Defense Department funded technology that allowed early users to communicate with one another and to share one another's computing resources. Established in 1969 as the U.S. Defense Department's Advanced Research Project Agency Network (ARPANET), this networking strategy at first connected a very small number of research institutions.

For years the number of computers ("nodes") on the network remained severely limited. At that stage, it has been described as a plaything shared by scientists who were willing to put up with the arcane language this early network required of them. (Early users report that the network was as popular among scientists for the early "e-mail" it enabled them to share as for the extra computing power it afforded.)

Here is a complete, four-node map of the "Internet" months after it was first devised, but barely thirty years ago:

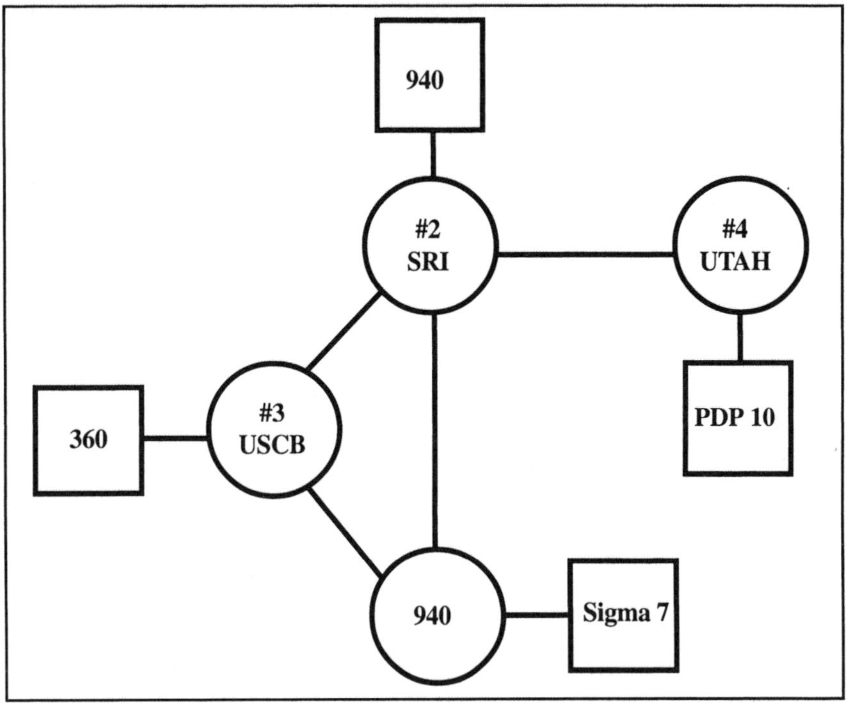

Schematic of Four-Node ARPANET, soon after the network was established.

By the 1970s, as more networks came to be connected to the ARPANET, network architects promoted the value of accepting a single networking standard. TCP/IP (Transfer Control Protocol/Internet Protocol), a suite of protocols initially outlined by Cerf and Kahn[13] in 1974, was adapted as that single standard in 1983. Every computer connected to the Internet utilizes TCP/IP, with an agreed upon addressing scheme which uniquely identifies each machine.

The acceptance of this standard on a "packet switched" backbone enabled computers to be linked to one another in such a way that complex messages could be disassembled into small "packets" consisting entirely of ones and zeros. One remarkable consequence of this networking strategy, coupled with the processing capacity of recent personal computers, is that the wherewithal required for someone to become a *producer* of information on the Internet—as well as a *consumer*—is now widely available. The profound implications of this radical disintermediation are explored further in this paper.

The growth of the Internet has been so rapid that reliable estimates of the number of host computers (much less individual users) are no longer possible. One source estimates that the number of computers connected to the Internet with a unique address now approaches 175 million, more than 200 times the number a decade ago.[14] As expansive as the predictions of Internet growth have been, estimates typically have to be adjusted upwards.

The period from the first powerful but unreliable vacuum tube devices to the present level of penetration and dependence on microprocessors has spanned only a few decades, and yet in that time the reach of computerization has extended beyond anyone's ability to grasp.

Oh, the Things that It Brings

The potential of these developments for enriching education for all, and providing additional opportunities for traditionally disenfranchised groups, both in the United States and abroad, is enormous. Consider the following wide-ranging examples.

Deeper Learning Experiences

Among the most thoughtful and visionary implementations of information technology is the JASON Project. Now in its fifth year, JASON utilizes advanced information technologies not only to collect scientific data but also to enable schoolchildren connected via electronic links to experience environments that would otherwise be unavailable to them. "Expeditions" to Hawaiian mountain streams and volcanoes to rainforests and the deep ocean with Internet connections featuring audio and video, and designed with a keen sensitivity to the interests of children, provide immersion in worlds that have never been explored. These opportunities, including "real-time" Remotely Operated Vehicles (ROVs), soon to be equipped with force-feedback devices so children can "feel" the sand the vehicles touch, and inspire scientific curiosity and a "bonding with the environment," according to Robert Ballard, the leader of this assembly of projects.

Ballard, who has spent his life exploring the ocean depths and who promotes the educational and scientific advantages of these new approaches, says that being connected via the Internet is "better than being there—you can go deeper, farther, stay longer" without being hemmed in by the "limitations" of the human body.[15]

Considering the implications of this and other expansive deployments of information technology, some observers believe that the potentials of new technologies to reshape human experience and the ways we interact with the world and with one another are so profound that eventually these "interfaces" will compete with physical reality itself. Jeff Bezos, founder of Amazon.com, has made comparative statements one could never have conceived of a few years ago: "The physical world is still the best medium ever invented. It's a great way to do things. [However,] it does have a few unfortunate limitations."[16]

Telemedicine

The strategic deployment of information technology enables advanced but scarce medical resources to be made widely available. For example, heart patients who live far from appropriate specialists and who experience mobility difficulties can have their pacemakers monitored over the phone, with an affordable technician collecting data, and specialists available when abnormalities are detected.

In another example, a 1996 project at Charles R. Drew University in South Central Los Angeles launched a pilot telemedicine project in which people with eye problems are seen in local clinics by technicians and first year ophthalmology residents. The images are sent over high-speed digital lines to a board-certified ophthalmologist who can "speak to the patient over a real-time video connection, prescribe a treatment, and schedule a more intensive in-person examination if necessary." The model, which allows scarce specialists to make "highly accurate diagnoses," has been replicated in three additional clinics monitoring 2,300 people, "many of whom would otherwise have experienced severe visual impairment or blindness."[17]

International Relief Efforts

After Hurricane Mitch hit Central America in the fall of 1998, two thousand refugees of the disaster were gathered near a cultural center in a Honduran village, equipped with scanty shelter, food, and clothing. The center was able to send a fax to a non-governmental organization (NGO) in the capital about the desperate situation there. The wired NGO then submitted notice on a listserv, where the news reached a Washington D.C. group, the Committee for Honduran Relief, who responded with the news that they would send fifteen thousand dollars for relief supplies. The exchange took place within four hours.[18]

Because time is typically such a critical factor in disaster relief, increased efficiency of communication can simply save lives. Humanitarian aid efforts also increasingly depend on the technologies for inventory and distribution of relief supplies, as well as coordination between agencies. Healthnet, for example, has developed networks of healthcare professionals in Asia, Latin America, and Africa to help procure supplies cheaply, and to quickly share information in times of outbreak.[19]

In another major effort following the ravages of Hurricane Mitch, a cooperative venture is bringing solar energy, Internet access emphasizing wireless technology, and a variety of related services to remote Honduran villages. Starting with the "most poverty stricken and least accessible" village in the southern region of Honduras, and using satellite links to the Internet, solar-powered computers and solar generators, this joint venture between OnSat, the Honduran government, agencies of the United Nations and other parties, is attempting to demonstrate the health, educational, and related advantages that can flow even to the most isolated regions of Latin America once they have sustainable connections to the world's communications infrastructure.[20]

Solar-powered computers being delivered by burro to Honduran village

Maintaining Cultural Connections

The Internet has been utilized to establish a "strong virtual network" among the Tatar Diaspora, who have been dislocated under oppressive regimes since 1793. Entirely built and maintained by Crimean Tatars since the mid-1990s, their Internet presence has enabled participants to stay connected with one another, to publicize their cause through electronic discussion lists and Web sites, as well as facilitating their international fundraising.[21]

The diaspora has many faces: Mongolians working in a Wal-mart in rural Arkansas regularly come as a family to a public library to connect with their community of Mongols via websites and e-mail—outings and connections clearly important to them and otherwise unavailable.[22]

Giving Voice to the Underdog

Tehelka ("News. Views. All the Juice") investigates corruption in India and throughout Southeast Asia, publishing "well-researched, well-documented exposés" of "rot" in high places. Their information surely wouldn't be widely available if it weren't for the Internet. And they report proudly when their initially belittled investigative reports are vindicated in major media.[23]

Providing Locally Relevant Information

In Madhya Pradesh, India, a software developer and local government officials teamed up to establish Gyandoot, a program bringing needed information and economic opportunities to both small-scale entrepreneurs and rural villagers. The entrepreneurs each buy a computer, a printer, and a connection to a local Intranet from Gyandoot, and in turn sell locally relevant information they receive from the Intranet to customers paying nominal fees. The operation allows villagers to bypass middlemen to obtain crop prices for local markets, government records, and other information. Other services include e-mail, a net-based market for villagers who want to sell goods, computer classes, and even marriage broker services for parents wanting to find good matches for their children.[24]

In a project of the M.S. Swaminathan Foundation in Pondicherry, India, voice recordings (saved as MP3 files) are sent to a group of rural villages requiring those at either end to only know how to click, open, and listen to the messages sent. The technology has helped local villagers gain speedy access to doctors and veterinarians. Landless women obtain farm labor insurance, fishermen obtain warnings about weather conditions and fish migration patterns (potentially life saving information, they aver), and farmers get price information that helps them to bargain with unscrupulous middlemen.[25]

Other versions of community technology centers exist all over the world. They come in a variety of shapes and sizes with varying degrees of local control, community relevance, and participation. Examples of successful models flourish in such far-flung places as Niger, Uganda, and Senegal.[26]

Poverty Alleviation and Technology: Grameen Telecom

Grameen Telecom in Bangladesh provides perhaps the best documented example of using communication technologies for poverty alleviation. The company leases phones to rural women on credit, securing only a promise from the women that they will pay for the phone within three years. The women then use the phones as the basis of microenterprises, charging fees to villagers who use the phones to make business and personal calls. The women pay off the phones in monthly installments until they own them outright.

The project has brought telecommunications technology to parts of the country that were previously without telephone service. The connectivity has reportedly helped law enforcement efforts, as well as preparation for and response to natural disasters.

One fourth of the users of the phones are rural poor. Besides communicating with distant family members and friends, they use the phones to obtain medical information and to verify market prices for the goods they buy and sell (thereby reducing the likelihood they will be fleeced by unprincipled intermediaries). For the "phone-ladies" themselves, the devices have proven to be quite lucrative money makers. The effective deployment of the phones has helped some of the village women surmount traditional socioeconomic and cultural barriers, shaking up the status quo and giving a new group some economic clout. About 1,500 phone-ladies existed in Bangladesh in 1998 and Grameen's goal is to increase that number to 68,000 by 2007.[27]

Persistent Development of Affordable Devices and Thoughtful Implementations

In the developing world, *adaptation* of technologies is often preferred to the *development* of technologies, with an emphasis on how to achieve an appropriate level of benefit while minimizing costs so the technologies become affordable. A group of engineers from the Indian Institute of Technology in Bangalore, for example, recently introduced the Simputer, "the poor man's hand-held computer," specifically to meet the needs of rural villages. While not yet commercially available (they hope to license the technology to manufacturers for production by Spring 2002), the estimated cost for the device will be less than $200—within the budgets of some locally based NGOs, government agencies, and cooperative associations working on integrated rural development strategies.

The Simputer can run on AAA batteries, a more viable energy source in remote regions than a temperamental (or nonexistent) electricity grid. In a country where fifty percent of the population cannot read or write, the Simputer incorporates graphic and voice-based interfaces that would enable a user to translate English to a local language, which the computer would then read aloud to the user. The Simputer also allows numerous users to store their information separately (suitable for multiuse and multiusers in a village context).[28]

International Distribution Channels for Regional Goods Produced in Poor Countries

There are numerous examples of using the Internet to bring products from developing countries to markets around the globe. The Fair Trade Federation, Global Exchange, Crafts Center, PEOPLink, and GreenMarketplace.com are among the many organizations that advertise and sell products of the developing world on their sites. Some start up on their own and others benefit from strategic partnerships. Novica, in conjunction with *National Geographic*, for example, uses the

Internet to distribute hand-made goods from "1,700 extraordinary artists" in developing regions throughout the world (the Andes, Bali and Java, Brazil, Cuba, India, Mexico, Thailand, and West Africa).

Subsidization by social change organizations is still largely necessary to overcome the red tape and trust issues that would make international e-commerce sustainable in the market. And, despite the dot-com bottom out in 2001, there is hope that e-commerce may still have the potential to help reinvigorate developing economies. One successful example, according to a recent report by the United Nations Conference on Trade and Development, is Ethiogift.com, an Ethiopian company which generated fifty thousand dollars in revenues in 2000 by selling flowers, gifts, spirits—and sheep—online.[29]

Building More Personal Connections for Money Transfer

While the Internet hasn't spawned massive increases in new philanthropic giving, a few of the countless attempts to make use of the new medium are worth noting. The Hunger Site raised donations of over fifteen thousand metric tons of food between its inception in June 1999 and October 2001. Web surfers can simply "click" once a day on the site, and for each click, sponsors donate a cup of food to hunger relief agencies (in return for free advertising).[30] Netaid.org, a joint project of Cisco Systems and the United Nations Development Programme, raised over $3 million in two years to support poverty alleviation efforts, enabling them to provide information on poverty issues and a service linking online volunteers to organizations throughout the world.[31]

Local organizations, too, can overcome geography to reach distant donors by using the Web. Fundaschool, launched by the government of Madhya Pradesh, India, to fund the establishment of new schools in underserved areas. Donors can peruse descriptions of the schools, choose which one(s) they want to sponsor, and in return receive photographs of the children and their quarterly academic reports. Donors from as far away as the United States, Kuwait, and Switzerland funded more than 300 schools through this online effort, in effect using the horizontal medium to cut through the red tape of organizational hierarchy and impersonality.[32]

The Flip Side

These are but a few examples of the innovative use of new technology. By extension, observers often suggest that widespread computerization can only result in profound progress for all. Indeed, optimistic, world-shaping consequences of new technologies for "linking us together" and illustrating our "common humanity" have been predicted for hundreds of years. When the telegraph cable under the Atlantic was finished, for example, the *Times of London* opined that, "The Atlantic is dried up, and we become in reality as well as in wish one country. The Atlantic Telegraph has half undone the Declaration of 1776 and has gone far to make us once again, in spite of ourselves, one people."[33] Others foresaw the inevitable end of war—that the electric telegraph would "make muskets into candlesticks."[34]

But many of the efforts described above are pilot projects, whose consequences, replicability, and long-range viability are still largely unknown. And the disadvantages of the new technologies are to many equally profound, if less easily perceived, and illustrate that progress is by no means inevitable.

Free Computers Have Costs

In the midst of our working diligently in an earlier project to encourage computer companies to donate used equipment to small, local organizations to support their community building activities, a student who helped with the initial installations prepared a memo entitled "The cost of free computers." Robert LeBailly[35] achieved the critical distance on our activities to make several important points, including these:

> • The "free" computers were often given away *for a reason*—besides the tax breaks to the bequeathing companies, the computers were typically of an earlier generation, which can be a fundamental problem when software evolves so quickly that current applications cannot be run.
>
> • The machines were often incomplete, and not "quite" in working order, which implied either that money had to be found to repair them or human effort expended to get them to work. Merely assuring that the machines worked predictably and well could exhaust the resources of a small non-profit organization.[36]
>
> • More elusive, but perhaps more important, the gifts hardly ever included resources for additional personnel, and these machines typically went to organizations with few people and limited budgets. To the extent that personnel are redirected toward dealing with the machines rather than with their established mission, organizations may be deflected from the very reasons they were initially established. More insidiously, their work may evolve to become what the computers are capable of doing well, often undermining rather than facilitating the organization's core mission.

Implementation—Reading the Small Print

New technologies are often introduced as panaceas, with the expectation that they will not only solve existing problems, but will also launch organizations on highly desirable new paths.[37] We conducted one study focused on the impact of one of these new paths—telecommuting—in major organizations in the Puget Sound region of the state of Washington.[38]

The study turned out to be as much about the dysfunction of current office settings as about the potential of telecommuting. Sponsoring companies thought that high speed lines were required in order for a person to "telecommute" successfully from home, but in fact many telecommuters didn't use their "telecommuting" days to sign on to a company network. Instead, free of the meetings that interrupt focused work in the office, they used the day to "get work done." Office based co-workers sometimes reported that they, too, accomplished more on *other people's* telecommuting days, because those were days when meetings couldn't be scheduled. (In a perceptive early consideration of related issues, Weizenbaum describes how early computers arrived "just in time" to enable the overburdened U.S. welfare system to continue to deliver welfare checks without rethinking their mission.)[39]

Information Overload

An overwhelming variety of sources is available to information consumers at the click of a button, without any readily available guidelines to sort the wheat from the chaff. Internet search engines vary in the algorithms they employ, but none facilitate quality assurance. Searching for "holocaust" with various search engines, for example, will turn up from hundreds to thousands of sources, each list a cacophony of holocaust research, holocaust deniers, and idiosyncratic sources. Sorting the good from the bad, the verified from the unverified, the trivial from the profound, can be extremely perplexing—and ultimately impossible for most.

Even if we were able to choose among the sources sensibly, there's too much information, and it's coming at us too fast to absorb or to manage. The incredible pace of the information society sometimes seems to have rendered time—to ponder, to absorb, to deliberate—an endangered species.

To many observers, the ramifications of this overload are among the most significant of our modern age. Todd Oppenheimer[40] and others have argued, for example, that whatever the promise of computer and Internet access in schools, the reality typically is a shift from an emphasis on the capacity to learn to an emphasis on the glitzier features of the new technologies, often introduced without teaching the "information literacy" skills required to utilize these new tools effectively. Students are awash in unprocessed information, and teachers are deflected from their educational mission.

Psychologist David Lewis theorizes that these aspects of the information age may negatively impact our health. "Information Fatigue Syndrome,"[41] he suggests, may result in symptoms of tension, ill health, increased anxiety, poor memory, and poor attention span.

The health—even the survival—of the planet is also at risk. As we have noted, microchips are now embedded in an endless variety of devices, from cars to refrigerators—to weapons of mass destruction. Technology enhanced weapons with potentially earth-shattering consequences can be hidden in suitcases or travel thousands of miles in minutes, requiring world leaders—still mere humans—to make the most far-reaching decisions before they have the opportunity to process the information themselves, much less the opportunity for meaningful consultation.

Cultural Invasion

Ideally, the Internet can contribute to culture survival if cultural contexts (languages, images, etc.) are maintained. But with over seventy percent of the content of the World Wide Web in English, the demand for Western (and in particular, American) culture is only likely to increase. Furthermore, with the sheer number of voices competing for attention, it is unlikely that the small voice of a less spoken language will have any significant sway in the sea of information that is the Internet. Thus, for example, the Maori of New Zealand and some Native American groups believe that the Internet provides an opportunity for others to collect and distribute data on their cultures "with astounding speed"—information which can reinforce "the most negative stereotypes." A recent exploration of this issue argues that this "pillaging" is not deliberate, but a by-product of the imbalance in who controls this or any other new medium where histories and stories are disseminated by others "who have no stake in the integrity or survival [of other cultures]."[42] On the one hand, the Internet enables even the smallest, most isolated voice to get its message out. On the other hand, the din of competing messages, and speed with which "disinformation" can be spread by forces that may have little interest in preserving the legitimate message of these small voices, have multiplied as well.

Information Repression

While the Internet can be used to open up whole new information vistas, access is often suppressed or controlled in authoritarian or semi-authoritarian regimes. Some examples: The Burmese government prevents popular access to the Internet and forbids the use of fax machines and satellite dishes. Saudi Arabia and the United Arab Emirates utilize ambitious censorship schemes to control the political and social impact of the Internet.[43]

The Chinese government has been repeatedly lambasted for the ways in which it attempts to control the information available to its citizens. (The 1989 Tienanmien Square episode is often described as well known in the West only because of fax machines.) On September 10, 2001, after the Chinese were awarded the Olympics, a citizen (Zhu Ruixiang) was sentenced to three years in prison for forwarding e-mail news bulletins to twelve friends inside China. The messages were deemed "reactionary." E-mail messages are often destroyed and bulletin boards shut down because of complaints about the government imposing regulations which declare that it is "illegal to publish materials that negate the guiding role of Marxism and Leninism . . . go against the guiding principles, official line, or policies of the Communist Party... or...violate party propaganda discipline."[44]

Increased Resource Consumption

Quicker access to information seems at first blush to be an unalloyed positive. In a society predicated on competition, quicker information retrieval inevitably feeds back into the race for increased production. But, aside from its effect on the worker, who must produce ever greater quantities to stay competitive,[45] the quicker coordination of market forces also accelerates the pace of resource exploitation and, inevitably, environmental degradation.

Discerning the appropriate places to apply information is more important than indiscriminately increasing the speed with which we access it. If we continue to apply information as imperfectly as our markets and governments do now, the increased "efficiency" of information retrieval will continue to feed inefficiencies that exist within our economic systems, perhaps undermining our natural resource base beyond repair.

Inequality at Every Turn

The "digital divide"—the gap between those who have and do not have access to communications technologies—continues to receive widespread attention in the United States and abroad. Some take the minimization of this inequality extremely seriously, stating, for example, that access to digital technology is a human right. (In 2001, Estonia became the first country in the world to define access to the Internet as a fundamental right.)[46]

But meaningful access to these technologies implies a number of preconditions which much of the world is far from achieving. For those of us who are among the planet's most advantaged citizens, the Internet serves an endless array of functions—as an efficient postal service, an instantaneous mail order catalog, and the world's biggest library. Of course, to use it, one first needs electricity, telephone connectivity, access to a computer, and some skills. If one speaks English and is a middle or upper class resident of a developed country, the barriers are few. The less affluent might have to turn to a local public library for access, but information technology is nevertheless unavailable in many of the poorest parts of the world.

The information gap hardly began with current technologies. While the grand schemes described earlier in this paper are playing out, *an estimated 50 percent of the world's population has never used a telephone*. Contemporary investors cannot be expected to put much effort in bringing information technologies to the rural poor unless they believe it will further their own economic interests. Profits resulting from such ventures, if successful, would concentrate even greater amounts of wealth in the pockets of investors, by and large benefiting the wealthiest citizens and societies. In other words, extending the horizontal infrastructures of the information economy within the current rules of the market will continue to produce greater vertical power distances between rich and poor. As economic power becomes more concentrated, the outlook for the poor, whether related to the digital divide, the food and water divide, or the political representation divide, may continue to deteriorate.

Progress? It Depends on Where You Sit

In highly developed or in developing countries, in schools, businesses or in homes, it has been repeatedly demonstrated that the meaning of technology not only from the perspective of the group, but also from the perspective of individual users. A study of computer implementation in police departments[47] vividly illustrated that no matter how sensible the deployment of a new technology may be if one understands the stated organization mission, what seems to matter most is the meaning of the technology in the individual lives of its intended users. A Geographic Information System designed for the Chicago Police Department was apparently well received as a technique to enable patrol officers, detectives, and other police personnel to share what they had learned about crimes they were attempting to solve. But the police were far more reluctant to put information into the system than expected. Despite the rhetoric of sharing, officers were commended or promoted *as individuals* on the basis of crimes they solved *as individuals*, and the incentives for hoarding information vastly exceeded any incentives for sharing information with others who might then be able to solve the crime "on their own." Until these incentives are dramatically revised, large-scale use of this or similar systems remains unlikely.

As is made apparent repeatedly in Suchman's work,[48] one cannot understand the real value of information technology, for good or ill, without understanding it in the context of the organization and the individuals of which it is comprised. In short, it "depends on where you sit."

Case in Point: The Zapatista "Netwar"

On January 1, 1994 (the moment the North American Free Trade Agreement went into effect), the Zapatista uprising against the authority of the Mexican government in Chiapas, Mexico began. The events that followed have been described as the first "post-modern" revolution. Others describe it as the first "social netwar."[49]

Calling for the rights of indigenous peoples to self-determination, the Zapatistas used the new medium of the Internet to plead their case to international civil society, and they called the people of the world to come to Chiapas to bear witness to their claims. Defenders of human and indigenous rights swarmed on Chiapas, at times standing as physical buffers between the Mexican Army and peace negotiations. The Internet-enabled mobilization, and the public relations nightmare that it created for the Mexican government, almost certainly precluded the Mexican Army from using swift, overpowering force to suppress the insurrection. Instead, a protracted propaganda war, much of it waged online, ensued.

The netwar did not put an end to the violence, nor (yet) lead to the realization of the Zapatistas' demands for indigenous autonomy. But the movement did profoundly affect public discourse in Mexico, and influence the reactions of the Mexican government, newly sensitive to its image at home and abroad. Indeed, the Zapatistas' able use of the medium may have contributed substantially to the chain of events that eventually led to the ousting of the Institutional Revolutionary Party—which had held power since 1929—in the 2000 elections.

For the traditional patriarchy that had strong interest in maintaining the existing social order, the Internet was perhaps a threat. For the dispossessed indigenous who had been marginalized by that social order, it was an opportunity. Did the technology produce progress? It depends on where you sit.

The New Philanthropy and Information Technology (IT) Wealth

In the past twenty years, information technologies have created vast new fortunes. The new IT wealthy seem to bring with them new ideas and new ways of doing philanthropy. Rob Glaser's many years of work to help progressive organizations take advantage of the potential of the Internet is one significant example of this new philanthropic spirit, as is Bill Gates' effort to eradicate disease in developing countries.

The evolution of Bill Gates' philanthropy also seems to suggest an important opportunity. Gates says that at the outset of his endeavors, he was naive about the issues of poverty and development. At first, he had faith that technology could be the deciding factor to turn the tide in the fight against poverty. As people became wired, they would become empowered and be able to share in the wealth created by knowledge and informational tools.

But over the past six years, Gates visited many people in remote corners of the world and personally bore witness to the meager and bare existence within which many human beings spend their lives. Connected to the global economy by only the thinnest of strands, possessing only the most meager control over information and material resources, these poorest of the poor, the 1.7 billion living below a dollar a day, were not in a position to leverage computer technology to great benefit—not, that is, in ways that might leverage food, water, medical care, capital, and education. In a significant conference among IT experts committed to improving world conditions for the world's poorest citizens, Gates made his perspective evident:

> Pacing the room, waving his hands, he [Bill Gates] conjures up an image of an African village that receives a computer. "The mothers are going to walk right up to that computer and say, 'My children are dying, what can you do?'.... They're not going to sit there and like, browse eBay or something. What they want is for their children to live. They don't want their children's growth to be stunted. Do you really have to put in computers to figure that out?"[50]

Gates' "conversion" has shown that donors who are sincere in their efforts can learn the real needs of the poor, rather than imposing on them their own preconceived solutions.

But despite the presence of a number of new and active philanthropists, poverty is holding tight in the world. Meanwhile, the disparity between the wealthy and the poor is growing, not decreasing. Perhaps IT philanthropists could play a leading role by applying their leverage to foster social and systemic changes needed to better distribute wealth. In any regard, how the new rich choose to use their power and wealth will be critical in determining whether information technology—and the wealth it creates—ultimately leads to greater social progress.

Into the Future

Zapatista netwar chronicler David Ronfeldt posited four major forms of human social organization—the tribe, the institution, the market, and, the most recent, the network—that have developed (and continue to develop) in different societies at different points in history. As each new form of social organization is superimposed over earlier forms, new identities emerge, along with inevitable conflicts and loyalties. No form is intrinsically better or worse than the others, but with the emergence of each new form, the complexity of our organizational life grows and the palette from which we draw our identities is enriched.[51]

The complex interconnections of the Internet provide a tangible depiction of the complexity that governs the phenomenological processes of our world. We increasingly use the Internet as a model for reshaping our perceptions, institutions, and organizations to reflect our growing appreciation for and understanding of that complexity. By providing both a technological infrastructure and a metaphor for interconnectivity, the Internet has helped to accelerate the emergence of the "network" form of social organization at a breathtaking pace.

Rather than viewing the Internet as good or bad, it might be more useful to consider it as a catalyst of change in a long evolution that has both positive and negative consequences. The network form, besides being more democratic in the participatory sense, also brings the potential for greater anarchy.

On September 11, 2001, violent and destructive forces on a massive scale were unleashed in the United States, with consequences that will continue to evolve for decades. Information technology has been implicated in these events and their aftermath in many complex and telling ways. For example, according to an account in *USA Today* from June 2001, months before the event, U.S. officials knew that Osama bin Laden was posting instructions for terrorist activities in sports chat rooms and on pornographic bulletin boards, with the messages hidden in typically ignored bits of the X-rated pictures and on posted comments. Their exploitation of specific characteristics of the technologies led one agent to say "They're thwarting the efforts of law enforcement to detect, prevent and investigate illegal activities."[52] Also, apparently the "terrorists" who took over the three planes

- regularly used public access computers in Florida libraries (including some we study) to plan their attack on the World Trade Center,
- ordered their airline tickets over the Internet (via Travelocity), and
- moved out of one motel because management was unable to guarantee them a twenty-four hour connection to the Internet.

And lest we forget how important communication technologies are to the practice of warfare, the "smart bombs" which minutely targeted al-Qaeda forces in Afghanistan while avoiding most—but by no means all—civilians were microprocessor equipped and equipped with their own internal computers.

But among the many other examples of the use of communication technologies are these:

- The passengers on the plane which broke apart in a Pennsylvania field were apparently reassured of their safety by the hijackers, but learned through their cell phones of the crashes into the World Trade Center, which led them to confront the hijackers and to deflect the plane from its intended target.
- "Digital mementos" of the victims of the bombings (e-mail, phone messages) are being preserved as permanent keepsakes by their family and friends.

Interesting commentaries are also being written about how Osama bin Laden's network models the "consensual anarchy" of the Web—with small, loosely connected cells dispersed to every continent, communicating only as necessary, analogous to a spider web except for lacking a central strand whose elimination guarantees the destruction of the network as a whole.[53]

For some observers, the complexity and competing consequences of this new technological environment have been evident for some time. For example, in a 1999 report from the United States Commission on national security in the twenty-first century, the authors, led by former U.S. Senators Gary Hart and Warren Rudman, declared that because of new technology, coupled with persistent disparities in income throughout the world, "Americans are now, and will increasing become, less secure than they believe themselves to be."[54]

In a prescient commentary on the implications of the relative lack of access to new technologies, the report also speculated that "Increasingly, the pockets of poverty amid wealth will be more closely interlaced than today. Some regions of the world are still almost entirely devoid of the accoutrements of the information revolution; the huge and densely populated area within a circle drawn at a radius of 1,600 miles around Kabul is an example."[55]

In the post-September 11th world, the traditional hierarchies of the institution and market are not powerless; quite the contrary. They have taken measures to control the anarchy (and possibly the democracy) inherent in this new environment, engaging in their own "counternetwar." In the wake of the attacks, the U.S. Congress has passed an anti-terror bill granting unprecedented police authority for Internet monitoring, and thereby drastically altering our previous notions of what constitutes civil liberties. The government also established an agreement with the five major U.S. television networks not to air unedited video propaganda efforts of Osama bin Laden. The United States shut down Somalia's only Internet provider because its parent company's financial businesses may have been used to funnel money to al-Qaeda, leaving the people of that impoverished nation without access.[56] Furthermore, the U.S. government has considered the development of an alternative Internet to insulate essential government services from the possibility of cyberattacks.[57]

As the authors of the Hart/Rudman report suggest, new technologies will divide the world as well as draw it together.

In Summary

Modern telecommunication makes globalization both possible and inevitable—for good or ill. As Thomas Friedman has said about globalization, modern telecommunication via the Internet "has both empowering and enriching features and disempowering and impoverishing features, and it all depends on how you manage it."[58]

New technological discoveries at this point in history are inevitable. Massive capital investments, the arrangements formulated by powerful leaders in politics and business, and the retooling of our social structures over the past two centuries have created infrastructures that will be used to build new technologies, come hell (i.e., ozone depletion) or high water (i.e., global warming). Our ancestors rolled the dice, set the wheels in motion, and we will have a white whale of a time trying to hedge the bets they placed. As a society, we ride along on this slipstream, sometimes questioning the process, sometimes kicking the dirt, but mostly just burying our heads and hoping for the best. However we react, we almost certainly understand the tremendous difficulty of resisting technological development.

There is some hope that information technology will improve society; but it won't do it alone. Arundhati Roy offers us the haunting image of emaciated workers in Delhi, India laying fiber optic cable by candlelight.[59] The technology itself may be value-neutral, but in its implementation we reinforce whatever social patterns we weave into its use and distribution.

Champions of the market regard social progress as a serendipitous byproduct of successful investment. The guiding principle of investment, however, is the potential for profit. People invest money where there is money to be made, and the profit potential of information technology, despite the burst of the dot-com bubble in 2001, still looms large on the horizon.

Investment is targeted to serve markets that have money to spend. Most investment in information technology necessarily aims for markets with significant disposable income. Whether the poorest of the poor—those most in need of attaining some degree of progress—would ever benefit from these exigencies of the "free" market is a matter of great debate. After all, although it has been with us for well over a century, half of the world is still waiting for the telephone to trickle down to them.

NGOs and governments may intercede to overcome these market failures. In fact, such intervention is probably essential if information technology is to contribute to the progress of the poor. Policies that promote the research, development, and dissemination of technologies tailored to benefit the poor are critical to these efforts.

Still, harsh climatic conditions, lack of technical support, inadequate telecommunications and electrical infrastructures, susceptibility to theft, prohibitive cost, and the constant need for equipment upgrades will conspire to limit the spread of information technologies to many places in the world. Although numerous pilot projects seek to overcome these hurdles, important opportunity costs still must be considered before public or philanthropic dollars are allocated for these purposes. After all, without enough donor funding to go around, what will the priorities be: clean water, vaccines, or computer labs?

Clearly, new methods of analysis are needed to make these decisions. Just as clearly, those most affected—the poor themselves—need to be included in the decision making processes. Those who set the standards and regulations for information technology add their own visions to the social code, and those who define the social code define progress.

Progress is a subjective determination, inevitably tied to one's identity and priorities. From this subjective seat, at this juncture in history, human progress seems to depend largely on increasing equality of opportunity and outcomes. Perhaps information technology's contribution to progress—as far as the poor and marginalized are concerned—will not be decided by the technology itself, but within more inclusive and effective decision making processes that govern its development and use.

While technological change brings new opportunity to members of society, it also brings increasing vulnerability to the social order. Computer viruses are the most pesky and persistent reminder of that vulnerability. Corporate and governmental communication, educational systems, medical devices, weapons verification and control, all increasingly count on a stable Internet—the same telecommunications system that terrorists use to send both open and coded messages to us and to one another. New technologies ensure that more crucial information—much of it requiring rapid decision making—comes our way than even assigned experts have the capacity to absorb or process.

But corralling destructive forces while also unleashing creative potential and furthering opportunities for human communion is as delicate and unpredictable a matter in communication policy as it is in the human soul. Society has no distinctive advantage over the unpredictability of nature if it does not learn to avoid cataclysm as well as share its misfortunes and joys equally. Policy prescriptions that seek to support and balance these two delicate goals depend, again, on sensitive and enlightened deliberative processes. Whether humankind is up to the task of developing and promoting these processes remains to be seen.

Quite simply, information technology is no panacea for the world's social problems. These tools are ultimately only as useful as the justice and purposefulness with which they are used. A computer won't allow us to bypass fundamental issues of justice and equality. Just as new technologies may help raise awareness on these fronts, they can also be used to hide information, exploit it for destructive purposes, or bury it in a vast swamp of banality. Our awe with the new technology may divert us from attending to the rules and practices that, at the end of the day, provide the moral frame of our society.

Ultimately, a universal definition of progress is impossible; it depends on where you sit. But for most, progress would probably include commitments to greater justice and less human misery. Technology is in itself value neutral; it will simply reflect the values with which we imbue it. Government and World Bank officials, Microsoft and McDonald's executives, and others vested with any degree of economic and political power have choices in how they will implement their information technologies, and to what end.

So do we all. The potential of technologies to create progress depends largely on the framework we set through our laws and our personal actions—as well as some lucky caroms or divine guidance as we weave through the unpredictability of time and space.

On individual, community, and societal levels, we choose the memes we want to nurture and propagate. We must choose thoughtfully if we are to survive—and to progress.

Notes

* Many thanks to Leigh Anderson, Margaret Gordon, Seth Gordon, and Janet Looney for their assistance in preparing this chapter.

1. Robin Leidner, *Fast Food, Fast Talk: Service Work and the Routinization of Everyday Life* (Los Angeles: University of California Press, 1993).

2. Quoted in Tom Standage, *The Victorian Internet* (New York: Walker and Co., 1998), 28.

3. The French had developed a far inferior "optical telegraph" in the late 1700s. Some commentators have speculated that their insistence of holding on to the optical telegraph despite the clear advantages of the electric variety, just as they clung to their late 1970s networking device, the Minitel, while others embraced the later but superior TCP/IP infrastructure, worked against them in the long run.

4. James Carey, "Technology and Ideology: The Case of the Telegraph," *Prospects* 8 (1983): 303.

5. See also, "An Historical Analysis Relating Causes to Effects," in U.S. Congress, Office of Technology Assessment, *Global Communications: Opportunities for Trade and Aid*, OTA-IC-642 (Washington D.C.: U.S. Congress, U.S. Government Printing Office, September 1995), appendix A.

6. From Richard Kielbowitz, "The Role of Communication in Building Communities and Markets," contractor report prepared for the Office of Technology Assessment, November 1987 as cited in "An Historical Analysis Relating Causes to Effects," in U.S. Congress, Office of Technology Assessment, *Global Communications: Opportunities for Trade and Aid*, OTA-IC-642 (Washington D.C.: U.S. Congress, U.S. Government Printing Office, September 1995), 169.

7. Mechanical devices which interpreted ones and zeros, such as Babbage's Analytic Engine (c. 1834) are significant to a comprehensive history but beyond the space available to us here.

8. It is perhaps an exaggeration, but one often repeated, that when the ENIAC, the first general purpose, vacuum tube-based computer, was turned on at the University of Pennsylvania in 1946, the lights in Philadelphia went dim.

9. This estimate originally appeared in Gordon Moore's "Cramming More Components Onto Integrated Circuits," *Electronics* 38, no. 8 (April 1965): 114-17.

10. See Mike Tuck, "The Real History of the GUI," *SitePoint,* 1998-2002, at www.webmasterbase.com/article/511/28 (accessed 12 December 2001).

11. Alan Kaye, a computer visionary by anyone's definition, turned Watson's idea around by declaring "the best way to predict the future is to invent it."

12. Unknown source.

13. See Barry M. Leiner, et al., "A Brief History of the Internet" *Internet Society,* 2000, at www.isoc.org/internet/history/brief.shtml (accessed 12 December 2001).

14. Katie Hafner, "The Internet's Invisible Hand," *New York Times*, 10 January 2002, (G1). The numbers vary dramatically by country, with estimates of 102 million "active Internet users" in the United States, fives times as many as Japan, the closest rival country.

15. See jasonproject.org. Quotes from Robert J. Ballard interview by Steve Scher on "Weekday," KUOW, 94.9 FM, Seattle, 14 June 2001.

16. Charles Fishman, "Face Time with Jeff Bezos," *Fast Company* 43 (February 2001): 80. One commentator has said of Bezos: "He is in the enviable position of being able to condescend to what we used to call 'reality'" See James Gleick, "Stop Me Before I Shop Again," *New Yorker,* Volume 75, Number 12 (May 24, 1999): 42-49.

17. Morino Institute, *From Access to Outcomes: Raising the Aspirations for Technology Initiatives in Low-Income Communities* (Reston, VA.: Morino Institute, July, 2001), 11.

18. United Nations Development Programme, "Honduras hurricane victims saved by the web," *NetAid,* at www.app.netaid.org/WhatWorks/1.2.html?pillar_id=8&proj_id=110> (accessed10 December 2001).

19. United Nations Development Program, *Human Development Report, 2001* (New York: United Nations Development Program, 2001).

20. See www.onsatnet.com. With sponsorship from the Bill and Melinda Gates Foundation, related satellite-based technology is being used to bring telecommunications infrastructure to Native Americans in the Four Corners region of the Southwestern United States.

21. Altintas, Kemal "e-TATARS: Virtual Community of the Crimean Tatar Diaspora," paper presented at INET 2001, International Meeting of the Internet Society, Stockholm, June, 2001.

22. These data and other observations in libraries in this paper come from our assessment of the Gates Library Initiative, a major undertaking of the Bill and Melinda Gates Foundation to provide computers, software, training, and infrastructure for thousands of public libraries in the United States and Canada, with special emphasis on libraries serving poor communities. See Margaret Gordon, Andrew Gordon, and Elizabeth Moore "New Computers Bring New Patrons" *Library Journal* 126 (February 2001).

23. See <tehelka.com>.

24. Personal observation and interviews, 2000.

25. "Assessment of Impact of Information Technology on Rural Areas of India" *M.S. Swaminathan Research Foundation,* 2000, at www.mssrf.org/informationvillage/assessment.htm (accessed 10 December 2001).

26. Sabine Isabel Michiels and L. Van Crowder, "Discovering the 'Magic Box': Local appropriation of information and communication technologies (ICTs)" *Sustainable Development Department, Food and Agriculture Organization of the United Nations,* June 2001, at www.fao.org/sd/2001/kn0602a_en.htm (accessed 10 December 2001).

27. A. Bayes, J. von Braun, and R. Akhter, *Village Pay Phones and Poverty Reduction: Insights from a Grameen Bank Initiative in Bangladesh* (Bonn, Germany: Zentrum

für Entwicklungsforschung Center for Development Research, June 1999).

28. "The Simputer FAQ," *Simputer Trust,* 5 May 2001, at www.simputer.org/simputer/faq/ (accessed10 December 2001).

29. United Nations Conference on Trade and Development "E-Commerce and Development Report 2001" *United Nations Conference on Trade and Development,* 2001, at www.oneworld.net/cgi-bin/index.cgi?root=129&url=http%3A%2F%2Fwww%2Eunctad%2Eorg%2Fen%2Fpub%2Fps1ecdr01%2Een%2Ehtm (accessed 10 December 2001).

30. See www.thehungersite.com/cgi-bin/WebObjects/CTDSites.

31. See www.netaid.org/.

32. See www.fundaschool.org/.

33. Standage, *The Victorian Internet*, 83.

34. Standage, *The Victorian Internet*, 83.

35. Robert LeBailly, "The Cost of Free Computers," paper submitted to the Department of Sociology, Northwestern University, Evanston, Illinois, March 1985.

36. A contrasting example has proven to be highly informative: In the Gates Library Initiative we are currently assessing (see A. Gordon, M. Gordon, and Moore "New Computers"), a decision was made early on to design and then to provide "bullet proof computers"—computers which would continue to run and would "bounce back" to their initial configuration, resisting nearly any innocent or deliberate attempt to modify the contents or the "look and feel" of these public access computers. The fact that machines in isolated rural libraries were generally running flawlessly three years after installation, despite the variety of users and the modest technical skills of many librarians, testifies to the success of that aspect of the Library Initiative design.

37. A particularly trenchant analysis of these expectations is found in Joseph Weizenbaum, *Computer Power and Human Reason: From Judgment to Calculation* (San Francisco: W. H. Freeman, 1976).

38. Cy Ulberg, Andrew Gordon, and David Spain, "Telecommuting: Evaluation of Puget Sound Telecommuting Project," final report submitted to the Washington State Energy Office, June, 1993.

39. Weizenbaum, *Computer Power*, 31.

40. Todd Oppenheimer, "The Computer Delusion," *Atlantic Monthly* (July 1997): 45-62.

41. F. Heylighen, "Change and Information Overload: negative effects," *Principia Cybernetica Web,* 19 February 1999, at www.pespmc1.vub.ac.be/CHINNEG.html (accessed 19 December 2001).

42. Robyn Kamira, "I Sneeze—Therefore I Live! The Impact of the Internet on the Maori Culture," paper delivered at INET 2001, International Meeting of the Internet Society, Stockholm, June 2001.

43. Shanthi Kalathil and Taylor C. Boas, "The Internet and State Control in Authoritarian Regimes: China Cuba, and the Counterrevolution" *First Monday* 6, no. 8 (August 6, 2001).

44. "Lambda Bulletin on Anti-terrorism Measures, Chinese Censorship," *Cyber-Rights*

online, September 2001, at www.legalminds.lp.findlaw.com/list/cyber-rights/msg01391.html (accessed 10 January 2001).

45. See, for example, Barbara Garson, *The Electronic Sweatshop: How Computers Are Transforming the Office of the Future into the Factory of the Past* (New York: Simon & Schuster, 1988).

46. Andrew Meier, "Estonia's Tiger Leap to Technology?" *United Nations Development Program* at www.sdnhq.undp.org/it4dev/stories/estonia.html (accessed 10 December 2001).

47. Michael Maltz, Andrew Gordon, and Warren Friedman, *Mapping Crime in Its Community Setting: Event Geography Analysis* (New York: Springer-Verlag, 1990).

48. Lucy Suchman, "Anthropology as 'Brand': Reflections on Corporate Anthropology," paper presented at the American Anthropological Association annual meeting, San Francisco, November, 2000.

49. David Ronfeldt, John Arquilla, Graham E. Fuller, and Melissa Fuller, *The Zapatista "Social Netwar" in Mexico* (Santa Monica, Calif: Rand, 1998).

50. Sam Howe Verhovek, "Bill Gates Turns Skeptical On Digital Solution's Scope," *New York Times*, 3 November 2000, (A18).

51. For a fuller discussion of these issues, see Ronfeldt, Arquilla, G. Fuller, and M. Fuller, *The Zapatista.*

52. Jack Kelley, "Terror Groups Hide Behind Web Encryption," *USA Today*, 5 February 2001, (A5).

53. See, for example, Edward Rothstein, "A Lethal Web with No Spider," *New York Times*, 20 October 2001, (A13).

54. Gary Hart and Warren Rudman, *New World Coming: American Security in the 21st Century—Supporting Research and Analysis* (Arlington, VA: U.S. Commission on National Security in the 21st Century, 15 September 1999), 7.

55. Hart and Rudman, *New World*, 38.

56. "U.S. Shuts Down Somalia Internet" *BBC News,* 23 November 2001, at www.news.bbc.co.uk/hi/english/world/africa/newsid_1672000/1672220.stm (accessed 10 December 2001). See also, www.oneworld.net/cgi-bin/index.cgi?root=129&url=http://dfn.org/.

57. Allison Mitchell, "To Forestall a 'Digital Pearl Harbor,' U.S. Looks to System Separate from Internet," *New York Times*, 17 November 2001, (B7).

58. Thomas L. Friedman, "Evolutionaries," *New York Times*, (A21).

59. Arundhati Roy, "A Writer's Place in Politics," lecture on Alternative Radio, 15 February, 2001. Tape available at www.alternativeradio.org/tapes/sum-p-s.html#AROY1; also referred to in David Barsamian, "The Progressive Interview: Fiber Optics, Candlelight and Invisibility in Delhi: Convoys of the Digital Revolution," *The Progressive,* April 2001, at www.progressive.org/intv0401.html (accessed 25 February 2002).

Chapter 21

Toward Eliminating Poverty from the World: Grameen Bank Experience

Muhammad Yunus

A Short History of Grameen Bank

In 1974 Bangladesh was gripped by terrible famine. Previously, I used to get excited telling my students how economic theories provided the answers to economic problems of all types. I got carried away with the beauty and elegance of these theories. But now I was having doubts. What good were theories when people all around me were dying of starvation? I wanted to understand more about the real-life economics played out every day in the villages where people in my country lived. Fortunately, Chittagong University campus where I worked was right next to one of these villages, Jobra.

I did my best to learn about poor people and see their problems as they faced them. One such problem led me to the Grameen Bank idea. It was 1976. I kept seeing repeatedly how the poor people around the campus suffered because they could not find tiny amounts of money to carry out their livelihood activities, I thought of making a list of people who needed a small amount of money and the amount each needed. I came out with a list of forty-two people. They needed a combined amount of twenty-seven dollars. I was shocked and realized how far removed we were in the classrooms where we discuss national development plans costing billions of dollars. We don't even know that people suffer not for lack of large amounts of money but for amounts less than a dollar! I lent twenty-seven dollars out of my own pocket to forty-two people. They were totally surprised to get money so easy. That made me wonder, if I could make so many people so happy with such a small amount of money, why shouldn't I do more of it?

That's exactly what I did—I did more of it. I went to the local bank to arrange loans for these people. The bank managers refused my proposal on the grounds that the poor are not creditworthy, so I offered myself as a guarantor. It worked. People took loans from me and paid them back without any problem. I turned this into a research project to examine the possibility of designing a credit delivery system to provide banking services targeted at the rural poor.

The Grameen Bank Project (grameen means 'rural' or 'village' in Bangla language) came into operation with the following objectives: to extend banking facilities to poor men and women; to eliminate the exploitation of the poor by money lenders; to create opportunities for self-employment for huge numbers of unemployed people in rural Bangladesh; to bring the disadvantaged, mostly the women from the poorest households, into groups which they can understand and manage by themselves; and to reverse the age-old vicious circle of "low income, low saving, low investment," into a virtuous circle of "low income, injection of credit, investment, more income, more savings, more investment, more income."

The first project was successful in some of the neighboring villages between 1976 and 1979. With the sponsorship of the central bank of the country and support of the nationalized commercial banks, the project was expanded to cover several districts. In October 1983, the Grameen Bank Project was transformed into an independent bank. Today 92 percent of the shares of Grameen Bank are owned by poor rural women and men who are the borrowers of the bank. The remaining 8 percent is owned by the government.

Breaking the Vicious Cycle of Poverty through Micro-credit

Grameen Bank is owned by poor people and it works exclusively with poor people. Conventional banks are based on the principle that the more you have, the more you can get; if you don't have anything, you don't get anything. Grameen has literally turned this principle completely around. Grameen's principle is the less you have, the higher the priority you get in receiving loans from Grameen. If you have nothing, you get the highest priority.

The Grameen Bank is based on the voluntary formation of small groups of five people to provide mutual, morally binding group guarantees in lieu of the collateral required by conventional banks. At first only two members of a group are allowed to apply for a loan. Depending on their performance in repayment the next two borrowers can then apply and, subsequently, the fifth member as well.

The assumption is that if individual borrowers are given access to credit, they will be able to identify and engage in viable income-generating activities—simple processing such as paddy husking and lime-making, manufacturing such as pottery, weaving, and garment sewing, as well as storage, marketing, and transport services. Women were initially given equal access to the schemes, and proved not only reliable borrowers but astute entrepreneurs. As a result, they have raised their status, lessened their dependency on their husbands, and improved their homes and the nutritional standards of their children.

Intensive discipline, supervision, and servicing characterize the operations of the Grameen Bank, which are carried out by "bicycle bankers" in branch units with considerable delegated authority. The rigorous selection of borrowers and their projects by these bank workers, the powerful peer pressure exerted on these individuals by the groups, and the repayment scheme based on fifty weekly installments all contribute to the operational viability of this rural banking system designed for the poor.

The success of this approach shows that a number of objections to lending to the poor can be overcome if careful supervision and management are provided. For example, it had earlier been thought that the poor would not be able to find remunerative occupations. In fact, Grameen borrowers have successfully done so. It was thought that the poor would not be able to repay; in fact, repayment rates reached 97 percent. It was thought that poor rural women in particular were not bankable; in fact, by 1992 they accounted for 94 percent of borrowers. It was thought that the poor could not save; in fact, group savings have proven as successful as group lending. It was thought that rural power structures would make sure that such a bank failed; but the Grameen Bank has been able to expand rapidly, from fewer than 15,000 borrowers in 1980, to 2.4 million members by the beginning of 1999.

Estimates suggest that the average household income of Grameen Bank members is higher than their counterpart households and that there has been a sharp reduction in the number of members living below the poverty line. There has also been a shift from agricultural wage labor (considered to be socially inferior) to self-employment in petty trading. Such a shift in occupational patterns has an indirect positive effect on the employment and wages of other agricultural waged laborers. What started as an innovative local initiative has thus grown to the point where it has made an impact on poverty alleviation at the national level.

Why Women?

Procedures designed for the conventional banking system deliberately exclude the poor. This was my number one criticism of the banking system. My second criticism was that banks are also biased against women, not just poor women but all women. Of all the borrowers of all the banks in Bangladesh fewer than 1 percent are women.

When I began, I wanted to make sure that in my program 50 percent of the borrowers were women. So I would deliberately go and try to persuade the poor women to borrow money from the Grameen project.

At first they would run away from us. A woman would say, "Why don't you give the money to my husband, he is the one who knows how to use the money, I don't know anything about money." We would continue trying to persuade them, explaining that they might have ideas to earn money for themselves. It took months to get women into the group. It took six years to come to the level where, finally, half of our borrowers were women and the other half men. But after we reached that point, we saw that the money that went to the families through women brought much more benefit than money that went to the families through men.

First, women were very cautious with their money. They didn't want to waste any bit of it. One of the things which became apparent to me, and which I started to explain to allay their fears about borrowing, was that as poor women, they already possessed one very special skill—the skill to manage scarce resources efficiently. They could use this skill to also manage any money borrowed from the bank.

The second benefit we noticed is that when the mother is the borrower, the children become the immediate beneficiaries. Their social situation improves because with their mothers' support, they start going to school. In our experience, women have a longer vision than men. Men are more likely to enjoy what they've got right away, and they are generally more impulsive. But a woman is more likely to have a very consistent vision for the future. She wants a better life and to build her security for her and for her family.

Noticing these benefits we changed our policy of evenhandedness between men and women. We decided to prioritize women. We gave our staff incentives to give priority to women, and today 95 percent of our members are women.

When a woman starts handling money she becomes a decision maker. Once she starts making decisions about business, soon she starts making decisions about family matters and about social issues.

The birth rate in Grameen families is lower because, I believe, the woman takes control, becomes more assertive, and has the welfare of the family high on her list. Another positive change is that there is less domestic violence among people involved in our program, because when the woman is a provider herself it brings out a new kind of relationship within the family.

The poor in any culture need financial resources. Wherever you live, when you can finance your own activities you start to break out of the poverty cycle. This is particularly true for women who cannot get jobs for social reasons. Credit is used to create enterprises. These tiny enterprises created tiny successes. Once you achieve something you are ready to achieve more. Initially you are only worried about finding food. But once the food problem has been resolved then you start looking at your house, you start looking at your neighbors, and you start looking at your children.

Poverty Is Not Created by the Poor

If we are looking for one single action which will enable the poor to overcome their poverty, I would recommend credit. Money is power. I have been arguing that credit should be accepted as a human right. If we can come up with a system which allows everybody access to credit while ensuring excellent repayment—I can guarantee you poverty will not last long.

Poverty is not created by the poor. Poverty is created by the existing world system which denies fair chances to the poor. If we can ensure truly equal opportunities to everybody in the society there is no reason why poverty should linger around us.

The Grameen idea of micro-credit started spreading in other countries. The first serious Grameen replication program was initiated in Malaysia. This was followed by programs in the Philippines, Indonesia, Nepal, and India. Now there are hundreds of programs all over the world, both in developing and industrialized countries. The United States was the first industrialized country which put this program into use to address the recipients of public assistance. Later it was adopted by Canada, France, Norway, Sweden, Finland, Bosnia, and Poland. Recently Grameen has been invited to work in Kosovo.

Funding Micro-credit Programs

While we were trying to promote micro-credit for the poor to enable them to change their own lives, bilateral and multilateral foreign aid programs continued to disburse around fifty billion dollars a year to finance conventional infrastructure creating programs to fight poverty. We continued to appeal to policy makers to include micro-credit within their foreign aid package. In 1995, it created a multi-donor consultative group named the Consultative Group to Assist the Poorest (CGAP).

While CGAP brought micro-credit within the purview of serious consideration for official development assistance it has not been able to spur sufficient donor interest to build up significant outreach each year. However, it has made important contributions in drawing attention to many important operational and policy issues related to micro-credit, and to setting global standards.

To draw the attention of national and international policy makers and opinion-builders, a global conference, called the "Micro-Credit Summit," was organized in Washington D.C. in February of 1997. It turned micro-credit into an international movement. The Summit adopted a goal to reach 100 million of the poorest families with micro-credit, preferably through the women in those families, by 2005.

The Summit's goal will require a very large sum of money and the appropriate institutional arrangements to take the funds directly to the poor. Under the existing procedures multilateral international financial institutions give commercial or soft loans to governments, who in turn pass the money on to governmental micro-credit programs or non-governmental organizations. This has not been proven as an efficient method to channel micro-credit funds.

Expanding micro-credit programs rapidly will require finding a way to bypass or limit governments' involvement with donor money. It will also require administering funds with local, not donor, staff. A substantial amount of donor money gets spent on feasibility studies, appraisal missions, monitoring, supervision, and administration by expensive consultants and contractors, mostly from the donor countries. Besides the cost, it also creates the problem of hiring the wrong consultants. Since people with micro-credit experiences are very rare in the donor countries, people with conventional banking backgrounds are hired as consultants. These consultants quickly get busy in "fixing" the micro-credit programs by converting them into "proper" financial institutions.

As a result of the high costs involved in providing funds directly to micro-credit programs as well as the high costs (some justifiable, some not) incurred by many programs, a relatively small amount of these funds are actually provided as loans to the poorest. One way to efficiently deliver donor funds to micro-credit programs is to create non-governmental and sustainable wholesaler micro-credit funds (MCFs) at the local level. Donors can channel their funds to these MCFs which will initiate and support micro-credit programs within their areas of operation.[1]

In-country wholesaler micro-credit funds reduce overhead costs dramatically. The cost of delivering and monitoring a loan to a very poor woman in a Third World country village from a donor headquartered in Europe or North America is much greater than having a local MCF deliver the same loan. Through this mechanism, more donor money can go into the hands of the poorest as loans, rather than in the pockets of officials and the consultants as salaries, fees, and international travel.

The Micro-Credit Summit estimated that out of a total of U.S. $23 billion, U.S. $11.6 billion would be needed as grants and soft loans to reach 100 million families (the balance would come from commercial sources). This U.S. $11.6 billion could be mobilized by raising the percentage of overseas direct assistance going to micro-credit. I believe there would be considerable public support in donor countries for earmarking 5 percent of the foreign aid money from bilateral and mulitlateral sources for micro-credit, particularly if donors commit to making the bulk of this money available to the poorest people.

Information Technology Avenues to End Global Poverty

I believe that micro-credit and information technology (IT), with their combined strength, can become a very effective force to eliminate poverty from the world.

The number of people living on less than a dollar a day is now 1.2 billion. This number is going to double by the middle of this century if the present trend continues. This trend must be changed by the creative use of IT. The market will benefit immensely if the entire poor population can leave poverty behind and bring their productivity and creativity to the market place as producers and their purchasing power as consumers. IT and micro-credit can create an environment for the poor to give them the best opportunity to change their lives.

Information technology is going to change the world dramatically. IT is creating a distanceless world where communication is becoming instantaneous. It is helping economies expand at an unprecedented rate. Rich countries will continue to become richer and rich people will become richer faster than ever before. Within the framework of the free market economy rich countries and rich people are directing IT for their own purposes. Although IT can offer the most exciting possibility for overcoming poverty, this potential will remain vastly unexplored if we leave it to market forces.

IT skills have become central to competitive differentiation on the part of individuals and firms, those in the developing countries included. Programs for forming quickly-marketable IT skills among the poor in developing countries are crucial to empower them to compete in the emerging international division of labor. Remote production of infotech-enabled services will be a very large and rapidly growing part of such a division of labor between nations. This points to the imperative of drawing up an agenda for creating IT infrastructure and IT know-how in developing countries to facilitate the poor's access to IT-enabled economic expansion.

The combination of Internet technology and distributed production of services has opened up a real opportunity to tap into what experts believe would be a rapidly growing globalization of white-collar services. These services range from human resources to translation to remote-ticketing to monitoring business and home networks for security in real time. Outsourcing of IT-enabled white-collar services to mainly the developed country markets is believed to be worth on the order of $180 billion over the next decade. A large part of this can and will be located in poor countries of the world. And the poor know of this coming opportunity. They have a tremendous motivation to learn and adapt to the rigorous skills needed. What they don't have is an organized effort to promote their interest and explore the full potential of IT to get them out of poverty in a sustainable way.

Toward that end, we have created a family of companies around Grameen Bank, all with the objective of building an institutional support system for the poor to help themselves out of poverty. Some of these companies are IT related: Grameen Phone, a mobile telephone company; Grameen Telecom, takes mobile telephones to villages to help Grameen borrowers become telephone-ladies; Grameen Communications, brings Internet services to the rural areas where Grameen Telecom has brought mobile phones; Grameen Cybernet, an Internet service provider; Grameen Software Limited, a software company; and Grameen Shakti, a company bringing solar energy to villages without grid-energy (only fifteen percent of the population of Bangladesh has access to electricity).

IT offers a window of opportunity to integrate knowledge based techniques of production and distribution into the work and survival options of the poor in the world. IT can help improve the productivity of the working poor, both women and men, at work. IT can help the poor cope more effectively and cheaply to survive hazards and to access healthcare delivery systems. Education can be made enjoyable, life oriented, and promote social and environmental consciousness. IT can leap-frog a backward community or a family into a society fit for the new millennium.

We have the best chance mankind has ever had to end poverty in the world for all time to come. Let us not miss this opportunity.

Notes

1. I am familiar with the workings of two such wholesaler micro-credit funds in Banglasdesh: Palli Karma-Sahayak Foundation (PKSF) and Grameen Trust. PKSF disburses approximately U.S. $40 million a year to over 162 micro-credit start-ups and established programs. The World Bank provided U.S. $105 million to PKSF in its first loan, and $150 million in its second loan. Grameen Trust has been providing funding and technical support for the past eight years to a group of micro-credit projects in Asia, Africa, Europe, and the Americas, which has now grown to 138 projects in thirty countries.

Chapter 22

Progressing toward Environmental Sustainability

Alison Cullen and Christopher Bretherton

> We shall never achieve harmony with the land any more than we shall achieve justice or liberty for people. In these higher aspirations the important thing is not to achieve, but to strive. It is only in mechanical enterprises that we can expect that early or complete fruition of effort which we call "success."
>
> Aldo Leopold, 1953

The Goal of Environmental Progress

In the last two centuries, human civilization has extended its reach into all corners of the world. Human population has quadrupled in the last century, and mechanization has increased human capacity to exploit most natural resources enormously. In the process, pollution, degradation, and destruction of natural environments have mushroomed.

These concerns are leading to a growing consensus that the primary goal of environmental progress must be *environmental sustainability*—stabilizing the local and global impact of humanity on the natural world. The broad appeal of this goal rests on several arguments. The first is human nurture—it provides future generations with a world that can continue to meet their material needs. The second is stewardship—our natural world should be preserved for its own sake, as a retreat or aesthetic treasure, or as heritage. The third is precaution—that human disruption to complex natural systems may have unforeseen adverse consequences.

But will humanity actually proceed along an orderly track toward environmental sustainability? Or are we on a collision course with environmental catastrophe in the coming century? In this chapter we argue that meaningful progress will involve three elements all vigorously supported through intelligent public policy: information, values, and opportunities for action.

Comments on Environmental Sustainability

Like many attractive concepts, environmental sustainability is not very precise and can fit many visions. It does not posit a particular level of resource use or population or natural habitat preservation, of human equity or quality of life. Not all possible environmentally sustainable societies appear to constitute progress from our current state. Stone age hunter-gatherer societies of fifty thousand years ago were environmentally sustainable due to their low and nearly steady-state population culled by famine, disease, and war. In medieval Europe or China, a large fraction of land was brought under cultivation, and the social system was much more stratified, but again the overall structure of society and its environmental impacts were relatively steady for hundreds of years. Lester Brown's essay *Vision of a Sustainable World*[1] offered a tantalizingly achievable vision of a modern environmentally sustainable society, and Ernest Callenbach's book *Ecotopia*[2] offered a more radical and whimsical vision. Regardless of its exact form, the implicit goal of environmental sustainability today is a social framework, which will vary with locale and evolve with the society, sustaining qualitative improvements of both the lives of humans and our natural world.

A key question in the pursuit of environmental sustainability is the meaning of stewardship of our natural world. Even without human intervention, it is a constantly and sometimes rapidly changing system. Sixty-five million years ago, a catastrophic meteorite impact appears to have caused the extinction of most known forms of life and ushered in the age of mammals. Currently, human activities are causing mass extinction and ecosystem disruptions, but are unlikely to result in the annihilation of all forms of life. Viral and microbial drug resistance testifies to the ability of some life forms to thrive even in the face of our best efforts to destroy them. Although "ecosystem services" such as natural cleansing of anthropogenic waste are invaluable, the societal choice of how much to preserve of our natural world is at once a practical, aesthetic, and moral one, and subject to diverse reasonable opinions. Rapid cultural and technological evolution makes envisioning the relation between humanity and the natural world centuries into the future almost meaningless. Hence, conserving a limited resource to ensure current consumption levels for thousands of years may not be appropriate.

However vague, environmental sustainability does represent a radical change from current practice in most nations. In our everyday lives, we live by values of sustainability all the time, nurturing our own bodies, families, relationships, gardens, and farms (even as we collectively do this in an environmentally unsustainable way!). This reflects our awareness of the finitude of our lives and our dependence on other people and things for happiness and satisfaction. Ironically, the same awareness of finitude is not currently reflected in most nations' economic and social systems, which promote economic growth over concern for resource efficiency and waste minimization. An environmentally sustainable society must develop a social mechanism for defining acceptable levels of human impact on the natural environment, and of revisiting these levels as society and our understanding of the natural world evolve. To bring about such a society will require strong popular consensus for change, and political, business, and social leaders who provide form to the vision. Such a consensus will require most people to feel deeply that their lives or their children's lives will be improved by progress toward an environmentally sustainable society.

A Brief History of the Concept of Sustainability

Sustainability as a concept has long roots and a worldwide presence. Ancient writings such as the Koran, Torah, and Bible include many references to sustainability and a charge of responsibility for the well-being of future generations. In the nineteenth and early twentieth centuries the conservation movement embraced language which has become quite familiar today due to a focus on sustainability: "... down at bottom [conservation] policy rests upon the fundamental law that neither man nor nation can prosper unless, in dealing with the present, thought is steadily taken for the future.[3]

Before the first Earth Day in 1970, much of environmental protection worldwide revolved around land conservation, sustainable practices in land use, or the safety of products such as chemicals and pesticides. With the Brundtland Commission's report issued in preparation for the Rio Earth Summit, emphasis shifted to development with the goal of improving the human condition: "[Sustainable Development] is the complex of activities that can be expected to improve the human condition in such a manner that the improvement can be maintained."[4]

The motivation for sustainable community initiatives has come from many sectors, but perhaps most consistently from disillusioned environmentalists. National and international efforts have failed to solve global environmental problems, thus many have returned to local and regional efforts as an appropriate and manageable point of entry. "Agenda 21," which emerged from the Earth Summit in Rio de Janeiro in 1992, promoted community-oriented initiatives as the future focus of sustainability.[5] In the triad of sustainability principles—environment, economy, and equity—each element is necessary for sustainable future states. In this chapter we look specifically at environmental sustainability, a single strand in this rich tapestry.

Elements of Environmental Sustainability

> What is and is not sustainable depends on the number of people now and in the future, the demands made on the planetary system by those people, the system's physical and biological processes, and the investment society is able and willing to make to overcome constraints in the system.
>
> Gordon H. Orians, *Environment,* Nov. 1990

To assess progress toward environmental sustainability, we must examine the aggregate human footprint on the environment by considering a variety of human impacts. These can be broadly classified into population, resource use (water, food, energy, other natural resources), pollution and waste disposal, and inadvertent impacts on complex systems (climate change, reduced biodiversity). In industrialized countries, resource use goes far beyond basic needs for food, water, and shelter, making overall trends in per capita consumption patterns at least as vital a sustainability indicator as population. While we take a global view, we recognize that our world is composed of different localities in which some of these impacts may be much more acute than others. Only when and where all of these impacts are addressed can environmental sustainability be achieved.

Human Population

> The earth can scarcely provide for our needs; as our demands grow greater, our complaints against nature's inadequacy are heard by all. The scourges of pestilence, famine, wars and earthquakes have come to be regarded as a blessing to overcrowded nations, since they serve to prune away the luxuriant growth of the human race.
>
> Tertullian, c. 155-c. 220, *De anima*

A fundamental requirement for environmental sustainability is a stable human population. The human carrying capacity of the earth is debatable, and is dependent on technology and lifestyle choices. This might conceivably be increased to as many as forty billion if humans moved to a largely vegetarian diet.

Estimates of the human population ten thousand years ago are about five million, increasing by less than 1 percent per century, and limited by disease, accidents, war, and famine. After the agricultural transition, human population began to rise more rapidly, reaching about half a billion by 1650 A. D. The doubling time was 200 years, however, indicating a nearly stable population by modern standards.

Explosive population growth started around 1850 when human population was a billion. Growth accelerated through the mid-twentieth century, peaking at 2 percent a year before falling to 1.3 percent (a doubling time of forty years) by 2000, when human population exceeded six billion. Population growth is an unintended byproduct of one of the greatest achievements of modern times, the increase of life expectancy by control of lethal infectious disease through medicine and better sanitation. Disease and war continue. Millions died in two bloody world wars. In Africa alone, over six thousand lives are lost each day to the AIDS epidemic.[6] However, the recent decline in growth rate is mainly due to family planning.

Land and Water Use

> Woe unto them that join house to house, that lay field to field; till there be no place that they may be placed alone in the midst of the earth!
>
> Bible, Isaiah 5:

In an environmentally sustainable society, land is managed to sustain both humanity and nature. Almost the entire earth's land surface, except for areas such as Antarctica or the Sahara Desert, is under active human management. Despite pervasive human interference, some species find habitat in unexpected locations. Even an apartment building can support an ecosystem of cats, dogs, rats, pigeons, and cockroaches. However, many natural ecosystems cannot tolerate such disturbance and compete with human uses for land or water resources. Thus trends in human land and water use, such as agriculture, grazing, forestry, fishing, urbanization, and deliberate preservation of natural lands, have profound impacts on environmental sustainability.

Agriculture and Grazing

For the last fifty years, a little over one third of the earth's land surface has been used for agriculture. New cultivation has offset significant losses in land area due to urbanization and soil degradation.[7] Progress in farming methods and technology has doubled the average crop productivity of land since 1960, outpacing world population growth.[8] However, current practices of world agriculture are not fully sustainable. Some of the productivity increase has come from unsustainable irrigation practices, as well as the use of fertilizer and pesticide that has created serious water quality problems. Furthermore, three-quarters of all agricultural land has poor soil, quickly rendered unproductive by erosion on hillsides or rapid depletion of nutrients after the clearing of forests. Additionally, approximately one-quarter of the earth's land surface is grazed by domesticated animals. Intensive grazing can dramatically modify the natural ecosystem, and there have been few effective attempts to limit the environmental impact of grazing outside of parks in the developing and developed worlds alike.

Forestry

Sustainable forestry practices have the potential to maintain a fairly natural ecosystem. However, the world's appetite for wood and paper products appears insatiable. Paper use in particular has quadrupled over the past forty years, representing 20 percent of all wood products. Computers, far from making a paperless society, have increased demand by automating printing. Industrialized countries, whose own forest cover is approaching a steady state, import wood harvested in developing countries. This trend has hidden the problem from its creators. In some areas of the developing world, wood is a primary fuel. World forest cover (outside of tree plantations) has decreased by 40 percent since pre-human times and is currently decreasing by 0.4 percent a year. Over 90 percent of this forest loss is in the biologically rich tropical forests of South America, Asia, and Africa. Forest destruction is often rationalized as providing cleared land for agriculture and grazing, but only rarely sustains such uses for long.

Urbanization and Industrialization

In 1900, forty percent of the U.S. population and 10 percent of world population lived in cities; by the 1990s, these percentages had increased to 90 percent and 46 percent.[9] Although urban, suburban, and industrial areas occupy only 2 percent of global land area (and 5 percent of the United States), they impact the local environment acutely, especially with air and water pollution. Furthermore, an unsustainable trend in the United States is "urban sprawl" of low-density housing, commercial, and industrial development around cities. For example, from 1970 to 1990, the land area around Chicago was developed fourteen times faster than the rate of regional population growth.[10] Urban sprawl has contributed to a 60 percent increase in vehicle-miles traveled per person in the United States over the last thirty years.

Preservation of Natural Lands

In the last century, as humans filled the earth, many societies have recognized the desirability of preserving or managing some areas primarily in their natural form. The U.S. National Park system has expanded almost three-fold in the last thirty years, and 5 percent of land in the United States has been designated as wilderness. However, many natural ecosystems which compete with human land use, such as tallgrass prairie or wetlands, are under-represented. The "American Serengeti" that Lewis and Clark marveled at is no more, and tropical rain forests appear to be headed for a similar fate. Illegal timber harvesting, hunting, and collecting in "preserved" lands in developing countries emphasize the challenges of preservation without strong understanding and support by the local populace.

Air and Water Quality

Ill air slays sooner than the sword.

Ratis Raving, c. 1450

The sewer is the conscience of the city.

Victor Hugo, *Les Miserables,* 1862

Degradation of the air and water is an ancient societal problem. Upon seeing the pollution from Indian fires in the sixteenth century, Juan Rodriguez Cabrillo named the Los Angeles Basin the Bay of 10000 Smokes. The rapid urbanization of the twentieth century has highlighted the need for regulations to maintain breathable air and drinkable water. An increasingly stringent set of government regulations has been effective in controlling and often reducing acute air and water pollution in industrialized nations.

Air pollution around the new megalopolises in developing countries is far more acute, due to lax regulations. In Brazil and central Africa, fires lit to clear brush or forests fill the skies with smoke in the dry season. Contamination of water by untreated human and animal waste harms many freshwater ecosystems and poses a major health problem in much of the developing world, and seriously compromises many freshwater ecosystems such as the Ganges River in India.

There has been less progress in controlling pollution whose effects are felt far from its source, or when the source is distributed. For example, water pollution is attributable to multiple sources, including farm runoff, and damage to forests and lakes is the result of acid rain from distant sulfuric and nitric acid emissions. An anoxic "dead zone" in the Gulf of Mexico has rapidly expanded over the last decade to fill an area larger than New Jersey.[11] In that zone, fertilizer and sewage has promoted algal growth that removes all the oxygen from the water and leaves it largely uninhabitable by marine life. In addition, human emissions of nontoxic greenhouse gases such as carbon dioxide (e.g., from vehicles) and methane (e.g., from landfills and cows) are still rapidly rising.

Waste Disposal

Only want sets a limit to waste.

Latin proverb

Production of solid waste is a growing problem in industrialized countries, particularly in the United States where Americans generate six pounds of nonrecycled waste per person per day—three times the weight of the food we eat. In the developing world, the average is about fifty times smaller, due mainly to much lower consumption and more reuse of materials. In many industrialized countries, organized recycling programs have expanded dramatically in the last twenty years. While the United States currently recycles about two pounds of materials per person per day, the volume of nonrecycled waste has still increased 10 to 20 percent per person in the last thirty years. The sustainability of large-scale solid waste disposal practices, such as landfilling, incineration, ocean dumping, and isolation of radioactive waste, must be examined. All have environmental side effects, but the magnitude of the waste stream seems to be the larger problem for environmental sustainability.

The Oceans

> Life originated in the sea, and about eighty percent of it is still there.
>
> Isaac Asimov, 1988

While the oceans cover almost three-quarters of the earth's surface, the last century has demonstrated their finitude and the challenge of sustaining them as an international "commons." Here we consider only their role as a human resource, leaving aside their role in biodiversity, climate change, and waste processing. In the nineteenth century, sperm whales were hunted nearly to extinction worldwide, but the availability of most fish was limited not by their scarcity but by the labor required to catch them. In the last century, improved technology and an overbuilt world fishing fleet have led to massive regional over-fishing. This has decimated fish populations in formerly productive areas such as the Grand Banks off New England, belatedly leading to national and international restrictions on fishing in many regions. Even so, the current world fish catch of eighty-five million tons, providing 20 percent of the world's population with its primary protein source, is thought to exceed the sustainable yield of the world oceans.[12] Fish farming has grown rapidly, but waterborne waste and escaping fish may spread disease and ecological disruption in sensitive coastal zones, raising questions about its sustainability.

Climate

> For the first time in my life, I saw the horizon as a curved line. It was accentuated by a thin seam of dark blue light—our atmosphere. Obviously this was not the "ocean" of air I had been told it was so many times in my life. I was terrified by its fragile appearance.
>
> Ulf Merbold, West German space shuttle astronaut, *The Greenhouse Trap*, 1990

In 1896, the Swedish chemist Svante Arrhenius recognized the "greenhouse effect:" increasing levels of carbon dioxide should lead to a warmer climate by absorbing infrared radiation and reducing the efficiency with which the earth's surface radiates heat energy. Current computer models have suggested that a doubling of carbon dioxide would warm the earth's surface by four to eight degrees Fahrenheit. Since 1950, carbon dioxide has been increasing at roughly one percent per year, mainly due to the combustion of fossil fuels. At the current rate of increase, carbon dioxide will double from pre-industrial levels by 2050. In the past century, the worldwide average land surface temperature has increased almost two degrees Fahrenheit. According to scientific consensus, this is mainly a result of carbon dioxide increases.[13] Dirty combustion and other industrial processes can also produce a haze of small reflective aerosol particles that inhibit sunlight from reaching the earth's surface, but this is thought to counteract only a small fraction of greenhouse warming.

Perhaps the most serious human impact attributed to global warming is the disruption of normal patterns of temperature and rainfall to which land use planning is calibrated and human settlements are accustomed. Documented natural impacts include substantial glacial retreat, less pervasive snow cover and longer growing seasons in high-latitudes, thinning and retreating sea ice and permafrost, a slow rise in sea level, and heat-stress-induced "coral bleaching" over many parts of the tropical oceans. These impacts are expected to accelerate over the next fifty years, and changes in precipitation patterns may become more evident. Some models suggest major changes in the circulation of the Atlantic Ocean or nearly complete summertime melting of Arctic pack ice by 2050, both of which would cause dramatic climate change in certain areas.

Energy

> Considering the prices we've been paying, we haven't been wasteful of energy at all. We've simply been using it according to the way it's been valued in the marketplace.
>
> Bernard Gelb, *Newsweek,* 18 April 1977

The tremendous technological progress of modern industrial societies has been fueled by cheap energy. In the twentieth century most of this energy has been supplied by fossil fuels. Fossil fuels are far from a scarce resource; proven reserves of oil and gas have remained fairly constant as discovery and extraction techniques improve. Enough coal deposits exist in the United States and China alone to power the world for nearly a century. However, continued reliance on fossil fuels would likely bring on drastic greenhouse warming, threatening the sustainability of both human activities and natural ecosystems. Energy conservation programs have stabilized per-capita fossil fuel energy use for the past twenty years in most industrialized countries, but only a wholesale movement away from fossil fuel use can sustain a semblance of our current climate.

Nuclear power has become a significant energy source in countries such as

France, which now produces seventy percent of its electricity from nuclear plants. Still, concerns about nuclear waste disposal and reactor safety resonate with a public already educated in the enormous destructive power of nuclear weapons. In Europe, construction of new nuclear power plants is decreasing, while in the United States, no new plants have been certified for fifteen years. The sustainable alternative is renewable energy sources. Wind and solar power appear the most environmentally benign, but so far have been only locally deployed as they are currently several times more expensive than fossil fuels. Hydropower causes large-scale disruption of river systems and seems unlikely to become a dominant energy source.

Biodiversity and Habitat Preservation

> There is no historical precedent for conservation of a major resource as it became obvious that the resource was being wiped out. The response to precipitous declines in buffalo in the American West and blue whales in the oceans was to harvest both resources harder than ever, up to the point at which they were almost extinct—and it was no longer economically worthwhile to harvest them.
>
> Kenneth E. F. Watt, *Ecocide,* 1971

A marvelous aspect of our planet is its incredible diversity of life. All domestic plants and animals were selected by trial and error from the wild genome. As biotechnology advances further, so does our ability to learn from and make use of the amazing adaptations of other life forms. The "web of life" provides important metaphors for human societies, of complex feedback loops, selection, closed-loop design, as well as the ecoservices of processing our wastes, purifying our water, and conditioning our air.

Human activities are bound to disturb natural ecosystems, and not all humans feel strongly about the loss of other species. Nevertheless, one value of an environmentally sustainable society should be preserving the existing fabric of nature along with human society. Surely we should not be proud, then, of causing a mass extinction unrivalled since a meteorite devastated the earth sixty-five million years ago. Deliberate and inadvertent effects of human activities—overfishing, habitat destruction, degradation, and fragmentation, introduced or possibly genetically modified species, and bioaccumulation of toxic chemicals such as DDT—have decimated many species in this century. Biologists estimate that humans have raised extinction rates 100 to 1000 fold and that twenty-seven thousand plant and animal species vanish each year.[14] 20 percent of all freshwater fish species are either extinct or endangered. Two of the ocean's most biodiverse habitats, coral reefs and mangrove swamps, are already severely degraded and tropical rain forests are heading for the same fate. Given current trends, 50 percent of all pre-human multicellular species may be extinct by the end of the century.[15] Perhaps the most hopeful trends are our increasing knowledge about biodiversity and individual species, and the introduction of legal protection for endangered species.

Means of Progressing toward Environmental Sustainability

In the end, we conserve only what we love.
We will love only what we understand.
We will understand only what we are taught.
Baba Dioum, Senegalese poet

Human impacts on many natural systems have compromised sustainability and are continuing to increase rapidly. Who speaks on behalf of environmental progress, and how is it most effectively promoted? There is no central international body with the authority and will to bring about environmental sustainability. Environmental sustainability is achievable only through billions of everyday decisions in its favor by individuals, populations, and leaders in all sectors. Because both population and consumption patterns affect natural resource demands, public policies aimed at environmental progress may target either or both of these elements.

Personal choices affecting environmental sustainability—such as where and how to live, or whether to have children and how many—present a variety of tradeoffs, uncertainties, and risks. Individuals operate with a limited amount of information, sometimes distorted or wrong, about the implications of their actions. Personal values of the costs and benefits affect individuals' behavior. Decisions by local or global groups also reflect a spectrum of different individuals' knowledge, experiences, values, and opinions. Environmental progress requires effective information collection, synthesis, and delivery, changes in individual and collective values, or changes in the options and requirements for action. Without a reconciliation of economic and environmental goals through public dialogue and policy, progress toward environmental sustainability is unlikely. In the following sections, we discuss some approaches to environmental progress.

Improving the Information Base

The first and greatest knowledge, and also common to all men,
is the division and order of our environment.
Polybius, 130 B.C., *Histories*

Information about status and trends in environmental health, operations of planetary systems, and the implications of human actions and choices on environmental sustainability is critical to sound decision making. Scientists gather detailed information relevant to the environment, such as studies of individual animal and plant species, of ecosystem dynamics, atmospheric chemistry, or ocean circulation, and human impacts on all of these. Most of this research and monitoring is publicly funded and motivated by public interest. Computers have given scientists an unprecedented capability for modeling complex systems and their feedbacks.

However, few of us are directly involved in even the slightest fraction of this work. How do we as individuals learn about our environment? In today's world, we obtain information from such diverse sources as conversation, television, the Internet, schools, pricing schemes, and government mandated labels. This information is of varying quality. While the media cover scientific and technological findings, simplifying complex issues skillfully, they often focus on controversy, sensation, and extremes in order to maintain an audience. In many countries, the government filters and distorts public information channels. In fact, most of the world has little or no access to organized information.

Nevertheless, existing channels can be used to communicate environmental information. In the United States, school children learn about ecology, and have participated in environmental education programs stressing such behaviors as recycling, while the adult public has been targeted for specific consumer campaigns, such as the successful phase out of ozone depleting aerosol propellants. Innovative metrics of environmental sustainability and health such as vehicle miles traveled per person per year, cultivated acreage required to feed each citizen of a country, and fraction of land surfaces which are impervious, promote an increased understanding of what is meant by environmental sustainability.[16] Air and water pollution, endangered species and global warming are often in the news.

Has this barrage of information had an impact? While 80 percent of Americans consider themselves to be environmentalists, this is rarely reflected in their behavior. The environmental education movement has been fueled by the belief that if people were aware of wasteful or environmentally damaging behavior, progress would come naturally. This has proven true only in limited arenas such as recycling. Part of the problem is distinguishing between meaningful environmental choices and those with negligible impact, which requires the time and skill to sort through facts and opinions. The Union of Concerned Scientists has recently picked up the mantle of public education including a consumer's guide directed at identifying environmentally "meaningful" consumer choices.[17] They point out that a few major high impact decisions, such as one's selection of a house or car, can overwhelm the effects of low impact decisions made on a daily basis. Still, lack of information is not the only issue in the United States—for example, the environmental impact of sport utility vehicles (SUVs) has been well-publicized, yet they are still fashionable. Environmental sustainability will be achieved only if given a high priority. This will require a shift in values.

Values Shifts

When we talk about preservation of the environment, it is related to many

> other things. Ultimately the decision must come from the human heart, so I think the key point is to have a genuine sense of universal responsibility.
>
> Dalai Lama (Tenzin Gyatso) and Galen Rowell, *My Tibet,* 1990.

However strong our belief in the existence of environmental problems, these beliefs must compete with other values and with practical constraints, and may not lead to action. To ensure an environmentally sustainable future, sustainability must take precedence in individual and societal decisions.

Values come to us through a variety of ways, including through experience, by rote learning, and from friends and leaders we esteem. Shifts in values bring about profound changes not only in decision making at every level, but also in our perception of the costs and benefits of these changes. Values can thus ease delays in personal pleasure and allow some compensation with the belief that one is contributing to the greater good, enabling future generations to pursue happiness or justice. An individual's pleasure in selecting, using, or consuming environmentally friendly products may come to include the satisfaction that these products are associated with a smaller impact on the earth than the alternatives. Finally, the combined values of multiple individuals collectively influence institutional decision making.

Different groups have developed different understandings of the role of humans in nature. Some believe that the natural world exists in service of humankind. Others believe that humans are responsible as caring stewards of the earth. Still others extend what might be considered "human" rights to other species and ecosystems.

Individual behavior such as gardening or having children provides direct experience with sustaining life in the natural world. Involvement with environmental cleanup and stewardship (e.g., Adopt a Highway) may improve understanding of sustainability. Through such projects individuals experience directly the time and effort required to remedy environmental problems. They develop a sense of responsibility for environmental health and learn the importance of prevention over remediation. Direct experience with the natural world and its rhythms can also shape values and promote environmental awareness. Throughout recorded history humans have sought challenges in wild and remote settings as a path to personal growth. Experience with the natural world strengthens our appreciation of nature's intrinsic value and the place of humans.

The earth cannot sustain current levels of natural resource consumption in industrialized societies, especially if these levels are adopted worldwide. The availability of cheap products has led to consumptive behavior beyond the wildest imaginings of those who lived even 100 years ago. Further, individuals have increasingly valued personal gratification above social or communal goals, especially in the United States. To date neither government policies nor corporate leadership have promoted responsible consumption effectively, and in fact it may be argued that the reverse is true. Value shifts may have a major impact on consumption patterns, though this seems less likely given competition with powerful price incentives. Value shifts may also generate public support for market interventions to bring consumption patterns in line with sustainable levels.

Fostering Sustainable Resource Use—Opportunities and Requirements for Action

Each approach for bringing resource use into a sustainable balance has garnered friends and enemies either through its successes and failures, or by the creation of winners and losers. Any single approach is unlikely to prove completely effective given the current range of environmental challenges. Not surprisingly, in the past three decades environmental policies have evolved, and increasingly integrated approaches have become prominent.

Industrial Regulatory Approaches

With the formation of the U.S. Environmental Protection Agency (EPA) in 1970 and the enactment of the Clean Air and Clean Water Acts in 1972, pollution reduction was sought through vigorous command and control regulation. Pollutant emissions to air and water dropped drastically and major improvements in environmental quality ensued. Yet these changes have not been without cost. In 1994, expenditures on industrial pollution abatement approached twenty-nine billion dollars.[18] Command and control regulation can serve to level the playing field, enabling companies to be competitive while taking care of environmental resources that do not always translate into shareholder dividends. Command and control strategies such as mandating pollutant emission levels and banning products and processes have been successful in reducing environmental stresses in early stages. However, they have also been criticized for stifling innovation by prescribing technology rather than performance standards. In their stead pollution prevention, market-based incentives and natural capitalism evolved as attempts to meet the goals of environmental sustainability at lower cost. Still, regulatory controls are effective when environmental concerns are time sensitive or there is a potential for irreversible effects.

In response to the dissatisfaction with command and control regulation, pollution prevention programs began to appear in the 1980s. These programs are usually voluntary and often incentive-based. They allow businesses to identify the best means of minimizing pollution in the production process. At the same time, government mandated reporting requirements have become part of statutory law, e.g., the Toxics Release Inventory (TRI) of the Superfund Amendments and Reauthorization Act Title III. Careful analysis shows that voluntary programs may be most effective in combination with command and control or market-based incentives.[19] These latter tools serve to align a firm's economic interests with the desired voluntary actions. Consistent with this assertion, the results of the TRI program are mixed. Reductions in emissions of the "listed" chemicals have dropped predictably but unevenly across industrial categories. It is not known whether decreased overall chemical use at the source is responsible for this reduction in emissions or whether it is attributable to more effective filtering, trapping, and collection of toxics as they exit industrial facilities.

While pollution prevention was lauded, it was also criticized for its uncertain impact. Meanwhile, market incentives were suggested as a means of promoting the cost-effective attainment of specific government-mandated environmental goals. In 1988 Senators John Heinz and Timothy Wirth sponsored Project 88, which offered detailed guidance about the implementation of market-based approaches.[20]

In the Clean Air Act Amendments of 1990, a tradable permit program for sulfur dioxide emissions was introduced. Permits allowing the emission of one ton of sulfur dioxide per year were distributed to industry according to information about current operations. Based on industry predictions about the cost of reducing sulfur dioxide emissions, the permits were expected to trade in the range of $1,500 each. Emissions were reduced long before the target date, however, and permit values dropped rapidly. After ten years, permits were trading for about $100.

Market incentives also extend to efforts to tax and thus discourage inefficient use of natural resources. Levying such "eco-taxes" creates economic advantages for sustainable industries such as organic farming and eco-forests. The same reasoning might be applied in other areas such as the removal of government subsidies on unsustainable consumption at below market rates. Government subsidized energy and water rates do not align the user's incentives with sustainability. Similarly, allowing grazing and logging on public lands at a nominal cost leads to unsustainable behavior.

An interesting example of regulatory failure is the United States' inability to increase its Corporate Average Fuel Economy (CAFE) standards. CAFE standards were established during the 1975 energy crisis and were successfully tightened five years later. Across a manufacturer's fleet of vehicles the average fuel economy of each car is weighted by sales. Fines are levied on manufacturers whose fleet average violates a standard. Despite the existence of technology that would allow the manufacture of cars with three-fold or more fuel efficiency than those currently available, subsequent efforts to raise CAFE standards have been blocked by industrial groups. Meanwhile, high profit gas guzzlers have been promoted to consumers through intensive advertising, ironically with frequent inclusion of images of the wilderness that one can access behind the wheel of an off-road SUV.

Throughout the past thirty years industry has simultaneously fought tightening standards while showing interest in long-term environmental and economic sustainability. While tougher standards, such as limits on waste and pollutant emissions, affect existing processes and facilities, sustainability measures help develop cleaner, more efficient processes for the manufacture of better designed products. The former tends to hurt a firm's ability to compete while the latter is seen as a means to improve it. Both assertions are true in some contexts but neither holds across the board. In general, large companies are greening at greater rates than small and medium sized companies.[21] Smaller companies tend to view pollution prevention as prohibitively costly, at least in the near term, and with uncertain benefits over the longer term. These companies have difficulty making the necessary initial investment for a transition to sustainable practice.

Regulatory Approaches to Land Use

Beyond the industrial arena lies another key area of regulatory attention—land use planning. An environmentally sustainable society needs strong public policy which acknowledges the sometimes competing land use needs and goals of the diverse inhabitants of the planet. Humans have the ability to inhabit or exploit almost all areas on the planet. Humans naturally concentrate in areas with favorable conditions, such as a moderate climate and a water supply. As the earth's population has increased, however, and the transport of energy, food, and water has become more efficient, residential areas have sprawled beyond urban districts. At the beginning of the twenty-first century communities all over the planet are beginning to realize the importance of forethought to increase the efficiency with which residential, industrial, commercial, agricultural, recreational, and other land uses interact.

In localized areas progress toward sustainable land use is evident, such as recent improvements in sustainable forestry practices and stricter protection of wetlands. However in much of the world, urban sprawl and rapid development of resort communities in environmentally sensitive areas are often inadequately planned. Grazing, mining, and water rights derived from archaic laws, have encouraged resource exploitation. And few countries have policies or enforcement mechanisms in place that seem likely to lead to sustainable management of their forests.

Natural disasters such as Hurricane Mitch in 1998 can draw attention to poor land use practices. The magnitude of the damage was compounded by not only the severity of the storm, but also by existing problems such as flimsy houses and farms situated on steep slopes, deforestation, and a lack of emergency preparedness and infrastructure.[22] Emergencies such as this can be used to mobilize people and funding for both governmental and non-governmental organization (NGO) programs to improve land use policy (and other social policy) for long-term regional sustainability.

In the tropics, changes in land use may produce unintended regional climate changes by disrupting the heat and water balance at the land surface. If rain forests are replaced by more reflective and drier fields, belts of tropical thunderstorms may shift and cause regional drought. Resulting forest fires can exacerbate the problem. In such regions, potential climate change warrants consideration in land use policy.

There are multiple approaches to maintaining some areas as wilderness and devoting others to development for human purposes. For example, growth management boundaries may be set in order to concentrate growth and density in some areas while preserving openness in others. In the past twenty years, growth boundaries have had mixed success in the United States as developers press for access and prices of available property soar under limited supply. Large urban concentrations have led to acute pollution, and distanced humans from everyday contact with the natural world; however, they may still be the most environmentally benign configuration to support a large human population.

If dense populations are to be supported, efficient, coordinated transportation must be available. Effective planning of mass transit systems allows access to transportation to vast numbers of individuals while preserving land for other purposes. Sustainable high-density land use depends on the re-use of designated sections of land for housing and services, as in urban renewal and rehabilitation, rather than repeatedly developing and then discarding land parcels. The U.S. government took responsibility for its own role with a 1996 executive order that federal offices be sited in historic or urban locations.

The importance of land use planning in the preservation of biodiversity warrants further comment. A century ago, habitat seemed boundless in most of the world. Now, preserving biodiversity requires a deliberate decision by a government, private interest, or NGO, to set aside sensitive land and minimize human impacts. The value of protecting species is recognized worldwide—most countries have national parks or preserves which are managed partially for wildlife preservation (and often as a tourist attraction). However, in many of these managed areas, poaching and squatting are both rampant and lucrative. In tropical rain forests, many species have specialized niches and limited ranges, and may become extinct due to habitat destruction before they are even known. Governments are subsidizing, ignoring, or being overwhelmed by this habitat destruction, despite awareness of its consequences for biodiversity, all for economic development. Determined efforts to preserve individual species, such as whooping cranes, have been effective, as long as suitable habitat still exists. In the United States, the passage of the Endangered Species Act in 1966 represented a public consensus about preserving biodiversity. This consensus has endured despite well-publicized controversies pitting human plans against endangered species—Tennessee dam builders versus the snail darter, Washington loggers versus the spotted owl, or California vintners versus a rare salamander. A crucial aspect of maintaining biodiversity is recognizing and protecting sensitive habitats, which is rarely done with complete understanding of the ecological tapestry.

Technological Innovation

Throughout human history we find an abundance of examples of technological innovation increasing the efficiency of resource use. However, in many cases innovations have brought unforeseen environmental impacts. Perhaps the oldest examples are observed in agriculture. Much of the recent increase in crop productivity is due to new and continuing application of an ancient practice, irrigation, which allows more harvests per year and a higher yield of crop per harvest. The fraction of cropland that is irrigated has more than doubled over the last fifty years to seventeen percent, and this acreage provides forty percent of the world's food. It is unclear how sustainable this large-scale irrigation is. Intensive irrigation has already damaged twenty percent of the irrigated land by salination and competes with cities and natural river flow for water. In parts of India, China, and the United States, underground aquifers are being pumped for irrigation, lowering water tables as much as 1.5 meters per year. It is estimated that ten percent of the world's food production comes from irrigation which is depleting ground water and which may have to be abandoned within the next 50 to 100 years.

In addition to irrigation, several other innovations have helped increase productivity with unforeseen costs. Fertilizers and pesticides can increase productivity (at least temporarily) but are notorious contributors to water pollution. Genetically modified crops can provide superior productivity and disease resistance, but may have unforeseen interactions with natural organisms. Finally, more efficient and mechanized agricultural practices have reduced the need for farm labor, but have contributed to fossil fuel use.

Technological innovation also lies at the heart of "natural capitalism," which promises environmental sustainability without economic compromise.[23] Natural capitalism differs from conventional capitalism by explicitly valuing natural assets such as forests and oceans, ecosystem services such as air and water purification, and living populations. Advocates argue that this will lead to economic decisions that promote environmental sustainability naturally.

The current market does not attach appropriate value to natural assets, so why should businesses? First, assigning a high cost to natural resource consumption or waste production leads to new "closed-loop" designs and manufacturing approaches that lower costs by improving efficiency. Second, it encourages technologically innovative products or services with reduced environmental impact. This may position natural capitalists as leaders if natural resources become scarce or human society embraces environmental sustainability. Third, natural capitalism represents a congruence of economic and environmental values that satisfies leaders, employees, and customers. Advocates of natural capitalism suggest that these advantages will transform the business world rapidly without explicit market incentives or government subsidies encouraging resource use.

The lure of natural capitalism reducing consumption and waste is strong. Nevertheless, natural capitalism has had an impact only in limited niches. Natural capitalist companies may be able to market their "green-ness" successfully in the longer term. In the short term, they must usually compete by offering an innovative product at a competitive price. While there are many opportunities for this type of approach, firms must win over consumers, which will take time. Furthermore, natural capitalism in our current market economy can only succeed where new technologies allow both better resource efficiency and lower costs of production. In many industries, the wait for these new technologies may be longer than our environment can tolerate. For these reasons, technological development and natural capitalism seem much more likely to succeed if supported by public policy and appropriate incentives.[24]

Voluntary pursuit of sustainable practice has become entwined with a market incentive approach *within* some companies. British Petroleum-Amoco has made a voluntary public commitment to reduce global warming by reducing carbon dioxide emissions. As an added incentive to individual employees and plants, the company instituted an internal emissions-trading scheme. Individual business units which are able to cut emissions are entitled to sell vouchers representing that saving to units within the company unable to make the necessary reductions. The use of an intramural trading scheme ensures that the company meets its self-declared sustainability goals in the most cost-effective manner possible. Early reports show significant reductions already in place with the addition of control equipment whose cost will be paid by the internal trade.[25]

The energy generation industry is an excellent illustration of the possibility of using technological innovation to power progress. We suggested earlier that climate change considerations will likely force a transition away from fossil fuels within the next few decades. New technologies promise to lower the cost of this transition dramatically. Although the United States has great unexploited potential for renewable wind and solar energy generation and even export, both wind and solar technologies still cost two to four times as much as coal or gas-fired power plants under current accounting and require a lot of land. So far, the public and industry have not supported incentives to promote the use of solar and wind power, though this may change. Both wind and solar power technologies have become substantially more efficient over the past twenty years, and further improvement is likely. Wind farms now supply about 5 percent of the electrical demand of California. If North Dakota were covered by an array of wind turbines, it could (on average) supply the entire U.S. electrical demand with limited impacts on the underlying, predominantly agricultural, land use. Solar cells are broadly used in locations remote from the electrical grid, and massive deployment of solar cells or reflectors in the southwestern United States could supply most U.S. energy needs.

Fuel cells may provide a cost-effective and environmentally attractive alternative to gasoline or batteries for mobile power generation, particularly for transportation. Fuel cell technology—harnessing the energy released from cleaving the bonds of molecular hydrogen—has traveled the long road from a nineteenth century British research laboratory, through the twentieth century space program, to the promise of twenty-first century commercial use. Liquid-hydrogen based fuel cells, whose only byproducts are heat and water, are now under commercial development. Initially, the liquid hydrogen will be created using energy from fossil fuels, but it can also be created using renewably generated electricity to give nonpolluting "clean power."

By the middle of the twenty-first century, other potential energy technologies could become viable on a large scale for an advanced environmentally sustainable society. Natural or genetically modified oil-bearing plants could harness the natural power of photosynthesis. Nuclear fusion, while not strictly renewable, could theoretically supply almost unlimited energy from a naturally occurring heavy isotope of hydrogen. However, the extraordinary difficulty of containing a hot, dense plasma for long enough to generate substantial fusion energy has already perplexed a generation of originally optimistic physicists. Fusion seems unlikely to become a technologically feasible, economically viable power source within the next fifty years.

Economic Development

In many parts of the developing world the roadblocks to environmental sustainability are linked more to economic "development" (planned economic growth) than to a balance of appropriate policy instruments or environmental regulation. In fact for many policy makers, such development is synonymous with progress, resulting in improvements in quality of life such as increased purchasing power, better health, and cleaner living and working environments, and better prospects for survival of children. In developing countries the desire for a better life, and sometimes simply for life itself, may overwhelm sustainability considerations. In addition, developing countries have rapidly growing urban populations, sometimes requiring them to resort to large food imports. This leads to intense pressure to earn foreign currency and provide additional employment by increasing exports. The most easily developed export is often natural resources such as timber, extracted in a rapid and environmentally unsustainable manner.

A major trend of the past fifty years has been the globalization of commerce and the rise of multinational corporations. Conventions such as the Global Agreement on Tariffs and Trade and the World Trade Organization, aim to produce an efficient and fair system of international trade with minimal tariffs and political linkages. While this has spurred international trade and capital investment, it has been at best a mixed blessing for environmental sustainability, especially in less industrialized but resource-rich countries.

Unfettered trade lowers consumer prices and benefits corporations by stimulating demand for remotely produced natural resources. An American consumer may be largely unaware of the environmental costs associated with a table made with mahogany logged in Indonesia, and any guilt pangs are assuaged by its low price. Meanwhile, much of the profit may flow to investors back in America—stimulating further demand. The Indonesian government endorses this process in the name of exports, jobs, taxes, and often kickbacks. Meanwhile, the forest is rapidly degraded or destroyed, as there is little or no incentive for sustainable logging, with the monetary capital not tied to the land.

Multinational corporations need to maintain a positive image to sell their products, however. Environmentalists occasionally expose controversial practices by companies and leverage a change in its international operations. For instance, Starbucks Coffee now sells a "shade-grown" coffee from traditional tree-shaded plantations, more hospitable to native bird life than open-bush plantations. European consumer resistance is causing a delay in the adoption of genetically modified crops in many parts of the world. Modern news media and the Internet have improved the ability of environmental groups to publicize environmental problems in remote locations, shaping consumer opinion more easily. Furthermore, multinational manufacturers, such as major automobile corporations, may introduce energy and resource-efficient manufacturing plants to developing countries. As a last example, tradable permit systems, e.g., for emissions of CO_2, would allow multinational corporations with access to efficient energy-generation technologies to deploy them at lower net costs in developing countries, allowing them to leapfrog into a relatively technologically advanced state. Such contributions by multinationals may lead to extraordinary progress but cannot become a reality without more explicit linkage between economic opportunity and environmental sustainability.

Non-governmental Organizations

Nonprofits and non-governmental organizations (NGOs) have supported many aspects of public policy development for environmental sustainability. Traditional roles of NGOs, including raising awareness and money, have been supplemented by more active roles in management. For example, NGOs have played an important role in supplying family planning education and services in resource-poor developing countries.

NGOs have also organized powerful constituencies on all sides of the policy spectrum. The result has sometimes been to polarize discussion about environmental issues and foster gridlock, while in other instances NGOs have provided a substantial impetus for public policy change. At international meetings on global warming, population, the status of women, and international trade, NGOs are playing an increasingly vocal role.

One area of notable success for NGOs is land preservation. Especially in developed countries, land banking is facilitated by NGOs, which often can take better advantage of short-lived land acquisition opportunities than governments. Land banking increasingly serves as an alternative to governmental protection. NGOs may also manage the lands after acquisition. In developing countries, NGOs promote both knowledge and preservation of sensitive ecosystems. In many cases these efforts are overwhelmed by pressure on habitat, yet some may serve to slow the loss of biodiversity, buying time while other approaches become effective.

Green Metrics

Environmental sustainability requires constraints on economic growth and resource consumption. Governments play a major role in macroeconomic policy-setting through taxes and subsidies, international trade and investment, monetary policy, and collecting and providing economic information. How do governments measure the success of economic policies? The single most widely publicized metric is a measure of the scale of the economy, the gross national product or GNP, which is the aggregate monetary value of goods and services produced. Government and economic leaders proudly proclaim how they have "expanded the economy" as GNP rises.

Herein lies the fundamental conflict between environmental sustainability and current economic policies. Optimizing economic policy to maximize GNP growth will tend to maximize rather than minimize resource consumption. The depletion of environmental resources is not counted against a country's GNP while investments in pollution control and cleanup are counted positively in the calculation. Of course, most policy makers have a multifaceted view of economic policy which also weights other statistics such as distribution of income and jobs, but GNP has a disproportionate influence. Hence, "green" economists have proposed macroeconomic metrics and accounting systems which attempt to account for the environmental and social impacts of economic change better (while remaining objectively quantifiable and based on available information). Typically, these metrics account for "natural capital" such as standing tree stocks, possibly including valuations for ecoservices such as water or air purification, for recreation, or for biodiversity. In addition, they focus on improved quality of life as opposed to measuring economic size. An example is Daly and Cobb's (1994) Index of Sustainable Economic Welfare (ISEW).[26] The ISEW in the United States increased from 1950 to 1970, but has decreased since then despite GNP growth.

So far, green metrics and accounting have not caught on, even as international agencies such as the World Bank have begun to consider environmental sustainability when funding development projects. One possible reason is that "green" metrics encapsulate an implied trade-off between economic growth and external constraints on the economy. Most economists are more comfortable disaggregating the internal measure (GNP) from the external constraints and optimizing GNP subject to these constraints.

Environmental Sustainability and Risk Management

Progress toward environmental sustainability requires societal decisions about what environmental problems are most pressing and what approaches to these problems are most appropriate. These decisions require an assessment of the benefits, risks, and costs associated with different alternatives. Policy analysis tools, such as risk or cost-effectiveness analyses, provide a framework for discussing such decisions, especially when multiple stakeholders are involved. Risk assessment attempts to characterize multiple dimensions such as risk magnitude (which is often uncertain) and the uneven and uncertain distribution of the costs and benefits of risk reduction alternatives, presenting a substantial challenge to public policy. Given the multiple dimensions characterizing human and planetary risks, assessment may be performed piecemeal across the various alternatives, leading to suboptimal public policy decisions. In this section, we discuss two examples of how perception of risks and costs has influenced aspects of public policy relevant to environmental sustainability. Solid waste management provides an example of incomplete comparison of risk across alternatives, resulting in the persistence of management strategies which may impede progress toward sustainability. Climate change policy demonstrates how uncertainty about risks and costs may serve to paralyze those making high-stakes decisions.

A broad spectrum of interested parties vigorously debate waste management decisions. One example of such public debate in the United States surrounds municipal waste combustors (MWCs). In 1986 there were 111 MWCs which incinerated 5 to 10 percent of the municipal solid waste stream in the United States. As landfills reached capacity and open space dwindled in the mid 1990s, as many as 200 communities had plans to build MWCs. However, by 1995 most of these facilities were cancelled under heavy public opposition. Concerns over health centered not on the magnitude of risk but on the acknowledgement that a risk existed.

From the early 1980s scientists have reported the presence of dioxin in MWC ash. This finding raised public concern, since dioxin acts as a potent carcinogen in animals, and is acutely toxic. Meanwhile, health risk assessments explored MWCs in isolation without comparing them to alternative waste management options. Consequently, these risk assessments never served as a basis for national policy making or as a means for weighing alternatives for waste disposal in a common framework. Ironically, health risks associated with landfill disposal may exceed those associated with disposal by incineration.[27] The importance of comparative risk assessment across the full range of alternatives cannot be overstated.

Some oppose incineration in an attempt to shrink waste generation by restricting disposal options. Trends in the United States have not demonstrated the effectiveness of this approach however. While MWC sitings have reached a virtual standstill, and recycling programs enjoy public support, the remaining volume of waste, largely destined for landfills, has not been reduced.[28] Policy approaches to shrinking the waste stream such as packaging mandates have only begun to receive serious attention on a large scale.

An example of public policy challenged by uncertain, but potentially severe and irreversible risk, is the threat of global warming. Reports of the Intergovernmental Panel on Climate Change (IPCC) in 1990, 1995, and 2000 helped publicize the science of climate change. They established an international scientific consensus that human-induced climate change is being detected, and is comparable to model predictions. The IPCC reports noted continuing uncertainties in modeling, and admitted that temperature projections have uncertainties of at least 50 percent. Nevertheless, they promoted worldwide concern that led to the 1997 signing of the Kyoto Protocol, which prescribed reduction of overall carbon dioxide emissions.

In Europe, many industrialized nations have increased efforts to promote energy efficiency and a transition away from fossil fuels. In the United States and most developing countries, however, per capita fossil fuel consumption continues to rise. Congress has actively opposed the Kyoto Protocol and has limited discussion of policies to reduce domestic carbon dioxide emissions. This opposition appears to have three main bases. The first lies in skepticism about the reality of global warming. The second is skepticism about the impacts of global warming on society. The third basis is a perception that reducing carbon dioxide emissions would have enormous economic and social costs. Uncertainty about these costs is much larger than uncertainty about the relation of climate change to greenhouse gases. These uncertainties have lead to a failure to act to counter global warming.

Fostering Population Stabilization

> People are everywhere. Some people say there are too many of us, but no one wants to leave.
>
> Charles Schultz, *Peanuts,* 23 January 1971

Population growth is a key challenge to environmental sustainability. It has proven particularly sensitive, intertwining education, values, and policy intervention. Population has stabilized—even declined—in most developed countries due to general education, ease of access to contraception, and the status of women. In developing countries, many religions and some governments overtly oppose contraception and family planning, while others have not given it high priority. Efforts to reduce population growth have been most successful in countries which actively support it through voluntary or incentive-based programs. Voluntary programs focus on public information campaigns, calls for socially conscious limitation of family size, and easy access to birth control. Family planning may be encouraged indirectly with programs targeted to the improvement of the status of women or the provision of post-natal health care aimed at decreasing infant mortality. In addition, policies geared toward promoting economic development may discourage large families for financial sustainability. Incentive-based programs have included forced abortions, payments for sterilization, or penalties such as denial of services or educational opportunities as with China's famous one-child policy. The latter programs have generally met strong social resistance when they have not been aligned with local values or appear discriminatory. China's policy, though an overall success, was resented and sometimes ignored in rural areas.

Overall, voluntary measures, coupled in some areas to economic development, have been more effective than forced measures. Both nonprofit groups and many governments in developing countries have tried to extend rudimentary public health care, including basic family planning education and services, to broad segments of the population. Since 1969, the United Nations Population Fund has led this effort. The 1994 Cairo conference promoted the status of women in family planning. These efforts and others have nearly halved average family size over the last forty years in less developed countries, even while more coercive approaches in some locations have been failures.

What will happen in the next century? In the industrialized world, which comprises one-fifth of the world's population, birth rates have dropped below the replacement level and population has begun to stabilize. These countries tend to have high levels of education, access to contraception, and accept a strong role for women in family planning.

This transition is not evident in most developing countries, however. About one-quarter of the world's population lives in countries where families average four or more children (e.g., in Rwanda the average is eight). Poverty and social structures in these countries have limited access to and use of contraception; mortality rates, though high, have dropped far more than fertility. Some believe that rapid population growth has helped perpetuate low wages, continued poverty, and increased social inequity both within and between nations. World population is projected to reach eight to ten billion by 2050, but the evolution of family size in the most rapidly growing countries will affect this greatly. Under optimistic scenarios, world population could stabilize by the latter half of the twenty-first century. Without stabilization, progress toward environmental sustainability seems unimaginable regardless of what other avenues are pursued.

Powering Progress

> The profligacy of the 20th century has led humanity into a bottleneck of overpopulation and shrinking natural resources. Through this bottleneck humanity and the rest of life must now pass.
>
> E.O. Wilson, 2000

Above, we have explored deliberate approaches that could lead toward environmental sustainability. To date, progress has been limited. What will make society move more seriously toward fostering this goal? The avenues discussed below range from accidental twists of fate to strategic steps by individuals and groups.

Extreme events and crises attract attention, educate, and bring about rapid and radical change. For some resources, systems, and species, irreversible damage is dangerously close or even at hand. Yet a notable lack of concern pervades many human choices and behaviors which impact environmental health profoundly. In stark contrast to this is the fear associated with visible natural disasters such as volcanic eruptions, earthquakes, and tsunamis. This fear may motivate people to live in historically safer locations and upgrade building codes. Similarly, graphic media coverage of natural crises, including some for which humans are responsible, has been effective in mobilizing behavioral change. For example, consumer preferences turned away from CFC-based aerosol propellants almost overnight with the broadcast of satellite images of the ozone hole on the evening news.

The easy availability of alternate technologies for aerosol propellants accelerated this transition. While the rise of technology may be blamed for environmental degradation it can also help solve environmental problems given appropriate incentives. It can lead to more efficient use of resources and reduce waste. It is now possible to produce cars which are safe, comfortable, and efficient, traveling 80 to 100 miles on a gallon of gas.[29] We know that energy can be generated cleanly by harnessing solar, water, and wind power. Still, these technologies have yet to hit primetime.

The current system forces companies to focus on profits while consumers concentrate on prices. Despite promises of long-run competitive advantage and pricing, designs for supercars and green energy languish on high-tech drawing boards, or in small-scale operations. Policy changes and incentives, such as tougher fuel economy standards or prices that incorporate the full social cost of products, could change this, but they have been blocked by disputes about costs. In the end, a three pronged approach involving education, values, and technical innovation holds the best promise for progress.

The most comprehensive force for any change is leadership. Human leaders may command attention and motivate followers by charisma, by example, or by force. A loved or respected leader has the power to remove impediments to progress. Leaders can shape human values by example, as did Gandhi, or by persuasion, as did Rachel Carson, who shaped the values of a whole generation with her warning of the possibility of a *Silent Spring*.[30] Leaders often excel at communication and thus have the ability to educate individuals and groups about the implications of their actions. And finally leaders can create new options and alternatives simply by believing in them or by convincing others of their possibility. For example, Amory Lovins provides rare insight to the task of creating alternatives, through technological improvement, to environmentally damaging products and services human society consumes. Political leaders in democratic countries tend to be reactive, not proactive, so environmental progress usually comes as a response to persuasive arguments arising from outside of government.

A recent opportunity for environmental leadership confronted William C. Ford Jr., chairman of Ford Motor Company. In May 2000, the company released a report acknowledging that the company's line of sport utility vehicles (SUVs) is responsible for the emission of large amounts of carbon dioxide to the atmosphere, as well as for "undue" health and safety risks to occupants of other vehicles. This unusual statement was in keeping with the company's public commitment to social responsibility and Ford's personal values. And yet there are limits to what can be expected from corporate leadership. Ford's shareholders would have revolted if it announced that it would discontinue the manufacture of SUVs, and was instead turning its advertising skill to educating consumers and marketing more environmentally friendly vehicles.

The voluntary assumption of social responsibility by corporations is a complex affair. The case of Ford Motor Company is a striking example of the dilemma faced by environmentally progressive companies in a competitive marketplace. Ford has pursued process changes to ensure that their manufacturing is as efficient as possible, with a minimum of waste produced. If Ford stopped making SUVs, a less socially responsible company would fill the void, ultimately resulting in the production of additional manufacturing and energy waste for the same output of cars. Wall Street has had little reaction, noting that although these public statements would be unlikely to increase the company's value, they would not likely result in a decrease.[31] Only appropriate public policy intervention and regulation saves companies from this dilemma by raising overall minimum environmental standards and rewarding progressive companies.[32]

Multinationals may become channels of environmental progress as well. This is unlikely to happen, however, unless governments in developing countries, the WTO and other international organizations, and consumers worldwide demand more explicit linkage between economic opportunity and environmental sustainability. These changes will require a confluence of international economic and environmental values that will come only after many individual nations have more fully embraced environmental sustainability as a guiding principle.

We believe that environmental progress will be more rapid in a world at peace, in which social inequities are being addressed, and in which overall quality of human life is improving. One might argue that resource consumption would increase under these conditions, but we believe that any such impact would be overwhelmed by improved opportunities for education and development of sustainable values, and increased availability of resources to safeguard the environment.

Recent years have brought some progress, especially in addressing localized issues. Many environmental disasters have been averted or reversed, such as severe contamination of air, water, and soil, or near-extinction of some species. In many cases, these changes have resulted from an increased awareness of the gravity of the situation. Human values have been evolving along with an appreciation of what sustainability requires of us. While this evolution will proceed at different rates within different populations, we believe that society will indeed progress toward environmentally sustainable decision making. Such change must be seeded on a local scale and supported at every level as it grows.

Notes

1. L. Brown, C. Flavin and S. Postel, "Vision of a Sustainable World," in *The Worldwatch Reader*, ed. Lester Brown (New York: Norton, 1991).

2. Ernest Callenbach, *Ecotopia*, (New York: Bantam Books, 1975).

3. Theodore Roosevelt (1858-1919), *The Outlook*, 27 August 1910.

4. Brundtland Commission (World Commission on Environment and Development), *Our Common Future* (New York: Oxford University Press, 1987).

5. United Nations, *Agenda 21 Program of Action from Rio* (New York: United Nations, 1993).

6. L. Brown, "Africa Is Dying—It Needs Help," Worldwatch Institute Issue Alerts, 2000, at www.worldwatch.org/chairman/issue/000718.html (accessed July 2000).

7. Worldwatch Institute, *State of the World 2000*, ed. L. R. et al. (New York: W.W. Norton, 2000); Population Reference Bureau, *World Population Data Sheet* (Washington D.C.: Population Reference Bureau, 1999).

8. Worldwatch Institute, *State of the World 2000.*

9. World Bank, *World Development Indicators 1999* (Washington D.C.: World Bank, 1999).

10. Lamont C. Hempel, "Conceptual and Analytic Challenges in Building Sustainable Communities," in *Toward Sustainable Communities: Transition and Transformations in Environmental Policy*, ed. D. Maxmanian and M. Kraft (Cambridge, Mass.: MIT Press, 1999).

11. C. Safina, "Cry of the Ancient Mariner," *Time* (April-May 2000): 38-41.

12. Worldwatch Institute, *State of the World 2000.*

13. Inter-governmental Panel on Climate Change. "IPPC Second Assessment Report," 1995, at www.ipcc.ch/cc95/cont-95.htm (accessed July 2000).

14. USAID, Center for Population, Health and Nutrition, *From Commitment to Action* (Washington D.C.: USAID, 1999).

15. E. O. Wilson, "Vanishing Before Our Eyes," *Time* (April-May 2000): 29-34.

16. Sustainable Seattle, "Indicators of Sustainable Community," (Seattle, Wash.: Sustainable Seattle, 1998).

17. M. Brower and W. Leon, Union of Concerned Scientists, *Consumer's Guide to Effective Environmental Choices* (New York: Three Rivers Press, 1999).

18. D. Press and D. Mazmanian, "Understanding the Transition to a Sustainable Economy," in *Environmental Policy: New Directions for the 21st Century*, 4th edition, ed. N. Vig and M. Kraft (Washington D.C.: Congressional Quarterly Press, 2000).

19. K. Harrison, "Talking with the Donkey: Cooperative Approaches to Environmental Protection," *Journal of Industrial Ecology* 2, no. 3 (1999): 51-72.

20. R. Stavins and B. Whitehead, *The Greening of America's Taxes: Pollution Charges and Environmental Protection*, Policy Report No. 13 (Washington, D.C.: Progressive Policy Institute, 1992).

21. Press and Mazmanian, "Understanding the Transition."

22. D. Sarewitz and R. Pielke, Jr., "Breaking the Global-warming Gridlock," *Atlantic*

Monthly (July 2000): 55-64.

23. P. Hawken, A. Lovins, and L. H. Lovins, *Natural Capitalism* (Boston: Little Brown, 1999).

24. G. Daily and B. Walker, "Seeking the Great Transition," *Nature* 403 (January 20, 2000): 243-45.

25. J. Carey, "A Free Market Cure for Glaobal Warming," *Buisiness Week* (May 15, 2000): 167-69

26. H. Daly and J. Cobb, *For the Common Good*, second edition (Boston: Beacon Hill Press, 1994).

27. A. C. Cullen and A. Q. Eschenroeder, "Coping with Municipal Waste," in *The Greening of Industry*, ed. Graham and Hartwell (Cambridge, Mass.: Harvard University Press, 1997).

28. Worldwatch Institute, *State of the World 2000*.

29. Hawken, Lovins, and Lovins, *Natural Capitalism*.

30. R. Carson, *Silent Spring* (Boston: Houghton Mifflin, 1962).

31. K. Bradsher, "Ford is Conceding in S. U. V. Drawbacks," *New York Times*, 12 May 2000, (1).

32. Daily and Walker, "Seeking."

Bibliography

Select Readings on Progress

Pre-Twentieth Century

Comte, Auguste (1798-1857). *System of Positive Policy, by Auguste Comte*. London: Longmans, Green and Co., 1875-1877.

Condorcet, Marquis De (1743-1794). *Esquisse d'un Tableau Historique des Progrès de l'Esprit Humain* (Outlines of an historical view of the progress of the human mind: being a posthumous work of the late M. de Condorcet). London: printed for J. Johnson, 1795.

Darwin, Charles (1809-1882). *On the Origin of Species by Means of Natural Selection*. London: Murray, 1859.

———. *The Descent of Man and Selection in Relation to Sex*. London: Murray, 1871.

Hegel, Georg Wilhelm Friedrich (1770-1831). *Hegel's Philosopy of Right*, translated with notes by T. M. Knox. Oxford: Clarendon Press, 1942.

———. *Lectures on the Philosophy of History, by G. W. F. Hegel*, translated by J. Sibree. London: G. Bell and Sons, 1902.

Kant, Immanuel (1724-1804). "Idea of a Universal History from a Cosmopolitical Point of View," in *Principles of Politics*. Ed. and trans. by William Hastie. Edinburgh: T and T Clark, 1891.

Machiavelli, Niccolo (1469-1527). *Discorsi Sopra la Prima Deca di Tito Livio* (Discourses on Livy). Trans. by Harvey C. Mansfield and Nathan Tarcov. Chicago: University of Chicago Press, c1996.

————. *Principe* (The Prince). Trans. by Harvey C. Mansfield. Chicago: University of Chicago Press, 1998.

Marx, Karl (1818-1883). *Capital*. Trans. by Eden and Cedar Paul. London: Dent, 1957.

Marx, Karl and Friedrich Engels (1820-1895). *The Communist Manifesto [by] Karl Marx [and] Friedrich Engels*. Trans. by Samuel Moore. Harmondsworth: Penguin, 1967.

Mill, John Stuart (1806-1873). *Principles of Political Economy: and Chapters on Socialism*. Ed. by Jonathan Riley. Oxford: Oxford University Press, 1994.

————. *On Liberty*. Ed. by Gertrude Himmelfarb. Harmondsworth: Penguin, 1974.

Nietzsche, Friedrich (1844-1900). *Thus Spoke Zarathustra: A Book for All and None*. Trans. by Thomas Common. New York: Gordon Press, 1974.

Rouseau, Jean Jacques (1712-1778). Discours sur l'Origine et les Fondements de l'Inégalité Parmi les Hommes. English (A discourse on inequality). Trans. by Maurice Cranston. Harmondsworth: Penguin Books, 1984.

Smith, Adam (1723-1790). *An Inquiry into the Nature and Causes of the Wealth of Nations by Adam Smith*. New York: P. F. Collier and son, 1901.

Spencer, Herbert (1820-1903). *Social Statics; or the Conditions Essential to Human Happiness, Specified, and the First of Them Developed*, revised edition. New York: D. Appleton, 1882.

————. *The Man Versus the State*. Caldwell, Id.: Caxton Printers, 1940.

Turgot, Anne-Robert-Jacques, baron de l'Aulne (1727-1781). *Turgot on Progress, Sociology and Economics: A Philosophical Review of the Successive Advances of the Human Mind, On Universal History [and] Reflections on the Forma-*

tion and the Distribution of Wealth. Trans. and ed. by Ronald L. Meek. Cambridge: University Press, 1973.

Twentieth Century

Almond, Gabriel, Marvin Chodorow, and Roy Harvey Pearce. *Progress and Its Discontents.* Berkeley: University of California Press, 1982.

Boulding, Kenneth. *Human Betterment.* Beverly Hills: Sage Publications, 1985.

Bury, J. B. (1861-1927). *The Idea of Progress; an Inquiry into Its Origins and Growth.* London: Macmillan, 1920.

Gastil, Raymond D. *Progress: Critical Thinking about Historical Change.* Westport, Conn: Praeger, 1993.

Manuel, Frank E. *The Prophets of Paris.* Cambridge: Harvard University Press, 1962.

Marx, Leo and Bruce Mazlish, ed. *Progress: Fact or Illusion?* Ann Arbor: University of Michigan Press, 1996.

Melzer, Arthur M., Jerry Weinberger, and M. Richard Zinman, ed. *History and the Idea of Progress.* Ithica, N.Y.: Cornell University Press, 1995.

Niebuhr, Reinhold. *Faith and History: A Comparison of Christian and Modern Views of History.* New York: C. Scribner's Sons, 1949.

———. *The Nature and Destiny of Man: A Christian Interpretation.* New York: C. Scribner's Sons, 1941.

Nisbet, Robert A. *History of the Idea of Progress.* New York: Basic Books, 1980.

Spengler, Oswald. *The Decline of the West.* New York: A. A. Knopf, 1932.

Wagar, Warren W. *Good Tidings: The Belief in Progress from Darwin to Marcuse.* Bloomington, Ind.: Indiana University Press, 1972.

Wager, Warren W., ed. *The Idea of Progress Since the Renaissance.* New York: John Wiley and Sons, 1969.

Index

Author Biographies

C. Leigh Anderson

Associate professor at the Daniel J. Evans School of Public Affairs, University of Washington. Professor Anderson is an economist with research and teaching interests in international economic development, particularly microfinance, and trade and environmental policy. She has recently published articles in *World Development*, the *Journal of Economic History*, and the *International Review of Law and Economics* on these topics.

Richard N. Brandon

Director of the Human Services Policy Center, University of Washington. Brandon oversees research projects which focus on multi service-sector problems such as the health and welfare of children, improving training and collaboration across service occupations, and the effective use of public communications to improve policies for children and families. His current area of concern is the financing of high quality care and education for young children. He has served as staff director of the U.S. Senate Budget Committee and as a consultant to the Carnegie Commission on Science, Technology, and Government, the American Association of Retired Persons, Fannie Mae, as well as state and local governments and non-governmental organizations.

Christopher Bretherton

Professor of atmospheric sciences and applied mathematics at the University of Washington. Professor Bretherton's research focuses on atmospheric convection, boundary layer cloudiness, and numerical modeling. He is currently editor of the *Journal of Atmospheric Sciences*.

Daniel Chirot

Professor of sociology and international studies and chair of the International Studies Program at the University of Washington. Professor Chirot is the author of books on Eastern Europe, social change, the politics of tyranny, and on ethnic conflict in the modern world. The most recent are *Modern Tyrants, How Societies Change*, and a book he co-edited with Martin Seligman, *Ethnopolitical Warfare*. Currently, he is working on a book about political massacres and genocides.

Ruth Schwartz Cowan

Professor of history and chair of the Honors College at the State University of New York at Stony Brook. Professor Cowan is a historian of science, technology, and medicine with a special focus on the ways in which scientific, technical, and medical developments affect women. She is the author of five books, among them, *More Work for Mother: The Ironies of Household Technology from the Open Hearth to the Microwave* and *A Social History of American Technology*. Cowan has served as president of the Society for the History of Technology and on numerous advisory and editorial boards, including the Smithsonian Council. She has also been a Senior Fulbright Scholar and a Guggenheim Fellow.

Mihaly Csikszentmihalyi

The C. S. and D. J. Davidson Professor of Psychology at the Drucker School of Management, Claremont Graduate University. Professor Csikszentmihalyi has written several books and many articles on the topic of human happiness, creativity, satisfaction, and fulfillment including the widely acclaimed *Flow, The Evolving Self, Creativity, Talented Teenagers,* and *The Psychology of Optimal Experience*. Csikszentmihalyi is a fellow of the American Academy of Arts and Sciences, The American Academy of Education, has twice been a Senior Fulbright Fellow, sits on a number of boards, and has attracted considerable interest outside academia through articles for *Newsweek, Psychology Today, Omni, Wired, The Washington Post, Chicago Tribune,* and *The New York Times*.

Alison Cullen

Associate professor of public affairs at the Daniel J. Evans School of Public Affairs, University of Washington. Professor Cullen has served as a technical consultant to the Natural Resources Defense Council, the Environmental Defense Fund, and on the Risk Assessment Advisory Committee for the State of California. She is currently on the advisory board of the Program on the Environment at the University of Washington and the executive committee of the National Center for Research in Statistics and the Environment. In 1998 she received the Outstanding

Young Scientist Award from the International Society of Exposure Analysis.

Martin Daly and Margo Wilson

Professors of psychology at McMaster University. Professor Daly and Professor Wilson have co-produced numerous articles and books on human behavior in evolutionary perspective, including *Homicide* and *The Truth About Cinderella: A Darwinian View of Parental Love*. They are co-editors-in-chief of *Evolution and Human Behavior*. Daly and Wilson are also members of the MacArthur Foundation's Norms and Preferences Network, an interdisciplinary group of distinguished researchers concerned with developing a better model of Homo economicus. Their research extends from economic decision making in seed-eating desert rodents to sexual proprietariness, risk-taking, and violence in humans. In 1998, Daly and Wilson were elected Fellows of the Royal Society of Canada.

J. Patrick Dobel

Professor of political science at the Daniel J. Evans School of Public Affairs, University of Washington. Professor Dobel is the author of many academic articles on public ethics as well as articles in journals of opinion. His books *Compromise and Political Action: Political Morality in Liberal and Democratic Life* and *Public Integrity* study the reality of ethics in public life. He has chaired the King County Ethics Board and has served as a consultant on management, leadership, and ethics issues to numerous public and nonprofit agencies.

Daniel J. Evans

Perhaps best known as Governor of the State of Washington from 1965 to 1977, Senator Evans has demonstrated a lifetime commitment to public service. He entered politics as a member of the Washington State House of Representatives, where he served from 1956 to 1965. In 1983, after the death of Senator Henry "Scoop" Jackson, he was appointed and then elected to the U.S. Senate. In 1989, he chose not to run again. Senator Evans is active with a large number of community and non-profit organizations. He chaired the National Academy of Science's Commission on Policy Options for Global Warming, and co-chaired with former President Jimmy Carter a delegation to monitor the elections in Nicaragua. In addition, he serves on numerous corporate and civic boards, including Puget Sound Energy and the Nature Conservancy.

Andrew C. Gordon

Professor of public affairs at the Daniel J. Evans School of Public Affairs, University of Washington. Professor Gordon has published many articles in the areas of bureaucratic information sources and distortions; microcomputers and public policy; and community organizations. He co-wrote *The Politics of Social Program Evaluation* and edited *Public Access to Information.* Gordon is currently working with the Bill and Melinda Gates Foundation on programs that deal with the digital divide.

Margaret T. Gordon

Professor of public affairs and dean emeritus at the Daniel J. Evans School of Public Affairs, University of Washington. Professor Gordon is the author of *The Female Fear* and has published multiple articles in the areas of the news media and the public's declining trust in government; the news media and public policy making; and women's fear and self-protective behaviors. Gordon serves on numerous boards, is a member of the National Selection Committee for the American Government Innovations Awards, and former president of the National Association of Schools of Public Affairs and Administration.

Robert Heilbroner

Norman Thomas Professor of Economics at the New School for Social Research. Professor Heilbroner is author of the widely read book *The Worldly Philosophers*, he has served as vice president for the American Economic Association, and he holds seven honorary degrees. Heilbroner's awards include the Guggenheim Fellowship, the Veblen-Commons Award from the Association for Evolutionary Economics, and Scholar of the Year (1994) from the New York Council for the Humanities.

David A. Hennes

Senior Planning and Development Specialist for the City of Seattle's Department of Finance. Mr. Hennes has worked as a teacher, researcher, and fiscal and policy analyst for university, governmental, and non-governmental organizations. His research work has largely revolved around the economic and organizational effects of institutional change.

Alex Inkeles

Professor emeritus of sociology at Stanford University and senior fellow at the Hoover Institution. Professor Inkeles is the author of numerous books and more than 150 articles on sociology and social psychology. His most recent volumes include *One World Emerging? Convergence and Divergence in Industrial Societies* and *National Character: A Psycho-Social Perspective*. Inkeles has been a Fulbright scholar, a Guggenheim Fellow, and has received the Grant Squires Prize from Columbia University.

Charles Johnson

Novelist, essayist, critic, philosopher, illustrator, screenwriter, and playwright, Professor Johnson holds an endowed chair, the Pollock Professorship for Excellence in English at the University of Washington. Johnson has written over twenty screenplays for PBS, including "Booker" which received the international Prix Jeunesse Award and a 1985 Writers Guild Award. He received the 1990 National Book Award for *Middle Passage*, a National Endowment for the Arts grant, a 1998 MacArthur Fellowship, and a Guggenheim Fellowship. Johnson was named as one of the ten best short story writers in America in a survey conducted by the University of Southern California. His fiction appears in *Best American Short Stories* and the *O. Henry Prize Stories*.

Albert R. Jonsen

Professor emeritus of ethics in medicine at the University of Washington. Professor Jonsen's recent books include *A Short History of Medical Ethics* and *The Birth of Bioethics*. Jonsen was chair of NABER, the National Advisory Board on Ethics and Reproduction, and a member of the National Research Council Committee on AIDS Research. He served as commissioner on the National Commission for the Protection of Human Subjects of Biomedical and Behavioral Research and on the President's Commission for the Study of Ethical Problems in Medicine.

Marc Lindenberg

Dean and professor of public affairs at the Daniel J. Evans School of Public Affairs, University of Washington. Professor Lindenberg's recent books include *Going Global: Transforming Relief and Development NGOs*, *The Human Development Race*, *Democratic Transitions in Central America,* and *Managing Adjustment in Developing Countries and Managing Development: The Political Dimension.* He served as senior vice president of CARE USA between 1992 and 1997. Lindenberg serves on numerous boards including Oxfam America, the Desmond Tutu Peace Foundation, and the Washington Red Cross. He has also worked as an advisor to past presidents Monge of Costa Rica, Barletta of Panama, Cerezo of Guatemala, and Maljuad of Ecuador.

Hubert Locke

Marguerite Corbally Professor of Public Service and dean emeritus at the Daniel J. Evans School of Public Affairs, University of Washington. Professor Locke is the author and editor of several books and numerous chapters in publications dealing with race, criminal justice, religion, and public policy. He is a member of the board of trustees for the Bullitt Foundation, the National Council on Crime and Delinquency, and the Pacific School of Religion, and is former chair of the Washington State Sentencing Guidelines Commission.

Janet W. Looney

Associate Director of Program Development at the Daniel J. Evans School of Public Affairs, University of Washington. In 1999-2000, she served as program director for The Progress Project: Rethinking Progress and Human Development. Looney has published articles and conducted applied research on welfare reform, urban education reform, community development, and disability and workforce policies. She has also developed and implemented outreach programs for professionals and for the general public on a variety of public policy issues.

Tom Martin

Graduate student at the Daniel J. Evans School of Public Affairs, University of Washington. In 2000, Mr. Martin spent six months as a consultant with CARE India, where he researched and assessed the potential of information technologies for the organization's programs, and developed a pilot project for a computer resource center in Uttar Pradesh. Previously, he served as development director for Bread for the City in Washington, D.C., and as communications and research associate for the Institute for Local Self-Reliance, also in Washington, D.C.

Scott L. Montgomery

Geologist, writer, and independent scholar in the history of science. Mr. Montgomery is the author of numerous scientific papers, as well as several books and many articles and essays related to the history of science, science education, and socio-cultural studies of science. His recent works include *Minds for the Making, The Scientific Voice, The Moon and the Western Imagination, and Science and Translation: Movements of Knowledge through Cultures and Time.* He has received several awards for his writing and was a 1999 National Endowment for the Humanities Fellow. His current research involves studies of art and science in the medieval and early modern periods.

San C. Ng

Assistant to the dean for research, teaching, and consulting on NGOs and international development at the Daniel J. Evans School of Public Affairs, University of Washington. Ms. Ng obtained her Masters in Law (International Development), Masters in Public Affairs, and Certificate in International Development from the University of Washington. Prior to graduate school she worked for CARE helping to manage an HIV program in Thailand, setting up a China office and raising funds. Prior to her international development work she was a court attorney in Singapore.

Elinor Ostrom

Arthur F. Bentley Professor of Political Science and co-director of the Workshop in Political Theory and Policy Analysis at Indiana University. Professor Ostrom is a fellow at the American Academy of Arts and Sciences and is also co-director at the Center for the Study of Institutions, Population, and Environmental Change (CIPEC). She was president of the American Political Science Association and has written several books including *Governing the Commons, Rules, Games, and Common Pool Resources* and *Competition and Cooperation: Conversations with Nobelists about Economics and Political Science.* She has served on many boards including the Committee on Human Dimensions of Global Change for the National Academy of Sciences and the Research Advisory Committee for the U.S. Agency for International Development.

Charles Tilly

Buttenweiser Professor of Social Science at Columbia University. Professor Tilly's recent books include *Roads from Past to Future, Work Under Capitalism* (with son, Chris Tilly), *Durable Inequality, Dynamics of Contention* (with Doug McAdam and Sidney Tarrow), and *Stories, Identities, and Political Change.* His honors include the Common Wealth Award (1982), election to the National Academy of Sciences (1983), and honorary doctorates from Erasmus University (Rotterdam), the University of Paris, the University of Strasbourg, the University of Geneva, and the University of Toronto.

Muhammad Yunus

Founder and managing director of the Grameen Bank, Bangladesh. Professor Yunus is world renowned for helping to develop microcredit lending programs for the poor. He has received many international awards including: Ramon Magsaysay Award (1984) from Philippines; Aga Khan award for Architecture (1989) from Switzerland; World Food Prize (1994) from the United States; Help for Self-Help Prize (1997) from Norway; the Prince Austurias Award for Concord (1998) from Spain; Ozaki (Gakudo) Award (1998) from Japan; Indira Gandhi Award (1998) from India; Rotary International Award for World Understanding (1999); and King Hussein Humanitarian Leadership Award (2000) from Jordan. Yunus was the first chair of the Policy Advisory Group of CGAP (Consultative Group to Assist the Poorest) and he recently published his autobiography, *Banker to the Poor: Micro-Lending and the Battle Against World Poverty.*

Richard O. Zerbe, Jr.

Professor of public affairs and adjunct professor of law at the University of Washington. Most recently, Professor Zerbe is the author of *Economic Efficiency in Law and Economics,* which has been recognized as a path-breaking contribution to the nature and meaning of economic efficiency. He has published over one hundred books and articles including a recent jointly authored article on the effect of culture in the California gold fields. Zerbe is editor of *Research in Law and Economics* and is a founding member of the American Law and Economics Association. He has been offered a Fulbright Chair and has served as a consultant to the Federal Trade Commission and other government agencies.

William Zumeta

Professor of public affairs and education and associate dean of the Daniel J. Evans School of Public Affairs, University of Washington. Professor Zumeta has published widely in the areas of higher education policy and finance and policies relating to advanced training in science. He is the author of *Extending the Educational Ladder* published by Lexington Books. His work has been supported by the Lilly Endowment, Pew Charitable Trusts, the Sloan Foundation, the National Science Foundation, and the U.S. Department of Education among other government agencies and national organizations. Zumeta serves on various national committees, advisory panels, and editorial boards including the National Research Council, National Center for Public Policy and Higher Education, National Education Association, *International Public Management Journal*, and the *Journal of Public Administration Research and Theory.*